ISSN 1529-7446

BEACHAM'S GUIDE TO LITERATURE FOR YOUNG ADULTS

volume 14

GALE GROUP

™

THOMSON LEARNING

Detroit • New York • San Diego • San Francisco
Boston • New Haven, Conn. • Waterville, Maine
London • Munich

Mark W. Scott, *Publisher, Literature Product*

Scot Peacock, *Managing Editor, Literature Product*
Frank Castronova, Lisa Kumar, *Senior Editors*; Katy Balcer, Kristen A. Dorsch, Marie Lazzari,
Thomas McMahon, Ira Mark Milne, Pam Revitzer, Jennifer Smith, Colleen Laine Tavor, *Editors*;
Alana Foster, Shayla Hawkins, Motoko Fujishiro Huthwaite, Arlene M. Johnson, Thomas Wiloch,
Associate Editors; Jennifer Kilian, Anita Sundaresan, Daniel Toronto, Carol Ullmann, *Assistant
Editors*; Anna Marie Dahn, *Administrative Assistant*; Joshua Kondek, *Technical Training Specialist*

Dwayne Hayes, *Managing Editor*

Susan M. Trosky, *Content Director*

Maria Franklin, *Permissions Manager*
Edna Hedblad, *Permissions Specialist*
Lori Hines, *Permissions Associate*

Mary Beth Trimper, *Composition Manager*
Stacy L. Melson, *Buyer*

Barbara J. Yarrow, *Manager, Imaging and Multimedia Content*
Randy Bassett, *Imaging Supervisor*
Robert Duncan, Dan Newell, and Luke Rademacher, *Imaging Specialists*
Pamela A. Reed, *Imaging Coordinator*
Leitha Etheridge-Sims, Mary Grimes, and David G. Oblender, *Image Catalogers*
Robyn V. Young, *Project Manager, Imaging and Multimedia Content*
Dean Dauphinais, *Senior Editor, Imaging and Multimedia Content*
Kelly A. Quin, *Editor, Imaging and Multimedia Content*

Library of Congress Catalog Card Number 89–18048

ISBN 0–7876–5182–6

ISSN 1529–7446

Printed in the United States of America

10 9 8 7 6 5 4 3 2 1

INTRODUCTION

◆

Since the first three volumes of *Beacham's Guide to Literature for Young Adults* were published in 1989, selecting which literary works to cover has been a long and difficult process. The series editors originally began with a list of over four thousand titles; we then pared this list to about one thousand titles. In paring this second list even further, we had five main considerations: 1) Is the title a popular one that young people like to read? 2) Does the work possess literary merits or social themes that warrant calling it to the attention of young readers, their parents and teachers? 3) Is the work a classic that had over time won a permanent place in young adult literature? 4) Is the title a critically acclaimed work that had won awards, such as the Newbery Medal? 5) Is the book appropriate for a junior high or high school audience?

Scholars, teachers, and librarians offered practical advice about what books were of particular interest to young adults, and each of the titles included in this series meets at least three of the criteria mentioned above. The titles included in the series represent a cross-section of the complex world of young adult literature. Volumes 1–3 cover mainstream novels and short story collections, historical novels, classics, biographies, autobiographies, and nonfiction. Volume 4 covers science fiction, adventure novels, myths, epics, and mysteries. Volume 5 covers fantasy and gothic novels. Volumes 6–8 include novels, biographies, autobiographies, and other nonfiction published since 1980. Volume 9 continued the focus on contemporary fiction and nonfiction.

Beginning with Volume 10, the series returned to its basic tenet of covering works of fiction and nonfiction—both contemporary and classic—that have been widely recognized as important books for young adult readers. The titles we have included vary in reading difficulty and maturity of subject matter, so that there are many titles appropriate for junior high, as well as high school students. We have included titles that have been widely recognized and reviewed, including Newbery Award and Honor Book recipients, but have also included some authors who have been overlooked in the review process. We hope that by including them here, they will begin to gain the recognition they deserve.

Since the publication of the first volumes of *Beacham's Guide to Literature for Young Adults*, we have discovered that the audience for the series is large and diverse. It includes involved readers who want to know more about their favorite books and authors; students who are researching term papers and book reports; teachers preparing classes; librarians building collections and selecting books for their patrons; parents seeking appropriate reading material for their children; and college students and professors developing ideas for curriculum designs. An easy-to-follow format had to be devised that provides the clarity that younger readers require, while providing detailed information and depth of thought to satisfy the interests of more experienced readers. Especially useful to teachers planning thematic segments, and to students writing papers and reports, is the appendix that groups titles by themes. There are thematic appendices at the end of Volume 3, in Volumes 4 and 5, and at the end of Volumes 8 and 9. The cumulative index in the current volume provides easy access to authors and titles for the entire series. Each formatted article is divided into the following sections.

ABOUT THE AUTHOR

The basics of the author's life are laid out here, with particular attention to the events that shaped the writer's work or sensibilities. This section also discusses the author's critical and popular success.

OVERVIEW

This section, which provides a snapshot of the plot and characters, is intended to generate student interest in reading the book, and to give teachers and librarians a quick guide to the subject matter.

SETTING

Many books for young adults are intended to acquaint them with places they have never been and cultures they have never experienced. Novels about faraway lands, futuristic worlds, historical times, the inner city, and the farm all serve to transport readers into the unfamiliar, helping them to broaden their outlook and to understand similarities and differences of other cultures. The "Setting" section acquaints readers with the special aspects of the setting (including additional historical background to explain the merits or weaknesses of a historical novel), as well as showing how the author uses place and time to develop themes and characterizations.

THEMES AND CHARACTERS

This section explains how the themes and characters are woven together to create a unified work of art, and it establishes the groundwork for understanding the characters' motivation and actions. Because some books are more thematically complex than others, the length of the "Themes and Characters" section varies accordingly. The object of this section is to give insight into a work's literary merits by taking an in-depth look at how well rounded the characters are, how plausible they are, and how well they fit into the work's themes. This section is intended to provide serious critical treatment, thereby enriching a reader's appreciation of the literary work.

LITERARY QUALITIES

The "Literary Qualities" section analyzes the techniques authors use to communicate with their readers. It also introduces students to literary devices such as foreshadowing and archetypes. In explaining the skill behind the artistry, this section shows the reader how to become a more thoughtful critic.

SOCIAL SENSITIVITY

Often books for young adults are controversial. For instance, some old classics for young readers contain racist undercurrents that were overlooked in less enlightened times. On the other hand, since the 1960s the subjects that books for young adults treat have broadened to include topics that were once thought to be strictly for adults, such as sex, drug addiction, and hatred toward one's parents. Some young adult books are very violent, others are intensely frightening, and still others express doubts about the morals and ethics of religion, science, or society. The "Social Sensitivity" section analyzes the social context and explains how the sensitive aspects of the book fit in with its setting, themes, characters, and plot. The "Social Sensitivity" section may alert adults to sensitive issues, but it does not attempt to judge or censor material, including "reality" topics like nuclear war, sexuality, broken homes, racism, religious faith, and a host of other "real world" issues.

TOPICS FOR DISCUSSION

This section provides a list of topics and questions designed to stimulate classroom discussion. For students conducting research on their own, these questions serve to guide the reader toward the most important elements of theme and character.

IDEAS FOR REPORTS AND PAPERS

This section is designed to lead readers toward ideas for additional reading assignments, writing assignments, and in-class presentations. Its purpose is to help students think about their topics and to offer them some guidance as to what approaches to the book could be effective. It provides suggestions for simple reports as well as complex term papers. Librarians will find this section useful in guiding students who are searching for report topics.

RELATED TITLES/ADAPTATIONS

This section discusses books by the same author that share similarities with the main title, or by other authors dealing with the same themes or characters. Often these books form part of a series, such as the Tillerman cycle by Cynthia Voigt. This section is useful to students who are writing a comparative analysis paper, or who are seeking another title by an author they liked. If a title has been adapted to stage, radio, television, or film, this section compares the adaptation to the original title.

FOR FURTHER REFERENCE

In some cases, there is a wealth of published material on a particular author or a particular title; in those cases, the "Further Reference" section guides the reader to the most helpful sources. On the other hand, some of the titles have not been widely reviewed, which limits the bibliography.

RELATED WEBSITES

This section lists websites that contain information about a particular author or title. Each citation includes a brief summary of the website's contents. In some cases, the date that the site was last known to be active is provided.

It is heartening that *Beacham's Guide to Literature for Young Adults* provides much new material that cannot be found elsewhere, but it also serves as an indication of how very much more work needs to be done in studying the many meritorious works in young adult literature.

ACKNOWLEDGMENTS

ADAMS, DOUGLAS. A cover of *The Hitchhiker's Guide to the Galaxy*, by Douglas Adams. Ballantine Books, 1995. Reproduced by permission of Random House, Inc. / Adams, Douglas, 1993, photograph by Frank Capri. Archive Photos, Inc. © Frank Capri/SAGA. Reproduced by permission.

APPLEGATE, K(atherine) A(lice). Spalenka, Greg, illustrator. From a cover of *Everworld: Enter the Enchanted*, by K. A. Applegate. Scholastic, Inc., 1999. Copyright © 1999 by Katherine Applegate. Reproduced by permission. / Spalenka, Greg, illustrator. From a cover of *Everworld: Realm of the Reaper*, by K. A. Applegate. Scholastic, Inc., 1999. Copyright © 1999 by Katherine Applegate. Reproduced by permission. / Applegate, K. A., photograph. AP/Wide World Photos. Reproduced by permission.

BAMBARA, TONI CADE. Taddei, Richard, illustrator. From a cover of *Gorilla, My Love*, by Toni Cade Bambara. Vintage Contemporaries, 1992. All rights reserved. Reproduced by permission of Vintage Books, a division of Random House, Inc.

BARRON, T(om) A. Sweet, Darrell K., illustrator. From a cover of *The Merlin Effect*, by T. A. Barron. Tor Books, 1996. Illustration copyright © 1995 by Anthony Bacon Venti. Reproduced by permission. / Barron, T. A., photograph by Currie C. Barron. Reproduced by permission of T. A. Barron.

BAT-AMI, MIRIAM. Mosberg, Hilary, illustrator. From a jacket of *Two Suns in the Sky*, by Miriam Bat-Ami. Front Street / Cricket Books, 1999. Jacket © 1999 by Hilary Mosberg. / Bat-Ami, Miriam, photograph. Reproduced by permission.

BROYARD, BLISS. Javorek, Mary, photographer. From a cover of *My Father, Dancing*, by Bliss Broyard. Harcourt, Inc., 1999. Copyright © 1999 by Bliss Broyard. Reproduced by permission. / Broyard, Bliss, photograph by Marion Ettlinger. Reproduced by permission of Marion Ettllinger.

CERVANTES SAAVEDRA, MIGUEL DE. Title page of *Don Quixote*, 1605. Corbis-Bettman. Reproduced by permission. / de Cervantes Saavedra, Miguel, photograph.

CHEKOV, ANTON. Chekhov, Anton, photograph. The Library of Congress.

CONTRIBUTORS

◆

Without the expertise and generosity of the hundreds of contributors to this series, the depth of criticism now available to young adult readers, their teachers, librarians, and parents would not have been possible. To all of our contributors, past, present, and future, we gratefully acknowledge your contributions.

Contributors whose analyses appear in this volume are:

Emily Alward

Tamra Andrews

Kirk H. Beetz

Vicki Cox

Ellen Donovan

Melanie C. Duncan

Paula Johanson

Patrick Jones

Marilyn A. Perlberg

Evelyn Perry

Robert Redmon

Susan Swords Steffen

Harriett S. Williams, Ph.D.
University of South Carolina

CONTENTS

BEACHAM'S GUIDE TO LITERATURE FOR YOUNG ADULTS

ARMAGEDDON SUMMER

Novel

1998

Authors: Jane Yolen and Bruce Coville

◆

Major Books for Young Adults

Armageddon Summer, 1998

◆ ABOUT THE AUTHORS ◆

The award-winning *Armageddon Summer* represents the first collaborative effort of prolific authors Jane Yolen and Bruce Coville. Both are primarily fantasists whose publishing credits reflect a strong interest in literature for children and young adults. The life stories of both authors include a childhood love of books and writing in which family influences play a part. Yolen particularly claims an interest in religious matters that developed in her early years. Although both authors are equally responsible for *Armageddon Summer*, they agree that Yolen conceived the idea and led the way.

Yolen was born in New York City, New York, on February 11, 1939, into a Jewish family gifted in storytelling and writing. Her father, Will Hyatt Yolen, worked as a journalist and publicist and wrote books and radio scripts. Her mother, Isabelle Berlin Yolen, liked to write stories and develop puzzles and acrostics (taking the first or last letter of a word and creating a word or phrase from that). Encouraged by her parents, Yolen read fairy tales and studied music at an early age. She wrote the musical for her first-grade class. As an eighth-grader at Hunter, a New York school for gifted girls, she composed a paper in rhyme, as well as wrote a nonfiction piece about pirates and a seventeen-page western novel. Yolen's first book *Pirates in Petticoats*, published in 1963, grew from these efforts.

During her high school years in Westport, Connecticut, Yolen pursued her writing and won an English prize. At this time she also developed her lasting interest in diverse religions. She was impressed by the Quaker religion when an adored cousin-in-law gave her a copy of the journal of George Fox, its founder. She attended church with a Roman Catholic friend. The observances became a source for the rituals Yolen later wove into her stories and fairy tales. She once noted that *The Magic Three of Solatia*, published in 1974, is a blend of Jewish, Quaker, and Roman Catholic elements. Yolen has published a number of books, including novels

Jane Yolen

and a children's biography of George Fox, that reflect her enduring interest in religious subjects.

Yolen attended Smith College, where she took courses in religion, and graduated with a bachelor of arts in 1960. She received a contract for her first book in 1962, the year she married computer science professor David Stemple. Their three grown children have all collaborated with Yolen on songs and books. Yolen's background also includes a master's degree in education in 1976 from the University of Massachusetts and doctoral work in children's literature. Yolen has gained a reputation as an editor, critic, lecturer, and educator as well as the creator of short stories, nonfiction books, novels, poems, plays, fairy tales, and songs. She has served in important capacities in the Society of Children's Book Writers and Illustrators and the Science Fiction Writers Association, among other groups. She has received numerous awards, including the Mythopoeic Society Award, a Christopher

Medal, and the University of Minnesota's Kerlan Award.

Although best known for fantasies and highly innovative literary fairy tales, Yolen continues to conceive books with serious religious themes. News stories about millennialist groups led Yolen to the idea for *Armageddon Summer*. When she decided to proceed with the novel, she contacted Coville, a longtime close friend, to write alternating chapters with her. By then he also had received numerous literary honors, including numerous state children's choice awards. The authors enjoyed writing together in a competitive spirit. According to Yolen, she and Coville resemble the major characters Marina and Jed whose episodes they supply in the novel. Yolen went through Marina's spiritual passage; Coville, who is a Unitarian, went through Jed's.

Coville was born May 16, 1950, in Syracuse, New York. His father, Arthur J. Coville, was a traveling sales engineer and his mother, Jean Chase Coville, an executive secretary. Coville nurtured his imaginative spirit by playing in the woods and buildings on his grandparents' dairy farm near Phoenix in central New York. He began to love books when his father read him a "Tom Swift" novel. Besides the "Tom Swift" books, Coville avidly read *Mary Poppins, Dr. Dolittle,* the "Hardy Boys" and "Nancy Drew" series, *The Black Stallion,* and all sorts of comics. He began to enjoy writing when a sixth-grade teacher assigned a long story and let each student choose the topic.

Coville was in his late teens when he realized that he wanted to write books in order to give children the reading pleasure he experienced at their age. In 1969 he married artist Katherine Dietz, with whom he has had three children. She has illustrated many of his books since the first one they sold, *The Foolish Giant,* published in 1978. Since then Coville has published numerous books as well as musical plays. He taught elementary school before becoming a full-time writer. He and Yolen share the philosophy that young people can be educated through literature that contains mythic elements. Both authors also believe that there is a dearth of stories for young people that deal honestly with religious faith. *Armageddon Summer* represents an effort to fill the gap they perceive.

◆ OVERVIEW ◆

Inspired by the approach of the millennial year 2000, *Armageddon Summer* is the gripping story of two teenagers embroiled in family breakups and fanatical predictions that the world is coming to an end. Major characters Marina Marlow and Jed Hoskins meet when each accompanies a troubled parent to Reverend Beelson's armed encampment of Believers. There, while the Believers prepare to watch apocalyptic fires destroy everyone except their group, Marina and Jed struggle to come to terms with their own beliefs and the loss of control over their lives. The teenagers grow in self-awareness and compassion while they build a romantic friendship that helps them cope.

◆ SETTING ◆

The novel is set in Massachusetts during the year 2000. References to Massachusetts place names, like the Emily Dickinson Homestead in Amherst, reflect the locale. References to products like Coke and Pepsi, and to computers and the Internet, enhance the novel's atmosphere of contemporary realism.

Although the novel begins with Marina's and Jed's recollections of earlier times with their respective families, it primarily covers a three-week period that ends July 27, the day Reverend Beelson predicted Armageddon will begin. The main action takes place in the Believer retreat on Mount Weeupcut, in a wooded area normally reserved for recreational camping by the day or week. The area is reached by a narrow blacktop that turns into a dirt road spiraling up the mountainside. Marina describes the place as "pretty wild, pretty cold," inhospitable even in the summer. Its remoteness conforms to Reverend Beelson's characteristic sense of isolation from a sinful world.

A quarter of a mile up from the encampment of Believers, above the timberline, is the rugged, rocky mountaintop itself. It is significant thematically as a place apart from the Believers spiritually as well as physically. Jed often withdraws to a mountaintop cave to think in private, and Marina can usually find him there. In this meeting-place the two share their thoughts, especially their religious doubts, and develop their budding relationship. Here too Jed escapes with his laptop computer, one of the technological advances that Reverend Beelson forbids.

The encampment below, where the teenagers spend most of their time, is equipped with facilities that are typical of wilderness-use areas. There is a historically interesting log cabin called Cut House, which Reverend Beelson renames The Temple. Four rooms inside open onto a "Great Hall." One room contains a generator to produce electricity and a wood-burning stove on which to cook. An artesian well provides water. Beside the site's four primitive bathrooms, long trenches dug by the Believers serve as privies for 144 members. Tents arranged in rings around Cut House serve as living quarters.

The realistic camp setting lends credibility to the group's activities and rituals. Their religion includes "Capital Letters for Everything," according to Jed. Besides The Temple, there are The Place of Eating and The Place of Greeting. A big signboard records the number of arrivals in the cult. Accurate records are necessary since Reverend Beelson's claims that the Scriptures limit salvation to 144. Early arrivals are called First Families. Persons who seek late entrance are Last-Minute Christers. Before each meal, Believers attend church. Besides listening to fiery preaching about doom and destruction, they sing, shout, dance, sway, clap hands, and cry.

Men and women meet separately for daily Bible study. Labor is divided by gender as well and honors the Believer slogan: "Remember That Work Is Prayer Made Visible." Women known as Lady Angels clean and cook, although food often consists of canned food and lumpy oatmeal. Lady Seraphim provide day care for the youngest children. Marina is one of the big-girl Cherubs assigned to do anyone's bidding. Jed helps Angel men construct the electrified fence that he finds ominous. Also ominous are the armed Angels, the big, strong men assigned to guard the camp with rifles and semiautomatic weapons.

◆ THEMES AND CHARACTERS ◆

Fourteen-year-old Marina Marlow and sixteen-year-old Jed Hoskins are strangers to each other when the novel begins, but their relationship soon becomes the novel's focal point. Integral to it are overlapping themes that reflect upon the overall complexity of life. These include family dynamics and religious faith as well as alienation and maturation. Specific family issues involve spousal infidelity, separation, and child abuse. The Believer religion raises specific questions of fanaticism, charismatic leadership, and the nature of faith and its relationship to science.

Marina and Jed bond because of stressful circumstances. Marina's particular situation interrelates thematic aspects of family and religion. Marina's mother Myrna, a Believer, leaves her husband behind with his girlfriend and takes their six children to the encampment. While Marina tries passionately to accept her mother's faith in an imminent Armageddon, she vacillates and thinks in terms of "maybe." She is especially troubled because she turns fourteen on July 27, the forecast day of Armageddon.

Marina is intensely thoughtful and inclined to pray and worry about her absent father, her mother, and why Believers "should be saved and not anyone else." While Marina often ponders the nature of God and morals, she is guided by the remembered sayings of her former teacher, Mrs. Lathery, and even more by the poems of Emily Dickinson. Marina seeks Jed's company to discuss Armageddon and "be sure of things again." Jed supplies the rational perspective Marina sorely needs, while she provides him with someone intelligent to talk.

Unlike Marina, Jed never wavers in his spiritual stand against these "religious maniacs." Jed, alienated from the group, acknowledges religion merely to ask: "Please, God—get me out of this nuthouse!" Despite the sneer on his face and sarcastic approach, Jed is bright, self-searching, and deeply caring. While he considers prayer a fruitless endeavor, he is keenly, almost religiously inspired by the natural universe. Whenever he enjoys his assigned camp work, it is because he likes the outdoors and connecting with people.

The situation of Jed, like that of Marina, addresses issues of spousal infidelity and abandonment as well as responsibility and maturation. When the novel begins, Jed has already learned to take charge. He goes to the encampment to watch over his father, who disintegrated emotionally when Jed's mother ran off with another man. Although his mother abandoned him as well as his father, until the novel's end Jed longs deeply for her. Jed makes lists when he mentally sorts through a problem, a tactic his mother used which reminds him of her.

The actual process of maturation is seen primarily in Marina, who confronts child neglect and abuse in her own family. The camp behavior of Myrna Marlow is far from the motherly ideal, which forces Marina to take increasing responsibility for her five younger brothers. Marina becomes a surrogate mother, especially to three-year-old Leo. In the end, as in the case of Jed, Marina appears as the responsible adult in the family. She also has her relationship with Jed partly because her mother, who declares him a "devil-boy," is seldom present.

Myrna Marlow and Jed's father, Mr. Hoskins, who is not prominent in the narrative, are significant to the religious theme. Their ties to Reverend Beelson, the novel's defining religious character, relate specifically to issues of fanaticism and charismatic leadership. Myrna Marlow follows the Reverend with her eyes, calls him "beautiful," and talks to him as though he is God. Jed notes that the eyes of his father, once set on "perma-sad," are bright and happy because of the large, charismatic Reverend with his "deep, moving cello of a voice."

Jed pronounces the Reverend's sermons rather un-Christian, since they portray non-Believers as "people with greasy souls" who "will crackle when they burn." Still Reverend Beelson, though a "nutcase" according to Jed, evokes compassion when violence looms against outside forces. The Reverend is caught in a trap of his own making. He feels responsible for those who trusted his beliefs. Jed sympathizes with the fear and loneliness he sees in the Reverend's eyes, while Marina realizes that Armageddon is made by man, not God.

Another theme linked to Reverend Beelson and his religion is the nature of family. On Mount Weeupcut, worldly kinships are dissolved so that Believers can be "Brethren," "Sistern," a "Family" of Angels chosen to start the world anew. On this basis Myrna Marlow abandons her children to the group.

A theme of science and religion arises from this approach. Little Leo, Marina's special concern, becomes ill from neglect and lack of sanitation. Just as Reverend Beelson forbids the conveniences of laptop computers and television sets, he resists the modern medicine that Leo needs. The case of Leo raises serious questions about responsibility and child endangerment when a parent's beliefs reject modern medical care available to ill youngsters.

The theme of science and faith is also developed in the character of Grahame, Marina's ten-year-old, wisecracking brother. Grahame is "naturally curious" and oppressed by the rule against television because he cannot watch the science program *Nova*. His endless recitation of scientific facts initially annoys Marina. As the day of Armageddon nears, Grahame undergoes a change that affects Marina as well. He begins to read the Bible and recite from it. Marina realizes that a reliance upon scientific facts and numbers is the way her brother makes himself feel safe, and she learns to respect the tactic.

Besides these characters, the novel includes a cast of lesser figures who contribute to various aspects of its themes. Marina's suffering fellow Cherub Jillian is thematically interesting because she too undergoes a process of self-realization and maturation. Jillian also wonders what to believe, and she questions Marina in her habitual "bizarre little half sentences." Later, in time of crisis, Jillian speaks clearly and displays like Jed and Marina the independence and courage required of teenagers when family and society fail them.

Mr. Hoskins, like Mr. Marlow, is a loving, flawed father. He weeps for the fiery fate of his daughter Alice, a psychology major left behind at college, while he subjects his son Jed to unwitting participation in acts that ensure a lasting sorrow of remembrance. Other Believer parents include

David and Melinda, whose baby Agnes especially exemplifies the helplessness of children. A Believer related to the issue is Mrs. Parker, who pities Leo and disapproves of the way Myrna Marlow treats her children.

Thematic issues of family separation and the value of science are addressed in "tattered" Charlie, number 144 to arrive and Reverend Beelson's own long-lost, grownup son. As an experienced nurse who cares for Leo, Charlie has a hospice background and complicates the question of health care by pronouncing modern medicine "only a so-so miracle at best." Like others in the group, Charlie is a likable and sympathetic character. Ultimately, the teenagers mature in understanding that life is complex and there are no easy answers.

◆ LITERARY QUALITIES ◆

In *Armageddon Summer,* chapters alternate between the viewpoint of two characters who speak in first-person narration. Yolen wrote for Marina and Coville for Jed. The result is an impressive sense of focus, as each character brings a different perspective to the same events. Because the authors are well matched, their characters' distinctive voices achieve equal depth and strength.

The chapters written in the voices of "Marina" and "Jed" are often interspersed with brief pieces that present additional perspectives on characters, setting, and action. The first, for example, constructed as an excerpted FBI file, supplies information about Reverend Beelson's past. Drafts of letters written by Myrna Marlow shed additional light on her character and that of her husband, Harmon. Texts of sermons delivered by Reverend Beelson provide insight on the nature of his preaching. Such pieces as these and others allow the reader to know what cannot be reported by Marina and Jed, but they do not disturb the flow of the story.

The novel features rounded characters and believable dialogue. Serious themes are lightened by humorous touches. The dialogue of Grahame, for example, incorporates joking remarks. The interposed radio interview with a scholar features the repartee of a fun-loving announcer. Action is fast-paced and moves swiftly from family backgrounds to the characters' departures for Mount Weeupcut, the novel's major setting. The authors employ characters' recollections to facilitate almost immediate entry into the major action, which builds for several weeks that end on the day of the predicted Armageddon. The novel culminates in bursts of dramatically realized insights as well as action.

Figurative language lends power to the writing. Jed describes the outsiders' disruption of the inspirational Last Day ritual with a volley of images: "with shrieks that sliced through my newfound joy like razors of fire, they burst through the door." The day's lasting impact is depicted in words that mimic the violence of gunfire: "It keeps bursting back on me in little pieces, shreds of memory that explode in the middle of a thought." Marina's narrative, too, is laced with imagery. Marina observes a "red flower" that "blossoms" on a woman's sweater. The red smear is blood. The peaceful nature of escape is conveyed by Marina's going "out into a night as dark as chocolate cake with candles made of flickering stars."

There is symbolism in the mountaintop setting to which Marina and Jed flee. The higher location signifies their spiritual journey upward and away from stifling beliefs they cannot accept, and ultimately it is a path followed by all of the novel's young characters. The blood that Mr. Hoskins causes to spatter on Jed's Last Day robe represents the taint the son will bear because of his father's foolish act. Leo's illness is suggestive of the fires of Armageddon. Leo suffers the dehydration and fever that intense heat would cause.

Jed's laptop frequently reappears, especially on the mountaintop, to signify that a technologically advanced society exists outside the encampment. Eventually the laptop is the means by which the emotionally enslaved Myrna Marlow returns to the world of reality. The laptop's cell-phone provides the means to get help. Numbers become a recurring reference point, beginning with Reverend Beelson's insistence that 144 Believers will be saved. Eventually Marina seeks refuge in numbers. She counts minutes, hours, and days as a means to regain some control over her life. Finally, the teenagers resort to numbers in order to be sure that they save all of the children in their care.

◆ SOCIAL SENSITIVITY ◆

In *Armageddon Summer*, Yolen and Coville address tough religious, social, and family issues with honesty and sensitivity. While they depict teenagers and children who are victimized, they are sympathetic to the adults who are responsible. Characters like Marina's parents, Jed's father, and Reverend Beelson appear rounded, motivated, and understandable. Within that sensitive context, the authors broach problems of teenage pregnancy, abortion, alcoholism, and AIDS. They also raise questions about religious cults and fundamentalist ideology. The novel includes scenes of violence and parental neglect, but the authors depict their teenage characters in salutary terms of achieving personal growth and social awareness.

Marina's story begins with hard-hitting issues of unwanted teenage pregnancy and habitual infidelity. Myrna Marlow quit high school because she was pregnant with Marina. She rejected an abortion at the insistence of Marina's father Harmon, who

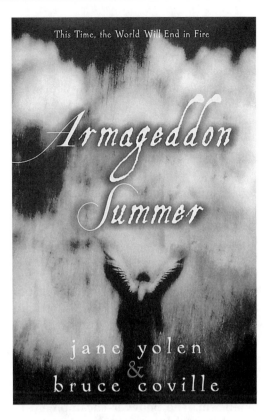

Book jacket illustration by Cliff Nielson for *Armageddon Summer* by Jane Yolen and Bruce Coville.

wanted children very much. Through knowledge of her mother's past, combined with word of Reverend Beelson's plan to pair off new "Adams and Eves," Marina comes to understand how a teenager might not be ready to bear children. She can view her father's alienation in terms of her mother's lack of readiness for marriage.

Jed understands the anguish an extramarital affair can cause. His mother's infidelity drove his father to find solace in alcohol. The authors sensitively depict Jed yearning for his mother and recalling how he cared lovingly for his drunken father. In addition, the authors also show that the flawed fathers of Marina and Jed love their children. Marina's mother remains a difficult parental figure, but she is shown to achieve greater maturity and independence by the novel's conclusion. In the meantime, her irresponsible behavior furthers her daughter's maturation. Jed's particular reflections about these various problems, as well as polluted air, hunger, and crime, indicate a growing understanding of how people can get caught up in ideas like those preached by Reverend Beelson.

The authors depict the Believers in sensitive terms. They appear to be naïve or troubled but generally nice people. Reverend Beelson is depicted sympathetically as a father who lost a son to AIDS. He rejoices when another son returns to him. He is sincere in his convictions and devastated by the turn of events on Armageddon day. The authors complicate the question of Reverend Beelson's responsibility by depicting confused or foolish outsiders at his gate. Nonetheless, they do not whitewash the dangers of charismatic appeal and religious fanaticism. The Believer encampment is armed and fortified. The novel includes violent scenes which children witness. Jed sees his father shoot a person. He then copes with news of his father's violent death.

The Believer religion raises another issue, which the authors again treat with sensitivity to both sides. In accordance with Reverend Beelson's order, Mynra Marlow removes her children from school and teaches them at home. Although she is a high-school dropout, she is depicted as having been an excellent student who can handle essential subjects. However, her poorly written draft and letter to her husband reflect the potential problem with home schooling when a parent is less than qualified. Myrna also has no interest in teaching science, although she provides her son Grahame with the books he asks for.

Positive aspects of home schooling are conveyed through major characters. Marina, who has been taught at home since seventh grade, thinks often of her favorite teacher but never misses her classmates. She has many new friends and pen pals by means of the Internet. Jed remembers that his mother wept when the governor had armed guards placed in schools throughout the state. She wept again when the governor ruled that even kindergarten children had to be checked for weapons.

Ultimately the authors raise questions about a gamut of contemporary issues, including religion, with sensitivity to the fact that teenagers need realistic presentations. Realism extends to dialogue that infrequently incorporates a profane expression. The authors demonstrate sensitivity to gender equality in their portrayals of Marina and Jed as well as Charlie, a male nurse. They present the teenagers' relationship in healthy terms of growing friendship rather than frivolous attraction. The characters emerge more tolerant of others. They have a heightened appreciation of each other and a greater awareness of pitfalls to avoid in life. While neither has found the answer to religion, each has a grasp on faith.

◆ TOPICS FOR DISCUSSION ◆

1. Characterize Marina's religious journey in the novel. Does she resolve her search for religious understanding?

2. In spite of his irreverent attitude, Jed likes the Believers personally. At one point he even prays with Reverend Beelson. Is Jed ever really inclined to become a Believer? Characterize his religious outlook throughout the novel. Has he changed by the conclusion?

3. Why does Myna Marlow leave for Mount Weeupcut? Has she good reason to leave Harmon Marlow?

4. Compare Marina to her mother. Who seems more mature at the beginning of the novel? At the end?

5. How does Jed handle the problems with his father? Is his approach a good one?

6. An excerpt from a July 22 sermon by Reverend Beelson includes the words: "We must defend our Family." What does "Family" mean to the Believers?

7. Why does Mrs. Marlow think Jed is a "devil's child"? Does it seem reasonable for her to change her mind about him at the conclusion?

8. Characterize Reverend Beelson's leadership. Is his type a danger to society? Has the Reverend any good qualities?

9. Is there a satisfactory explanation for Charlie's arrival as number 144, or is this a coincidence in the novel? Is Charlie's relationship with his father clearly defined?

10. Law enforcement officers and family members who gather outside the Mount Weeupcut fortification consider the Believers to be kidnappers. Is this assessment accurate?

11. How important to plot and theme is the setting of Mount Weeupcut?

12. What humorous elements does the novel contain? Are they effective?

13. Why does Marina feel that Jed must be the one to tell Reverend Beelson about the parents and authorities who are coming to get the children? Why does she know that Jed "had to go the rest of the way alone"?

◆ IDEAS FOR REPORTS AND PAPERS ◆

1. *Armageddon Summer* reflects Yolen's particular interest in the technique of telling a story from different perspectives. Select at least five of the items interpolated among Marina and Jed's alternating chapters, and indicate how each contributes to an understanding of events, themes, or characters in the novel. Treat Myrna Marlow's "first draft" and "letter sent" as one item. Do the same for Reverend Beelson's several sermons and the inserted conversations following chapters thirty-four and thirty-six. Does the technique enhance the novel?

2. Many critics hail Emily Dickinson as one of the geniuses of American poetry. Explore accounts of Dickinson's life and ideas and consider references to her and the quoted lines of her poetry in the novel. Based upon your research, write an essay that links Dickinson to Marina. Why does Marina find comfort in thinking about Dickinson and her poetry?

3. Could the novel have a better ending than an exchange of e-mails between Marina and Jed? Should the authors have brought the two of them together in the final scenes? How would you end the novel, and why?

4. American history is peppered with accounts of millennialist groups or cults considered dangerous by mainstream society. In recent decades, for example, much publicity was given to the People's Temple of Jim Jones in Guyana and the Branch Davidians of David Koresh in Waco. Research one of these groups or another like it, and compare your selection to the Beelsonite Believers.

5. Read Yolen's *The Gift of Sarah Barker*, another novel with a basis in religion, and compare it to *Armageddon Summer*. How are the novels similar in technique, theme, characterization? Do they differ in significant ways?

6. Yolen and Coville employ mythic elements in their writing. Marina thinks about "maybes" in regard to Ms. Leatherby's reference to the mythic snake Ouroborus. Marina relates her religious understanding to the word: "Maybe." Research the mythic Ouroborus. How does Ouroborus relate to Marina's thoughts about the Believers?

7. What is the origin of the word "Armageddon"? How does its original meaning apply to Reverend Beelson's interpretation and events at the conclusion of the novel?

8. Yolen's interest in religion led her to study the Shakers, or the "Shaking Quakers," who flourished in America in the last half of the nineteenth century. Characterize the Shakers. Can you find any similarities to the religion depicted in *Armageddon Summer*?

9. Is religion or family the focus of the novel? Or is the relationship between Marina and Jed most important?

◆ RELATED TITLES ◆

Yolen is the author of other novels which explore the subject of religion. A novel she published in 1966, *Trust a City Kid* written with her friend Anne Huston, recounts a boy's experience on a farm owned by Quakers. *The Gift of Sarah Barker*, published in 1981, is based upon the history of American Shaker communities. Some aspects of the novel are similar to *Armageddon Summer*, among them the technique of alternating viewpoints and the theme of a mutual attraction between teenagers. Major characters Sarah and Abel seek each other's company in a religious community dedicated to celibacy and strict obedience. Yolen also explores questions of religious leadership and community in her adult fantasy *Sister Light, Sister Dark,* published in 1988.

Armageddon Summer was adapted for audiocassette in 1999 by Recorded Books, narrated by Kate Forbes and Johnny Heller.

◆ FOR FURTHER REFERENCE ◆

"Coville, Bruce." In *Contemporary Authors New Revision Series,* vol. 22. Detroit: Gale Research, 1988. Biographical entry notable for Coville's comments about the importance of mythic patterns in his children's books.

"Coville, Bruce." In *Something about the Author,* vol. 77. Detroit: Gale Research, 1994. Biographical overview including Coville's comments about his career development and approach to children's literature.

Yolen, Jane. *Touch Magic: Fantasy, Faerie and Folklore in the Literature of Childhood.* New York: Philomel Books, 1981. Contains argument for tough heroines and bold confrontations with evil in children's literature.

"Yolen, Jane (Hyatt)." In *Something about the Author,* vol. 75. Detroit: Gale Research, 1994. Biographical overview.

◆ RELATED WEBSITES ◆

Bruce Coville Web Site http://www.bruce-coville.com. February 15, 2001. Resource for Coville's life, books, and writing tips.

Jane Yolen Web Site http://www.janeyolen.com. February 15, 2001. Valuable resource for details about Yolen's life, books, and awards.

Marilyn A. Perlberg

ATHLETIC SHORTS

Short Stories

1991

Author: Chris Crutcher

◆

Major Books for Young Adults

Running Loose, 1983
Stotan!, 1986
The Crazy Horse Electric Game, 1987
Chinese Handcuffs, 1989

Athletic Shorts: Six Short Stories, 1991
Staying Fat for Sarah Byrnes, 1993
Ironman, 1995
Whale Talk, 2001

◆ ABOUT THE AUTHOR ◆

Chris Crutcher is one of the most honored young adult novelists, having won the prestigious Margaret A. Edwards Award for Lifetime Achievement from the Young Adult Services Library Association, an award from the Assembly on Adolescent Literature for significant contributions to young adult literature, and the Intellectual Freedom Award from the National Council of Teachers of English. Pretty amazing for a self-professed academic underachiever who often tells the story of how he read only one book—*To Kill a Mockingbird*—cover-to-cover during four years of high school.

Crutcher was born on July 17, 1946, in Dayton, Ohio; he is a middle child. He says that they all arrived in Cascade, Idaho, a small lumber and logging town of less than 1,000 people, while he was still an infant.

His father, John, had been a B-17 pilot in World War II. Crutcher described his father as "deliberate and extremely patient, though he could be a little hard to please." Like the father in the story "Goin' Fishin'" from *Athletic Shorts,* his father "always thought I was a little too frivolous and I always thought he was a little too serious." He grew up in a dysfunctional household where he often took the role of the caretaker— "my mother was a pretty significant alcoholic through my junior high, high school, and college years."

His family were all readers, although Crutcher preferred to play sports or watch television. Getting good grades was also not high on his list of priorities, which made him a direct opposite of his older brother, the valedictorian of his class. When assigned to do book reports, Crutcher, rather than reading the book, would borrow an old report of his brother's, misspelling a few words in order to make it appear to be his own work before he turning it in. Failing that, he would also complete book report assignments by inventing authors and stories, getting the names of characters from the Boise, Idaho phone book.

His other writing as a teenager normally came in the form of "punishment" writing, although one of these essays caught the eye of a teacher who invited him to write a column for the school newspaper called "Chris' Crumbs." Crutcher found high school a good place to be a stand-up comic, although his other passion, as would surface in all of his books, was sports. During an interview, Crutcher told Heather Vogel Frederick that in a small town like Cascade that "it didn't matter if you were a good athlete or not. You tried out for the football team with a stethoscope—if you could breathe you could play." Although Crutcher loved sports, he admitted that he was not a star and that "my characters are always much better athletes than I was."

It would be in college that Crutcher would excel as an athlete in swimming, reaching the small college nationals at Eastern Washington State College. Very much a product his times, Crutcher was "rebellious as hell—I mean rebellious with ideas—and I really enjoyed it." After graduating in 1968 with a bachelor's degree, majoring in psychology and minoring in sociology, Crutcher and a friend took a cross-country trip, landing them eventually in Dallas, Texas, where he worked construction. He returned to Washington, earning a teaching credential. After another short stint as a manual laborer, Crutcher began his teaching career at Kennewick Dropout School in Kennewick, Washington. When funding for the school ended, Crutcher was moved to the regular high school as a social studies teacher.

After three and half years, Crutcher left Washington to work in the inner city of Oakland, California, where he worked in an alternative school. Crutcher notes that the school was "the toughest place I've ever been." He started as a teacher, but after taking his various concerns about the school to the top administrator of the school, he was named the director of the school. Despite success at the school, Crutcher, having grown up in a rural small town, wanted to escape the urban environment. Crutcher left the school in 1981, returning to the Northwest. Despite vowing not to get involved in another emotionally demanding profession, within six months he took the job as the coordinator of the Spokane Child Protection Team, a group handling tough child abuse cases.

While student teaching in 1970, Crutcher stayed with Terry Davis, a former classmate from Eastern Washington State College. They became reacquainted when both were living in the Bay Area, Crutcher working in the school at Oakland while Davis was on a fellowship at Stanford University, in the process of becoming a writer. They would run together and talk about writing. A year later, Davis visited Crutcher and challenged him to work on a story for publication. During the time between leaving the job in Oakland and moving to Spokane, Crutcher started work on his first novel *Running Loose*. After finishing it, he sent a copy to Davis. Davis loved it and sent it on to his agent who accepted it within a week and shortly thereafter sold the book. The book was not written specifically as a young adult novel because Crutcher "didn't know there was such a thing." The editor at Greenwillow, Susan Hirshman, convinced Crutcher to clean up the language and the book was soon published receiving rave reviews.

That *Running Loose* was not written as a young adult novel is hard to believe. It tells the story of Louie Banks, a high school senior who plays on his school's championship football team. He quits the team, however, over a moral issue and finds little support outside of his girlfriend. He is devastated by her death in a car accident, but through the help of a caring Coach, he channels his emotions into running and starts his journey to winning back his life from grief. The title and message of "running loose" echoes Pony Boy's cry of "stay gold" from *The Outsiders* some twenty years previous. The book is rich in detail about the small town of Trout, Idaho, modeled after Crutcher's own Cascade. The book would introduce readers to Crutcher's world of small towns in the Northwest, introspective male athletes who are in the process of becoming heroes in every sense of the word, the dichotomy of caring adult characters along with those who border on pure evil, and big themes about trust, truth, and morality. *Running Loose,* like every other Crutcher book, was named a "Best Book" by the Young Adult Library Services Association.

Crutcher followed *Running Loose* with *Stotan!* Based on his experiences as a college swimmer. *Stotan* (someone who is a cross between a Stoic and a Spartan and able to face a task with steely eyed determination), tells the story of four high school swimmers. Less plot driven than *Running Loose, Stotan!*'s characters' damaged lives are the real story. The book's deeply scarred characters were an outgrowth of Crutcher's work as a child and family therapist, first for the Community Mental Health clinic in Spokane and then in private practice. Crutcher explains the connection between his work as a therapist who hears stories, and a novelist who writes them: "what I do as a therapist is listen to somebody's story and look for that thread, the pieces that run through his or her life that have meaning; [I try to] find the truth and the lies and bring them to the surface. As a writer, when I'm telling a story, I do it in reverse. Rather than taking it in, I'm writing it down, but I'm looking for the same truths and the same lies."

Similarly, Crutcher finds connections between his own life as an athlete and the sporting passions of his protagonists. He states, "one of the things I like about sports is that rules are clear. I use sports in young adult fiction to talk about the rules of life." Sports would play a lesser role in Crutcher's next book *The Crazy Horse Electric Game,* as the focus is what happens to a great young athlete after he suffers an injury, which affects his ability to compete in sports, but also to communicate. This novel, set primarily in an alternative school, draws heavily from Crutcher's work at the Lakeside School. The book's major theme is about dealing with expectations.

Crutcher's next career, as a therapist dealing with child abuse cases, would serve as the backbone of his next novel *Chinese Handcuffs.* Sports drama again takes a back seat to the real life trauma of the two main characters: Dillon, who witnesses his brother's suicide, and Laurie who is a victim of sexual abuse. The book's complex plot, heavy themes and relentless exposing of the pain in his characters led it to be his most controversial novel, although it was still named a Best Book for Young Adults.

Crutcher followed the intensity of *Chinese Handcuffs* with *Athletic Shorts,* a collection of stories. Only one story, "A Moment in the Life of Angus Bethune," had been previously published, while the others were new, although each focused on a character from a Crutcher book. Another departure followed as Crutcher published *The Deep End,* an adult mystery novel featuring a child therapist looking into the case of a missing child. Child abuse is once again the major subject of the book, which won rave reviews and, according to Heather Vogel Frederick, was one of the four books President Clinton purchased while Christmas shopping one year.

Swimming is the sport of choice for Eric, aka Moby, the main character in Crutcher's next novel, *Staying Fat for Sarah Brynes*. The book again focuses on familiar themes, such as child abuse, includes the "good" adult and "evil" adult dichotomy, and was yet another award winner. *Ironman*, his next young adult novel, also featured a vicious adult character, this time the father of the main male protagonist Bo Brewster. Unable to communicate with his father, or other adults, Bo pens letters to TV personality Larry King which make up the bulk of the book describing his triathlon.

Around the time of *Ironman*, Crutcher made the difficult decision of leaving the mental health profession to become a full-time writer. Ironically, after turning out a book a year, Crutcher took over five years in between *Ironman* and the novel *Whale Talk*. In between, Crutcher worked on a screenplay for *Staying Fat for Sarah Brynes*, several short stories for young adult collections, as well as a yet to be published novel that would be his "most autobiographical" book. He also had completed a novel about school shootings, but he says that after Columbine "there was no way in the world my story could come out and not look like exploitation." Some of the characters and a few scenes, however, would be used in *Whale Talk*. *Whale Talk* centers on multi-racial main character (TJ) who is embattled on two fronts. At school, he runs afoul of the athletic department when he forms a swimming team, while his work in the community with abused children lead to a deadly conflict with an abusive father.

Whale Talk is very much a Chris Crutcher novel, in terms of style, tone, but mostly in the themes he is exploring. While the book entertains, it mostly teaches. The teaching comes, as in all Crutcher novels, not so much from an adult authority figure, but from the characters as they search for the truth in their own lives. He told the audience when accepting the Margaret Edwards Lifetime Achievement Award that "For me

to know my characters, I needed to get out of their way and let them tell their own truths; respect them and present them for who they were. In the end my job was to celebrate it all, the ghastly with the glorious, because one could not exist without the other."

This getting out of the way, Crutcher notes, includes being true to the language the kids use, the hurt they feel in their lives, and sometimes by showing the harshness of the world, which he considers, however, to be a fair place. His view is "life is exactly fair; people are not fair and relationships are not predictable either. Life *is fair*, though."

Although sports is the outward element of every Crutcher novel, it is the conflict of real life that is his main concern with an intention of using his stories to allow readers to make connections in their own lives. Crutcher's intent is to tell stories that allow readers to recognize themselves in his books. "We are all connected," he says. From conflict comes connections, as characters from Louie Banks in *Running Loose* through T. J. in *Whale Talk*, are tested. More than simple books about identity, Crutcher is looking for heroes in his fiction. He states that "having a character stand-up for himself is one of the common themes in my writing. There is no act of heroism that does not include standing up for oneself."

From those acts of heroism come, what Terry Davis called Crutcher's "healing vision." Davis, Crutcher's friend and mentor, talks about the role of a therapist and that of a storyteller, Crutcher's preferred term for himself rather than writer or artist. After quoting Crutcher, talk about the horrors he has seen in therapy, and the limits of what can be done to repair damaged lives, Davis ties the two strands together, and in doing so, gets to the very essence of Chris Crutcher as therapist, storyteller, and child advocate: "what does a storyteller do to correct the damage the therapist says he can't fix? He tries to get people to see in new ways. He presents a new vision of the world. A healing vision."

The healing vision in Crutcher's book has won over not only young adult readers, but also professionals working in the field of young adult literature, such as professors, English teachers, and librarians. As mentioned, Crutcher has received awards from the three largest professional associations for his body of work, while individual titles have all been awarded with honors. Every Crutcher title has been named a Young Adult Library Services Association "Best Book" while five titles: *Athletic Shorts, Chinese Handcuffs, Ironman, Running Loose,* and *Staying Fat for Sarah Byrnes* were all named "The Best of the Best" during a preconference at the American Library Association's Annual Conference in 2000. Librarians selected the one hundred titles they consider to be the best books for young adults from the last half of the twentieth century; no other author had five books named.

Crutcher lives in Spokane, Washington and, according to all his book jackets, plays "old man basketball" as well as running in marathons, weight training, and running his dogs. His process for writing is also quite rigorous. He says that normally it takes him a year to write a book, but that the novel is "in good shape after about seven months into the process . . . I revise as a I write, sort of chapter by chapter. I read what I have written out loud and make some changes." Crutcher reads a limited amount of young adult literature, particularly admiring the work of his friend Terry Davis, as well as that of another friend Will Weaver. He is impressed with relatively new authors, such as Christopher Paul Curtis and Rob Thomas, while also admiring the works of adult novelists Kurt Vonnegut, Pat Conroy, and Tim O'Brien. He told Carter that he tries to balance his life between writing, working with families, and traveling to speak at schools and conferences.

◆ OVERVIEW ◆

Athletic Shorts is a collection of six short stories, five of them published for the first time in the collection. The common thread to those five stories is they all contain characters from Crutcher's novels. Petey, Johnny, and Telephone Man reappear from *The Crazy Horse Electric Game.* Lionel from *Stotan!* reemerges, as does Louis Banks from *Running Loose.* All the characters, except Telephone Man, are athletes. The stories about Lion and Louie do not directly involve sports, while the climatic scenes of the stories about Petey and Johnny both take place on the wrestling mat. Only Angus Bethune is a new character, although the story had appeared in a collection of young adult short stories. Crutcher writes an introduction to each story, as well as a foreword. In the foreword, he notes that readers ask him about the fate of his characters after the book ends, writing in the introduction to the volume that "my stories don't stop because I stop writing them, but my participation in them does . . . I present the characters to you, the reader. What happens next is up to you." Yet, he also admits some characters have lingered with him and the stories give him a chance to check in on them, in some cases providing stories after they have appeared, while in one case "Goin' Fishin'" featuring Lion from *Stotan!,* the fiction provides the "back story." The plots in each story all lead to a decision by the protagonist: Angus on how to handle a bully, Johnny and Telephone Man on how to confront their fathers, and Lion on how to confront his past. The stories are not about plot, or even characters, they are mostly about delivering Crutcher's message about kids doing their best in tough situations.

The stories in *Athletic Shorts* primarily take place in small towns of Montana. The exceptions are "Telephone Man" which is set in Oakland and "Angus" which is set at Lake Michigan High School. The city and state are not given. The settings are important in all the stories, since many of them have to do with issues of honor, shame, and embarrassment. While these are key issues in young adult life, in small town life, they take on even more importance because "everyone" knows. Everyone would know if Petey loses his wrestling match to Chris Byers, if Johnny Rivers loses his match to his father, if Lion is unable to come to terms with Neal, but in particular the story about Louie Banks in "In the Time I Get" is where the sense of place is most important. Playing on stereotypes of small town bigots, Crutcher puts his character in conflict with that town's values when he befriends a young man dying of AIDS. The story might not have impact if it was set in Oakland, but Louie's decision, as well as the history everyone knows about him, means more in the small town atmosphere. Not that bigotry is limited to small towns as Crutcher demonstrates in "Telephone Man," a story set at Oakland, California's inner city One More Last Chance High School, the setting for most of *The Crazy Horse Electric Game.* The characters such as Hawk and Lam, are street kids in every sense of the word.

♦ THEMES AND CHARACTERS ♦

As usual, Crutcher has created, or in this case, often recreated a cast of well-developed characters. He provides them with motivation, an obstacle or decision, and then lets the characters work it out. In the short story format, there are fewer characters than in his popular novels. Each story features the main character (male) as the protagonist, a family member (a father) or peer (a bigot) as the antagonist, and a "moment of truth" in which the Crutcher character becomes a hero.

Angus Bethune is one of Crutcher's most unique creations: an overweight teenager with two sets of gay parents. Angus's story centers around his joke election as king of the senior ball which involves a dance with the queen, Melissa, a girl Angus has had a crush on for years. Told in first person, Angus's voice is one of almost constant bemusement, given the circumstances of his life. The main theme of this story, which runs through most of the other stories, is about prejudice and acceptance as Angus stands up for himself. Crutcher's hero theme is hard at work when Angus defends his family to a drunken fearful bigot. Being so different, in size and background, the theme of acceptance weighs heavy on Angus. Not so much about acceptance by another group or his classmates, although Melissa's kindness toward him is touching, the story is about Angus himself learning to accept his life as it is. Thus, the story is ultimately about pride. Angus simply wants his "moment," noting that "when you're different, on the down side, you learn to live from one scarce rich moment to the next, no matter the distance between. You become like a camel . . . storing those cool watery moments in your hump."

Those same themes about acceptance, pride, and a "heroic" moment are found in the next story featuring Johnny Rivers, the wise-cracking best friend of Willie Weaver from *The Crazy Horse Electric Game*. Tired of being beaten down by his father, both physically and emotionally, Johnny decides to confront him head-on by challenging him to an amateur-wrestling match. His father was a great student athlete in the town of Coho and a wrestler at the University of Oklahoma. Crutcher doesn't tell his reader, but next to Iowa State, the University of

Oklahoma has a strong tradition of turning out championship NCAA grapplers. Johnny's emotions toward his father are mixed at best, and he has second and third thoughts about going through with the match. Yet, he does and he wins the match. His anger overcomes him and as he is turning towards his father to pin him, he thinks "screw you dad" but feels empty after the fact. At the story's end, the father and son reconcile as Johnny's father comes to the realization that he has treated his own son as his dad treated him. The story is about getting off the train of history.

Johnny provides the comic relief in "The Other Pin" which features Petey, also from *The Crazy Horse Electric Game*. Petey is almost a stereotypical underweight underdog who plays sports for fun and excitement, not knowing of the challenges to his character that he might encounter. In many ways, this story mirrors that of Angus as Petey is faced with a moment that could lead to utter public humiliation when he is assigned to tangle with a girl wrestler at the next wrestling meet. Crutcher announces the theme of story in his introduction: "humiliation breeds character" and the story, like the other two, is about a moment of truth when he has to tangle with Byers. Yet, Crutcher is having fun here, throwing a light story in the middle of this collection as Chris and Petey, neither of whom want the match and find they do want to be with each other, conspire against their coaches to "work" the match.

The farce of "The Other Pin" is opposite in tone to the next story "Goin' Fishin'," perhaps deliberately. This could be why Crutcher placed them next to each other. The character of Lion was well established in *Stotan!* as a bit of an oddball, both an athlete and artist. In this story, Lion recounts the death of his parents and younger brother in a boating accident, and comes face-to-face with the young man whom

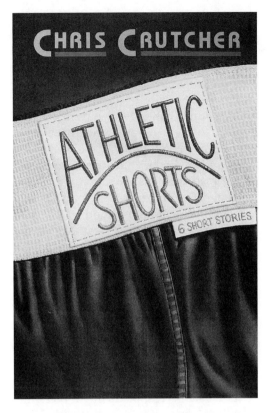

Book cover illustration by Bryce Lee for *Athletic Shorts: Six Short Stories* by Chris Crutcher.

caused the accident. Lion is pulled in opposite directions: one side still so angry seeking if not vengeance than at least a reckoning, while the other side, wants closure, mercy and compassion. In writing the story, Crutcher says that the Lion character (who would show up in the novel *Ironman* as an adult), became "instantly richer . . . he had to go through all of that pain when his lost parents." The theme of "Goin' Fishin'" is dealing with the loss: the moment Lion decides not to forgive Neal, but then at least tries to help him.

In helping Neal, however, Lion is really helping himself overcome his grief and move on with his life. At one point in the story, he tells his friend Elaine, who also appears in *Stotan!* and is a friend of Neal in this story, that if he ever stops hating Neal, he thinks he will die. It is not his grief hanging onto him and weighing him down; it is his anger. The classic Crutcher choice scenes soon emerge as Elaine, more or less, tells Lion that he must decide: to stay friends with her or to continue hating Neal, but she won't be a party to his anger any longer. It is when she tells him to "think," the very same words Lion's dad would always say to him, that he realizes his dilemma. He values Elaine's friendship so much, for it has been her and his swimming buddies that have kept him alive since the death of his parents, that he is willing to pay any price to retain it. Like Louie Banks in *Running Loose,* Lion's life was changed dramatically in just a moment, by a random freak accident over which he had no control. Crutcher's message in both books is how young people deal with loss and pain, often by "letting it go" (the theme of *Chinese Handcuffs*) is the most important story of all.

Louie Banks reappears in "In the Time I Get," the final story of the book which seems, in some ways, almost like a continuation of *Running Loose.* Once again, Louie has to stand up against the prejudice of his small town, and once again, he will lose someone he cares for. Much like Lion battles a war within himself between mercy and anger, Louie is balancing between an old friend and his new one. Near the beginning of the story, Louie meets Darren, a young man who knows that Louie has endured the death of his girlfriend. Knowing this, Darren tells Louie that he has AIDS. At first repulsed by what he assumes is Darren's sexual preference, Louis comes to realize that what matters most is the possibility of death. Yet, as the story goes along, the real issue is not death, but as in the Angus story, is dignity.

Just as in *Running Loose,* Louis is faced with a choice between siding with bigots (in this case his lifelong friend Carter) or doing "the right thing," which is staying Darren's friend in the face of Carter's homophobia and taunting. The conflict of forces is dramatized in a scene where Darren, who has told Louie that no one has touched him once they learned he has AIDS, reaches his hand out. Louis hesitates, if only for a moment, and then clutches his hand. At that exact moment, Carter walks in the door and sees the two of them, seemingly holding hands. The simple act of the human touch takes on tremendous importance.

In almost every Crutcher novel or story, his protagonist becomes a better, stronger, healthier, and more complete person not just by achieving something, but also by giving something up. In some books, what they must surrender is their pain; in "In the Time I Get," Louis must let go of his prejudice, knowing in doing so, he will be sacrificing a friendship of great value. Just as he stands up to his coach, Louie stands his ground against not just Carter, but against prejudice, fear, and hate.

"Telephone Man" is the odd story out here, set not in a small town, but in urban Oakland. Yet, the lessons about prejudice and the universality of father-son conflicts, fit in with the other tales. Picking up on the Telephone Man (Jack is his real name but no one calls him that) character, Crutcher recounts the fateful scene from *The Crazy Horse Electric Game* where he is beaten by the Asian gang, only to be saved by Hawk, an African-American student. Telephone Man has been taught by his father to hate minorities; African Americans in particular. Thus, when Hawk saves him, and as he reflects upon his daily encounters with Andre, the African-American principal of One More Last Chance High School, Telephone Man's views about race are challenged.

What a person believes, about themselves and about others, is the central theme running through all the stories in *Athletic Shorts.* All of the young men in these stories face, more or less a moment of truth. What they believe will determine how they behave. In many cases, they need to reject what others believe, in particular the views of parents and peers, to "do the right thing." What the right thing is, as these stories indicate, is not always easy to see, and almost always hard to do. These stories are the best example of Crutcher's "heroic creed" as he explains:

> Having a character stand up for himself .... is usually the hardest thing to do because it is embarrassing for one thing ... Heroes stand up when it's easier to sit-down. They are visible when it's easier to be invisible. Superman is *not* a hero; he is invulnerable. Since he cannot be hurt, he is not brave ... If you cannot be hurt, if you are not in danger, then you are not a hero.

◆ LITERARY QUALITIES ◆

Working in the short story format, Crutcher's style is very storytelling, very straightforward. Although there are illusions to the past, there are few flashbacks. Diaries, letters, and other techniques are not used. All the stories are told in the first person, except "The Other Pin" which is the least dramatic and personal of the stories and is told in the third person. The characters are, as always in Crutcher's work, very introspective as they make their way through the moral and emotional minefield of adolescence. Yet, it is primarily through dialogue and interaction with other characters that readers learn most about the truth in each character. The dialogue is very sharp, often witty, and rings true. In some cases, such as "Telephone Man," this results in harsh language and racial slurs. The characterization is strong for all the main characters, but also in the new and secondary characters. In particular, the fathers in "Goin' Fishin'" and "The Pin" who seem, based on interviews, close in some ways to Crutcher's own father, loom very large. The adult characters do not take on the "good" or "evil" personas of the adults found in other novels, but rather, except for these two stories, stay in the background.

Humor is of course used with great effect. Angus makes fun of himself, before others do, while Johnny is a joke machine. The Telephone Man's "incident" involving Bisquick and strawberry shampoo is recounted, and the ending of "The Other Pin" is quite funny, yet there is little humor in the two stories about death: "Goin' Fishin'" and "In the Time I Get."

The most outstanding literary quality here is Crutcher's own voice used in the foreword and introductions. In these short essays, Crutcher lays out his themes, reasons for writing, and even guides readers toward what they might (should?) think. The messages emerge not only in Crutcher's voice, but also in the results of the confrontations that are pivotal within every story. Every story builds to a moment of truth where the character needs to decide what is the "right thing" and, unlike his novels which often do not end happily, the characters here seem to make the right call.

◆ SOCIAL SENSITIVITY ◆

The themes in Crutcher's book always deal with social situations and moral dilemmas. The issues of racism and tolerance, born in the first pages of *Running Loose* from 1986 through every page of 2001s *Whale Talk*, play heavy in Crutcher's books. What does it mean to hate? Why do people hate? But more importantly, how do people stand up to or against prejudice? Those are the questions many of these stories attempt to answer. In particular, Crutcher seems most concerned with racial prejudice and homophobia. "In the Time I Get" deals with the issue head on with if not anger, then with a hard-nosed look, while Angus takes a more humorous, although not less effective look, at the same theme.

Hate, anger, and resentment occur not just in society at large, but in families, as Crutcher demonstrates in "The Pin." The role of family, in particular of fathers, is crucial to every story, in particular "The Pin" and "Goin' Fishin'." That fathers are the issue is no surprise; while there are female characters in this book, the issues are often about what it means to be a man. In many ways, that is the only theme that runs through every story. Is Angus a man if his parents are gay? Is Johnny a man if he lets his father dominate him? Is Petey a man if he might lose to a girl in a wrestling match? Is Lion a man if he cannot move beyond his hate for the person who killed his father? Is Jack a real man, not just a Telephone Man, if he continues to believe his father's lies? Can Louis be a man if he befriends a gay man dying of AIDS? Sports is not Crutcher subject matter; masculinity is.

◆ TOPICS FOR DISCUSSION ◆

1. Do Crutcher's introductions to the stories and foreword to the collection add or subtract from the experience of reading the book?

2. How believable is the ending of "The Other Pin?" What could have been some other alternate endings?

3. Most of these stories were written over a decade ago. Do the hateful attitudes, in particular about homosexuals and African Americans held by characters in these stories, still ring true? Has the United States made any progress in reducing racism and homophobia?

4. In "The Pin," Johnny wonders if he should have lost. Would he have been right in making that decision?

5. In "Goin' Fishin'," Lion must confront Neal, the person responsible for killing his parents. How believable is this scene?

Does Lion seem ready to show mercy? Why or why not?

6. If Crutcher's main characters are the heroes of each story, then who are the villains? Why are they villains? Do you need a "bad guy" in order to have a "good guy"?

7. Although Petey and Chris work out a farce to end their match like one found on TV, most amateur wrestlers look upon professional wrestling with distain? Why is this? Why has pro-wrestling gained so much popularity and why do so many people rip it apart?

8. How would the characters in the different stories interact with each other? What if Angus transferred to school in Coho? How would Johnny and Petey treat him? Would Lion and Louie be friends if they were the same age?

9. These stories all feature male protagonists with the issue of masculinity serving as an over-riding theme. Are there any strong female characters? How are they portrayed? Do any of these stories speak to the concerns of adolescent girls?

◆ IDEAS FOR REPORTS AND PAPERS ◆

1. Rent the video *Angus*, then compare and contrast it with the short story. How is it different? Better? Worse?

2. There are two allusions to the WWF (World Wrestling Federation). Research the history of professional wrestling in the United States, focusing in particular on the role of the WWF in the past twenty years in dominating the industry.

3. Angus is the child of two sets of gay parents. Research gay parents, in par-

ticular focusing on the effects on children. What are some of your findings?

4. AIDS is mentioned in two stories. Research the recent advances made in AIDS medical research. How has society's attitude towards people with AIDS changed over time?

5. There is an allusion in "The Pin" to the book *Vision Quest* by Crutcher's friend Terry Davis. Read *Vision Quest*, then compare and contrast Davis's and Crutcher's style, themes, plots, and characters.

6. Both Angus and Louie confront homophobia. Research homophobia, in particular how it has been manifested in "gay bashing" incidents.

7. Chris is a female athlete competing in a male sport. Research the rise of female sports, in particular looking at high school and college women who have played on all male teams.

8. A street gang plays an important role in the story "Telephone Man." Research youth gangs, looking both at the history of young gangs and the various measures used in communities to combat youth violence caused by gangs.

9. The collection was criticized for "reeking of political correctness." What does that term mean? Research the debate about political correctness, focusing in particular on political correctness in relation to media.

10. Choose one of the characters in these stories, and then go back and read the novel in which they originally appeared. Has Crutcher been consistent? Does the character seem the same as when they first appeared? How are they similar? How are the different?

◆ RELATED TITLES/ADAPTATIONS ◆

Athletic Shorts was adapted as an audio book by Recorded Books in 1995. Narrated by Frank Muller, this is an unabridged version of the book, running over four hours. The short story "A Brief Moment in the Life of Angus Bethune" was adapted in 1994 by Jill Gordon as a screenplay. The film from the screenplay was released as *Angus* to mixed reviews in 1995. Despite an appealing tagline ("For everyone on the outside looking in . . . your moment has arrived!"), a popular soundtrack featuring "hot" bands at the time such as Goo Goo Dolls, Weezer, and Green Day, plus Academy Award winners George S. Scott and Kathy Bates in major roles, the film lost money, grossing less than five million dollars. Readers of *Athletic Shorts* who like the short story format have lots of choices, but most popular would be *Ultimate Sports: Short Stories by Outstanding Writers for Young Adults* edited by Don Gallo (Delacorte, 1996). The Angus story appears in the collection *Prejudice: Stories about Hate, Ignorance, Revelation, and Transformation* edited by Daphne Muse (Hyperion, 1995). "Angus" first appeared in the Donald Gallo edited story collection *Connections: Short Stories By Outstanding Writers for Young Adults* (Delacorte 1989). Other Gallo collections, such as *Time Capsule: Short Stories about Teenagers Throughout The Twentieth Century* (Delacorte, 2000) and *On the Fringe* (Dial Books, 2001) also contain stories by Crutcher. Readers of the Louie Banks story ("In the Time I Get") would be interested in novels dealing with AIDS such as *Until Whatever* by Martha Humphreys (Clarion, 1992),*Night Kites* by M. E. Kerr (HarperCollins, 1987) and Theresa Nelson's *Earthshine* (Orchard, 1994). Those fascinated by the wrestling stories would be interested in *Wresting Sturbridge* by Rick Wallace (Random House, 1997), and, of course, *Vision Quest* by Terry Davis (Viking, 1979). A novel about another female wrestler like in "The

Other Pin" is the focus of *There's A Girl in My Hammerlock* by Jerry Spinelli (Aladdin, 1994). Jacqueline Woodson's *Wonder Boys* (Bantam, 2000) and Harry Mazer's *When the Phone Rang* (Scholastic, 1985) would appeal to readers moved by "Goin' Fishin'," a tale of a teenage orphan. *Out of the Ordinary: Essays on Growing Up with Gay, Lesbian, and Transgender Parents* edited by Noelle Howey (St Martin's, 2000) as well as the novels *Jack* by A. M. Holmes (Vintage, 1990) and *From the Notebooks of Melanin Sun* by Jacqueline Woodson (Point, 1997) are related to the Angus story.

◆ FOR FURTHER REFERENCE ◆

Brown, Jennifer. "PW Talks with Chris Crutcher." *Publishers Weekly* (March 12, 2001): 92. Short interview focusing on novel *Whale Talk* and Crutcher's reactions to rash of school shootings.

Bushman, John. "Coping with Harsh Realities: The Novels of Chris Crutcher." *English Journal* (March 1992): 82–84. Brief plot summaries of each novel, but also, a focus on themes and characters in each book make up the majority of the essay. Quotes from the novels are used to illustrate the themes of each novel.

Carpenter, Marilyn. "A Conversation with Chris Crutcher." *New Advocate* (Summer 2000): 201–12. Long interview where Crutcher discusses his novels, his themes, and his passion for truth-telling, and focuses on the novel *Whale Talk*.

Carter, Betty. "Eyes Wide Open." *School Library Journal* (June 2000): 42–45. In the wake of winning the Margaret Edwards Award, Crutcher answers questions about the themes in his books, his goal in writing for teenagers, and his life growing up.

"Chris Crutcher." *Children's Literature Review,* Volume 28. Detroit: Gale, 1992. Long sketch contains a short summary of Crutcher's themes and reprints excerpt for a long article based on an interview with Crutcher. Sketch also provides excerpts for general critical works and reprints parts of reviews for each novel.

"Chris Crutcher." *Contemporary Authors Online.* Detroit: Gale Group, 2000. Based on the print source *Contemporary Authors,* an excellent compilation of information about Crutcher including list of writings, further readings about the authors, as well as quotes from the author.

Crutcher, Chris. "Healing Through Literature." In *Authors Insights.* Edited by Don Gallo. Portsmouth: Boynton/Cook, 1992. A thoughtful essay where Crutcher lays out his vision of writing, in particular its role in helping young people's lives.

Crutcher, Chris. In *Journal of Youth Services in Libraries* (Summer 2000): 17–19. Crutcher talks about his own childhood, the importance of story, and the role of novelists in the official version of his award acceptance speech.

Crutcher, Chris. "R*E*S*P*E*S*T: For Kids, for Adolescence, for Story." *Voices from the Middle* (December 1999): 17–19. Essay by Crutcher arguing for more respect by teachers for literature for young adults. Bulk of essay concerns Columbine High School as Crutcher reflects upon that incident as it reflects upon his writing and his beliefs about respecting teenagers.

Davis, Ann-Marie. "Chris Crutcher" in *Children's Books and Their Creators.* Edited by Anita Silvey. Boston: Houghton Mifflin, 1995. Short essay relating Crutcher's novels to his life experience.

Davis, Terry. "A Healing Vision." *English Journal* (March 1996): 36–41. Almost a summary of his book on Crutcher, Davis examines the themes in Crutcher's novels. Looking at the connection between Crutcher's work as a therapist and his career as a novelist, Davis examines the "connectedness" of characters in his the novels.

Davis, Terry. *Presenting Chris Crutcher*. New York: Twayne Publishers, 1997. Part of the *Presenting Young Adult Authors* series, this is a critical and biographical look at the Crutcher from his friend, mentor, and fellow young adult author Terry Davis. Davis examines each Crutcher title, including an entire chapter on *Athletic Shorts*, focusing on the characterization and themes. Essential reading for a fuller understanding of Crutcher's work.

Ericson, Bonnie O. "Chris Crutcher" in *Twentieth-Century Young Adult Writers*, first edition. Detroit: St. James Press, 1994. Short essay focusing on the role of sport in the works of Crutcher. Beginning with a quote from the author, the article provides short descriptions of each work, as well as discussing themes, literary techniques, and possible reader responses to his work.

Frederick, Heather Vogel. "Chris Crutcher: 'What's Known Can't Be Unknown.'" *Publishers Weekly* (February 20, 1995): 183–184. Describing Crutcher as a "ferocious child advocate," Frederick discusses Crutcher's works based on an interview. Crutcher describes his writing process and also discusses his own teen years.

Gallo, Don. Review of *Athletic Shorts*. *ALAN Review* (Fall 1991): 34. Very strong review pointing out Crutcher's skills in creating attractive, sensitive characters and development through provoking situations.

Gallo, Donald R., editor. *Speaking for Ourselves: Autobiographical Sketches by Notable Authors of Books for Young Adults.* Urbana: National Council of Teachers of English (1990). Crutcher reflects on his books, characters, but mostly on his intentions as a writer for young people.

Greenway, Betty. "Chris Crutcher: Hero or Villain?" *ALAN Review* (Fall 1994): 25–28. Describes the negative response to Crutcher's books from attendees at the young adult literature conference, includes student parodies of Crutcher's writings.

Jenkinson, Dave. "Presenting Chris Crutcher." *Emergency Librarian* (January–February 1991): 67–71. Based on an interview, this article examines Crutcher's works and in particular the writing process. Crutcher discusses the characters from his novels, as well as comments on the themes and autobiographical elements in each book.

Kozikowski, Thomas. "Chris Crutcher" in *Authors & Artists for Young Adults*, Volume 9. Detroit: Gale Research, 1992. Lengthy profile based on secondary materials and an interview with Crutcher.

Krumbein, Sue. Review of *Athletic Shorts*. *Voice of Youth Advocates* (April 1992): 26. Long review which briefly recounts the plot of each story, but focuses mostly on the story "Telephone Man." The reviewer notes that the book lives up to the "high standards" people have come to expect of Crutcher.

Lesesne, Teri S. "Banned in Berlin: An Interview with Chris Crutcher." *Emergency Librarian* (May–June 1996): 61–63. Interview with Crutcher by a young adult literature professor focusing on themes, such as the role of heroes, and on characters.

McDonnell, Christine. "New Voices, New Visions: Chris Crutcher." *Horn Book* (May 1988): 332–335. Short essay focusing on the connections between Crutcher's background and the situations in his works.

Also, examines the role of sports in his works.

Morning, Todd. Review of *Athletic Shorts*. *School Library Journal* (September, 1991): 278. Very strong review calling the book a "winning collection" which will touch teens deeply and make them want to read Crutcher's novels.

Nilsen, Allen Pace and Ken Donelson. Review of *Athletic Shorts*. *English Journal* (November 1992). Mixed review calling the collection "three definite winners, one close-call, and two well-fought losses."

Review of *Athletic Shorts*. *English Journal* (April 1992): 85. Long unsigned review which dubs the book a "great collection" for high school students. The only review to call "Goin' Fishin'" the strongest story in the book.

Review of *Athletic Shorts*. *Journal of Reading* (October 1993): 152. Short very positive unsigned review focusing on the messages in the stories, as well as Crutcher's strong writing.

Review of *Athletic Shorts*. *Publishers Weekly* (August 23, 1991): 63. Short positive unsigned review discusses the themes found in the stories, and notes how Crutcher is fighting against the stereotypical image of uncaring and unthinking athletes.

Senick, Gerald. "Chris Crutcher" in *Something about the Author*, Volume 99. Detroit: Gale Research, 1999. Updates earlier profile in Volume 52 of the series. This sketch provides information on Crutcher's career, awards and honors, adaptations, and a long essay focusing on each title, augmented with quotes from the author.

Sheffer, Susannah. "An Adult Reads Chris Crutcher." *The ALAN Review* (Spring 1997): 10–11. An adult reader responds to the novels of Crutcher, recommended to her by her twelve-year-old daughter, in particular focusing on *Chinese Handcuffs* and *Staying Fat for Sarah Byrnes*.

Smith, Louisa. "Limitations on Young Adult Fiction: An Interview with Chris Crutcher." *The Lion and the Unicorn*. (Spring 1992): 66–74. Interview with Crutcher discussing all aspects of his careers, but with particular attention to his writing process.

Spencer, Pam. "YA Novels in the AP Classroom: Crutcher Meets Camus." *English Journal* (November 1989): 44–6. Compares the themes in the works of Crutcher with those found in "classics" and advocates for teachers to use more YA literature in the classroom.

Sutton, Roger. Review of *Athletic Shorts*. *Bulletin of the Center for Children's Books*. (December 1991): 87. Mixed review which is critical of Crutcher's didactic tone in not only the stories, but also in his foreword and introduction to each story.

Vasilakis, Nancy. Review of *Athletic Shorts*. *Horn Book* (September 1991): 602. Very strong view noting the powerful characterization, realistic dialogue, and handling of major themes in young adult literature/young adult life. Special attention is paid to the stories featuring Angus Bethune, the Telephone Man, and Louie Banks.

Weaver, Matthew. "Chris Crutcher's Balancing Act: Cool Old Guy Meets Brash Young Writer." *Voice of Youth Advocates* (August 2001): 182–185.

Zvirin, Stephanie. Review of *Athletic Shorts*. *Booklist* (October 15, 1991): 428. Strong review focusing in particular on the Angus Bethune and Telephone Man stories. The reviewer notes that Crutcher's themes have great young adult appeal, his plots are straightforward and easy to follow, and his writing achieves a great balance between humor and poignancy.

◆ RELATED WEBSITES ◆

"Author Feature–Chris Crutcher." *Carmel Clay Public Library Young Adult Department.* http://www.carmel.lib.in.us/ya/crutcher.htm Short summaries of each Crutcher novel including a discussion of themes and subjects.

"Author Profile: Chris Crutcher." *Teen-Reads.Com* http://www.teenreads.com/authors/au-crutcher-chris.asp Good in-depth interview with Crutcher, focusing on the connection between his work as a therapist and as a storyteller. Also includes Crutcher's views about how teachers can better connect with students, and about the use of classics in the classroom.

Chris Crutcher Web Site. http://www.aboutcrutcher.com Author's official website contains biographical information, links to more resources, and essays by Crutcher regarding school violence.

Crutcher, Chris. "On Writing Sports Fiction." In *Literature for Today's Young Adult Online* http://occ.awlonline.com/bookbind/pubbooks/nilsen_awl/chapter5/custom1/deluxe-content.html Crutcher talks about the role of sports in his novel, and the reason his main characters engage in athletic pursuits.

Cunfer, Sue. "Learning about Chris Crutcher." *School of Communication, Information, and Library Studies at Rutgers University* http://www.scils.rutgers.edu/special/kay/crutcher.html Nice overview of Crutcher's works with excerpts from reviews, lists of awards, and links

Patrick Jones

BEYOND DREAMS

Short Stories

1995

Author: Marilyn Reynolds

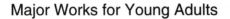

Major Works for Young Adults

True-to-Life series
Telling, 1989
Detour for Emily, 1993
Too Soon for Jeff, 1994
Beyond Dreams, 1995 (short stories)

But What about Me?, 1996
Baby Help, 1998
If You Loved Me, 1999
Love Rules, 2001

◆ ABOUT THE AUTHOR ◆

Marilyn Reynolds was born on May 17, 1935, in what is now Toronto, Canada. She has worked as a library assistant, a teacher, and a writer in addition to raising three children, now grown. Reynolds has written for both children and adults and has published essays and short stories in newspapers, journals, and literary magazines. Her books for young adults generally center around the struggle to meet challenges, with her characters often making difficult decisions to change the course of their lives.

Reynolds has published several books about teenage challenges, all published in a series called "True-To Life Series from Hamilton High." *Beyond Dreams* is the third book in this series and the only collection of short stories. Reynolds has received the most recognition for her young adult literature, and her frank treatment of controversial subject matter has brought her both praise and criticism. *Too Soon for Jeff* and *Detour for Emily* have both been named American Library Association Best Books for Young Adults, though they have also been the object of several banning attempts. Reynolds' books do cover sensitive subject matter, but they also discuss topics that the author knows touch the lives of teenagers from all walks of life. While working in an alternative high school, she was able to talk to young people every day who struggle with problems similar to those of the characters she creates.

Reynolds lives in Sacramento, California, and continues to teach and write. She relies on input from her students to add

Marilyn Reynolds

depth and substance to her stories and to help her dig deep into the minds of teenagers in crisis situations.

◆ OVERVIEW ◆

Beyond Dreams is a collection of short stories that focus on high school students facing difficult challenges. Each of the six stories deals with a crisis, including school failure, domestic violence, drunk driving, teen pregnancy, racism, and the aging of a close relative. These themes hit home for many of Reynolds' readers who have either found themselves in similar circumstances or know someone who has. The characters in the collection must learn to make sense of the world around them and determine the best course of action to pull them out of their slump and better their lives. The pro-

tagonists in all the stories have found themselves on a much different path than they imagined in their dreams. However disturbing the subject matter, Reynolds gives her readers a hopeful message. She creates characters with the common sense and the motivation to overcome their hardships, and they succeed. With a little help from friends and caring adults, they manage to make sensible decisions and get themselves back on track.

◆ SETTING ◆

The backdrop for this book and the other books in the "Hamilton High" series is an urban, racially diverse high school in Southern California. All of the stories do not take place within the school however. Reynolds sometimes removes her characters from this environment to bring the reader into their personal dilemmas. In "Only If You Think So," the first of the six stories, Jason, the protagonist, has left Hamilton High because of poor grades and moved to Sojourner High School, a school his father calls "Loser High." Reynolds takes readers into Jason's dysfunctional home to shed light on how Jason came to view himself as a loser in the first place.

Clearly, Reynolds uses this setting both to emphasize the odds Jason is up against and to help him recognize his motivation to beat these odds. It would be all too easy for Jason to fall into the same pattern his father fell into, sitting in front of the television all day with a hostile attitude, but Jeff wants something more out of his life. He sees what his father has become, and finds refuge at Sojourner High. It is there that he meets with caring adults who help him get on the right track and give him the opportunities he needs to succeed.

Through the course of the novel, Reynolds takes readers inside other dysfunctional homes. In "Baby Help," the protagonist

Melissa lives with her abusive boyfriend, Rudy, their two-year-old baby, Cheyenne, and Rudy's mother, Irma. The home setting again is one Melissa needs to break out of, but until she realizes the danger behind Rudy's abuse, she finds it easier to live in what she once considered a "stable" environment than to branch out into the unknown world alone. But all of the characters are heading out into the unknown world, and they all discover that there is help out there if only they learn to accept it.

◆ THEMES AND CHARACTERS ◆

Perhaps the primary theme in *Beyond Dreams* is the importance of turning challenging situations into opportunities. This is the theme that links all the stories and all the characters in the collection. Reynolds' protagonists all find themselves in situations that challenge their emotional health and require them to confront the unknown. They must recognize their ability to deal effectively with threatening situations and accept the challenges these situations present. As well, they must learn to develop the critical thinking skills necessary to overcome their difficulties, both internal and external.

"Baby Help" focuses on Melissa, a seventeen-year-old mother living with her abusive boyfriend, their two-year-old daughter, and her boyfriend's mother. Melissa fell in love with Rudy at a young age, and having never felt wanted before, she developed a warped sense of what true love is all about. Rudy showers Melissa with affection, but eventually she finds his possessiveness frightening. As she gradually realizes that Rudy cannot control his anger and that she is a victim of abuse, she moves toward self-actualization.

For most of the story, Melissa is planning to marry Rudy rather than leave him. Slowly she begins to grasp what the future will hold for her and her baby if they remain with Rudy in their dysfunctional home. Rudy gets drunk and hits Melissa, and time and time again she makes excuses for him. But she finds it more and more difficult to cling to the image she has of a stable family for Cheyenne, one with two loving parents, and in her case, a doting grandmother. It takes Melissa a long time to redefine what she considers stability and to reevaluate her definition of love.

Melissa's unfamiliarity with love makes it difficult for her to give up her ideal, even when she recognizes that Rudy has a cruel streak and a violent temper. She constantly struggles to convince herself that because Rudy can be so sensitive and loving sometimes he truly does love her and will never abuse her again. Melissa is a victim in more ways than one. Reynolds gives enough background into her past to help readers recognize the cycle of abuse and understand why Melissa thinks and reasons the way she does. Melissa felt unloved and unwanted as a child, so when Rudy came along and showered her with attention, she fell easily into a trap. Rudy himself is in this same trap. His father was abusive and his mother put up with it. Irma tells Melissa that she must learn when to keep her mouth shut, and she must learn when to stay out of Rudy's way. But clearly Melissa is more intelligent than to follow that advice. Reynolds gives her the foresight to recognize the danger of remaining in this vicious cycle.

Melissa's situation is not unlike the situations of the other protagaonists in this collection. They all face different crises, but they all find the resolve to break out of their unhealthy life and move toward actually obtaining the life they imagine. In "Only If You Think So," Jason must break his pattern of failure and find the motivation it takes to succeed. In "For Ethan and Me," Christina must take a different path than she took in the past in order to make a better life for herself and her son in the future. In "What If," Paul must come to terms with the fatal accident that killed his best friend Gabe, and with the fact that he cannot change what happened. None of these protagonists can change what happened. But they can influence what is to come. Reynolds lets readers know that often times, one must feel trapped before recognizing the need to change directions.

For Melissa, this recognition comes gradually. Readers begin to wonder for a while if she will ever come to define herself as an abused partner, or if she will ever find the courage it takes to break out of the cycle and prevent herself from becoming another abused wife. But readers do understand that she is capable of reasoning. Reynolds gives her the common sense to pull away from Rudy and Irma, and she gives readers the knowledge that Melissa is much stronger than either one of them. The entire time she is making up stories to cover up the truth behind her bumps and bruises she constantly evaluating her situation. Rudy and Irma, it appears, never got that far. They remain constantly in turmoil. Reynolds allows readers to see Melissa's turmoil and to witness her change of attitude. Readers watch as she becomes more aware and more determined to better her situation.

Reynolds introduces another young mother in "For Ethan and Me." This story focuses on Christina Calderon, a character from *Too Soon for Jeff*, one of the earlier books in Reynolds' "Hamilton High" series and one that won praise from reviewers. In the first book, Christina becomes pregnant and gives birth to a son named Ethan. In "For Ethan and Me," the baby is just two years old when she gets pregnant again. Christina appears to be a responsible young adult in "For Ethan and Me," working hard to take care of her son, complete her schooling, and even teach other young adults about safe sex. But unfortunately, Christina neglected

to practice what she preached. She knows that she can afford neither the financial nor the emotional strain of raising another child, so this time, she decides to have an abortion. The story centers around this difficult decision and the emotional process Christina must go through in order to accept her decision as the right choice.

Christina and Melissa are able to make wise decisions because they have been empowered by information. They are learning to be responsible parents, and they have access to the information to help them through the trials of raising a child while still children themselves. Reynolds gives her readers several messages here. She lets them know that however hopeless a situation may seem, it is possible to take control and obliterate the hopelessness. She makes readers aware that there is help available. Reynolds discusses the social programs for abused partners and for teenage mothers, and emphasizes that there are caring people working for these programs who can offer guidance during difficult times.

Motherhood changed both Melissa and Christina in ways that led them to act more sensibly and responsibly than they had in the past. As soon as they accepted the responsibility of being in control of others, they saw the necessity of taking control of themselves. This is also true for Jason in "Only If You Think So." Responsibility gives him the motivation he needs to help himself out of his slump. When the story begins, Jason already has the motivation to succeed in baseball, but he has given up on his dream because he considers himself an academic failure. He also has the ability to influence others and become a role model, but he is hostile to adult authority and school in general. Jason alters his attitude when he takes responsibility for others. He begins to care about others and himself. This is also true for Josh in "Uncle Tweetie." Eighty-seven-year- old Uncle Tweetie moves in to Josh's room just after his older brother moved away to college and Josh thought he would finally have his own space. This elderly man presented Josh with the challenge to keep a lid on his anger and resentment, but ended up teaching him important lessons about love and selflessness.

Teachers come in all shapes and sizes. Uncle Tweetie is aging and uneducated. Making matters worse, he has annoying habits that drive Josh crazy. Clearly, he presents a challenge for Josh to find something meaningful in what he considers to be a stifling situation. Cheyenne presents a similar challenge to Melissa in "Baby Help," but like Uncle Tweetie, she ends up teaching Melissa about love and selflessness. She also gives Melissa the motivation to recognize her own self worth. Caught in a trap with Rudy, Melissa has trouble protecting her own autonomy. But when Rudy threatens Cheyenne, it spurs her into action. She has no trouble recognizing that her daughter's independence and safety is worth protecting, and while fighting for Cheyenne, she ends up fighting for herself as well.

Beyond Dreams is about choices. It is about the power of will and determination. It is about accepting personal responsibility. Melissa takes responsibility for herself when she decides to leave Rudy. Christina takes responsibility for herself when she decides to have an abortion. Jason takes responsibility for himself when he decides to succeed in school. Once these characters realize that they have choices, they take control of their lives and renew their hope for fulfilling their dreams. Jason realizes that he chose to fail in school, and he can similarly choose to suceed. Melissa realizes that she chose to remain with Rudy, and she can also choose to leave him.

In "What If," Paul finds himself in a situation where he did not decide to be. When the story opens, Paul is lying in a hospital bed unconscious, the victim of a drunk driver who carelessly ran Paul and his best friend Gabe off the road. Gabe was killed instantly, and Paul finds himself looking back and wondering if there was anything he could have done to change what happened. Paul has no difficult decision to make other than to accept what happened, because nothing he can do can alter the path he must take after the accident. He must come to terms with the his friend's death and the events that led up to it. He must choose to do this, rather than let the question of "what if" continue to torment him.

Paul can make the choice to put the past behind him and move on. Each of the characters in the collection finds an acceptable resolution to their problems, though readers know that they will have more problems in the future. Melissa will struggle being a young mother on her own, and Christina will have to come to terms with her abortion. Jason has a long way to go before he can graduate, and Paul will always have to deal with losing his best friend. But people can choose to fail or to succeed; that seems to be Reynolds' message. She succeeds in conveying the complexity of her characters' situations without making them seem hopeless.

The odds seem insurmountable for some of the characters, yet they do manage to surmount them. Reynolds takes these teenagers through the process of identifying their problem, analyzing their choices, and coming to terms with what they need to do to better their lives. For Jason, it is a matter of finding his niche. His niche is baseball. He has always excelled at it, but gave up any hope of playing baseball because he flunked out of Hamilton High. Fortunately for Jason, he has another chance. He is not handed that chance, but rather guided on how he can make it happen for himself.

Trinh, known by her English name Tammy to her friends at school, faces a dilemma that seems different from those of the other characters. She is struggling to come to terms with her split identity, trying to be American and speak English at school and trying to be Vietnamese and speak Vietnamese at home. The story appears to be about racism, but more adequately it is about the process of self-identity and self-acceptance that all teenagers experience. Trinh has the added confusion of trying to reconcile two cultures and find a place in both. Trinh's American friends have trouble understanding the cultural mores of Vietnamese families, and her mother and brother demand a different kind of loyalty from Trinh than her American friends can comprehend.

As the story progresses, readers understand more about the conflict Trinh feels and receive crucial information about her past. Trinh has long been troubled by a disturbing dream that creeps slowly into her consciousness and gradually explodes an awful truth she must come to accept and understand. Like the other characters in the story, Trinh's determination to accept this challenge leads her to a fuller understanding of human nature and of her true self.

The characters in *Beyond Dreams* are all likeable individuals who have compassion and integrity. They have faith in human nature and they respect others, but they must learn how to have faith in themselves. These characters truly wish to surmount their difficulties and better their lives, and though they remain stuck for a while, they manage to pull themselves up, change directions, and head down a more promising path. Reynolds' characters are on a journey, and they have come across some serious stumbling blocks. But this is typical of any journey to self-discovery. The travelers must learn to accept difficult decisions as challenges, and they must learn how to look out for themselves.

◆ LITERARY QUALITIES ◆

In writing *Beyond Dreams*, Reynolds is faced with the dual task of developing separate voices for each of her stories and advancing themes that unify her collection. She develops separate voices by varying her literary techniques and narrative styles and by alternating between male and female narrators. She relates each of the character's stories in first person, allowing readers insight into the characters' thought processes. The protagonists in each of these stories undergoes a transformation during the unraveling of their tales, and the first person narration helps readers understand the characters' changing thoughts and emotions. The transformation process is one unifying theme in the collection. So is the process of evaluation, as Reynolds analyzes the ways in which people face challenges and deal with turmoil. Because Reynolds succeeds at distinguishing each of her characters as unique individuals, readers witness the reasoning process from different viewpoints and see the ways that individual people move themselves out of crisis. The characters in all these stories are reflective, and they are believable because most readers can understand the confusing thought processes that plague individuals during difficult times.

In several of the stories, Reynolds uses foreshadowing to hint at what it will take for her protagonists to make the decisions they need to make in order to lead happier lives. Early in the story "Baby Help," Melissa relates the emotions she experienced one time when Cheyenne fell into the deep end of a swimming pool. Melissa, unable to swim, jumped in immediately to save Cheyenne. "Any time my baby needs help," she says, "I'll be there, even if it means risking my own life. That's how I know I love her more than myself." This remark allows readers to surmise that Melissa will leave Rudy, and that she will do so when she realizes that Cheyenne is in danger. Melissa puts up with Rudy's abuse time and time again, but just one incident of Rudy abusing Cheyenne spurs Melissa to action. As she said, she loves Cheyenne more than herself. Just as in the pool incident, she did not hesitate one moment to save her daughter from a dangerous situation and her maternal protectiveness kicked in when she witnessed Rudy slowly undermining Cheyenne's self-esteem. Once Melissa realized that Rudy's controlling behavior could potentially destroy her daughter's resolve, making the decision to move out came just as naturally and instantaneously as jumping into the pool.

While foreshadowing helps readers see the path these characters will take in the future, flashbacks help readers see the path they traveled in the past that led them to where they are now. In "What If," Paul remembers the years before the accident when he developed a close relationship with Gabe, and he flashes back to just before the accident when he had a few beers, failed to recognize that Gabe was not wearing a seat belt, and failed to protect his friend from the drunk driver who ended Gabe's life. Alternating between detailing the present and flashing back to the past helps readers understand how Paul must deal with this tragedy. He has to dissect his life in order to put it back together. Dwelling on the "what if's" after tragedy occurs is a natural part of the grieving process, and defining the tragic event in relation to what occurred before and after helps him put the incident in perspective. It also helps readers see how it is both possible and necessary to evaluate a crisis and work through it in order to get past the devastation and move toward self-actualization.

Paul's turmoil in "What If" conveys a powerful message about the horrors of drunk driving, and Christina's turmoil in deciding what to do about her unwanted pregnancy coveys a powerful message about

Book cover for *Beyond Dreams* by Marilyn Reynolds.

the consequences of unprotected sex. Reynolds has been criticized for both her raw language and her controversial subject matter. But she is a master at creating realistic dialogue that helps convey teenage confusion and helps explain their fears and desires. Think about the significance of the title *Beyond Dreams*. All these characters have dreams, but it is their determination and strength that helps them get beyond dreaming and create their own reality. Think about the title "What If." "What if I had made a different choice?" is the inevitable question of anyone who wishes he or she could change what happened to make things go wrong. It is also a necessary question, and those who analyze that question in their minds find it an affirmation of the availability of choices. Any one can change their lives if they want to badly enough, Reynolds tells her readers. She also tells them, as the title "Only If You Think So" implies, that they will remain in a losing situation only if think they are losers. But if they understand they have other options, they can in fact become winners.

One way Reynolds helps her characters move in the right direction is by allowing them to recognize their ability to reason and their faith in the mind's strength. Another way she helps them is by teaching them responsible behavior. She incorporates important lessons naturally into the dialogue, such as revealing to her characters tips for responsible parenting and information on social programs available to teens in trouble, and by encouraging discussions that lead high school students to identify and evaluate the effect of racist attitudes. Clearly, Reynolds wishes to teach her readers morals and help them learn how to be responsible, caring adults. Yet her writing never appears preachy. Her natural, flowing dialogue and her sensitivity toward her characters' emotions help teen readers relate the problems these fictional high schoolers have to problems of their own. Her ability to get into her characters' minds and expose both their strengths and their weaknesses helps anyone who reads her book evaluate their own strengths and weaknesses and gives them the positive message that though they cannot change past mistakes, they can change past behaviors.

◆ SOCIAL SENSITIVITY ◆

Reynolds' book teaches young adults about morality and responsibility. The characters she creates seem real and their emotions convincing because many teens understand the crises these characters face and they need to read about ways of dealing with them. Reynolds incorporates in-

formation on personal and social responsibility into the text without seeming preachy. She makes us realize the difficulties of teen pressures and the likelihood of falling into difficult traps. It is all too easy, Reynolds recognizes, to feel trapped by crisis situations and to start defining yourself as a loser.

Teenagers who find themselves in these situations often feel that they have to fight stereotypes. Reynolds helps her teenager readers (as well as Jason himself) understand that Jason is not a loser because he has been on a losing track for a while, and she helps them understand that Christina and Melissa are not unable to become responsible parents because they failed to act responsibly in the past. Fortunately, most of the characters in the book have adults in their lives who do not judge them but help them fight stereotypical images of teens in trouble. Reynolds underscores the ability of adults to help, but she also gives her protagonists good minds and the ability to find their own strength. She clearly conveys the message that no matter how difficult the crisis, people do have the ability to remold their lives, even though they cannot change the past. She lets her readers know that even people who feel trapped in hopeless situations can decide their own futures, create their own happiness, and break past patterns that have kept them from realizing their dreams.

Reynolds covers universal themes in her book that teenagers from all walks of life often understand intimately. Drinking and driving, racism, school failure, unwanted pregnancy, partner abuse, and the intrusion of an aging relative are all issues that teens understand can affect their own lives. These are issues familiar to teens, whether they attend urban, ethnically mixed high schools or not. All teenagers hear about the dangers of drunk driving and the importance of safe sex, but Reynolds' characters drive the seriousness of these issues home.

Reynolds is never condescending toward her characters or critical of their situations, but rather she is compassionate and she gives her characters credit for their ability to make good decisions.

Not only does Reynolds' book cover pertinent social issues but her stories speak to both males and females. She also presents a multicultural cast of characters. Several critics have recommended this book for "reluctant readers," for those who may respond to this kind of writing because they may recognize these characters from their own lives and understand the relevance of their situations. But despite its nearly universal appeal, Reynolds' books and other books that deal with sensitive subject matter have often been the subject of banning attempts. Some parents wish to protect their children from these situations and they believe books such as *Beyond Dreams* make controversial issues such as teenage sex and abortion seem all too common and even acceptable. But working in an alternative school, Reynolds knows the reality of these situations and recognizes the need to raise the consciousness of her readers about how they can deal with them. Her stories are both cautionary and thought provoking; they teach critical thinking, foster personal development, and teach responsible behavior. They give readers the message that there are consequences to their actions, but they still have control. She educates and empowers her readers by suppling information on social programs for pregnant teenagers and for abused wives and girlfriends. The author introduces other avenues troubled teenagers can explore to help themselves out of trouble and prevent their lives from spiraling downward.

◆ TOPICS FOR DISCUSSION ◆

1. What influences did Melissa have in her life that Irma did not have in hers

that may have led to Melissa's ability to leave Rudy?

2. Why was it so easy for Melissa to mistake Rudy's obsessiveness as love and so difficult for her to understand it as abuse?

3. What effect do you believe the "innocent" racial epithets had on Trinh's perception of herself?

4. What do you see as a turning point for Josh in "Uncle Tweetie"?

5. Do you think Christina made the right decision in choosing to have and abortion? Why or why not?

6. Do you think Reynolds' primary purpose of writing these stories was to teach moral lessons?

7. Several of Reynolds' books have been the subject of banning attempts. What, if anything, do you consider controversial about *Beyond Dreams*?

8. Which character do you find most appealing and why? Identify the way that character learned to cope with his or her problem.

9. Discuss the notion of a "cycle of abuse" as it appears in "Baby Help." Do any of the other characters in the collection have to break a cycle?

10. Reynolds uses foreshadowing in "Baby Help" to hint at what may happen to Melissa in the future. Talk about foreshadowing as a literary device and discuss how Reynolds uses it in the other stories in her collection.

◆ IDEAS FOR REPORTS AND PAPERS ◆

1. Write a persuasive paper in answer to one of the three questions Melissa must answer in her class on teen parenting. Research teen pregnancy in the United

States. What do you discover through your research?

2. Choose one of the stories and compare and contrast the adult influences on the teen character's life. Discuss which adults helped these characters and which ones hindered them.

3. Compare and contrast Melissa and Christina, who find themselves in similar situations. Discuss how motherhood has changed their attitudes about life and led them to take responsibility for themselves as well as their children. Do you know anyone your age who is a mother? Interview her and discuss your findings.

4. Choose one character and analyze the thought process that occurs in the character's mind as he or she comes to a resolution of the problem. When you are faced with a difficult choice or problem, how do you go about finding an answer? How do some of the people you know solve their problems?

5. Discuss the various ways Trinh feels torn between cultures. Are her thoughts unusual for children of immigrants? Research Vietnam and the Vietnam War. What can you say about the people, the culture, and the land?

6. Discuss the subtle ways people discriminate against others.

7. What is an epiphany? Do you think any of the characters in the collection have an epiphany? Who does and why?

8. Compare how America's culture treats it's elderly with, for example, cultures in Mexico or Japan. What are some of the differences and/or similarities you find in how the elderly are treated and cared for?

9. What are some of the statistics on teen alcoholism? Why do you think teens drink alcohol? What part do you think their parents, peers, and society play in the consumption of alcohol?

◆ RELATED TITLES ◆

Beyond Dreams is the Reynolds' "Hamilton High" series. Christina appears in an earlier book in the series titled *Too Soon for Jeff*, a story in which Reynolds sheds light on the teen pregnancy issue from the young father's point of view. Another book in the series, *Detour for Emmy*, also deals with teen pregnancy. As ninth grader Emmy's pregnancy turns her world upside down, she learns to accept the consequences of her actions and take responsibility for her future. Her book *Love Rules* features a young lesbian who comes out to her family and friends and must learn to deal with the intolerance she encounters after she does so. *Baby Help*, published after *Beyond Dreams*, continues Melissa's story and turns it into a novel. In the novel, Melissa has moved to a group home, but returns to Rudy only to face more problems and more dangers.

For those interested in Melissa's story, another book that deals with an abusive boyfriend is "Past Forgiving," by Gloria Miklowitz. The protagonist of this book is a fifteen-year-old girl named Alexandra who must learn the danger in remaining with Cliff, her boyfriend who is obsessive and jealous, then eventually, physically abusive.

Chris Crutcher is another young adult novelist who focuses on teenagers dealing with crisis situations. Crutcher's *Athletic Shorts* is a collection of six short stories that feature characters from his novels and that center around the theme of finding courage to get through trying situations. His *Chinese Handcuffs* deals with teenage parenting, sexual abuse, and suicide; and his other titles such as *Crazy Horse Electric Game* and *Stotan!* also introduce serious problems that challenge the main characters. Crutcher and

Reynolds have both been criticized for covering disturbing and controversial subject matter. But both of these authors succeed in raising the consciousness of young adults by allowing them to read about these situations and understand how to deal with them.

◆ FOR FURTHER REFERENCE ◆

Farber, Susan R. Review of *Beyond Dreams. School Library Journal* (September, 1995): 220.

Napp, Rosemary. Review of *Beyond Dreams. Book Report* (January–February, 1996): 49.

Reynolds, Marilyn. In *Something about the Author Autobiography Series*, vol. 23. Detroit: Gale, 1996. Reynolds provides an essay about her life and insight into her thoughts and works.

Triner, Jeanne. Review of *Beyond Dreams. Booklist* (November 15, 1995): 548.

Tamra Andrews

THE BLACK STALLION

Novel

1941

Author: Walter Farley

◆

Major Books for Young Adults

The Black Stallion, 1941
The Black Stallion Returns, 1945
Son of the Black Stallion, 1947
The Island Stallion, 1948
The Black Stallion and Satan, 1949
The Blood Bay Colt, 1950
The Island Stallion's Fury, 1951
The Black Stallion's Filly, 1952
The Black Stallion Revolts, 1953
The Black Stallion's Sulky Colt, 1954
The Island Stallion Races, 1955

The Black Stallion's Courage, 1956
The Black Stallion Mystery, 1957
The Black Stallion and Flame, 1960
Man O' War, 1962 (fictionalized
  biography)
The Black Stallion Challenged!, 1964
The Black Stallion's Ghost, 1969
The Black Stallion and the Girl, 1971
The Black Stallion Legend, 1983
The Young Black Stallion, 1989

◆ ABOUT THE AUTHOR ◆

Walter Farley built his career upon a love of horses that began in early childhood, when he played with a black horse toy. *The Black Stallion* reflects this love and several other aspects of Farley's life. Much like the novel's teenage hero Alec Ramsay, young Farley rode horseback near his home in Flushing, New York. He often visited the nearby Belmont racetrack, site of Alec's fictional workouts with the stallion. Farley spent as much time as he could with an uncle who trained horses for shows and races. Characters in *The Black Stallion* are surely patterned on people Farley met during these times. The awe inspired in Alec by the stallion recalls the boyhood reaction of Farley to the legendary racehorse Man O' War, whose stable he visited with his father on a summer trip to Kentucky.

As a boy, however, Farley never could own a horse or travel the way Alec did. Instead, Farley wrote *The Black Stallion*. Its subsequent success enabled him to realize the dreams of his boyhood. Farley published more than thirty books, almost all focused on horses. *The Black Stallion* was the first in a series of novels that continue to

Walter Farley

enjoy enormous success. Millions of books featuring the black horse and his counterpart, the island stallion Flame, have sold over the years in various editions and adaptations. There have been translations into more than twenty languages. *The Black Stallion* and *The Black Stallion Returns* were adapted into Francis Ford Coppola motion pictures, for which Farley served as consultant and promoter.

The Black Stallion had its beginnings in stories Farley wrote as a boy in Syracuse, New York, where he was born on June 26, 1915. His parents, Isabell Vermilyea Farley and Walter Farley, relocated the family to the New York City area when their son was in his teens. Farley loved horses, sports, and writing. He developed drafts of the novel during his student years at Erasmus Hall High School in Brooklyn, where he was on the track team. He continued to work on the novel as a student at Mercersburg Academy in Pennsylvania.

Farley worked briefly for an advertising agency. He attended Columbia University, where he completed his manuscript with a professor's guidance. Random House published *The Black Stallion* in 1941 to reader acclaim. Months later Farley entered the United States Army. He spent much of World War II as a reporter for the Army publication *Yank*. In 1945, the year Farley married Rosemary Lutz, *The Black Stallion Returns* was published. When Farley received his Army discharge in 1946, he embarked upon a full-time writing career. He began to develop the "Black Stallion" books into a series. He also created a new series about an island-dwelling, flame-colored stallion. The first book in *The Island Stallion* series was published in 1948.

The Farleys, who first settled on a Pennsylvania farm, later established a residence in Florida horse country with their four children. Farley traveled and owned horses. He hobnobbed frequently with the sports reporters, trainers, jockeys, and other racing professionals he liked to write about. Besides novels, he developed easy-to-read books. Farley was a strong promoter of children's reading programs. He and Rosemary Farley were instrumental in the development of the public library in Venice, Florida. Months before Farley's death on October 16, 1989, a Literary Landmark was established there. Farley proved by his life the validity of advice he often gave to young people. He blended talents and interests to forge a career, so that he always had the fun of writing about the horses he loved.

◆ OVERVIEW ◆

A teenager named Alec Ramsay befriends a wild stallion of exotic beauty in Farley's novel. From an Arabian seaport to a New York farm, Alec and the stallion—called

The Black Stallion

simply "the Black"—forge a relationship that causes other characters to marvel. Alec achieves growth and self-realization as he struggles to control a horse whose winning characteristics continue to enthrall readers.

◆ SETTING ◆

The exotic opening setting sustains theme and characterization in significant ways. Alec enters the novel in a situation that demonstrates his capacity for independence. He is a passenger on the steamer *Drake*, headed toward the Gulf of Aden and into the Red Sea. Alec is returning alone to New York after a stay with his Uncle Ralph in India. The black stallion first appears in a setting that conjures images from the *Arabian Nights*. Alec's steamer docks to take the stallion aboard at a small Arabian seaport. The locale establishes the aura of mystery that clings to the stallion and foreshadows the "strange understanding" that soon develops between him and Alec.

Ships at sea, foreign ports of call, and outdoor settings distinguish approximately the first third of the novel, as Alec and the stallion pursue their journey together to New York. The outdoor settings are critical in evoking a larger-than-life sense of the stallion. They reveal Alec's courage and determination when his ship is wrecked in a storm. Alec is plunged into the sea with the stallion, who swims for a considerable time. The two reach an uninhabited island, where again the stallion proves to be an unusual life-saving force. The island is especially important, since it is here that Alec solidifies his relationship with the Black.

Alec comes to terms with wild nature in both the stallion and the environment. The island is small, perhaps two miles around, and largely barren. The few existing trees and bushes are inadequate for shelter. The reader may wonder when a snake appears for the stallion to kill, since the island is

depicted as devoid of wildlife. The landscape includes an abandoned bird's nest and a hollow turtle shell. Sand, intense heat, and scattered patches of burned-out grass also characterize the island. Its features provide a perfect backdrop to Alec's demonstration of courageous self-reliance, since food and shelter must be found through ingenuity. Readers who are familiar with Daniel Defoe's fictional character Robinson Crusoe will recognize one of Alec's literary antecedents.

The natural setting of the island explores the issue of an interdependency between humans and animals. Even the wildest of animals is vulnerable and requires human help, and the stallion must respond to Alec's overtures in order to eat. A theme of value in education is highlighted here as well, since Alec is forced to recall what he learned in high school about the edible properties of a kind of seaweed called carragheen.

The island experience, which lasts for nineteen September days, lends a timeless and somewhat mythic quality to the narrative. Otherwise, the novel evokes a more leisurely time in history. Alec reaches the island after weeks at sea. The modern reader, accustomed to air travel, will note that Alec spent four weeks by ship to reach India in the first place. Back in the United States, trains are the foremost means of travel. Alec uses a train toward the novel's close in order to reach Chicago.

Once Alec arrives home, the action is set primarily in or near the New York City suburb of Flushing. The setting represents a shift toward greater realism, except that Alec's extraordinary relationship with the wild stallion remains. Flushing in the year 1941 is a town with open fields rather than a hectic part of a vast metropolitan area. The Ramsay family dwelling is a typical middle-class house, complete with kitchen, bedrooms, and living room with shaded lights and comfortable furniture. Alec's room includes "familiar high school banners hanging on the walls."

Two blocks from the Ramsay house is the run-down Halleran estate, and it is here that Alec and the stallion spend most of their time. The Halleran house is used to accommodate tourists, but behind it and down a gravel road are a barn and field. In these facilities Alec stables and trains the stallion. Additional workouts occur during the night at nearby Belmont track, the original facility rather than the rebuilt one that stands today.

◆ THEMES AND CHARACTERS ◆

Red-haired and freckle-faced Alexander Ramsay, known as Alec, begins his relationship with the black stallion on board the ship. Alec pities the stallion and entices the animal with handfuls of sugar, a kind act that no one else attempts. The stallion has proved to be dangerous, likely to kill, and determined to batter down the walls of his stall. Alec persists because he dearly loves horses, and the Black is unlike any he has seen. The novel's thematic center is the relationship that forms between the caring, determined teenager and the unruly stallion. Layered into this relationship are themes of courageous self-reliance and maturation, beauty, nature, education, cooperation, and—on the other hand—competition.

The theme of maturation develops through Alec. Although he displays independent qualities when the novel begins, he becomes stronger as events unfold. Alec is largely defined by his ability to relate to the Black, who frees and exalts him. He feels "different" atop the Black, "like being in a world all his own." Companioned and empowered by the Black, who at the same time needs him, Alec develops unusual self-reliance on the island. He is brave, hopeful, and patient in the face of adversity. He wastes little time in regret or philosophical pondering. Instead, he concentrates on making nature supply shelter and food. When Mrs. Ramsay greets her son in New York, she marvels at the new, "calm, self-reliant look" in his eyes.

Themes related to nature and beauty are developed through the Black. The stallion behaves in many ways that are normal for a horse, but he possesses incredible powers. When he runs at Belmont, an observer exclaims that he "made the track record look like it was made by a hobbyhorse!" The Black reflects the duality of nature, beautiful and helpful and yet dangerous. He has "a wonderful physical perfection" with a "savage, ruthless spirit" to match. Because the Black represents the wild, free, and unconquerable side of nature, he forces Alec to continue to grow. "I'll control him— one of these days."

Alec's maturation is also fostered by Henry Bailey, the only other human character of any prominence. Henry, a retired jockey who facilitates Alec's desire to keep and train the Black, is more than just a surrogate father. He is a confidant who validates Alec's maturation by suggesting that they "work together just like partners." While Alec's father encourages responsibility by having his son do chores to pay for the stallion's upkeep, ultimately it is Henry who passes along the torch of manhood. Before the match race that dominates the novel's concluding scenes, Henry tells Alec: "Well, kid, you're on your own now." Henry speaks as a mentor, and in this capacity he reflects the theme of education.

The value of school is a given in the novel. Its importance to life is shown when Alec can identify, prepare, and eat island carragheen as a result of a remembered biology class experiment. At Flushing, Alec displays concern about his grades and is depicted in school. Before the match race, Mr. Ramsay has concerns for his son's fulfillment of school requirements. Alec agrees to race "under one condition—that I stay until I finish my exams."

Henry's helpfulness and Mr. Ramsay's acquiescence exemplify the theme of cooperation that permeates the novel. Conflict is not centered in problems among characters, who are largely stereotypical, but in Alec's struggles to overcome raw natural forces and to control the Black. Mr. and Mrs. Ramsay—both minor figures—offer no real objection to Alec's sessions with Henry and the Black. They seem strangely willing to let Alec keep and ride a stallion described as "untamable." The novel's other characters, mostly very minor, generally love horses as Mr. Ramsay does, marvel at the Black, and smooth Alec's way.

The attitude of huckster Tony, owner of the Black's stablemate Napoleon, is typical of helpful minor characters. Tony shows no animosity toward Henry and Alec when he is told that old Napoleon, who must work daily to pull a cart of produce, has spent his nighttime hours going along to the Belmont track. When asked whether Napoleon might accompany the Black to the Chicago match race, Tony seeks no remuneration and considers it a vacation for his horse.

The spirit of cooperation is bound up in a theme it seems to contradict, that of one-upmanship or competition. From the beginning of their relationship, the dangerous Black so dazzles everyone that he gives Alec a competitive edge. Minor characters Whiff Sample and Bill Lee, Alec's high-school pals, reflect the theme by admitting that they fear the Black. Experienced match-race jockeys appear happy to confirm Alec's superiority. The same attitude characterizes Mr. Volence and Mr. Hurst, owners of the match-race horses Sun Raider and Cyclone. While Alec basks in his winning powers astride the Black, Henry voices the spirit that defines other characters: "We all should be mighty proud of him."

◆ LITERARY QUALITIES ◆

Farley employs a variety of techniques that keep the reader's attention focused upon the black stallion and Alec's relationship to him. Among these are repetition, the use of superlatives in narrative and dialogue, the incorporation of symbolic and mythic elements, and recurring motifs of color and contrast. The narrative is structured so that exotic features are balanced by settings and details that are commonplace. The novel features dramatic adventures. Alec experiences a shipwreck, a swim for dear life, an inhospitable island, a series of rides astride an unruly stallion.

The stallion enters the novel in the midst of action made more effective by third-person description from Alec's point of view. Alec notices a throng of milling Arabs and hears a whistle—"shrill, loud, clear, unlike anything he had ever heard before." He sees a "mighty black horse" engaged in rearing, with forelegs striking out at the air. The horse continues to scream and rear, bolt and plunge. Once in his shipboard stall, the horse crashes his legs into wood and sends it flying. Through a similar action scene when quarantined in New York, Farley reinforces the idea of the stallion's powerful character.

The scene of the storm that wrecks Alec's ship is filled with drama and suspense. It begins with the ship's nighttime lurch that throws Alec to the floor. Farley employs the senses—sight, hearing, touch—in this scene as he does elsewhere in order to build excitement. Thus Alec sees lightning flashes, hears shouts, feels his face hot and sticky with blood after a sharp crack that shakes the ship and again throws him, stunned, to the floor. The subsequent battle with waves sets Alec on the island with the Black in a situation of dramatic contrast. Alec feels the stillness—"no birds, no animals, no sounds."

The effect is to build the mystique that surrounds and differentiates the castaways.

Superlatives help to sustain the mystique. Besides introducing the stallion in an unusual locale accompanied by dramatic action, Farley initially depicts him as "a giant of a horse" with a head that is "beautiful, savage, splendid." The stallion is also depicted as "wild," "ruthless," "powerful." Farley foreshadows the mystery that surrounds the origin of the stallion by depicting him as "too big to be pure Arabian." The use of Alec's point of view enhances the description, which is repetitive: "a wild stallion—unbroken, such as he had read and dreamed about!" Repetitious use of such vivid descriptive words and synonyms for them evoke wonder and sustain the perception throughout the narrative.

Dialogue that reflects reactions of characters is a particularly effective method by which Farley reinforces the reader's perceptions of the stallion. "He's too wild," a sea captain says. "He's a beauty," a police officer says. Alec's mother comments fearfully that the Black is "dangerous." The reaction of Alec's friend Whiff is typical: "Boy, he's the biggest horse I ever did see and what a mean look!" The unusual quality of Alec's relationship with the Black is reinforced by dialogue. A ship's captain considers "almost uncanny" the way Alec gets along with "a wild beast like that, a killer." The sailor Pat confirms that the relationship is "one of the strangest things" he has ever seen. Henry remarks that the Black and Alec play the "strangest" game.

Characters also refer to the Black as a "devil." The Black is in many ways a creature of symbolism and myth. In an early chapter, the stallion appears "as if by magic" to crew members of the rescue ship after they hear "an inhuman scream." It is significant also that the stallion's presence seems to provoke cooperation from anyone who might thwart Alec's purpose. Alec's watery pursuit at the end of the stallion's rope is the stuff of myth and legend. It evokes the sea chase after a symbolic white whale in Herman Melville's *Moby Dick*.

In addition, Alec is preoccupied with a stallion he never really names, except to call it the Black. The color black, which reflects no light, is another way in which Farley sustains an aura of mystery and symbolism. Farley employs other colors as well. Stablemate Napoleon is gray, a neutral color. The horse has a "quieting effect" on the Black. The match-race horses, red Cyclone and chestnut-gold Sun Raider, are bright in contrast to the Black. Farley employs the starkly contrasting colors of black and white in an important recurring motif that emphasizes the stallion and related themes. Alec first sees the horse in terms of black and white. The Black's eyes are covered with a white scarf. On the island, Alec sees the stallion standing beside a boulder "as if an artist had painted the Black on white stone."

Contrasts of black and white particularly integrate with the thematic concept of nature's dark side opposed to youthful innocence that must change and grow. Alec often wears white that stands out against the Black's body. He does so in a scene at Belmont, when he experiences a loss of control over his mount who runs "wild and free." Alec clings to the Black, white shirt "standing out vividly" again the black body. In another scene set two nights later, Alec retains control wearing a black sweater. Guided by the white fence, Alec lets the stallion run until they become a "black blur." The Black slows when he sees the quieting, "gray form" of Napoleon.

Farley employs contrast in settings as well, which include exotic and mundane locales. He balances the Black's extraordinary characteristics by portraying him with unremarkable elements of tack. Details related to racing lend verisimilitude, such as

Henry's memorabilia of silver cups, newspaper clippings, jockey's clothes and cap. Slower-paced episodes balance dramatic scenes, although Farley never loses sight of elements that generate mystery and excitement. He threads a suspenseful wait for a letter about the Black into chapters when Alec's life "became as regular as a time clock."

Farley builds excitement into the concluding match race in several ways. He begins before it occurs by limiting knowledge of the Black's involvement to a few characters. The uninitiated repeatedly wonder who the "mystery horse" is. Farley also depicts preparations in terms that stress Alec's trouble controlling the Black. In a rare shift away from Alec's viewpoint, Farley enhances the thrill of the actual race by employing the perceptions of a network sports commentator. The device permits a recapitulation of the Black's dangerous qualities. "That boy sure can stick on a horse. What a struggle is going on out there, folks!" Farley cleverly condenses the governor's post-race speech. He depicts Alec catching sight of his parents with Henry and forgetting to listen. "The governor kept talking. . . . Finally the governor was through."

Book illustration by Keith Ward for *The Black Stallion* by Walter Farley.

◆ SOCIAL SENSITIVITY ◆

Farley's sensitivity to the needs of young readers undoubtedly accounts for much of *The Black Stallion*'s timeless appeal. There is little opportunity for boredom in a novel that unfolds at a fast pace and builds to a thrilling conclusion. The subject matter involves the typical wish for a pet, and Farley's hero Alec succeeds admirably as the owner of a winning horse. Alec is highly attractive as well because he gains the approval and respect young people need so much from peers, parents, and adults in the world at large. While the 1941 novel incorporates a few social attitudes that have dropped from favor, Farley's positive overall presentation diminishes their significance.

Farley displays particular sensitivity to the emotional process of maturation he depicts. Within the context of a unique relationship with an animal, Farley constructs a supportive atmosphere in which Alec can "try his wings" and build self-confidence. No authority figure blocks Alec's way as he proceeds with the Black, a symbol of adult responsibility and freedom. His parents especially acquiesce in letting Alec have a horse known to be untamable. In this way, Farley deftly handles the desire often seen in teenagers not only to be free but to rebel by courting danger in some form. In spite of early scenes that confirm the stallion's potential to kill, ultimately Farley confines the danger within the parameters of a competitive sport.

Farley delicately treats the subject of teenage rebellion by involving his protagonist in a mild conspiracy. Alec sneaks out while his parents are asleep to go to the racetrack with his friend Henry, a mature and supportive adult who is well able to serve as a guardian. Farley gently depicts teenage independence by having Alec hobnob with a number of respectful and approving adults, such as sportswriters and racetrack professionals. Alec is rarely shown in the company of his peers, since becoming an adult is what matters in this novel. However, Farley makes it clear that Alec has school friends who respect him.

The educational process is distasteful to many young people, and Farley seldom shows Alec at school. His approach is nonetheless very positive. Alec is understood to be a concerned student. His sole act of defiance at school is to continue sprinting down the hall when a person in authority calls out for him to stop. Henry considers school to be important in Alec's life. "We'll show your folks that you can raise a champion race horse and get good marks at the same time!" The relationship between Alec and Henry is important for the positive image it conveys of the respect and harmonious exchange of information between generations. Alec gains immeasurably from Henry's teaching and friendship, and Henry recaptures lost youth as his pupil fills his shoes as a winning jockey.

Henry comments, however, on having raised two girls who presumably could not follow in his footsteps. The 1941 novel is notable for a dearth of female characters. Mrs. Ramsay, if viewed in the context of modern standards for gender equality, may appear as a subservient as well as minor figure. She is stereotypically depicted as a homemaker who provides griddle cakes and sausages. "I'll have to tell your father," she says, if Alec neglects his studies. Mrs. Ramsay's departure alone to visit her sister in Chicago seems to reflect a time of separate and complementary spheres for men and women.

Farley's portrayal of family life emanates from a time when most parents stayed together. Teenagers like Alec worked for allowances at home rather than paychecks from outside employers. The portrayal is nonetheless very positive. *The Black Stallion* is a sensitive novel that stresses timeless human values. Alec has universal appeal as a character who persists to realize his dream. He surprises family members, friends, and the country at large by succeeding at something that—as Henry tells Mr. Ramsay— "no one else in the world can do!"

◆ TOPICS FOR DISCUSSION ◆

1. Characterize Alec before and after he meets the Black. Does he change in any way?

2. Are the Ramsays a typical American family? Give details to support your answer.

3. Tony comes down the street at the precise moment that Napoleon is needed to calm the Black. Mrs. Ramsay is in Chicago at the time of the match race. What other coincidences can you think of? Are there too many to be credible?

4. Almost every exchange of dialogue in the novel relates to the black stallion. Is this technique overdone? Explain your answer.

5. What are the Black's best qualities? What are the worst? Does the Black seem to behave realistically?

6. Does it seem reasonable for Mr. and Mrs. Ramsay to let Alec keep a dangerous horse and ride bareback until spring?

7. Which character is more important, Alec or the Black? Or is each of equal interest to the reader?

8. The novel gained so much popularity in the 1940s that Black Stallion Clubs began to be formed. Why is a dangerous horse an appealing character?

9. Excluding Henry, rank in order of importance to Alec four supporting human characters in the novel. Why do you rank them this way?

10. For the first third of the novel Alec appears in unusual situations and locales. Is the remainder of the novel less exciting because it is set primarily in New York and Chicago?

11. Compare Henry to Mr. Ramsay. How important is Henry? Is he interesting and likable apart from his role as Alec's helper?

12. Alec surmounts difficult problems to bring the Black to New York and race him. Would you characterize Alec as a lucky fellow, or someone whose efforts bring him success?

13. Although Pat and the captain of Alec's rescue ship are sailors and Joe Russo and Jim Neville are sportswriters, do these two sets of characters differ in any other significant way? If so, how?

◆ IDEAS FOR REPORTS AND PAPERS ◆

1. Read at least part of Daniel Defoe's *Robinson Crusoe* and two or three short commentaries on that long novel. Compare Defoe's treatment of the incidents with Farley's *The Black Stallion*. Are the two novels more alike or different?

2. What characteristics do Arabian horses possess? Find information about three or four other kinds of horses, and explain how they differ from Arabians.

3. Read Farley's nonfiction book *How to Stay Out of Trouble with Your Horse: Some Basic Safety Rules to Help You Enjoy Riding* (published in 1981) and investigate several other instructional sources on the subject. How accurate is *The Black Stallion* in light of the facts about riding a horse for pleasure?

4. What realistic elements does the novel include? What unrealistic ones appear? Is *The Black Stallion* more a work of realism or fantasy?

5. Compare *The Black Stallion* with Anna Sewell's *Black Beauty* (1877) or Marguerite Henry's *King of the Wind* (1948) or *Born to Trot* (1950). Comment in particular on realism, plot, and general interest of the novels.

6. How are racehorses bred and trained? Does the Black's life significantly resemble the actual experience of a racer? Consult Farley's biography *Man O' War,* if you wish.

7. What aspects of the novel would you change if you gave it a modern setting? Include details about the region near the Gulf of Aden and ships as well as American life.

8. Farley largely omitted female characters from this novel, but there is an important one in *The Black Stallion and the Girl.* Read the novel and assess its accuracy in light of the role women currently have in professional racing. Do they work as jockeys? If so, have any gained as much prominence as male jockeys?

9. Read John Steinbeck's novella *The Red Pony* (1945). Is it easier to identify with Steinbeck's major character Jody or with

Farley's Alec? Which major character grows up more in the course of his story?

10. View *The Black Stallion* motion picture of 1979 and compare it to the novel. How are they alike and different? Which has greater appeal?

◆ RELATED TITLES/ADAPTATIONS ◆

The Black Stallion launched a series of novels featuring Alec Ramsay and his adventures with horses, primarily the Black and his offspring. Alec grows to adulthood in the course of the series and gains in depth as well, according to some critics, as a result of Farley's maturation as a writer. Notable novels include *The Black Stallion Returns* (1945) and *Son of the Black Stallion* (1947). These novels center upon Alec's loss of the Black to the Arab sheikh who owns him. The sheikh provides the Black's first colt as compensation. The Arab's daughter returns the Black to Alec in *The Black Stallion and Satan* (1949). Alec races the colt in this novel and finds out if the Black can outrun him. Another representative novel is *The Black Stallion's Filly* (1952), which concerns the efforts of Henry Bailey and Alec to train and race the Black's daughter. *The Black Stallion Mystery* (1957) depicts a search in Arabia for the Black's sire.

In *The Black Stallion and the Girl* (1971), Alec hires a female horse trainer and insists upon keeping her in spite of opposition from those around him. The novel is significant as a memorial to Farley's daughter Pamela, who died at the age of twenty in an auto accident. *The Young Black Stallion* (1989), prequel to *The Black Stallion*, traces the horse's life as a colt in Arabia. It is significant as Farley's last novel, written with the help of his son Steve Farley.

Anyone who enjoys *The Black Stallion* will be interested in the flame-colored horse introduced in Farley's *The Island Stallion*

(1948). The series protagonist, Steve Duncan, discovers Flame in a secret valley when he accompanies a friend to a Caribbean island. *The Black Stallion and Flame* (1960) brings the horses of both series together on a desert island after the Black and Alec undergo a plane crash in the Caribbean. In *The Black Stallion Challenged!* (1964), Steve Duncan proposes a race between the Black and Flame. Although not part of the series, *Man O' War* (1962) is of interest as a fictionalized account of the legendary American racehorse Farley saw as a boy. *The Horse-Tamer* (1958), though not about Alec Ramsay, concerns an adult protagonist's efforts to prevent the mistreatment of horses.

Steve Farley, who helped his father complete *The Young Black Stallion*, is the author of his own contemporary novels about horses. Besides carrying on the tradition in *The Black Stallion's Shadow* (1996) and *The Black Stallion's Steeplechaser* (1997), Steve Farley is the creator of a series of novels featuring Danielle Conner and her adventures with horses. In the first novel, *The Young Black Stallion: The Promise* (1998), Alec Ramsay reappears as a jockey who plans to buy the Conner property.

There are many adaptations of *The Black Stallion*. Robert Genin developed *The Black Stallion: A Comic Book Album* (1983) illustrated by Michel Faure. *Big Black Horse* (1953, 1955) is one of several easy-to-read adaptations for children. Other titles include *The Black Stallion: An Easy-to-Read Adaptation* (1986) and *The Black Stallion Beginner Book* (1987), a primer that adapts only the shipwreck and rescue scenes from the original novel. *The Black Stallion Picture Book* (1979) is illustrated with photographs from the Francis Ford Coppola motion picture released by United Artists.

The motion picture of *The Black Stallion*, which starred Kelly Reno as Alec and Mickey Rooney as Henry, appeared in 1979 to critical acclaim. Carroll Ballard directed; and

Melissa Mathison, Jeanne Rosenberg, and David D. Witliff wrote the screenplay. The film deviates from the novel most notably in its depiction of Alec as an eleven-year-old boy instead of a teenager. An MGM/UA videotape is available. An MGM Home Entertainment DVD, released in 1997, is available with English, French, or Spanish audio tracks or with subtitles in those languages. Seabrook Productions and Alliance International produced a television series based on *The Black Stallion* for The Family Channel. Titled *The Adventures of the Black Stallion*, the thirty-minute episodes featured Richard Cox as Alec and Mickey Rooney as Henry in plots of adventure and horse races.

◆ FOR FURTHER REFERENCE ◆

"Farley, Walter." In *Contemporary Authors New Revision Series*, vol. 84. Detroit: Gale Group, 2000. Favorable overview of critical commentary with personal information and lists of books and awards.

"Farley, Walter." In *Something about the Author*, vol. 43. Detroit: Gale Research, 1986. Biographical overview including significant quotations by Farley about his life, work, and purpose.

◆ RELATED WEBSITES ◆

The Black Stallion http://www.theblackstallion. com. February 2, 2001. Valuable resource for Farley's biography and *The Black Stallion* book, series, and motion picture.

Walter Farley Literary Landmark http:// www.venice-florida.com/community/ education/farley.htm. February 2, 2001. An overview of Farley's life and importance to the Venice Public Library and to literature for young people.

Marilyn A. Perlberg

A BOY AND HIS DOG

Novella

1969

Author: Harlan Ellison

◆

Major Books for Young Adults

Web of the City, 1958
Spider Kiss, 1961
Gentleman Junkie, 1961
Ellison Wonderland, 1962
I Have No Mouth & I Must Scream, 1967
From the Land of Fear, 1967

Love Ain't Nothing But Sex
  Misspelled, 1968
A Boy and His Dog, 1969
All the Lies That Are My Life, 1980
Vic and Blood: Chronicles of a Boy and
  His Dog, 1989

◆ ABOUT THE AUTHOR ◆

The author was born Harlan Jay Ellison on May 27, 1934, in Cleveland, Ohio. In grade school when his father died, Harlan endured a childhood in poverty, raised by his widowed mother. Young Harlan spent a restless boyhood on the road working at odd jobs. When he became old enough to earn a living, Ellison supported his mother. Ellison has written warmly of his Jewish parents, particularly his mother, and has quoted her Yiddish expressions, which have had a colorful influence upon his writing all his life.

As a young man, Ellison went to Ohio State University from 1953 to 1954, before moving to New York City to work as a writer. To gain background for his first major novel, dealing with juvenile delinquency, he took an assumed name and ran with a youth gang in Brooklyn's dangerous Red Hook sections for ten weeks. In 1957, he was drafted into the United States Army, training at Ranger School at Fort Benning, Georgia, and serving two years at Fort Knox, Kentucky, and Camp Brekenridge, Indiana. Since leaving the military, he has been a writer in many genres.

Ellison's writing career has spanned nearly fifty years. His works have been translated into twenty-six languages and have sold millions of copies. He has drawn attention to the art of writing by performing the remarkable feat of writing stories in the windows of bookstores (in Paris, London, New York, Boston, Los Angeles, San Francisco, New Orleans and elsewhere),

Harlan Ellison

International Horror Critics at the 1995 World Horror Convention.

Perhaps Ellison's summarizes his own life best in the afterword to his book *The Essential Ellison*, "For a brief time I was here; and for a brief time I mattered."

◆ OVERVIEW ◆

Vic and Blood, a boy and his dog, look out for each other in a hard, cruel world some years after a nuclear war. Through a telepathic link, they communicate at least as effectively as through speech. They work to meet each other's basic needs for survival: food, companionship, and the relief of despair or boredom.

Blood's efforts to educate Vic are not as successful as he would like; Vic would far rather that Blood used his keen sense of smell to find him a girl. During this search they enter a small, rough community of desperate people who prey on each other. Blood does locate a girl, and together Vic and Blood track her out of a jury-rigged cinema. The girl, Quilla June, is seemingly not afraid of Vic or his rough ideas of sex—though she ought to be. He tracked her down with the intent of raping her several times before either murdering her or abandoning her to die. His plan is interrupted by an attack, and Vic and Blood have to fight several desperate toughs for their lives.

After they escape, Quilla June reveals where she has come from: an underground community in a nuclear fallout bunker, as Blood and Vic had guessed. Quilla June insists that Vic come alone with her inside the bunkered community, leaving Blood outside. The people of the hidden community welcome Vic, but also enslave him as a sperm donor for their young women, as they have no healthy young men. This entrapment was their intent when Quilla June was sent out.

stories that have gone on to win major awards and literary prizes. He has covered and written about civil rights marches, riots, antiwar demonstrations, and other scenes of civil unrest. His two books of essays on television, *The Glass Teat* and *The Other Glass Teat*, have sold millions of copies and have been used in media classes in more than 200 American universities.

He has won more awards than any other living writer for his over seventy-five books, 1700 stories, essays, articles and newspaper columns, two dozen teleplays, and one dozen motion pictures. He has won the Hugo, the Nebula, the Bram Stoker Award, the Edgar Allan Poe Award, the Georges Melies fantasy film award, the World Fantasy Award for Life Achievement, the Writers' Guild of America Award, as well as the Silver Pen for Journalism by PEN, the international writers' union. He was presented with the first Living Legend Award by the

However, the leaders of the community did not expect Quilla June to revolt when she is not made part of the ruling committee. She kills her parents and others while helping Vic escape from bondage and leave the underground community.

At the hidden entrance, Vic finds that Blood is still waiting for him, though it has been days. Blood is weak from starvation.

Vic cannot keep alive both this girl, who is ignorant of the outside world, and the dog who has saved his life many times. He knows which of them will be a faithful companion for heart and mind as well as helping him survive. He has to choose which he must kill to feed the other.

"A boy loves his dog."

◆ SETTING ◆

The story is set in Arizona, in an unspecified post-apocalyptic time, after what appears to have been a thoroughly devastating nuclear war and environmental disaster. A reasonable guess at the calendar date could be around the turn of the twenty-first century, more than ten years but less than thirty years after the disaster. Vic and Blood wander through a landscape that is desolate, where little approximating food grows. The few people they meet are all trying desperately to survive on scavenged canned goods, and are willing to fight and kill for less than a meal.

It would be hard for either the dog or boy to survive for very long alone in the small town they enter. Far from being a helpful community, the people are preying on each other. Vic and Blood are no better: when they find a woman with her throat cut by rapists and thieves, Vic is upset that they have killed her already. She could have been raped a few more times. Hers is not an uncommon fate, and Vic is not unusual for a young rover.

The community where Quilla June lives seems much better at first glance. In this town, the genteel culture of the American Midwest has been re-created. Security is better in the underground bunker, and the people seem to be leading more civilized, cooperative lives. It is not apparent at first that Vic has been manipulated into entering the bunker, and for what reasons. Though this community may seem utopian in contrast to the outside world, it is no ideal place for Vic.

◆ THEMES AND CHARACTERS ◆

Harlan Ellison's personal beliefs about the ethical and moral behavior of humans in their various interactions have been made very clear in *A Boy and His Dog*, and time and again in the themes of his fiction, and overtly in his nonfiction writing. Ellison outlines the themes he writes about in this story, in a quote from *The Harlan Ellison Hornbook*: "My philosophy of life is that the meek shall inherit nothing but debasement, frustration and ignoble deaths." Ellison goes on to say

> that there is security in personal strength; that you CAN fight City Hall and WIN; that any action is better than no action, even if it's the wrong action; that you never reach glory or self-fulfillment unless you're willing to risk everything, dare anything, put yourself dead on the line every time; and that once one becomes strong or rich or potent or powerful it is the responsibility of the strong to help the weak BECOME strong.

The author has made his personal beliefs the themes of this short novel. Through the experiences of Vic, the reader is shown that meek people do suffer and die, that Vic does find some security in his personal strength and his struggles against attacks in the communities he enters, that Vic is willing to take great risks to stay close to Quilla

June, and finally that Vic decides to help his weak friend Blood survive, though he has no such compassion for Quilla June.

Though Vic is barely eighteen years old, it is clear when the story begins that he has been on his own for years. It is also clear that he could not have survived this long without the dog Blood. Not only are they an effective team for finding food and water and other essentials of life, but they converse together and give each other their attention and loyalty.

The dog is a far more complex and interesting character than the boy. Blood is better educated, from his training and experience and telepathic links with other men in the past, though it is not hard to be better educated than Vic, who is in many respects a feral child. As a medium-sized dog, Blood is tough and strong, a good partner for a skinny young man. With Blood's guidance, Vic is capable and knowledgeable in the hunting and scavenging skills needed to survive in this dangerous environment.

The reader might ask why Blood needs a human companion at all . . . but the boy finds them food, tends their hurts, can fire a gun, and can fight to defend his partner in the dangerous world that post-apocalyptic Arizona has become. But even more than that, Vic is someone to talk with and teach. Blood needs that, and he needs a human for him to be loyal to above all else. In that, he is clearly still a dog, for all his memory and conversation and telepathy. He is not a wolf, which hunts its own food and resists domestication by humans.

Even with an experienced dog as his guide, Vic makes choices that are less than wise. His idea of long-term plans is raping a girl more than once before leaving her for dead. It is apparent that Vic does not have sophisticated skills for human interaction. Quilla June has come looking for someone exactly like him, and even as young and

ignorant as she is, she can manipulate him sufficiently for her community's plans.

Vic is not much troubled by the notion of finding a girl in a rough wreckage of a town, where she has no right to be; Vic merely assumes that she has snuck out of a safer bolthole to risk a little danger. That she is bait for a trap to entice him into her sheltered community does not even occur to him. Even when Vic learns of the reason Quilla June was sent out as bait for a young, healthy man, he is still not alarmed at first.

In fact, he rather liked the idea of being kept as a stud for the young women of this sheltered community—if allowed to couple with them as he expects. Being a sperm donor has considerably less appeal, particularly when his donations are taken by force. And once several of the young women become pregnant, Vic's life expectancy would be zero, as he would no longer be needed. Once again, Vic has found a human community where people are surviving at each other's expense.

The development of the character of Quilla June takes two unexpected turns. Far from being merely a stupid innocent who is risking the dangers of the outside world for excitement, Quilla June is revealed as a conspirator sent out to entice a virile and healthy young man into her secure community, using her body as bait. She is even more resolved to bring Vic in after he survives the fight, during which he proved his strength and dexterity and intelligence, rather than merely settling for returning with a possible new pregnancy.

But when she does not profit as much as she wished from her daring, Quilla June will no longer consent to be manipulated by the ruling committee of her community or her parents. She glories in the slaughter of her own parents and is willing to kill others as she rescues Vic from bondage. She has chosen a partner of proven superior survival abilities, and wants to go with Vic to form a team of two in the cruel surface world.

What she does not understand is that there is no place in that devastation for a man and a woman to live together in peace, or even to exploit each other for mutual benefit for more than a few days (as would be far more likely, for Vic and Quilla June). There are few women surviving the roving gangs and solos, and no safe places but the rare underground bunkers like the one she and Vic have escaped. Dogs like Blood can track a woman by her scent, no matter how well she may disguise herself or a companion might defend her. A solo rover like Vic would probably not be able to scavenge enough resources for the two of them, and would certainly not be able to defend her for long against the inevitable series of attacks from other desperate men, alone or in gangs.

Compassion and true love triumph as the story ends. But it is Vic's compassion for his true friend Blood, not the conventional love of woman, which triumphs.

◆ LITERARY QUALITIES ◆

There are clearly some autobiographical elements in Vic, who is the emotional offspring of the young, frustrated Harlan Ellison. The author manages to write the story from the viewpoint of an ignorant young man, one who would be a sociopath and very likely a convicted criminal in an ordinary real-world community. It is probable that Ellison drew on his experience as a young man running with a teen gang in Brooklyn, when creating the character of Vic.

Somehow Ellison shows readers that Vic has committed horrifying crimes and intends to do so in future, while simultaneously making it clear that Vic is the product of his environment and almost completely ignorant about other possible ways to

behave—*without excusing his crimes*. Vic knows he is not a "nice" person. He does not seem to know how anyone can care for anyone else. It would seem that what the boy needs most of all is to learn about love and interdependence; and when he realizes what he knows, Vic is able to affirm that love and interdependence.

That he does so by choosing his faithful dog, Blood, over the conniving Quilla June is the stroke of genius that earned *A Boy and his Dog* the Nebula Award from the Science Fiction Writers of America.

Edgar Rice Burroughs would have written in a fortuitous lizard-beast for his hero to kill, to feed the loyal dog and the chastened girl. Theodore Sturgeon would have written of Vic's vigil over the dying dog, while the girl leaves and runs into other rovers, who rape and kill her (as Vic had intended to do when they met). Only Ellison could make this ending more honest and natural; it is thoroughly horrifying for the reader.

This story is not an easy, effortless read. It can be an upsetting or emotional experience for the reader. Ellison intends his writing to be a commentary on life, and to encourage introspection as well as action among his readers. For this story and others, and for his nonfiction writing, he has faced hecklers, raving phone calls, obnoxious letters, and death threats.

◆ SOCIAL SENSITIVITY ◆

In Ellison's writing, and especially in this story, characters who harm or exploit others are carefully written so that it is clear that these characters are not good people, nor are they happy or admirable or worthy of emulation. The reader may come to understand what it feels like to be that person, but is not expected to want to be that person.

Characters in *A Boy and His Dog* can and do fight to defend themselves or their associates, and this is portrayed as necessary but to be avoided when possible. The risk of death or injury is very high, when all parties are desperate for survival; and there is little or no medical treatment for injuries.

It is very apparent that the author intends for the reader to see the difference between the violence that Vic commits to defend himself and Blood (and Quilla June, whom he regards as an exploitable short-term resource rather than a companion) and the unnecessarily malicious rape, theft, and murder that goes on among the surface-dwelling people, Vic included.

The author also makes a clear depiction of the subterranean town, where a thin veneer of genteel behavior conceals a hypocritically savage exploitation. Vic is not the only character that the reader may condemn for his crimes (even though he knows no other way for humans to interact). The people in the underground town know what cooperative behavior is necessary for a human community, but they send an ignorant teenage girl out into a wilderness of desperate thieves and murderers. They can afford to lose one of their girls after all, and choose not to risk one of their few experienced grown men (who might have been able to move through the upper town more safely) to engage Vic as an ally instead of a dupe. Once they have a healthy young man in their bunker, rather than honestly hiring Vic as a stud or welcoming him into their families, they continue to conspire to make him a captive and rape him repeatedly. He is just another exploitable short-term resource, and this community is just another group of desperate people living at the expense of others.

Violence leads to impasse, or a meaningless repetitive struggle stripped of purpose and meaning. The committee of Quilla June's community missed an excellent opportunity for renewal when they locked Blood out and enslaved Vic. A safe environment of cooperative people educated by Blood and seeded by the healthy children of a man adopted to become an advisor of the committee could have sustained itself in diversity and vigor for another twenty years before emerging to the surface, ready and capable of dealing with the tough sparse remnants of a depopulated world.

A Boy and His Dog outlines precisely the possible future feared by many people during the 1950s, 60s, and 70s. Stories in settings like this one were elemental in focusing public attention on the necessary effort to prevent nuclear war and environmental disasters. In the 1960s, no one published stories with champagne being drunk at Checkpoint Charlie as the Berlin Wall was torn down, a real-life situation for which Ellison did not envision in his fiction.

◆ TOPICS FOR DISCUSSION ◆

1. What expectations does a reader bring to a story?

2. What could the title *A Boy and his Dog* lead a reader to expect? Did the author probably intend this? What is the result?

3. In what ways is Vic like any boy of his age?

4. In what ways has he been shaped by his environment?

5. When does the reader realize that Blood is a dog, not a human?

6. Is Blood a "person"? Does he behave like a reasoning being?

7. Why is Blood making an effort to educate Vic? What good can the learning he imparts do for Vic? Or is it for his own benefit as well?

8. Was Vic wrong with his assumption that Quilla June was searching for danger and excitement?

9. What was Quilla June hoping to accomplish by luring Vic to her community?

10. Was choosing to save Blood rather than Quilla June an easy decision for Vic?

1. So many people in this story ruin and waste whatever comes to hand, including other people. What is Ellison saying about human nature, even after disaster? Is there any chance for redemption, for individuals or humanity?

2. If Vic had been born the year that you were born, in your neighborhood, how would his life be different from the story? Is Vic entirely a product of his upbringing? What sort of childhood would be necessary for Vic to be a different person? Is he capable of being better or worse than he is?

3. There is a common saying that "Everyone is entitled to an opinion." One of the statements Ellison has made several times in his speeches and essays, including his nonfiction book *The Glass Teat* is: "Everyone is entitled to an 'informed' opinion." What significance does this modification of the cliche have for you? How do the opinions of the character Vic in this story change as he becomes more informed about the world around him? How does Vic's opinion of Quilla June change as he learns her motivations?

4. Define the terms "utopia" and "dystopia." Are there any utopian elements to any community in this story? When, in general, does a utopia become a dystopia? When does Vic realize that he has not yet found a utopia?

5. What similarities and differences can you find between this novelette and *Gulliver's Travels* by Jonathan Swift? Does it matter that Vic has a faithful companion, while Gulliver travels alone? What do each of these travelers learn about the communities they visit?

6. Imagine what Vic would own and carry on his person or in a pack. What clothing would he have that would suit post-apocalyptic Arizona? What tools and weapons would be most useful? Draw a sketch of Vic as you imagine him, and itemize a list of his possessions. What do you think would be sensible additions to his equipment, which Vic does not possess?

7. What talents has Vic managed to accrue, with and without the help of Blood? What necessary skills is he lacking, in your opinion? What will be his eventual fate, sooner or later, without these skills?

8. At the time the story was written, how possible did it seem that the world would suffer from nuclear war and environmental disaster that Ellison postulates? Why are fewer "after the nuclear war" stories and novels being published? What is the currently popular crisis for science fiction writers? How and why do these fashions in literature change as time passes?

A Boy and His Dog was adapted for a feature film, released in 1975. The director worked uncommonly closely with the author, and Harlan Ellison has never been so satisfied before or since with the conversion of his writing to a visual medium. The film stars a young Don Johnson as Vic and an excellent dog actor as Blood, who earned a Patsy Award for his work. The film is available on video in libraries and video stores. Rated R, the film is completely unsuited for young viewers and is upsetting for many adults. It is comparable in many respects to Stanley Kubrick's film version of *A Clockwork Orange.*

Ellison has written a version of the story for the comic book scripts *Vic and Blood 1* (Mad Dog) 1987, *Vic and Blood 2* (Mad Dog) 1988, and *Vic and Blood* (NBM) 1988 (collected volume in color).

Two further stories have been written by Harlan Ellison to extend this novelette to a full-length novel called *Blood's a Rover.* In the center piece, Blood is unable to save Vic, who falls into despair because of his murder of Quilla June and no longer sustains the constant effort necessary to survive. In the final portion of the novel, Blood finds a new human partner, a girl rover. The novel does not survive the viewpoint shift as well as a reader could hope, such as in Ellison's story "Pretty Maggie Money-Eyes" in which viewpoint shifts are handled brilliantly.

◆ FOR FURTHER REFERENCE ◆

Bleiler, Richard, editor. *Science Fiction Writers,* 2nd edition. New York: Scribner's, 1999. Includes an excellent biographical essay on Harlan Ellison and his multi-genre writing.

Ellison, Harlan. *The Essential Ellison.* Omaha: Nemo Press, 1987. A collection of eighty-six selected works, including fiction, essays, and reviews.

Ellison, Harlan. *The Glass Teat.* New York: Ace, 1970. A collection of essays commenting on the impact of television.

◆ RELATED WEBSITES ◆

Harlan Ellison Web Site http://www.harlanellison.com. October 19, 2001. The official Web site of Harlan Ellison, giving information about the author's life and works. It also provides a list of themes for his stories.

Paula Johanson

CONFESSIONS OF AN UGLY STEPSISTER

Novel

1999

Author: Gregory Maguire

◆

Major Books for Young Adults

Lightning Time, 1978
The Daughter of the Moon, 1980
Lights on the Lake, 1981
The Dream Stealer, 1983
The Peace and Quiet Diner, 1988
I Feel Like the Morning Star, 1989
Lucas Fishbone, 1990
Seven Spiders Spinning, 1994
Missing Sisters, 1994

*Wicked: The Life and Times of the Wicked
    Witch of the West*, 1995
Oasis, 1996
Six Haunted Hairdos, 1997
Five Alien Elves, 1998
Confessions of an Ugly Stepsister, 1999
The Good Liar, 1999
Crabby Cratchitt, 2000
Four Stupid Cupids, 2000

◆ ABOUT THE AUTHOR ◆

Gregory Maguire was born on June 9, 1954 in Albany, New York. He came from a family of writers, his father a journalist and speech writer and his mother a poet. Maguire and several of his siblings all grew up to be professional authors. He quite naturally developed a love for books at an early age, and in addition to being an avid reader, he kept a journal and wrote several stories, beginning when he was just a young child. Maguire attended Catholic schools and read about saints and angels, and soon found himself fascinated with stories of fantasy and magic.

Though he has written some realist fiction, Gregory Maguire is best known for producing fantasy, science fiction, and creative renditions of fairy tales. Maguire says that his fascination with magic led him to look for magic in everyday life, and after discovering a pond that seemed to him like a magical world, he wrote his first fantasy adventure; a multi-volume series entitled "The Chronicles of Filiaan." Though "The Chronicles of Filiaan" was never published, the experience of writing it propelled him into the career he would eventually pursue. He graduated from high school and attended State University of New York where he majored in English, then enrolled in a children's literature program in Massachusetts. While studying in this program, he published his first novel, a children's story called *Lightning Time*. *Lightning Time* was well received by the critics and Maguire was well on his way to a literary career. He wrote more children's books, took a teaching position in the children's literature program at Simmons College, and enrolled in a doctorate program at Tufts University.

Maguire has a love for the creative arts, and today composes music and works in the visual arts in addition to writing books. He was the artist-in-residence at the Blue Mountain Center, the Isabella Stewart Gardner Museum, and the Hambridge Center and has enjoyed a prolific career as a writer of fantasies, science fiction, and historical novels. His two young adult novels: *Wicked: The Life and Times of the Wicked Witch of the West* and *Confessions of an Ugly Stepsister* both received rave reviews and were made into ABC miniseries. Maguire is a founding member of Children's Literature of New England, a non-profit charity, and under the auspices of this charity he co-edited an anthology of lectures entitled "Origins of the Story: On Writing for Children." In addition to writing fiction, Maguire also writes book reviews for the *New York Times*, *Horn Book*, and other journals, and he speaks about children's literature at conferences and at schools. He has received honors and awards from prestigious literary organizations such as the National Council of Teachers of English and the American Library Association.

◆ OVERVIEW ◆

Confessions of an Ugly Stepsister is a retelling of Perrault's classic "Cinderella". It's a fantasy only in a sense: the story itself has no magic, yet suggestions of magic permeate the text. This Cinderella story has the same characters as the original, but the perspective is reversed. Maguire tells his story from the viewpoint of one of the stepsisters, Iris, who is neither ugly nor evil, but multi-faceted and ordinary. Maguire's Cinderella is part fairy tale, part historical romance, and part lesson in morality. It's not solely about Iris, but about her mother, a woman named Margarethe Fisher who leaves England after the death of her husband and arrives in Holland with her daughters, Iris and Ruth, homeless and hungry. The women find shelter with a painter and work with a tulip merchant, and the story progresses into a politically-correct tale of love and life. Maguire reworks the fairy tale into a realistic myth that empowers women and that blurs the divisions between beauty and ugliness, good and evil.

◆ SETTING ◆

Confessions of an Ugly Stepsister is set in Holland in the seventeenth century and begins when Margarethe and her two daughters arrive in the town of Haarlem during Holland's tulip mania. Maguire describes the surroundings in detail, using art and flowers to create a colorful backdrop, which allows readers to see the fallacy of appearances. Throughout the novel Maguire challenges our preoccupation with physical beauty, and he uses the setting to emphasize beauty's ephemeral nature. The town thrives on a commodity of fleeting beauty but all too soon the tulip market collapses. The seventeenth-century setting during Holland's tulip craze left those who once relied on physical beauty to sustain them searching for something of substance that can endure the test of time.

Setting the story in seventeenth-century Holland puts the events in historical perspective. This is accomplished largely by bringing to the surface the emphasis on aestheticism prevalent during this time in history. It was a time when Calvinistic doctrine had taken hold in Holland, and when Rembrandt and other Dutch masters were transforming a culture by creating colorful landscapes that began to replace the religious paintings of times past. When Margarethe and her daughters first arrive in the city of Haarlem, they find that color dominates the landscape. Maguire captures the landscape in images. He does this both by describing the sights and smells of the city and by introducing Schoonmaker into the plot and leading Margarethe and her daughters into his studio. These women are searching for beauty that goes far beyond appearances, yet physical beauty surrounds them. Schoonmaker re-creates it. This aesthetically appealing world lures the three women into a place of artifice, however, and they must learn to see the truth behind appearances.

Schoonmaker's art in a large way defines the setting and the setting aptly depicts the world of contrasts Maguire wishes to create. That Schoonmaker wishes to paint Iris against the backdrop of wildflowers means that he wishes to contrast the plain with the beautiful. He fills his studio full of lovely pictures but hides pictures of monstrosities in the back room. Haarlem is a land of contrasts, and so too is the setting of the traditional fairy tale. Haarlem comes alive when colorful flowers characterize the land, but it dies when the color fades and the flowers die. In fairy tales everything is divided into black or white, good or bad, a world full of color or a world of grayness. So the vivid images Maguire creates help sustain the idea that the land is magic and the story is a fairy tale. The pictures Schoonmaker creates capture the dichotomy inherent in fairy tales but also reveal the impossibility of such a dichotomy in the real world.

Confessions of an Ugly Stepsister is an adult fable of sorts, which examines the nature of evil and the deception of appearances. The novel contains two interwoven plots. The first plot involves Margarethe's struggle against poverty and her mission to find a husband—a prince, of course—for Iris, the most eligible of her two daughters. The second plot revolves around a struggling Flemish painter named Luycas Schoonmaker and his attempt to make a name for himself in the art world. Both plots in the novel focus on the definition of beauty and shed light on the saying "Beauty is in the eye of the beholder."

The story begins when Margarethe and her two daughters, Iris and Ruth, arrive destitute in Holland. They have just fled England after the tragic death of Margarethe's husband, who we later learn was brutally murdered by his neighbors. Margarethe is on a mission to make a life for herself and her daughters, and after discovering that the grandfather with whom they hoped to stay had passed away, suddenly find themselves homeless and hungry. Margarethe manages to find shelter with an artist named Luycas Schoonmaker, however, then eventually marries a wealthy tulip merchant named Cornelius van den Meer and meets with Maguire's Cinderella.

Maguire's Cinderella actually surfaces earlier in the novel, before Margarethe becomes the girl's stepmother. Margarethe and her daughters are wandering the streets and see a strangely lovely girl peeking through a window. The girl attracts the newcomers with her beauty, as does the colorful land, but later when Maguire exposes the complexity of this Cinderella we see that she does not conform to the fairy tale image of the beautiful maiden. Maguire makes it known that Clara, this Cinderella, has mystery surrounding her. Rumor has it in fact, that she may be a changeling. It's interesting that Clara asks if Ruth is a changeling when she first sees her through the window. These two girls appear to recognize in each other a kindred soul. A changeling cannot be confined to one realm, or in other words, cannot be categorized into good or bad, black or white. Physical beauty does not confine Clara to the realm of good nor does plainness confine Ruth to the realm of evil. Both of these characters emerge as real people, struggling to find their place in a world that creates divisions between extremes.

Reality hits hard for Margarethe and her daughters when they find themselves homeless on the streets of Haarlem. They are inundated with bright colors and delicious smells yet their world is full of grayness and hunger. Margarethe longs for a beautiful life and Maguire gives her motivation to create a fairy tale. She is ambitious, but haunted by her past and frustrated by her dire circumstances. After her husband's murder, she and her two daughters fled from the house immediately, with no money and no belongings, and headed for her grandfather's home only to find that he had passed away.

Soon after their arrival in Holland, however, the three women encounter Schoonmaker who agrees to take the women in if Iris will pose for a painting. Iris resists at first but eventually consents, and readers are thrust into a world of images that either conform or fail to conform to someone's definition of beauty. Readers quickly grasp the idea that appearances are not as they seem, and that society places value on what they deem to be a standard of physical loveliness.

Schoonmaker's paintings are complex and disturbing, and Iris, in her plainness, seems an unlikely model for a portrait artist to choose. But it appears that Schoonmaker sees in Iris some kind of tragic beauty that only he can recognize. Schoonmaker is a primary character in the novel and referred to simply as "The Master," alluding to the Dutch master Rembrandt. Rembrandt, like Schoonmaker, turned to portraiture when he lost large amounts of money in religious commissions due to the political and social upheavals of the time period. Schoonmaker struggles to secure his place as an artist in seventeenth-century Holland and to reconcile society's concept of beauty with his own. When society demanded painting lovely religious pictures, he felt compelled to chronicle "God's mistakes." Then as the political environment changed in Holland, Schoonmaker was commissioned to paint the lovely Clara, yet he also longed to paint Iris, who is referred to as "a study in human ordinariness." Maguire uses Schoonmaker to illustrate how people are expected to conform to society's standards of physical beauty and often fail to recognize true beauty when they see it. Early in the novel, Margarethe says to The Master, speaking of the idols in the Roman chapel: "Does all of this painted beauty serve any purpose?" Then the Master replies: "Who can say what purpose beauty serves?" As the novel progresses, Clara, Iris, and the other characters lead us to realize that beauty may serve no purpose at all, and that appearances merely mask truths that many people may not recognize.

Margarethe's "plain" daughter Iris is meant to be the focus of Maguire's tale, not the beautiful Clara, Maguire's Cinderella. Iris is intelligent and not truly ugly, so Margarethe considers Iris the key to securing her future. Margarethe is an opportunist and she plans to marry Iris off to a prince—so surely enough, a prince makes his appearance. Though traditional fairy tale motifs define this novel, the characters stray far from the fairy tale mold. The characters are not one-dimensional but complex, and it appears clear early on that a royal marriage between Iris and a prince will never occur.

As in traditional tales, *Confessions of an Ugly Stepsister* examines familiar literary themes such as the price of love, the loss of innocence, and the nature of evil. Aspects of the original fairy tale surface immediately. Not only does the husband Margarethe wishes for Iris happen to be a prince, but the plot builds to a climactic grand ball given by Marie de' Medici, the former Queen of France. As it turns out, it is Clara, not Iris, who marries the prince, and Iris falls in love with the painter's apprentice. Maguire cleverly crafts his story so that magic permeates the novel, yet nothing truly supernatural ever occurs. The children speak of changelings, fairies, wicked witches and cows that give milk made of pure gold. Schoonmaker, (The Master) refers to Clara as a changeling and Iris and Ruth wonder if she could possibly be something so strange and mysterious. Maguire tells us that "a changeling is said to be deficient of something essential, either memory, or sense, or mercy." It appears that Schoonmaker recognizes her deficiencies. He longs to paint her, and he calls her "Haarlem's hidden beauty [and] a witness to the weirdness of this world."

Clara is in many ways Iris's counterpart. Clara is the daughter of the tulip merchant Cornelius van den Meer, and as time goes by, Margarethe begins to clean house for this man and Iris is hired on as a companion to Clara. Unlike Iris, Clara is beautiful and mysterious, and much like the fairy tale Cinderella, she is timid and reclusive. She hates her new family, and when her father marries Margarethe, she retreats to the kitchen, sits by the cinders, and immerses herself in household chores.

Maguire challenges several stereotypes in his novel, including the image of stepparents as mean and abusive. In this story, it is not Margarethe who subjugates Cinderella; instead, it is Cinderella herself. What if this familiar character creates her own misery, Maguire seems to be asking. Clara feels safe in the kitchen and she asks Iris to call her Cinderling or Ashgirl. In Maguire's tale, Cinderella is not victimized by her stepmother nor her stepsisters, but rather she chooses to isolate herself in the kitchen, and she chooses to create work for herself.

The relationship between Iris and Clara is complicated, which naturally follows Maguire's development of complex characters and his realistic rendition of the tale. These two young women are contrasting characters in many ways; they are not diametrically opposed like the real Cinderella and her stepsister, because in reality divisions are not so black and white. There's a gray area that fairy tales neglect by intentionally making their characters extreme opposites in order to maintain the strict dividing line between good and evil. Clara and Iris are each a blend of good and evil, their personalities molded by their life experiences.

Maguire touches on numerous themes in his book, including betrayal and deception, the loss of innocence, the search for personal identity, and the ways in which people cope with pain and sorrow. These themes all paint a realistic portrait of life. His characters seem like real people searching for the truth in life and trying to make their way through life's complexities. The theme of betrayal goes hand in hand with the notion that appearances can be deceiving. Maguire's "fairy tale" revolves around a world of wealth and artifice.

◆ LITERARY QUALITIES ◆

The most obvious literary quality of the novel involves Maguire's use of motifs from the familiar fairy tale, including the ball, the lost slipper, the visit from the prince, the cinders by the fire, and so forth. Maguire includes these motifs, but he rearranges them to build suspense and keep readers wondering how this Cinderella tale will unfold. We do not know that Maguire's tale will end in the same way Perrault's did, and in fact, we have trouble identifying the main character. The story is told from Iris's perspective, yet in third person narrative, and when all is said and done, Clara and Margarethe appear just as strong as Iris as characters.

Maguire's characters differ from their fairy tale counterparts, yet they seem to embody the same concepts. The character of Luycas Schoonfield, for instance, embodies the theme of creation just as does the fairy godmother in the original tale. As an artist, he is a natural creator, but, unlike a fairy godmother, he creates by will and not by magic. He also has a striking resemblance to Rembrandt, whose influence permeates the novel. Rembrandt, like Schoonmaker, gained recognition as a portrait artist after he suffered from the devaluation of religious paintings. He also turned to landscape artistry and created fantasy landscapes of the Dutch countryside. Rembrandt was also known for experimenting with extremes of light and dark and throughout the novel Maguire uses descriptive language to reveal the contrast of light and dark in the "fairy tale" he intends to create.

The heavy emphasis on art and beauty helps establish Maguire's theme of artifice. Maguire uses numerous metaphors in the novel; the preoccupation with appearances, for instance, is revealed through the town's obsession with tulips. The symbolism of the tulip permeates the novel. The story takes Iris, Ruth, and Clara from childhood to adulthood, metaphorically blooming like the tulips that grow throughout Haarlem. Iris is the name of a flower, and Iris and Clara both can be compared to the young

blossoms. Tulips are objects of beauty; they are admired for their beauty and marketed for their beauty, but they do not last. Beauty does not last, Maguire is telling us, and he expresses this metaphorically with the crash of the tulip market.

◆ SOCIAL SENSITIVITY ◆

Maguire's book is a politically correct Cinderella story, and as such, it challenges our tendency to equate beauty with good and ugliness with evil. Maguire undermines our preoccupation with physical beauty, and he challenges the ways in which evil is presented to children in classic tales. Just as he did in his first book, *Wicked*, Maguire stresses the notion that girls don't have to conform to society's definitions of beauty in order to be good, kind people. He takes the premise of the traditional Cinderella story and reverses it, maintaining that mythic archetypes—such as the ugly, mean stepsister and the beautiful Cinderella—psychologically damage young children by conditioning them to believe that physical beauty leads to happiness.

Confessions of an Ugly Stepsister emerges as a commentary on love and society and an analysis of the notions of good and evil. Maguire removes the extreme dichotomy of good and evil, and he does this by blending the characteristics of beauty and ugliness, kindness and maliciousness and by creating multidimensional characters that cannot be confined to stereotypical molds. In the book, Cinderella (Clara) is physically beautiful, and because of this, she is not expected to learn any skills but rather is conditioned to believe she can get by on her looks alone. Maguire forces us to question whether physical beauty is a gift or a curse; he reverses the notion by making Clara's beauty an affliction rather than an asset.

In order for Maguire's Cinderella to be classified as a true fairy tale, it would seem that the story must contain some embodiment of evil. Margarethe is more evil than her daughters are, yet even she is not truly evil but simply bitter and self-serving. She is greedy for money, but not without reason. She is disturbed because of her husband's brutal murder, and ambitious and self-serving because she has no choice but to provide for herself and her two daughters.

What Maguire intends to do is to explain the circumstances that Perrault described in the fairy tale. He changes the setting, he gives the characters complexity, and in a sense, he reverses their situations. In making this reversal and in developing multifaceted characters, Maguire empowers the women in his book. The Cinderella in the original tale is subjugated and has no voice, but this Cinderella chooses to be reclusive. She controls her own life, just as Margarethe controls hers when she makes the choices to create the kind of life she wants. By giving his characters depth and substance and allowing them the capacity for both good and evil, Maguire not only creates believable characters, but he removes the victimization of women that occurs in many traditional fairy tales.

◆ TOPICS FOR DISCUSSION ◆

1. Do you feel sympathetic toward Clara? Why?

2. Who do you consider the heroine in the story and why?

3. Talk about Maguire's portrayal of Prince Charming.

4. Identify some of the common elements in fairy tales. Do you consider *Confessions of an Ugly Stepsister* a fairy tale? Why or why not?

5. What is your opinion of the ending of this book? Is it a "happily ever after" ending?

6. What does the setting add to the story?

7. Can you identify evil characters and good characters in Maguire's book?

8. What kind of a person is Margarethe? What kind of ideals does she embody?

9. The Master says, "the true consequence of beauty . . . is devotion." What does he mean by this?

◆ IDEAS FOR REPORTS AND PAPERS ◆

1. Take a fairy tale, other than "Cinderella," that you believe undermines a woman's self-perception and explain what can be done to transform the archetypes.

2. Read Gail Carson Levine's *Ella Enchanted* and compare what Levine attempts to accomplish in this story with what Maguire attempts to accomplish in *Confessions of an Ugly Stepsister*.

3. Beginning with a definition of satire, discuss the literary devises Maguire uses to satirize the traditional "Cinderella".

4. Write an in-depth character analysis of Iris.

5. Discuss the purpose of the images Maguire evokes by developing the themes surrounding the painter and the tulip merchant. How do these images of art

and nature contribute to Maguire's message?

6. Discuss the theme of magic in the novel and elaborate on how Maguire uses magic (or the lack of it) to tell his tale.

7. Discuss the dynamics of the relationship between Iris and Clara.

8. Discuss the familiar motifs found in Maguires story, such as the glass slipper, the ball, etc., and compare the presentation of these motifs to those in the original fairy tale.

9. In the original fairy tale, Perrault presents numerous messages that Maguire challenges. One of them is the equation of beauty with good and ugliness with evil. What are some of the other messages derived from the original tale and how does Maguire counter them?

◆ RELATED TITLES/ADAPTATIONS ◆

The tale of Cinderella has been one of the most widely studied fairy tales of all time, and it has enjoyed numerous variations and numerous retellings. Most notably among these is the work of Gail Carson Levine, who wrote a series of books called the "Princess Tales Series." *Ella Enchanted* is arguably the most noted of Levine's books, and it tells the humorous story of Ella of Frell who was bestowed with the "gift" of obedience at birth. Like Maguire, Levine gives Ella the challenge of breaking this spell, which turns out to be a curse rather than a gift. All of the books in Levine's "Princess Tales Series" challenge politically incorrect stereotypes. *The Fairy's Mistake* is a spoof on the fairy tale "Toads and Diamonds," *The Princess Test* is a spoof on "The Princess and the Pea," and *Princess Sonora*

and the Long Sleep is a spoof on "Sleeping Beauty."

Another modern version of "Cinderella" is a book by Margaret Peterson Haddix entitled *Just Ella* (1999). In this book Ella is also "cursed" with obedience, and though she does win her prince, she does not do so with beauty alone. Like *Ella Enchanted, Just Ella* is a comedy, and an attempt to give Cinderella depth and substance.

Another rendition of the Cinderella is a story by David Henry Wilson entitled *The Coachman Rat* (1990). Wilson's story has been described as "a dark fantasy," and is told from the perspective of the coachman.

Maguire's *Wicked: The Life and Times of the Wicked Witch of the West* should be of interest to anyone who enjoyed *Confessions of an Ugly Stepsister*. This book tells the Wizard of Oz story from the viewpoint of the Wicked Witch and again challenges the traditional conceptions of evil and good.

◆ FOR FURTHER REFERENCE ◆

Bernheimer, Kate. *Mirror, Mirror on the Wall: Women Writers Explore their Favorite Fairy Tales.* New York: Anchor Books, 1998. Twenty-five contemporary women writers discuss how traditional fairy tales affect women. The essays are scholarly and include how fairy tales influence self-esteem and emotion.

Bettelheim, Bruno. *The Uses of Enchantment: The Meaning and Importance of Fairy Tales.* New York: Vintage Books, 1975. Bettelheim, a child psychologist, discusses the value of fairy tales. He focuses on their timeless themes and how these stories educate children and mold their emotional selves.

"Maguire, Gregory." In *Authors and Artists for Young Adults*, Volume 22. Detroit: Gale Research, 1997. This series gives a lengthy profile of the author's life and work and includes quotes from the author as well as a list of works cited.

"Maguire, Gregory." In *Something about the Author*, vols 28 and 84. Detroit: Gale Research, 1982 and 1996. Author profile as well as quotes from the author providing pertinent information about the author's writing career.

Tamra Andrews

DISCOVER THE DESTROYER

Novel

2000

Author: K. A. Applegate

◆

Major Books for Young Adults

The Story of Two American Generals:
*   Benjamin O. Davis, Jr. and Colin L.*
*   Powell*, 1992
The Boyfriend Mix-Up, 1994
Sharing Sam, 1995
Listen to My Heart, 1996

Boyfriends and Girlfriends series,
**   including:**
Zoey Fools Around, 1994
Lucas Gets Hurt, 1998
Claire Can't Lose, 1999
Who Loves Kate, 1999

Animorphs series, including:

The Message, 1996
The Stranger, 1997
The Reunion, 1999
The Prophecy, 2000
The Ultimate, 2001

Everworld series
Search for Senna, 1999
Land of Loss, 1999
Enter the Enchanted, 1999
Realm of the Reaper, 1999
The Destroyer, 1999
Fear the Fantastic, 2000
Understand the Unknown, 2000
Discover the Destroyer, 2000
Inside the Illusion, 2000

◆ ABOUT THE AUTHOR ◆

Katherine Alice Applegate is simultaneously one of America's most famous authors and one of America's most mysterious. She guards her privacy, as does her publisher, Scholastic, which has brilliantly marketed her Animorphs and Everworld series with astounding success. Applegate was already a well-established writer of books for young readers, mostly romance novels, when she proposed the Animorphs series to Scholastic, where the proposal was met with enthusiasm. She wanted to write a series of books that showed how the world might look from the perspectives of different animals; the result has been a series of fascinating novellas for readers from late elementary school to junior high school.

K.A. Applegate

After moving around the United States several times, the Michigan-born writer now resides in Minneapolis. Over a hundred of her books have been published, and she has written them at an amazing pace. Begun in 1996, her Animorphs series numbered over forty books plus several spin-offs by 2001. Her series intended for adolescents, Everworld, begun in 1999, numbered nine volumes by the end of 2000. Sally Lodge, in *Publishers Weekly*, quotes Applegate, "A series writer has to develop plotting and pacing that become a well-oiled machine. You don't have the luxury of spending a year on a book and absolutely cannot indulge in writer's block. Yet I knew I had to write in perfect language and choose just the right images, to make sure that my middle readers fell in love with the characters and returned again and again.". The two hundred letters from young readers Applegate receives per week, as well as the one hundred emails she receives per day from youngsters, attest to the success she has had in reaching her intended audience. They love her characters.

In spite of the success of Applegate's writings, they have received scant attention in the press, perhaps because of a prevailing view that books written so quickly cannot be worth writing about, or perhaps because of the immense difficulty in keeping current with all the books Applegate publishes. In spite of the great pace at which Applegate has written her books, they tend to be of higher quality than other mass-market writings. In the Animorphs series the perspectives of characters as animals, whether fleas or birds, are artful and informative. The Everworld novels offer fine introductions to the mythologies of the world. In both series, the suspense is captivating and the characterizations are sharp but well-rounded; the books are page-turners, I-can't-go-to-bed-until-I-finish tales of adventure.

Applegate does not shy away from the tough questions about growing up and building sound, honest relationships with others. For instance, the nonseries title *Sharing Sam* deals with the prospect of a close friend dying and how to love in spite of the pain. In Everworld, the relationships among the principal characters are essential to the appeal of the novels. The art of characterization is one that Applegate has mastered, and it is perhaps the most important reason her rapidly-written works stand as good literature as well as entertaining reads.

◆ OVERVIEW ◆

Everworld is filled with wonders such as giant gods, knives that can cut through anything, and even, somewhere, a being so fearsome that he eats gods. *Discover the Destroyer* increases the wonder, displaying a land of greedy fairies, a dragon larger than a small town, and rubies that replace hearts. Applegate's achievement in *Discover the Destroyer* is occasionally astonishing, always entertaining, and often funny. Indeed, despite the chaos and destruction that seem to be permanent companions of David, Christopher, April, and Jalil, *Discover the Destroyer* may be the funniest novel of the "Everworld" series. In any case, the teenagers try to cope with finding jobs, studying for exams, and avoiding being eaten, burned, or fed to Ka Anor, the god eater, whose presence is closer than ever before.

◆ SETTING ◆

The laws of gravity do not apply in Everworld as they do on earth. This bothers David to some degree; his is a calculating mind that balances his heroic impulses with good sense. For instance, he climbs onto Nidhoggr, a dragon so vast that David, a big guy, can crouch behind one eyebrow ridge and be completely hidden from sight: "And then, with wings at once so vast and tiny, he began to fly. Straight up. A blue whale flying directly vertical with only the leisurely flapping of wings that might, might on a good day have lifted my Buick." The four teens have coined an abbreviation for such things that defy logic: "WTE," which stands for "Welcome to Everworld."

David and his companions find themselves with ruby hearts instead of real hearts, a gift from Nidhoggr, who says that the ruby hearts will burn them to death in six days if they do not recover the magical objects stolen from him by leprechauns: "Nidhoggr had been robbed. Four items had been taken from his treasure. A stone, a spear, a sword, and a cauldron were missing." Finding the stolen objects means journeying into the land of the fairies, a territory surrounded by high walls, with gates guarded by fairies who are willing to accept bribes to let people pass. Borrowing a little bit from Mark Twain's *A Connecticut Yankee*

in King Arthur's Court, Applegate creates a land in which some copper wire, wooden posts, and, to Christopher's delight, free-market capitalism hold the answers to recovering Nidhoggr's stolen goods, and the teenagers' real hearts.

David is suspicious of Fairy Land. "Too pretty," he says. "That's what I kept thinking. Too neat, too orderly, too well kept. The yellow bricks had even been cleaned of manure. They sparkled wet with a recent washing." It is as if Fairy Land were calculated to attract visitors with well-designed, squeaky-clean settings.

◆ THEMES AND CHARACTERS ◆

David returns as the narrator for *Discover the Destroyer,* after narrating the first novel in the series, *Search for Senna.* Finding Senna has not been a great problem; she tends to show up wherever the quartet of teens are going. But finding her complicates matters, because she seems to be perpetually in trouble and she is treacherous, ready to sell out anyone to get what she wants. What *does* she want? She has suggested that she would like to rule Everworld, but is she serious? In any case, she betrays April and continues to have a mysterious magical hold on David's emotions, "[Senna] had that power, that I knew. The power to confuse men's minds and appear to be anything," he observes. His determination to save a friend, April, from Ka Anor finally motivates him to say no to her, resulting in Senna's screaming anger: "The shrieking, out-of-control rage was like nothing I'd ever seen," David says.

David has his own anger to deal with. At the start of *Discover the Destroyer,* he is outraged that Christopher, April, and Jalil distrust him: "How many times had I come through for them, for us all? How many times had I stood out from, not alone maybe but out on the line, out at the point where danger pressed closest?" This is part of a long rant about what he has managed to accomplish in Everworld, and he is hurt that he is distrusted.

The others have reasons for mistrusting David Levin. He notes that "Senna was never really a part of us [the quartet]. A part of me, yes." His insistence on playing the hero for Senna has made the others think that his judgment cannot be trusted where Senna is involved, and he knows his judgment favors Senna, a witch so distasteful that a ruby could not replace her hard heart—only a diamond would do, according to Nidhoggr. In *Discover the Destroyer*, David's already well-rounded characterization becomes even more complex. Not only does he realize that Senna has an influence on his desires, he realizes that Everworld has hold of his imagination: "How would I live now? How would I go through the motions, the school, the tests, the college, the jobs, the life, the already-tired life that awaits me?" he asks of his life in the Old World, the Earth. The other teenagers may yearn for warm, comfortable beds and showers, but David relishes the challenges of Everworld. Nothing about the Old World interests him as much as the smallest details of Everworld. Besides, chapter nine of *Discover the Destroyer* suggests that he has horrors on earth to flee from that are more terrible to him than even Hel herself, something about a molestation when he was at camp that he tries to bury deep away from his thoughts.

A man of action, David is paradoxically pleased when Nidhoggr switches the teenagers' hearts for rubies and sets a six-day deadline. "At least a goal," he remarks, "a compelling need, a unifying, simplifying ambition." He should know better. Of the four narrators of the Everworld novels, David seems to have the most insight into what is going on, perhaps because he is open to Everworld's possibilities whereas the others resist and resent Everworld. For instance, he notes, "Cynicism is a weak force in Everworld. It was one of our very few advantages." This is a sharp, incisive thought and one of the fundamentals about those who live in Everworld: they are hopeful, ever seeking to accomplish something. This, David realizes, leaves them susceptible to exploitation by someone less hopeful but more practical.

Further, David has more insight into himself than the others have into themselves. In the next novel in the series, *Fear the Fantastic*, Christopher seems to fail to recognize how his ethnic and sexist jokes alienate others: he is defensive about their reactions to him. On the other hand, David is ruthless in his self-analysis. Not only does he realize that Senna has an unusual influence over his behavior, but he notices that he has other limitations. He tells Jalil, "I don't know what the hell I'm doing. I'm in the middle of a tornado here." At the same time, he berates Jalil: "You want me to lead, then when it hits the fan you bail out on me." Even though Jalil, Christopher, and April tend to oversimplify David and David's emotions—portraying him as a gung-ho adventurer—David's narration reveals that he is a complicated young man whose heroism is born amid much self-doubt and the realization that he is often in over his head. "If I was a leader I was doing a piss-poor job," he says after one of the group's many disagreements. "We were fragmented," he adds, "disunited. And I was just one of the fragments. We seemed incapable of working together. Each of us was a unit, none of us part of a team." He is capable of a deep understanding of the motivations of others, and he realizes that to survive, he and the others need to work together. Much of Everworld is devoted to the theme of leadership, and the theme is complex because of the depiction of David, who is ruthless in his self-analysis as well as insightful into the problems he faces as a leader.

An important theme for *Discover the Destroyer* is greed. Jalil recognizes its power for the fairies, and he is cynical enough to take advantage of that power. "I mean," he says, "that's the thing about greed. Enough is never enough. Even too much isn't enough." Nidhoggr has already shown the hold greed has on him: even when buried in tons of riches, he cries over the loss of four stolen items. In Fairy Land, desire for wealth overrides other concerns. "You had to admire Jalil's mind," David says, showing his own tendency to analyze the strengths and weaknesses of others. "There wasn't a lot of sentimentality getting in the way." Further, David notes that "Jalil has a good, sharp eye for self-interest."

Like Jalil, Christopher recognizes the possibilities in the greed of the fairies, but where Jalil's analytical mind just sees the greed as something to be dispassionately exploited, Christopher revels in the give-and-take of bargaining and relishes the dynamics of the business of trade. He seems at home among the merchants.

In *Discover the Destroyer*, David's relationship with April presents special problems. He likes to think in terms of being part of a team, and in spite of his recognition that the four teenagers often function as separate units, he thinks of them as jointly his responsibility. This is where Senna miscalculates. She has managed to persuade David to protect her from heart-eating gods, from the queen of hell, and even from a huge dragon, but when she declares that April is the "witch," and not herself, she defies something essential to David's nature. She has betrayed a team member. He has already noticed that "April hates Senna. Hates. And hate isn't an emotion that comes lightly or easily to April." He does not know why April hates Senna, but Senna's blunt betrayal of her half-sister may hold a clue. In any case, in an awkward scene, David punches Senna, knocking her out, enabling him to get her out of his way while he contrives to free April from the dungeon of the King and Queen of Fairy Land, who have sold her to the Hetwan, the servants of Ka Anor.

Fairy Land has many wonders, including a castle whose towers are actually missiles designed to shoot down a dragon, but its people are the greatest wonders. Take, for example, the nymph Idalia:

> She was green. Not a little green, a lot green. I could see the color because she glowed like a paper candle lantern. Like she was filled with neon gas. She glowed the green of a spring leaf. Her skin, her face. Her hair was a darker green, like the same leaf in late summer. Her eyes, I didn't see them at first, couldn't because they darted this way and that, but when they paused for a microsecond they were yellow. Sunflower yellow.

She is youthful, "But a definite young woman, not a girl." In spite of her beauty, David insists, "I wasn't attracted to Idalia. More like I was embarrassed."

More menacing is the Hetwan who purchase April from the King and Queen of Fairy Land: "He was taller than the fairies but just as slightly built. His eyes were those of an exceedingly large fly. He had wings folded against his back. His mouth was ringed by three small, jointed arms that never seemed to stop reaching for and grasping invisible food from the air."

Yet, more important than the Hetwan, more important than the nymph, even more important than the Queen, who actually rules Fairy Land, is a fairy named Ambrigar, a fellow who spends his days in the marketplace buying and selling goods, including copper wire. It is fun to watch Christopher launch into his sales pitch about the telegraph and to watch Ambrigar slowly realize what he can do with a telegraph. Perhaps Fairy Land, maybe all of Everworld, will become linked by telegraph, like King Arthur's Britain in Twain's *A Connecticut Yankee in King Arthur's Court*.

Another impressive character is Nidhoggr, the enormous dragon who lives under hell. The Hetwan wish to get him out of the way so that they can invade hell, in order to capture Hel and other immortals to feed to Ka Anor. Nidhoggr may be greedy and too sentimental about his treasure, but he is not stupid, and he is not a willing victim. Still, greed is his weakness. For instance, he says to David, "Witches are never anything but trouble. Their hearts are hard. I'd have had to use a diamond to exchange for [Senna's] heart." David finds this amusing, realizing that the only reason Senna was spared from having her heart taken from her was that the old dragon was too cheap to use a diamond.

◆ LITERARY QUALITIES ◆

David really is not a whiner, not down deep, but if there is a weakness in *Discover the Destroyer*, it is David's excessive indulgence in teenaged angst: "Pleasure fades, gets old, gets thrown out with last year's fad. Fear, guilt, all that stuff stays fresh." Part of this is motivated by his bad memories of childhood. David's memories are nothing compared to what Jalil has to go through with his mental illness, and regrets over no longer getting a thrill out of skating down a parking ramp seem way too childish for the active, even exuberant personality of David.

On the other hand, Applegate's craftsmanship is evident in the construction of *Discover the Destroyer*. It begins with a life-or-death problem for the teenagers, the replacement of their hearts by rubies that will go bad in six days, then passes through one thrilling event after another, to end in a good cliffhanger: "We had entered the land of Ka Anor."

Perhaps what is most admirable about *Discover the Destroyer* is the mix of the characters. Because David is the narrator, each teenager is given a major role. In contrast, the reader notices that when Christopher narrates *The Land of Loss*, he tends to focus almost entirely on himself. In *Discover the Destroyer*, David shows off his leadership skills and finally stands up to Senna over an issue that is important to him—doing right by his companions, especially April, who has been betrayed by Senna. Jalil gets his due not only as the cynical manipulator but also as the scientifically minded member of the group; the success of the telegraph depends on his knowledge. Indeed, the very idea of building the telegraph depends on his being one of the teenagers.

Christopher's brightest moment so far in the "Everworld" series, including his own narrated novel, *Land of Loss*, comes when he wheels and deals with Fairy Land's entrepreneurs. His usually dispirited tone changes to one of excitement and pleasure when he dives into his salesmanship: "It's called a telegraph. And that's only the beginning, my brother, because, see, the same technology can warn you if bad weather is coming or tell you if there's an enemy army heading your way. It can be used to send messages to your people far away." It is good to see this happy side of Christopher, and it is this spirited tone that makes *Discover the Destroyer* a special, exciting novel.

◆ SOCIAL SENSITIVITY ◆

The issue of child molestation is touched on briefly in chapter nine, but it is too murkily presented to be more than a hint at one of the bad memories David wishes to leave behind in the Old World. The chapter is such a marked departure from the tone and content of the rest of *Discover the Destroyer* that it may stand out as a special problem for some readers.

Of greater significance to *Discover the Destroyer* is the theme of greed. Christopher views the economy of Fairy Land as robustly capitalist, and talks confidently about the law of supply-and-demand with Ambrigar. But David also sees Fairy Land as phony, a fake place prettied up to attract people who have money to spend or have profitable business to take to Fairy Land. David likens his impression to visiting the botanical gardens in Chicago, implying a place that is artificial.

◆ TOPICS FOR DISCUSSION ◆

1. Would you have bargained with Nidhoggr for Senna? Why or why not?

2. How well do David, Christopher, April, and Jalil work together in *Discover the Destroyer*? Are they a team?

3. Why does David insist on saving April from the Hetwan?

4. What does David's punching Senna say about his personal development in the Everworld series?

5. How dangerous does Senna seem at the end of *Discover the Destroyer*?

6. Why does Nidhoggr live up to his side of the bargain he makes with David at the end of *Discover the Destroyer*?

7. Are there dreamlike passages in *Discover the Destroyer*? What do they reveal about the characters?

8. How does David overcome his self-doubts?

9. Will Ambrigar make a success of his telegraph business?

10. How good a salesman is Christopher?

11. Why does Applegate make Fairy Land seem artificial?

12. Why would David admire Jalil's cynicism?

13. What does David's illness tell about what can happen in Everworld?

14. What special qualities does David bring to his narration of *Discover the Destroyer*? How do they color his account of events and his descriptions of places and characters?

15. By the end of *Discover the Destroyer*, what have the Everworld novels revealed about the Hetwan? What does this suggest about what the teenagers will discover in the land of Ka Anor?

◆ IDEAS FOR REPORTS AND PAPERS ◆

1. What characteristics does Nidhoggr have in common with the dragons of medieval European folklore? Or in common with the dragon in *Beowulf*? Or in common with dragons in Norse mythology?

2. What is rationalism? What are its strengths? What are its weaknesses?

3. Compare the narratives of *Discover the Destroyer*, *Realm of the Reaper*, *Enter the Enchanted*, *Land of Loss*, and *Search for Senna*. Are there notable differences in how the stories are told? Are there notable similarities? What does this tell you about Applegate's artistic achievement in *Discover the Destroyer*?

4. Draw a map of the city in Fairy Land, showing where every place is, including the palace and the market.

5. Draw or paint a picture of the marketplace, paying special attention to how its layout would encourage business dealings.

6. Compare the introduction of the telegraph to King Arthur's Britain in Mark

Twain's *A Connecticut Yankee in King Arthur's Court* with the introduction of the telegraph to Fairy Land in *Discover the Destroyer*. What is Twain's purpose in his novel? Is it similar to or different from Applegate's purpose in *Discover the Destroyer*?

7. What is the law of supply-and-demand? How does it apply to the fairy society in *Discover the Destroyer*?

8. Christopher calls the fairy economy capitalist. Is it really capitalist? Why or why not?

◆ RELATED TITLES ◆

Applegate likes to experiment, and her novels tend to be lively exercises in ideas and techniques. In the case of Everworld, she creates a place where the world's ancient mythologies coexist, and she has fun creating adventures that involve mixing the mythologies. For the "Everworld" series, she creates four adventurers who are snatched from fairly ordinary teenaged American lives, although Jalil's psychological problems are somewhat out of the ordinary. Through these characters, she experiments with techniques of narration by having each one narrate a novel. David narrates *Search for Senna*, which introduces Vikings, Loki, and Norse mythology. Jalil's *Realm of the Reaper* delves more deeply into Norse myths about life and death and the underworld than *Search for Senna* does. It also tells of hell and where Thor is to be found. Christopher's *Land of Loss* focuses more on Aztec mythology than Norse mythology and introduces the Coo-Hatch, aliens from yet another world. April's *Enter the Enchanted* tells of the survival of Arthurian culture in Everworld and shows that the various cultures and their gods know about each other and mix with one another. In *Discover the Destroyer*, David returns as the narrator, showing much more insight into what is happening in Everworld than the other narrators have.

The personality of each narrator shows through in the telling of each book, and David explains how each teenager brings useful personal attributes to their adventures in Everworld. The shifting of narrators allows Everworld to be described through David's love of action and interest in logistics, through Christopher's acidic humor and tendency to see below the surface of events to find what is really going on, through April's good sense and practicality, and through Jalil's analytical mind that finds the logic linking events.

The novels also continue to introduce mythologies, and in the process, Applegate creates a new mythology of her own. Here, human endeavors are placed in a vast cosmic scheme in which everyone is important, even though in any individual novel they may seem like pawns. Once the youngsters meet Merlin in *Land of Loss*, the grand contest of universe-shaking powers begins to reveal itself, and dreams really do seem more real than real life. *Discover the Destroyer* advances the unifying plot of the "Everworld" series by showing how the Hetwan are insinuating themselves into the politics of Fairy Land, as well as revealing how tough David, Christopher, April, and Jalil have become.

◆ FOR FURTHER REFERENCE ◆

"Applegate, Katherine (Alice)." In *Authors and Artists for Young Adults*, vol. 37. Detroit: Gale, 2000. A biographical essay with comments on Applegate's life and work.

"Applegate, Katherine (Alice)." In *Something about the Author*, vol. 109. Detroit: Gale, 2000. An essay that includes biographical information about Applegate and information about her writing.

"NYC Radio Station Celebrates the Season." *Publishers Weekly* (January 17, 2000): 26. Mentions the marketing of the "Everworld" series.

Review of *Search for Senna. Publishers Weekly* (June 21, 1999): 69. In this review the critic says, "With her blend of accessible story and mythological cast of characters, Applegate is sure to attract a host of new fans."

"Scholastic's Animorphs Series Has Legs," *Publishers Weekly* 244, 45 (November 3, 1997): 36–37.

Kirk H. Beetz

DON QUIXOTE

Novel

1605 and 1615

Author: Miguel de Cervantes Saavedra

◆

Major Books for Young Adults

Don Quixote, 1605 and 1615
Three Exemplary Novels, 1952 (translated by Samuel Putnam)

◆ ABOUT THE AUTHOR ◆

Miguel de Cervantes Saavedra, the Spanish novelist, dramatist, and poet, is
regarded as a literary peer of Shakespeare.
Born in Alcala de Henares, Spain, in 1547,
Cervantes came from a good though often
poor family.

Little is known of his youth or education
except that in 1568 Cervantes was a student
of the Madrid humanist Juan Lopez de
Hoyos, who edited an elegiac volume on
the death of Queen Isabel de Valois, to
which Cervantes contributed some verses.
Possibly fleeing arrest, Cervantes went to
Naples and then Rome in 1569; there in the
service of Cardinal Giulio Acquaviva, he
studied Italian literature and philosophy,
which were later to influence his work.

In 1570 he enlisted in the army and fought
in the naval battle of Lepanto (1571), in
which he acquitted himself with distinction, receiving a wound that permanently
crippled his left arm. He was extremely
proud of his role in the famous victory and
of the nickname he had earned, *El manco de
Lepanto*. As Cervantes was returning to Spain
with his brother on the galley *El Sol* in 1575,
the ship was captured by Barbary pirates,
and the two brothers were taken to Algiers
as slaves. Miguel remained in captivity for
five years, eventually becoming the property of the viceroy of Algiers. After many
romantic, if futile, efforts to escape, he was
ransomed for five hundred ducats by the
Trinitarian friars in 1580, a cost that brought
financial ruin to himself and to his family.

Having returned to Spain, Cervantes married Catalina de Salazar y Palacios in 1584,
fathered an illegitimate daughter, and in
1587 secured employment as a purchasing
agent for the navy in Seville until 1597. In
this capacity, he traveled throughout the
country, often becoming involved in dis-

Miguel de Cervantes Saavedra

improved considerably, however, after the publication of the first part of *Don Quixote* in the same year, when he was fifty-eight. Although Cervantes's previous literary efforts had met with little success, this book immediately caught the fancy of the reading public.

Moving to Madrid, he devoted his last years to writing. Cervantes did not enjoy financial security until he became the protege of the Count of Lemos in 1613. A spurious Part II for *Don Quixote* appeared in 1614, probably encouraging Cervantes to complete the second volume which appeared in 1615.

In his later years Cervantes wrote other works of fiction, including *Novelas ejemplares* (1613), twelve original tales of human passions drawn from his own experience and molded by his mature craftsmanship. Some of these stories in themselves prove him one of the great literary masters.

It should be noted that various translators, including Samuel Putman (in 1949) and J. M. Cohen (in 1950), use the English letters "x" or "j," according to different conventions, when translating the Spanish consonant pronounced as an unaspirated "h." Accordingly, the title of Cervantes' most famous work is variously spelled in English *Don Quixote* or *Don Quijote,* and either way is pronounced "Don Kee-ho-tay."

Cervantes himself realized that he was deficient in poetic gifts, a judgment confirmed by later generations. Aside from his plays, his most ambitious work in verse is the *Viaje del Parnaso* (1614), an allegory which consists largely of a rather tedious though good-natured review of contemporary poets. *Los trabajos de Persiles y Sigismunda* (1617) is a verse romance, which Cervantes thought would be either the worst or the best book in the Spanish language. Though some critics have boggled at the fantastic geography of its early scenes and the incredible adven-

putes with communities reluctant to part with their crops; on one occasion, he was excommunicated for seizing grain that belonged to the church. His unbusinesslike methods resulted in deficits, and twice he was imprisoned for debt.

Cervantes's reputation as one of the greatest writers in history rests almost entirely on his novel *Don Quixote* and on his twelve short stories known as the *Novelas ejemplares.* His literary production, however, was considerable. His first published work was an effusive pastoral romance in prose and verse, *La Galatea,* published in 1585. Between 1582 and 1587, he wrote more than twenty plays, only two of which survive.

In 1605 Cervantes and his family, who were then living in Valladolid, were accused of complicity in the death of a young nobleman. They were later absolved, but the records of the case give evidence of the poverty and wretchedness of Cervantes's mode of existence at the time. His position

tures of its characters, others have praised its polished style.

Regardless of its merits, the *Persiles* will be remembered, if only for its dedication and prologue. Addressed to the Count of Lemos, the dedication was signed on April 19, 1616, just four days before Cervantes's death. Quoting an old ballad, *Puesto ya el pie en el estribo* ("one foot already in the stirrup"), Cervantes took leave of his patron and of the world with the same gallantry and grace that characterized both his life and his work.

◆ OVERVIEW ◆

A retired and impoverished gentleman named Alonzo Quixano lived in the Spanish province of La Mancha. He had read so many romances of chivalry that he decided one day to revive the ancient custom of knight-errantry. Changing his name to Don Quixote de la Mancha, he had himself dubbed a knight by a rascally publican whose miserable inn he mistook for a castle.

For armor he donned an old suit of mail which had belonged to his great-grandfather. Then upon a bony old nag he called Rosinante, he set out upon his first adventure. Not far from his village he fell into the company of some traveling merchants who beat the mad old man severely when he challenged them.

Back home recovering, he was closely watched by his good neighbor, the village priest, and the barber. Hoping to cure him of his fancies, the curate and the barber burned his library of chivalric romances. Don Quixote, however, believed that his books had been carried off by a wizard. Undaunted, he set out on the road again with an uncouth rustic named Sancho Panza as his squire, promising to make Sancho the governor of the first island he would conquer. As the mistress to whom he dedicated his deeds of valor, he chose a buxom peasant wench famous for her skill in salting pork. He called her Dulcinea del Toboso.

The knight and his squire had to sneak out of the village under cover of darkness, but in their own minds they presented a brave appearance: the lean old man on his bony horse and his squat, black-browed servant on a small donkey, Dapple. The don carried his sword and lance, Sancho Panza a canvas wallet and a leather bottle.

Traveling together, Don Quixote and Sancho had many adventures. The knight challenged windmills and flocks of sheep and faced other similarly spurious dangers. The pair ended up in Barcelona, after making the acquaintance of many people who told interminable stories, after being repeatedly hoodwinked and beaten, and after having behaved in a thoroughly embarrassing manner in their journey across Spain. Sancho did eventually get to rule an island, for a week, before he resigned.

After his last defeat, Don Quixote went back home, determined next to follow a pastoral shepherd life. He quickly declined, and before he died, he renounced as nonsense all to do with knight-errantry, not realizing that in his high-minded, noble-hearted nature he himself had been a great chivalrous gentleman.

◆ SETTING ◆

The novel is set in Spain, Cervantes's homeland, through which he traveled during his youth and middle years. There are many autobiographical elements in *Don Quixote.* Cervantes clearly put his experiences as a student, as a captive of pirates, and also as a government purchasing agent to good use when composing the adventures of a poor and mad nobleman.

The novel provides a cross-section of Spanish life, thought, and feeling at the end of the chivalric age. In fact, the whole fabric of seventeenth-century Spanish society is detailed with piercing yet sympathetic insight in a thousand pages of close-set type. Although Cervantes meant his novel to be a satire on the exaggerated chivalric romances of his time, it has been interpreted as an ironic story of an idealist frustrated and mocked in a materialistic world. It can also be seen as a veiled attack on the Catholic church and on contemporary Spanish politics.

The contrasting figures of Don Quixote and Sancho Panza, the visionary idealist and the practical realist, symbolize the duality of the Spanish character. With its variegated assortment of minor characters, shepherds, innkeepers, students, priests, and nobles, the novel also gives a panoramic view of seventeenth-century Spanish society.

The work has been appreciated as a satire on unrealistic extremism, an exposition of the tragedy of idealism in a corrupt world, and a plea for widespread reform. Set as a fictional satire, this novel could say many uncomfortable things about the real world with less offense than a manifesto would make. This masterpiece presented to the world an unforgettable description of the transforming power of illusion, and it had an indelible effect on the development of the European novel.

◆ THEMES AND CHARACTERS ◆

Among the innumerable characters in this novel there are three who are most prominent: Don Quixote, Sancho Panza, and Dulcinea.

Alonso Quixano is a gaunt country gentleman, kindly and dignified. His mind is so crazed by reading romances of chivalry that he believes himself called upon to redress the wrongs of the whole world. Changing his name to Don Quixote de la Mancha, he is knighted by an innkeeper whose miserable hostelry he mistakes for a castle. As his lady love, he chooses (without telling her) the peasant girl Aldonza Lorenzo, whom he names Dulcinea del Toboso. His madness is almost entirely internal to begin with, but that soon changes.

Don Quixote sallies forth into the world, but after several mishaps, he returns to his home. Undaunted, he asks Sancho Panza, an ignorant rustic, to be his squire and promises to reward him with the governorship of the first island they conquer. Riding Rosinante, a nag as bony as himself, Don Quixote sets out a second time, accompanied by Sancho on his donkey, Dapple.

During his travels, Don Quixote's overexcited imagination blinds him to reality: he thinks windmills to be giants, flocks of sheep to be armies, and galley-slaves to be oppressed gentlemen. Sancho is not subject to the same follies as his master; but as a servant subject to a madman he suffers the consequences of the Don's madness and, wilfully simple, does not use his own sense enough to compensate. It is almost as if this life following the whims of a madman is not too much different from his role as a peasant, subject to the will of a landowner.

Toward the end of the novel, Sancho is named governor of the isle of Barataria, a mock title given to him by some noblemen whose only aim is to make sport of the squire and his master. He governs well for a week before abdicating as invaders approach. It is a vindication for Sancho, who is proved by that week and that abdication to be not entirely simple after all.

As for the Don, after being bested in a duel with the Knight of the White Moon, in reality a student of his acquaintance in disguise, Don Quixote, tired and disillusioned, returns to La Mancha and, shortly before his death, renounces books of knight-errantry. In the end, he has been beaten by his own delusion.

Quixote had intended to retire to a pastoral setting, to give "full scope to his amorous sentiments." These have been directed throughout the novel to a woman he hardly knows, Aldonza Lorenzo, daughter of Lorenzo Corcuelo. She is just a country wench, but Quixote has adorned her with the name Lady Dulcinea del Toboso and also with a beauty she has never possessed. "I am enamoured," he tells Sancho early in Book One of the novel, "for no other reason but because it is necessary that knights-errant should be in love." On one level he knows her to be what she is, and yet "I paint her in my fancy, according to my wish." All his exploits were committed in her name, though she neither knew nor cared.

"I know her very well," replies Sancho to his master's statement.

> And I dare say that she can throw an iron bar as well as any the strongest lad in our parish. I vow, by the giver, 'tis a wench of the mark, tall and stout, and so sturdy withal, that she will bring her chin out of the mire, in despite of any knight-errant, or that shall err, him that shall honour her as his lady. Out upon her! What a strength and voice she hath! . . . And the very best that is in her is that she is nothing coy; for she hath a very great smack of courtship, and plays with every one, and gibes and jests at them all.

This is one woman who exists independently of the illusions a man may or may not hold about her.

The fulsome language used here to describe Aldonza/Dulcinea is employed time and again throughout the novel, as new characters are introduced and their own stories are told, whether priest or captive, in detail that becomes at times tiresome. This book is not a modern adventure film which cuts to the chase. In *Don Quixote*

Cervantes claims to have set out to destroy the books of chivalry. But readers may wonder whether his novel is not one more book of chivalry.

If you look for chivalric scenarios in everyday life, like Quixote, says critic David Quint in *The Modern Language Quarterly*, you will find not a castle but an inn, not a princess but the innkeeper's daughter, not a king or chatelaine but an innkeeper, who will demand to be paid. This novel juxtaposes three levels of narrative realism: the unreal, conventional fantasy of the chivalric romances; the captive's true adventure story that is touched by the miraculous, but nonetheless flesh-and-blood; and the portrait of rural Spain, the impoverished world of road and inn that Part I of *Don Quixote* takes place in and that the narrator presents in the new naturalistic style of the novel.

The realism of the world of the inn—that is, the novelistic world—encroaches on the other levels as well, through money. In different ways, to be sure, both don and squire regard free hospitality as due recompense for their knightly calling. But Quixote could not leave the inn if Fernando and the curate did not pay his bills. Money— particularly the money required in exchange for hospitality—measures the distance between the heroic, aristocratic world of Quixote's fantasy and the modern, material world through which he moves in the novel.

Buying your way out of captivity is hardly heroic; it is like settling your bill before you are allowed to leave an inn. There is implicit here a retrospective critique of Spain's crusading mission during her great century, when spiritual goals might too easily yield to material ones and human lives and freedom be exchanged for money. Cervantes, five years a captive in Algiers before being ransomed at a cost that beggared him and his family, knew this all too well.

Quint suggests that Cervantes owed much to Italian poet Lodovico Ariosto when he created the novel *Don Quixote*. He derived from Ariosto's *Orlando Furioso* both the narrative technique of interlace, which places multiple story lines next to one another, and Ariosto's particular use of it to juxtapose and intermingle hitherto distinct narrative genres.

Cervantes' debt to Ariosto goes beyond his occasional imitation of whole episodes from the *Furioso*. According to Quint, Cervantes learned from Ariosto how to juxtapose apparently different stories that turn out to be so many variants of a single plot, and Cervantes makes readers begin to feel that there are really only two stories available in literature: that of the worldly career and that of idolatrous male jealousy, both having something to do with marriage.

When Cervantes interlaces that other universal solvent of genres—prose—the novel is born.

◆ LITERARY QUALITIES ◆

The first part of *Don Quixote*, which may have been conceived while Cervantes was in prison, was first printed in 1605 in Madrid by Juan de la Cuesta. In 1614 a second part was published by an unknown author who used the pseudonym Alonso Fernandez de Avellaneda. This bit of plagiarism, though not an unusual practice at the time, spurred Cervantes to complete his own sequel, which appeared the following year and is usually considered superior to the first part.

The unabridged *Don Quixote* is over a thousand pages. The book was probably never intended to be read in the modern manner: that is, straight through. The reader would be wise to read an adaptation or an abridged version before tackling this massive tome. Reviewer Amis suggests that group or family recitations of a chapter a

night were, in all likelihood, the most that Cervantes expected anyone to manage. His epic is epic in length only, according to Amis; it has no momentum, no pace, no drive. Like an anthology, it simply accrues. Amis acknowledges that the book bristles with beauties, charm, and sublime comedy; it is also, for long stretches, inhumanly dull. In contrast, many critics have said that *Don Quixote* is the best novel in the world, beyond comparison.

The author took a decade to recover from the first part of *Don Quixote* before completing and publishing the second, Amis observes. Alas, modern readers often find themselves eyeing the fortress of Part II as soon as they turn the last page of Part I.

Since throughout the novel Cervantes constantly uses the technique of saying everything (at least) twice, it is appropriate that the second half should be a mirror image of the first—with one important reversal. Both in the real world and in the novel, Part I has been published, to international acclaim. The knight has not read the novel and awaits news of its reception with suitable diffidence. Predictably, his adventure has been criticized—the digressions, the "inadvertencies" (whereby, for instance, Senora Panza is given three different Christian names), the remorselessness of "those infinite drubbings"—but the Don is now famous, if for all the wrong reasons. "Sallying out once again with his squire, he is universally humored and hoaxed by a colluding reality," Amis concludes. "His baseless imaginings of Volume I are, through a series of elaborate deceptions (often as cruel and gratuitous as the beatings the Don earlier dispensed), given sham life in the observable world. Don Quixote was driven mad by books; now he enters a reality driven mad by Don Quixote."

Miguel de Cervantes' avowed purpose was to ridicule the books of chivalry which were popular even in his day, but he soared beyond this satirical purpose in his wealth of fancy and in his irrepressible high spirits as he pokes fun at social and literary conventions of his day.

Declaring his expertise in knight-errantry, Don Quixote asserts that "My absolute faith in the details of their histories and my knowledge of their features, their complexions and their deeds and their characters enable me by sound philosophy to deduce their features, their complexions, and their statures." This declaration affords a key to understanding the novel, for it demonstrates both the literal and the symbolic levels of the novel—and the distinction between those levels is crucial. The literal level is superficial; it reveals the obvious. The symbolic level deals, as all good literature must, with values. Don Quixote's declaration must be considered on both levels, and in context, lends insight into the novel as a whole.

On the literal level, the inventory of the Don's library, made just before the books were burned, reveals the extent of his collection. Later, there is evidence, in a very lucid and pragmatic statement for a presumably insane old man, of Don Quixote's having read Machiavelli, followed by the Don's citation of the misfortunes which befell his hero, Amadis of Gaul. Yet, on the literal level, Don Quixote's mastery of chivalric lore seems to serve only as a rationalization for his ill-luck.

On the symbolic level, more questions are raised than are answered. Quixote claims to have reached a "sound philosophy." But, is reliance on reading alone—as he has done—a valid basis for understanding reality, as the Don avers? In lieu of a clear-cut answer, Cervantes offers a paradox. Early in the text, the Squire has never read any histories because he is illiterate; but later, trying to divert the Don's attention with a story, Sancho, under questioning, admits

Title page of *Don Quixote* written by Miguel de Cervantes Saavedra.

that although he had not seen the person in question, "the man who told me this story said it was so true and authentic. . . . I could swear on my oath that I had seen it all."

The issues of verisimilitude and credibility are not really resolved in this novel. Consequently, these issues generate further questions about distinctions between reality and fantasy. Sancho represents empirical, commonsensical reality; the Don stands for whimsy and unfettered imagination. Whose view of the world is more accurate? Cervantes is ambiguous, at best, about the answer.

Cervantes' novel is a complex web of tangled skeins, subject to many interpretations, and is unequivocally judged by many literary authorities to be the finest Spanish novel ever written and one of the greatest works in world literature.

The novel has been subject to Marxist analysis and to psychoanalysis among many other interpretations. Most analysts find much here to praise, as does linguist Elizabeth A. Spiller, for example. She says in the *Modern Language Quarterly* that

> If *Don Quijote* as a whole narrates the literary-historical transformation of the romance into the novel, the Sierra Morena episode extends this analysis to the larger question of how reading practices changed during the early modern period. In this episode each character—from Gardenio to the illiterate Sancho—becomes in some sense a reader of romance. In the succession of their readings, Cervantes encapsulates a literary history of how romance reading changed during the previous hundred years.

Another issue raised on the symbolic level involves the possible immorality of reading "too many" books. This may be a veiled protest against the Index of Prohibited Books of the Catholic Church. The literal lesson emphasizes the corruptive power of books (and, therefore, education); however, the symbolic implication—given Cervantes' sympathetic treatment of Don Quixote—is that books and education are liberating influences on the human psyche. This epic novel may be a parody of the Church's monopoly of literary matters in the Middle Ages, with the uninhibited don a reproach to the insensitive, book-burning priest. Teachers using this book in a Catholic school may want to do extensive reading on the topic of the Index before writing lesson plans.

Don Quixote becomes a tragic figure toward the end of the novel, but not for the failure of his philosophy; rather, it is society's failure to accommodate a deviation from the norm. Cervantes did not make the Don contemptible nor did he treat him with contempt. Although the Don strives to push time back, his efforts are depicted as noble. He evokes popular sympathy for this underdog who defies all odds and is broken in the attempt.

◆ TOPICS FOR DISCUSSION ◆

1. What is a quest?

2. What noble goals does Don Quixote actually achieve on his journey?

3. What does Sancho Panza achieve? Is he entirely a figure of ridicule?

4. What role do women play in Don Quixote's fantasies?

5. How do the women Don Quixote actually meets figure in the story Cervantes tells?

6. How did Don Quixote fall into his delusion? Is there some way he could have been less vulnerable to his fantasy?

7. What virtues did Don Quixote or Sancho actually embody by the end of their adventures? Is this sufficient to make up for their foolishness?

8. Is Don Quixote's delusion a rare thing? Does it matter if you consider the time in which he is supposed to have lived?

9. What would be some modern equivalents to some of Don Quixote's delusions?

10. What modern writers in English are the cultural equivalent of Cervantes? What about writers in other languages?

1. Gustave Dore painted a scene from *Don Quixote*, which he titled *Don Quixote and Sancho Panza*. Carefully observe a copy of this painting. Can you tell which scene is being portrayed? What humorous elements can you find? What is Dore portraying as honestly heroic?

2. Create a detailed ink drawing (or painting) of a scene from *Don Quixote*. Include with it a written copy of the scene which is being illustrated. List several of the people and items which you have shown in the picture, with annotations explaining why you have included them, or styled them as you did.

3. Compare the two epic series of fantasy novels *The Belgeriad* and *The Malloreon* by David and Leigh Eddings with *Don Quixote*. Apart from the sheer size of these epics, what similarities can you find? Do the Eddings manage to impart a sense of humor to their work, as Cervantes does? What political commentary can you find in common between these works? In what ways is ridicule used by the Eddings and Cervantes?

4. Compare the two epic series of fantasy novels *A Man of His Word* and *A Handful of Men* by Dave Duncan with *Don Quixote*. What are the moral strengths of Duncan's protagonist Rap? How can he be contrasted to the wandering mad don? Where in Duncan's work does the reader get the sense of time passing and characters growing and maturing? How is this stronger than in Cervantes' work?

5. Was it necessary for Don Quixote to take on the mantle of chivalry in order to accomplish a quest? What alternatives did a gentleman of that era have? Could alchemical studies or setting up a *salon* have sufficed to meet his needs and goals?

6. What modern behaviors are cultural and contemporary equivalents to the quest? How can young people—or old people, for that matter—satisfy the urge that was felt by Don Quixote?

7. If Don Quixote was an old man in 1970s America, to what sort of delusion might he have fallen? What about in 1950, or the year 2000? What might he have done instead of read chivalrous romances? What journey might he have taken, for what imagined reasons? Using a short story format, try to make your story a modern version of this old man's folly and adventures.

8. Is Stephen King a modern equivalent to Cervantes? How could one arrive at this opinion? Is sheer volume of creative output the most essential quality for that likeness? What other qualities as a writer are necessary? What works of Cervantes are most celebrated since his death? What works of Stephen King are likely to receive critical attention?

9. What are the usual intents and purposes of a publisher who re-releases a classic book by a long-dead author? For what reasons is a classic book adapted or abridged? What are some of the positive and negative aspects to a comic-book version of a classic book?

10. Compare a film adaptation of *Don Quixote* to the film *The World According to Garp*. Both films, by necessity, are abridgements or excerpts from books too large in scale to present as films in their entirety. How satisfactory is the excerpt or abridgement when compared to the original? How does the director change the focus of the narrative when selecting portions of the original text? How is the experience of the reader/

viewer changed by the adaptation of the story? Does this technique of film adaptation work better with the contemporary story or the classic one?

◆ RELATED TITLES/ADAPTATIONS ◆

There are dozens of adaptations of the novel or portions thereof, some of which are intended for children or young adult readers. There are also many audiocassette readings of abridgements and adaptations of the novel. Any major city public library will have references to dozens of them and will have several on its shelves.

There are many video versions of the novel or adaptations of it. *The Man of La Mancha,* a musical by Dale Wasserman, Joe Darion, and Mitch Leigh, is available in many public libraries and video stores.

There are no sequels to *Don Quixote,* but Cervantes wrote a collection of *Exemplary Novels,* all much shorter and all showing his characteristic style and flair. Samuel Putnam has translated some of these under the title *Three Exemplary Novels.*

Readers who have enjoyed an abridged version of *Don Quixote* would probably also find a great deal of pleasure in *The Three Musketeers* by Alexandre Dumas or *Candide* by Voltaire. For stories of chivalry, Sir Thomas Mallory's *La Morte d'Arthur* is to be recommended, though it has less humor than anything by Cervantes.

◆ FOR FURTHER REFERENCE ◆

Amis, Martin. "The Adventures of Don Quixote de la Mancha." *The Atlantic* (March, 1986): 104. A frank assessment of *Don Quixote* as unreadably dull, taken as a whole.

"Cervantes, Miguel de." In *Benet's Reader's Encyclopedia,* 3rd ed. New York: Har-perCollins, 1987. A brief, but informative, biography.

De Cervantes, Miguel. *The First Part of the Delightful History of the Most Ingenious Knight Don Quixote of the Mancha.* Translated by Thomas Shelton. New York: P. F. Collier & Son, 1909 (62nd printing, 1969).

De Cervantes Saavedra, Miguel. *Three Exemplary Novels.* Translated by Samuel Putnam. New York: Viking, 1950. These three novels are considered by some easier to read and enjoy than *Don Quixote.*

"*Don Quixote,* 1605, 1615." In *Benet's Reader's Encyclopedia,* 3rd ed. New York: HarperCollins, 1987. Summary of the book.

Forcione, Alban K. *Cervantes, Aristotle, and the "Persiles."* Princeton, NJ: Princeton University Press, 1970. A discussion of how Cervantes' "Persiles" merits by being derivative of Aristotle.

Hart, Thomas R. *Cervantes and Ariosto: Renewing Fiction.* Princeton, NJ: Princeton University Press, 1989. A detailed comparison, complete with quotes from *Don Quixote* and *Orlando Furioso* in the original Spanish and Italian as well as English translations. The author's thesis is that Cervantes was consciously derivative of Ariosto.

Johnson, Carroll B. *Madness and Lust: A Psychoanalytical Approach to "Don Quixote."* Berkeley: University of California Press, 1983. A psychoanalytical interpretation of the character and the novel.

McKeon, Michael. *The Origins of the English Novel 1600–1740.* Baltimore: Johns Hopkins University Press, 1987. Includes a Marxist analysis of Quixote.

Quint, David. "Narrative Interlace and Narrative Genres in Don Quijote and the Orlando Furioso." *Modern Language Quarterly* (September, 1997): 241. Another article which praises Cervantes' genius lavishly for not only being influenced by Ariosto but having the wit to turn to prose when his talents at poetry were insufficient.

Spiller, Elizabeth A. "Cervantes avant la Lettre: The Material Transformation of Romance: Reading Culture in Don Quijote." *Modern Language Quarterly* (September, 1999): 295. An interpretation of reading as a different cultural experience for modern readers than in Cervantes' day.

Paula Johanson

ENTER THE ENCHANTED

Novel

1999

Author: K. A. Applegate

◆

Major Books for Young Adults

The Story of Two American Generals:
  Benjamin O. Davis, Jr. and Colin L.
  Powell, 1992
The Boyfriend Mix-Up, 1994
Sharing Sam, 1995
Listen to My Heart, 1996

Boyfriends and Girlfriends series,
  including:
Zoey Fools Around, 1994
Lucas Gets Hurt, 1998
Claire Can't Lose, 1999
Who Loves Kate, 1999

Animorphs series, including:

The Message, 1996
The Stranger, 1997
The Reunion, 1999
The Prophecy, 2000
The Ultimate, 2001

Everworld series
Search for Senna, 1999
Land of Loss, 1999
Enter the Enchanted, 1999
Realm of the Reaper, 1999
The Destroyer, 1999
Fear the Fantastic, 2000
Understand the Unknown, 2000
Discover the Destroyer, 2000
Inside the Illusion, 2000

◆ ABOUT THE AUTHOR ◆

Katherine Alice Applegate is simultaneously one of America's most famous
authors and one of America's most mysterious. She guards her privacy, as does her
publisher, Scholastic, which has brilliantly
marketed her Animorphs and Everworld
series with astounding success. Applegate
was already a well-established writer of
books for young readers, mostly romance
novels, when she proposed the Animorphs
series to Scholastic, where the proposal was
met with enthusiasm. She wanted to write a
series of books that showed how the world
might look from the perspectives of different animals; the result has been a series of
fascinating novellas for readers from late
elementary school to junior high school.

After moving around the United States several times, the Michigan-born writer now resides in Minneapolis. Over a hundred of her books have been published books, and she has written them at an amazing pace. Begun in 1996, her Animorphs series numbered over forty books plus several spin-offs by 2001. Her series intended for adolescents, Everworld, begun in 1999, numbered nine volumes by the end of 2000. Sally Lodge, in *Publishers Weekly*, quotes Applegate, "A series writer has to develop plotting and pacing that become a well-oiled machine. You don't have the luxury of spending a year on a book and absolutely cannot indulge in writer's block. Yet I knew I had to write in perfect language and choose just the right images, to make sure that my middle readers fell in love with the characters and returned again and again.". The two hundred letters from young readers Applegate receives per week, as well as the one hundred emails she receives per day from youngsters, attest to the success she has had in reaching her intended audience. They love her characters.

In spite of the success of Applegate's writings, they have received scant attention in the press, perhaps because of a prevailing view that books written so quickly cannot be worth writing about, or perhaps because of the immense difficulty in keeping current with all the books Applegate publishes. In spite of the great pace at which Applegate has written her books, they tend to be of higher quality than other mass-market writings. In the Animorphs series the perspectives of characters as animals, whether fleas or birds, are artful and informative. The Everworld novels offer fine introductions to the mythologies of the world. In both series, the suspense is captivating and the characterizations are sharp but well-rounded; the books are page-turners, I-can't-go-to-bed-until-I-finish tales of adventure.

Applegate does not shy away from the tough questions about growing up and building sound, honest relationships with others. For instance, the nonseries title *Sharing Sam* deals with the prospect of a close friend dying and how to love in spite of the pain. In Everworld, the relationships among the principal characters are essential to the appeal of the novels. The art of characterization is one that Applegate has mastered, and it is perhaps the most important reason her rapidly-written works stand as good literature as well as entertaining reads.

◆ OVERVIEW ◆

The situation in Everworld grows ever more complicated for April, David, Christopher, and Jalil. The greatest complication comes in the form of Galahad, a knight of King Arthur's Round Table. The problem he presents is that in Arthurian literature his character is the blending of more than one mythological figure. In Everworld, this results in his sometimes being confused in his memories, as if he were more than one person. This seems to be a clue as to what is actually happening in Everworld, but April and her companions do not have much time to think about it.

Loki is the giant, angry god of Norse mythology. In the "Everworld" series, he reappears in all his cunning and all his fury, bringing with him mayhem and destruction. He is very good at destruction. There are limits to his power, frightful though it is, and Merlin knows something about how to frustrate Loki. As if the teenagers do not have enough to worry about, dragons make their appearance and unleash some of their destructive power. Not even the great castles of Galahad can shield April and the others from the symphony of destruction sweeping though Everworld.

According to April, "There was magic here [Everworld]. Not magic like, 'Ah, the moonlight was magic.' Magic as in cause and effect didn't always cause or effect. The magic that negates all human knowledge, that invalidates ten thousand years of human learning." Especially disturbing to her are the variations in the effect of gravity in Everworld. "If gravity could come and go, wax and wane, then things could fly when they could not possibly fly." This exemplifies one of April's special contributions to the "Everworld" series. She insists on maintaining a firm grasp of earth-style reality, comparing it to, and highlighting Everworld's unique qualities. Everworld is, as she says, "a place apart, a place not touching reality, isolated."

In *Enter the Enchanted*, April deals with the sometimes unpleasant realities of being the only Earth girl other than Senna in Everworld. She is relieved to find herself untouched in Galahad's castle; in Loki's castle and New Tenochtitlan, she was in danger of suffering many indignities. In the lands of Galahad, courtly courtesy reigns, and women are treated with respect. It is a land of magnificent castles, broad meadows, fine forests, and happy people. Yet, disaster follows April and her companions, and there are menaces such as Loki and remote menaces such as the one that threatens to kill Everworld's gods.

◆ THEMES AND CHARACTERS ◆

As much fun as they have been as narrators of *Search for Senna* and *Land of Loss*, David and Christopher do not seem to grow as much in those novels as April does in *Enter the Enchanted*. April O'Brien narrates *Enter the Enchanted*, and as she tells the story of the events that befall her and her companions after the dragon attack that ends *Land*

of Loss, she tells of an internal personal struggle for control of herself. She engages in a fundamental reassessment of who she is and who she ought to be. This reassessment involves her view of how women should behave and be treated, as well her view of herself as either a victim waiting to be victimized, or someone who takes action to help herself.

When, near the end of *Enter the Enchanted*, April watches Loki's trolls advance on the scant fortifications defended by what is left of Galahad's followers, April says, "Soon the trolls would rush and crush and drive the men before them and pour in on us and what was I going to do, stand there and scream, 'Save me, save me' when there was no one left alive to save me?" The experiences April has endured have stripped away much of her civilized veneer, leaving the real April exposed. In *Land of Loss*, Christopher admits that he was terrified by his experiences. He had to choose to overcome his fear or perish. April, too, has had to deal with her fear, but her morally superior attitude to those around her has taken a pounding, as too often others have done her fighting for her. She must choose who she really wants to be, the victim Senna sneers at, or an activist in her own life. "I started walking," she says. "Knees knocked. Stiff. Forcing my body to move, and then seeing, as though from far off, that movement had become automatic. Forward. Closer. No longer even involved with the act of moving, the choice made, now could not be unmade." April makes her choice about herself. This is what the main theme is about, taking responsibility for oneself, and *Enter the Enchanted* is April's story of difficult, complex growth. Although her growth is still incomplete at the novel's end, she notes that once she has taken her first steps the choice cannot be undone.

Each of the narrators believes events in Everworld have been particularly tough on him or her. This is symptomatic of self-centeredness, but it is a useful trait for each to have, because it contributes to Applegate's intention of having each novel uniquely reflect the individual narrator. April has her own special concerns, partly originating in her immersion in cultures—Viking, Aztec, and Arthurian—in which men tend to be the bosses and women stand a fair chance of being victims of violence. "I threw back the covers, a sudden, convulsive gesture," she declares. "I sighed. I still had my clothes on. A weird little outfit consisting of the clothes I'd been wearing down at the lake and the odds and ends I'd picked up from Vikings and Aztecs." This brief passage is a model of concision, of saying much with few words. It sets out her situation nicely; describing her clothes goes a good way toward describing how well-off she is. Beyond that is the subtext of her relief in being clothed, a point that she emphasizes by later repeating it: "Things couldn't be too bad: I was in a feather bed and had my clothes on." In literature, nudity can be an expression of a character's vulnerability; having her clothes on gives April a sense of security she would not otherwise have had in a strange place. It also means that she was not molested.

April is in a castle. David tells her that it is "Galahad's castle. Or one of them. I think he has more." April soon finds herself in a contest for David: not fighting for a boyfriend, but fighting because she fears he has lost control of his mind. "He [David] was her [Senna's] puppet. She might as well have her arm inserted up his butt." When Senna asserts that she is the only person who can enable April, David, Christopher, and Jalil to return home permanently, rather than only during their sleep, April demands that Senna release control of David. That Senna concedes to April's demand is important not only because she allows David to think for himself, but because it is an unspoken admission that she really does control his mind at times.

Thus, Senna's character is further developed in *Enter the Enchanted*. She becomes more than Loki's victim, dragged to Everworld to do his bidding—she is an active part of events. Although she is good at pretending to be the defenseless female who needs protection from big, strong males, she is, in fact, a deadly earnest player in Everworld's crisis. Christopher believes her to be a manipulator of minds in *Land of Loss*, but she could have been simply exerting the effect of her good looks on males who, according to April's view, are governed by rampaging hormones. In *Enter the Enchanted*, she makes it clear that she has used April and the others, even though she insists that she is one of them. April rejects that idea because Senna is too much the puppeteer and not enough the companion.

April seems resistant to Senna's mind control, and much of *Enter the Enchanted* focuses on April's contest of wills with Senna. She tries to persuade David to defy Senna: "'She lies to us, David,' I said. 'Uses us. I don't know how, I admit that, but she does, she is. She's using us right now, or else planning to.'" This makes April a danger to Senna, whose response is to taunt April and to threaten her. Even though April is willing to believe that only Senna can get her home, she finds herself "wondering which was worse: Senna alive, or Senna dead?" This suggests that April may be willing to sacrifice her chance to get home in order to prevent Senna from doing something monstrous such as letting Loki go to Earth. There is much courage in a person who believes "[Senna] was something different from me. Greater than me," yet stands her ground against Senna. Indeed, April has a good grasp of reality, in spite of the battering she has taken in a world where earthly physical laws are often disregarded. When Senna shows that she can misjudge people by saying to April, "You've decided you believe in me," April snaps back, "I believe in the same God I've always believed in, and guess what, that's still not you, Senna." Score a victory for April in the contest of wills.

The contest for Senna broadens in *Enter the Enchanted.* Loki had his own designs on her in *Search for Senna,* and he still does in *Enter the Enchanted,* but another great power enters the contest, Merlin:

> And in walked the old man with the once-blond hair and beard. He wore a robe, dark blue, but not the goofy curly-toed slippers you'd expect on some goofy book wizard. He wore boots crusted with mud and pants tucked in at the top, also muddy and only now beginning to dry. There was a sword at his side.

Applegate's Merlin is a man of action, symbolized by mud on the boots and the sword. The mud means that he is willing to get dirty, to get into the muck as April has, in order to get what he wants, and the sword means that he is willing to take action. Although he speaks of helping people, the reason he wants to control Senna is kept vague—he is not someone who gives away his plans.

Of all the people April and the others have met so far, Merlin has the best chance of standing up to a god like Loki. In *Search for Senna,* David describes Loki as huge. Typical of his point of view, David focuses on how formidable an adversary Loki would be. This contrasts with April's point of view: "He [Loki] was handsome, that's what was weird about him. Lustrous blond hair, high cheekbones, and perfect teeth. He could have been a model. He could have been a movie star." That Loki could be attractive is an important idea, because it suggests that violence is not the only means of persuasion available to him. The passage also shows something of how Applegate makes each narrative in the Everworld novels

unique to the individual narrator. In this case, the different narrators focus on different details about someone they both describe. Yet, handsome or not, Loki reveals himself in all his rampant evil when fighting breaks out between his forces and those of Galahad.

There is much to admire in Galahad, and April is just the right person to notice the warmth of his personality, as well as his strength of character. At dinner, she notes:

> Galahad was calm, assured, soft-spoken once we were past his bellowed demand for "Food!" His eyes were often downcast, not sad, but thoughtful. He smiled, but not in derision, only in welcome. He sat tall in his chair, arms held wide, open, inviting, an equal at least in his body language. When he spoke, he met the eyes of the person he spoke to, listened attentively, nodded appreciatively.

April may be forgiven for liking Galahad more than most of the other people he meets. She eventually learns that he is not just talk and good feelings; when it comes to treating people well he is willing to fight and to die for them.

Enter the Enchanted is April's novel, and her companions tend to be background figures. David is often too trusting, but he proves to be a magnificent fighter when called upon to fight the trolls. Christopher makes wisecracks and tries to stand and fight if he can. Jalil is the analyst. There are hints of what his narrative in the next novel will be like when he says of his home world, "We live in a superstitious age. People's heads full of mush." His supercilious attitude ends up annoying just about everyone.

◆ LITERARY QUALITIES ◆

Maintaining interest in a story line that transpires over a series of novels is chal-

Book cover illustration by Greg Spalenka for *Enter the Enchanted* by K.A. Applegate.

the audience's appetite for more adventures in Everworld. For example, Loki says, "The thousand years of the prophecy are almost done." What prophecy? The only way to find out is to continue reading. Direct threats can also heighten tension and interest: "As we came to Everworld, we can return to the Old World [the Earth]," Loki declares. Then there is the matter of the invasion of Everworld: "Ka Anor is the god-eater, he will kill you all, one by one, and the Hetwan will exterminate all the free peoples, and that will be an end to Everworld," shouts Merlin. The prospect of a cosmic conflict involving all the quarrelsome, complex gods of Everworld against someone called a "god-eater" promises great action and thrills to come. Further, there is Merlin's declared hope to unite all of Everworld to fight Ka Anor and save Everworld. Although this sounds grand, as Loki points out, Merlin's last attempt resulted in the death of King Arthur. Merlin does not have a good track record for fighting evil. So, what is it to be? Is there to be a unified front, an invasion of the Earth, or two invasions, not only of Earth but of Everworld, too? Applegate promises excitement to come with well-placed remarks, declarations, and threats.

When April catches David with his shirt off Applegate employs literary irony (the audience of a literary work, in this case a novel, knows more about what is going on than the characters do). In the case of April in *Enter the Enchanted*, we the audience understand more about what April is talking about than she does. Her criticism of men as immature and guided by their hormones turns on her when she fails to recognize that looking at David's attractive chest is obviously not something only a guy would do, because she is in fact doing exactly that—staring at a chest. As the audience, we are aware of her feelings and reaction, even if she is not aware.

lenging. One good way to do it is with foreshadowing, but Applegate is faced with the challenge of dropping the tantalizing phrases of mysteries to be solved and action to come without compromising her fictional narrator, April. So, the author does this in part by having characters mention their plans or worries in vague terms, for example, Merlin shows himself to be actively involved in the contest for possession of Senna without giving away exactly what he means to do with her. That he is an enemy of Loki does not mean that he is a friend to April or to earth, although he drops hints about wanting to protect Earth.

Cryptic remarks by characters is another way to foreshadow future events and whet

◆ SOCIAL SENSITIVITY ◆

In *Enter the Enchanted*, April is in a man's world, a patriarchal society in which noblemen such as Galahad are in charge. This will not always be the case in other novels, but in *Enter the Enchanted*, it is a special concern for April, especially since events in New Tenochtitlan, in *Land of Loss*, have shown the depravity to which people can sink in Everworld. Therefore, it is only natural to be happy to find when she awakens in Galahad's castle that she has been unmolested. It is comforting to her to discover that Galahad expects women to be treated well.

Through the first three novels of Everworld, April has been concerned about differences between men and women and a bit uncomfortable about her own sexual feelings. She has manifested her concern by criticizing all men, accusing them all of being governed by hormones and afflicted by immaturity. In *Enter the Enchanted*, she shows that much of her problem in dealing with her male companions comes from her own confusion about what are right and wrong feelings to have. For instance, when she knocks on David's door and he opens it and is only wearing pants, April's eyes are drawn to David's chest. She resists looking at it, while trying to focus on talking with him, but her thoughts stray to *"I said, don't look at his chest, it's tacky. It's the kind of thing a guy would do."* If one has read *Search for Senna* and *Land of Loss*, then one knows that David is big and athletic, and his chest might reasonably attract admiring looks. Yet, April feels unready for her sexual emotions and tries to set them aside—and evidently she fails. She probably should be forgiven for this, because just as she claims that men have been raised to go to war, so she has been raised with social dogma that does not necessarily apply to real life. It is taking her time to sort through what she wants to be true, what she feels, and what should be true.

Her comment on men is a curious one, probably meant to show just how far her prejudices go. She remarks, "[Men had] been raised from birth with the understanding that the day might come when they would have to go to war." She offers this comment not as a condemnation of men, although in an offhanded way it is, but as an explanation for her own paralysis as Loki's trolls approach her. "And for me, for all women, it wasn't that way. I had never played the video games, the mock battles, never run the fantasies through my head, never channel-surfed and felt the draw to stop at every battle scene." If the readers of this passage are thoughtful ones, they will note that April's premise is fundamentally wrong. In life, America has many brave, heroic women in the military; they must have thought about going to war. Further, many women play video games. What April is doing is denying her own individual problems by saying that "all women" are just like she is. This may be at the root of her objections to David, Christopher, and Jalil—not that they suffer from congenital male stupidity, but that they have points of view that vary from what she wants them to think.

◆ TOPICS FOR DISCUSSION ◆

1. Was killing off Galahad a good idea? Will you miss him?

2. Galahad is a mixture of mythological figures. What does this imply about the other denizens of Everworld?

3. What accounts for April's sometimes sexist attitude?

4. When does April save the lives of her companions?

5. How dangerous is Senna to April?

6. Does David accept April's claim that Senna somehow controls his mind? Why or why not?

7. Is Merlin on the side of good or of evil, or some other side altogether? How do you know?

8. How good is April at describing battles? What is significant about her perspective during the battles?

9. Are there dream-like passages in *Land of Loss*?

10. In *Land of Loss*, Christopher suggests to April that she is overly concerned with "Political Correctness." Does she seem that way in *Enter the Enchanted*?

11. In what ways does April change during her narrative in *Enter the Enchanted*? How well does she adapt to her situation in Everworld?

12. Why would the dragon kill Galahad? What does this say about the dragon? What might it foreshadow for contact with dragons in later novels?

◆ IDEAS FOR REPORTS AND PAPERS ◆

1. What does Loki mean when he says that Merlin got careless and cost King Arthur his life?

2. The Galahad of *Enter the Enchanted* is the combination of more than one figure, according to April. What are the mythical origins of the knight now known as Galahad?

3. In the Middle Ages, what rules were supposed to govern the conduct of knights toward women?

4. Who is Merlin? In what ancient stories is he found? Based on the stories about him, how may he be expected to behave in Everworld?

5. What are trolls? Where do they come from? Why would they be in Loki's army?

6. Does April sound like a teenager? Where does she sound most realistic, and where does she sound more like Applegate?

7. Compare the narratives of *Enter the Enchanted*, *Land of Loss*, and *Search for Senna*. Are there notable differences in how the stories are told? Are there notable similarities? What does this tell you about Applegate's artistic achievement in *Enter the Enchanted*?

8. Draw a map of an ancient British castle, showing how the rooms would be laid out, and note the different places where April would have been and where the action in *Enter the Enchanted* takes place.

9. Loki changes size in *Enter the Enchanted*. Is this something that happens in Norse myths?

10. What are the common characteristics of dragons in medieval European folktales? Are any of these characteristics reflected in *Enter the Enchanted*?

◆ RELATED TITLES ◆

Applegate likes to experiment, and her novels tend to be lively exercises in ideas and techniques. In the case of Everworld, she creates a place where the world's ancient mythologies coexist, and she has fun creating adventures that involve mixing the mythologies. For the "Everworld" series, she creates four adventurers who are snatched from fairly ordinary teenaged American lives, although Jalil's psychological problems are somewhat out of the ordinary. Through these characters she experiments with techniques of narration by having each one narrate novels: first David for *Search for Senna*, then Christopher for *Land of Loss*, then April for *Enter the Enchanted*, then Jalil for *Realm of the Reaper*, and the cycle is repeated through the subsequent novels.

This can be disconcerting. David is a very engaging narrator, and losing his storytelling voice for *Land of Loss* is disappointing, although Christopher manages to make *Land of Loss* his own novel. In *Enter the Enchanted*, April proves to be an engaging narrator who is frank about her concerns and about what she observes, especially in the behavior of others. She whines a little bit, blaming others when events do not go according to her hopes. The personality of each narrator shows through in each book, and April proves herself to be an appealing figure, courageous and thoughtful. The shifting of narrators allows Everworld to be described through David's love of action and interest in logistics, through Christopher's acidic humor and tendency to see below the surface of events to find what is really going on, through April's good sense and practicality, and through Jalil's analytical mind that finds the logic linking events.

The novels also continue to introduce mythologies, and in the process, Applegate creates a new mythology of her own. Human endeavors are placed in a vast cosmic scheme in which everyone is important, even though in any individual novel they may seem like pawns. Once the youngsters meet Merlin in *Land of Loss*, the grand contest of universe-shaking powers begins to reveal itself, and dreams really do seem more real than real life. *Enter the Enchanted* advances the story of Everworld by showing how Merlin views

Senna, how Loki hopes to achieve his goals, and how the mythological figures of Everworld may be like Galahad, products more of human imagination than earthly substance.

◆ FOR FURTHER REFERENCE ◆

"Applegate, Katherine (Alice)." In *Authors and Artists for Young Adults,* vol. 37. Detroit: Gale, 2000. A biographical essay with comments on Applegate's life and work.

"Applegate, Katherine (Alice)." In *Something about the Author,* vol. 109. Detroit: Gale, 2000. An essay that includes biographical information about Applegate and information about her writing.

"NYC Radio Station Celebrates the Season." *Publishers Weekly* (January 17, 2000): 26. Mentions the marketing of the "Everworld" series.

Review of *Search for Senna. Publishers Weekly* (June 21, 1999): 69. In this review the critic says, "With her blend of accessible story and mythological cast of characters, Applegate is sure to attract a host of new fans."

"Scholastic's Animorphs Series Has Legs." *Publishers Weekly* (November 3, 1997): 36–37.

Kirk H. Beetz

FANTASTIC BEASTS AND WHERE TO FIND THEM

Novel

2001

Author: J. K. Rowling

◆

Major Books for Young Adults

Harry Potter and the Philosopher's Stone,
  1997 (also published as *Harry Potter
  and the Sorcerer's Stone*)
*Harry Potter and the Chamber of
  Secrets,* 1998

*Harry Potter and the Prisoner of
  Azkaban,* 1999
Harry Potter and the Goblet of Fire, 2000
*Fantastic Beasts and Where to Find
  Them,* 2001
Quidditch Through the Ages, 2001

◆ ABOUT THE AUTHOR ◆

J. K. (Joanne Kathleen) Rowling was born in Gloucestershire, England on July 31, 1966. She attended Exeter University and worked as a teacher in Edinburgh, Scotland and in Portugal before publishing her first Harry Potter book in 1997. She wrote this book while she was a single mother supported by public assistance, unable to work and pay for child care at the same time. After the publication of this first book, entitled *Harry Potter and the Sorcerer's Stone,* Rowling's situation changed from rags to riches. The first three books in her seven book series sold over 30 million copies, they were printed in 35 languages, and Rowling earned over $400 million.

Rowling has received numerous awards for her Harry Potter books, and because of her tremendous success stimulating children to read, she was awarded an honorary doctorate from St. Andrews, Scotland in 2000. Because Rowling's Harry Potter books dominated the top slots on the *New York Times* Best Seller list, the decision was made to create a separate best seller's list for children's books. This of course, was an honor to Rowling as well as a boon for children's authors. Rowling is an inspiration for children's authors. She achieved stardom with her first published book, she sold Warner Bros. the film rights to her first two books, and she sold all seven volumes of Harry Potter's adventures as a series, each volume focusing on one year of Harry's training at the Hogwarts School of Witchcraft and Wizardry. The publication of

J. K. Rowling

Quidditch Through the Ages and *Fantastic Beasts and Where to Find Them* came about after the British charity Comic Relief, dedicated to helping poor children all over the world, asked Rowling to write something for them. They suggested a short story at first, but Rowling instead suggested the idea of producing two of Harry's textbooks from the Hogwarts School. Not surprisingly, these two "textbooks" achieved remarkable success. They are distributed all over the world, and most of the money from these titles goes to charity.

◆ OVERVIEW ◆

Fantastic Beasts and Where to Find Them is a spin-off from the books in Rowling's Harry Potter series and is intended to be one of the books Harry and his friends use themselves. This book is among Harry Potter's own schoolbooks, with *Fantastic Beasts and Where*

to Find Them purportedly written by Newt Scamander, an expert in "magizoology." This book is a bestiary, hailed as the most complete listing of imaginary creatures available and containing both familiar beasts, such as unicorns and dragons, and unfamiliar ones, such as Flobberworms and Mackled Malaclaws. Rowling lists these beasts in alphabetical order and provides detailed information about each one, as well as including a rating indicating how dangerous each of these beasts is to non-magic folks, or Muggles. Rowling intended for these books to seem like real textbooks, textbooks that readers of the "Harry Potter" books may already find familiar. *Fantastic Beasts* was mentioned in Rowling's first book, *Harry Potter and the Sorcerer's Stone,* where it was required reading for first-year students in the Hogwarts School of Witchcraft and Wizardry.

◆ SETTING ◆

The setting of the book is truly within the fantasy world Rowling created for Harry Potter and his friends; a place where witches and wizards and magical beings of all sorts exist side by side with ordinary beings. When Rowling brought Harry Potter and his friends to life, she created a world in which children of all ages found themselves immersed, and where they could hold on to their childhood belief in magic. It is in this world where Rowling's fantastic beasts live, seventy-five species in all, in addition to ten separate species of dragon. Rowling is adept at sustaining her fantasy. She describes the habitat of these creatures as if they existed in the real world, informing readers that the Leprechaun lives only in Ireland, for instance, and that the Tebo lives in the Congo and Zaire. All of these creatures can materialize in Harry Potter's world, however, though often times only the wizards can see them. Newt Scamander, in his introduction, explains one reason why Muggles, or ordinary folks, rarely see them. Muggles fear magic, he explains, so they are under the illusion that these creatures exist only in the imagination. The setting of the book, therefore, is the imagination, and any reader who finds himself captivated with Rowling's books lives in the imagination as well.

This book is unconventional in that it is not intended as a listing of mythological creatures as such, but it is intended as a listing of creatures presumed by those engrossed in Harry Potter's magic world to actually exist. If there were a theme to be identified in the book it would have to be simply the validation that magic exists, and the underlying belief that wizards can encounter any of the creatures that grace these pages at any time.

In addition to the beasts themselves, the characters in the book are the Harry Potter characters who give these beasts reality. Included are Harry Potter, his friend Ron Weasley, Newt Scamander, Professor Dumbledore (who wrote the Foreword), and all of the peripheral characters who add validity to Rowling's world. Harry's friend Hagrid, for instance, also appears, as do Dumbledore's wife, Porpetina, and their pet Kneazles: Hoppy, Milly and Mauler.

Kneazles are just one of the seventy-five types of creatures listed in the bestiary. The entry for each type of creature attempts to validate the creature's existence by including a description of the its characteristics and habitat and an explanation of its relationship with wizards. Each entry also includes a Ministry of Magic (M.O.M.) classification rating how dangerous the creature is, whether it is essentially harmless, or whether it is a "known wizard killer" and "impossible to tame or domesticate." The

horrendous Nandu who Harry and Ron encounter in *Harry Potter and the Chamber of Secrets,* the Knarl who Muggles often mistake for a hedgehog, and the demonic Nogtail who resembles a stunted piglet are just a few of the fantastic creatures listed in the bestiary. The footnotes provide additional information and refer the reader to other fictional books, written by other fictional authors, which add to the scholarly tone of the book.

Fantastic Beasts and How to Find Them is written for Muggles, non-magical people who share the world with wizards but who have no power and therefore no knowledge of how to interact with powerful creatures. Dumbledore, in the Foreward, explains why this book is now offered to Muggles for the first time. In Harry Potter's world, the book can be found in the households of nearly every family that practices wizardry, Dumbledore tells readers. He says that the book is in its fifty-second edition, attesting to its usefulness and importance as a scholarly textbook.

Newt Scamander, the fictional author of this book, can perhaps be considered the book's primary "character" because it is his knowledge of "magizoology" that qualified him to write the bestiary and it is Rowling's knowledge of him that allows him to do it. Scamander, of course, is simply a pen name for J. K. Rowling, but his character existed in her mind and in her other books long before this book was published. Rowling provides information about Scamander's life and work on a page entitled "About the Author." This "author" purportedly collected the information for the book while traveling abroad during research trips for the Dragon Research and Restraint Bureau. Scamander appears in the book *Harry Potter and the Sorcerer's Stone* as a known expert in "magizoology," which is defined as "the study of magical beasts." He worked for the Beast Division of the

Ministry of Magic in the Department of the Regulation and Control of Magical Creatures for many years, but is now retired and living in Dorset.

Just as Rowling uses the character of Scamander to write the book, she uses the character of Albus Dumbledore to relate the book's purpose. Both of these characters are familiar to Harry Potter fans. Dumbledore is the headmaster of Hogwarts School of Witchcraft and Wizardry, and Scamander chose him to write the Foreword. In this section Dumbledore informs readers that the book supports Comic Relief, that this is a facsimile of Harry's personal copy, and that this book is now being offered to Muggles for the first time. Rowling fills Dumbledore's Foreword with facts that sustain the fantasy and keep readers captivated by her magical world. It says, "Wizards wishing to make additional donations [to Comic Relief] should do so through Gringotts Wizarding Bank (ask for Griphook)". It also says that the book carries a "Thief's Curse," and that Muggles should be assured that "the amusing creatures described hereafter are fictional and cannot hurt you."

◆ LITERARY QUALITIES ◆

Newt Scamander (a.k.a. J. K. Rowling) wrote *Fantastic Beasts and Where to Find Them* in encyclopedia format, thus giving it a stamp of reality. Rowling uses numerous devices to make her book a credible representation of Harry Potter's actual schoolbook. First and foremost, Rowling does not identify herself as the author, but rather she identifies one of the characters from her fictional world as the author. She also includes graffiti, scribbled in the book's margins by Harry and Ron, to give substance to her characters and to maintain the suspension of disbelief.

◆ SOCIAL SENSITIVITY ◆

The wide appeal of Rowling's books and the success she has had in creating a world of magic influenced this author to create this "textbook" and its companion book, *Quidditch Through the Ages. Fantastic Beasts and Where to Find Them* is geared to people of all ages, and to Harry Potter fans specifically, but also to anyone who peruses any kind of bestiary or mythological reference book and to anyone who finds themselves captivated by the idea that a world may exist that is not readily recognizable to humans. *Fantastic Beasts* serves as an actual bestiary, providing information about unicorns and kelpies and many other creatures that appear in myths and legends around the world. Even people who have never read a "Harry Potter" book will find many of these beasts familiar.

On first inspection, it appears that *Fantastic Beasts and Where to Find Them*, as well as *Quidditch Through the Ages*, is an effort on Rowling's part to cash in on her fame. Due to the popularity of her "Harry Potter" books, Rowling probably knew that people would read anything connected to Harry Potter. Furthermore, the timing of these two textbooks was perfect: they were published in 2000 when no other Harry Potter books could be seen on the horizon. Though these two books certainly boosted Rowling's popularity, she wrote them for charity and not for profit. Proceeds from both *Fantastic Beasts and Where to Find Them* and *Quidditch Through the Ages* support Comic Relief, a British charity founded by a group of comedians to help needy children around the world.

◆ TOPICS FOR DISCUSSION ◆

1. Do you think that J. K. Rowling wrote this book and its companion book pri-

marily to increase her stardom or primarily to help the British charity Comic Relief? Explain.

2. Who would you identify as the primary characters in this book, the mythological beasts or Harry Potter, Ron Weasley, Professor Dumbledore, and Newt Scamander?

3. Why do you suppose Dumbledore says in the foreword that the creatures in the book are imaginary and can not hurt you?

4. Do you think the A-Z format of the book hinders Rowlings' ability to be creative? Why or why not?

◆ IDEAS FOR REPORTS AND PAPERS ◆

1. Explain the devices Rowling uses to make this bestiary appear to be real.

2. J. K. Rowling's "Harry Potter" books have been so successful that readers in the United States often purchase copies of the British editions over the Internet rather than wait for the American editions to be published. This has caused much controversy, however. Research the issue of "marketing territory infringement" and voice your opinion on it the issue as it relates to Rowling's books.

3. Discuss the ways in which Rowling develops the character of Newt Scamander.

4. Rowling's books have received criticism from some Christian fundamentalists who believe that the Harry Potter books promote Satanism. Research this issue and describe the reasoning behind this claim.

5. Explain the term "suspension of disbelief" and relate it to Rowling's writing.

◆ RELATED TITLES ◆

Quidditch Through the Ages, the companion book to *Fantastic Beasts and Where to Find Them*, is another of Harry Potter's schoolbooks. This one not Harry's own copy, but purportedly borrowed from the library of Harry's school, the Hogwarts School of Witchcraft and Wizardry. Quidditch is a game of wizards and witches, something like soccer but played in the air on broomsticks, and this book provides a history of the sport and details accounts of past matches.

In addition to *Fantastic Beasts and Where to Find Them*, numerous other bestiaries have been published over the years, though most of them serve as general listings of creatures in myths and legends throughout the ages. Books such as *The Book of Beasts* by T. H. White, *Treasury of Fantastic and Mythological Creatures: 1087 Renderings from Historic Sources* by Richard Huber, and *Gurps Bestiary* by Steffan O'Sullivan, et al., all serve the purpose of identifying imaginary creatures people might encounter as they read myths and legends from different parts of the world.

Many of the beasts in Rowling's book appear in these other bestiaries as well, though many of them are unique to her own books and the magic world she creates for Harry Potter and his friends. David Day attempted to do something of this same thing with his *Tolkein Bestiary*, published in 1984. This book lists imaginary beasts that appear in J. R. R. Tolkein's *The Hobbit* and *Lord of the Rings*. In addition to imaginary beasts, Day's book includes races, nations, deities, fauna, and flora unique to the Middle Earth and the Undying Land, the mythical worlds Tolkein created in his works.

◆ FOR FURTHER REFERENCE ◆

Bethune, Brian. "Fun and Games with Harry." *MacLean's* (March 19, 2001): 50.

Review of *Fantastic Beasts and Where to Find Them.*

Cooper, Ilene. Review of *Fantastic Beasts and Where to Find Them. Booklist* (May 1, 2001): 1683–1684.

Gleick, Elizabeth. "The Wizard of Hogwarts." *Time* (April 12, 1999): 86. Discusses Rowling's success as an author, gives a bit of biographical information about her, and provides information on the appeal of her books.

Gray, Paul. "Magic 101." *Time* (March 19, 2001): 77. Review of *Fantastic Beasts and Where to Find Them.*

Jones, Malcolm. Review of *Fantastic Beasts and Where to Find Them. Newsweek* (March 19, 2001): 62.

"Rowling, J(oanne) K(athleen)." In *Contemporary Authors*, vol. 173. Detroit: Gale, 1999. Biographical information about Rowling.

Tamra Andrews

FORTY ACRES AND MAYBE A MULE

Novel

1998

Author: Harriette Gillem Robinet

◆

Major Books for Young Adults

Jay and the Marigold, 1976
Ride the Red Cycle, 1980
Children of Fire, 1991
Mississippi Chariot, 1994
If You Please, President Lincoln, 1995
Washington City Is Burning, 1996

The Twins, the Pirates, and the Battle of New Orleans, 1997
Forty Acres and Maybe a Mule, 1998
Children of the Haymarket Struggle, 2000
Walking to the Bus Rider Blues, 2000
Missing from Haymarket Square, 2001

◆ ABOUT THE AUTHOR ◆

Harriette Gillem Robinet was born July 14, 1931, in Washington, D.C. She is the daughter of Richard Avitus and Martha Gray, both teachers. She spent her childhood in Arlington, Virginia, where her maternal grandfather had been a slave under General Robert E. Lee. She attended the College of New Rochelle in New York and received her master's and doctorate degrees from Catholic University of America in Washington, D.C. She lives with her husband, McLouis Robinet, in Oak Park, Illinois. Before turning to writing in 1962, she worked as a bacteriologist in Children's Hospital, Washington, D.C., a medical bacteriologist at Walter Reed Army Medical Center, a research bacteriologist at Xavier University in New Orleans, Louisiana, an instructor in biology for the U.S. Army, and as a civilian food bacteriologist. She has six children and four grandchildren. A son afflicted with cerebral palsy has influenced Robinet's writing, as the protagonists in her first two books, *Jay and the Marigold* and *Ride the Red Cycle* must triumph over physical handicaps.

◆ OVERVIEW ◆

Twelve-year-old slave, Pascal, is reunited with his runaway brother, Gideon, who brings news that all slaves have been freed. Pascal, Gideon, and eight-year-old Nelly flee their master's plantation, searching for the forty acres and a mule General Sherman has promised the ex-slaves. En route to Georgia, they meet poor white travelers,

Harriette Gillem Robinet

site among the trees, for example, she surrounds the children with "the gurgle of the ditch," "mosquito whines and cricket chirps." She writes that "sunbeams danced on their faces, and the scent of broken pine branch spiced the air." Robinet makes Gideon's parcel of land seem like an Eden. "Wind-dancing willows" line the lake and creek. "Grass and wildflowers blanketed the land. Meadowlarks flashed yellow feathers, singing as they flew across the flowers. Red-winged blackbirds called from cat-nine-tails at the creek. The land smelled clean and fertile and good."

◆ THEMES AND CHARACTERS ◆

Robinet fleshes out this specific episode of the Reconstruction with a quintet of characters, each having strengths and weaknesses. Pascal, a twelve-year-old slave with a crippled leg and arm, is the likable narrator of the story. He is charming as he amuses Nelly and Judith, his two friends, with terrible puns. His generosity and kindness towards the poor, white Bibbs family has great appeal. Falling asleep in the cotton rows or sneaking away from the field are realistic reactions to the fatigue, hard work, and withering Georgia sun. The reader quickly empathizes and identifies with him.

Pascal progresses from a tag-along little brother to a problem solver. His quick thinking saves Gideon after he falls through a dilapidated bridge. He also rescues Gideon from a confrontation with a white man. A clever youth, Pascal asks Michael and Judith to play near Green Gloryland so that others might think that whites own the farm. Night riders who would burn the crops on freed slaves' farms, thus pass by, fooled by Pascal's trick.

However, Pascal has a big responsibility as narrator in the story. He must tell the reader much of what happens before the story actually begins, either by conveniently

bigoted ne'er-do-wells, and night riders. During this six months of the Reconstruction, the children and their new friends claim their promised land, plant crops on it, and attend school. But all the while, they fear retaliation by resentful white Southerners. Finally, the family is evicted from their farm, Green Gloryland. As the story unfolds, each character seeks and amends individual definitions of freedom.

◆ SETTING ◆

By mentioning that a treat for Pascal was an uneaten biscuit his mother picked up from the Master's plate, that he slept in a shanty with six other people, or that no one had hugged him since his mother's death, Robinet brings the reader face to face with the realities of plantation life from which Pascal escapes. Robinet is at her best describing rural environments. At a camp-

remembering the past or by summary. Some reviewers feel that Pascal sees and remembers just too much for his age, and notice that his moralizing seems a bit forced. As freed slaves flee the burned down Jubilee Town, he wonders, "Brother? Sister? Yes . . . in bad times and good we all be family. He was looking for three brothers, but maybe he belonged to a bigger family."

Pascal's older brother, Gideon, enters *Forty Acres and Maybe a Mule* as a brittle militant. Slaves on the plantation think the sixteen-year-old has always been a "sound-off" and are surprised he has not gotten himself killed for his outspokenness. Pascal remembers that previously, Gideon put burrs under the overseer's saddle so his horse will throw. Gideon plans "slow downs" for the young slaves in the fields. He is rebellious and insolent to hostile whites.

Though he cruelly calls his brother "crooked leg" and eight-year-old Nelly "good for nothing," he does possess a softer side. He tells Pascal to stay out of town and protect Nelly while he finds out about the Freedmen's Bureau. He reasons, "Just in case some white man get mad. I'll do the finding out." He offers food to other ex-slaves and asks Mister Freedman, an ex-slave they come upon, to join his troupe for supper. He is emotionally overcome when he obtains the farm land. When it is taken from him, he cries again.

Nelly is an eight-year-old with "biscuit-tan skin color and full moon eyes of honey brown." An orphan, she joins the brothers' search for land. At first, she is so frightened all she can do is twist her braids and wait for Pascal's reassurance and protection. Later, when Gideon returns from town beaten up, she tends his cuts and holds a wet rag to his swollen face. Gradually she acquires a larger matriarchal role, suggesting she and Pascal fish, giving food to Pascal (actually, stuffing it into his mouth like a baby), and sewing pockets on his clothing.

More importantly, her imaginative insight lifts their spirits. She tells Pascal to pick up a pretty pebble to appreciate "the glory of the earth" and urges him to make his shadow dance. She answers Pascal's question about dreams and wishes. "We living out the dream of every slave what ever been borned. Landowners of the prettiest farm on God's green earth."

Pascal provides the wit. Gideon provides the will. Nelly supplies the imagination for their new life. Mister Freedman, as the only adult in Pascal's ever-increasing family, brings adult skill to the enterprise of farming. He suggests clearing the land by burning instead of plowing. He knows how to build a house, complete with front porch and hidden escape routes. When they lose Green Gloryland, he dismantles the house and reassembles it on the Bibbs' place. He will survive after the farm is given to whites by his carpentry skills.

The Bibbs family, who eventually settle on adjacent land, seem to be color blind. From their first meeting, they treat the freed slaves well. They see the freed slaves as individuals seeking a dream, just as they do. They regret the injustices that fall on Pascal's family when they lose Green Gloryland.

The characters in *Forty Acres and Maybe a Mule* consider the many nuances of freedom. Throughout much of the book, their definition requires owning land. Gideon first introduces the notion when he returns to the plantation with the news. He says, "President Lincoln freed us slaves two years ago. And better still, now we gonna have our own land."

The characters then embellish this requirement with the other trappings of freedom. Pascal concludes freedom means there will be no more running errands, fanning breezes, or shooing flies for the Master. Nelly believes freedom also means no more whippings at the whipping tree. Daydreaming, Pascal says "every morning we gonna rise up singing, and every night we gonna laugh till the moon rise, and the stars sing 'Glory to God.'" Mr. Freedman thinks eating biscuits for breakfast every day of the week is part of freedom.

In another discussion, they reach deeper definitions of freedom. Mr. Freedman says, "Freedom is all about having dignity. I don't have to feel shame." Gideon adds, "I think freedom be all about owning land and having people look at you with respect."

Once the makeshift family settles on their forty acres, freedom includes an education, an ability to make money, and a house with a front porch. But by the book's end, they have lost the land, the farmhouse, and its front porch. Faced with the loss of all these material things, the family arrives at a larger definition of freedom. Their new definition is internal—one based on what each person believes about himself. Pascal tells Nelly, "Freedom be here, like you said. Can't nobody take it away." Later he tells her ". . .we can BE free. We can do what be good and right."

Another theme of the book concerns survival. Gideon and Pascal's mother was shot because she fought injustice with confrontation. Gideon would be well on the way to same fate if it were not for Pascal's wiser counsel. He tells Gideon, "Sometime we got to talk nice to white folks and just accept things to stay alive." He seems to realize that the actions of ignorant white folks matter little when you already have the gift of freedom in your heart.

◆ LITERARY QUALITIES ◆

There is no doubt why this book is entitled *Forty Acres and Maybe a Mule*. The phrase, first mentioned on page four, is the refrain to the ex-slaves' song of freedom. It appears in practically every chapter as the goal Gideon hopes to achieve, as the dream they attain in Georgia, and as the vision they lose when their farm is confiscated.

Robinet expands facts text books would cover in three or four paragraphs. The entire *Forty Acres and Maybe a Mule* personifies one family's application of General Sherman's Field Order No. 13. Pascal and Nellie bring the reader along with them into the town where freed slaves are enveloped in the Black Codes and required to sign work contracts.

Robinet chooses three trees to symbolize the effects of the Civil War and Reconstruction on Pascal and his expanded family. The whipping tree on the plantation, the Ghost Tree on Green Gloryland, and the apple seedlings the Bibbs give them represents the past, present, and future for the liberated slaves.

By the book's end, Robinet ironically makes Pascal and Gideon switch attitudes towards injustice that befalls them. Once quiet and acquiescent, Pascal is outraged by the loss of the farm. Once a fighter and rebel, Gideon grasps at the hope of a new farm on Sea Island.

Throughout the story, Robinet uses rural colloquialisms like "living high on the hog" and "when push comes to shove," explaining their literal meaning within the action of the story. She replaces "are" and "was" in the freed slaves' conversations with "be," as in "When he said his mama be Jerusalem City, I knew he be our brother. When I told him I be Gideon, his baby brother, he smiled and died." Reviewers have praised Robinet for her ability to capture the rich language used by the freed slaves, adding to the historical context of the novel.

◆ SOCIAL SENSITIVITY ◆

Robinet's story ably dramatizes the atrocities of plantation life and the South's continuing hatred of its freed slaves. The plantation master and overseer are despicable. Night riders lynch hard-working farmers simply because they are ex-slaves. Ne'er-do-wells in carriages malign President Lincoln's policies.

Through the events surrounding Pascal, readers see that neither war nor law change social attitudes. The legislation first gave and then took away the ex-slaves' land grants. Similarly, Pascal's story has no happy ending. As Robinet points out in her Author's Note, out of 40,000 freed slaves who were awarded farm land, all but 1,565 lost the land. By 1877, most of the land returned to the hands of the former slave owners. Northern troops, Abolitionists, and even the Supreme Court abandoned the cause of freedom for the ex-slaves.

Book cover illustration by Bessie Nickens for *Forty Acres and Maybe a Mule* by Harriette Gillem Robinet.

◆ TOPICS FOR DISCUSSION ◆

1. Gideon is sixteen years old and Pascal is just twelve. Cite ways Robinet makes Pascal seem more mature than his brother.

2. On their journey to find forty acres and a mule, what other facets of freedom do the children discover?

3. How does the City family, the name Pascal and friends give themselves, change their idea of freedom by the end of the novel?

4. Describe what schooling was like in the novel in terms of discipline, subjects studied, and the attitude of the students. Compare this to today's education.

5. How does Miss Anderson, the school teacher, change her ideas of her students and what she should be teaching them by the end of the novel?

6. In the novel, three trees are very important: the whipping tree, the Ghost Tree, and the apple tree the Bibbs give Gideon and Gladness. Discuss what each tree symbolizes for the freed slaves.

7. Discuss the ways Robinet keeps the Bibbs' family, the school teacher, and the Freedman's Bureau's representative from becoming stereotypes of the vengeful whites.

8. Discuss the ways that Gideon and Pascal have exchanged viewpoints about the injustices that controlled their lives.

9. Explain how Pascal and Gideon have changed after farming their own land.

1. Research the circumstances surrounding the assassination of President Lincoln. What similarities have others found in the the the assassinations of McKinley and Kennedy.

2. Compare and contrast the land provision programs of Reconstruction and Homestead Act.

3. The Bibbs family is hit by typhoid. What are its symptoms, its cause, and treatment? Is it a serious health threat today?

4. Freed slaves were not considered equal to their white neighbors. In the 1896 *Plessy v. Ferguson* Supreme Court decision, the highest court ruled that separate schools for blacks were permissible, so long as the facilities were of equal quality. Investigate the 1954 Supreme Court ruling in *Brown v. Board of Education* which finally changed that policy.

5. Investigate the terms of contracts signed by indentured servants who lived in Colonial America and those of the Black Codes of the South after the Civil War. How were they alike? How were they different?

6. Investigate the following two Supreme Court rulings which impacted the lives of African Americans. First discover how and why the Supreme Court reversed the 1875 Civil Rights Act in 1883 and then research how and why that ruling was again reversed in 1964.

7. Who were the Abolitionists? What contribution did they make to the Civil War and to the Reconstruction when the war concluded?

Robinet takes young readers into the drama of other historical events, including the War of 1812 (in Washington, D.C., and New Orleans), the Civil War, the Great Chicago Fire, and the early civil rights movement. Each story is told through the lives of young children. *Children of the Fire* (1991) deals with Chicago's catastrophic event. Virginia, a young slave serving President Madison in 1814, uses her position to help slaves escape in *Washington City Is Burning* (1996). *The Twins, the Pirates, and the Battle of New Orleans* takes a look at the War of 1812 through the eyes of young brothers Pierre and Andrew who hope to find their father, one of Jean Lafitte's pirates. In *If You Please, President Lincoln*, Robinet dramatizes another obscure fact in history: Lincoln's proposed colonization of slaves after the Civil War. *Walking to the Bus-Rider Blues* centers on the early civil rights movement after Rosa Parks refused to relinquish her seat in Montgomery, AL.

Isaacs, Kathleen. Review of *Forty Acres and Maybe a Mule*. *School Library Journal* (November, 1998): 128. Isaacs lauds Robinet for humanizing with Pascal, and his adopted family, a "little-known piece of American history."

Lempke, Susan. Review of *Forty Acres and Maybe a Mule*. *Booklist* (January 1–15, 1999): 879. Lempke praises Robinet's ability to blend her historical knowledge with feelings of her characters into a "fine historical novel."

"Robinet, Harriette Gillem." In *Contemporary Authors*, vol. 42. Detroit: Gale, 1994.

"Robinet, Harriette Gillem." In *Something about the Author*, vol. 104. Detroit: Gale, 1999. Biography of Robinet's career and life.

◆ RELATED WEBSITES ◆

Harriette Gillem Robinet Web site http://www.
hgrobinet.com. October 20, 2001. The author's Web site gives a brief biography,
list of awards, and summary of her books.

Vicki Cox

GATHERING BLUE

Novel

2000

Author: Lois Lowry

◆

Major Books for Young Adults

◆ ABOUT THE AUTHOR ◆

Two time Newbery Medal winner Lois Lowry was born March 20, 1937, in Honolulu, Hawaii. Her father, Major Robert E. Hammersberg, was a dentist serving in the same army hospital where Lois was born. Lois's mother, Katherine, was a schoolteacher. Lois has an older sister, Helen, and a younger brother, Jon.

In 1940, the Army moved the Hammersbergs to New York, and in 1942, after the outbreak of WWII, Lois's father was posted to the Pacific theater. Lois's mother then moved Lois and her sister to Amish Country in Pennsylvania to live near her mother's family. This early, prolonged separation from her beloved father and the very close relationships that it engendered between Lois, her mother, and her two siblings strongly influenced many of the books that she would later write.

Jealous of her older sister's newly learned skill and fascinated by the relationship be-

Lois Lowry

tween letters and sounds, Lois learned to read when she was only three years old. Lois has always liked doing things on her own terms and in her own way. Even as a very young girl, she preferred reading to the more typical children's games and pastimes. Partly because of her exceptional reading ability, Lois was allowed to skip second grade and graduated from an all girls' high school at the age of sixteen. Even then she knew she wanted to become a novelist.

When Lois was nineteen, she dropped out of college to marry an young naval officer, becoming Lois Lowry. She has four children and many grandchildren, many of whom would figure prominently in Lois's many novels. In 1973, at the age of thirty-six, Lois finally received a college degree. She began publishing short stories soon after. Her first novel, *A Summer to Die*, about a teenager's struggle to come to terms with her older sister's death, was published in 1977. Illustrating the many parallels be-

tween Lois's own experiences and her stories, Lois lost her own older sister to cancer when Helen was just twenty-eight. Loss of a loved one is a frequent theme in Lowry's novels. Lowry was divorced at age forty, just as she was beginning her writing career.

Lowry's many succeeding novels continue to chronicle the lives of typical adolescents who have found themselves in exceptional times or situations. Notable among these are the several novels featuring her precocious teenage protagonist, Anastasia Krupnik, whom Lowry claims she patterned after her two "quite nutty" daughters. In addition to patterning many of her characters after family members and friends, Lowry's novels are often partly autobiographical in nature. For instance, *Autumn Street* is about how a character named Elizabeth Lorimer moves into her grandfather's house in Pennsylvania at the outset of WWII, just as Lowry herself had done. Lowry has always had an affinity for animals, especially horses and dogs. All of Lowry's novels involve animals in some way, often a dog, like Branchie in *Gathering Blue*.

Lowry claims she always starts a book knowing how it will begin and how it will end. She writes on a regular basis, whenever she is at home. She advises others who want to write for young people to read as much as possible, reflecting her own life-long love of books and reading.

◆ OVERVIEW ◆

Gathering Blue, published in 2000, offers a disturbing yet hopeful view of the future that challenges readers to reflect critically on the social values and political directions of the present. It is the story of Kira, an extraordinarily talented young girl who finds herself suddenly orphaned and taken to live in a mysterious government compound near the center of her village. There she meets other equally talented and crea-

Gathering Blue

tive children, and together they discover the truth about themselves, their parents, and their society. In the end, Kira learns that in order for her village to survive and to prosper, she must overcome her own fears and break down age-old patterns of superstition and isolation so that she may "gather the blue."

◆ SETTING ◆

Gathering Blue is set in a non-specific, dystopian (anti-utopian) future. Sometime in the distant past, a terrible catastrophe has occurred, forcing a once socially and technologically advanced civilization into a rapid disintegration that the people in Kira's village call the "Ruin." Fragments of that civilization survive in small, isolated enclaves of simple, superstitious people ruled by local oligarchic (governed by few) "Councils," whose primary task is to preserve a memory of the past and to guide the future of their people. It is in one of these enclaves that the action of *Gathering Blue* takes place.

Gathering Blue begins in the "Field of Leaving," as Kira awaits the "diggers" who will come to bury her mother once her mother's spirit has been given sufficient time to exit her body. The setting is a medieval-like village, isolated from the rest of the world by a dense and forbidding forest inhabited by awful beasts and creatures of the night. Life in the village is primitive and hard. Space is at a premium. The people in Kira's village live in small huts crudely built of tree limbs and mud, and are engaged in a day-to-day struggle for survival. The village people grow vegetables in small gardens and the village men hunt wild animals in the fields outside the village. The women carry water from the nearby river. There is no tolerance for people with physical handicaps who can no longer contribute their share of work to the good of the community. Those who are injured or diseased are removed from the village and taken by the "draggers" to the field outside the village to die.

After her mother's death, Kira becomes a ward of the "Council of Guardians." The compound to which Kira is taken to live is called the "Council Edifice." The Council Edifice is an island of safety, comfort, and mysterious anachronism. Outside the Edifice, there is hunger and primitive living conditions. Within the Edifice there is hot and cold running water, soap, and many of the personal comforts that we associate with a more modern setting. It is the only remaining structure from a time before the "Ruin," an event in the village's history that, some time in the distant past, nearly destroyed the civilization that evolved into Kira's culture. It is never made clear to the reader how wide-spread that destruction was, or whether it was of natural or man-made origins.

Within the village there is a subculture called the Fen. People who live here do the dirtiest, most difficult work of the village. Even though life in the village is difficult for all the people, for the people in the Fen it is all the more distressing, even more crowded, even more noisy, even more dirty. One of the young protagonists in the story, Matt, lives there. The children in the Fen are treated harshly by their parents and grow up quickly. At nine, Matt is, for all intents and purposes, on his own. His mother does not grow concerned when he disappears for days at a time. Matt has somehow found Kira and they have become friends. Before Kira's mother died, Kira regularly told stories to the children of the village, including Matt.

◆ THEMES AND CHARACTERS ◆

Kira is lucky to be alive. Babies born with deformities such as Kira's crooked leg are almost always taken away from the mother and left in the field outside the village to die; it is the Way of her people. The Way is harsh and impersonal. The Way is their law. It demands that everyone in the village be able to work, to contribute, to earn the right to live. Those that can not are weeded out and disposed of. However, due partly to a stubborn mother, partly to an influential grandfather, and partly to her own stubborn refusal to be separated from her mother, Kira survives to grow into an intelligent and talented young woman. Both Kira's grandfather and her mother are respected people in the village. Kira's grandfather had once been a member of the Council of Guardians, the ruling body of the village. Kira's mother, Katrina, had a special and valuable talent. She knew how to extract dyes from plants and how to embroider colorful images into the weave of the otherwise colorless, prosaic textiles that are the norm in the village. Because of Katrina's skills, she is chosen to maintain the "Singer's Robe," a unique and very important ceremonial garment worn only once a year at a celebration called the Gathering.

One of the significant themes in *Gathering Blue* is the way society reacts to people with handicaps. The people in Kira's village shun and resent handicapped people. Villagers who become handicapped, either through injury or disease, and children who are born with physical imperfections are almost always condemned to death. There seems to be no compassion or sympathy for others. The people seem only concerned with their own well being and survival.

Another significant theme is control. In the village, the instruments of control are the Council of Guardians and the bell in the tower of the Council Edifice. The bell tells the people when to start work, when to stop, and when to gather for meetings, when to celebrate, and when to arm against danger. The Council of Guardians is the governing body of the village. The Guardians control the tower bell, interpret and enforce the Way, mediate disputes, and preserve the history of the people. The Guardians live and meet in the Council Edifice, an ancient stone structure in the center of the village. The Edifice is the only structure known to survive the Ruin. It was once a church, and the guardians have adopted a role similar to that of clergy. Once a year, the people of the village are called to the Edifice for a Gathering, where they hear the story of their history sung to them by the Singer. As the Singer sings the narrative, he points to corresponding places on the Robe where the story is embroidered. In his hand, he holds a staff into which the same story has been carved in relief. The "Ruin Song" tells the way it has always been, demonstrating a never-ending pattern of ruin and rebuilding, perpetuating the Way and validating the role and the authority of the Guardians.

The Guardians also use fear to control the people and discourage them from venturing away from the isolation of the village. They perpetuate a lie that there are awful beasts lurking in the forests and fields surrounding the village. In truth, the most ferocious animals are rabbits and deer. They use force to protect their secret. Annabella, one of Kira's teachers, and a symbol of learning and wisdom, dies mysteriously after telling Kira the truth about the beasts of the forest.

Control is also evident in the rigid separation of the classes, the definition of strict male and female roles, and the isolation of family units. Women had certain jobs like making cloth, raising children, and tending the family garden. Men had different jobs like being a butcher and going on hunts to gather meat for the village. Only certain people were allowed to learn reading and writing. Kira was frightened and felt guilty when she realized she was inadvertently learning to read Thomas's record of plants and dyes. The most privileged and educated people in the village were the Guardians.

Jamison, the Guardian responsible for identifying and then guiding the young artists brought to the Edifice, best represents the theme of control and the role of the Guardians in village life. On the surface he is kind and genuinely concerned. He acts as an advocate for the children and visits them regularly. However, Jamison is also the Guardian that seems to the be most responsible for the sudden deaths of their parents and of Annabella. This manipulative, subversive duality characterizes the role of government in *Gathering Blue*.

Perhaps the most significant theme of *Gathering Blue* is creativity and artistic expression. Creativity is presented as an almost supernatural influence on those who have been gifted with it. The monotony of day-to-day existence and years of struggle for simple survival has systematically siphoned imagination and creativity out of the people of the village. The Council of Guardians recognizes the power of creativity and attempts to channel it to suit their needs, to shape a new future. To that end, children who demonstrate creative talent are orphaned and then brought to live in the Council Edifice, where their creative talents are put to work creating a future that fits the only pattern they know, that of the "Ruin Song". The parents of Kira, Thomas, and Jo all died immediately prior to their being brought to live in the Edifice.

Kira grew up helping her mother and learning her mother's craft. She also made herself useful gathering scraps of cloth from beneath the looms in the weaving sheds. Though she was crippled and walked stiffly with a stick, she managed to do her share of work and was liked and respected by those who knew her. One day, while practicing the art of embroidery on a small scrap of cloth, Kira's fingers and the bone needle in them seemed to begin to work on their own, as if the patterns and images appearing in the cloth were the work of the cloth itself. Though she could not explain it to anyone, that magical scrap of cloth became Kira's muse and advisor. It seemed to communicate with her, giving her direction and inspiration. When Kira was brought to the Edifice, she was put to work first repairing the Singer's Robe as her mother had done, and then restoring it. After coming to work in the Edifice, Kira's connection with her magical scrap of cloth started becoming weaker and weaker.

Thomas is another young person who has been brought to live in the Edifice. His talent is wood carving. Thomas demonstrates his artistic talent and creativity at a very young age and lives and works in the Edifice most of his life. He is told his parents were killed in a storm. Thomas's fingers, like Kira's, seem to have a mind of their own when carving. Like Kira's scrap of cloth, Thomas keeps his first truly creative wood carving with him at all times. Also like Kira's cloth, the piece of wood represents his creative instincts, guiding and inspiring him, both personally and artistically. Thomas is put to work restoring the Singer's Staff, a wooden rod with the entire history of the world carved into it. Thomas notices that the more he carves the Singer's Staff, the less his special piece of wood seems to speak to him.

The youngest of the artists living in the Edifice is Jo. Jo is little more than an infant when her parents died and she is brought to the compound. Kira discovers Jo locked in her room in another section of the Edifice after hearing her crying in the night. Jo is to be the new Singer, replacing the aging, existing Singer who is, like Jo, held prisoner somewhere within the Edifice and who is released once a year to sing the Ruin Song at the Gathering. Jo's talent for music and singing emerges when she is very young. It is as though she had been born with the ability to sing and to create songs. Her songs are beautiful and fresh. They bring happiness and hope to those who hear them. In the Edifice she is forced to memorize the old songs, the songs of the Robe and the Staff. Once again, the creative and artistic energy of the children is stifled by measures that seem to be designed to perpetuate the status quo and continue to validate the Way.

After learning the old songs and restoring the old stories in embroidery or wooden relief, Kira, Thomas, and Jo are told they are to complete the Song, the Robe, and the Staff by creating the future, a future guided by the past and the Way, a future much like the present.

Hope is added to the mix of themes in *Gathering Blue* by the pluck, the innocence and the imagination of the young protagonists. Kira offers her stubborn belief in herself, a strong compassion for others, and in a dream of a better, brighter, more colorful future. Thomas, the wood carver, demonstrates a candid openness, an unqualified friendship, and a willingness to explore new ideas and challenge accepted truths. Matt, the precocious, totally fearless, dirty-faced boy from the Fen who challenges authority and accepted beliefs to protect Kira's belongings after her mother's death and to bring her the blue from an inconceivable "yonder," brings his energy, his bravery, and his willingness to go where none have gone before along with selfless dedication and loyalty to friends.

◆ LITERARY QUALITIES ◆

The most remarkable literary quality reflected in *Gathering Blue* is its readability. The language is chosen carefully so as not to insult young readers or adults while at the same time providing access for younger

or less experienced readers. As is typical in her novels, Lowry uses dialogue as a key element in her character and plot development. The story is told from the third person, limited omniscient point of view, allowing the reader inside the mind of the main protagonist, Kira. Lowry also relies upon devices like foreshadowing, inference, allusion, careful diction, integrated motifs, and figurative language to enhance and enable her telling of *Gathering Blue*.

Lowry doesn't overuse the technique of foreshadowing; however, she does use it skillfully. Kira's resolution to rebuild her burned cottage in the face of almost insurmountable odds hints to her continued resolve and her eventual decision to stay in the village and work to build a new future for the people, also in the face of daunting obstacles. Her penchant for storytelling foreshadowed the role she will eventually play in creating a new future for her people.

Readers are asked to make many inferences as they negotiate the plot of *Gathering Blue*. One example is the role of Jamison in the deaths of Kira's parents and of Annabella. Not until the end of the story is the connection made directly, when Kira's father tells the story of his disappearance. However, throughout the book, clues and references are made that point to his complicity. Readers are led to assume he is not all that he seems and that he may have a dark side. Another example of inference is found in the description of the Edifice. References to colored glass in the windows, an enormous chamber, a bell in a tower, and the cross-like "object of worship" all lead the reader to infer that the Edifice was once a church.

Several allusions are made that add texture to the mood of the story and help the reader better understand situations and plot elements. For instance, Lowry's use of the word Way to refer to natural law and Kira's requisite four days of mourning are reminiscent of Navajo culture. Additionally, the

Ruin Song makes unmistakeable references to stories from the Bible and to events in recent history such as the great wars and the destruction of modern cities.

Magical inspiration is a motif integrated into the characters of Kira, Thomas, and Jo. Each discovers their artistic talent in an almost supernatural flood of creative inspiration. Kira and Thomas maintain a unique relationship and even a kind of dialogue with the products of their first creative experience, Kira's scrap of embroidered material and Thomas's piece of carved wood. This magical quality fits neatly into the near medieval context within which the story is set and adds to its charm. It also invites the possibility of more magic that will break down the walls of ignorance and isolation and somehow lead the village into a better future.

Lowry uses careful diction and colloquial expressions to tie the village and its people to the reader by using contemporary expressions like "hubby" for husband. Using old, out of use words like "tyke" help establish the mood of decay. The speech of the people from the Fen is filled with non-standard expressions to illustrate their separation from mainstream life in the village and to give them additional color and depth. Lowry uses double negatives, calculated errors in verb tense and pronoun usage, and other non-standard expressions such as "filched," and "iffen" to make Kari's wayward young friend from the Fen, Matt, believable and complete. Jo's use of expressions like "kissie" and "wavie" help her character take on a sense of freshness and innocence.

Lowry makes sparing but effective use of figurative language in her writing, using personification like "whisper a breeze" and metaphors like "centered fragments of her childhood life" to add depth of meaning and imagery to her narrative. Onomatopoetic words like "clatter" used to describe the

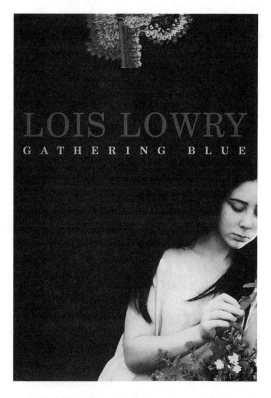

Jacket photograph by Lois Lowry for *Gathering Blue* by Lois Lowry.

sound of the looms in the weaving shed enhance the readers' understanding and their overall reading experience.

◆ SOCIAL SENSITIVITY ◆

Lowry demonstrates a sensitivity to people with handicaps and the way they are often resented by "normal" people in the world, either because they are seen "not to contribute" or because they are shown special consideration for their handicaps that others are not. Kira has been taught to be ashamed of her deformity, but she refuses to let it make her less of a person. Like many other people with handicaps, her physical weakness is compensated by her mental resolve and her extraordinary talents.

Gathering Blue also demonstrates that there are many people in the world who see past a person's handicap. In this story, Thomas never seems to notice that Kira has a crippled leg; and Kira's friend Matt seems determined to find ways to help her compensate for her infirmity. Often in the narrative, Kira or someone else mentions that it is doubtful that she will ever find a mate. Matt even attempts a little matchmaking with a boy from outside the village. However, readers may be lead to imagine that Kira is missing something, and that she might find romance close at hand, in the person of her new friend and fellow artist, Thomas.

In *Gathering Blue*, Lowry shows some lack of concern for those who are typically forgotten by mainstream society, the people who live on the "wrong side of the tracks." In this case, the wrong side of the tracks is the Fen. She portrays these people as being less articulate, filthy, and loud and tasks them with the least desirable jobs in the village. They are violent and greedy. The people of the Fen are portrayed as poor parents who mistreat their children and allow them to wander about with little or no supervision. When Kira goes to the Fen looking for Matt, she finds that Matt's mom does not know or seem to care where her nine-year-old son is, only that he stole some food when he left. "Good rid to him," is her comment when Kira asks about his absence.

Gathering Blue also addresses child abuse. Children in this story are often neglected and abused, valued only for what they can contribute to the family and to the village. They are "taken," moved and traded from family to family as best benefits the community, with no regard for their feelings or their needs. Children who are born weak or deformed are immediately taken to the field and put to death. Children who get sick or injured suffer the same fate. Children have no rights, and adults in the story take ad-

vantage of them whenever they can, like Vandara, the woman who took Kira's land to build a pen to corral the neighborhood children.

◆ TOPICS FOR DISCUSSION ◆

1. What kinds of catastrophes, natural or man-made, could have brought about the destruction of an entire civilization, sending it back to a primitive state, like that of *Gathering Blue*?

2. Why might Kira's village remain in ruin, never regaining the glory and sophistication it once seemed to enjoy?

3. In what ways is the funeral ceremony at the beginning of the story alike or different than those we know?

4. When did you begin to suspect that Kira's mom did not die of a disease. When did you begin to suspect that her father is not killed by beasts? What clues are there?

5. How does the Way, the law that governs life in the village, seem similar and different from the laws that govern our lives?

6. How do the Guardians maintain control over the people in the village?

7. The Edifice is the only structure to survive the Ruin. What do you think it is before the ruin? How might it be significant that this building is the only one to survive? What clues are given that reveal its previous role?

8. How are Kira, Thomas, and Jo different from all others in the village?

9. Why have Kira, Thomas, and Jo been taken to live in the Edifice? Why are they not given to another family like other children who have been orphaned?

10. How is life in the Edifice different from life in the village? Why do you suppose this is true?

11. How is Anabella different from the other adults in the story? What forbidden truth did she reveal to Kira?

12. Why does the Gathering seem like a religious ceremony of some kind? What are the similarities and differences? What do you suppose is the purpose of the Gathering?

13. Why do you think the Singer is in chains? What might that symbolize?

14. Besides gathering plants that can be used to make blue dye, what symbolic meaning might be attached to the title, *Gathering Blue*? What is it that Kira is really seeking to add to the fabric of life in the village?

15. Why do you think Kira decides to remain in the village rather than leave to live with her father in the much nicer place where he has come to live?

◆ IDEAS FOR REPORTS AND PAPERS ◆

1. Describe a scenario leading to a man-made catastrophe that could result in the kind of destruction found in *Gathering Blue*. Is war the only possible cause? Could the ruin have been brought about in an ecological disaster of some kind? How about some form of accident?

2. What natural catastrophes could cause such complete and wide-spread destruction and ruin? Write a story about surviving such a catastrophe and what life might be like in the aftermath.

3. Compare *Gathering Blue* to other books or stories you may have read that present an unflattering, pessimistic view of the future. What do they have in common? What do you think is their purpose?

4. What role does color have in our lives? Do certain colors have special meaning to us, symbolize certain things? Do some colors affect the way we think and feel?

5. How are gifted children treated in our society? Are gifted children sometimes taken from their parents so that their talents may be nurtured and "harvested" in ways similar to that in *Gathering Blue*?

6. We cherish and celebrate our freedom. Were the people of the village free? Do you think they thought they were free? What makes a person free? Are there different kinds and degrees of freedom?

7. What kind of people do you consider handicapped? How do our laws protect the handicapped? Are handicapped people still discriminated against in any way? How do handicapped people compensate for their handicap?

8. What is creativity? Can creativity be taught, nurtured, or cultivated? Is it a gift? Are creative people born with some special quality that allows them to create new ideas and new ways of seeing and understanding the world?

9. Can art really change the world, make it better? How?

◆ RELATED TITLES ◆

In 1995, Lowry published the Newbery Medal winning novel, *The Giver*, which represented a rather significant departure from her previous writing. *The Giver* is a science fiction novel about life in a highly structured, future society where all the physical and emotional challenges in life have systematically been eliminated. The safety and security of the people are ensured by regimented ignorance enforced by a form of government reminiscent of George Orwell's *1984*. No one has to make difficult choices or to even be aware there are such choices. The plot centers around Jonas, who has been chosen to be the successor to the Giver, the one member of the society who still knows and remembers all the pain, the wonder, and the triumph of life before. As the apprentice to the Giver, Jonas learns many truths that no one else knows about life in his society. He must then decide what to do with this knowledge.

With *Gathering Blue*, Lowry continues the dystopic theme set by *The Giver*, painting a much different, but equally disturbing future. As in Steven Vincent Benet's short story, "By the Waters of Babylon," something terrible has gone wrong, throwing a once sophisticated culture back to a near primitive state. The past is so distant and alien that extraordinary measures must be taken to preserve the history and traditions of the people in the hopes that they will once again rise to greatness. Like Jonas in *The Giver*, the young protagonist of *Gathering Blue* is chosen to be the agent of that social memory and must find ways to overcome isolation and the loss of a loved one.

◆ FOR FURTHER REFERENCE ◆

"Lois Lowry." In *Authors and Artists for Young Adults*, vol. 32. Detroit: Gale Research, 2000, pp. 79–87. *A recent, useful, rather complete biographical essay.*

"Lowry, Lois." In *Contemporary Authors*, vol. 70. Detroit: Gale Research, 1999, pp. 311–315. *Recent, useful resource.*

"Lowry, Lois." In *Contemporary Authors*, vol. 13. Detroit: Gale Research, 1984, pp. 333–336. A bit dated, but includes an interesting interview with Lowry.

Lowry, Lois. *Looking Back: A Book of Memories*. Boston: Houghton Mifflin Company, 1998. Unusual autobiography crafted around pictures from Lowry's past.

Robert Redmon

GO ASK ALICE

Novel

1971

Author: Beatrice Mathews Sparks

◆

Major Books for Young Adults

Key to Happiness, 1967
Go Ask Alice, 1971
Jay's Journal, 1979
It Happened to Nancy, 1994

*Almost Lost: The True Story of an
    Anonymous Teenager's Life on the
    Streets*, 1996
Annie's Baby, 1998

◆ ABOUT THE AUTHOR ◆

Beatrice Mathews Sparks was born on January 15, 1918, in Goldberg, Idaho. A Mormon and an active member of the Church of Jesus Christ of Latter-Day Saints, Sparks attended the University of California at Los Angeles and Brigham Young University in Utah, and has worked as a youth counselor, a teacher, a music therapist, a public speaker, and a writer. She continues to write books as well as columns for several periodicals, spreading her messages to teens around the country. Sparks became interested in young adult problems when she began working with troubled teens in 1955. She has spoken to teens in crisis all over the country—in the Utah State Mental Hospital where she worked as a music therapist, at Brigham Young University where she taught continuing education courses, and on a cross-country trip

with her husband where she had the opportunity to talk with more than a thousand teenagers from all walks of life. Sparks was apparently touched deeply by the pain young people experience and the challenges they face on a day to day basis. She began writing books that deal with kids in crisis and that focus on how these kids cope with problem situations.

Sparks has written four "diaries," of which *Go Ask Alice* is the most popular. The book became a cult classic in the seventies, at the height of the drug culture, and its poignant message hit home for many teens who themselves found drugs titillating and nearly impossible to resist. *Go Ask Alice* and Sparks' other books all send powerful messages to young adults. By focusing on topics such as drug abuse, occult magic, suicide, homosexuality, and pornography, she hopes to educate kids, she says, and inform them that they have choices and can control the outcome of their life. *Go Ask Alice* has retained its popularity despite numerous attempts to ban the book from schools. Since its publication in 1971, it has been published in sixteen languages and has been made into a motion picture.

◆ OVERVIEW ◆

Go Ask Alice is written as the diary of a fifteen-year-old girl's day-to-day struggle with drug addiction. Created during the height of the drug era, the girl could be anyone from this time who found him or herself seduced by the mind-altering affects of marijuana, LSD, bennies, dexies, and heroin. When the book begins, the author of the diary is an ordinary teenager with ordinary teenage concerns. She is an innocent, yearning to see what life has to offer her, and she falls in with a group of kids headed on a destructive path. Wanting desperately to be part of the popular crowd, this "innocent" girl discovers drugs, and very quickly her addition becomes uncontrollable. The girl spirals downward and finds herself trapped in a world of pushers, prostitutes, and runaway teens too stoned and too out of touch with reality to find their way back home.

Go Ask Alice became a cult classic in the 1970s, revealing the inner thoughts of a teen in turmoil and detailing her attempts to pull herself out of her drug-induced haze. Though the story was widely criticized as a "complete fabrication" and dismissed as propaganda, its message remained powerful. The book took the romance out of the drug culture that so dominated the 1960s and 70s, and is hailed still today as a groundbreaking book on teenage drug addiction.

◆ SETTING ◆

The girl who wrote this "diary" lived in two different worlds, the real world and a fantasy world. The real world encompasses her home with her parents, her home with her grandmother, the homes of parties she attends with her friends, the streets of San Francisco and Berkeley, and eventually, a psychiatric hospital ward. The fantasy world encompasses all she sees and believes in her hallucinations. The girl thinks and acts differently when she resides in each place. At the beginning of the book, the girl lives in the real world, and she is unhappy there. She has not yet learned how to feel comfortable with herself or how to create her own contentment, so she seeks to find contentment elsewhere, in another world. She wants to escape the real world as she knows it and find a place where she can be someone else.

This girl becomes a different person once she discovers "wonderland." In this fantasy world, her senses are heightened and she feels uninhibited and free. This world is the world within her head; it is not real, but it seems real, and this world comes to life only as she retreats into her drug-induced hallucinations. Readers cannot help but see the comparison between the fantasy world and Lewis Carroll's *Alice's Adventures in Wonderland*. Everything is distorted and crazy in wonderland; but it is there where she feels fantastic.

Sparks contrasts these two worlds in part by emphasizing the conflict within the girl's mind. She is happy and free in her fantasy world, then once she returns to her real world, she swears she will never return to "wonderland" again. By emphasizing the vast difference between the girl's life when she is straight and the girl's life when she is stoned, Sparks sets apart reality from fantasy. This girl moves back and forth from place to place, from reality to hallucination, trying desperately to find her place.

She cannot possibly reconcile the two worlds, so she becomes confused. Will she come back to reality or retreat further and further into "wonderland"?

◆ THEMES AND CHARACTERS ◆

This diary of an unnamed teenager begins just before the girl's fifteenth birthday, September 16th, year unknown. It begins with the sentence "Yesterday I remember being the happiest person in the whole earth, in the whole galaxy, in all of God's creation. . . . Now it's all smashed down upon my head and I wish I could just melt into the blaaa-ness of the universe and cease to exist." In this sentence, the girl is referring to something that happened at school that humiliated her, but it exposes her insecurity, her emotional vulnerability, and her rather typical feelings of teenage angst. Readers understand that Roger is the girl's boyfriend, and that he hurt her deeply when he failed to show up for a date. The girl appears to be the typical American teenager in many ways. She is raised in the middle class, and she has typical teenage concerns. She worries about her weight and about boys and friends. She is curious about sex. She dreams of having a husband and a family someday. But these early diary entries seem perhaps overly dramatic. This girl has low self-esteem, and it appears that she views Roger's rejection of her as a validation of her own feelings of inadequacy.

By the second short diary entry readers get a clearer picture of the girl's insecurity. She feels unattractive, lacks confidence in her friendships, and seems to be unhappy with her life. Though most adolescents struggle with feelings of insecurity and experience ups and downs, for this girl the ups and downs seem a bit extreme. She exhibits many characteristics typical of drug users.

However, when the book begins the girl is innocent. Then over the course of her writing, readers witness a corruption of that innocence as this troubled teenager, in her longing to feel accepted, dives headfirst into a world she finds both fabulous and frightening.

Early on in the book, the girl's writings show signs of an addictive personality. This girl seems to be overly concerned with her weight and self-conscious about her appearance, appearing to have somewhat of a food addiction. She fits the stereotype of the troubled child destined to flirt with danger. She so longs for acceptance that she is particularly susceptible to peer pressure, and she wants desperately to change her lifestyle and be a part of the popular crowd. Careful examination of the girl's character permits readers to recognize the danger she will inevitably fall into, particularly because of her ambivalence about her life. At times in her early writings she expresses an interest in many things, her friends and her religion for instance, and she looks forward to Christmas with a refreshing childhood excitement. Then quickly she reverses stances. She says that she seems to be "kind of losing interest in everything." She has no interest in school, seemingly because she feels unattractive and unpopular. This makes her susceptible to feeling worthless, and perhaps even prone to depression.

The girl's personality changes drastically during the course of the book. As she gets further and further into the drug life, "she develops a crass attitude, and becomes paranoid." This change begins rather abruptly after she experiences drugs for the first time. While staying with her grandmother for the summer, she is thrilled to be invited to a party with the popular kids, and she eagerly prepares for what she hopes to bring about a change in her life. Certainly her life changes after the party, but it turns out to be quite different from anything she could have imagined. In a dangerous game called "Button, Button, Who's Got the Button," the girl unknowingly takes her first hit of LSD, and this is the catalyst for her loss of innocence.

The acid trip the girl experienced that night confuses her just as much as it enchants her. Because she had no idea she was given acid and certainly no idea what to expect, she at first feels afraid that she might have been poisoned, but then she quickly relaxes into the wondrous world that seems to open up to her before her very eyes.

Reliance on drugs comes quickly after that first night, though she tries to tell herself that she will never take drugs again. This experimentation then becomes a pattern, and before readers know it, she tries all kinds of substances, pushing drugs for her boyfriend, and even selling drugs to young children in elementary schools. The girl has a problem with her behavior, but she seems to have no willpower to stop it. Soon, in addition to doing drugs, she starts having sex with many different men, always when she is in an altered state.

The girl lost her virginity one night while she was tripping with her boyfriend Bill "one last time." This first sexual experience was all a part of her drug trip—she could not separate the two. Then the regrets sink in. She had wanted Roger, not Bill, to be the first. She worries about becoming pregnant and fears that Bill will think she is easy. Beginning to hate Bill and her new friends and her summer home with her grandparents, the teenager wants to go home. She says in her diary that she is "living with doubts and apprehensions and fears that [she] never dreamed possible." These doubts, apprehensions, and fears cause her to take her grandfather's sleeping pills to relax. Soon readers find out that she regularly relies on sleeping pills and tranquilizers to help her deal with her stress. The equation

of sex with drugs means that Alice seeks out both for the same reasons—escape, pleasure, altered states, and the need to remove oneself into a fantasy world. Soon, like Alice in Wonderland, the world in which she finds herself is nothing like the one she knew before.

The girl's boyfriend Richie is a frightening portrait of the kind of person this confused young girl finds appealing. The girl thinks she is in love with Richie, but he has a controlling personality, treating her with little or no respect. Readers understand that he only uses her to push his drugs. The girl knows it too, deep down, but she continues to deny it. She claims to be disgusted with her life but is unable to reverse it. When the girl finds Richie having sex with his roommate Ted, however, the haze lifts a little, and she finally gets the courage to leave him. Unfortunately her decision as to how to do it leads her into more trouble, more drugs, and farther away from self-contentment.

The girl makes a decision with her friend Chris, who has also vowed to mend her ways. The two decide that the only way they can change their lives and get off the drugs is to run away to San Francisco, a poor choice in the height of the drug era, but the girls do go to San Francisco and they pledge to stay clean. The diarist writes a note to her parents to say goodbye and scribbles a note to the police to turn in Richie, before getting on a bus with Chris. Despite their intentions, soon after arriving in San Francisco they get involved in the drug scene once again. The girl writes in her diary about the party they attended, saying that as soon as she smelled the pot at the party, she immediately wanted "to be ripped, smashed, torn up as I had never wanted anything before." At that moment, despite her original intentions when she moved to San Francisco, the girl wanted desperately to be a part of this drug crowd.

"Last night was the worst night of my shitty, rotten, stinky, dreary —ed-up life," the girl writes in her diary. Readers learn that she and Chris did heroin with a girl named Sheila and her boyfriend, and they fell prey not only to the drugs but also to a trap set by these new friends, who raped the girls and treated them "sadistically and brutally." Again the girls profess to look out for each other, realizing that doing drugs makes people out of control. The girl's entire world has become a downward spiral into a land where everything is distorted and unreal. The ecstasy of sex and drugs is just an illusion. "All my life I've thought that the first time I had sex with someone it would be something special, and maybe even painful, but it turned out to be just part of the brilliant, freaky, way-out pattern. I still can't quite separate one thing from another," the girl writes in her diary. At one point she refers to being brainwashed by Richie, and she clearly has been brainwashed by the entire drug culture. It robbed her of her innocence. At the beginning of the book, the girl had a healthy teenage curiosity about sex and an entire world of pleasure to explore. By the time she arrives at Berkeley, however, she says that she has never had sex without drugs.

Sparks makes a point to underscore the conflict that rages within the girl's mind. After each of her drug experiences, she vows never to do them again. Then she is seduced by the drugs again, and each acid trip makes her feel totally uninhibited and wonderful. She likens her experience with torpedoes and speed to "riding shooting stars through the Milky Way, only a million, trillion times better." Then she feels guilty for doing these drugs the next day. This kind of flip-flopping is typical of addiction. The girl is curious (just like Alice in Wonderland) and so she will always have to fight the urge to flirt with danger. She likes how uninhibited drugs make her feel,

but then she hates herself afterward. She engages in these internal battles constantly. Nevertheless, after her experience on her own in California, she appears ready to change her life. She goes home to her parents in December of that year, for Christmas.

The girl's parents play a very small role in the book. They are underdeveloped as characters. Readers know how the diarist feels about them but very little about how they feel about her. The emphasis here is clearly on the thoughts, feelings, and attitudes of this metaphorical "Alice."

The girl's attitude truly seems to change when she returns home from California. Soon her diary reveals that she is back with her old friends, and is being harassed and physically "abused" because one of them wants her to get him some pot. Then the next thing readers know is that the girl is in the hospital in horrible shape, apparently from an overdose of something one of these old "friends" gave her to teach her a lesson. It is a sad story what happens to "Alice." She says at one point that she became "old and hard." By the end of the book, she is dead. The message Sparks wished to convey became clear. The life of a drug addict is a frightening and tragic one.

◆ LITERARY QUALITIES ◆

Sparks wrote *Go Ask Alice* in a diary format, which proved to be an effective way to convey her message, whether or not the "diary" was real. Sparks assumed the perspective of a teenage drug user realistically, using teenage language and parroting teenage concerns. She likewise leaves blanks to omit names and make her diary more convincing. It is interesting to read the first sentence of girl's first diary entry again after finishing the book. This first sentence alludes to the ups and downs drug users experience every day. The quote on the back of the book foreshadows what will become of this unnamed girl. "After you've had it," the quote reads, "there isn't even life without drugs."

There is a little girl quality about Alice; the way she speaks, the way she reasons, the expressions she uses. The author of her diary lets her teenage protagonist convey thoughts that adults wish to pass on to teenagers without preaching at them. For instance, the girl writes in her diary that she realizes that what she has heard about drugs came from people like her parents who obviously did not know what they were talking about. That people who do LSD are not "low-class, unclean [and] despicable." They are regular kids, children within her own socio-economic group. This seems to be one of the author's messages.

Perhaps the most obvious literary devise Sparks uses is the allusion to Louis Carroll's *Alice's Adventures in Wonderland*. The title alludes to Carroll's character, and the teenager "author" of the diary recognizes the connection as well. "It's a completely new world I'm exploring, and you can't even conceive the wide new doors that are opening up before me," she says. "I feel like Alice in Wonderland. Maybe Lewis G. Carroll was on drugs too."

Go Ask Alice was written long after *Alice's Adventures in Wonderland*, and after the rock group Jefferson Airplane wrote the song "White Rabbit," which also alluded to Carroll's book as well as added to the interpretation of that book as a portrayal of a drug-induced hallucination. In *Alice's Adventures in Wonderland*, the young girl ingested some strange substance, or mushroom, as the song says, and then spiraled down the rabbit hole to a fantasy world where nothing was as it seemed. In what kind of world does the girl in *Go Ask Alice* find herself? It is not reality, but pure fantasy. It is a world

both frightening and fabulous, like a hallucination. This girl also ingests strange substances, spirals downward, and finds herself in a world where nothing is as it seems.

Close examination of *Go Ask Alice* reveals that several presumptions have been made about this book that Sparks may never have intended. It is presumed that Alice died of an overdose for example, yet Sparks says only that the cause of the girl's death was unknown. Furthermore, it is widely presumed that Alice is the name of the girl who wrote the diary, and the movie *Go Ask Alice* did in fact feature a girl named Alice as the main character. Nevertheless, Sparks never names the author of the diary at all. In fact, it seems that she wished to keep this girl unnamed. "Alice" it appears, is no one in particular, but simply a symbol for the drug culture and for any one of millions who found themselves caught in its trap. In this sense, the diarist is Alice, for she too is a symbol.

In the book, the girl does encounter the true Alice, the symbolic Alice, who is simply some girl sitting stoned on a street curb at Berkeley. At this point in the story, the author of the "diary" is wandering the streets aimlessly, and like millions of other runaways, lost in a strange land with no idea what day it is or what direction she is heading. "Then I talked to Alice, who I met just sitting stoned on the curb," the girl writes in her diary. "She didn't know if she was running away from something or running to something, but she admitted that deep in her heart she wanted to go home." This passage seems to encapsulate Sparks' message. Anyone who falls into the "wonderland" of drugs lives in a state of confusion and longs to find their way out. The Alice on the street corner, like the diarist in Sparks' book, fell down the rabbit hole as surely as Louis Carroll's Alice did, and she too found herself living in "wonderland." This "wonderland" seems to represent a hallucinatory state where everything is an illusion and nothing seems to make any sense at all.

◆ SOCIAL SENSITIVITY ◆

Some reviewers suggest that the book is too moralistic, perhaps, parroting the typical warnings that parents and drug counselors typically use to scare kids away from drugs. For this reason, *Go Ask Alice* has received mixed reactions. Many teens that read the book loved it, considering it both frightening and realistic. Others commented that it was propaganda, obviously written by an older person outside the world of drugs who made it sound frightening on purpose. Many were outraged to discover that Sparks wrote the book and not the girl they came to refer to as "Alice." Some teenagers simply refused to believe it.

Readers must to ask themselves if it really matters who wrote this book. Is the message powerful enough that the book is effective whether it is true or not? Or it so unrealistic that it refutes the author's intentions? Is it realistic that the girl first trips without knowing it, and that her friends become so cruel as to harm her? Is it realistic that she lives such an extreme life, becomes a pusher so quickly, and even pushes drugs to grade school kids? Though at the time it was written, *Go Ask Alice* took the romance out of the drug culture hailed by the hippies of the 1960s and 1970s, today's readers may not consider it a realistic portrayal of teenage drug use.

◆ TOPICS FOR DISCUSSION ◆

1. How do you feel about the fact that *Go Ask Alice* was passed off as a true diary? Do you feel that this was deceptive? Do you feel that it made Sparks' message more poignant?

2. Do you believe this is a typical experience for someone who gets involved in drugs?

3. Who is Alice?

4. Do you think the ending of the book made sense? Was it a surprise to you that the girl died after seemingly getting her life together? Was it ever clear exactly how she died?

5. What clues, if any, led you to believe that this diary was not truly written by a fifteen-year-old girl?

6. Describe the girl's relationship with Richie. Why do you suppose she is willing to settle for this?

7. Did you understand the incident that finally put the girl in the hospital? What happened? How do you suppose the girl died—from an overdose of what drug?

8. What was the most disturbing part of the book to you and why?

◆ IDEAS FOR REPORTS AND PAPERS ◆

1. Compare *Go Ask Alice* to Lewis Carroll's *Alice's Adventures in Wonderland*.

2. Analyze the lyrics of the Jefferson Airplane song "White Rabbit." Relate them to this anonymous girl's experience with drugs.

3. *Go Ask Alice* was a highly controversial book and the subject of banning attempts by parents and school districts. Explain why you think the book was so objectionable and give your opinion on censorship.

4. Columbia University has started a Web site called *Go Ask Alice*, which provides young readers a resource for some of the questions they may have. Explain the genesis of this site and how the

book inspired teens to address these issues.

5. Compare and contrast the glamorous with the frightening in the world of drugs, as portrayed in the book.

6. Write a character analysis of the anonymous girl who wrote the diary. What do we know about her? Is she rebellious, self-confident, or easily influenced? Why do you suppose she was so easily lured into the drug world?

7. Chronicle the changes in the girl's personality and temperament as she moves from an innocent to "old and hard" as she describes herself.

8. The girl who wrote this diary exhibits some of the typical traits of someone with an addictive personality. Use examples from the book to explain how this anonymous girl fits this mold.

9. From the time of the book's publication, it has been presumed that "Alice" is the name of the girl who wrote the diary. Do you think this is true? Explain who you think Alice really is and what significance it has to Sparks message.

10. Choose one of the other "diaries" written by Sparks. What do you think about the message of these books?

◆ RELATED TITLES/ADAPTATIONS ◆

A made-for-television movie version of *Go Ask Alice* was released in 1972. Directed by John Korty, the movie starred Jamie Smith Jackson as Alice and William Shatner as Alice's father. Andy Griffith, Mackenzie Phillips, and Robert Caradine also made guest appearances in the anti-drug movie.

Sparks wrote a series of four "anonymous" diaries, all of which attempt to educate young adults about the dangers they

face and convey the message that falling into destructive patterns can destroy lives. *Go Ask Alice* was the first of these diaries, and undoubtedly the most popular. *Jay's Journal* is about a young boy who gets involved with a satanic cult. *Almost Lost* is about a teenager's life on the streets. *It Happened to Nancy* is about a young girl who is raped and contracts AIDS, and *Annie's Baby* is about a pregnant fourteen-year-old and her abusive boyfriend.

Melvin Burgess's *Smack* (published in England as *Junk*) is another book about teenage drug use, this time about heroin addiction. Unlike *Go Ask Alice, Smack* is not passed off as a true account, but rather as an example or a realistic portrayal of a teenager's life as an addict. "Smack," American slang for heroin, was popular with the punk rockers in England in the 1980s, and it centers on a young girl named Gemma. Gemma, her boyfriend Tar, and eight other teens narrate the story, as their lives intertwine and they become caught in the heroin trap.

Beauty Queen, by Linda Glovach, is another "diary" of a teenage heroin addict. Sam, the protagonist, becomes a topless dancer to make money to support her drug habit, and she eventually dies of an overdose.

◆ FOR FURTHER REFERENCE ◆

Homstad, Wayne. *Anatomy of a Book Controversy.* Bloomington: Phi Delta Kappa Education Foundation, 1995. Nonfictional account of one school district's controversial efforts to ban *Go Ask Alice.*

Nilsen, Alleen Pace. "The House That Alice Built: An Interview with the Author Who Brought You *Go Ask Alice." School Library Journal* (October, 1979).

"Sparks, Beatrice Mathews." In *Contemporary Authors,* vol. 97. Detroit: Gale, 1981. A brief entry containing biographical information about Beatrice Matthews Sparks and a critical introduction to her work.

"Sparks, Beatrice Mathews." In *Something about the Author*, vol. 44. Detroit: Gale, 1986. A brief entry containing biographical information about Beatrice Matthews Sparks and a critical introduction to her work.

Tamra Andrews

GOOSEBERRIES

Short Story

1916

Author: Anton Chekhov

◆

Major Books for Young Adults

In the Twilight, 1887
The Black Monk and Other Stories, 1903
The Kiss and Other Stories, 1908
Stories of Russian Life, 1915
*Russian Silhouettes: More Stories of Rus-
    sian Life,* 1915
The Steppe and Other Stories, 1915

The Bet and Other Stories, 1915
The Tales, 1916–1923 (thirteen volumes)
Nine Humorous Tales, 1918,
*The House with the Mezzanine and Other
    Stories,* 1920
Selected Short Stories, 1951

◆ ABOUT THE AUTHOR ◆

Anton Pavlovich Chekhov was born on January 17, 1860, in Taganrog, a city in southern Russia. He was one of six children born to Evgeniya and to Pavel Chekhov, a strict religious man who owned a grocery store and who was physically abusive with Anton and his two older brothers. Though Anton had a depressing childhood, he was educated at an early age and apparently well-read. He earned a medical degree from Moscow University in 1884, then began practicing medicine at the Zemstvo Hospital in Vosklressensk.

About the same time Chekhov entered medical school, he began writing for publication. At this time he wrote for newspa-

pers and humor magazines, primarily to earn money, and he published comical short stories under the pseudonym Antosha Chekhonte. In a short time, Chekhov realized his passion for writing and launched his literary career. It was during the second stage of his writing career that he became famous. Chekhov was heavily influenced by the political views of Leo Tolstoy, specifically by his rejection of materialism and his concern with alleviating the suffering of the peasants. Tolstoy's influence on Chekhov became obvious in this second set of stories, published after 1886 under his true name. Later, when Chekhov rejected Tolstoy's views, this rejection was reflected in Chekhov's works including his short story "Gooseberries."

Anton Chekhov

After Chekhov abandoned his medical career to write, he enjoyed a prolific writing career. Though he wrote almost six hundred short stories, he is primarily noted for his plays—seven full-length plays and ten one-act plays. He also wrote sketches, anecdotes, theater reviews, critical essays, journal articles, cartoon captions, jokes, and two novels. Chekhov's work had an enormous influence on both Russian and foreign writers, including such names as James Joyce, Virginia Woolf, and Ernest Hemingway, and many of his works have been adapted for both stage and screen. Before Chekhov's death from tuberculosis in 1904, he was awarded the Pushkin Prize from the Division of Russian Language and Letters of the Academy of Sciences for his collection of stories titled *In the Twilight.* He was selected as an honorary member of the Russian Academy of Sciences, and for a brief time he served as president of the Society of Lovers of Russian Literature.

◆ OVERVIEW ◆

The second in a set of three short stories referred to as "The Little Trilogy," "Gooseberries" is a parody set in the Russian countryside in the 1890s. Ivan, the narrator of the tale, and his friend, Burkin, are tired from a long day of hunting in the country when it begins to rain, and the two seek shelter in the home of their friend Pavel, a local landowner. After bathing in the river and settling comfortably in the country estate, the three men eat dinner, and Ivan tells Burkin and Pavel the story of his brother Nikolai's life.

Chekhov juxtaposes the present situation of Ivan telling this story in Pavel's home with the past situation Ivan explains in Nikolai's life. Ivan launches into a monologue in order to explain his own views on land proprietorship. Ivan is clearly moralizing as he tells his story, and he blatantly discounts Nikolai's happiness as simply an illusion. Some critics have argued that "Gooseberries" is a story in which Chekhov advocates Tolstoy's humanistic views and other critics have argued that it is one of the stories in which he rejects them. But Ivan certainly appears to serve as Chekhov's spokesperson. Ivan concludes his story, the three men retire to bed, and the reader is left to interpret the author's message.

◆ SETTING ◆

The story opens with a description of the Russian countryside on a rainy day. Chekhov at first describes the scene as gray and dull, conveying the feelings of monotony that plague the Russian people and the general sense of isolation they experience. The still country setting of the story plays a crucial role in conveying Chekhov's message. Contradictions appear almost immediately. On the first page of the story the country is described as both gray and dull and serene and refreshing. Ivan himself embodies this contradiction. It is he who reverses his opinion of the setting, and it is he who takes great pleasure in bathing in the cool river water and settles quite comfortably in Pavel's country estate.

Shortly after Ivan and Burkin arrive at Pavel's home, Ivan launches into his story of his brother Nikolai, who like Pavel is also the owner of a country estate. Ivan appears to be condemning Nikolai's materialism and the idea that he secured his own comfort while others continue to suffer, yet all the while Ivan himself is enjoying the peaceful serenity of Pavel's estate. The hypocrisy of Ivan's views suggests a conflict between social responsibility and the desire for personal comfort. As Chekhov juxtaposes the peaceful country setting Ivan so enjoys with the moralistic tale he relates to his friends, the incompatibility of social consciousness with personal happiness becomes one of the central ironies of Chekhov's tale.

◆ THEMES AND CHARACTERS ◆

"Gooseberries" is a slow-moving, seemingly plotless story devoid of action. The conflict appears only in Ivan's mind, not in the story itself, and Burkin, Pavel, and even Ivan himself remain passive characters throughout the tale, as Ivan delivers his moralistic speech on the evils of land proprietorship. Chekhov's characters are often passive, introspective people who live quiet and discontented lives. Nikolai seemingly represents the Chekhovian character who appears to be self-centered yet is misunderstood by others, and Ivan seemingly represents the melancholy and desperate man searching for the meaning of true happiness.

Ivan is a veterinary surgeon, a medical man like Chekhov himself, and his brother Nikolai is a retired landowner. Nikolai is revealed to readers only through Ivan who tells the story of how Nikolai spent his life pursuing his dream of owning a country estate and growing gooseberries. Nikolai apparently grew up in the country but went to work in the city when his family had to sell their estate to pay their debts. But Nikolai never stopped longing for the country, and he invested all his time and energy and into making his dream of country life a reality.

According to Ivan, Nikolai's life has been a waste and his dream nothing but an escape from reality. Ivan believes that instead of retreating to the peace and quiet of the country, one should actively work for the betterment of society. To illustrate the error in Nikolai's ways, Ivan relates how his brother became stingy and selfish and how he married an elderly rich widow for money then deprived her of food and comfort. When the woman dies, Nikolai is able to buy three hundred acres of land and settle into the country life he always dreamed of.

It appears that Nikolai certainly is a selfish and miserly man who, unlike Tolstoy, and Chekhov during a large part of his life, has little concern for improving the lives of the peasants. Ivan tells how his brother treats the peasants badly and how he believes that most of them are not yet ready for education and that corporal punishment for these people is often justified. In condemning Nikolai's way of life, Ivan argues that living in pursuit of personal happiness makes a person blind to the suffering of others and in fact prolongs the suffering of others as these selfish people advocate demeaning practices such as corporal punishment and denial of education. Ivan ends his "speech" by imploring Pavel never to become a selfish landowner like Nikolai is, but to instead try to work for the betterment of society.

On the surface, it clearly appears that Nikolai and Ivan advocate opposing political views and embrace opposing moral values. But a closer character analysis leads readers to question this appearance and to analyze Chekhov's message. Ivan seems to be a realist and Nikolai an idealist, yet readers have to question whether Nikolai's happiness is truly the illusion Ivan thinks it is or whether Ivan himself is living the illusion. After Ivan warns Pavel against the evils of land ownership and implores him not to ignore societal concerns in the pursuit of personal happiness, he appears to contradict himself. Just as in the beginning of Chekhov's tale, Ivan changes his opinion of the countryside as a place of tedium to a place of luxury, he now changes his opinion once again. He relates how his visit to his brother's estate changed his mind completely and how now he too wishes to live with this illusion of the country. Ivan wonders how people can deceive themselves into being happy. Yet he himself is not happy, and Nikolai certainly appears to be.

What launches Ivan into his monologue and what stirs him to condemn the country lifestyle is the memory of his visit to Nikolai's estate and Ivan's amazement when Nikolai believed his gooseberries to be delicious when they were actually hard and sour. Ivan seems to make the point that Nikolai became so obsessed with his desire for personal happiness that he lost touch with reality, or that he created his own reality based solely on illusion. When Ivan visited his brother, he clearly saw that Nikolai believed he was living out his dream. Yet unlike the dream, Nikolai's estate did not have a pond, it had only a polluted river, and it had no gooseberry bushes at all until Nikolai planted them. It is the belief that Nikolai is deluding himself and the realization that he is happy with so little that so depresses Ivan, finding it necessary to tell Burkin and Pavel his story. Both the story itself and the framework Chekhov sets for Ivan's telling of the story advances the themes of disillusionment and isolation. The author appears to be saying that the isolated life one has in the country leads to an isolation from society's concerns. This country lifestyle then, is nothing but self-serving, and it is just an escape from the harsh realities of life. Through Ivan, Chekhov is telling readers that Nikolai proved this to be true when he dedicated his life to the pursuit of his own personal happiness with no regard for the happiness of others.

◆ LITERARY QUALITIES ◆

The narrator of "Gooseberries" is presumably Chekhov himself. He makes Ivan his spokesperson, hailing the benefits of moderation and stressing the danger in retreating from life and ignoring the needs of the masses. Chekhov himself was a realist, and Ivan appears to parrot what is known about Chekhov's views. While Chekhov was once an avid supporter of Tolstoy's anti-materialism, he gradually rejected this doctrine. In "Gooseberries," Chekhov's ambivalence seems apparent. Ivan both denounces Nikolai's materialism and wallows in the pleasures of country life.

"Gooseberries" is comprised of two separate parts, which can be labeled the narrative and the anecdote. It is a story within a story, a format that allows Chekhov to interweave the past with the present and create a framework for setting forth his series of contrasts. Chekhov contrasts the two landowners, Pavel and Nikolai, and by doing so he contrasts realism with idealism, activism with passivity, and involvement versus isolation. Using Pavel to represent the kind and caring landowner and Nikolai to represent the isolated and unaffected man, Chekhov clearly sets apart the plight of the masses from what he considers the selfish bourgeois class and their fruitless existence.

Chekhov has been labeled a master ironist, and in "Gooseberries" the first apparent irony is that Pavel's farm is so much like Nikolai's yet Ivan views them differently.

The second irony is that Nikolai's dream of happiness is only an illusion, that his desire for "the simple life" involved disregarding the needs of others and creating his own reality. Nikolai's gooseberries are obviously a symbol, both a symbol of country life and, to Nikolai, a symbol of an idyllic life and of bourgeois success, both of which to him, equate with happiness. Nikolai believes he is living a life of personal contentment and the life of a self-made man. It is also ironic that the image of the self-made man typically contrasts with the image of the proprietor of an estate. But Nikolai is both and can not embody one of these images without condemning the other.

The gooseberries not only serve as the central symbol in this story, but they also illustrate Chekhov's art of exaggeration. Chekhov often exaggerates to prove his point, and Nikolai's obsession with gooseberries as well as his belief that his own gooseberries are delicious is a satirical commentary on the power of denial and the human propensity to delude oneself. But "Gooseberries" is labeled a parody and not a satire, and the most simple definition of a parody is the use of exaggeration to make something appear ridiculous.

◆ SOCIAL SENSITIVITY ◆

Chekhov clearly uses Ivan's speech as a vehicle to defend his stand on social issues of concern in Russia in the late 1800s. Education of the peasants and the mistreatment of the peasants by the bourgeois class were primary issues at this time, and Chekhov appears to be laying these issues out for evaluation.

Chekhov was criticized for his lack of social consciousness and noted for first supporting, then rejecting, the views of Leo Tolstoy, the famous Russian novelist and noted religious thinker. The influence of Tolstoy is apparent in "Gooseberries." Tolstoy believed that society was corrupt and that one could retreat from this corruption and enjoy a simple life in the country. Tolstoy proposed that people should not worry about society but strive instead for their own peace and happiness, and through this general sense of contentment society would begin to improve. Chekhov, at the time he wrote "Gooseberries," discounted Tolstoy's ideas as unrealistic, and he obviously used Ivan's story of Nikolai to express his disenchantment with Tolstoyism. But Ivan's speech reveals Chekhov's ambivalence. Ivan was so distressed at witnessing Nikolai's smug happiness in the face of others' suffering that he himself appeared to discount the entire notion of happiness. Many critics have interpreted this story as a direct commentary on Tolstoy's story "How Much Land Does a Man Need?" In both Tolstoy's story and in Chekhov's, the protagonists desire material wealth, and both of them "die" in the pursuit. In Tolstoy, the hero physically dies just as he is about to obtain his dream. In Chekhov, Nikolai experiences a spiritual death. Having led his entire life in pursuit of personal satisfaction, he loses his humanity and compassion. Ivan feels deeply disturbed by the kind of happiness Nikolai experiences, and he forces his audience to engage in a personal analysis on the meaning of happiness.

◆ TOPICS FOR DISCUSSION ◆

1. Is the ending of the book satisfactory? Can you identify a climax to the story?

2. What purpose does Pelageya serve in the story?

3. In the last part of the story, what does the image of Ivan's pipe symbolize to you?

4. The story both begins and ends with the image of rain—at first pounding down on the land and in the end tap-

ping on the windows in Pavel's estate. What does this image convey to you?

5. How does Nikolai's first appearance in Ivan's story compare with Pavel's first appearance in Chekhov's narrative?

6. What do you think Chekhov wished to achieve by creating a slow moving, seemingly plotless story lacking in action?

7. What do you consider to be Nikolai's greatest "crime?"

8. Why do you think Ivan is so hostile toward his brother?

9. What purpose does Burkin serve in the story and how much does Chekhov reveal about him?

◆ IDEAS FOR REPORTS AND PAPERS ◆

1. Discuss the symbolism in the novel; specifically of the gooseberries, the rain, and the pipe.

2. It has been said that one of Tolstoy's central themes is the alienation of modern man from his natural environment. Discuss this theme as it relates to Chekhov's "Gooseberries."

3. It has been said that "Gooseberries" is a direct commentary on Tolstoy's short story "How Much Land Does a Man Need?" This story says that a man only needs six feet of earth in which to be buried. Read this short story, analyze this quote, and explain how Chekhov comments on this view in "Gooseberries."

4. To quote Ivan: "Behind the door of every contented, happy man, there ought to be someone standing with a little hammer and continually reminding him with a knock that there are unhappy people, and that however happy he may be, life will sooner or later show him its claws." Explain what

Ivan meant by this and comment on what this quote means to you.

5. Assuming that Ivan speaks for Chekhov, write an essay on Chekhov's views on happiness.

6. "Gooseberries" is the second in a trilogy of short stories that have unifying themes. Read the first story, "The Man in a Shell," and the third story, "About Love" and discuss the themes you find in all three stories.

7. Extend the concept of stillness and isolation to encompass the concept of death. Do you recognize any death symbolism in the story? Discuss the theme of death, the symbols of death, and comment on what you believe Chekhov appears to be saying by advancing this theme.

◆ RELATED TITLES ◆

Gooseberries is the middle story in a trilogy of Chekhov's tales, the first titled "The Man in a Shell" and the last titled "About Love." All are united in theme, particularly on the theme of isolation and escape from life. They also all comment on Tolstoy's short story "How Much Land Does a Man Need."

◆ FOR FURTHER REFERENCE ◆

"Chekhov, Anton." In *Contemporary Authors,* vol. 124. Detroit: Gale, 1988. A biographical essay with information about Chekhov's work.

"Chekhov, Anton." In *Short Story Criticism,* vol. 28. Detroit: Gale, 1998. Contains extensive excerpts from individual critical reviews of "Gooseberries."

"Chekhov, Anton." In *World Literature Criticism.* Detroit: Gale, 1992. The essay about

Chekhov discusses the critical response to his works and provides some biographical information.

"Chekhov, Anton Pavlovich." In *Something about the Author*, vol. 90. Detroit: Gale, 1997. An essay that includes biographical information about Chekhov and comments on his work.

Hahn, Beverly. *Chekhov: A Study of the Major Stories and Plays*. Cambridge: Cambridge University Press, 1977. Hahn's book gives an overview of Chekhov's work. It discusses the development of his writing style and themes through the course of his career as a short story and play writer.

Johnson, Ronald J. *Anton Chekhov: A Study of the Short Fiction*. New York: Twayne, 1993. This introduction to Chekhov's short stories includes a critical analysis of "Gooseberries." It discusses Chekhov's narrative and point of view in the story, as well as his social conscience and his beliefs regarding freedom and happiness.

Pritchett, V. S. *Chekhov: A Spirit Set Free.* London: Hodder & Stoughton, 1988. Pritchett's work contains biographical information on Chekhov and critical analysis of his works, particularly of his short fiction. It serves as a good introduction to Chekhov's works and provides a basis for further study of his views and themes.

Tamra Andrews

THE GRASS DANCER

Novel

1994

Author: Susan Power

◆

Major Books for Young Adults

The Grass Dancer, 1994
Strong Heart Society, 1997

◆ ABOUT THE AUTHOR ◆

Susan Power was born in Chicago, Illinois, on October 12, 1961, to a Caucasian father and a Sioux mother, and is currently a member of the Standing Rock Sioux tribe. She attended high school in Chicago, where she became active in the Native American movement, then she continued her education at Harvard/Radcliffe where she earned a bachelor's degree in psychology. Power says that she was inspired by her parents, both as a writer and as an activist. Her father, now deceased, worked as a salesman at a publishing house. Her mother is a Sioux who came to Chicago from her reservation at the age of sixteen, became editor of the University of Chicago Law Review, founded the American Indian Center in Chicago, and became a civil rights activist. Both parents told their daughter stories and read to her as a young child. Because storytelling was an important part of her childhood, Power considers writing an oral

experience, and she draws heavily on storytelling techniques in her novels. Her mother's activism encouraged Power's interest in civil rights issues affecting Native Americans and other groups, and the need for Indian lawyers led her to obtain a law degree from Harvard in 1986. But Power abandoned law to become a writer. She needed a creative outlet, and she wished to incorporate into her writing both the oral traditions and the socio-political concerns that played a large role in her cultural identity.

Power has worked variously as a storyteller, a secretary, a technical writer, and an editor. She also has given lectures, written poetry and short stories for literary journals, and conducted writing seminars. She began writing fiction at the University of Iowa Writers' Workshop where she earned a master's of fine arts in 1992, and it was there that she began writing the short stories which eventually became chapters of

Susan Power

together combine to reveal complex relationships between members of the Sioux community and their spirit ancestors. The stories begin in the early 1980s and move backward over one hundred years, to 1864 when the two most vivid characters, Red Dress and Ghost Horse, lived and fell in love. Legends and folk motifs help to document Native American culture and consciousness. The novel chronicles the pains and hardships of modern life on a Plains Indians reservation, and it tells the story of connections among generations and how long deceased ancestors continue to affect the lives of the living.

◆ SETTING ◆

The primary setting of *The Grass Dancer* is a Sioux Indian reservation in North Dakota. Though the Native American setting helps define what life is like for rural Indians, it also serves as a model of society as a whole, which underscores the more general human experience of Power's characters. Some of the scenes are uniquely Native American, including the powwows, for instance, as are the images of sweats and other Indian rituals like the grass dance itself. Power uses these outdoor ceremonies and scenes to underscore the connection her people feel with nature, but she also uses the natural settings to distance Native American philosophy with that of urban whites.

What makes the setting of *The Grass Dancer* particularly unique is that Power's characters inhabit two worlds. They inhabit both the Anglo and the tribal worlds in one sense, but they also inhabit both the world of the living and the world of the dead. So Power seems to define the Native American "setting" as a spiritual realm, a realm where ghosts and spirits move about as freely as do living beings. Nature and nature imagery are crucial to Power's defini-

The Grass Dancer. She considers her stories not to be uniquely about the Native American experience, but simply about human nature and human experience. She says that her degree in psychology helped her create complex characters and gave her insight into human behavior. *The Grass Dancer* won the Ernest Hemingway Foundation Award for first fiction in 1995. Since then, Power has written *Strong Heart Society*, a novel about three Native Americans living in Chicago, and she is also working on another novel, titled *War Bundles*, about the Native American experience.

◆ OVERVIEW ◆

The Grass Dancer is a novel that interweaves the lives of people living on a Dakota Sioux Indian reservation. It is a portrait of Native American culture depicted in chapters, each of which serves as a story in itself, but

The Grass Dancer

tion of spirit. The significance of the grass dance, for instance, lies in its ability to define movement in the world. In Native American thought, movement means life force, and the fact that the grass dancers in the novel imitate the movement of the grass and try to become one with nature demonstrates their willingness to accept the notion of connecting spirit. As the characters relate to the world around them, they stay in touch with the spirituality that defines their lifestyle and which they must retain in order to fight the dissolution of their culture.

◆ THEMES AND CHARACTERS ◆

Power deals with complex themes and creates characters whose depth and substance is revealed slowly through each individual story. In developing her characters and in expanding their stories, she not only presents a history of the Sioux community, but she creates a world where past, present, and future meld together to create a group consciousness, or an ever present notion of connecting spirit. The dead ancestors are just as "alive" in the minds of the living characters as the living characters are alive to each other. Ancestors continue to exist as spirits, and they continue to inhabit the world in memories and dreams. Their experiences also exist in memories and dreams, and through this strange, immutable bond that connects all the members of the tribe, these experiences that occurred long ago continue to impact the experiences of those living today.

The novel begins with a powwow and with a grass dance, powerful symbols of Indian spiritualism. The scene involves a beautiful young woman named Pumpkin who comes from the city but who dances seductively at the reservation powwows and who captivates a seventeen-year-old boy named Harley Wind Soldier. Harley falls instantly in love with Pumpkin, and

the two spend the night together, convinced that they were meant to be together forever. The next day, however, fate intervenes, and Pumpkin is killed in a tragic car accident. Harley is devastated. He is struggling to come to terms with another tragic accident that years before had left his father and brother dead and his mother unable to speak a word. As Power reveals more and more about the past, readers begin to wonder if these two accidents were truly accidents at all or if they were the effects of powerful magic. Gradually, it becomes clear that these two incidents have some mysterious connection. Powerful people come into focus in the novel, and magic and mystery emerge as one of Power's primary themes.

Throughout the novel and in the stories to follow, Harley reemerges as a character and so does Pumpkin. The circumstances surrounding the accident become clearer. Power unravels the secrets in her characters' lives by moving back through generations to explain how past people and events continue to play a role in present day life. Details about Pumpkin's character and Harley's character emerge through the telling of additional tales. The crash, it appears, did not exist as a single incident, but only existed in relation to other events that had occurred in the past and that will occur in the future. This is one example of how Power conveys a sense of Native American time; she represents people and events as part of cyclical time and continuing motion.

Pumpkin and Harley Wind Soldier are simply two of a long cast of characters whose lives intermingle in Power's mind and in readers' imaginations. One of the most striking elements in Power's book is that some of the strongest characters are not living people at all but spirit ancestors. This reveals the significance of spirit ancestors in Native American thought, and likely in Power's own belief system as well. It appears obvious that Power knows Native

American spirituality intimately, and that is what enabled her to create powerfully real ancestral spirits.

The story of Red Dress and Ghost Horse emerges as a primary plot in the novel and one that underscores the notion of spirit in Native American consciousness. While some of the living characters seem rather undefined, Red Dress and Ghost Horse appear larger than life. Arguably the most poignant character in the novel is Red Dress, the spirit ancestor of Charlene Thunder who, like Pumpkin, falls in love with Harley Wind Soldier. Red Dress died fighting the European invaders in 1864, but she lives on in nature, as a grove of plum trees it is said, and she remains present in the lives of Charlene and the other people in the Sioux community and continues to exist in their memories and influence their lives. Red Dress appears to Harley Wind Soldier during a vision, one of the ways Power reveals the presence of spirits. Red Dress is so powerful a spirit that her people can feel her presence in the world around them. "I am memory. I tell them when they're sleeping," she says. Like memory, she keeps the past alive and she gives the living a spiritual link with history. Not only does Red Dress represent memory, but also the interconnectedness of all things, the spirit that exists in all creatures. Her presence also attests to the important role of women in tribal culture.

The struggle to preserve Native American culture influenced Power to become active in the civil rights movement. Power fought for her people's traditions, and Red Dress continually reminds her people of the importance of keeping tradition. The grass dance is but one powerful tradition, and through Red Dress, Harley learns the symbolic meaning of the grass dance he performs at powwows. He must remember the steps, she tells him, because as long as he does, he will help to preserve the culture and continue to help his people resist Anglo influence. The grass dance, as a symbol of tradition itself, attests to the notion of movement as a life force.

Critics have often labeled Power's style of writing "magical realism," but Power herself argues that she simply told her story the way it is. She sees her characters as individuals, and their spiritual beliefs just a part of who they are. These characters acknowledge the presence of a world that can not be seen or felt, but only perceived. Memories, dreams, and visions offer insight into that world and infuse her characters' lives with magic.

Operating on the notion that magic exists and that communication exists between different worlds, Power equips her characters with supernatural abilities. Mercury Thunder is the reservation witch, for instance. She is not a medicine woman exactly; that is, one who practices good magic, but rather, she practices black magic, and she tends to use her powers for selfish reasons. When Mercury Thunder exercises her powers, it leads to tragedy. So everyone in the reservation fears her. In a world infused with power, it seems logical that Power should touch on the use and abuse of power, and the effects of good and bad magic.

It is this pervasive belief in magic that makes gods and ancestors real characters in Power's book. Wakan Tanka, the Great Spirit, seems real to Herod Small War, and Herod feels the presence of Wakan Tanka beside him when he communes with nature. Herod Small War is a Yuwipi, an interpreter of dreams, and he "tries to bring his community into harmony with the spiritual world." He clings to tradition. He starts the day off with a sweat, a ritual used by his people to help them isolate the spirit within them and see into other worlds. Herod Small War and other characters in *The Grass Dancer* who cling to these rituals and who put faith in tribal stories keep their culture alive, helping to preserve Native American identity. The pervasive belief in the significance of tribal history and in the ghosts and spirits that continue to exist from bygone eras has much to do with the reliance on myths and legends that permeate Indian societies.

The individual stories that comprise *The Grass Dancer* read like living myths. Through the telling of tales, Power presents a clear picture of Native American life. But she also uses the Sioux community as a microcosm of all societies as a whole. She explores the universal themes of love and jealousy, poverty, illness, and injustice, yet she shows how the Sioux face these challenges as a unique people. She paints a picture of the Sioux community as an extended family—connected by spirit and by common cause, and tied to each other through living legends that continue impact their actions.

Though Power certainly conveys the message that the Sioux fight many of the same battles as any other people fight, she also conveys the message that the injustices inflicted on Native Americans was and is an assault on their identity. Those who tried to bring Christianity to the Sioux led an assault on their spirituality. It is revealed in the novel that Red Dress intentionally misinterpreted the message of a Jesuit priest who was trying to convert the tribe to Christianity. She claims that she has a dream about what will become of the tribe if they lose their sense of tradition. Disaster will happen, she sees in the dream, and her people will lose their cultural identity. Power speaks of Red Dress as the true "grass dancer" of the novel. The grass, Power says, represents the preservation of culture. So does Red Dress. Red Dress represents connectedness as she embodies the past and its effect on the future. She continually reminds her people of the importance of tradition and the importance of continuing

their struggle against oppression, prejudice, and the destructive effects of colonization.

◆ LITERARY QUALITIES ◆

The plot moves in reverse chronological order, beginning in the early 1980s. Power is a storyteller, and she uses storytelling techniques in her novel to emphasize the influence of oral tradition on her people. She interweaves the lives and tales of multiple characters not only to portray the complex relationships between members of the Sioux tribe, but also to highlight their belief in the interconnectedness of all things.

Power's circular plot moves back 100 years from the 1980s, then back to the present day. Each chapter serves as a short story in itself, but as Power reveals the relationships between people and events, the stories come together and readers get a sense of the consequences between seemingly random acts. This interconnectedness helps the audience gain an understanding of Native American time as a continuum, circular rather than linear, with life and death simply part of the same cycle. Power reveals the Native American belief of a connecting spirit by using recurring characters and related tales, and by mingling the life and death of the dead with the life and death of the living.

Powerful nature imagery pervades the novel, helping readers understand the connection between human beings and nature. This oneness of spirit defines Native American philosophy. Power contrasts the Apollo moon landing, for instance, with Margaret Many Wounds "dancing on the moon," with dancing on the moon serving as a metaphor for her death and the connection of her spirit with the spirit of nature. Power weaves historical events such as the Apollo moon landing and the nineteenth-century Great Plains drought into her narrative to help define the co-existence of the real world and the spiritual realm. She creates both a living history and a living philosophy of her people.

The symbolism of the grass dance is crucial to Power's message. In the novel, Power emphasizes the harmonious relationship the Native Americans have with nature, and their belief that one unifying spirit unites all living things. She stresses the connection between woman and nature, for instance, as Red Dress exists as a grove of plum trees. Mary Ellen Quinn, who reviewed *The Grass Dancer* for *Booklist*, says that the strongest characters in the novel are women, and perhaps this has something to do with the symbolic connection between women and nature. Power uses the seductive Pumpkin performing her grass dance, and the grass dance itself, to emphasize movement and life force. In the Native American consciousness, neither humans nor nature ever die, but continue to exist as spirits.

Magical realism is a theme that emerged in fiction written in the mid-twentieth century. It is generally associated with Latin American writers, but it is actually more of an international movement. It is based on the assumption that magic must be inexplicable and uncontrollable, and a natural occurrence within people and within their environment. The people who experience magic exist within a real world where magic is simply a part of the reality. Magical realism incorporates elements of folklore and myth into otherwise realistic fiction, helping define cultures in which folklore and myth continue to play a large role in philosophical beliefs.

Though Power argues that she does not use magical realism as a literary device but simply as a way to identify the beliefs of her people, magic does appear in the novel. It also undermines the Western belief that connects truth with fact and imagination with falsehood. Those who embrace the notion of magic in the world do not deny or question its existence. So writers such as Power give magic the status of reality and use it to explain superstitions and oral traditions. Because Power considers magic an accepted reality for her characters and for the Native Americans she knows in her own life, she considers the label "magical realism" simply a cultural interpretation of Native America, a term coined by people outside Native America who have difficulty understanding the implications of an acknowledged spiritual presence in the world.

In *The Grass Dancer*, spirits reveal themselves to living people through memories, visions, and dreams. Power emphasizes the significance of these "otherworldly" experiences. The philosophy of her people assumes a harmonious relationship between the natural and the cosmic spheres, and that relationship appears to be based on dream connections. Dreams, like memories and visions, connect the natural world with the spirit world. They reveal the presence of power to make things happen—such as the ability to cure the sick, to communicate with animals, plants, and nonphysical beings or to influence the will of another human being. Because Power's characters affirm the Native American belief in a "magic" world and because they believe in the power of a universal connecting spirit, they view myths and legends as living history. Power uses visionary language because Native American philosophy naturally links vision and myth.

◆ SOCIAL SENSITIVITY ◆

Power presents a picture of Sioux life that combines the spiritual, the socio-political, and the historical bases of Native American philosophy. The beliefs of her people are threatened in white America, she believes, as is the very survival of her culture. It appears to be necessary for her to tell the story of her people from their unique viewpoint of a culture in transition. She presents important historical movements from a Native American perspective, using the spiritual beliefs of her people to help readers see historical change in a new way.

Magical realism emerges in the literature of cultures where myths, legends, and ritual religious practices are a part of everyday life. It involves participation in both human and cosmic realms. Whether or not Power uses magical realism as a literary device, her mingling of magic and reality does serve to distance Native American life from Anglo life. That Power's characters cling to their belief in magic, and indeed continue to practice magic, illustrates their resistance to internal colonization and the resulting dissolution of their identity. The conflict between white and Native American becomes evident. Power has felt the effects of assimilation, and she understands how it undermines Indian identity. This occurs day-to-day on the reservations and in the city. In the character of Pumpkin, Power tackles the plight of the urban Indian. In Pumpkin's essay on the "plight of the urban Indian" she speaks of her anxiety about going to college. "I will have to put aside one worldview—perhaps temporarily— to take up another. From what I have learned so far, I know the two are not complementary but rather incompatible, and melodramatic as it may sound, I sometimes feel I am risking my soul by leaving the Indian community."

Powers deals with the threat to Native American religious and socio-political views effectively and makes it clear that Native Americans continue to struggle against attempts to undermine their traditions. A grandfather in the novel, Herod Small War, speaks to the water, "I was just saying to Wakan Tanka that I haven't forgotten Him. I didn't go the way of the steamer and the great piano. I listen for His voice and the music He makes in the water and through the wind." Herod Small War clings to the old spiritualism. To the character in *The Grass Dancer*, Christianity seems like an assault on his gods.

◆ TOPICS FOR DISCUSSION ◆

1. Discuss the symbolism of the grass dance.

2. Discuss Pumpkin's essay on "The Plight of the Urban Indian." Talk about the conflict she feels.

3. Powers succeeds in painting a picture of modern day Native American culture. She gives insights into the thoughts and concerns of tribal people. What do you feel are some of the primary concerns facing Native Americans today?

4. How does Pumpkin's attitude as an urban Indian differ from Charlene's view?

5. Choose several names from the novel and discuss their significance. Who are some of the strongest characters in the novel and why?

6. Discuss the significance of visions in tribal consciousness, remembering the daily sweats performed by Herod Small War.

7. After reading the novel, do you feel that Powers revealed more about Native American nature or about human nature in general? Think about the Native American community as a microcosm for society as a whole.

8. How do you perceive the significance of magic in the novel?

◆ IDEAS FOR REPORTS AND PAPERS ◆

1. Using examples from the novel, discuss the significance of nature in Native American thought.

2. Discuss the practice of ancestor worship in Native American thought. Touch on the practice in other traditional societies as well to help clarify the concept.

3. Using examples from the novel, discuss magical realism. Do you believe that Powers uses magical realism as a technique? Why or why not?

4. Discuss the symbolism of Red Dress and Ghost Horse.

5. Choose one of the socio-political concerns Powers covers in the novel and detail how she chooses to shed light on the problem.

6. Discuss the notion of tribal time and connectedness.

7. Choose one chapter from the novel and discuss how it works as a story in itself and how it fits as a piece of the whole novel.

8. Discuss the different "grass dancers" in the novel and what the grass dance means to them.

9. Write a characterization of one of the people in the novel and discuss how Powers uses that character to advance a theme.

10. Do you think Anglo Americans have rituals? If so, compare them to Native American rituals. What are some of your discoveries?

11. Compare Native American philosophy toward nature with that of Caucasian Americans. Are they vastly different? Are there any similarities? Explain.

◆ RELATED TITLES ◆

In addition to *The Grass Dancer*, Power has written *Strong Heart Society*, which depicts Native American life in urban Chicago. *Strong Heart Society* offers an insider's view to the Native American experience as well as unique insights into the human thoughts and concerns. She is also working on her third book, *War Bundles*, which centers on three Native American characters, each from a different background—Dakota, Winnebago, and Potawatomi.

Power has often been compared to Louise Erdrich, a Chippewa writer who Power says influenced her writing a great deal. Erdrich writes about the Chippewa reservations in North Dakota, and she too weaves the lives of her characters together, blending the past, present, and future to give a sense of the time continuum inherent in Native American thought. Visions and witchcraft are powerful forces in both Power's book and in Erdrich's books. Perhaps most closely related to *The Grass Dancer* is Erdrich's *Love Medicine*. This book also centers on life on an Indian reservation, consisting of a series of seemingly unrelated chapters that come together to form a colorful history of two families over five decades. Like Power, Erdrich also creates a multitude of characters and spins a web of relationships and secrets among them.

Linda Hogan, James Welch, and Leslie Marmon Silko are several other authors who write on Native American life and deal with themes that emphasize the preservation of Native American tradition and culture. Linda Hogan's *Power: A Novel* is a coming-of-age novel about Omishito, a sixteen-year-old Taiga girl who witnesses the killing of her clan's totem animal. In this book Hogan underscores the threats that endanger Native Americans spirituality, and she uses magical realism to help define the philosophical views of her characters. Omishito's aunt tells her tribal stories—mythomagical stories of transformations that occurred in a time when human and nonhuman beings lived together in harmony. These stories help Omishito make sense out of the present and to feel the power and unseen forces in the world

Leslie Marmon Silko's novel *Ceremony* centers around Tayo, a young half-white Laguna Indian on a search for self-identity. A World War II veteran, Tayo becomes emotionally distraught after the war and rediscovers his connection to the land and to ancient tribal rituals.

James Welch's *Medicine River* features the story of a boy and his best friend living in a Native American community and dealing with the hardships that plague their people. Like Power, Welch also gives insight into the human condition by interweaving the characters' lives and actions, and by dealing with family relationships.

◆ FOR FURTHER REFERENCE ◆

Grapman, Jackie. Review of *The Grass Dancer*. *School Library Journal* (May, 1995): 136.

Henighan, Stephen. Review of *The Grass Dancer*. *Times Literary Supplement* (December 2, 1994): 22.

"Power, Susan." In *Contemporary Authors*, vol. 145. Detroit: Gale, 2000. A biographical essay that includes information about Power's life and work.

"Power, Susan." In *Contemporary Literary Criticism*, vol. 91, Detroit: Gale, 1996. Provides biographical information about Power and critical commentary on her novel.

Quinn, Mary Ellen. Review of *The Grass Dancer. Booklist* (August, 1994): 2024.

Thornton, Lawrence. Review of *The Grass Dancer. New York Times Book Review* (August 21, 1994): 7

Walter, Roland. "Pan-American (Re)visions: Magical Realism and Amerindian Cultures in Susan Power's 'The Grass Dancer,' Giaconda Belli's 'La Mujer Habiitada,' Linda Hogan's 'Power,' and Mario Vargas Llosa's 'El Hablador.' *American Studies International* (October, 1999): 63. Roland discusses the concept of magical realism both as literary mode and as a cultural practice in the Americas. He related magical realism to *The Grass Dancer*, as well as to other works of Native American literature.

Tamra Andrews

GREAT EXPECTATIONS

Novel

1861

Author: Charles Dickens

◆

Major Books for Young Adults

*The Posthumous Papers of the Pickwick
Club*, 1836–1837
Sketches by Boz, 1837
*The Life and Adventures of Nicholas
Nickleby*, 1837–1839
*Oliver Twist, or the Parish Boy's Prog-
ress*, 1838
The Old Curiosity Shop, 1841
*Barnaby Rudge: A Tale of the Riots of
'Eighty*, 1841
*The Life and Adventures of Martin
Chuzzlewit*, 1842–1844

A Christmas Carol, 1843
*The Personal History of David
Copperfield*, 1849–1850
A Child's History of England, 1852–1854
Bleak House, 1852–1853
Hard Times: For These Times, 1854
Little Dorrit, 1855–1857
A Tale of Two Cities, 1859
Great Expectations, 1861
The Mystery of Edwin Drood, 1870
 (concluded by Leon Garfield, 1980)
A Child's Dream of a Star, 1871

◆ ABOUT THE AUTHOR ◆

Charles John Huffam Dickens was born
February 7, 1812, in Portsmouth, England. He was the son of John Dickens, a
clerk in the Navy Pay Office, and Elizabeth
(Barrow) Dickens. Young Dickens was taught
at home by his mother, and attended a
Dame School (a school in which the rudiments of reading and writing were taught
by a woman in her own home) at Chatham
for a short time, and Wellington Academy
in London. Later, he further educated himself by reading widely in the British Museum.

Dickens's father was incompetent at managing money, and was eventually sent to
debtor's prison. Attempting to support herself and the younger children in more modest quarters when they had to leave the
family home, Mrs. Dickens tried to set herself up as the principal of a girls' school, but
no one enrolled any children to be taught
by her. Dickens was sent at age twelve to
work in a run-down part of London, in a
business owned by a family friend, sticking
labels on bottles of boot-black; he lived in a
small, humble rooming house nearby. For
months his only recreation was depressing

Charles Dickens

Sunday visits to his father in debtor's prison. This life horrified him, giving him belly cramps and lasting nightmares. Even the friendship of a poor boy named Fagin who tended Dickens when he was sick at work was not enough to relieve his shame.

After some months the family's income was recovered to a small extent, but it took the intervention of another family friend before young Dickens's parents brought him to Kent to live with the family. It simply had not occurred to them to remove their twelve-year-old son from miserable employment in a slum.

These few months had a profound affect on young Dickens's life. Afterwards he strove to be a gentleman, to escape what he had learned of poverty. He considered a career in the theatre, but took up writing and discovered that he had a natural talent—and what he wrote, he could sell to earn a respectable living.

For the rest of his life, Dickens avoided that run-down part of London where he had lived and worked in misery for months. Even as an adult, a successful author and editor, he told no one about those experiences. His children noticed that if Dickens had to walk through that district, he would grimly hold their hands and proceed out of the area as quickly as possible, never saying a word. It was not until his literary executor asked some searching questions that Dickens broke silence, only once, in the last years of his life. The core of feelings that was the genesis of his celebrated novels *David Copperfield, Oliver Twist*, and *Great Expectations* was revealed only after the author's death.

Dickens enjoyed a career as a novelist, journalist, court reporter, and editor. He was editor of *London Daily News* in 1846, founder and editor of *Household Words* from 1833–1835, and of *All the Year Round* from 1859–1870. He was also a talented amateur actor, and presented public readings of his works, beginning in 1858. He acquired a grand home in Kent, called Gad's Hill, which he had aspired to own since boyhood.

Dickens fell in love many times as a young man, but he married Catherine Hogarth in April, 1836 and together they raised ten children. Some of their descendants have gone on to their own literary careers. He and his wife separated in 1858, when he was spending a great deal of time in London. Later they divorced, probably at least in part because Dickens had fallen in love with Ellen Ternan, an Irish actress.

In 1865, Dickens survived a train wreck which left his first-class carriage dangling from a railway bridge. By all reports, Dickens calmed his travelling companions (his mistress Ellen Ternen and her mother), got them all safely off the train and then went to the aid of many injured and dying passengers. Eventually, Dickens retrieved his current manuscript from the railway carriage as it swayed from the bridge, before leaving the scene. Afterwards, he suffered from a great fear of train wrecks but continued to travel for lectures and readings.

He died of a paralytic stroke, at Gad's Hill, Kent, England, on June 18, 1870 and was buried in Poet's Corner of Westminster Abbey, near Chaucer and Shakespeare.

◆ OVERVIEW ◆

The orphaned Philip Pirrip, who calls himself Pip, was raised by his harsh sister Mrs. Joe and her kind husband Joe Gargery, a blacksmith. Wandering through the marshes near his home one day, Pip encounters a ragged stranger who demands that Pip bring him food and a file to remove the chain that binds his leg. Pip complies with this request. Later Pip sees him struggling with another stranger before they disappear from view. The man Pip had helped is later captured by the police, but promises to repay Pip for his aid.

Miss Havisham, an eccentric old lady who lives in a huge mansion, asks that Pip come to visit her. All of the clocks in her dark, dusty house are stopped on the hour that the man Miss Havisham planned to marry abandoned her. She still wears her now-yellowed wedding dress, and the moldy wedding cake still stands on a table in her room, inhabited by a colony of spiders. A frequent visitor at the mansion, Pip talks with Estella, Miss Havisham's haughty young ward. Eventually he is paid a small sum and told it is time for him to become Joe's apprentice.

One day someone breaks into their home and Pip's sister, Mrs. Joe, is injured with a great blow to the back of the head. A kind young woman named Biddy moves from the village into Joe's home to help take care of Mrs. Joe and the household. Biddy believes that it was Orlick, a contemptuous employee of Joe's, who injured Mrs. Joe. Biddy also fears that Orlick is falling in love with her. Pip continues to work for Joe. Every year on Pip's birthday, the youth visits Miss Havisham. Pip is constantly regretting his desire for a more comfortable lifestyle, and regrets also his infatuation with Estella.

Pip is surprised and pleased when a London lawyer, Mr. Jaggers, brings him to London to be educated, become a gentleman, and eventually come into an inheritance; Pip assumes that Miss Havisham is financing this plan to groom him as a proper husband for Estella. In London, Pip rooms with an agreeable young man named Herbert Pocket, a distant relative of Miss Havisham.

Pip associates with a group of young dandies who call themselves the Finches of the Grove, the most prominent of which is a cad named Bentley Drummle. When the still-devoted Joe comes to visit him, Pip is embarrassed by his brother-in-law's crude ways and treats him unkindly. Miss Havisham informs Pip that Estella will be moving to London and that she wants Pip to fall in love with her. But after her arrival in London, Estella is courted by Drummle.

Pip receives an unexpected visit on his twenty-first birthday from the convict whom he had met so long ago in the marshes. The man, whose name is Abel Magwitch, reveals that he has been the boy's benefactor all along, having grown rich after being banished to Australia. He has come back to witness Pip's progress even though his own life is endangered by his illegal return to England. Pip is initially repulsed by Magwitch's coarseness yet realizes how much he owes him; he decides to try to help Magwitch in any way he can. Magwitch is using the pseudonym Provis to avoid detection. He also reveals that the man with whom he had struggled in the marsh and who still vows to destroy him is the villainous Compeyson, who, coincidentally, is also the man responsible for the abandonment of Miss Havisham by her fiance Arthur on their wedding day. Determined to chastise Miss Havisham for allowing him to believe that she was his benefactor, Pip visits her. He learns that Estella is engaged to Drummle and that Miss Havisham had carefully trained her young ward to break the hearts of as many men as possible, as vengeance for the desertion she herself had experienced. As a result, Estella is a cold and detached young woman, unable to love or feel compassion. On a final visit to Miss Havisham's house after Estella's wedding, Pip finds the mansion on fire but is unable to save Miss Havisham, who perishes.

Pip and young Herbert Pocket scheme to help Magwitch escape to France, but just as they have secured him aboard a boat, Compeyson appears and the two men fight, eventually struggling in the water. Magwitch kills his enemy and is immediately apprehended by the police; he dies in prison, but not before Pip recognizes his pity and love for his benefactor. Pip becomes seriously ill and Joe arrives to nurse him back to health, giving Pip an occasion to realize the value of his old friend's constancy and love. Mrs. Joe has since died, and Joe has married the Gargery's former servant, Biddy. Still despondent over having lost Estella, Pip establishes an importing business with Herbert.

Eleven years later he returns to visit Joe and also the spot where Miss Havisham's mansion once stood. He finds the widowed Estella also wandering there; she has become a warmer, more compassionate person over the years. The two leave together, and appear destined for happiness together. In Dickens's original version, Pip and Estella part with the understanding that they will probably never see each other again, but in the revised version, Dickens's makes the ending more optimistic by implying that they will, indeed, have a future together someday.

◆ SETTING ◆

This novel is set in England, contemporary with the time of its writing. The action takes place in a country village built on marshy land, and in London, which is far more distant spiritually from the village than physically.

Pip becomes familiar with the homes of people of varying incomes. The humble home of Joe Gargery, the blacksmith, is where Pip is raised. The Gargery house and its furnishings are simple, but decent; by contrast, the inadequate foster care given young Pip by his grown sister is unnecessarily stingy and cruel. But the comparative wealth of Miss Havisham has not made her grand house a comfortable home, nor filled it with wonders. Her refusal to move on from the moment she was jilted has resulted in a house that is a gothic horror of spiders' webs and dust.

In London, Pip finds homes that are not so much a source of comforts both physical and emotional, as a theatre for play-acting. From pretend-castles to a lawyer's absolute domain, to even his young gentleman's digs, Pip is in place after place where the concerns of the rest of the world do not intrude. It would seem that the greatest freedom of a gentleman is the freedom in his home to do no practical work, and to entertain himself there as its absolute master.

◆ THEMES AND CHARACTERS ◆

G. K. Chesterton said: "It is the real unconquerable rush and energy in a character which was the supreme and quite indescribable greatness of Dickens." By the time the reader finishes several chapters and has met what would seem to be enough major characters for any novel, new characters are introduced, some of whom (though minor roles) are crucial to the final story, and have important relationships with Pip and other major characters.

Young Phillip Pirrip, also known as Pip, is shaped by his changing circumstances. He is an orphan who never knew his dead parents or brothers, raised by his sister and Joe Gargery at Joe's workshop on the marshes near a country village at some distance from London. For a child in constant fear of punishment, Pip learns to lie rather convincingly. A sensitive boy, he is frequently beaten or starved and verbally abused by his sister, although he keeps only one secret: that he once stole food and a file to give an escaped convict, a crime he is certain will be his doom.

Pip is intimidated by the hideous Miss Havisham and by the lovely Estella. Even though Estella is his own age, Pip feels dominated by the girl and obeys Miss Havisham's order to *love her*! When Pip learns that he has an anonymous benefactor who will provide for his education in London, he eagerly leaves his apprenticeship with Joe behind, certain that his patron is Miss Havisham who is preparing him to become a gentleman worthy of marrying Estella. His hunch is supported by his long-standing belief that he deserves more in life than becoming a blacksmith like Joe. Furthermore, the lawyer who pays Pip's allowance is also Miss Havisham's lawyer.

However, in London, Pip's tutor, Mr. Pocket, turns out to be ineffectual, and Pip finds himself without adequate training for any profession to fit his new social class. Pip is made conceited and mean by his good fortune; but he always remains a good fellow, with a desire to do right, and with warm feelings. He also discovers that all of his old expectations have been wrong. Even so, learning this seems to be his best education.

For Pip, who spends much of his life either daydreaming or defending himself, such a change of heart seems heroic enough to set things right again. However, except for risking his own life to save Miss Havisham, Pip is not really a hero. In the end, he redeems himself by forgiving Miss Havisham, and requesting that she make her young relative Herbert Pocket her heir. He realizes who his true friends are when all of his expectations and money are gone. He is reunited with Joe and Biddy, and his kindness to Herbert Pocket is repaid.

The minor characters in *Great Expectations* are a motley crew. Among those not to be admired is Bentley Drummle, the rich and sulky leader of the dandified Finches of the Grove (and thus the epitome of Pip's misguided early notion of a gentleman), who marries and violently mistreats Estella. Others include Miss Havisham's relative Sarah Pocket, a withered, sharp-tongued, snobbish woman who resents Pip's ascent to her own elevated social class; Old Bill Barley, the father of Herbert's fiancee Clara, a gouty and drunken old man whose habit of surveying a nearby river with a telescope is a remnant of his former career as a sailor; Mr. Pocket, Herbert's father and Pip's tutor, who teaches him only the mere rudiments of education since as a gentleman he won't need to know much; and Molly, Mr. Jaggers's strange, silent housekeeper, who turns out to have been a murderess, Magwitch's mistress, and Estella's mother.

Another of these minor characters is Mr. Wopsle. A man who accompanies Pip and Joe across the marsh the night the police first catch the escaped convicts, Mr. Wopsle has seen both Magwitch and Compeyson. This is important much later in the story; when Mr. Wopsle has left the countryside for London to act in the theater, he recognizes the second convict, Compeyson, sitting behind Pip in the audience. With that knowledge, Pip knows that Compeyson is still alive and that he must get Magwitch out of the country as soon as possible before Compeyson finds him again.

Minor characters are used by the author to bring in news and important developments, and to keep the story revolving around its major character, Pip. Pip is not the best person in the novel, nor even a very admirable boy or young man. But he eventually learns to see what is good in the people around him, and through Pip's realizations, the author is stating his opinions about the absolute worth and relative worth of people like his characters.

The gentle, loving, soft-spoken, wise, and efficient Biddy is Pip's tutor before Mrs. Joe is injured and Biddy moves into the Gargery home to take care of the house. After Mrs. Joe dies, she marries Joe Gargery. Though Pip at one point might be interested in marrying Biddy if it weren't for her lowly social status, he later comes to realize that Biddy's true worth as a person far outshines any artificial class distinctions.

Far less worthy, though a gentleman, is Arthur, Miss Havisham's suitor who once jilted her. Before the novel begins, he has fallen in with the villainous Compeyson and his schemes. However, unlike Compeyson, Arthur has a conscience; he dreams of Miss Havisham dressed in white at his bedside and dies of fright. He and Compeyson had once schemed to get Miss Havisham's fortune, but at the last moment, with the wedding cake on the table and Miss Havisham dressed in her bridal finery, Arthur jilted her; presumably he could not carry through with the plan. He also functions as a parallel character with Bentley Drummle.

Compeyson is the man who arranges Miss Havisham's engagement with Arthur. He also testifies in court against Magwitch in an earlier scheme that failed, after which Magwitch is banished from England and exiled to Australia. Compeyson is the second escaped convict out on the marsh the

night that Pip first meets Magwitch, and he eventually dies fighting with Magwitch during their second capture years later.

Part of the fall-out from the jilting of Miss Havisham is the adoption of Estella by Miss Havisham at the age of two or three. She has been taught to reject all who love her; this is Miss Havisham's vengeance for her being jilted by Arthur. About the same age as Pip, Estella acts much older and snubs him more often than merely ignoring his attempts at friendship or love. In this, she is quite honest with Pip, for she has been raised to brush off love, and to reject it later in order to watch the man suffer. Miss Havisham's success in raising a cold-hearted beauty is too much for her, however, for Estella can feel no love for the old woman either. Thus, Estella can only refuse Pip whenever he confesses his love. Instead, she tells him that she will ruin the man she does marry and why not, when she cares for no one? When she becomes engaged to Bentley Drummle, Pip cannot talk her out of marrying such a brutal man. In the novel's revised ending, when Estella meets Pip years later she has had a daughter (also named Estella) by Drummle, who has died. Estella has survived, bent and broken by the doomed marriage. She never knew who her parents were because Miss Havisham led her to assume that they were dead. More tragically, Estella has never learned to care about anyone's happiness, not even her own.

A far more caring person is Joe Gargery, Pip's uncle and surrogate father, but also a fellow-sufferer from his wife's nasty temper and violent behavior. He is a rough, strong working man who keeps his emotions to himself. Whenever Joe had tried to protect young Pip from his sister's abuse, she not only hit Joe too but hurt Pip the more for it. Joe gladly takes Pip on as his apprentice at the forge and misses him terribly when Pip leaves for London, but will not stand in the way of Pip's good fortune. After Mrs. Joe is attacked, he nurses her with the help of Biddy, whom he marries after Mrs. Joe dies. He also lovingly nurses Pip back to health in London. An uneducated man, he learns enough about writing from Biddy to leave Pip a letter to say goodbye, misspelling his own name Jo as Pip had done as a child.

Of all Dickens's many characters in the novel, Joe is one who does not change, remaining tough yet childlike in love. His weakness is a tendency to look on the bright side, which seemed foolish to Pip as a teenager. The ways in which the other characters treat Joe provide insight into their own weaknesses: Pip is ashamed of him, Estella makes fun of him, and Jaggers is stunned when Joe refuses to accept money for the loss of Pip from his shop. In spite of Joe's hard life, he remains good-natured and devoted to Pip and Biddy.

Joe's first wife is a large, menacing woman. Mrs. Joe Gargery prides herself on raising Pip by hand, which is a sorry pun on the way she hits the child and her husband whenever she is not verbally attacking them. Her favorite instrument, The Tickler, is a stick that is worn smooth from caning Pip, regardless of his behavior. The bodice of her apron is stuck through with pins and needles, a true metaphor for her character. Only Orlick stands up to her, and she never recovers from his savage attack. She spends her last days in the tender care of Joe and Biddy, no longer vicious but in a state of childlike happiness.

There is no happiness for the novel's true eccentric. Always dressed in the wedding gown in which she had once planned to be married, Miss Havisham is colorless, from her hair to her single faded white shoe. She wants Pip and Estella to act out her love-turned-to-hatred for the man who jilted her on their wedding day. She has left the house untouched, even the items on her dressing table. The great room across from her cham-

Book illustration by Frederic W. Pailthorpe for *Great Expectations* by Charles Dickens.

ber is likewise untouched; the cake, now eerily covered with spiders and dusty cobwebs, is in the middle of the long dining table. Her wish that this table be cleared only when she is dead (so that she may be laid on it for her wake) is granted when the old lady's clothing accidentally catches on fire.

She is saved by Pip who rolls her in the tablecloth from the great room. Before she dies, she honors Pip's request to make his friend, Herbert Pocket, her heir, amazed that Pip wants nothing for himself. Her nightmares of dying without forgiveness are laid to rest when she dies with Pip's kiss on her wrinkled forehead.

There is little forgiveness for crime in the time the novel is set. All Londoners on the wrong side of the law know Mr. Jaggers is the lawyer with the best chance of keeping them out of Newgate Prison. Jaggers will not take a case he cannot win, or if his fee cannot be paid, and says so. He has moved many a judge and jury to tears with his courtroom drama. Outside the court, he never lets down his guard. Since he is Miss Havisham's lawyer and is bound by Pip's unnamed benefactor's desire to remain unknown, Jaggers bolsters Pip's belief that Miss Havisham is his benefactor.

Jaggers can be contrasted with his clerk, Wemmick. A true friend to Pip in London, John Wemmick is a dual personality. In London, where he is a chief clerk at Jaggers's law office, Wemmick is as coldly business-minded as his employer. However, he takes a liking to Pip and invites him to his house, a miniature castle complete with a tiny moat, drawbridge, and a cannon that Wemmick fires each evening because it delights his deaf father. In his own odd household, Wemmick becomes close friends with Pip, who grows to value their friendship deeply. Wemmick keeps one ear open at all times at the office to determine the best time to get Magwitch out of the country, and Wemmick sends word to Pip when he thinks the London underworld is unaware. Also, Wemmick thinks so much of Pip that Pip is the only wedding guest at the marriage of Wemmick and Miss Skiffins. Even so, when Pip sees him at the office, Wemmick is curt and businesslike again. Wemmick keeps both of his worlds separate from each other.

Another stereotype is Wemmick's parent, who is old and deaf, and he responds to almost all conversation by smiling and yelling, "All right, John!" In his odd house and landscape, the elderly parent is relaxation and comic relief for Pip, who enjoys visiting Wemmick's place as a world apart from the threats of London.

One of Wemmick's and Jagger's clients, Abel Magwitch is also known as Pip's convict and as Provis, his benefactor. In trouble from the day he was born, Abel Magwitch is an orphan like Pip but without Joe or any loving family member to befriend him. All he can recall of his early days is his name.

Banished to Australia, he tends sheep and saves his money to one day make an English gentleman of the boy named Pip who once was kind to him while he was running from the police on the marshes. When he re-enters Pip's life in London, Magwitch holds the key to many mysteries. As Provis, he spends many happy hours with Pip, in spite of Pip's discomfort at learning that his benefactor has not been Miss Havisham, but a criminal.

Magwitch is the link between more characters in the novel than anyone but Pip himself. Magwitch dies content to have lived out his dream of creating in Pip the respectable man that he himself could never be, as well as assuring that his former crime partner and arch-enemy Compeyson drowns. In his last days, Magwitch reveals to Pip the confidence scheme that he was drawn into with Arthur and Compeyson. However, it is only after Magwitch's death that Pip discovers that Magwitch was also Estella's father.

Jaggers's maid Molly who serves dinner to Pip, has the scars of shackles on her wrists. As her lawyer, Jaggers once saved her from being sent to Newgate Prison, and he shames her in front of Pip to remind her of her old life, her reform, and her alternative to serving in his house. At another dinner with Mr. Jaggers, Pip is fascinated by Molly's hands for another reason. He has seen them somewhere before. Eventually, Pip notices other resemblances between Molly and Estella and forces a stilted admission out of Jaggers that Molly was once married to a convict and that Jaggers arranged for their child to be adopted by a rich woman. Taken together with Magwitch's story, it is obvious that Molly was Magwitch's wife and Estella's mother.

Magwitch worked hard and achieved his goals, while Molly gave up their daughter to be raised in hopes of a better future, then worked as an honest maid. By contrast, Orlick is a character with no redeeming qualities. After being fired by Joe for insulting Mrs. Joe, Orlick bears a grudge against Pip. Years later, when Orlick lures Pip to the limekiln out on the marshes and ties Pip up, he tells Pip of the scene of his attack on Mrs. Joe's skull with a convict's (Magwitch's) leg irons he found on the marsh. Since Pip brought a file to Magwitch to remove his shackles, Orlick's deed may be only the delayed result of Pip's childhood crime of aiding a convict. However, help arrives and Orlick is arrested before Pip is harmed. These convolutions of motives, actions and consequences are pretty much standard throughout the novel; no act happens in isolation, as everything has eventual consequences and relates back to Pip and his circle of acquaintance, and his own less-than-happy life.

The warmest among Pip's circle of acquaintance is his roommate in London, Herbert Pocket, who is also his best friend. Herbert nicknames Pip "Handel" because it is the name of a famous man, as a compliment to Pip. An easygoing youth and not bright, Herbert is nonetheless loyal and persevering. While they are students together, Herbert tries to help Pip figure out where all of their money is going. Later, he invites Pip to share in his inheritance, before finding out that Pip is the reason for it. Herbert is the receiver of Pip's only request of Miss Havisham for money. Tolerant and kind, even to the irritating alcoholic and gout-ridden Mr. Barley, Herbert falls in love with and marries the equally kind and patient daughter Clara Barley. Also, he is trusted with helping Pip try to get Magwitch out of England. Herbert's most heroic hour is finding Orlick's letter that Pip had dropped and rushing off to save Pip at the moment that Orlick would have surely killed him. At last, Herbert provides a job for Pip when all of his fortune is gone. In the original ending of the novel, Herbert names his son Pip.

The two different endings to the novel have gathered much critical attention. In the original serial ending, which Dickens revised on advice from his friend, novelist Edward Bulwer-Lytton, Estella marries a benevolent doctor after the death of her first husband and she and Pip have one melancholy but friendly meeting years later. In the ending that Dickens decided to use when the novel was printed as a book, the two walk off hand in hand, apparently destined for marriage. Some critics claim that the latter ending is in keeping with Dickens's general hopeful nature, while others claim that it represents an unfortunate concession to his audience's desire for a happy ending and is true to neither Pip's nor Estella's character.

◆ LITERARY QUALITIES ◆

"The very title of this book [*Great Expectations*] indicates the confidence of conscious genius," said an un-named critic in a review. ". . .The most famous novelist of the day, watched by jealous rivals and critics, could hardly have selected it, had he not inwardly felt the capacity to meet all the expectations he raised." The critic had read this novel and all of Dickens's previous works, in installments, and was impressed by "the felicity with which expectation was excited and prolonged, and to the series of surprises which accompanied the unfolding of the plot of the story."

Dickens succeeded perfectly in stimulating and baffling the curiosity of his readers. In *Great Expectations,* he seemed to attain the mastery of powers which formerly more or less mastered him. He could not, like Thackeray, narrate a story as if he were merely looking on, a mere "knowing" observer of what he describes and represents; he therefore took observation simply as the basis of his plot and ran with his own particular talent for characterization. In this novel, Dickens was in the prime, and not in the decline of his great powers.

Dickens always had one weakness, and this novel is strongly marked with it. He would exaggerate one particular set of facts, a comic side in a character, or a comic turn of expression, until all reality faded away, and the person became a mere frame for an elaborate, fluttering construction. Miss Havisham is an example of Dickens's exaggeration.

But what was the peg on which the entire novel, this elaborate fluttering construction, was hung? It may have been the January 1850 issue of *Household Narrative of Current Events*.

In a January 1850 issue of *Household Narrative of Current Events* appeared an account of Martha Joachin, who always wore white after her suitor committed suicide in front of her. Also in that issue was a description of the transportation of convicts to Australia, and the story of a woman whose gown is set on fire. Peter Ackroyd suggests in his biography *Dickens* that the germ of the novel may have been planted by Dickens's casual reading of some journalism eleven years before he began writing the serial. "It is possible to understand how heterogeneous themes and ideas seem to attach themselves one to another, acquiring fresh power and resonance as they do so; it is in this very act of combining, perhaps, that the story itself begins to emerge," says Ackroyd. "As if storytelling itself were part of the process of consciousness rather than some neatly defined and independent activity."

It may be that storytelling, for Dickens and others, is a way of creating a pattern from random data fortuitously lodged in our consciousness. Whether Dickens overtly intended to combine these particular elements into an epic-length novel (incorporating elements of his own experience as a frustrated boy) cannot be determined; he

left no notes outlining his plan. But it is fascinating to look from the viewpoint of a reader over a hundred and forty years later, at a popular novel still in print, written by a man very nearly as self-centred as Pip, and to have some understanding of where he got his ideas.

This work, Dickens's second-to-last complete novel, was first published as a weekly series in 1860 and in book form in 1861. Early critics had mixed reviews, disliking Dickens's tendency to exaggerate both plot and characters, but readers were so enthusiastic that the 1861 edition required five printings. Victorian-era audiences appreciated the melodramatic scenes and the revised, more hopeful ending.

Modern critics have little but praise for Dickens's brilliant development of timeless themes: fear and fun, loneliness and luck, classism and social justice, humiliation and honor. Some still puzzle over Dickens's revision that ends the novel with sudden optimism, and they suggest that the sales of Dickens's magazine *All the Year Round,* in which the series first appeared, was assured by gluing on a happy ending that hints Pip and Estella will unite at last. For some, the original ending is more realistic since Pip must earn the self-knowledge that can only come from giving up his obsession with Estella. However, Victorian audiences eagerly followed the story, episode by episode, assuming that the protagonist's love and patience would win out in the end. Modern editions contain both denouements allowing the reader a choice.

In this novel, Dickens surpasses his previous works in one point. This is "a more profound study of the general nature of human character than Mr. Dickens usually [portrays]," decently distinct from *David Copperfield,* according to G.K. Chesterton. "Pip thinks himself better than every one else, and yet anybody can snub him; that is the everlasting male, and perhaps the everlasting gentleman. Dickens has described perfectly this quivering and defenceless dignity. . . how ill-armed it is against the coarse humour of real humanity. . . the humanity of Trabb's boy," Chesterton insists. In describing Pip's weakness, Dickens is as true and as delicate as Thackeray, but Thackeray and others also possessed a quick and quiet eye for the tremors of mankind. "George Eliot or Thackeray could have described the weakness of Pip. Exactly what George Eliot and Thackeray could not have described was the vigour of Trabb's boy."

◆ SOCIAL SENSITIVITY ◆

Dickens has been praised for having created in Pip a decidedly unheroic hero, a figure who, while basically good, must learn to recognize and conquer serious weaknesses within himself. As the young Pip grows from a powerless dreamer into a useful worker and then a moderately educated young man he reaches an important realization: grand schemes and dreams are never what they first seem to be. Pip himself is not always honest, and careful readers can catch him in several contradictions between his truth and fantasies. In chronicling the maturation of its likeable young hero, whose great expectations prove illusory, the novel promotes generosity, friendship, and love rather than the shallow virtues of wealth and social status.

It is generally acknowledged that Dickens based Estella, who has been called his most sexually viable female character, on the Irish actress Ellen Ternan, who eventually became his mistress. Pip's helpless attraction to Estella and the mingled hopelessness and intensity of his love for her mirror the emotions reportedly experienced by the author when he fell in love with Ternan. It should not escape the moral analyst that Dickens eventually divorced his wife over his love affair with Ternan. Among

his personal moral choices, Dickens left behind much that is worthy of discussion.

Charles Dickens never lost an awareness of his own experiences working as a boy, bottling boot-black, but he spoke of these days and his emotional horror, only once to his trusted friend and executor John Foster. With that knowledge, it is easier for the reader to understand the origins of the characters Pip, David Copperfield, and Oliver Twist—created by Dickens to give voice to young children like he had been.

Dickens was always acutely aware of the suffering endured by the poor, and made every endeavor as an adult not to be poor. His novels were the first modern codification of the concept that children ought not to be put to tedious, repetitive work at an early age, but should be helped to grow and learn and play. Dickens was not a political activist, nor did he campaign for child welfare laws. He brought these issues to the hearts and minds of his readers through his popular fiction, rather than writing overt autobiography or political tracts. His novels were part of the process by which it became common in much of the world to believe that all children, not only those of the wealthy, should be given education and leisure to play; that children who do labor should be given work less onerous and shorter in duration than adults; and ultimately that it is as abominable to deprive children of care, comfort and education as it is to deny them adequate food and shelter.

◆ TOPICS FOR DISCUSSION ◆

1. What are labor practices and working conditions?

2. How does social status at birth affect a child's future? What effect did it have in Dickens's lifetime?

3. From where does Pip get his expectations?

4. What does Pip do with his expectations? Are they so well-formed as to be called ambitions, or plans?

5. What influence does being paid by the word have upon an author?

6. How does a popular author reflect the mores of his or her culture?

7. What is least admirable about Pip? When is he most virtuous? Does he know when he has done right or wrong?

8. How much does young Herbert Pocket actually accomplish? Is he as worthy a young man as he could be? Where does his loyalty and generosity come from?

9. What expectations does Estella have? Does she accomplish what she expects? Has she achieved peace by the novel's end?

◆ IDEAS FOR REPORTS AND PAPERS ◆

1. What human miseries are avoidable, by honest individual effort, by luck and by community resolution? What human miseries are unavoidable, and can only be partially remedied after the fact?

2. Compare *Great Expectations* with *Jack Maggs* by author Peter Carrey. What does Carrey do with the character of Abel Magwitch that is a fulfillment of the character as invented by Dickens? What changes does Carrey ring on Magwitch in his creation of Jack Maggs? Is this appropriation of character a sensible comment on post-colonial attitudes? How does Carrey reinvent the "felon history" of Australia, which seems a necessary assumption of Dickens's time?

3. Why does Dickens populate this novel so thickly with characters, most of whom are not aristocratic to any degree? Is he making a statement by writing about working people, and villagers, and peo-

ple with small ambitions? What statement could he be making about gentlemen and other people of moderate status?

4. What are virtues in a character by Dickens? What are vices in his characters? Does the author portray any true heroes in this novel? What does Pip achieve in his life that is worthy? What errors does he commit?

5. Choose a minor character from the novel *Great Expectations*. Make notes on that character's physical traits as described by Dickens, and her/his typical actions or gestures or behaviors. Sketch the character as shown in one of the scenes from the novel. Prepare the sketch for display as a triptych, flanked with a copy of the scene and your list of the character's traits. Can other people who have read the novel identify the character from your sketch alone?

6. Draw a "family tree" chart linking the various characters of the novel *Great Expectations*. Show which characters have links both to Pip and to each other. Will you differentiate between blood ties and friendships? Close contact or rare meetings? How will you depict the association of Magwitch with his criminal colleagues? What sort of links can you show on your chart?

7. Are there any characters in the novel *Great Expectations* who interact only once with Pip and never with any other characters? Are the many characters Dickens depicts for us isolates, or are they interconnected with each other and not merely Pip?

8. As the novel *Great Expecations* progresses, is Pip interacting more with positive characters who mean to do well for him and themselves, or with negative characters who are cruel? Does he consciously imitate any other char-

acters, in attitude or behavior? Who has the greatest influence upon him?

9. Compare the novel *Great Expecations* with an English translation of the novel *Don Quixote* by Miguel de Cervantes Saavedra. Discuss what similarities you find, apart from sheer length: the legions of characters, multiple small incidents, the author's sense of humor. Do you find any evidence that Dickens may have read *Don Quixote* in translation?

10. Compare Dickens with modern authors of the late-twentieth century. Who among the popular authors is much like Dickens? How do these authors make use of available media and technology, as Dickens did?

11. The popular novelist Stephen King has gone to great efforts to emulate the literary successes of Dickens. Compare and contrast their work ethics, the scope of their bodies of work, and the literary merit of their most popular novels.

◆ RELATED TITLES/ADAPTATIONS ◆

There have been several adaptations made for audio, feature films and video of Dickens's novels, including *Great Expectations*. In 1947 Jean Simmons and John Mills appeared in a film version of *Great Expectations*. Another film version was a feature more recently on the Disney Channel.

There is a Monty Python sketch set in a bookshop which includes dialogue about Dickens, imaginary authors with phonetically similar names, and novels with titles that are spoonerisms (a transposition of usually initial sounds of two or more words [as in tons of soil for sons of toil]) of Dickens titles. It is a thoroughly amusing sketch with no foul language; it is eminently suitable for audio or video play for young adults.

Motion pictures based on *A Christmas Carol* have been shown since 1913. The most acclaimed version is the Alistair Sim film made in 1951 and still shown on television today. The film *Scrooged* which stars Bill Murray is another adaptation.

On television in recent years Masterpiece Theatre has shown *David Copperfield* and *A Tale of Two Cities.* Mobil Showcase has featured *Nicholas Nickleby* (which was also presented as a nine-hour show on Broadway).

◆ FOR FURTHER REFERENCE ◆

Ackroyd, Peter. *Dickens.* London: Sinclair-Stevenson Ltd., 1990. p. 886.

Barnard, Robert. "Imagery and Theme in Great Expectations," *Dickens Studies Annual* (1970): 238–51. Barnard describes Dickens's symbolic use of prison and animal imagery to suggest the transference of guilt from one character to another.

Carey, Peter. *Jack Maggs.* New York: Alfred A. Knopf Inc., 1998

Chesterton, G. K. "Great Expectations" in *Appreciations and Criticisms of the Works of Charles Dickens.* New York: E. P. Dutton & Co. (1911): 197–206. Reprinted in *Nineteenth-Century Literature Criticism,* Vol. 26. Detroit: Gale Research, 1990. An unimpeachable analysis of the novel, likening Dickens's talents to those of Thackeray.

Dickens, Charles. *Uncollected Writings from Household Words, 1850–1859.* London: Allen Lane, 1969. Text from issues of the serial *Household Words,* edited and largely written by Charles Dickens.

A review of *Great Expectations. The Saturday Review.* (July 20, 1861): 69–70. Reprinted in *Nineteenth-Century Literature Criticism,* Vol. 26, Detroit: Gale Research, 1990. In this mixed evaluation of *Great Expecta-*

tions, the reviewer praises the story as original and often powerfully written, but faults the work for its extremely rapid pace and frequently exaggerated comic scenes and characters.

Paula Johanson

GULLIVER'S TRAVELS

Novel

1726

Author: Jonathan Swift

◆

Major Books for Young Adults

Gulliver's Travels, 1726
A Modest Proposal, 1729 (essay)

◆ ABOUT THE AUTHOR ◆

Jonathan Swift was born in Dublin, Ireland on November 30, 1667. He was, or was alleged to be, the posthumous child of Jonathan Swift, a minor law official of the King's Inn, Dublin, and his wife Abigail Erick. His childhood was in some ways unusual—as a year-old baby he was brought to England, while his mother remained in Ireland, and when he was brought back to Ireland a year or two later, his mother returned to England, leaving young Jonathan to be raised by his uncle Godwin Swift. Though his parents were poor, young Jonathan was given the best education that could be had in Ireland. His uncle Godwin paid for him to attend Kilkenny Grammar School and later Trinity College, yet Swift later said of him that "He gave me the education of a dog." Any study of Swift's life will show several such mysteries, many of which have never been explained.

At age fourteen in 1682, young Jonathan entered Trinity College in Dublin. It was the only university in Ireland, with a few hundred students, most in training to become clergymen. Swift did not like the provost, and read more history and poetry than his formal studies. Graduating in 1685, when he was eighteen, Swift obtained his bachelor of arts degree only by a special concession. He stayed on for a year, intending to obtain his master's degree, but the civil war in England seemed likely to spread to Ireland, and Swift left for England, where he visited his mother.

In 1689 he lived at Moor Park in Surrey, in the household of Sir William Temple, a scholar and a prominent Whig statesman. Swift worked there as Sir William's secretary and as tutor to an eight-year-old girl named Esther Johnson. This girl was allegedly the daughter of one of the stewards, but there is some evidence that she was actually Sir William's illegitimate daugh-

Jonathan Swift

mother and of his mentor, he left the Whigs and joined the Tory party. His literary reputation grew also, through his friendship with Pope, Addison and Steele. He edited the Tory paper, *The Examiner,* and wrote a series of articles and pamphlets discrediting the Whig party and party-leaders. He had high expectations of being made a bishop, but this did not come to pass. Instead, at the age of forty-six in 1713, Swift was installed as Dean of St. Patrick's Cathedral in Dublin. When Queen Anne died, the Whigs came into power with the Hanover dynasty, and Swift regarded himself as in exile in Ireland.

During the latter thirty years of his life, Swift wrote his most enduring works of literature and politics, and *Gulliver's Travels.* His time at the center of power enabled him to discern the kind of political writing which can exert the most influence, and being cut off from the center of power gave Swift time to write. He wrote a series of political pamphlets called the *Drapier's Letters,* speaking out against the mercantilist policy by which English manufacturers and merchants profited at the expense of Irish interests. When the first pamphlet was printed anonymously, the printer was prosecuted but the jury refused to convict him; though a substantial reward was offered, no Dubliner betrayed Swift.

His most famous writing against the English landlords in Ireland was the pamphlet *A Modest Proposal.* This is indispensable reading for any student of justice, history, or social planning.

He helped Dublin tradesmen with interest-free loans, he persuaded his dear friend Stella to endow a Dublin hospital and he left his own money to found another hospital for the mentally afflicted. Swift outlived Stella and Esther van Homrigh, another woman friend, and most of his literary friends; loneliness made him sad and bitter. He died in 1745, having outlived

ter. It is also possible that she was Swift's half-sister, or other illegitimate relative through the Temples. She became Swift's dear friend and correspondant for all her life, and he called her Stella.

Swift took his master's degree at Oxford, was ordained and worked as a curate (a clergyman in charge of a parish) in Kilroot, County Antrim. In 1696 and 1697 he lived at Moor Park, writing his first two books which were published in 1704. Both raised his literary reputation, but the first (*A Tale of a Tub*) later sank his political fortunes. From 1700 to 1707 he lived mostly in Ireland, as a chaplain and vicar. On the death of Sir William Temple in 1699, Swift became Esther Johnson's protector; she and her relative Rebecca Dingley came to live in Ireland near Swift.

During the next decade, Swift's political influence increased. After the deaths of his

Gulliver's Travels

his hearing, his physical and his mental health, and was buried in St. Patrick's Cathedral, near Stella's tomb.

◆ OVERVIEW ◆

In Part I, Lemuel Gulliver describes how he began undertaking voyages as a ship's surgeon, and ended up during one voyage shipwrecked in Lilliput, a land where the people are twelve times smaller than in England. He makes careful observation of the habits and politics of the people of Lilliput and the neighboring nation of Blefuscu. Eventually he is able to make seaworthy a boat brought ashore by the sea, and he returns to England, where he profits handsomely from the sale of a few Lilliputian cattle and sheep.

In Part II, another voyage takes Gulliver to Brobdingnag, a land where every living being is twelve times larger than in England. The people there and their king are far more moral and practical than they are political or war-like. He becomes the friend of the king and queen, and of a nurse assigned to care for him. When a bird carries off a box in which Gulliver is being transported and drops it into the sea, Gulliver is found by a ship and returns to England.

Part III was written last of the four. In this section, Gulliver visits the islands of Laputa, Balnibarbi, Luggnagg, Glubbdubdribb, and Japan. Laputa, the Flying Island, is an allegory of the court and government of George I. The center piece of the satire is the Academy of Projectors, which is partly directed at the scientists of the Royal Society and the Dublin Philosophical Society. Through meeting the rare struldbrugs, immortal humans withered by time and loss of faculties, Gulliver loses his fear of a natural death. Once again, Gulliver eventually returns to England.

In Part IV, Gulliver journeys to the land of the Houyhnhnms, rational horses, and the Yahoos, appallingly irrational humans. In this most complex section, Swift speaks out on the subjects of war, colonization, and ethics. The Houyhnhnms are what men could be if they lived reasonably, and the Yahoos are what men will become if they are not controlled by a strict but human morality. When Gulliver eventually returns to England, he leads a rather isolated life, enjoying the company of horses living on his property.

◆ SETTING ◆

Gulliver's journey to Lilliput and Blefuscu in Part I is a close allegory of the political events of the last years of Queen Anne's reign and the first years of George I's. In Lilliput, Home Politics are depicted as a struggle between courtiers wearing High Heels and Low Heels, comparable to the Whig and Tory parties of Britain. As well, Gulliver learns of a schism over the question of whether to break soft-boiled eggs at the small or big end. When part of the population resisted the king's edict to change the end they break, civil war resulted. Thus, in a supposedly foreign setting, Swift satirized the religious schism created by Henry VIII's break with the Roman Catholic Church, leading eventually to the English Civil War and the Glorious Revolution.

After parodying his own lands so thoroughly, Swift turned in Part II to creating a more idealized country. The Brobdingnagians live with abundant resources and honest government, and Gulliver could have been even happier there if he had been more like these generous giants. His own fault of greed and advancement of self and country at the expense of others were truly foreign here, more foreign than the European-style countryside.

Swift invented the name Laputa—probably meaning "whore"—for the flying island of Part III. Though the place comes off badly in Swift's story, the idea of an island floating in the sky off the coast of Japan has a romantic appeal. Flying islands are not original to Swift, but he was the first to attribute scientific principles to its flight, according to science fiction writer Isaac Asimov. *Gulliver's Travels* may be notable as the first work of fiction in the Western world to feature Japan as a setting, though Japan is mentioned in passing in earlier fictional works, and was also discussed in travel writing (of which this work is a parody).

The lands Gulliver finds in Part III are contemptible in many ways, where "in order to feed the Luxury and Intemperance of the Males, and the Vanity of the Females, we sent away the greatest Part of our necessary Things to other Countries, from whence in return we brought the Materials of Diseases, Folly, and Vice, to spend among ourselves." These islands are not good places for destination vacations.

The land of the Houyhnhnms seems a utopia by contrast, except that the human-like Yahoos who live there are bestial. This is clearly, at least in part, because they are treated as beasts and given no training or education. In this fourth part of the novel, Swift is making clear his belief that an idyllic life is possible for all the inhabitants of a country if the people are resolved to treat each other, masters and servants and even cattle, well. Great Britain could be Utopia if humans behaved like Houyhnhnms, we learn from Swift, and even Yahoos could be less miserable if helped to be their best.

The author was a gentleman scholar and enjoyed conversations and correspondence with other learned men. The scientific knowledge of his day was available to Swift, through his education and his later experience with other scholars. He used this knowledge to make this imaginative story plausi-ble in many respects. The reader willingly suspends disbelief in the notion of tiny people or giants or immortals, because the stories are internally consistent and employ some considerations of scale or natural, observable phenomena. The Brobdingnagians have food animals and plants of a size appropriate to their scale, and the finest, lightest fabrics they weave are like tough sailcloth to Gulliver, for example.

Swift had clearly read several travel novels, and probably *Robinson Crusoe* before and while writing *Gulliver's Travels*. He captures perfectly the English perspective towards foreign places in the world, as well as a sense of wonder that such exotic places do exist to be found by a drab, profiteering bourgeois opportunist like Gulliver.

◆ THEMES AND CHARACTERS ◆

A knowledge of English politics at the time Swift was writing will make several of the characters more understandable, but is not essential for enjoyment of *Gulliver's Travels* as a fantasy. The civil war between those who break their eggs at the big end and those who do so at the small end is a masterful parody of the reasons nations go to war. Today, the terms "Big-Endians" and "Little-Endians" have come into common use, to describe any conflict over trivial differences, adhered to with religious zeal. Adherents in a modern computing conflict over byte order in messages have actually self-identified themselves as "Big-Endians" and "Little-Endians."

The character of Lemuel Gulliver is not an autobiographical construct; but the more admirable and sympathetic elements in his nature, particularly his daring, make him rather a version of Swift's friend Bolingbroke.

Gulliver goes on these journeys, not for a love of travel or far places, but to earn a handsome living from what he brings back. Though skilled and inventive, Gulliver is in it for the money. With a keen eye, he makes detailed observations of the regions he visits and the people who live there, and usually their behaviors, dwellings and cattle as well. The reader is made well aware of Gulliver's opinions as to the relative and absolute merit (so far as he is concerned) of all that he observes. He has an unforced arrogance that is British and Euro-centric by nature, and it is a wonder to the modern reader that he does not end up suffering the fate of Captain Cook, an historical English explorer who had many similar traits (who was eaten by Hawaiians after an ill-mannered tour of many Pacific islands).

Gulliver, and the other characters, do not have to be thought of as versions of historical persons. It is not necessary to know that the Emperor of Blefuscu is a parody of Louis XIV of France, or that the "Bigendian exiles" from Lilliput are meant to represent the followers of the Stuarts. The heir to the throne in Lilliput favours High Heels, much as the heir to the English throne favoured the Opposition at that time.

Swift invented the term Lilliput, the name of one of the two diminutive kingdoms in Part I. The people in Lilliput and Blefuscu were about six inches tall and everything else in their lands was made to the same scale (one inch to one foot). The term "Lilliputian" for something tiny or in miniature has passed into the general language, as has Brobdingnagian.

Brobdingnag is the nation of giants visited by Gulliver in Part II. The people are sixty feet tall and everything else in their land is sized in proportion, on a scale of one foot to one inch. Though the giants of Brobdingnag are repulsive to look at closely, they are sound in their politics in many ways. The king of that land felt "whoever could make two ears of corn or two blades of grass to grow upon a spot of ground where only one grew before, would deserve better of mankind, and do more essential service to his country than the whole race of politicians put together." The king of Brobdingnag is not only much like Swift's mentor, Sir William Temple, he is both a Tory mouthpiece and a humanist, and possibly Swift's ideal of a good monarch.

Yahoo was invented by Swift as the name of the race of de-evolved humans Gulliver encounters in the Land of the Houyhnhnms, in the last part of the book. The term is now commonly used to describe people who behave like louts and brutes.

Swift had little patience for people who behaved badly. He wrote in Part III, speaking ironically,

> I am not in the least provoked at the Sight of a Lawyer, a Pick-Pocket, a Colonel, a Fool, a Lord, a Gamester, a Politician, a Whore-Master, a Physician, an Evidence, a Suborner, an Attorney, a Traitor, or the like: This is all according to the due Course of Things: But when I behold a Lump of Deformity, and Diseases both in Body and Mind, smitten with Pride, it immediately breaks all the Measures of my Patience.

He populated the novel with scandalous characters of all kinds, and did not hesitate to show the reader the less positive aspects of his protagonist Gulliver.

Though he was not a student of medical science, Swift wrote an excellent clinical description of Alzheimer's disease, a degenerative disorder of the central nervous system that causes progressive decline in memory and dementia during mid- to late-adult life, in Gulliver's journey to Luggnagg in Part III. Swift described some of the struldbrugs, near-immortal natives as follows:

> They have no remembrance of anything but what they learned and observed in their youth and middle age, and even that is very imperfect. . . . In talking they forget the common appellation of things and the names of persons, even of those who

are their nearest friends and relations. For the same reason, they never can amuse themselves with reading, because their memory will not serve to carry them from the beginning of a sentence to the end; and by this defect they are deprived of the only entertainment whereof they might otherwise be capable . . . neither are they able . . . to hold any conversation (farther than a few general words) with their neighbors. . . . They were the most mortifying sight I ever beheld.

Swift devotes far more time and energy in *Gulliver's Travels* to a rather lengthy discussion (half the novel) of Gulliver's voyages to the lands of Lilliput, where humans grow only to six inches, and to Brobdingnag, a nation where the humans grow to 60 feet and higher. Swift chose those sizes because they were a handy factor of twelve: the Lilliputian foot corresponds to the Gulliverian inch, while the Gulliverian foot is merely a Brobdingnagian inch. Swift had no doubt spent most of his life doing conversions of twelves because of the English systems for measuring length and money.

Though Swift's ideas for a simple scaled-up human (the Brobdingnagians) and a scaled-down one (the Lilliputians and Blefuscites) are interesting, we know from the ratios of surface area to volume, and the properties of bones and organs, that these creatures are very different from humans. The Brobdingnagians are heavier and more ponderous than elephants and dinosaurs, and the Lilliputians are all blind (or at least have very grainy vision)!

Knowledge of allometry (relative growth of a part in relation to whole) can lead to some interesting questions about how the Lilliputians and Brobdingnagians might use behavioral modifications to keep themselves alive. Teachers wishing to discuss *Gulliver's Travels* with their classrooms in terms of allometry might wish first to read *Diatoms to Dinosaurs: The Size and Scale of Living Things* by Christopher McGowan.

◆ LITERARY QUALITIES ◆

Swift entertained no notions that his work had merit merely because it had been written. In Part III he had Gulliver admit: "I found how the World had been misled by prostitute Writers, to ascribe the greatest Exploits in War to Cowards, the wisest Counsel to Fools, Sincerity to Flatterers, Roman Virtue to Betrayers of their Country, Piety to Atheists, Chastity to Sodomites, Truth to Informers." He worked very hard with this book not only to parody travel writing (*Robinson Crusoe* had just been published about the time that Swift began serious work on *Gulliver's Travels*), and to satirize the politics of his age, but to point out human folly in many forms.

This is not really a children's book, but it has been seen as a children's story right from the start: little people, big people, a floating island, talking horses . . . it's an easy assumption to make. There was no distinct literature for children at the time the book was written and whatever came to hand may have been drafted to the purpose.

Over time what was considered fit reading for children has changed, as Professor J. R. R. Tolkien observed. Most modern children's and school editions of *Gulliver's Travels* are edited in one way or another. For younger children, the tale is often retold in a simpler, modern idiom, and some episodes, sometimes the whole third and fourth books, are eliminated. School versions sometimes use Swift's original text and include all four parts, but remove the elements considered inappropriate for young readers.

The tenets of modern science were still emerging while Swift was writing, and like Cervantes before him and H. G. Wells after, Swift incorporated elements from cutting-edge science and technology into his fiction. Modern science fiction writers count Swift among their early ranks, not only for his sociological speculations but the astronomical elements in *Gulliver's Travels*.

The fourth planet out from the Sun, Mars, has two moons. They are named Phobos (meaning "fear") and Deimos (meaning "panic"); appropriate companions for Mars, the God of War. Over a hundred and fifty years before the moons' discovery in 1877, Swift "predicted" their existence in *Gulliver's Travels*, in Gulliver's journey to Laputa.

> They [the Laputians] have likewise discovered two lesser stars, or satellites, which revolve about Mars, whereof the innermost is distant from the center of the primary planet exactly three of its diameters, and the outermost five; the former revolves in the space of ten hours, and the latter in twenty-one and a half; so that the squares of their periodical times are very near the same proportion with the cubes of their distance from the center of Mars, which evidently shows them to be governed by the same law of gravitation that influences the other heavenly bodies.

How could Swift have known the moons were real? He described Phobos's orbital period as ten hours (very close to the real figure of 7.6) and Deimos's as 21.5 (close to the real 30.2). Both seem to be very lucky guesses. Had Swift read the works of the astronomer Johannes Kepler?

In his essay, Lee Krystek wonders how Swift was able to predict the existence of the moons and the period of their orbits.

> Some have seriously suggested he had psychic powers. More likely, though, Swift may have employed the same logic as the French writer Voltaire did a quarter century later when he also predicted two Martian moons. Voltaire knew that the inner planets, Mercury and Venus, had no moons, and that the outer planets, Jupiter and Saturn each had many. Earth had one. It seemed likely to Voltaire that Mars, that next out from Earth, probably had at least two. Even if Swift had employed the same logic to figure the number of moons his

Book illustration by Arthur Rackham for
Gulliver's Travels into Several Remote Nations of the World by Jonathan Swift.

estimate on the duration of their orbits was still startlingly accurate.

As a scholar, Swift conversed and corresponded with many men of letters and education. It is likely, just as likely as Krystek's guess, that one of Swift's acquaintances had handled a telescope. The moons of Mars are visible, when Earth and Mars are at their closest points in their orbits, through the kinds of telescopes that were then being made.

The publishing of scientific discoveries was not consistent and standard at that time. As well, Galileo had been tried for heresy by the Inquisition for his published statements concerning his observations of the moons of Jupiter and his resulting theories about our solar system being centered on the Sun, not the Earth—and at least one of those "published" statements existed in only a couple of hand-written copies being proof-read by Galileo's associates. After Galileo's experiences it would be very understandable if some other gentleman scholar would turn a telescope on Mars, but not commit his observations to writing. Scholars do talk together, however, and they do put into their works of fiction the truths they and their associates have observed, truths which even a Protestant activist clergyman like Swift might hesitate to state in a scientific essay.

◆ SOCIAL SENSITIVITY ◆

Swift had high intentions to remedy some of the ills of the world through writing this work. He took care to put words in Gulliver's mouth and in accounts of his journeys, which made it clear that Gulliver was not to be mistaken for a kind and gentle man, nor one who was politically considerate of his fellow man.

Kathleen Smith writes of Gulliver's conversations with the King of Brobdingnag:

Gulliver's pomposity, lack of feeling, complacent amusement at the king's lack of political acumen, all are expressed in his way of writing; and they suggest man's readiness to become accustomed to wrong, to cruelty, if it is in his interest to do so. Gulliver's account shows us, in its revelation of the responses of this representative human being, how easily we blind ourselves, by national pride, by excuses of political necessity, and so on, to the immorality and cruelty of our actions as individuals or as nations.

Though Swift was a hero of the disaffected Dubliners, and through his *Drapier's Letters* managed to defeat the English government single-handedly over a matter of currency reform, his greatest work of letters, *Gulliver's Travels,* had no perceptible influence on the political scene of 1726. This is the most striking example of a work of close and detailed political reference failing to succeed as a tract for the times.

Gulliver's Travels is sometimes spoken of as a polemic against certain forms of government. Though Swift is now held up as an Irish hero and possibly the first spokesman for what was to become Sinn Fein (political party responsible for the Republic of Ireland's independence from Britain), he lived before democracy became a fashionable axiom. In his time it was believed, and may have been true, that society could be served best by the *reasonable* administration of power concentrated in the hands of qualified leaders.

Swift wrote in Part I

... Providence never intended to make the Management of publick Affairs a Mystery, to be comprehended only by a few Persons of sublime Genius, of which there seldom are three born in an Age: ... Mistakes committed by Ignorance in a virtuous Disposition, would never be of such fatal Consequence to the Publick Weal, as the Practices of a Man whose Inclinations led him to be corrupt, and had great Abilities to manage, and multiply, and defend his Corruptions.

William Alfred Eddy says of Swift:

When he satirized existing governments, which was often, he attacked not the theory but the abuse of authority. When he castigated bishops and prime ministers it was because they were unintelligent or corrupt ... Swift championed the Irish against unscrupulous exploitation, but he feared the tyranny of anarchy even more than the divine right of kings. With practical realism he looked about him on a world which at best was pretty bad, and he supported the lesser of evils. That his allegiance was never blind his satires prove conclusively.

As Swift said in Book IV of *Gulliver's Travels*: "My principal Design was to Inform, and not to amuse thee."

◆ TOPICS FOR DISCUSSION ◆

1. What is the difference between satire and parody?

2. What are the two kinds of satire commonly recognized?

3. What does the author intend to arouse in the reader by using satire?

4. What is the point of describing the quarrel between Lilliput and Blefuscu over which end to open a soft-boiled egg?

5. How do we see Gulliver differently after the Lilliputians propose to blind him?

6. How does he see himself differently after arriving in Brobdingnag?

7. What is patently improbable about a hoofed race (the Houyhnhnms) being masters of a race with nimble hands (the Yahoos)?

8. What is patently ridiculous about the flappers striking their masters' ears and mouths *after* a remark has been addressed to their masters?

9. What is completely impossible about a human body growing to be dozens of feet tall?

10. What is completely non-functional about a human body growing to be only six inches tall?

◆ IDEAS FOR REPORTS AND PAPERS ◆

1. If a modern equivalent to *Gulliver's Travels* were written today, what nations would be satirized, instead of England and France? What political and personal attitudes would be satirized? How

would Swift's tone be changed by contemporary language patterns? Would the end result be popular fiction?

2. Write a short essay much like Gulliver's journey to the land of the Houyhnhnms, in which humans are the unintelligent servants of automobiles. What are the towns like in this land? How do the domesticated humans serve the automobiles? How do the master cars treat their humans—as stock animals, pets, or commensals? What obvious differences will you make clear between this fantasy land and the real world, and what similarities?

3. Now that the entire globe has been mapped, where can we look for places sufficiently "remote" to be different from our familiar homes? Is mere travel what we need, whether by plane, boat, or on foot? How can we find cultures sufficiently different from our own to be exotic?

4. Which modern writers are comparable to Swift for their subjects, styles, and published works? On what do you base this assessment?

5. What are the origins of the flying island legends? How has Swift adapted these legends to his own story? Could there be any connection to the aboriginal Canadian Cree myths of creation?

6. How is Swift's political satire in his description of Lilliput effective in terms of when he lived? How understandable is the political commentary in modern terms? How necessary is the political element if some adaptions and abridgements trim it almost entirely?

7. What makes a book suitable for young readers? Is it subject matter, format, or style? In what ways is *Gulliver's Travels* suitable as children's literature? In what ways is it inappropriate?

8. Make a map or a globe modeling the Earth as described in *Gulliver's Travels*. Trace out the routes that Gulliver's ships would have taken on the voyages. Include an annotated list and marks indicating the various places Gulliver visits. Are extra continents or large islands necessary to fulfill Swift's descriptions, or can existing landmasses be assigned to be named Lilliput, Luggnagg or Blefuscu?

9. Discuss Gulliver and his views on colonialism, manifest destiny and the white man's burden. Is Swift taking up a "pro" or a "con" stance on these British cultural tendencies in *Gulliver's Travels*? Is he making some sort of commentary on the British Empire?

◆ RELATED TITLES/ADAPTATIONS ◆

Considering how many people know Swift's tale only as a charming children's fantasy, it is a tricky question whether or not it is better to introduce children to a more appropriate adaption of Swift or wait until they can appreciate the real thing. Among the better adaptions is the Grosset & Dunlap edition of *Gulliver's Travels*. ("Revised and slightly abridged for readers of our time.") It has a brief introduction, is somewhat upfront about what has been deleted, merges parts III and IV, but otherwise makes a decent presentation of the story. This edition is, in its way, a classic and is still in print.

Certainly *The Borrowers* by Mary Norton owes its genesis to Gulliver's adventures in Lilliput, as the sci-fi movie thriller *Attack of the 50-foot Woman* does to his adventures in Brobdingnag. There are other literary offspring of *Gulliver's Travels* in H. G. Wells' *Food of the Gods,* and in the modern film *Honey, I Shrunk the Kids* and its sequel *Honey, I Blew Up the Baby.*

The reader might look upon the "Hundred Worlds" literary development of the first *Star Trek* television series by producer Gene Roddenberry as a modern literary offspring of *Gulliver's Travels.*

◆ FOR FURTHER REFERENCE ◆

Bloom, Harold, editor. *Modern Critical Views: Jonathan Swift.* New York: Chelsea House, 1986.

Donoghue, Denis, editor. *Swift Revisited.* Cork: The Mercier Press, 1968. A collection of a series of five lectures aired on Radio Telefis Eireann in 1967, part of the Thomas Davis series of lectures on Irish life.

Eddy, Wiliam Alfred, editor. *Swift: Satires and Personal Writings.* London: Oxford University Press, 1932. A generous selection of Swift's best work in prose and verse, favoring lighter satire over political tracts. Contains selections from *The Journal to Stella.*

Ehrenpreis, Irvin. *Swift: The Man, His Work, and the Age,* Vol. 2. London: Methuen & Co, Ltd., 1967. A biography with political commentary.

McGowan, Christopher. *Diatoms to Dinosaurs: The Size and Scale of Living Things.* Island Press, 1994. A useful guide for anyone wondering why humans aren't sixty feet tall, or why mice have bigger eyes for their size than elephants do.

Tolkien, J. R. R., "On Fairy-stories", *Tree and Leaf.* London: Allen & Unwin, 1964. Essential reading for any student of fantasy writing. Based on a lecture by Tolkien, this is short but takes time to think through later.

Williams, Kathleen. *Profiles in Literature: Jonathan Swift.* London: Routledge and

Kegan Paul, 1968. Excerpts of Swift's satiric writings with brief explanatory introductions.

◆ RELATED WEBSITES ◆

Jaffe, Lee. *Jaffe Bros. Web Site* http://www.jaffebros.com/lee/gulliver/index.html. December 12, 2000. A useful website with analysis and discussion of *Gulliver's Travels* and Jonathan Swift, by amateur and professional scholars.

Krystek, Lee. "The Mysterious Moons of Mars." *Museum of Unnatural History* http://unmuseum.mus.pa.us/marsmoon.htm. 1997. A discussion of Swift's odd detail about the moons of Mars being discovered by people of Laputa.

Paula Johanson

HARRIET BEECHER STOWE AND THE BEECHER PREACHERS

Biography

1994

Author: Jean Fritz

◆

Major Books for Young Adults

The Cabin Faced West, 1958
Brady, 1960
San Francisco, 1962
Story of Eli Whitney, 1962
I, Adam, 1963
Early Thunder, 1967
George Washington's Breakfast, 1969
Cast for a Revolution, 1972
And Then What Happened, Paul
   Revere?, 1973
Why Don't You Get a Horse, Sam
   Adams?, 1974
Who's That Stepping on Plymouth
   Rock?, 1975
Where Was Patrick Henry on the 29th of
   May?, 1975
Will You Sign Here, John Hancock?, 1976
What's the Big Idea, Ben Franklin?, 1976
Stonewall, 1979
Brendan the Navigator, 1979
Where Do You Think You're Going,
   Christopher Columbus?, 1980
Traitor: The Case of Benedict

Arnold, 1981
Homesick: My Own Story, 1982
Can't You Make Them Behave, King
   George?, 1982
The Double Life of Pocahontas, 1983
China Homecoming, 1985
Make Way for Sam Houston!, 1986
Shh! We're Writing the
   Constitution, 1987
China's Kong March: 6,000 Miles of
   Danger, 1988
The Great Little Madison, 1991
Great Adventure of Christopher Colum-
   bus, 1991
Just a Few Words, Mr. Lincoln, 1993
Jean Fritz: 6 Revolutionary War Fig-
   ures, 1993
Surprising Myself, 1993
Around the World in a Hundred
   Years, 1994
You Want Women to Vote, Lizzie
   Stanton?, 1995
Why Not, Lafayette?, 1999

Jean Guttery was born in Hankow, China, on November 16, 1915. Her parents, Arthur and Myrtle Guttery, were missionaries for the Young Men's Christian Association (YMCA). Around 1928, she and her family left China to escape the warfare that swept through country in the aftermath of the revolution that removed the old monarchy and replaced it with a fragile civilian government. While in China, she kept a notebook of her thoughts and observations that later served as a basis for writing about China. Guttery's writings about her own life reveal a nostalgia for China.

After she graduated from Wheaton College in 1937, she took a job with an advertising agency in New York, but left it to work for a textbook publisher, Silver Burdett Company. She married Michael Fritz on November 1, 1941, just in time for him to be called to military service and sent to San Francisco, after Japan bombed Pearl Harbor, marking America's entrance into World War II. In 1953, she and her husband and their son and a daughter moved to Dobbs Ferry in New York. There, she found a job as a librarian, creating a children's literature section.

During the 1960s, Fritz researched the history of the American Revolution, resulting in a work intended for grownups but suitable for teenagers, *Cast for a Revolution* (1972), and several works for young readers such as *Will You Sign Here, John Hancock?* (1976) that have gone through many reprints, including one in 1999. Although she has written distinguished fiction, Fritz is drawn to biography, particularly lives presented in context with the history of their times. She was nominated in 1982 for the Laura Ingalls Wilder Award for her lifetime of writing, but did not win until 1986. Although published after Fritz won that award, *Harriet Beecher Stowe and the Beecher Preachers* may be the most universally praised of her books. Certainly it and her other publications since then have been as vibrant with life and thought-provoking as any of her writings.

Fritz has been nominated for awards such as the National Book Award many times, winning some of them. The Children's Book Guild gave her its honor award in 1978 for her many historical writings. In 1982, her autobiography *Homesick: My Own Story* was named a Newbery Honor Book and a *Boston Globe-Horn Book* Honor Book, and it won the American Book Award (what the National Book Award was called for a brief period). *The Double Life of Pocahontas* won the *Boston Globe-Horn Book* Nonfiction Award for 1984, and *The Great Little Madison* won the same award in 1990. The Madison biography also received the Orbis Pictus Award from the National Council of Teachers of English.

◆ OVERVIEW ◆

There was much more to Harriet Beecher Stowe than the writing of *Uncle Tom's Cabin*, but such is the stature of that book as one of the most influential novels ever published, and anyone who studies Stowe's life is likely to emphasize the writing of her novel. Given that the novel is part of the curricula of many schools, discussing it would be one of the primary tasks of a biographer. Further, modern attitudes toward the novel are very mixed, with some people trying to ban the book from schools, and others hailing the book as one of America's best. Thus, Fritz sets for herself the twofold task of explaining how the novel came to be written and why it became almost instantly influential, making Stowe one the world's most famous writers in a matter of months.

Fritz identifies Stowe's family life and Stowe's reading as the principal influences on how Stowe became a writer and on the subjects she chose. According to Fritz, writing was a form of liberation for Stowe, who felt painfully constrained by her father's view of what was proper for women to do, and *Harriet Beecher Stowe and the Beecher Preachers* is a study of how the liberation that writing brought Stowe turned into passions for the liberation of others and for fiction that condemned unreasonable restrictions on the freedoms to speak and act as one chooses. Fritz's prose is lively, her research sound, and her blending of quotations from letters and other sources into her narrative of the remarkable life of Stowe is masterful.

Jean Fritz

◆ SETTING ◆

Harriet Beecher was born on June 14, 1811 in Litchfield, Connecticut. Her father was Lyman Beecher, one of the most famous Americans of his time. He was a religious minister who preached a strict Puritan view of Christianity; he pressed his sons to become ministers, too, and he lamented having daughters, who at the time were not allowed to preach because to do so was thought to be unladylike. From her Aunt Mary, Stowe heard harrowing tales of how slaves were mistreated in Jamaica. Aunt Mary had been married to a Jamaican planter but she fled him and Jamaica because she could not tolerate his abuse of slaves.

In 1816, her mother died; in 1818 her father remarried. Her stepmother remained cold and distant from Lyman Beecher's children, but she was an efficient manager of his household. At age fourteen, in 1825, Stowe begins teaching in her eldest sister Catherine's school. Her move in 1832 with her father and other family members to Cincinnati takes her to where she would establish herself as a professional writer, and where she would gather firsthand accounts of slavery. While there, she began to publish essays and short stories based on people she had met through her father.

Cincinnati had periodic outbreaks of cholera, and unhealthy living conditions took many lives, including those of people close to Stowe. The second wife of Lyman Beecher died in July 1835. Stowe had formed a close friendship with Calvin Stowe and his wife, and when his wife died, she and Calvin were drawn together by their common interests in literature and current events. They became engaged in November 1835, and in January 1836, they married. Calvin proved to be a steadfast supporter of Stowe's literary ambitions.

In 1850, the Stowes moved to Brunswick, Maine. On September 12, 1850, the Fugitive Slave Act became law. It placed a bounty on runaway slaves in free states and encouraged private parties to hunt them. Stowe, who had been a moderate on the issue of slavery, hoping for a peaceful phasing out of slavery in the United States, became an abolitionist because of the new law, although she was unwilling to go so far as to advocate violence to end slavery.

On March 20, 1852, Stowe's novel *Uncle Tom's Cabin* was published and became an instant best-seller, going through several printings in just a few months. It was also pirated overseas, especially in England, for which she received no money. The royalties from her American publisher proved to be enough for her to supply her family with comforts and to make her financially secure, to the relief of her husband Calvin, who constantly fretted over the previous lack of money. She moved her family to Andover, Massachusetts, into what she considered a better house.

In 1853, Stowe visited England, then continental Europe. From the moment she stepped off her ship in England, crowds surrounded her, then politely moved out of her way. Stowe's fame is such that people just wanted to see her, the great writer of *Uncle Tom's Cabin*. Although shy, she accepted the attention in good humor.

In 1864, Stowe moved her family to Oakholm, in Hartford, Connecticut, where she lived for many years, with her daughters helping her in her social work. The Civil War ended in 1865, which is when Fritz ends *Harriet Beecher Stowe and the Beecher Preachers*. Her husband Calvin died in 1886, ending a remarkable love affair and domestic partnership and Stowe died in 1896.

◆ THEMES AND CHARACTERS ◆

Harriet Beecher Stowe was born into an intense family, ruled by its patriarch, her father, Lyman Beecher, a Puritanical preacher proud of his ability to make his audiences feel the flames of Hell as he spoke. According to Fritz, "He knew what everyone ought to be, and he made no bones about it." He also knew what people ought not to be, and women ought not to be preachers. He was trying to father as many Beecher preachers as possible, making the birth of any daughter a disappointment to him. In Fritz's analysis, Stowe spent much of her life trying to be the boy her father always wanted.

Lyman Beecher suffered "fits of depression," during which he would shovel sand in his basement from one side to the other, trying to work the melancholia out of himself. His depressions were sometimes so severe that he would lose the ability to speak for weeks at a time. In one fashion or another, his neuroses were visited upon most of his children.

For instance, his son "Calvin was a lifelong procrastinator who at times could only be called lazy." He was not alone in sometimes finding it impossible to work, to even move. Eventually, Stowe's closest brother George killed himself, seeming to do it for no particular reason, although he had suffered from depression all his life and had struggled to live up to his father's expectations. Indeed, in *Harriet Beecher Stowe and the Beecher Preachers* none of Lyman's children quite live up to his expectations, even those who were industrious.

His eldest child Catherine, in Fritz's view, came closest to fulfilling Lyman's views on women. Although she was a vigorous founder of schools, she was accepting of her role as a domestic organizer—bossing the other children around much of the time, even long after they were all adults. His son Henry Ward Beecher became the most famous of the sons, a truly dynamic preacher, but his emphasis on the Gospel was different from his father's—where Lyman's audience felt fire, Henry Ward's felt love. Except perhaps for Catherine, none of Lyman's children accepted his demanding view of God, each finding in the Bible a forgiving Lord. Even Stowe, who tried to please her father as much as she could, did not accept his Puritanical teachings. Fritz finds evidence early in Stowe's life of an admiration for the

Episcopalian view of Christianity; still, she waited until her father was dead before formally joining the Episcopalian Church.

Taken as a group, the children of Lyman Beecher formed one of the most remarkable families in American history. They influenced religion, the arts, and society throughout the United States, from the North to the Midwest to the deepest South to the East, they left their marks on numerous states and on national affairs. Henry Ward Beecher and Stowe were especially sought out by politicians, royalty, religious leaders, and social activists; Stowe's views were even entered by Senators into the Congressional Record.

Stowe herself is a difficult figure to understand. In her were contradictions of personality and social views that biographers have found difficult to explain, usually with only indifferent success. For instance, Stowe was determined to be the ideal of the domestic wife, no matter how badly the role suited her, and she devoted much of her time to running her husband and children's lives. Yet, she was an independent-minded person who read widely and formed her own opinions on political, social, and religious issues. She struggled to pursue her interest in writing while trying to manage a large household and often put her literary work on hold while planning her household's affairs. If she had not married an unusually open-minded man, implies Fritz, there is no telling whether she would have ever become as important as she did.

"Calvin often felt sorry for himself. Here he was, he sighed, feeling poorly, abandoned to a life of domestic disorder. Calvin couldn't stand anything out of place. He objected to furniture being rearranged. He hated to see a newspaper scattered helter-skelter on the floor." He was prone to panic, and money worries depressed him. Stowe took his complaints in stride, saying facetiously, "I really pity you in having such a wife." For all his woes and weaknesses, Calvin brought to the marriage a good mind and a great heart; he seemed to have always supported Stowe in her work and to have said to her that her work was more important than her domestic life. According to Fritz, his encouragement was constant and firm; however fussy he might be in other matters, he was clear in his devotion to his wife and to her ambitions.

Perhaps ambition is the most important factor she learned from her father. He had towering ambitions; in *Harriet Beecher Stowe and the Beecher Preachers*, he foresees a nation united in his personal view of God, as preached by himself, his children, and perhaps their children, as well. By the time she was a young adult, Stowe had already determined to preach with the written word; she had been delighted when an essay of hers had been read publicly (not by her) and that her father had liked it. Abolitionism had not originally been an interest of hers. Her essays and stories tended to be character studies based on the many unusual people who had visited her father.

"Stowe had hated the idea of slavery ever since she'd been a little girl and Aunt Mary, her mother's sister, had run away from her husband, a planter in Jamaica, because she couldn't stand to see how his slaves were treated," notes Fritz. But the horrifying tales of how slaves were abused had not inspired a novel. Like her father and many others who wanted slavery abolished, she saw compromise as the way to settle the issue of slavery in the United States. They saw slavery as an institution that would fade away.

What stirred Stowe to write *Uncle Tom's Cabin* is not entirely clear in *Harriet Beecher Stowe and the Beecher Preachers*. A voracious reader with opinions on almost any subject, Stowe may have been discouraged by United States Supreme Court rulings making slaves from slave states still slaves if brought by

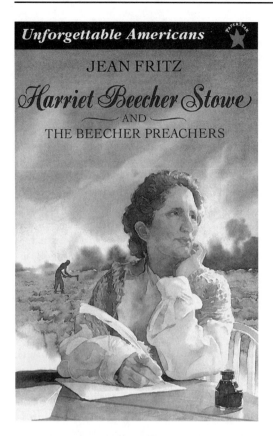

Unforgettable Americans

JEAN FRITZ

Harriet Beecher Stowe
— AND —
THE BEECHER PREACHERS

Book cover illustration by Ellen Thompson for *Harriet Beecher Stowe and the Beecher Preachers* by Jean Fritz.

their owners to free states. In Fritz's view, the Fugitive Slave Law passed by Congress may have radicalized Stowe, turning her from a gradualist to a fervent abolitionist. This shift in her views does not seem to have been immediately evident to her family and friends. The novel actually began as a novella meant to be serialized in only a few parts in a newspaper (the popular belief that it was too controversial for book publishers is implicitly denied in Fritz's account—it began as a serial). "It seemed to her," says Fritz of Stowe, "that the book [*Uncle Tom's Cabin*] had always been there. All she had done was find it and take down the words." She drew on her extensive

reading and on the many people she knew who were familiar with slavery, both pro and con. Stowe's narrative, constructed from many sources, fell together in an impassioned account of brutality and degradation presented with clarity and bluntness, united with a fashionable literary style that made her novel unique. It became clear early on in writing her proposed novella that it was going to be much longer than anticipated, but her editors accepted this. It was considered by many to be a masterpiece in the making.

Stowe "was shy and short (five feet at her tallest), and she considered herself plain," notes Fritz, yet she responded to the firestorm of praise and protest *Uncle Tom's Cabin* elicited with grace and fortitude. As the daughter of the passionate Lyman Beecher, she was no stranger to controversy. Perhaps she learned from her father how to respond to criticism by citing chapter and verse, but when Southern newspapers called her a liar (and more vile words), she wrote a "key" to *Uncle Tom's Cabin*, citing her sources for the events recounted in her book. When she traveled, she found herself the object of respectful but intense scrutiny. Rather than shrink away, she let people have their look.

The full extent of the influence of *Uncle Tom's Cabin* and Stowe's other writings is hard to measure. It is possible that Stowe influenced the course of America's most devastating war. That she also opened vast new avenues for women writers is probable. As far as Fritz is concerned, Stowe invented the protest novel, which would mean countless American writers since her time have been influenced by her literary innovation. Fritz insists that

in almost any list today of ten books that have changed the world, *Uncle Tom's Cabin* will appear. Harriet Beecher Stowe was a towering figure in her time, and although Lyman Beecher might not have admitted it, she was the best preacher of them all.

Harriet Beecher Stowe and the Beecher Preachers is not a biography of adulation. Instead, it is a careful reconstruction of what Stowe's life was like, with care taken to explain some of the complexities of her seemingly contradictory nature. It is likely that Fritz admires Stowe, but the tone of her biography is even, allowing Stowe's life to seem as though it is telling itself.

Any reader is likely to notice that a large chunk of Stowe's life, the period after the Civil War, is only sketched in *Harriet Beecher Stowe and the Beecher Preachers*. The reason for this may be a limitation on the biography's length. Publishers tend to shy away from young adult biographies that are over 50,000 words in length in the belief that young adults may be put off by something long. Of greatest interest to most young readers would be Stowe's rise to fame and influence, and *Uncle Tom's Cabin* would be Stowe's publication of greatest interest. Fritz covers these ably. Even so, Stowe's influence on literature and society extended well beyond her protest against slavery, and the "Afterword" only sketches what her life and career were like in the late-nineteenth-century.

♦ SOCIAL SENSITIVITY ♦

"Without realizing it, Harriet Beecher Stowe had written America's first protest novel, the first book written against a law," declares Fritz about *Uncle Tom's Cabin*. *Harriet Beecher Stowe and the Beecher Preachers* traces the development of Stowe's social consciousness and how its development affected her writing. Key to Fritz's reasoning is the influence of Stowe's father, Lyman Beecher, then one of the most famous people in America. Fritz unveils irony in Lyman Beecher's efforts to get his sons to follow him, for his sons abandoned his unforgiving Puritanical view of Christianity for a more loving view of Christ, with the ultimate irony being found in the success of a daughter at preaching through writing that far exceeded that of any of his sons. Fritz cites letters in which Stowe says that she will preach through her writing; she would be the ideal son, the boy her father wished she was.

It is very interesting how strong-willed, self-motivated daughters emerged from a family life in which female domesticity was emphasized. One daughter went about the United States founding schools, and Stowe developed her own independent view of how a woman may interact with her society. Fritz notes that Stowe took great care to fulfill her domestic obligations to first her father's family and later to her husband and children, although Fritz detects stress in Stowe, believing she would have forgone some of her duties if she could have.

Stowe was blessed with a husband who wholeheartedly supported her work as a writer, even making domestic concessions so that she could have privacy and time to write. Perhaps from his respect for his wife's working and likely from Stowe's own example, they had remarkably independent daughters, two of whom not only fulfilled their domestic obligations to their mother by caring for her as she grew old, but became influential suffragists.

Uncle Tom's Cabin is a striking condemnation of the abuse and debasement of a human being by other human beings, and it realistically depicts the language of racism and slavery of the time. In *Harriet Beecher Stowe and the Beecher Preachers*, the word "nigger" shows up in conversations (for example, "I never see a nigger yet I couldn't bring down in one crack"). Such foul language was typical of the era, and it would be almost impossible to present an honest analysis of Stowe's emergence as an abolitionist without noting the debased attitudes represented by such language that she and almost any American of the time would have encountered.

does she overcome his attitude? How does Stowe's father's prejudice affect her work?

◆ TOPICS FOR DISCUSSION ◆

1. Why would Fritz abruptly end her biography of Stowe after the end of the Civil War?

2. How does the "Afterword" help you to better understand Stowe's life? What does it leave you wondering about?

3. How did Stowe's family influence her life and her work? How did Stowe benefit from being a Beecher? How was being a Beecher a disadvantage for her?

4. Why was Stowe at first disappointed with President Lincoln? What happened during their meeting that changed her mind?

5. Why were some Southerners angry about *Uncle Tom's Cabin* when it was first published?

6. Why would the phrase "an Uncle Tom" become a pejorative slur used against some African Americans in the 1950s and 1960s?

7. Was Stowe "the best preacher of them all"? How does Fritz show this?

8. Does *Harriet Beecher Stowe and the Beecher Preachers* show why some feminists would have ambivalent feelings toward Stowe? What about her life, career, and attitudes would put off some feminists?

9. Is it really possible for any one novel to start a war? What were the other factors related to Stowe's work that Fritz mentions as influences on the start and course of the war?

10. How does Stowe deal with her father's prejudice in favor of boys? How much

◆ IDEAS FOR REPORTS AND PAPERS ◆

1. Do some of your own research on Harriet Beecher Stowe and compare her to others who have fought for freedom and equality. What are some of the contributions and changes that they have made? Are their efforts still felt today?

2. Some Southerners were angry about *Uncle Tom's Cabin*. Who hated it? What did they write about it? What did they threaten to do to Stowe?

3. What is the history of the character of Uncle Tom in *Uncle Tom's Cabin*? How is someone like him viewed today?

4. What were Stowe's views on giving women the right to vote? What may have been her influence on efforts to enfranchise women? Research the suffragists. Do you think it was especially hard for Stowe, being that she was black and a woman living during a time that viewed both as second class citizens?

5. What did Abraham Lincoln think of Harriet Beecher Stowe? What is the history of their relationship?

6. It is possible that *Uncle Tom's Cabin* kept England from joining the Civil War on the side of the Confederacy. What is the history of the novel's influence on England's popular attitudes toward American slavery and how did it affect the English government?

7. Why have people tried to ban *Uncle Tom's Cabin* from schools and libraries? What is the history of efforts to ban the novel?

8. Stowe wrote a book that explained her research and sources for the events in *Uncle Tom's Cabin*. What is the title of this book? Read it and critique it. Does it have any unsubstantiated claims? Does it do a good job of supporting the depiction of slavery in *Uncle Tom's Cabin*?

9. Harriet Beecher Stowe became the most famous member of the Beecher family. How did she handle being in the public eye from 1865 until her death? How much privacy did she have?

10. Stowe's daughters Eliza and Harriet never married, instead spending most of their lives working with their mother. What did they accomplish? What were their lives like? Were they happy?

◆ RELATED TITLES ◆

Suzanne M. Coil's *Harriet Beecher Stowe* (1993) and Norma Johnston's *Harriet: The Life and World of Harriet Beecher Stowe* (1994) are two of the most recent young adult biographies of Stowe. Coil attempts to cover Stowe's entire life, while emphasizing the writing of *Uncle Tom's Cabin*. She plainly admires her subject. Johnston tries to place Stowe's achievements in the context of her time, using Stowe to illustrate attitudes of the time toward women, writers, and social protest. Robert E. Jokoubek's *Harriet Beecher Stowe* (1989) is for somewhat less advanced readers than the books by Coil and Johnston. Jokoubek ably recounts the basic facts of Stowe's life, although not with the style and vigor found in *Harriet Beecher Stowe and the Beecher Preachers*.

Joan D. Hedrick's *Harriet Beecher Stowe: A Life* (1993) is a full-length biography of Stowe written for adults. Hedrick offers a feminist interpretation of Stowe's life, but sometimes seems to strain to put a modern feminist spin on Stowe's devotion to domestic life. An aspect of the lives of the Beechers not often covered in biographies is their sojourning in Florida, but John T. Foster and Sarah Whitmer Foster's *Beechers, Stowes, and Yankee Strangers: The Transformation of Florida* (1999) discusses their efforts, along with those of others, to make post-Civil War Florida into an ideal state, where all races could live freely and without conflict.

Marie Caskey's *Chariot of Fire: Religion and the Beecher Family* (1978) and Charles H. Foster's *The Rungless Ladder: Harriet Beecher Stowe and New England Puritanism* (1954) examine Stowe's religious beliefs. Caskey does a good job of explaining how Stowe's views differed from those of her father. Capturing not only Stowe's religious thinking but the whole of her complex personality in a biography is a challenging task, but Edward Wagenknecht's *Harriet Beecher Stowe, the Known and the Unknown* (1965) comes close to showing how Stowe could contain within herself a powerfully independent mind and yet embrace the traditional tasks of domestic motherhood.

◆ FOR FURTHER REFERENCE ◆

Burns, Mary M. *Horn Book* 70, (September–October 1994): 606. About *Harriet Beecher Stowe and the Beecher Preachers*, Burns declares in her review, "Written with vivacity and insight, this readable and engrossing biography is an important contribution to women's history as well as to the history of American letters."

Margolis, Sally. *School Library Journal* 40, (September 1994): 227. This review praises *Harriet Beecher Stowe and the Beecher Preachers*.

Review of *Harriet Beecher Stowe and the Beecher Preachers*. *Publishers Weekly* 241, (August 8, 1994): 450. The reviewer notes, "Fritz's picture of Stowe . . . isn't so much that of an influential writer as it is of a woman struggling to make her voice heard in a family where boys were seen as assets and girls as, simply, not boys." This brief review declares that Stowe "shines through" in *Harriet Beecher Stowe and the Beecher Preachers*.

Rochman, Hazel. Review of *Harriet Beecher Stowe and the Beecher Preachers. Booklist* 90, (August 1994): 2036. In her review, Rochman criticizes *Harriet Beecher Stowe and the Beecher Preachers* for having "no source notes." Otherwise, "Fritz quietly dramatizes a momentous truth: this woman wrote a book that, for all its flaws, changed the world."

Kirk H. Beetz

HARRISON BERGERON

Short Story

1961

Author: Kurt Vonnegut, Jr.

◆

Major Books for Young Adults

Player Piano, 1952
The Sirens of Titan, 1959
Mother Night, 1961
Cat's Cradle, 1963
God Bless You, Mr. Rosewater, 1965
Welcome to the Monkey House, 1968
   (short stories)
Slaughterhouse-Five, 1969
Happy Birthday, Wanda June,

1972 (play)
Breakfast of Champions, 1973
Wampeters, Foma and Granfalloons, 1974
   (essays)
Slapstick, 1976
Jailbird, 1979
Palm Sunday, 1981 (essays)
Deadeye Dick, 1982
Timequake, 1997

◆ ABOUT THE AUTHOR ◆

Kurt Vonnegut, Jr. was born on November 11, 1922, in Indianapolis, Indiana, the third child and second son of Kurt Vonnegut and Edith Lieber Vonnegut. The Vonneguts were successful architects, and they and the Liebers were respected members of the Indianapolis community for generations. Kurt was born into a large and supportive extended family.

Vonnegut was turning nine years old when the social and economic fortunes of his family changed radically. His father had no clients during the Great Depression and so endured a decade of unemployment. His mother, heiress of a now depleted fortune, lost her elegant possessions and was unable to afford exclusive private schooling for her younger son. The older children, Bernard and Alice, had attended exclusive private schools, but Kurt enrolled in Public School No. 43 and later attended Shortridge High School. The country's economic collapse changed his childhood and education with lifelong results.

Although Vonnegut grew up among a family that endured depression (most notably his father, sister, and grandfather) and came to suffer from depression himself as an adult, another great influence upon his childhood was his uncle Alex Vonnegut,

Kurt Vonnegut, Jr.

fraternity Delta Upsilon, is to this day an interested alumnus, and uses it as a frequent metaphor in his novels and essays.

Vonnegut was the managing editor on the student newspaper at Cornell, as he was on his high school paper. Working as a journalist delivering essential news to his community gave him strong links to his fellow students.

On advice from his father and brother Bernard, Kurt had enrolled in courses for a career as a biochemist. At that time, the sciences seemed his best prospect; his brother had earned a doctorate from the Massachusetts Institute of Technology and was becoming an internationally renowned atmospheric physicist who invented a rain-making process by seeding clouds with silver iodide crystals. He admired his brother all his life, writing in his book *Wampeters, Foma and Granfalloons,* "I thought scientists were going to find out exactly how everything worked, and then make it work better. I fully expected by the time I was twenty-one, some scientist, maybe my brother, would have taken a color photograph of God Almighty—and sold it to *Popular Mechanics* magazine."

But midway through his junior year he caught pneumonia and was forced to drop his classes; losing his student standing made him subject to military service. On enlistment, he was sent to the Carnegie Institute of Technology and then to the University of Tennessee to be trained as a mechanical engineer. When he served overseas, however, it was to be as an advance infantry scout.

In 1944, he went home on leave to visit his family on Mother's Day. Tragically, that day his mother committed suicide. Days later, he was sent overseas to join the 106th Infantry Division in England.

On December 22, 1944, he was captured by the Wehrmacht during the Battle of the Bulge, and interned as a prisoner of war

who taught him to enjoy socialist ideals and the finer, simpler things in life. Alex was a valuable counterbalance to the sadness and depression Kurt would be exposed to in his young life.

Though his mother hoped for sufficient funds to transfer him to a private school, he was glad to find friends at the public school and never forgot the lessons he learned in junior civics class. All his life, he has held dear his beliefs in social equality and the value of kindness. At college in Cornell University in upstate New York, Vonnegut found many of his early experiences repeated and socially confirmed. According to Jerome Klinkowitz in his analytical work *Kurt Vonnegut,* this young man

> discovered that the fraternity and sorority system could offer him not only a place to hang his hat but also an extended family with scores of artificially construed but none the less helpful brothers and sisters, and even a housemother. He pledged the

in Dresden. This supposedly open city was nonetheless destroyed in Allied firebombing on February 13, 1945, and few of the city's 250,000 inhabitants survived. Vonnegut never forgot what his war experiences taught him of the Allies and of the German war machine. These experiences influenced his future writing, particularly his novel *Slaughterhouse-Five.*

After his repatriation by the Red Army and a summer convalescing in Indianapolis, Vonnegut married his childhood sweetheart, Jane Cox; he later wrote a story about the day he asked her to marry him, "The Long Walk to Forever," which appears in his story collection *Welcome to the Monkey House.*

In 1945 Vonnegut enrolled in the University of Chicago's graduate anthropology program, though he had not completed a bachelor's degree. He completed his course work for a master's degree, and drafted three rejected theses comparing industrialized societies and primitive groups, a method of study that was not acceptable in this field until years later. In 1947 he left Chicago without a degree; years later, the sociology department studied Vonnegut's novel *Player Piano* and, on the strength of the sociological themes of the book, awarded him a graduate degree.

On leaving the university, Vonnegut took employment as a publicist for the Research Laboratory of General Electric in Schenectady, New York, where his brother worked as a scientist. While writing press releases and mingling with scientists, other ex-soldiers who attended college on the GI Bill, and their wives, Vonnegut became as skeptical of the corporate good life as he had become of the army, and vented his frustration by working on a novel and writing short stories. He sent his short works to the popular family magazines of that time.

In his book *Timequake,* Vonnegut described his own good luck that "for the first thirty-three years of my life, telling short stories with ink on paper was a major American industry." Although by 1951 he had a wife and two children, it made good business sense to quit his job as a publicity man for General Electric, forgoing the security of a company-sponsored health insurance and retirement plan. He could make more money selling stories to the *Saturday Evening Post* and *Collier's.* At that time, Vonnegut could mail off a story to his agent with reasonable confidence that one of the many magazines hungry for fiction would pay him something for it. He also had a contract with a major New York publisher for his "get-even" novel, *Player Piano.*

But not long after Vonnegut moved family from Schenectady, New York, to Cape Cod, Massachusetts, television began to dominate the entertainment industry. Vonnegut commuted to Boston, working for an industrial advertising agency, then became a Saab automobile dealer, and then taught high-school English in a private school. His son, Mark Vonnegut, an author and doctor, was asked by a reporter what it had been like to grow up with a famous father. His reply (as quoted in Vonnegut's book *Timequake*) was: "When I was growing up, my father was a car salesman who couldn't get a job teaching at Cape Cod Junior College."

On the death in 1958 of his sister, Alice, from cancer, some few hours after the death of her husband from an accident, Vonnegut and his wife Jane adopted three of Alice's four children and raised them with their own three. The loss of his sister a year after their father's death brought an emotional maturity to Vonnegut's writing. It was at this point that he began to write as if he were addressing one person—perhaps his late sister—and his work reached a radical new level of artfulness and depth.

After a long separation, Vonnegut divorced his first wife in 1979 and married Jill

Krementz, a photographer. He became a popular speaker and lecturer, and in 1988 his symphony *Requiem* was performed by the Buffalo Symphony. He adopted his daughter Lily in 1992.

In 2000, a cigarette Vonnegut left smouldering in an ashtray started a fire which burned down much of his East Side Manhattan brownstone. The one-time volunteer firefighter tried to extinguish the blaze on his own, and ended up in a hospital for almost three weeks, suffering from smoke inhalation. To recuperate, he moved to Northampton, Massachusetts, where several of his children and grandchildren live. At this time Vonnegut spent two semesters as writer-in-residence at Smith College. The experience was positive for him and the campus: not only did he spend hours with students on their own writing and give guest lectures, but he read poems and told jokes at local cafes, exhibited his artwork at a local gallery, and scatted as the lead vocalist of "Special K and His Crew." He also is spending time writing a new novel, something he never expected to do again.

◆ OVERVIEW ◆

"Harrison Bergeron" is set in a future America, when everyone is equal according to Constitutional Amendments, and agents of the Handicapper General enforce the equality laws. George and Hazel Bergeron are watching television at home, discussing George's handicaps that make him equal to her and their fellow citizens, and their son's arrest for suspicion of plotting to overthrow the government.

Young Harrison is only fourteen, but he is a strong and handsome young man who breaks out of custody and into the television station. On camera, he announces his rule as Emperor: "Even as I stand here crippled, hobbled, sickened, I am a greater ruler than any man who ever lived! Now watch me become what I can become!" He throws off his handicaps and chooses as his Empress a dancer who steps forward to join him. He removes her handicaps, and the handicaps of the studio musicians. Together Harrison and his Empress dance a transcendent dance—until the Handicapper General, Diana Moon Glampers, enters the television studio and shoots them both dead instantly with a double-blast of her shotgun. Glampers reloads and tells the musicians to get their handicaps back on.

While Hazel and George witness their son's death, they both forget why they are so sad.

◆ SETTING ◆

The story is set in the year 2081, in a middle-America very understandable by contemporary readers of October 1961, when the story was first published in *The Magazine of Fantasy and Science Fiction,* or 1968, when it appeared in the collection *Welcome to the Monkey House.* In this story there are television shows with stars much like George Burns and Gracie Allen, there is striving for social equality, and there is sufficient leisure time for ordinary working folk to watch television from the comfort of their own homes. But the television shows are populated by dancers and musicians and announcers aggressively equalized by handicaps such as heavy weights, ugly masks, and noise-making hearing aids, as is one of the two viewpoint characters, George.

The frightening extent to which the Handicapper General goes to maintain this crippling version of "equality" makes the story seem at first to be set in a fantasy world, or an alternate reality. But if one is aware that the author is an international traveler who has spent time in American public schools and universities, in the army, and in a prisoner-of-war camp in Germany, and has conversed with Nazis, Biafrans,

Communists, and his Cape Cod neighbor, all on their own home turf, the Handicapper General's final solution is possibly the least unrealistic element in the story.

Far more unreal is the way Harrison's parents immediately forget why they are sad, and the sound of a riveting gun in George's ear-radio leads them into a verbal exchange echoing comic lines popularized by comedians George Burns and Gracie Allen, from the closing dialogue of their television show. The simultaneous familiarity and inappropriateness of the dialogue make this story an unsettling experience for the reader.

◆ THEMES AND CHARACTERS ◆

This is a fairly typical story from the early part of Vonnegut's writing career. What critic Conrad Festa says of Vonnegut's writing is particularly true for "Harrison Bergeron": "The early satire is primarily concerned with the evils of technology and the follies of the American way of life."

"The year was 2081, and everybody was finally equal," is how the story begins, as told from a limited omniscient, impersonal point of view, more like a camera than a human narrator.

> They weren't only equal before God and the law. They were equal every which way. Nobody was smarter than anybody else. Nobody was better looking than anybody else. Nobody was stronger or quicker than anybody else. All this equality was due to the 211th, 212th, and 213th Amendments to the Constitution, and to the unceasing vigilance of agents of the United States Handicapper General.

These equality laws are enforced by agents of the Handicapper General, called H-G men, an allusion to the American slang term from the 1940s and 1950s of referring to Federal Bureau of Investigation and Secret Service officers as G-men, the G standing for government.

People are told they are made equal by handicapping devices which bring them down to the normalcy level in the story, which is actually below-average in intelligence, strength, and ability. These devices include weights to stunt speed and strength; masks, red rubber clown noses, or thick glasses to hide good looks and to make seeing difficult; and radio transmitters implanted in the ears of intelligent people, which emit a variety of sharp noises three times a minute to prevent sustained thought. The stated intent is so that nobody will have an advantage over anybody else.

Perceptive readers will see through the fallacy: if everyone were truly equal, the various handicaps would not be necessary. The story remains silent about the fate of those who fall below normal, except to say that television announcers all have speech impediments. There are no "equalizing" attempts to elevate anyone to normal or average.

Although he is only fourteen years old, the title character, Harrison Bergeron, stands seven feet tall and is an athlete who bears heavier handicaps and more grotesque masking devices than anyone else. He is so intelligent that, at the beginning of the story, the Handicapper General has Harrison arrested "on suspicion of plotting to overthrow the government."

That is exactly what Harrison tries to do when he escapes from custody. But instead of going to the Legislature, he goes to the television station to publicly declare himself Emperor. He selects a ballerina as his Empress, not a social leader; and rather than going out into the world to free the oppressed, the two dance on camera. "Neutralizing gravity with love and pure will," the couple leaps high enough to kiss the ceiling and float there in mid-air, kissing each other. They remain suspended until

Diana Moon Glampers, the United States Handicapper General, enters the television studio and blasts the couple out of the air with a double-barreled ten-gauge shotgun.

Harrison's actions suggest that power does indeed corrupt, or at least, ability does. Upon his escape, Harrison repeats government errors by trying to establish himself as the sole, unelected, source of authority. Had his rebellion succeeded, he would have forced people to break the current law by making them remove their government-imposed handicaps. It is clear that he would have become a tyrant, imposing his will by his strength and intelligence, because of how he deals with the musicians in the television studio. He first removes their handicaps (without asking), states that he will make them "barons and dukes and earls" if they play their best, and then physically intimidates them into trying harder to please him. Harrison may transcend the grotesque state he was forced to endure, but he has only found and reveled his strength and ability—he has not achieved greatness.

Harrison's father, George Bergeron, bears multiple government-imposed handicaps which repress his "way above-normal" intelligence. He refuses to remove any of them, however, for he believes that social and individual competition would inevitably cause civilization to regress back into the "dark ages," when there was competition. George and Hazel, his wife, witness Harrison's rebellious act on television, but afterwards cannot remember why they are sad. George wears birdshot weights and a mental handicap radio in his ear that receives a "sharp noise" transmission every twenty seconds, designed "to keep people . . . from taking unfair advantage of their brains."

Harrison's mother, Hazel Bergeron, wears no mental or physical handicaps as she possesses normal intelligence, appearance, and strength. In this story, however, normal seems to suggest that one is weak and simple, or unable to fathom anything beyond that which is superficial. Hazel's dialogue with her husband, George, recalls the comedic team of George Burns and Gracie Allen. She takes a naïve interest in George's handicaps and encourages George to remove a few lead balls from his handicap bag, at least just when he is home from work, to lighten his load. Hazel's suggestion to bend the rules leads George to defend their society and its laws.

Although Diana Moon Glampers, the United States Handicapper General, appears only briefly toward the end of the story in order to quell Harrison's rebellion, her presence pervades the story. As Handicapper General, she ruthlessly maintains law and order without due process. Glampers herself is not fully described in the story. As for her appearance, the reader is told only her gender, not her race or age or expressions. It is significant that she is not handicapped by wearing a bag of lead shot, or an ugly mask, or an ear-radio. Since everyone of superior strength or beauty or intelligence is aggressively equalized, Diana Moon Glampers is clearly neither strong and graceful, nor good-looking and smart. A Handicapper General who brings all capable people down to her level is even more frightening than an evil genius avoiding the Equality Laws.

The character Diana Moon Glampers also appears in Vonnegut's novel *God Bless You, Mr. Rosewater*. However, it is not essential to read the novel in order to better understand this story, or the character of Glampers within the story. It does not take much analysis to understand the motivation of someone who uses a double-barrelled shotgun to eliminate superior talents and opposition.

Critic Carl Mowery says in an essay on "Harrison Bergeron" that Vonnegut's experiences during World War II, and then as an employee at General Electric, caused him to question many of the power structures in the United States: the government, corporations, the military, and bureaucracies in general. "He was most concerned with situations in which the individual was a victim of oppression, and any society that reduced the individual to a mere number, or that limited the individual's opportunities to improve," says Mowery. "Vonnegut did not believe that everyone could be better, but that everyone should have the opportunity to try." Clearly, this was Vonnegut's primary theme for the story.

Some critics have complained that Vonnegut cuts to the chase in his fiction, skimping on character development and making overt statements about motivation rather than writing with sophisticated grace to show the readers, not explicitly tell them, why his characters do what they do. But Vonnegut himself spoke on this topic in his book *Timequake*, through his alter-ego character Kilgore Trout, a science fiction writer. "'If I'd wasted my time creating characters,' Trout said, 'I would never have gotten around to calling attention to things that really matter: irresistible forces in nature, and cruel inventions, and cockamamie ideals and governments and economies that make heroes and heroines alike feel like something the cat drug in.'"

Vonnegut adds, even more overtly: "Trout might have said, and it can be said of me as well, that he created caricatures rather than characters. His animus against so-called mainstream literature, moreover, wasn't peculiar to him. It was generic among writers of science fiction."

◆ LITERARY QUALITIES ◆

"I always had trouble ending short stories in ways that would satisfy a general public," Vonnegut notes in *Timequake*. "In real life, . . . people don't change, don't

learn anything from their mistakes, and don't apologize. In a short story they have to do at least two out of three of those things, or you might as well throw it away." Vonnegut admits he could handle that much. "But after I had a character change and/or learn something and/or apologize, that left the cast standing around with their thumbs up their asses. That is no way to tell a reader the show is over." In his salad days (youthful indiscretions—heyday), Vonnegut sought the advice of his then literary agent as to how to end stories without killing all the characters, and was told that nothing could be simpler. "The hero mounts his horse and rides off into the sunset." This story, "Harrison Bergeron", is clearly one of the ones where the author was willing to kill off a few characters.

Any cursory study of Vonnegut's fiction will reveal that the author starts and stops his stories *in media res*, that is, in the middle of things, with little or no attention paid to such literary devices as introductions, denouements, character development, or foreshadowing. This story is no exception. Vonnegut does not show the readers his characters and let the audience learn what they do in their world. Instead, he flat-out tells readers everything up front, in words of one and two syllables whenever possible.

"From the beginning of his professional writing career, Vonnegut demonstrated a strong inclination to write satire," says critic Conrad Festa in *Vonnegut in America*. "Stories such as 'Harrison Bergeron' [and others] fit easily and recognizably into the satiric genre. . . . Furthermore, the satiric objects in those works are easily identifiable and familiar, and their satiric significances are obvious. Judged solely on his early fiction, Vonnegut emerges as a somewhat traditional satirist," Festa concludes. "Were he to have continued writing in that way, we all would have joined hands long ago to slam down the lid on his box." While it is difficult to call Vonnegut's later writing more sophisticated, his later use of satire is certainly even less traditional than in this story.

When this story first appeared in *The Magazine of Fantasy and Science Fiction*, it was Vonnegut's third publication in a science fiction magazine following the drying up of the once-lucrative weekly family magazine market where he had published more than twenty stories between 1950 and 1961. The story received no critical attention, however, until 1968 when it appeared in Vonnegut's collection *Welcome to the Monkey House*. Initial reviews of the collection were less than favorable, with even the more positive reviewers commenting negatively on the commercial quality of many of the stories.

By the late 1980s, however, "Harrison Bergeron" was being reprinted in high school and college literature anthologies. "Popular aspects of the story include Vonnegut's satire of both enforced equality and the power of the Handicapper General, and the enervating effect television can have on viewers," says Joseph Alvarez. According to him, this futuristic story deals with "universal themes of equality, freedom, power and its abuses, and media influence," and "continues to evoke thoughtful responses about equality and individual freedom in the United States." He also suggests that "Harrison Bergeron" likely draws upon a controversial 1961 speech by then Federal Communications Commission chairman Newton Minow titled "The Vast Wasteland," a reference to a supposed dearth of quality in television programming.

Vonnegut rarely wrote short stories after the 1960s, preferring to write novels which brought him more income. "I still think up short stories from time to time, as though there were money in it. The habit dies hard," Vonnegut commented in *Timequake*. "All I do with short story ideas now is rough

them out, credit them to Kilgore Trout, and put them in a novel."

◆ SOCIAL SENSITIVITY ◆

In his book *Fates Worse Than Death: An Autobiographical Collage of the 1980s*, Kurt Vonnegut reflected on a 1983 speech he gave at the Cathedral of St. John the Divine in New York City:

> American TV, operating in the Free Market of Ideas ... was holding audiences with simulations of one of the two things most human beings, and especially young ones, can't help watching when given the opportunity: murder. TV, and of course movies, too, were and still are making us as callous about killing and death as Hitler's propaganda made the German people during the frenzied prelude to the death camps and World War II. ... What I should have said from the pulpit was that we weren't going to Hell. We were in Hell, thanks to technology which was telling us what to do, instead of the other way around. And it wasn't just TV.

With these words, Vonnegut is speaking on ideas he used in his story "Harrison Bergeron." In this story, television desensitized Hazel Bergeron, Harrison's mother, to the murder of her own son, which she witnesses while watching television. She does weep over what she sees, but is so numbed by watching television, that she cannot remember why she is crying.

In this story, Vonnegut shows readers that he was deeply affected by Newton Minow's famous 1961 speech about television programming, called "The Vast Wasteland." Minow specifically mentioned violence as a contributor to this wasteland. Near the end of the speech, talking about programming, Minow pleaded for imagination, not sterility; creativity, not imitation; experimentation, not conformity; excellence, not mediocrity. He added, "The power of instantaneous sight and sound is without precedent in mankind's history. This is an awesome power. It has limitless capabilities for good and for evil."

In "Harrison Bergeron", Vonnegut uses some of the ideas Minow discussed, particularly when he portrays television as a desensitizing, numbing, and definitely a thought-stifling—rather than thought-provoking—medium. When Harrison goes to the television station instead of to the Legislature to start his revolution, Vonnegut illustrates that awesome power Minow describes in his speech. Vonnegut seems to say that Harrison's power to reach the people and make a new reality (declaring himself emperor) stems from controlling television. Clearly, the government, or at least the Handicapper General, also understands that power.

Joseph Alvarez points out in his overview of "Harrison Bergeron" that Vonnegut gives his reader "a futuristic United States of America in which minds have been so softened or desensitized by television and other forces (fear of enemies) that the people give up their individual rights and aspirations, presumably for the good of the whole society." This sacrifice of the individual for the good of society does not improve conditions for the above average or even the average citizens. The equality standard seems to have been set well below the 1961 average. "In the resulting power vacuum," Alvarez adds, "a ruthless central government created by legislation controls people's lives, which have become as meaningless as if they were machines or automatons. . . . What really is lost in such a process is beauty, grace, and wisdom."

It cannot be argued that in this satirical short story Vonnegut is speaking out against equality before the law and civil rights. Karen and Charles Wood make this clear in *The Vonnegut Statement:*

Lest readers think that Vonnegut endorses by satire a continuation of the status quo

ante (or current conditions) in relation to equality, that is, legal and customary inequality, he has commented publicly that he learned social equality through his attendance at public schools of Indianapolis. Later in life, he endorsed legal equal opportunity on at least two different occasions.

During the Soviet Russian period of *glasnost,* or openness, Vonnegut referred favorably in essays and speeches (mentioned in *Wampeters, Foma and Granfalloons*) to the current American *glasnost* experiment of trying to offer women and people of color the same social regard enjoyed by white men.

Alvarez feels that Vonnegut clearly decries the kind of competition related to social Darwinism. "Vonnegut has championed a free market of ideas and has fought censorship against his own books, and for writers in other countries whose works are suppressed by their governments." Vonnegut has done fairly well as a writer competing in the marketplace of ideas, in Alvarez's opinion: "even though he does not believe he has received fair critical treatment during his later years. In essence, he has complained that critics expect writers always to write their best; they cannot be allowed to write a bad or even mediocre book." It is to Vonnegut's credit that he did not let writing a bad or even mediocre book keep him from writing about the most important ideas that came to his mind.

◆ TOPICS FOR DISCUSSION ◆

1. What is equality? Can you come up with various definitions?

2. Reread the moment of the transcendent kiss between Harrison and the dancer. What would this scene be like from the viewpoint of one of the musicians? How would he or she react to the sudden arrival of the Handicapper General?

Rewrite this scene from the musician's viewpoint, including emotional reactions for the characters as well as their physical actions.

3. Describe a beautiful human being. Can you come up with various definitions?

4. How do the Handicapper General and her agents "equalize" citizens?

5. Are there any positive results to the Equality Laws they enforce?

6. What is a transcendent experience? What effect does one person's transcendent experience have on others?

7. What sort of leader do the people of 2081 need?

8. What sort of leader does Harrison Bergeron set himself up to be?

9. As the Handicapper General is an appointed figure, not an elected one, she does not need to worry about being re-elected. What does she have to fear instead?

10. What sort of justice is the Handicapper General dealing out in the America of 2081?

◆ IDEAS FOR REPORTS AND PAPERS ◆

1. What is "equality" as defined by the American Bill of Rights? By the civil rights movement during the 1960s in America? How do these definitions compare to the Equality Laws in this story, and how they are enforced by the Handicapper General?

2. How can an individual's superior talents and strengths be of benefit to her or his family, neighbors, and fellow citizens? How can superior talents and strengths be a negative experience for an individual, or a community, rather than a benefit?

3. Compare the story "Harrison Bergeron" to a short story by Stephen King, perhaps "The Raft." Both authors are American, male, white, and attended college. What distinct differences and similarities can you detect in these two stories? How do the authors' writing styles differ? What can you say about the characters each author creates? How would Stephen King have written the story "Harrison Bergeron"?

4. Draw pictures of each of the major characters in "Harrison Bergeron", and include with each a series of notes describing what elements you took from the story and what elements you decided from your own impressions of the characters. Will you use television and movie actors as your models, or people around you?

5. What is the difference between the words "alike" and "equal"?

6. How useful is this fantasy story when considering real events and motivations? Is this story a good tool for beginning a dialogue on equality and civil rights? Find a relevant article in a newspaper or magazine and explain how it relates to the situation in "Harrison Bergeron."

7. How useful is this story for a beginning author to read? Annotate this story as you would for a writer's workshop, pointing out areas where you would revise characterization or suggesting ways to rephrase sentences which tell the reader what to know rather than showing the reader something to think about.

8. What systems of handicapping are used in sports such as golf and horse racing? Are these handicaps effective? How are they regarded by the people participat-

ing in these sports? What is the long-term effect?

9. What systems of handicapping are used in employment programs or government granting programs? Are these handicaps effective? How are they regarded by the people participating in these programs, or wishing to participate? How valid are any complaints?

◆ RELATED TITLES/ADAPTATIONS ◆

The short story "Harrison Bergeron" was adapted for video by Showtime and released on video in 1995. The production starred Sean Astin and Christopher Plummer. The director, Bruce Pittman, was nominated for Canada's Gemini award for "Best Direction in a Dramatic Program or Mini-Series." Readers might wish to examine other short stories from *Welcome to the Monkey House,* the collection in which "Harrison Bergeron" was republished.

◆ FOR FURTHER REFERENCE ◆

Abel, David. "Vonnegut Redux: Lost Man on Campus." Reprinted in *Edmonton Journal* (June 3, 2001): E13. An interview with Vonnegut and several English professors and students from Smith College, showing that Vonnegut is writing again and continuing to spread his satirical viewpoint on life and literature. This insightful article includes several excellent quotes from Vonnegut and his associates.

Alvarez, Joseph. Entry on "Harrison Bergeron." In *Exploring Short Stories.* Detroit: Gale, 1998. A critical commentary on the story, with useful character summaries, discussing "Harrison Bergeron" in light of Vonnegut's own beliefs about conditions in American society.

Festa, Conrad. "Vonnegut's Satire." In *Vonnegut in America: An Introduction to the Life and Work of Kurt Vonnegut.* Edited by Jerome Klinkowitz and Donald L. Lawler. New York: Delacorte Press, 1977. An essay on how Vonnegut's use of satire as it changes over time.

Klinkowitz, Jerome. *Kurt Vonnegut.* London: Methuen, 1982. An analysis of Vonnegut as a contemporary writer, largely through the discussion of his major novels. A readable, light biography as well as literary analysis. This book is highly-recommended to young adult readers trying to understand Vonnegut's motives as well as his fiction.

Mowery, Carl. Overview of "Harrison Bergeron." In Overview of *Exploring Short Stories.* Detroit: Gale Research, 1998. A discussion of the ways Vonnegut uses satire to attack the idea of forced equality.

Vonnegut, Kurt, Jr. *Fates Worse Than Death: An Autobiographical Collage of the 1980s.* New York: Delacorte, 1990.

Vonnegut, Kurt, Jr. *Timequake.* New York: Delacorte, 1997. A rewrite of a "Kilgore Trout" novel manuscript, with abundant self-referential essay material, some of which is worked over as "creative non-fiction" and some of which is identified as speculation on an imaginary future, five years after the novel's publication. Of interest mostly to Vonnegut fans.

Vonnegut, Kurt, Jr. *Wampeters, Foma and Granfalloons.* New York: Delacorte, 1981. An essay collection which ought to be on high-school reading lists throughout the West. A discussion-provoking work, *Wampeters, Foma and Granfalloons* features Vonnegut's plainspoken ideas.

Wood, Karen and Charles Wood. *The*

Vonnegut Statement. New York: Dell Publishing, 1973. A scholarly literary discussion of Vonnegut and his writings, with more attention to formal prose and literary structure than the subject ever indulged in himself.

Paula Johanson

HARRY POTTER AND THE GOBLET OF FIRE

Novel

2000

Author: J. K. Rowling

◆

Major Books for Young Adults

Harry Potter and the Sorcerer's Stone
  (Book 1), 1998
Harry Potter and the Chamber of Secrets
  (Book 2), 1999
Harry Potter and the Prisoner of Azkaban
  (Book 3), 1999

Harry Potter and the Goblet of Fire
  (Book 4), 2000
Harry Potter Schoolbooks: Quidditch
  Through the Ages, 2001
Harry Potter Schoolbooks: Fantastic
  Beasts and Where to Find Them, 2001

◆ ABOUT THE AUTHOR ◆

Joanne Kathleen Rowling was born on July 31, 1965, in Gloucestershire, England. The daughter of Peter and Anne Rowling, an engineer and laboratory technician, she developed her interest in literature and writing during her childhood in rural southwestern England. In addition to her parents buying books, mostly British children's classics, and reading aloud to Joanne and her sister Diana, Rowling created fantasy tales about rabbits, one of her favorite animals, to amuse her sister. Rowling enjoyed roaming the countryside near her home, viewing historical sites and castles that sparked her imagination. She also played with neighbor children named the Potters. Their games often involved fantastical elements such as pretending to be wizards and witches much like Rowling's fictional protagonist and his friends.

◆ OVERVIEW ◆

Harry Potter and the Goblet of Fire is J. K. Rowling's fourth Harry Potter book in what is expected to be a series of seven. Like the books before it (*Harry Potter and the Sorcerer's Stone, Harry Potter and the Chamber of Secrets,* and *Harry Potter and the Prisoner of Azkaban*), *Harry Potter and the Goblet of Fire* opens during Harry's summer vacation from school. After the first few chapters, the reader returns to Hogwarts School of Witchcraft and Wizardry with Harry and his two best friends, Ron Weasley and Hermione Granger. It is at Hogwarts that the main action of the novel takes place. *Harry Potter* and the *Goblet of Fire* describes Harry's, Ron's, and Hermione's fourth year at Hogwarts, and by now we are not surprised to find it framed by the end of summer at the beginning of the novel and by the beginning of summer at the end of the novel. It is also not a surprise that, despite these frames, the bulk of the novel is devoted almost entirely to an academic setting.

And yet, there is a disappointment that familiarity can sometimes bring to readers desirous of new material and technique. Indeed, of Rowling's *Harry Potter and the Goblet of Fire,* noted horror novelist Stephen King writes: "[We] may be a little tired of discovering Harry at home with his horrible aunt and uncle (plus his even more horrible cousin, Dudley, whose favorite PlayStation game is Mega-Mutilation Part 3), but once Harry has attended the obligatory Quidditch match and returned to Hogwarts, the tale picks up speed." While King has a point regarding the redundancy of the novel's frames, he is right in suggesting that "the tale picks up speed," for Rowling cannot be described as lacking in innovation(however loyal she is to the traditions of the fantasy genre). In *Harry Potter and the Goblet of Fire,* Rowling borrows the innovation of human development to keep her work strong. Earlier Harry Potter books use the Muggle (nonmagic) world as a backdrop for the magical world and a springboard for understanding and evaluating Hogwarts as a fantastic, parallel sociopolitical system. But this measure is no longer sufficient. Like the child-hero Harry (now 14 years old), the reader of J. K. Rowling's series craves to know more about the larger adult world that Harry will soon be entering.

For both protagonist and audience, and in keeping with classic British fantasy for young adults (especially the fantasy of C. S. Lewis), this larger world is the world of civil service and old school ties. It is the world of the Ministry of Magic and of adult characters more steeped in the recent history of the magic world—and all the policies, preferences, and politics that adult worlds involve. Happily, Rowling does not skimp on her description of the adult world, nor does she undermine the playful humor offset by wisdom with which she shapes the Harry Potter books. Wisely, rather than forcing Harry and the reader to enter into and successfully negotiate the adult magic world, as soon as the academic year begins, Rowling brings the adult magic world to Hogwarts, to Harry, and to us via the Triwizard Tournament. As Headmaster Albus Dumbledore explains:

> The Triwizard Tournament was first established some seven hundred years ago as a friendly competition between the three largest European schools of Wizardry: Hogwarts, Beauxbatons, and Durmstrang. A champion was selected to represent each school, and the three champions competed in three magical tasks. . . . There have been several attempts over the centuries to reinstate the tournament . . . none of which has been very successful. However, our own departments of International Magic Cooperation and Magical Games and Sports have decided the time is ripe for another attempt.

With the Triwizard Tournament comes the adult magic world (yet another challenge for Harry, who, despite being underage, is chosen as a competitor), the usual adjustments of a 14-year-old boy (namely friendship, romance, and puberty), and the political intrigues and devastating gravity surrounding the evil Lord Voldemort's use of the Triwizard Tournament to "rebirth" himself.

◆ SETTING ◆

Before readers of J. K. Rowling's *Harry Potter and the Goblet of Fire* return to the familiar setting of Hogwarts School of Witchcraft and Wizardry, they are first given a glimpse of the gray areas to which the fourth Harry Potter book expands: the boundary worlds that span the nonmagic Muggle world and the magic world. True to her talent for providing examples and provoking comparative thinking by describing the parallels between the Muggle and the magic, Rowling shows us both of these boundary worlds in the first ten chapters (158 pages) of her mammoth 37-chapter (734-page) novel.

Harry Potter and the Goblet of Fire opens in the village of Little Hangleton—a conservative Muggle town in rural England. We learn that the infamous villain of the Harry Potter books, Lord Voldemort ("He Who Shall Not Be Named"), is hiding out, regaining strength, and planning his return to power. Rowling distances her readers from this active threat by describing it as a dream: "Harry lay flat on his back, breathing hard as though he had been running. He had awoken from a vivid dream with his hands pressed over his face. The old scar on his forehead, which was shaped like a bolt of lightning, was burning beneath his fingers as though someone had just pressed a white-hot wire to his skin." But readers well acquainted with Rowling's series know that Harry Potter's burning scar is no dreamy matter—it hurts when Voldemort is nearby or feeling particularly hateful towards Harry. The threat is real and the distance between our hero and the villain is not so great as we would like to believe. In the meantime, the reader must expect that Voldemort's appearance in the Muggle world is a matter of much concern. The well-intentioned witches and wizards (primarily those working in the various departments at the Ministry of Magic) are devoted to making sure that the magic world does not intrude upon, or interfere with, the Muggle world. Rowling describes this from Harry's Muggle-raised,

but magic-informed, perspective in the opening chapters of *Harry Potter and the Goblet of Fire*: the Ministry covers up the (seemingly foolish) claims of inappropriate and dangerous goings-on in the village of Little Hangleton. Here, Rowling's penchant for parallel and oppositional description is exercised. The Ministry cover-up is told from the perspective of Harry, the young initiate, and from the vantage point of a new setting, the Quidditch World Cup, in chapters 2–9 of Rowling's text.

Chapters 2–9 showcase J. K. Rowling's gift for ingenious, imaginative detail, allowing her to describe once again the magic world that delights both her youngest and her oldest readers. Harry and his good friend Hermione Granger (Muggle-born and -raised), and their magic-born friend Ron Weasley (along with the Weasley family), use a portkey to travel to the Quidditch World Cup—an amusing parallel to World Cup Soccer. The Cup matches are held on a deserted moor ("it's very difficult for a large number of wizards to congregate without attracting Muggle attention"). Their portkey ("unobtrusive things . . . [that] Muggles . . . just think is litter," and one of "two hundred portkeys placed at strategic points around Britain") is a "moldy-looking old boot" located at the top of Stoatshead Hill. While on Stoatshead Hill, Harry and his friends meet Amos Diggory and his son Cedric, a Hogwarts schoolmate. Once transported to the moor, they are in greater company, and only some of that company is familiar (Ministry friends and colleagues, school chums, famous figures in the magic world).

Able to slip comfortably past the campsite director ("Mr. Roberts's eyes slid out of focus, his brows unknitted, and a look of dreamy unconcern fell over his face. Harry recognized the symptoms of one who had just had his memory modified"), Harry, Hermione, and the Weasley family set up camp. Their camping accommodations look rather cramped and apparently substandard, but are appropriate because they do not call attention to the party. However, in the world as Rowling describes it, things are not always as they initially appear: "Harry bent down, ducked under the tent flap, and felt his jaw drop. He had walked into what looked like an old-fashioned, three-room flat, complete with bathroom and kitchen." Other wizards shun the need for a low profile so close to Muggle territory and travel to the Quidditch World Cup with ostentation—and sometimes with a misinformed sense of style:

> [Right] behind a pair of men . . . were having a heated argument. One of them was a very old wizard who was wearing a long flowery nightgown. The other was clearly a Ministry wizard; he was holding out a pair of pinstriped trousers and almost crying with exasperation . . . .
>
> "You can't walk around like that, the Muggle at the gate's already getting suspicious—"
>
> "I bought this in a Muggle shop, said the old wizard stubbornly. Muggles wear them."
>
> "Muggle *women* wear them, Archie, not the men, they wear *these*. . . . "
>
> "I'm not putting them on, said old Archie in indignation. I like a nice healthy breeze 'round my privates, thanks."

While the beauties of Rowling's setting lie in a landscape of rich and thorough imagination, their literary effectiveness is the result of Rowling's ability to translate the setting via characterization—particularly via such characters as Harry and Hermione. Rather than "discovering" the world (as the characters of Lewis Carroll's and C. S. Lewis' fantasies often do—which then involves most of the plot), or having to explain and describe the fantastic setting for us (as is often the case in the novels of J. R. R. Tolkien), Harry's and Hermione's translations allow the reader to see the magic world as fresh and new, and as quickly and effectively as possible. Like the novels of T. H. White, Rowling's works invite the reader into a fantastic landscape that refuses to compromise the intricacies of the plot—and this natural and charming development and inclusion of sophisticated matter is always a boon in young adult literature.

This translative characterization is a facet of the Harry Potter books from the first (*Harry Potter and the Sorcerer's Stone*), in which it is used to fully describe Hogwarts School of Witchcraft and Wizardry. But here, in Book 4, Hogwarts remains the primary setting and is the familiar landscape to which we return following the Quidditch World Cup and the disturbing events that take place there. The Hogwarts School of Witchcraft and Wizardry is a traditional English boarding school located in the fairy-green countryside well beyond London. The meddlesome caretaker, Mr. Filch, and his cat, Mrs. Norris, carefully monitor the building, and the grounds are kept well by the beloved Keeper of Keys and Grounds (and Hogwarts dropout) Rubeus Hagrid. During the long-standing tradition of the Sorting Ceremony, first-year Hogwarts students are separated into four houses (Gryffindor, Hufflepuff, Ravenclaw, and Slytherin), each with its own proud history, alumni, and secret traditions. The faculty, respected scholars and authority figures, are removed from the emotional and interpersonal experiences of their students; the curriculum is carefully structured and deliberately traditional; classes are taken by year and with students from other houses. Residents of each house have points given and taken away for academic achievement, behavior and deportation, and athletic competition, and the points accumulate toward the goal of winning the much-coveted house cup at the end-of-year feast.

Hogwarts is a world all its own; a non-Muggle world. Students arrive by a train taken from platform nine and three-quarters at King's Cross Station. During the journey they snack on candies and amuse themselves by trading cards of famous witches and wizards from packages of Chocolate Frogs. The campus is located inside a moat and the building is a castle. The house dormitories are in the four round towers located at the corners of the building and accessed by secret passwords that open portrait holes. The Sorting Ceremony stars a Sorting Cap that reads the new students' minds before assigning them to the appropriate house. The access portraits to the houses have a frustrating tendency to visit other paintings in the castle, thereby foiling the stealthy return of many an erring student, who also find that Filch and Mrs. Norris are not the only "caretakers" to avoid. Peeves the Poltergeist will insist on reporting students out of bed after hours, and the other ghosts (Nearly Headless Nick and the Bloody Baron among them) have loyalties to certain houses. The faculty members also have allegiances—as well as curious (possible threatening) involvement with the adult, magic world. Coursework is difficult and requires much study. The sport of choice is Quidditch, a fast-paced game loosely resembling polo, played on flying brooms.

The setting of Hogwarts School of Witchcraft and Wizardry in the Harry Potter books is a setting at once comfortingly traditional and offbeat. Rowling also masterfully uses duality in her descriptions of the apprentice magic world of the Hogwarts students as compared to the adult magic world for which they are preparing, or the whole of the magic world as compared to the Muggle world. To the reader, things seem to be somewhat familiar, but given a brilliant twist that makes them totally different from the norm. Accepted Hogwarts students walk through a wall in order to reach platform nine and three-quarters at King's Cross Station. Tapping a brick behind the Leaky

Cauldron pub three times with your magic wand will open it to Diagon Alley, the shopping center of the magic world. Diagon Alley is also the only place "in" London where prospective students can get everything they need—from the uniform to course books and other equipment. The Ministry of Magic works to ensure that Muggles remain ignorant of the actuality of the magic world. And the commonplace systems of the Muggle world amaze and confound witches and wizards. The layering of experiences and perspectives in Rowling's text work to keep the reader both grounded and aware. As such, the reader enjoys a setting that has been wonderfully and completely imagined, described, and realized by J. K. Rowling in the Harry Potter books.

◆ THEMES AND CHARACTERS ◆

As the characters mature throughout J. K. Rowling's Harry Potter books, they become more savvy and more aware of the very complex and political nature of their world. This savvy awareness, as we might expect, results in a development and complication of theme. Thus, Book 1, *Harry Potter and the Sorcerer's Stone,* we move between the two fixed points of Privet Drive in the Muggle world and Hogwarts School of Witchcraft and Wizardry in the magic world. The parallel and doubling becomes more demonstrative of the Muggle world and more descriptive of the magic world in Book 2, *Harry Potter and the Chamber of Secrets,* and Book 3, *Harry Potter and the Prisoner of Azkaban,* and is ultimately expanded to the many levels of intrigue and circumstance in Book 4, *Harry Potter and the Goblet of Fire.* As a result, though *Harry Potter and the Goblet of Fire* is very much a novel about loyalty, the idea of loyalty is necessarily complicated. Loyalties, and likewise allegiances, while desired, are slippery, suspect, and unsure in this novel.

Most of the magic world, it seems, is divided into two groups: the good (generally, but not technically, lead by Professor Albus Dumbledore, Headmaster of Hogwarts) and the evil (under the control and influence of Lord Voldemort). For those readers familiar with the Harry Potter books, this is old territory, and it furthermore involves a longtime grudge between Voldemort and his child-nemesis, Harry Potter. Loyal readers of the series have witnessed the escalation of this grudge, but its history—even that predating the Harry Potter books—is thoughtfully outlined towards the beginning of each novel.

The story goes: Lord Voldemort's once-healthy regime brutalized the magic world and victimized many innocents (magic and Muggle alike). Voldemort personally murdered Harry's parents, leaving Harry an orphan, but he was unable to kill Harry— even as an infant. The first three Harry Potter books describe Lord Voldemort's continuing return to power and Harry's uncanny ability to thwart his evil. At the end of Book 4, *Harry Potter and the Goblet of Fire*, however, Voldemort's return to power is unfortunately realized. Lord Voldemort's "subjects" return to Lord Voldemort's service once they see the Dark Mark, which is released at the Quidditch World Cup and appears on their forearms. There is a great disturbance as the Ministry of Magic is thwarted with back talk and befuddlement— no one knows whose allegiance lies where and every action is a threat (for every action might indicate a return to, and strengthening of, Lord Voldemort's evil regime). Book 4, *Harry Potter and the Goblet of Fire*, is very much a novel about good, evil, and loyalty, and we are given to understand that, however black-hearted, abused, or bewitched, evil, too, has its loyal members. Some of Voldemort's loyal supporters are not a sur-

prise such as Wormtail and Lucius Malfoy, but most of Voldemort's supporters are characters new to the series: Igor Karkaroff, the Headmaster of Durmstrang; Ludovic "Ludo" Bagman, the Ministry's Head of Magical Games and Sports; and Bartemious Crouch, Jr., the presumed-dead son of the Head of the Department of International Magic Cooperation.

Loyal, too, are those who have fought with Professor Dumbledore against the evil Lord Voldemort: Inerva McGonagle, a faculty member at Hogwarts, and Sirius Black, Harry's godfather (currently on the run due to Wormtail's escape in Book 3). But most realistically unsettling are those characters whose loyalties are not readily apparent (like Severus Snape, the Potions master who is believed to have switched allegiances from evil to good, and Mad-Eye Moody, who helps Harry throughout the Triwizard Tournament) as well as those characters who, though not evil, have questionable agendas that create serious obstacles for good (Rita Skeeter, the gossip columnist for *The Daily Prophet*, and Cornelius Fudge, the Minister of Magic who functions in an abject state of denial).

Our protagonist, Harry Potter, and his two best friends, Ron Weasley and Hermione Granger, are asked to negotiate this increasingly complicated sociopolitical world and, likewise, to establish their own parallel loyalties. Suffering from jealousy over Harry's fame and recognition, Ron stops speaking to him. Relentlessly, Hermione encourages Harry and Ron to make up, though her encouragement does not effect change. It is only when Harry faces the dangers of the first task in the Triwizard Tournament (stealing from a dragon's nest) that Ron becomes convinced that Harry needs—and deserves— his friendship. Other tests of loyalty, allegiance, and friendship are less dire but still significant: Hermione, tired of not being recognized and appreciated as a young

Harry Potter and the Goblet of Fire

woman, accepts Viktor Krum's invitation to the Hogwarts formal ball despite mutual romantic feelings between her and Ron. Harry holds a grudge against the other Hogwarts champion, Cedric Diggory, when Cedric successfully woos Harry's love interest, Cho Chang.

To their credit, however, and in keeping with the spirited wisdom of J.K. Rowling's books, these young characters are quick to put aside petty conflicts in an ongoing effort to support that which is good—whether in the interest of friendship (as do Harry and Ron and Ron and Hermione) or to benefit their beloved Hogwarts (as do Harry and Cedric). And it should be noted that putting aside his own glory for that of Hogwarts is Cedric's last living act, which makes it all the more significant, appropriate, and profound.

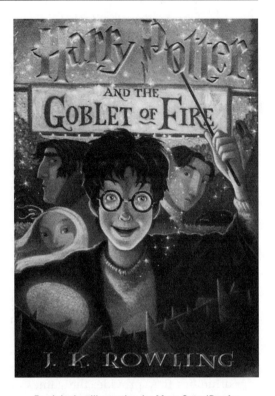

Book jacket illustration by Mary GrandPre for *Harry Potter and the Goblet of Fire* by J. K. Rowling.

◆ LITERARY QUALITIES ◆

There are seven (planned) books in the Harry Potter series, and this allows us to consider the fourth book, *Harry Potter and the Goblet of Fire,* as a halfway point—a benchmark in the series. As such, it is compelling that *Harry Potter and the Goblet of Fire* closes with a chapter entitled "The Beginning." Since the novel describes the evil Lord Voldemort's return to human form, his regaining of full magical powers, and his reentry into the magic world as a "rebirth," the reader is left to assume that—now that good and evil seem unfortunately well balanced—the real action of the series is about to start. Once again, Rowling draws parallels: now that evil has the strength of good, the battle may begin. Thus, the end chapter of *Harry Potter and the Goblet of Fire* is the series' halfway point. It marks the start of the battle between good and evil that characterizes fantastic fiction and sig-

nals the beginning of the hero's coming-of-age that classifies young adult literature. But the use of traditional themes refuses to undermine the innovation with which we credit J. K. Rowling. Book 4 defines itself in accordance with, and in opposition to, classic British fantasy for the young adult (Lewis Carroll's Alice books, C. S. Lewis' Narnia chronicles, J. R. R. Tolkien's *Hobbit* and *Lord of the Rings,* T. H. White's *The Once and Future King*).

If closing her fourth book with "The Beginning" allows J. K. Rowling to distance herself and her art from the pressures of canonical fantasy as literary precedent, it also enables her to describe the first three Harry Potter books as precedent for the fourth. Therefore, we may evaluate classic young adult fantasy (especially British fantasy) as the precedent for Book 1, but we must evaluate Books 1, 2 and 3 as the precedent for Book 4. The first half of Rowling's series is the precedent for the second half of the series.

The familiar motifs of a railway journey, a reflective device, games of logic, and an academic setting with familiar fantastic characterization in *Harry Potter and the Sorcerer's Stone* draws on such masters as Lewis Carroll, C. S. Lewis, J. R. R. Tolkien, and T. H. White. These very categories are then broadened and individualized in the subsequent Harry Potter books (*Harry Potter and the Chamber of Secrets* and *Harry Potter and the Prisoner of Azkaban*). In *Harry Potter and the Goblet of Fire*, the railway journey to and from Hogwarts School of Witchcraft and Wizardry has become a standard motif in fantastic literature as well as in Rowling's series; the reflective device has been expanded to ghost images and the reflexive opportunities they provide; the games of logic have been multiplied—and given greater mythic roots—as characters battle dragons, fight off sea creatures, and run a maze in the Triwizard Tournament.

If we are to understand the end of *Harry Potter and the Goblet of Fire* as "The Beginning" of the rest of the series, we might predict that the Harry Potter books will feature increasingly more sophisticated struggles between good and evil, and that they will draw on the motifs of classical (and not just classic) literature—both traditionally seen as appropriate for young adults.

◆ SOCIAL SENSITIVITY ◆

In the past, such eminent critics as Jack Zipes have criticized J.K. Rowling for a perceived lack of political correctness (which is often inappropriately confused with social sensitivity). The argument stands that quality art should not be judged according to its perceived level of political correctness—not even when the literary art has been created for a young adult audience. This consideration is complicated by the defense that Rowling's use of both tradition and innovation is within the "safe" remove of a fantasy setting. But that argument must necessarily be placed alongside the critical notion that young adults form opinions and expectations of their world based, in part, on their reading material and that, therefore, they do not gain the positive socialization from fantastic literature that they do from realism. It must be noted, however, that in fantasy—as in Rowling's Harry Potter books—it is the parallels that inform the reader, and the parallels are no less powerful than the bald truths that realism offers. Indeed, for many readers, and especially for nonlinear thinkers, fantastic parallels can provide a more accurate reflection of how they process their world.

It is a phenomenon of popularity that writers exposed to such arguments and defenses on their behalf might betray the strain of that exposure in their art, and J. K. Rowling seems no more impervious to this phenomenon than any writer. To her credit, however, Rowling shares her strain with us in her usual, tongue-in-cheek and self-aware manner. Within the pages of *Harry Potter and the Goblet of Fire*, Rowling pokes some fun at her critics on behalf of her supporters—thereby raising her above exposure to the debates regarding her art that threaten to undermine the quality of that art. While discussing Hermione's attempt to release the tea cozy-wearing house elves from bondage and to ensure their equal rights and payment, the young protagonists sympathize with Dobby the house elf and discover that (contrary to Ron's brother Percy) they would rather work for an honest person with a sense of humor than an earnest person without one:

"I'd still rather work for him than old Crouch", said Ron. "At least Bagman's got a sense of humor."

"Don't let Percy hear you saying that," Hermione said, smiling slightly.

"Yeah, well, Percy wouldn't want to work for anyone with a sense of humor, would he? . . . . Percy wouldn't recognize a joke if it danced naked in front of him wearing Dobby's tea cozy".

While it is clear that J. K. Rowling has a sense of humor (specifically here, a sense of humor about the criticism leveled at her work), it is also clear that she is listening to her critics. This has its benefits as well as its drawbacks. For example, Hermione raises a consciousness regarding the treatment of lower and indentured economic classes (especially those categorized by race), and Rowling does an impressive job of describing the complicated psychology of the abused subordinate. But the discerning reader will note that the liberation of house elves is dropped from the plot of the novel once it is no longer useful in classifying the good characters from the evil. As a result, its potential social effect is significantly weakened.

Likewise, the same may be said of other race-related prejudices in the novel, such as Harry's interracial romantic feelings for his classmate Cho Chang (which is lighthearted, unstated, but also unrequited). In a similar vein, Hagrid and Madam Maxim attempt to hide their interracial parentage but, although ogres are feared, despised and ostracized by the magic world, Hagrid and Maxim only suffer mere—and fleeting—ribbing from the gossip columnist Rita Skeeter. Thus, though Rowling's treatment of more socially sensitive aspects of the (parallel) magic world describes her politics, responds to her critics, and amuses her supporters, the textual dismissal of these aspects calls into question whether that treatment is a political gesture or a literary com-

mitment. But neither the political gesture nor the literary commitment is a requirement for quality art and Rowling herself has a magic for parallelism and doubling. So, it seems our consideration of social sensitivity in *Harry Potter and the Goblet of Fire* must be satisfied by the introduction of these aspects and the assumption that they will continue to shape, and to take shape in, subsequent Harry Potter books. Let it be a lesson in Transfiguration.

◆ TOPICS FOR DISCUSSION ◆

1. Who do *you* think won the Triwizard Tournament? Harry? Credric? Both? Neither? Why?

2. If the other two champions, Fleur Delacouer and Viktor Krum, were students at Hogwarts, to which house would they belong (Gryffindor, Hufflepuff, Ravenclaw, Slytherin)? Why?

3. In every one of the Harry Potter books, J. K. Rowling introduces us to interesting magical objects. In *Harry Potter and the Goblet of Fire,* one such object is the Pensieve. If you could "forget" (at least temporarily!) any one of your memories by putting it in a pensieve, which one memory would it be and why?

4. In *Harry Potter and the Goblet of Fire,* some house elves, like Dobby, want to be free; other house elves, like Winky, do not want to be free. How might Hermione help Dobby without hurting Winky? What more should—or could—be done? What should be less emphasized? What might Hermione do instead?

5. To date, four of the seven Harry Potter books have been written and/or published. Can you predict what might happen in the next three books that

have not been written? Are there any clues in *Harry Potter and the Goblet of Fire*?

◆ IDEAS FOR REPORTS AND PAPERS ◆

1. The Harry Potter books are set in England, but the author, J. K. Rowling, lives in Scotland. What has the relationship between England and Scotland been throughout history?

2. The Quidditch World Cup tournament resembles the World Cup tournament in soccer. Research the (soccer) World Cup and explain it in your report.

3. Research the idea of school tournaments. Does your school have one? Why or why not? Which schools do have one and how do they resemble the Triwizard Tournament in *Harry Potter and the Goblet of Fire*?

4. Hogwarts students take the train to school from London. Research the London Underground and the British railway system (especially King's Cross railway station). Which came first, the Underground or the railway? What is the connection between the Underground and the railway? What routes do they follow? Can you find any maps and timetables using the Internet?

5. J. K. Rowling had been a school teacher and was a single mother when she started writing the first Harry Potter book, *Harry Potter and the Sorcerer's Stone*. Research the author in order to find out more about her. What kinds of insights has she given in interviews? Are there any parallels between the author's life and her books?

6. So far, there are four Harry Potter books: *Harry Potter and the Sorcerer's* Stone, *Harry Potter and the Chamber of Secrets, Harry Potter and the Prisoner of Azkaban,* and *Harry Potter and the Goblet of Fire.* Read one (or more!) of the Harry Potter books and compare it/them to the latest book, *Harry Potter and the Goblet of Fire.* What has changed? How have characters and story lines changed?

7. The Ministry of Magic functions like the British Ministry. The Ministry is part of the British parliamentary system. Research the governmental systems of Britain (the Ministry and Parliament) and compare and contrast them to the Ministry of Magic in the Harry Potter books. Just how similar (and/or different) are they?

◆ FOR FURTHER REFERENCE ◆

Del Negro, Janice M. *Bulletin of the Center for Children's Books* (October 1999): 68. This review of *Harry Potter and the Prisoner of Azkaban* summarizes the novel's plot and recommends the book because "Rowling's characterizations are succinctly evocative and often slyly funny, ensuring that readers develop a fondness for her players, care what happens to them, and come back for more."

Hainer, Cathy. "Third Time's Another Charmer for 'Harry Potter.'" *USA Today,* (September 8, 1999): 1-D. Positive review of *Harry Potter and the Prisoner of Azkaban* which "scores another home run." Provides hints about plot twists.

Maughan, Shannon. "The Harry Potter Halo." *Publishers Weekly* (July 19, 1999): 92–94. Comments on how the Harry Potter novels have encouraged young readers to purchase other hardback editions of children's literature and increased library patronage. Discusses the cultural phenomenon of Harry Potter and the saga's impact on literacy and bookselling prior to the release of *Harry Potter and the Prisoner of Azkaban* in the United States.

Lists recommended novels similar to the Harry Potter books.

Mitnick, Eva. *School Library Journal* (October 1999): 128. This review of *Harry Potter and the Prisoner of Azkaban* praises the novel, stating "Isn't it reassuring that some things just get better and better? Harry is back and in fine form in the third installment of his adventures at Hogwarts School of Witchcraft and Wizardry." This reviewer admires the complexities of Rowling's plot and "non-stop" pacing and "stunning climax," concluding that "This is a fabulously entertaining read that will have Harry Potter fans cheering for more."

Parravano, Martha V. *Horn Book* (November–December 1999): 744–745. Recommends *Harry Potter and the Prisoner of Azkaban* because "all the elements that make the formula work are heightened." Notes the cultural impact of the Harry Potter saga, suggesting that "All current reviews of Harry Potter books should probably be addressed to some future audience for whom Harry is book rather than phenomenon; at the moment, reviews seem superfluous." Parravano also states "For the record, then, O future reader, this latest installment in Harry's saga is quite a good book."

Publishers Weekly (July 19, 1999): 195. This review of *Harry Potter and the Prisoner of Azkaban* asserts "Rowling proves that she has plenty of tricks left up her sleeve in this third Harry Potter adventure" because of the "genius of Rowling's plotting. Seemingly minor details established in Books 1 and 2 unfold to take on unforeseen significance, and the finale, while not airtight in its internal logic, is utterly thrilling." Concludes that "Rowling's wit never flags" and the "Potter spell is holding strong."

Schafer, Elizabeth D. *Beacham's Sourcebooks for Teaching Young Adult Fiction: Exploring Harry Potter.* Osprey: Beacham Publishing, 2000. A comprehensive, interdisciplinary analysis of the Harry Potter books which elaborates about literary components of the series. Includes a detailed chapter development analysis and discussion questions and suggested activities and projects for *Harry Potter and the Prisoner of Azkaban.* Provides citations for diverse resources, including reviews and websites, about Rowling and the Harry Potter series.

Evelyn Perry

THE HITCHHIKER'S GUIDE TO THE GALAXY

Novel

1980

Author: Douglas Adams

◆

Major Books for Young Adults

◆ ABOUT THE AUTHOR ◆

Douglas Adams was born March 11, 1952, the son of Christopher Douglas, a management consultant, and Jane Donovan, a nurse. Adams was a recipient of an honors degree in English Literature from St. John's College, Cambridge, in 1974. He began his writing career as a scriptwriter for radio and television comedies. For a time, he supported himself with odd jobs ranging from cleaning chicken houses to guarding the royal family of Qatar.

"I was lying drunk in a field in Innsbruck and gazing up at the stars," he says of the inspiration for his most famous story. "It occurred to me that somebody ought to write a hitchhiker's guide to the galaxy." His idea, first conceived as a radio series, was developed for the British Broadcasting Company. The 1978 series gradually won an enthusiastic following. Pan Books approached Adams to novelize his scripts. *The Hitchhiker's Guide to the Galaxy* sold one hundred thousand copies the first month and eventually sold two million copies in England alone. Across the Atlantic Ocean, similar success followed with a radio series on National Public Radio and a television version of the book.

Adams added four books to "The Hitchhiker's Guide to the Galaxy" series: *The Restaurant at the End of the Universe* (1980), *Life, the Universe and Everything,* (1982), *So Long, and Thanks for All the Fish* (1984), and *Mostly Harmless* (1992). Tired of the series, Adams coauthored *Last Chance to See* with zoologist Mark Carwardine in 1990. In a departure from the "Hitchhiker" books, it recounts their journey to see seven endangered species. He also developed a detective series which includes *Dick Gently's Holistic Detective Agency* (1987) and *The Long Dark Tea-Time of the Soul* (1988).

◆ OVERVIEW ◆

Moments before the earth is demolished to make way for a "hyperspacial express route," Arthur Dent is rescued by Ford Prefect, an alien who is disguised as an out-of-work actor. Prefect, who has become Dent's friend of several years, has been stranded on Earth while researching the planet for the revised version of the electronic book, *The Hitchhiker's Guide to the Galaxy*. The pair's misadventures as they ricochet from a Vogon spaceship, to the *Heart of Gold* state-of-the-art spaceship, to the planet factory, Magrathea, form the book's prime focus: satire.

◆ SETTING ◆

Though initially set in England, the majority of the story takes place in space, either in spaceships or on the planet Magrathea. With Adams creating his own worlds, cultures, creatures, and vocabularies, his satire fillets science fiction clichés and the human condition.

Dent and Prefect find themselves in two ships very unlike the usual spare and futuristic spaceship of science fiction genre. Just as the earth is vaporized, they use a "transformational beam" to board the spaceship of a Prostetnic Vogon Jeltz. In the ship's galley, Dent first sees dirty dishes and dirty alien underwear scattered about. Sitting on mattresses that have been grown and dried from the Sqornshellous Zeta swamps, Dent is not comforted by Prefect's reassurance that "very few have ever come to life again."

The *Heart of Gold* is the second ship to pick up the pair. In Adams's world, this ultimate space-age transportation is shaped like a running shoe and has its own sales brochure. Giving it an Improbability Drive, which powers the ship through every point in the universe, Adams creates scenes within the ship which combine elements of an Andy Warhol painting with Walt Disney's "Fantasia."

Finding Magrathea had been a high priority of many previous space explorations. When the characters accidently discover it, Prefect ranks its drab and desolate exterior somewhere below "cat litter." They learn its interior is three million miles across and that Magrathea's inhabitants used to make planets inside it.

The Hitchhiker's Guide to the Galaxy includes five characters: Arthur Dent, Ford Prefect, Zaphod Beeblebrox, Trillian (Tricia MacMillan), Slartibartfast, and Marvin, the robot. Though all are likable enough, they are one-dimensional creations who merely react to circumstances rather than handle them.

Arthur Dent is hardly the customary space hero. He has no answers, no solutions, and exhibits no bravery. The only thing he actually does is lie down in the mud in front of bulldozers intent on demolishing his home. During crises in space, he curls up in the fetal position, screeches "Huhhhhggggnnnn," falls asleep, or asks for a cup of tea.

Adams has said, "Arthur Dent is to a certain extent autobiographical. He moves from one astonishing event to another without fully comprehending what's going on. He's the Everyman Character—an ordinary person caught up in some extraordinary events."

Zaphod Beeblebox sums Arthur up quite well when other aliens propose to replace Arthur's brain with an electronic one. "You'd just have to program it to say 'What?' and 'I don't understand' and 'Where's the tea?'" he responds.

Arthur's sardonic one-liners in the face of the catastrophe provide much of the humor in *The Hitchhiker's Guide to the Galaxy*. For example, after being told by Ford Prefect that they are safe in a Vogon Constructor Fleet spaceship, Arthur says, "This is obviously some strange usage of the word safe that I wasn't previously aware of."

Ford Prefect accepts Dent for what he is, and the two are good friends. Prefect is a roving researcher for the electronic book, *The Hitchhiker's Guide to the Galaxy*. After being stranded for fifteen years on Earth, he expands its guidebook description from

Douglas Adams

"harmless" to "mostly harmless." He spends his time crashing university parties, drinking, or trying to pick up girls. As Arthur mourns the loss of Earth and its inhabitants, Prefect tries to reassure him by saying, "You just come along with me and have a good time. The Galaxy's a fun place."

Prefect does not get very upset about any kind of peril, including his impending demise in the vacuum of space. As trouble appears, his first defense is to simply talk his way out of it. Ironically, Prefect cannot understand why humans talk so much, but decides if they do not continually exercise their lips, their brains start working. Zaphod Beeblebrox should be, as a space creature with three arms and two heads, a villain. Instead he turns out to be Ford Prefect's semi-cousin, President of the Imperial Galactic Government, and mostly harmless himself. He is an adventurer, but is barely capable of piloting the spaceship he has stolen.

Trillian is an attractive human who Dent once tried to pick up at a party. As Zaphod Beeblebrox's companion, she does little but fiddle with the spaceship's controls and stand behind someone, anyone, during dangerous situations. Her most important contribution in the book is to bring two white mice (actually "hyperintelligent pandimensional beings" who first commissioned the creation of Earth) into the *Heart of Gold* spaceship.

Marvin is a prototype robot. Zaphod Beeblebrox calls him "the Paranoid Android," and Dent labels him "an electronic sulking machine." The first thing he says is, "I think you ought to know I'm feeling very depressed." Marvin is depressed, despairing, hopeless, abject, and wretched throughout the novel. Some reviewers credit him to be a satiric statement against the "me-first generation."

Slartibartfast functions in *The Hitchhiker's Guide to the Galaxy* to give information. An award-winning fjord designer, he fills in missing information for Arthur and the readers. He explains Magrathea's history and explains that space travelers commissioned the creation of the Earth in order to find the Ultimate Question for the Ultimate Answer.

Adams has said, "I'm not a science fiction writer, but a comedy writer who happens to be using the conventions of science fiction for this particular thing." Adams quickly deflates the arrogant notion that Earth and human kind are somehow pivotal to the universe. Earth is so obscure in the largeness of space, its entry in Ford Prefect's *The Hitchhiker's Guide to the Galaxy* is just barely discernible, listed above "Eccentrica Gallumbits, the triple-breasted whore of Eroticon 6."

The computer in science fiction is always in control by virtue of its unerring logic. On the other hand, the *Heart of Gold*'s computer is merely brash and cheery, and completely defenseless in protecting its ship. It can only sing "When You Walk through the Storm" as nuclear warheads approach. It wants a relationship with its programmers, and it possesses a matriarchal back-up personality which cautions Arthur and his companions to stay "all wrapped up snug and warm, and no playing with any naughty bug-eyed monsters."

As a comedy writer, he turns the laugh toward religion, nonviolence, alcohol, dollar-a-day guide books, philosophy, science, and poetry in seeming random fashion.

◆ LITERARY QUALITIES ◆

Adams's satire is not bitter. *The Hitchhiker's Guide to the Galaxy* is mostly about fun—fun with words, fun with genre, fun with television, and fun with human nature.

A great deal of Adams's humor depends on the unexpected. The coveted *Heart of Gold* spaceship is shaped like a running shoe. Nuclear warheads, attacking the space ship, unexpectedly turn into a bowl of petunias and a sperm whale. Adams's satire pokes fun at Scripture as well as the notion that monkeys left with a typewriter will eventually pound out a Shakespeare play.

Adams frequently employs the technique of flashback. As Arthur knows nothing of events in space, filling him in on past events provides the reader with similar information. Adams accomplishes this with a variety of vehicles, including footnotes and narration. Entries in the electronic *Hitchhiker's Guide to the Galaxy* tell Arthur about Magrathea, and Slartibartfast explains the creation of Deep Thought and its mission to arrive at Life's Ultimate Answer.

◆ SOCIAL SENSITIVITY ◆

Adams's satire skewers several sacred icons of society: science, poetry, philosophy, and government. As Dent and Prefect romp through space, the various other characters and events act as vehicles for Adams's social commentary.

His technological wonders include the Sub-Etha Sens-O-Matic, the Paralyso-Matic bomb, the Babel fish translator, and Kill-O-Zap gun. With names sounding like something out of a comic book, they make it impossible to take the technology of his world seriously.

Adams takes to task society's fascination and dependence on computers. The computer on the *Heart of Gold* and on Marvin the robot should solve problems with unwavering, impersonal logic. Instead the spaceship's computer whines and breaks into song. Marvin is emotion on wheels. Two of the funniest sections in the book satirize poets and philosophers. The recitation of the poem "Small Lump of Green Putty I Found in My Armpit One Midsummer Morning" causes members of the audience to die of internal hemorrhaging. One listener survives by gnawing off his own leg. Captured by a Vogon, Arthur and Ford are strapped into Poetry Appreciation chairs, attached to "imagery intensifiers, rhythmic modulators, alliterative residulators and simile dumpers," and then forced to listen to Vogon poetry. Only Adams's view of philosophers and philosophy is more scathing. His philosophers are part of the "Amalgamated Union of Philosophers, Sages, Luminaries and Other Thinking Persons." More concerned with job security than finding meaning to life, they argue for rigidly defined areas of doubt and uncertainty.

Adams points to the governmental ineffectiveness. In his world, the primary function of the President of the Intergalactic Government is to draw attention away from power rather than exercise it. Civil service in Adams's world is manned by clods who are expert only at bludgeoning beautiful creatures to death.

Book cover illustration for *The Hitchhiker's Guide to the Galaxy* by Douglas Adams.

◆ TOPICS FOR DISCUSSION ◆

1. Why does this book continue to be popular, especially among college students and adolescents?

2. Adams's humor has been described as both sophomoric and as brilliant. Decide which term best describes Adams's work and justify your opinion.

3. How effective is Adams's use of the technique of flashback in the novel?

4. What unresolved questions or conflicts in *The Hitchhiker's Guide to the Galaxy* makes probable its sequel?

5. Compare and contrast Adams's portrayal of space alien creatures in *The Hitchhiker's Guide to the Galaxy* to those found in science fiction genre.

6. What science fiction clichés does Adams's satire target?

7. How does Adams sustain his generally upbeat and buoyant tone through the book?

8. What foibles of human nature does Adams take issue with in his book?

9. The space-age technology in *The Hitchhiker's Guide to the Galaxy* may have seemed far-fetched and bizarre in 1980. Which of the inventions that Adams includes have appeared in society two decades later? How do you explain this seemingly prophetic materialization?

10. Some critics find the characters in *The Hitchhiker's Guide to the Galaxy* interesting because of the way they react to challenging circumstances. Discuss each character's response to the attack by Magrathea's missiles.

◆ IDEAS FOR REPORTS AND PAPERS ◆

1. Much of the technology described in *The Hitchhiker's Guide to the Galaxy* as being science fiction is now part of our daily lives. Pick one of these three inventions—digital watches, hydroboats (vehicles which hover above water without touching it), and virtual reality games—and research the development of it.

2. Adams has described his main character, Arthur Dent, as a semi-autobiographical character. Research the real-life accomplishments of Adams and discover the similarities between the author and Arthur.

3. Just about the only action Arthur Dent ever initiates takes place in the first chapter when he lies down in front of the bulldozer. Research at least one person who advocated initiated passive resistance in modern history. Relate the circumstances which inspired it, and discuss the results of the disobedience.

4. Ford Prefect's *The Hitchhiker's Guide to the Galaxy* was published on a "sub meson electronic component." Investigate electronic publishing today, including the contemporary Rocketbook, and the arguments for and against this form of publishing.

5. Carl Sagan was a controversial scientist. Compare his views of the origin of the universe to those given in *The Hitchhiker's Guide to the Galaxy*.

6. For inventing the Infinite Improbability Drive a student scientist is awarded the Galactic Institute's Prize for Extreme Cleverness. Pick a Nobel Prize winner in one of the science or medicine categories. Research what contribution or discovery earned him or her such renown.

7. Marvin is a robot of unique qualities. Compare and contrast his capabilities, personality, and programmed functions to other famous robots such as Robby the Robot of "Lost in Space" television fame, R2D2 and C3PO of the "Star Wars" movies, or Hal in Stanley Kubrick's film *2001: A Space Odyssey*.

8. Investigate references in the Gospels that Adams parodies when Deep Thought announces it is only the second largest computer in the universe.

9. Read selections from the "Monty Python" television scripts and the books of Jonathan Swift and Kurt Vonnegut. Compare and contrast Adams to each of them.

10. Obtain *The Hitchhiker's Guide to the Galaxy* in radio script and/or television script form. Compare and contrast the effectiveness of these forms to the book.

◆ RELATED TITLES/ADAPTATIONS ◆

Adams five books in the "Hitchhiker" series sends his quartet of characters forward and backward in time after *The Hitchhiker's Guide to the Galaxy*. By programing the second largest computer in history to deliberate seven and one-half million years, they learn in *The Hitchhiker's Guide to the Galaxy* that the Ultimate Answer is 42. The problem they pursue through subsequent books is finding the Ultimate Question for the Ultimate Answer. In *The Restaurant at the End of the Universe,* they discover the true reason for Earth's existence. In *Life, the Universe and Everything,* their mission is to save the entire universe from Krikkit white killer robots. *So Long, and Thanks for All the Fish* recounts how Arthur finds true love, while in *Mostly Harmless,* Arthur searches for home and discovers his estranged daughter who herself is searching for the planet of her ancestors.

◆ FOR FURTHER REFERENCE ◆

"Adams, Douglas." In *Contemporary Authors: New Revision Series,* vol. 64. Detroit: Gale, 1998. A biblio-biograpical essay, including summaries of Adams's books with both positive and negative critical remarks.

Adams, Michael. "Douglas (Noel) Adams" In *Dictionary of Literary Biography Yearbook: 1983.* Detroit: Gale, 1984. Michael Adams summarizes both the life and works of Douglas Adams in a mostly positive critique.

Conly, Marc. "Douglas (Noel) Adams Criticism." *Bloomsbury Review* (May–June, 1989): 16–17. Interview with Adams.

Critchton, Jennifer. Review of *The Hitchhiker's Trilogy. Publishers Weekly* (January 14, 1983): 47–50. An in-depth interview with Adams including a publishing history of his book from radio script to trilogy.

"Douglas (Noel) Adams." *Contemporary Literary Criticism,* vol. 27. Detroit: Gale, 1984. After a short biographical sketch, fourteen reviewers critique Adams's books.

Langway, Lynn, Linda R. Prout and Edward Behr "Turn Left at the Nebula." *Newsweek* (November 15, 1982): 119. Adams's life and career is summarized. The reviewers like the "lunatic fringe" of Adams's writing.

Review of *The Hitchhiker's Guide to the Galaxy. New York Times Book Reviews,* (January 25, 1981): 24–25. Adams is praised for writing science fiction that appeals to readers outside the genre enthusiasts.

Vicki Cox

JOSH GIBSON

Biography

1995

Author: John B. Holway

◆

Major Books for Young Adults

Voices from the Great Blackball Leagues, 1975
The Pitcher, (with John Thorn) 1987
Blackball Stars, 1988
Black Diamonds: Life in the Negro Leagues from the Men Who Lived It, 1989
The Sluggers, 1989

Josh and Satch: The Life and Times of Josh Gibson and Satchel Paige, 1991
The Last .400 Hitter: The Anatomy of a .400 Season, 1992
Josh Gibson, 1995
Red Tails, Black Wings: The Men of America's Black Air Force, 1997

◆ ABOUT THE AUTHOR ◆

On November 12, 1929, John B. Holway was born to Edward J., an engineer, and Frances (Rimbach) Holway, in Glen Ridge, New Jersey. He eventually attended the University of Iowa, where he received his bachelor of arts degree in 1950. The following year he joined the United States Army, and while in the service he met his future wife, Motoka Mori, marrying her on October 15, 1954. The couple have four children, two boys and two girls. Holway reached the rank of first lieutenant in the army, but he left the service in 1956, whereupon he took a job with the United States Information Service (USIS). This job pro-

vided him with his primary source of income while he pursued his literary interests.

Holway began by writing about sports, publishing *Japan Is Big League in Thrills* in 1955 and *Sumo* in 1957. He published articles in several magazines such as *Look* and *American Heritage* before beginning to publish the books for which he is best known. His longtime hobby has been the Negro baseball leagues of the days when African Americans were excluded from the National League and the American League. As part of his hobby, he tracked down and interviewed former Negro league ballplayers and thereby amassed an enormous amount of information on the players, coaches, and owners for these teams. He recalls hunting down Satchel Paige and being told by a boy working in the front yard that no one named Satchel Paige lived in the house. A call to Paige's agent and a check for $250 changed the situation, and the next time Holway tracked Paige down the boy answered the door and led him to Paige. Holway's job for the USIS probably provided him with the wherewithal to pay for his expensive research.

The first book to result from Holway's investigations is *Voices from the Great Black Baseball Leagues,* published in 1975, featuring excerpts from interviews of those who played on Negro league teams. Holway also began to uncover many of the details of player biographies and player performances that now form the basis for information in such reference works as *The Baseball Encyclopedia,* edited by Rick Wolff and others. Holway's interest in history as well as baseball led to *Blackball Stars: Negro League Pioneers,* a gathering of articles published in magazines and of new profiles of some of the most famous players from the Negro leagues. This book marks the beginning of a string of historical books that have established Holway as one of the most prominent writers of history for general audiences. Holway's historical research has expanded beyond baseball and has resulted in what may be Holway's most popular title yet, *Red Tails, Black Wings: The Men of America's Black Air Force,* published in 1997.

◆ OVERVIEW ◆

Coretta Scott King's introduction to *Josh Gibson* notes that reading the stories of Gibson and other

> courageous men and women not only helps us discover the principles that we will use to guide our own lives but also teaches us to know the heroes and heroines of our history and to realize that the price we paid in our struggle for equality in America was dear. But we must also under-

stand that we have gotten as far as we have partly because America's democratic system made it possible.

It is asking much to make a star athlete an example of a people's struggle, but Holway narrows the focus to the realm of athletics and uses Gibson to show the state of affairs for African-American athletes during the Great Depression and World War II. Further, Holway emphasizes Gibson's humanity, his weaknesses as well as his strengths. An athlete as talented as Gibson could be made to look like a superman, with his titanic home runs making him seem a man of indomitable physical power, but Holway is honest with his audience, presenting Gibson as a remarkable athlete but a fallible man. Thus *Josh Gibson* is not a story of lifelong triumph but of success on the ball field marred by failure and despair off the field. His obsession with being paid what Babe Ruth was paid, even though he made more money than most people, may have led to the bad habits, anger, and despair that may have contributed to his premature death, just one year before the Cleveland Indians probably would have signed him to a major league contract to be Satchel Paige's catcher.

◆ SETTING ◆

Josh Gibson was born on December 31, 1911, in Buena Vista, Georgia, to sharecroppers Mark and Nancy Gibson. Gibson said that one of the best things his father ever did for him was move his family in 1924 to Pittsburgh, Pennsylvania, because he believed it gave him economic opportunities that he would not have had in the South. He considered his getting a good-paying job in 1927 at a Pittsburgh steel mill, which sponsored an amateur baseball team that he joined, an example of this. In 1929, the Crawford Colored Giants, a well-known black semipro baseball team, invited him to join their club. It was while playing for the Crawfords that he began to build his reputation as a home run hitter. Holway emphasizes the opportunities Gibson had to excel in Pittsburgh, while noting that Gibson lived in a working-class city where times became hard when the Great Depression began.

In spite of the hard times of the Depression, Gibson flourished. The Great Depression had devastated the Negro leagues almost the instant the crisis started, with many fans no longer able to afford a ticket to a ball game. Gibson became an important box office attraction, bringing in fans to see his enormously long home runs, and in 1930 The Homestead Grays of the National Negro League offered him a contract. He is said to have hit a home run to left centerfield and out of Yankee Stadium on September 27. The centerfield wall was about 480 feet from home plate at that time.

Although fellow players remembered him as a big, happy-go-lucky player, he actually suffered in the early years of fame after his wife Helen died just as he began to make a name for himself in the Negro National League. For most of the rest of *Josh Gibson*, Holway focuses on Gibson's on-field heroics and the slugger's movements around the United States and Latin America.

In 1932, he jumped to the Pittsburgh Crawfords of the Negro National League, beginning his pattern of chasing the biggest paycheck. It was his desire to be paid what he thought he was worth that may have most darkened his life as his career progressed. Holway hints that it may have had much to do with Gibson's increasing melancholia and eventual abuse of alcohol and other drugs, especially marijuana and perhaps heroine and cocaine. Major leaguers such as Dizzy Dean, would tell Gibson that he belonged in the major leagues, remarking that if Gibson and Satchel Paige would join the St. Louis Cardinals, which featured pitchers Dizzy himself and brother Daffy Dean, the Cards would win the pennant in July and they could go fishing for the rest of the season. Any efforts by major league ball clubs to sign Gibson during the 1930s were squelched by threats of economic sanctions by other ball clubs and the opposition of the commissioner's office.

Increasing Gibson's anger was the difference in how well he was treated in Latin America as opposed to America. In Mexico, he and other African-American ballplayers were treated like heroes, and their ability to socialize with whites contrasted markedly with how they were treated in segregated American states. Throughout the American South, Negro leaguers had trouble finding places to eat and places to use the toilet, and sometimes they just had to pack themselves into automobiles and race across a state to avoid being shanghaied by police into working in farm fields, harvesting crops. The stories of how Gibson and other players coped with segregation are sometimes funny, as when they send a light-skinned player into a restaurant for hamburgers, but generally sad, rueful tales of coping with abuse because of skin color.

In 1937, Gibson and other African-American baseball stars played for the Dominican Republic's Trujillo Dragons in a season that became notorious—Gibson and other Negro leaguers on the Dragons were given to understand that they could be shot if they did not win the championship for dictator Trujillo's team. They won and then fled the country. It is probably while playing in the Dominican Republic that Gibson was introduced to hard drugs. Other players remembered him sneaking off to public rest rooms and returning groggy, with slurred speech and his once bright and quick sense of humor gone.

From 1940–1941 Gibson played mostly in Latin America, most notably in Mexico, where he was treated like a hero, feasting in private homes almost every night. By then his bitterness had given him a resentful, dark personality. When the United States entered World War II, most of the Negro leagues' stars were drafted, but not Gibson, who joined the Washington Homestead Grays. By then, the old organized Negro leagues had been ruined by the Great Depression, and there were only brief organized schedules, with most of the surviving teams earning enough to stay in business by traveling all over the United States playing any kind of team that was willing, often local semipro or amateur clubs.

During the war years, against teams weakened by the military draft, which took many African American as well as major league stars, Gibson was a bright light of on-field achievement. His hitting skills overwhelmed many pitchers, but Gibson's emotional troubles made him unpalatable to major league baseball owners and general managers, even though his hitting could make winners out their teams. Having been excluded from the major leagues because of his race during the 1930s, Gibson was passed over to become the first African American to officially play in the major leagues in over forty years.

From baseball fields, the setting of *Josh Gibson* moves to the home of Gibson's mother. He had become very obese by 1946, so fat that he could not drop into a full catcher's crouch, but in 1947, Gibson lost weight alarmingly. He died, probably from a stroke, at home and in the company of his mother, on January 20, 1947. The legend begins that he died of a broken heart because the major leagues seemed to have passed him by. Biographer Holway suggests that Gibson would have been signed by the Cleveland Indians for the 1948 season, catching for Satchel Paige.

◆ THEMES AND CHARACTERS ◆

"Some people say Josh Gibson died of a brain hemorrhage. I say he died of a broken heart," claims Ted Page in *Josh Gibson*. Page had been an outfielder and teammate of Gibson, and the two had palled around for many years. Page reports Gibson's ill health, but remarks that the last he saw of Gibson, the big man still joked with him as he had when they played together. Holway gives to Page the chance to express what Satchel Paige and other players said of Gibson's death: He died of a broken heart.

Page is one of many colorful characters who populate *Josh Gibson*, as may reasonably be expected of an account of Gibson's flamboyant life. While these figures are not developed in depth, their interaction with Gibson is recounted in enough detail to make clear their importance in Gibson's life. For instance, there is Willie Wells, a brilliant shortstop and a dangerous power hitter in his own right, who invented the batting helmet by knocking the lamp off of a miner's helmet after pitchers kept throwing at his head.

Spoken of more often are the pitchers who had to face Gibson in ball games. There is Connie Rector, a "crafty" pitcher with a "tantalizing slow ball"; Joe Williams, "strictly a fireballer" who may have been the best pitcher of all; Chet Brewer, a "'sandpaper' artist," who made his pitches dance. (Pitchers often doctored baseballs in the Negro leagues.) Roosevelt Davis "was a wily cut-ball artist," and Bill Byrd was a "spitball specialist." Throwing fast balls to Gibson seems to have been a waste of effort, and pitchers threw off-speed pitches and "junk" pitches to him. In the book, Holway talks of Ted Trent who "had a legendary curve"; Ray Brown, who "had a dancing knuckleball to complement his fastball and curve"; Luis Tiant, Sr., who "was mainly a 'junkball' pitcher relying on slow curves, change-ups, and the like"; and Leroy Matlock, who "had almost perfect control."

These were the men charged with the task of getting Gibson out, a difficult task given that Gibson tended to hit balls to where no one could catch them. Indeed, Holway notes that Gibson hit more home runs than he had strike outs, an impressive feat for a free-swinging power hitter in any era. But among the pitchers Holway mentions, one stands out. As with other significant figures in *Josh Gibson,* he was interviewed by Holway, and he is allowed to tell about his relationship in his own words. He is Satchel Paige, the foremost celebrity of the Negro leagues, a man who drew fans of all ethnic groups by the tens of thousands to the games he pitched.

The sometime teammate and frequent antagonist of Gibson, Paige wanted every bit as much as Gibson did to be the first African American to officially cross the color line in major league baseball since the nineteenth century. Like Gibson, Paige expected to be paid well, and like Gibson, he was careless with his money, but he learned from his mistakes and learned how to profit from his celebrity. It is interesting to read Paige's remarks and to wonder about how Gibson might be remembered if he, too, had lived as long as Paige, being able to comment on his experiences as a ballplayer. As it is, Paige is remembered as a sage, as a man who intelligently worked his way through racism and discrimination to become important to the American community far beyond the boundaries of race and of baseball. In his playing days, he turned his confrontations into great shows, to the profit of not only Gibson and himself but of their teammates, as well.

Even though Paige is just about as colorful a sports figure as any America has ever had, Holway does not allow him to steal attention away from Gibson. In developing Gibson, Holway tries to paint a full picture of his development as a ballplayer. The common image of a tall, heavily muscled but somewhat clumsy man is belied by Holway's research. Yes, Gibson was tall and well built, and he hit tremendous home runs, but "Gibson could also run," and his high batting averages suggest that he had quick wrists and superior hand-eye coordination. Holway asserts that at his best, Gibson was a fast runner and a good defensive catcher who threw "light" balls that were easy for infielders to catch.

"He realized that he was just as good as Ruth. He changed from the Josh I knew— an overgrown kid who did nothing but play ball, eat ice cream, or go to the movies. He changed to a man who was kind of bitter with somebody, or mad with somebody," observes Ted Page. It dawned on Gibson that segregation was depriving him of the income a major leaguer with his talent would earn. Gibson's feeling that he was underpaid is emphasized in *Josh Gibson,* but curiously the fact that racism denied him the respect that was his due is not touched on. Money woes alone do not seem to adequately account for his changing from the all-American ideal of an athlete to a heavy drinker and drug abuser.

To his credit, Holway does not gloss over Gibson's decline and the role alcohol and other drugs had in it. Gibson seems to abuse drugs to dampen anguish, a belief that he was not being treated fairly. He seems to have released his frustrations on baseballs, which he hit with rare fierceness during the last several years of his life. He became famous beyond Negro league fans at the time he was passing his peak. Page thinks Gibson knew that his skills were declining, that he was not going to be able to show what he could do in the major leagues and make the money he should. Hard drinks and drugs hastened his decline: He became a very slow runner; his defense became weak, with poor throws.

Yet at the end, believing he had a brain tumor, unable to properly crouch behind home plate, and convinced that racists had defeated him and denied him his rightful place in baseball, he played his games with great vigor, making pitchers fear him until his sudden death from causes yet to be fully explained.

Holway brings passion and compassion to his account of Josh Gibson's life. It is hard for a baseball fan not to be passionate about a ballplayer who could have set records and raised the earned-run averages of major league pitchers, but who was denied his chance to showcase his skills in major league ballparks because of his skin's color. Holway is a classic fan who has devoted much of his life to the lore and history of baseball. Holway is plainly partisan in his account of Gibson, noting Gibson's athletic feats and comparing them to other, less gifted players, yet he is also honest about the uglier sides of Gibson's life.

In this honesty lies Holway's artistic achievement. His presentation of Gibson as a man among men is compassionate without being cloying; he reveals Gibson's humanity even while noting his exceptional ability. In part, this means that Gibson is not a role model for young adults. His almost desperate desire for money, his bitterness, his alcoholism, and his abuse of drugs are all presented plainly, all as aspects of an immature personality that never quite grew up. Yet, although Gibson is not a role model, Holway's presentation of him is a fine example of how a person may honestly appreciate an athlete. Instead of idolatry, sincere recognition of what Gibson managed to do, with firsthand accounts of Gibson's performances, is tempered with the recognition that Gibson's private behavior was self-destructive. The result is a portrait of an athlete to be admired for his determination and hard work, as well as his feats of strength and skill, yet to be regarded with dismay and sorrow because of his failure to cope with disappointments.

Racial prejudice is an issue throughout *Josh Gibson*. Holway presents Josh Gibson's life as one that was constantly influenced by his race and by the racial relations of the catcher's era. Gibson remarked that the best thing his father did for him was move him out of the South to Pennsylvania, away from the sharecropper's life and institutionalized segregation of the races. This does not mean that Gibson escaped racial discrimination, but it means that he had economic opportunities he probably would not have had if he had remained in Georgia. In Pennsylvania, he was able to get a job at a local factory. Although this curtailed his education, the job meant a chance to raise himself out of poverty. It also meant a chance to play baseball on an organized amateur club, which in turn meant a chance to show his talent.

Although Holway does not mention it, white baseball scouts seem to have noticed Gibson almost as soon as he joined the Crawford Colored Giants, and major league scouts and managers both chafed under the major leagues' antiblack restrictions that prevented them from signing ballplayers as talented as Gibson. He might have made the difference between second place and a championship for several major league clubs. The discrimination against African Americans was not written into the rules of the major leagues, and officials denied that there was any formal discrimination. Yet, major league Commissioner Kenesaw Mountain Landis had vowed that no African American would play in either the National League or the American League while he was in charge. The pressure was enough to prevent African Americans from playing (at least openly) on the teams John McGraw managed, even though he made it plain that he wanted to sign and play African-American ballplayers. Commissioner Landis's threats prevented team owners who wanted to improve their teams by fielding black stand-outs from signing them to contracts. It was not until Landis's successor Happy Chandler declared that baseball should not discriminate against any Americans of any background that Brooklyn Dodgers General Manager Branch Rickey, who would eventually sign Jackie Robinson, and others saw an opening for signing African Americans without fear of reprisal.

Holway does not go much into this background of racism, instead maintaining a steady focus on Gibson, but he does detail Gibson's own frustrations from playing segregated baseball. Characterized as an overgrown boy, full of fun and mischief, in his first several years in the Negro leagues, the years of being excluded from some hotels and restaurants, of having to drive automobiles pell-mell through Southern states out of fear of the police and out of need to find a bathroom that blacks would be allowed to use, seems to have wearied Gibson. Further, he played exhibition games against white major leaguers, many of whom told him he could play in the major leagues if only he were not black. Eventually, he was discovered by national magazines such as *Time,* and he became well-known as the greatest African-American slugger of the 1930s and 1940s. He became a big drawing card for ball games and as a result became one the highest paid Negro leaguers, but he believed he was not as well paid as he would have been in the major leagues and that he was not as well respected as he should have been. In Holway's account, he became bitter and angry, turning to alcohol and drugs to escape his anguish. Strong in body, but weak in spirit, Gibson despaired as he realized that his best years were behind him and that he would not be able to show what he could do in the spotlights of the major leagues.

Holway does not go into depth about what the racial discrimination of Gibson's time represented for American sports, but it is worth noting that team owners that refused to sign a superior athlete because of his race could not have been committed to fielding the best team possible. Racism meant more to them than winning. This means that major league clubs that sold tickets with the promise of trying to win championships were defrauding their customers. Not every owner or team could be accused of this, but those who wanted to sign Gibson and other black players were thwarted by the disapproval of most of the rest of the team owners such as Charles Comiskey, owner of the Chicago White Sox, who early in the twentieth century had moved owners to disbar a black second baseman John McGraw (then managing the Baltimore American League club) was fielding. Holway points out that most Americans, white as well as black, were denied the opportunity to see great ballplayers such as Gibson, because of baseball's color line.

◆ TOPICS FOR DISCUSSION ◆

1. Does Holway satisfactorily explain why Gibson abused drugs? What more would you like to know?

2. How does Holway show Gibson's decline from happy-go-lucky to bitter? How well does Holway trace the decline?

3. How well does Holway mix Gibson's exploits on the ball field with his life off the field?

4. Why does Holway emphasize Gibson's home runs?

5. Is Gibson an admirable man? What does Holway say about this?

6. Is Gibson an appropriate subject for a series on "Black Americans of Achievement"? Might young readers receive a false impression of what is considered admirable in a person?

7. What is the purpose of *Josh Gibson*? Does it fulfill its purpose?

8. Does Holway make it clear why Gibson was distressed over how much money he earned, even though he was very well paid during the Great Depression when compared to most Americans?

9. What factors, other than money, about being excluded from the National and American Leagues would have dismayed Gibson?

10. A man who became a bitter drug abuser would seem to have little to offer readers of his biography. What lessons, if any, can be drawn from Gibson's behavior?

11. What are some of the funniest passages in *Josh Gibson*?

12. Why did Paige earn more money than Gibson?

13. What were the hardest parts about playing in the Negro leagues? Why would players endure such hardships rather than quitting and finding another job?

◆ IDEAS FOR REPORTS AND PAPERS ◆

1. Josh Gibson refers to players and others involved in the Negro leagues besides Gibson. Choose one of them and research his or her life and then write a short biography of him or her. You may wish to imitate Holway's style, which emphasizes quotations from firsthand observers.

2. In what other books besides *Josh Gibson* and in what journalistic articles does Holway write about Gibson? How do his views grow and change over the years as he discusses Josh Gibson? Where does Holway come closest to capturing the real man behind the famous image?

3. African-American ball players had trouble finding service stations that would let them use their bathrooms. How widespread was this problem in those days? Was it exclusively a Southern problem, or were African Americans refused service because of their race in other regions of the United States?

4. Gibson played in many different ball parks for Negro league teams. Describe one of these ball parks as it would have looked when Gibson played in it and explain how a baseball player would have experienced the grounds.

5. Many African-American baseball players preferred to play in Latin American leagues. What was the appeal of Latin American baseball? How were the players from the United States treated in Latin American countries?

6. Josh Gibson had his start in organized baseball by playing for a factory team. Such teams were once common. What were they like? Who owned them? Who ran them? Why would many of them be integrated even though the major leagues were not?

7. What reasons did the executives of major league teams give for not hiring the likes of Gibson? Why would a team in contention for a pennant not want to hire a slugger who could hit any pitch 500 feet with great regularity?

8. In Gibson's day, there were major league ballplayers such as Ty Cobb who wanted nothing to do with African-American

players. Who were some of these players? What were their reasons for not wanting to play against African Americans?

9. Some major league managers and players wanted to include African Americans in the major leagues. Holway cites Dizzy Dean often as an outspoken exponent for admitting African Americans to the major leagues. Who were some of the other white players who wanted to include African American players? What did they try to do to open the major leagues to African Americans?

10. Some historians think that Gibson was done in by drug abuse. How prevalent were illicit drugs in baseball in the 1940s? Did they harm any other players?

11. How did Gibson make his way from factory worker to the Negro National League? Was this typical in his day, even for major leaguers?

12. There is more than one possibility for what killed Gibson. What are the possibilities? Which most likely is the reason he died? Could there be more than one reason?

◆ RELATED TITLES ◆

Josh Gibson is the unusual instance of a biography by the same author being the best source for additional information. Holway's *Josh and Satch: The Life and Times of Josh Gibson and Satchel Paige* (1991) goes into more detail about Gibson's love life and paints a fuller picture of his times in Latin America than does *Josh Gibson*. *Josh and Satch* is a dual biography in which the lives of Gibson and Satchel Paige are interconnected. In it, Paige learns to cope with racism, and with a sense of humor and a keen eye for business, he turns himself into

a folk hero who was admired and sought after for public appearances long after his playing days were over. In *Josh and Satch*, Gibson fails to cope with the same pressures that Paige handled well; he is an example of how the pressures of racism and celebrity could destroy a man, whereas Paige is an example of how good sense and a positive outlook can help someone overcome injustice. In it, personality determines fate.

Holway began his research of Negro league baseball by interviewing those who had been involved in the various Negro leagues. These interviews continued for many years before resulting in *Voices from the Great Blackball Leagues*, a 1975 collection of interviews. Young readers as well as grownups are likely to enjoy the down-to-earth stories told by players and others associated with the leagues. *Blackball Stars* (1988) is another major book by Holway on the Negro leagues. It is a gathering and rewriting of numerous articles Holway had published about Negro leaguers. It has short biographies of many of the players, owners, and executives involved in the creation of the leagues as well as involved in the playing of league games. *Blackball Stars* is somewhat earthier than *Josh Gibson*, featuring some off-color stories of ballplayers' romantic adventures. It is an excellent book and is suitable reading for teenagers.

◆ FOR FURTHER REFERENCE ◆

Holway, John B. "Not All Stars Were White." *Sporting News* (July 4, 1983): S14. Holway talks about the Negro leagues' 1933 All-Star Game, played in Chicago in August, in which Gibson represented the Pittsburgh Crawfords.

"Negro Leagues Register." In *The Baseball Encyclopedia*. Ninth edition. Edited by Rick Wolff, et al. New York: Macmillan,

1993, pp. 2609–2680. Although far from a complete listing of all Negro leaguers, this has the most authoritative statistics for many of the stars of the Negro leagues.

Kirk H. Beetz

LAND OF LOSS

Novel

1999

Author: K. A. Applegate

◆

Major Books for Young Adults

The Story of Two American Generals:
  Benjamin O. Davis, Jr. and Colin L.
  Powell, 1992
The Boyfriend Mix-Up, 1994
Sharing Sam, 1995
Listen to My Heart, 1996

Boyfriends and Girlfriends series,
  including:
Zoey Fools Around, 1994
Lucas Gets Hurt, 1998
Claire Can't Lose, 1999
Who Loves Kate, 1999

Animorphs series, including:

The Message, 1996
The Stranger, 1997
The Reunion, 1999
The Prophecy, 2000
The Ultimate, 2001

Everworld series
Search for Senna, 1999
Land of Loss, 1999
Enter the Enchanted, 1999
Realm of the Reaper, 1999
The Destroyer, 1999
Fear the Fantastic, 2000
Understand the Unknown, 2000
Discover the Destroyer, 2000
Inside the Illusion, 2000

◆ ABOUT THE AUTHOR ◆

Katherine Alice Applegate is simultaneously one of America's most famous
authors and one of America's most mysterious. She guards her privacy, as does her
publisher, Scholastic, which has brilliantly
marketed her Animorphs and Everworld
series with astounding success. Applegate
was already a well-established writer of
books for young readers, mostly romance
novels, when she proposed the Animorphs
series to Scholastic, where the proposal was
met with enthusiasm. She wanted to write a
series of books that showed how the world
might look from the perspectives of different animals; the result has been a series of
fascinating novellas for readers from late
elementary school to junior high school.

After moving around the United States several times, the Michigan-born writer now resides in Minneapolis. Over a hundred of her books have been published, and she has written them at an amazing pace. Begun in 1996, her Animorphs series numbered over forty books plus several spin-offs by 2001. Her series intended for adolescents, Everworld, begun in 1999, numbered nine volumes by the end of 2000. Sally Lodge, in *Publishers Weekly*, quotes Applegate, "A series writer has to develop plotting and pacing that become a well-oiled machine. You don't have the luxury of spending a year on a book and absolutely cannot indulge in writer's block. Yet I knew I had to write in perfect language and choose just the right images, to make sure that my middle readers fell in love with the characters and returned again and again.". The two hundred letters from young readers Applegate receives per week, as well as the one hundred emails she receives per day from youngsters, attest to the success she has had in reaching her intended audience. They love her characters.

In spite of the success of Applegate's writings, they have received scant attention in the press, perhaps because of a prevailing view that books written so quickly cannot be worth writing about, or perhaps because of the immense difficulty in keeping current with all the books Applegate publishes. In spite of the great pace at which Applegate has written her books, they tend to be of higher quality than other mass-market writings. In the Animorphs series the perspectives of characters as animals, whether fleas or birds, are artful and informative. The Everworld novels offer fine introductions to the mythologies of the world. In both series, the suspense is captivating and the characterizations are sharp but well-rounded; the books are page-turners, I-can't-go-to-bed-until-I-finish tales of adventure.

Applegate does not shy away from the tough questions about growing up and building sound, honest relationships with others. For instance, the nonseries title *Sharing Sam* deals with the prospect of a close friend dying and how to love in spite of the pain. In Everworld, the relationships among the principal characters are essential to the appeal of the novels. The art of characterization is one that Applegate has mastered, and it is perhaps the most important reason her rapidly-written works stand as good literature as well as entertaining reads.

◆ OVERVIEW ◆

Land of Loss is the second novel of Everworld, and while it can be read and enjoyed apart from the first book, *Search for Senna*, reading the first book would clarify why four high schoolers are fighting for their lives in an ancient Aztec city that is inhabited by a god who eats people's hearts. This is no ordinary god; this is Huitzilopoctli, a monster of evil. In *Search for Senna*, David describes him:

> He was shaped like a man. Blue, the blue of the sky late on a summer day. His face was striped horizontally with bands of blue and yellow. Around his eyes were glittering white stars, stars that seemed real and hot and explosive.

> Iridescent feathers grew from his head, spreading down across his shoulders and back. In his left hand he held a disk, a mirror that smoked and burned. In the right hand was a snake, a twisting, writhing snake that breathed fire and almost seemed an extension of his hand.

> His other hand, the one that held the mirror, dripped red. It dripped red and you knew, knew deep down, that it could never, would never be wiped clean.

This is why Christopher (the narrator of *Land of Loss*), April, and Jalil are afraid.

They are at first trapped in a city that serves the evil god.

Everworld is the place where the ancient gods of earth went eons ago, taking their followers with them, but leaving most of humanity behind. As Christopher explains, "Somehow, someway, for some reason, the old gods of Earth decided to abandon the real world. We didn't know why. Just knew that the gods of the Norsemen and the gods of the Greeks and the gods of the Aztecs and the Inca and the Egyptians and all the endless panoply of immortals, all decided they'd had enough of the real world. Our world." A terrifying being that consumes gods is headed for Everworld. One problem is that the gods are thinking of returning to earth, and the Norse god Loki is trying to open a way back to earth for himself and the other gods in order to escape. Once back on earth, they would reassert their rule over humanity. The blood sacrifices to feed Huitzilopoctli are merely one example of the horrors that would fall upon human beings. Somewhat nicer gods than Loki (such as Thor and Odin) have disappeared because of Loki's treachery, so it seems that Loki is not necessarily intent on taking all the gods back to earth; he may wish to take only the evil ones. (He will claim otherwise in *Enter the Enchanted*, but can his word be trusted?)

Christopher, David, April, and Jalil were drawn into Everworld when a giant wolf kidnapped Senna, who is, unbeknownst to them, a witch. They are all pulled into a vortex that seems to turn them inside out at first. It takes them much of *Land of Loss* to figure out what happened to them. Early on, they suspect that Senna exerts some sort of mind control over David, and perhaps Christopher, who was her boyfriend before David became her boyfriend. By the novel's end, they have put together some of the pieces of the puzzle that is Senna. She is a teenager on earth, but, in Everworld, she is the witch who is the key to opening the passage to earth for Loki, Huitzilopoctli, and others who live in Everworld.

◆ SETTING ◆

Everworld is a wonderful place for adventures, another one of author Applegate's remarkable imaginative creations. In *Land of Loss*, the narrative clarifies some of the background of the four youngsters: Christopher, David, April, and Jalil. They are from Chicago, and the lake where they were pulled into Everworld is Lake Michigan. One of the special complications in their adventures is that they are simultaneously living in both Chicago and Everworld. Whenever they fall asleep in Everworld, they merge with themselves on earth, and their memories mingle. At home, they are living their ordinary lives while their Everworld selves are struggling to stay alive. When they merge, they take advantage of the possibilities living lives on two different worlds at the same time offers: On earth, they research the cultures they have encountered in Everworld and try to find answers to questions they have about how to survive in Everworld. When they awaken in Everworld, they remember what they learned while back on earth. In addition, this comes in handy for keeping track of each other. When April is separated from the boys in the Aztec city, David suggests that they can find out where she is and how she is doing by going to sleep and asking her earthly self about her Everworld self.

After being captured by the minions of Loki, the youngsters escape Loki and join a Viking invasion of the Aztec lands across a sea from the Viking lands, until the Viking invasion is crushed by the gigantic god Huitzilopoctli, and they are taken prisoner. Part of the fun of *Land of Loss* is the ancient Aztec setting, with impressive temples, big stone walls built to keep out the jungle, and buildings that make up a thriving Aztec city, New Tenochtitlan. The jungle itself proves to be an interesting place, too. Not only does it have the standard obstacles to be found in a hostile jungle, but it has wandering aliens from outer space, the Coo-Hatch of the Third Forge.

◆ THEMES AND CHARACTERS ◆

"If I believed in hell," says Jalil, "it would be approximately like that city," New Tenochtitlan, the city of Huitzilopoctli. He may be forgiven his sentiments, given that people tried to sacrifice him to a blood-thirsty god there. He is the most fastidious of the four teenaged adventurers and resents the dirt, sweat, and other unpleasant aspects of Everworld. Less fussy, David remarks that not all of Everworld can be that bad.

But *Land of Loss* is Christopher Hitchcock's novel. He is the narrator of *Land of Loss*, and his point of view prevails throughout. He is a complex character who is fond of making long speeches to whomever will listen. Sometimes, eventually realizing, he talks even if no one is listening. It is "my own simple belief that we were screwed, screwed, utterly, irretrievably screwed by Senna Wales." Part of his complexity is that he is aware that Senna controls him in an unnatural way and resists her influence, yet sometimes gives in to her.

Senna manages to be the crux of *Land of Loss* (just as she is in *Search for Senna*), by being the person almost everyone wants something from. The gods want her power to open a way to earth and the youngsters she pulled with her from earth to Everworld want her to send them home. Diffident and mysterious in *Search for Senna*, she becomes menacing in *Land of Loss*. When April slaps Senna, Christopher closely watches her reaction: "Arrogance. That was it. The calm, superior sneering look of the two-hundred-and-fifty-pound linebacker who's just been punched by the ninety-five-pound gymnast." Even as Senna exerts her influence over Christopher, making him defend her against another of Everworld's menaces, he sees her face, "a vision illuminated by the dragon's fire. A smile. A killer's smile, as though the lips might stretch still further and reveal vampire fangs." She remains more a mystery than a developed character, but the hints Christopher gives of what she may truly be like add to the interest of *Land of Loss* and are some of the elements that make the novel a page-turner: Will we find out who she is? And what is her purpose?

Christopher's strength as a narrator is his ability to convey the complexities of the personalities of his companions. Even while he annoys his companions with his sarcastic witticisms, as well as his profound personal insecurity, he is sensitive to their points of view.

One of his potentially irritating traits is pontificating. He can burst into a lecture or tirade at any time. Even so, sometimes his speeches are Shakespearean—fascinating for their language and insights into his character: "Just scared?" he responds to David, who views fear as something to be overcome. "No. I'm not just scared. See, that makes it sound like some plain old everyday emotion. I'm terrified. Horrified. Overwhelmed with dread. I feel like my brain has been filled full of sewage and I'll never, ever be able to get it clean, like this stuff will eat me alive in my dreams, like I'll never see the world the same again. Scared? They want to eat us, you moron! They want to cut out our hearts and they almost did, you fool!" This is punchy prose—sharp, swiftly moving prose—and the images are stark, yet as metaphors they carry much meaning beyond their words. "My brain has been filled with sewage" conveys a weighty amount of emotion, speaking of a revulsion that is deeply dire; it is also a striking use of

Land of Loss

words, creating an image that is difficult to forget.

One reason why Christopher is bitter and sarcastic is his penchant for self-analysis, marred by self-hatred. Losing Senna as his girlfriend was a big blow to him back on earth, and his time in Everworld is not made easier by knowing that David is her preference for her "hero," the man who would best protect her. He is disgusted with himself for still yearning for her company. When he thinks of himself as being no more than a supporting character in her life, the hero's companion who is almost always killed in motion picture adventures, he reacts by making cutting jokes about other people, as well as himself, and picking fights. He comments on his antisocial behavior, "Or maybe I was just mad at good old Christopher. I was whiny, bitchy, snide, resentful, childish. Picking stupid fights. Acting like the kind of person I couldn't stand." This helps make him a tragic figure in *Land of Loss*, because just as he cannot entirely resist Senna's influence even though he knows about it, he cannot make himself be the man he wants to be, even though he is aware of the aspects of his behavior that are hurtful to himself as well as to others.

For *Search for Senna*, David seems like the logical choice for narrator. He is, after all, strong, tough, and given to performing heroic deeds. He is able to size up opponents, spot their strengths and weaknesses, and then take action. Further, he is adaptable, using whatever tools or weapons are at hand for whatever task he undertakes, and he frankly enjoys being on an adventure. This makes Christopher's narration a striking contrast to that of David. Adjusting is not something Christopher cares to do. He does not like adventuring; he does not like strange environments; he does not like people, either. His awareness of his own vulnerability helps to make him an attractive

character, his biting wit is sometimes funny, and he has a way with words that is pithy and pleasing. For instance, his remark to April, "How do you figure your life out when you're late for class *and* about to be sacrificed to a pagan deity?" is a good summary of the multiplicity of problems he and his companions must overcome. By the end of *Land of Loss*, he is learning to summarize his ideas like this: "Lesson number one in Everworld: There's them, and there's us. And any day we can keep them from destroying us, that's a victory."

In *Land of Loss*, April asserts herself more than she has before. She is active in trying to keep the four teenagers together in a group, and when others are losing their heads, she is usually keeping hers. She says to Christopher and Jalil, "David's not the hero. He's just a fool. A puppet. Like all of us. This is all Senna. It's all her. This is her game we're playing. We're all fools." Although she includes herself in the "fools" category, she seems resistant to the influence Senna exerts over the boys, which makes her an important part of the team. During *Land of Loss*, Christopher begins to admire her—foreshadowing events in later novels—and begins to value her as someone who will know when he is losing control of himself.

Applegate's novel is a story in which exciting events and new obstacles pop up everywhere as her characters progress through the tale. Perhaps one should not be surprised that after escaping imprisonment, saving a bunch of Vikings from having their hearts cut out, and fleeing a city of evil into a dark jungle, the teenagers would be set upon in their sleep by aliens from another world. The Coo-Hatch of the Third Forge are twenty to twenty-five in number and about the same size as men, but they have a face that is "a long, very long, maybe three-foot-long point, a hard cone, a needle, like an anteater who'd evolved to hunt for ants inside of concrete. Resting above, at the back of the needle were two eyes, enormous, blue-irised within dark red." Their bodies are bent so that their snouts are over their clawed feet, and they have four arms, "two brawny arms at mid-arc, two smaller, delicate arms jutting out just below the eyes." Had David described them, he might have assessed how dangerous they were. But Christopher, after being frightened, perceives something other than threat in them, even letting one take his axe. It turns out that these weird creatures are master metallurgists and are far more interested in trade and commerce than war.

In addition to giving a close-up look at the Coo-Hatch, *Land of Loss* introduces a new figure who foreshadows the introduction of a new mythology into the "Everworld" series—and with that mythology new complications to the mystery of Everworld. Christopher discovers a man rummaging about near the sleeping figure of Huitzilopoctli, who remarks about the sleeping god and gods in general that "the gods of war usually are rather dull." He is old but self-possessed and seemingly not concerned about the bloodthirsty god; he tells Christopher, "Call me Merlin." Merlin is a figure from the stories of King Arthur and the Round Table, leading the reader to believe that the arrival of a dragon is imminent.

◆ LITERARY QUALITIES ◆

When an author uses a narrator who cannot be a skilled writer, critics often complain that the narration reads like the author rather than the fictional narrator. For instance, one could suggest that Christopher's descriptions are vivid because Applegate actually writes them. Having mentioned this obvious argument, let me put it away. Applegate is no ordinary writer; even though she has written a huge number of books in a seemingly short time, she is a

conscientious writer, and in *Land of Loss* much of her talent for characterization is put on display. Key to her artistic success in this novel is her ability to let Christopher have his say in his way. Rarely is there even a hint that Christopher is not the person talking to the audience of *Land of Loss*. He has his limitations and has a tendency to see himself enclosed in a dark box, sometimes perceiving little that is around him. The incident when he cries while at a dead end is an example of this; whereas David is looking for a place to go, Christopher sees only the ending. His introspective nature and self-hatred cause him to burst out with long disquisitions about other people's faults, but he is intelligent and able to understand what others feel. David would not have recognized the evil, satisfied look on Senna's face as the dragon approached, but Christopher notices it because he cares about such matters. He knows enough about himself to see her for what she is even as he yields—as he knows he must—to her influence.

◆ SOCIAL SENSITIVITY ◆

The obvious social issues in *Land of Loss* arise from Christopher's sometimes angry intention to hurt others. For instance, he picks on David's Jewishness:

"Hey, David. You're a Jew, right?"

"Half Jewish," he said.

"Yeah? Well you know the word 'schmuck'? Did I pronounce that right? 'Schmuck'? Or maybe you'd prefer a good old-fashioned Anglo-Saxon word, you—"

"Back off," David warned.

This passage illustrates Christopher's self-destructiveness, because he knows better than to make mocking remarks about someone's ethnicity and to pick on someone like David, who is bigger and stronger than he is. When put in the context of the stress that at one point had Christopher crying at the dead end of a street, as well as Christopher's self-hatred, his taunting of David is just one more miserable outburst. But it also reveals an aspect of his character that goes beyond the normal anxiety of being a teenager.

Later in *Land of Loss*, Christopher touches on Jalil's ethnicity by suggesting that the situation in Everworld is like an adventure movie: David plays the hero who is supposed to save Senna, Christopher himself is the hero's best friend, April is the requisite female companion, and Jalil is the black companion. He notes that he and Jalil would be killed, and if a sequel to the movie were anticipated, then the female companion would die, too, so that a new one could be used in the next motion picture. Sensibly, April notes that their adventure is different from a movie, but Jalil objects to his characterization as the standard "black" man who is supposed to be killed. He and Christopher have nearly come to blows before, so Jalil deserves credit for being restrained in this scene and not striking Christopher. This scene is symptomatic of Christopher's tendency to express his anxieties out loud without thinking about what he is saying. Readers recognize that Applegate has Christopher talking nonsense, since many adventure movies do not follow the pattern to which he alludes.

April has many appealing qualities, including courage, good sense, and sensitive leadership, but she has a blind spot when it comes to characterizing men: "I don't know, maybe males aren't capable of ever really being adults. Maybe you're crippled by your hormones or something." Her attitude that she is the only grownup among a bunch of childish boys becomes wearisome after awhile, and it is as much of a cliche as Christopher's description of adventure movies. Applegate does not delve deeply into April's attitude toward male lack of maturity in *Land of Loss*, but she does let Christo-

pher have his say, "You know what, I'm sick of your 'better-than-everyone, my crap doesn't stink' attitude. In case you missed it, this isn't Political Correctness World, okay?" This is one more source of friction among the characters, who must learn to work together in order to survive. It is also an interesting complication that raises a good question about whether twentieth-century American cultural values can function under life-or-death stress—an issue that could have been explored in more depth in the Everworld series.

The treatment of Aztec culture may be an issue in reading *Land of Loss*, although it may prove to be no issue at all. In any case, Applegate sketches some brutal rituals of the religion of the ancient Aztecs, who engaged in horrendous human sacrifices in which they cut out the hearts of living human beings in order to offer blood to their gods. They would start wars with their neighbors in order to take prisoners— sometime by the thousands—to sacrifice. This is one reason many Native Americans, of what is now Mexico, helped the conquistadors conquer the Aztecs.

◆ TOPICS FOR DISCUSSION ◆

1. How trustworthy is Christopher? Do you trust everything he says in *Land of Loss*? Why or why not?

2. What are the sources of Christopher's insecurity?

3. Christopher cannot defy Senna's influence over him. Why not?

4. Why would Christopher be miserable in Everworld even while David is enjoying the adventure?

5. Why does Christopher hand his axe to Estett when Estett asks for it?

6. Is Christopher likable? Does it matter for the enjoyment of the story? Why?

7. Why does April put men down as childish? How might Senna exploit April's attitude towards the boys and toward men in general?

8. Is Senna a villain or a heroine in *Land of Loss*? Explain why you think she is or is not.

9. How does Christopher's attitude towards his companions affect what he says about them?

10. Why does Christopher handle his fear in a different way than David?

11. Why does Christopher dare to approach the resting Huitzilopoctli?

12. What does Merlin's presence in *Land of Loss* suggest about what will come in later novels in the "Everworld" series?

13. Is the ending of *Land of Loss* a good cliffhanger?

14. What does Christopher bring to his narrative that makes a special contribution to understanding the events in Everworld?

15. What do the Coo-Hatch contribute to the development of the plot in *Land of Loss*?

16. The Vikings do not make much of an effort to escape at the start of *Land of Loss*. Why not? What is the difference between them and Christopher, David, and Jalil that leads the boys to attempt escaping?

17. At one point in *Land of Loss*, Christopher admits that "at the moment logic was a tiny, faraway voice way, way back in my head." If he has moments like this, how can we trust him to tell the story as it actually happened?

18. What are dreamlike passages in *Land of Loss*?

◆ IDEAS FOR REPORTS AND PAPERS ◆

1. How accurate is the representation of Aztec culture in *Land of Loss*?

2. What was the Aztec ritual of human sacrifice that was like the one in *Land of Loss*? Why did they practice this ritual? Did they have other rituals of human sacrifice?

3. What did Viking raiders do when they invaded a town or city? What would they be doing to New Tenochtitlan in *Land of Loss*?

4. What was the layout for the city Tenochtitlan? How is this layout reflected in the descriptions in *Search for Senna* and *Land of Loss*?

5. What figure in Aztec mythology does Huitzilopoctli represent? How did Aztecs expect him to behave?

6. What is fatalism? Why would Applegate attribute it to the Vikings?

7. Who is Merlin? In what ancient stories is he found? Based on the stories about him, how may he be expected to behave in Everworld?

8. What would the temple in *Land of Loss* look like in Tenochtitlan? Where would the altar be? Where would the god be? In what room would Merlin have been discovered? You could draw a picture of the temple and label the places Christopher would have seen in *Land of Loss*.

9. Christopher suggests to April that "Political Correctness" is inappropriate for Everworld. What is political correctness, and why would Christopher think that put-downs of men would be con-

sidered politically correct? What ideas are introduced in *Land of Loss* by Christopher's remarks?

10. Compare the narratives of *Land of Loss* and *Search for Senna*. Are there notable differences in how the stories are told? Are there notable similarities? What does this tell you about Applegate's artistic achievement in *Land of Loss*?

11. What is Thor's hammer called? What is the Norse myth about how Thor acquired his hammer? What do Norse myths say about the hammer's power? Could it do what it does in *Land of Loss*?

◆ RELATED TITLES ◆

Applegate likes to experiment, and her novels tend to be lively exercises in ideas and techniques. In the case of Everworld, she creates a place where the world's ancient mythologies coexist, and she has fun creating adventures that involve mixing the mythologies. For the Everworld series, she creates four adventurers who are snatched from fairly ordinary teenaged American lives, although Jalil's psychological problems are somewhat out of the ordinary. Through these characters she experiments with techniques of narration by having each one narrate novels: first David for *Search for Senna*, then Christopher for *Land of Loss*, then April for *Enter the Enchanted*, then Jalil for *Realm of the Reaper*, and then repeating the cycle through the subsequent novels.

This can be disconcerting at first. David is a very engaging narrator, and losing his storytelling voice for *Land of Loss* is disappointing, although Christopher manages to make *Land of Loss* his own novel. Once the reader gets used to the rhythm of the shifting narrators, Applegate's experimentation becomes fun. The personality of each narrator shows through in the telling of each book. Everworld is described through David's

love of action and interest in logistics, through Christopher's acidic humor and tendency to see below the surface of events to find what is really going on, through April's good sense and practicality, and through Jalil's analytical mind that finds the logic linking events.

The novels also continue to introduce mythologies, and in the process, Applegate creates a new mythology of her own, in which human endeavors are placed in a vast cosmic scheme in which everyone is important, even though in any individual novel they may seem like pawns. Once the youngsters meet Merlin in *Land of Loss*, the grand contest of universe-shaking powers begins to reveal itself, and dreams really do seem more real than real life. Combine the heroic scope of the ambition for the Everworld series with exceptional characterizations and vividly realized scenes of action, and it is no wonder that Applegate's audience loves these books.

◆ FOR FURTHER REFERENCE ◆

*Authors and Artists for Young Adults,*vol. 37. Detroit: Gale, 2000. A biographical essay with comments on Applegate's life and work.

"NYC Radio Station Celebrates the Season." *Publishers Weekly* (January 17, 2000): 26. Mentions the marketing of the "Everworld" series.

Publishers Weekly (June 21, 1999): 69. In this review of *Search for Senna*, the reviewer says, "With her blend of accessible story and mythological cast of characters, Applegate is sure to attract a host of new fans."

"Scholastic's Animorphs Series Has Legs," *Publishers Weekly* 244, 45 (November 3, 1997): 36–37.

Something about the Author, vol. 109. Detroit: Gale, 2000. An essay that includes biographical information about Applegate and information about her writing.

Kirk H. Beetz

THE LESSON

Short Story

1972

Author: Toni Cade Bambara

◆

Major Books for Young Adults

Tales and Stories for Black Folks, 1971
(anthology of works by various
black authors)
Gorilla My Love, 1972 (short stories)

The Sea Birds Are Still Alive, 1977 (short
stories)
The Salt Eaters, 1980 (novel)

◆ ABOUT THE AUTHOR ◆

Toni Cade Bambara was an African American writer, film critic and teacher who conveyed her message about the necessity for social activism in the black community through authentic spoken voices, often those of feisty female adolescents. Toni Cade was born in New York City on March 25, 1939. Cade's mother, Helen Brent Henderson Cade, who reared her and brother Walter, was insistent that black history be taught in the schools her children attended, and she often visited classrooms to make sure that the curriculum was satisfactory. She also championed her daughter's independence, believing that there should be no differences in how boys and girls are raised.

Cade spent her most of her childhood in Harlem and Bedford-Stuyvestant in New York City. She studied theatre arts and English at Queens College and then went on to graduate study of African fiction at City College of New York (CCNY). Feeling obligated to improve her community, she pursued several helping professions in the city: social work in Harlem, program director at Colony House in Brooklyn, and recreational therapist at New York Metropolitan Hospital. Later, she returned to CCNY as a teacher of writing and fiction, working with under-prepared non-traditional college students who were entering college through open admissions programs. In the late 1960s she began to publish short fiction, most with strong black women as protagonists, in literary journals and in some popular magazines such as *Redbook*.

When she became a published author, Cade added her Grandmother's adopted surname, Bambara, as a tribute to the other woman who had been an important influence in her intellectual and emotional development. Bambara often refers to Grandma Dorothy as the woman who taught her critical theory and steeped her in the tradition of Afrocentric aesthetic regulations. In essays and in interviews, Bambara has acknowledged her debt to her mother and grandmother, as well as to an unofficial set of mothers, women from her community who collectively bonded together to empower and educate her. Many of her works of fiction explore the concept of debts that African-American children owe to community members who have collectively mothered, educated and empowered them.

Bambara was an editor before she became a full-fledged writer, compiling in 1970 an anthology entitled *The Black Woman*, dedicated to "the uptown mamas who nudged me to jest set it down in print so it gets to be a habit to write letters to each other, so maybe that way we don't keep treadmilling the same ole ground." In 1971 she produced a second anthology entitled *Tales and Stories for Black Folks*, which combines work by established black writers such as Langston Hughes, Alice Walker and Ernest Gaines with stories by several of her freshmen composition students. This book also contains black fairy tales, which demonstrate the richness of Black English while celebrating the black folk tradition. One of Bambara's own, frequently anthologized short stories, "Raymond's Run," is included in this volume. This story's heroine is an outspoken adolescent girl, the subject of many of Bambara's later stories that would appeal to young readers. "The Lesson," with its exceptionally strong female adolescent voices, first appeared in *Gorilla My Love*, published in 1972.

The next collection of short stories, *The Sea Birds Are Still Alive* (1977) focuses on life in black neighborhoods in big cities and experiments with non-traditional plot patterns. Bambara's novel, *The Salt Eaters* (1980),

uses jazz techniques, with narrators moving backward and forward in time. It was much admired by Toni Morrison, who championed the manuscript while serving as an editor at Random House.

Bambara remained active in her community and in wider issues of social justice until her death in 1995. Although she is known primarily for her fiction, she was also a successful documentary filmmaker and screenwriter. Two of her most enduring documentaries are *The Bombing of Osage Avenue*, about the police action in Philadelphia that burned out whole blocks in a black neighborhood, and *W.E.B. DuBois: A Biography in Four Voices*. Her fiction is frequently taught in literature classes from middle school to college. Her portrayal of the generational struggles between black parents and their children, her witty and outspoken protagonists, and her lifelong commitment to improving the lives of inner-city children keep her fiction from feeling dated.

◆ OVERVIEW ◆

Narrated in the voice of Sylvia, a pre-adolescent black girl, "The Lesson" is her version of a summer day trip organized by Miss Moore, a socially conscious spinster who is determined to teach eight children a lesson about the nature of money and how it is distributed in American society. In order to expose the children to the notion of class differences, Miss Moore, the self-appointed teacher, takes them from the "slums" in New York City to the upscale retail area on Fifth Avenue where they visit F.A.O. Schwarz, a world-famous toy store. Although the lesson Miss Moore attempts to teach is quite serious, the story is infused with sassy humor provided by the various children's honest and irreverent voices.

The story begins and ends in a predominantly black neighborhood in New York City, probably Harlem, but most of the action takes place outside and inside the Fifth Avenue toy store. The contrast between these two settings underscores Miss Moore's lesson in economic disparity.

Sylvia, the narrator, describes her neighborhood in the opening scene. She lives near all her cousins "'cause we all moved North the same time and to the same apartment and then spread out gradual to breathe." Although the children seem content at the beginning of the story, they resent the squalor that surrounds them as exemplified by the "winos who cluttered up our parks and pissed on our handball walls and stank up our hallways and stairs so you couldn't halfway play hide-and-seek without a god-damn gas mask." Evidently, it's one thing for the children to complain about their homes, but another for someone else to do so. When Miss Moore rounds them up to start the trip, she emphasizes their poverty. Sylvia complains, "And then she gets to the part about we all poor and live in the slums, which I don't feature." They then take two cabs to their destination.

As soon as the children alight from the cab, they sense that they are out of their element: "Then we check out that we on Fifth Avenue and everybody dressed up in stockings. One lady in a fur coat, hot as it is. White folks crazy." After ignoring Miss Moore's lecture and ogling the merchandise in the windows, Sylvia and her friends follow Miss Moore into the store. Their sense of uneasiness grows:

> Then the rest of us tumble in like a glued-together jigsaw done all wrong. And people looking at us. And it's like the time me and Sugar crashed into the Catholic church on a dare. But once we got in there and everything so hushed and holy and the candles and the bowin and the handker-chiefs on all the drooping heads, I just couldn't go through with the plan.

Not only does this new setting put the children on the defensive, it also presents Miss Moore another opportunity to remind them of what their homes lack. When Rosie asks what a $480 paperweight is used for, Miss Moore explains it is to "weigh paper down so it won't scatter and make your desk untidy." Figuring their mentor is "crazy or lying one," Junebug reminds her they don't keep paper on their school desks. Miss Moore uses the opportunity to contrast this environment with their own:

> "At home then," she say. "Don't you have a calendar and a pencil case and a blotter and a letter-opener on your desk at home?" And she know damn well what our homes look like cause she nosys around in them every chance she get.
>
> "I don't even have a desk," say Junebug, "Do we?"
>
> "And I don't even have a home," say Flyboy like he do at school to keep the white folks off his back and sorry for him. Send this poor kid to camp posters, is his specialty.

They return by subway to their familiar neighborhood, where they can all breathe easier for the finale of the lesson. "Miss Moore lines us up in front of the mailbox where we started from, seem like years ago, and I got a headache for thinkin so hard," Sylvia complains. Although Sylvia had feigned indifference to Miss Moore's lesson in the store, now that she is back in her element, she has regained control and plans to reflect on the lesson she has stubbornly resisted learning: ". . . I'm going to the West End and then over to the Drive to think this day through."

◆ THEMES AND CHARACTERS ◆

Sylvia, the narrator, is the central character, and it is through her consciousness that readers intuit the significance of the title, "The Lesson." Sylvia is smart, aggressive and the leader of the band of friends and cousins that prefers to spend their summer days "terrorizing the West Indian kids," by snatching "their hair ribbons and their money too." Not quite an adolescent, Sylvia is fascinated with experimenting with the lipstick her friend Sugar has stolen from her mother. Although she seems fearless on her own territory, she "feel funny, shame" when she realizes she is out of her element on Fifth Avenue. Sylvia has always been aware that she is poor, but she has been blissfully ignorant of how startling her disadvantages are until her world is contrasted with that of Manhattan's rich. She has always resented Miss Moore, "the nappy-head bitch and her goddamn college degree," but after the trip to Fifth Avenue, her anger spreads from Miss Moore to her friends, who have actually admitted to the older woman that they have "gotten" the lesson.

Her closest companion, Sugar, breaks ranks with Sylvia by responding to Miss Moore's probing questions about social justice:

> "Imagine for a minute what kind of society it is in which some people can spend on a toy what it would cost to feed a family of six or seven. What do you think?"

> "I think," say Sugar pushing me off her feet like she never done before, cause I whip her ass in a minute, "that this is not much of a democracy if you ask me. Equal chance to pursue happiness means an equal crack at the dough, don't it?" Miss Moore is besides herself and I am disgusted with Sugar's treachery.

Sylvia's parting of the ways with Sugar signals an ambiguous ending. When Sylvia uncharacteristically lets Sugar get ahead of her as they race down the block to spend the remaining taxi money they "forgot" to return to Miss Moore, she thinks, "She can run if she want to and even run faster. But ain't nobody gonna beat me at nuthin."

Miss Moore is the catalyst for Sylvia's angst and also for her newfound determination. Because all of the information readers get about Miss Moore is filtered through Sylvia's irreverent consciousness, she seems at first an uppity, quintessential busybody, "the only woman on the block with no first name." But it is evident that the other elders respect, if not like her: "She'd been to college and it was only right that she should take responsibility for the young ones' education, and she not even related by marriage or blood."

Miss Moore has a genius for finding teachable moments. After escorting her brood into the toy store, ". . . steady watching us like she waiting for a sign. Like Mama Drewery watches the sky and sniffs the air and takes note of just how much slant is in the bird formation," she stands back as Sugar and Sylvia study the price tag on a $1195 fiberglass sailboat. "Looking closely . . . like maybe she planning to do a portrait from memory," Miss Moore waits for the girls to intuitively grasp her lesson. Although Sylvia realizes the point ("Where we are is who we are Miss Moore always pointin out. But it don't necessarily have to be that way . . .'"), she "won't give her that satisfaction" of admitting this out loud. Sylvia's final refusal to publicly acknowledge Miss Moore's lesson about class-consciousness underscores Bambara's theme of generational conflicts in the black community.

Other characters—Big Butt, Rosie Giraffe, Flyboy, Q. T., and Junebug—provide primarily comic relief. On first viewing F.A.O. Schwarz, one child asks, "Can we steal?" Junebug delights in exploiting the humor in bodily noises and in turning Miss Moore's phrases such as "naked eye" into hilarious sexual references. However, Mercedes serves as a foil to the others, emphasizing the theme of inequitable income distribution. Only Mercedes is serious throughout the entire trip, undaunted by the riches before her, perhaps because her home is more upscale: "I have a box of stationery on my desk and a picture of my cat. My godmother bought the stationery and the desk. There's a big rose on each sheet and the envelopes smell like roses." Mercedes, though, seems to have missed the lesson about economic disparity. The others "shove her out of the pack so she has to lean on the mailbox by herself" when Mercedes longs to "go back there again when I get my birthday money."

Book cover illustration by Richard Taddei for *Gorilla, My Love* by Toni Cade Bambara.

◆ LITERARY QUALITIES ◆

The most significant literary technique Bambara employs in the story is the creation of an authentic preadolescent voice. Sylvia's point of view supplies the story with its humor and its irony. The opening line emphasizes why Sylvia voice is so important to the message: "Back in the days when everyone was old and stupid or young and foolish and me and Sugar were the only ones just right, this lady moved on our block with nappy hair and proper speech and no makeup." Sylvia's sass gives the narrative its fire and life. Sylvia can imitate her elders, and her description of her mother's expected response if the child were to ask for one of the toys is a vivid example: "I could see me askin my mother for a thirty-five-dollar birthday clown. 'You want a who that cost what?' she'd say, cocking her head to the side to get a better view of the hole in my head." Sylvia's calculated pretense of not understanding Miss Moore's purpose in taking the children on the trip also creates the ironic and ambiguous ending.

The story's structure is also notable. The opening scene and closing scene mirror each other, both taking place by the mailbox in the neighborhood. Sylvia considers Miss Moore and her ideas "boring-ass" at the beginning, but at the end she is think-

ing, hard, about what she has observed, and "something weird is goin on. I can feel it in my chest." It's important that the newly reflective Sylvia be standing in the same place as the child who, just hours earlier, was determined to remain blissfully uninformed.

◆ SOCIAL SENSITIVITY ◆

The primary social issue in this story is the disparity of wealth, especially in America's larger cities. Sylvia emphasizes this point as she contemplates the thirty-five-dollar birthday clown:

Thirty-five dollars and the whole household could go visit Granddaddy Nelson in the country. Thirty-five dollars would pay for the rent and the piano bill too. Who are these people that spend that much for performing clowns and $1000 for toy sailboats? What kinda work they do and how they live and how come we ain't in on it?

Another social issue the story tackles is the notion of inadequate parenting. Some of the neighborhood parents take very little responsibility for the whereabouts, much less the education, of their own children. This issue of parental failure is alluded to as Sylvia describes Aunt Gretchen:

> She was the main gofer in the family. You got some ole dumb s—— foolishness you want somebody to go for, you send for Aunt Gretchen. . . . Which is how she got saddled with me and Sugar and Junior in the first place while our mothers were in a la-de-da apartment up the block having a good ole time.

The children's lack of respect for Miss Moore and their habitual use of profanity combine to create a tone that some readers have found objectionable. The lack of respect is clearly a plot device, because everyone except Sylvia develops a more favorable attitude toward the older woman at the end of the story. However, the profanity, even though totally realistic, has created a problem for some teachers of younger students who want to teach the story but find the language problematic.

◆ TOPICS FOR DISCUSSION ◆

1. Why does Miss Moore take the children to a posh Fifth Avenue toy store?

2. What is the lesson Miss Moore is attempting to teach?

3. Why does Miss Moore refuse to tell the children what her point had been?

4. What is the effect of the children's use of vulgar language in the story?

5. How do Sugar and Sylvia react differently to the lesson?

6. Discuss the other children in the story. Are they presented as individuals?

7. What do you think Miss Moore's motives are in spending time with the children?

8. How is Miss Moore different from the other women in the neighborhood?

9. Compare how Bambara would describe Miss Moore with some of Sylvia's descriptions of her.

10. Discuss Sylvia's last words. What are various ways to interpret these remarks?

◆ IDEAS FOR REPORTS AND PAPERS ◆

1. Investigate the geography of the story. Get a map of New York City and plot the various sites on it.

2. Compare this story to other works of literature in which a child or pre-adolescent voice is used. Decide if the voice is consistently authentic. Are there any lines that sound as if written by an adult?

3. Investigate present-day disparities in living expenses in Manhattan and Harlem.

4. Discover the history of Harlem. What was the area like in its prime?

5. F.A.O. Schwarz has been featured in other works of literature and in several films. Research the store to see why it has captured the imagination of so many writers and directors.

6. Research the performance of children on New York City's mandatory assessment tests. What disparities remain in educational opportunities for children in different areas of the city?

7. Sylvia alludes to the fact that all of her family has moved to the city from the

South. Research this migration to discover when and why it happened as well as whether it continues today.

◆ RELATED TITLES/ADAPTATIONS ◆

Bambara's short stories often feature a hostile, powerful young black woman, and just as frequently, an older black woman appears as a mentor or guide. Most of the stories in *Gorilla My Love*, the anthology that contains "The Lesson," also feature female narrators. Many of them are young women who must confront experiences that force them to a new, often unwanted, awareness of life. From *Tales and Stories for Black Folks*, the most frequently anthologized of Bambara's stories, "Raymond's Run," also has as its heroine a young black woman who appears at first to be resentful and difficult. Her handicapped brother, Raymond, is both her greatest burden and her deepest love; her greatest pride is her own athletic ability. Although she can outrun everyone, and Raymond can barely run, it is only when she observes him in a race that she recognizes that the love is stronger than the resentment.

Although it is autobiographical rather than fictional, Maya Angelou's *I Know Why the Caged Bird Sings* has a great deal in common with "The Lesson" and "Raymond's Run" and is often taught in conjunction with Bambara's work. The voice of a young girl on the edge of adolescence and the often touching yet difficult experiences that nudge her toward adulthood are central to both Bambara's short stories and the first volume of Angelou's autobiography.

There are no film or audiocassette versions of "The Lesson," but David Michael Donnangelo, a contemporary artist, has produced what he refers to as a "narrative painting" illustrating the story. Depicting Sylvia standing outside the toy store window expressionless as she observes the birth-day clown and the sailboat, the painting aims to provide visual insight into this child's life and her social dilemma. The pictoral version is accessible online at http://members.tripod.com/DavidDonnangelo/Bibliography.html (last accessed November 20, 2001).

◆ FOR FURTHER REFERENCE ◆

Comfort, Mary. "Liberating Figures in Toni Cade Bambara's *Gorilla My Love*." *Studies in American Humor* 3.5 (1998): 76–96. This essay examines characters in all fifteen of the short stories in this collection.

Gidley, Mick. "Reading Bambara's 'Raymond's Run.'" *English Language Notes* 28.1 (September 1990): 67–72. Gidley provides an explication of the most frequently anthologized Bambara short story.

Hargrove, Nancy D. "Youth in Toni Cade Bambara's *Gorilla My Love*." *Southern Quarterly* 22.1 (Fall 1983): 479–93. This essay explores the young characters in this anthology.

Reuben, Paul P. "Chapter 10: Late Twentieth Century, 1945 to the Present—Toni Cade Bambara." *PAL: Perspectives in American Literature—A Research and Reference Guide.*

◆ RELATED WEBSITES ◆

URL: http://www.csustan.edu/english/reuben/pal/chap10/bambara.html (last accessed November 20, 2001). This web page offers a full bibliography of Bambara scholarship.

Harriett S. Williams, Ph.D.
University of South Carolina

THE MAN THAT CORRUPTED HADLEYBURG

Short Story

1900

Author: Mark Twain

◆

Major Books for Young Adults

*The Celebrated Jumping Frog of Calaveras
    County, and Other Sketches*, 1867
The Adventures of Tom Sawyer, 1876
The Prince and the Pauper, 1882
The Adventures of Huckleberry

Finn, 1884
*A Connecticut Yankee in King Arthur's
    Court*, 1889
*The Man That Corrupted Hadleyburg,
    and Other Stories and Essays*, 1900

◆ ABOUT THE AUTHOR ◆

Mark Twain was born Samuel Langhorne Clemens in Florida, Missouri, on November 30, 1835, the sixth child of John and Mary Clemens. In 1839, the Clemens family moved to the Mississippi River town of Hannibal, Missouri. Life in Hannibal centered on the river. Steamboats landed in Hannibal three times a day. Grand riverboats and giant barges traveled up and down the Mississippi, bringing with them the wonders of the world and a constantly changing but always colorful cross-section of humanity. Throughout his career as a writer and a humorist, Twain drew ideas and inspiration from the places, the people, and the events of his childhood. Clemens's pen name, Mark Twain, was taken from life on the river. It is a riverman's term meaning two fathoms of water, the minimum safe depth for steamboats negotiating the Mississippi.

Clemens's literary career began at an early age. Following his father's death in 1847, at the age of thirteen, Clemens went to work as an apprentice printer at the *Missouri Courier*, a local newspaper. His first written sketches were published when he was sixteen, while working for his brother Orion's newspaper, the *Hannibal Western Union*. Samuel Clemens spent his late adolescence and early adulthood traveling and writing, publishing articles in the *Saturday Evening Post* and the *Hannibal Journal* in addition to his brother's second newspaper, the *Keokuk Journal*.

Clemens's dream as a boy was to pilot a steamboat on the river. In 1857, when Clemens was twenty-one years old, he met a steamboat pilot named Horace Bixby. He

Mark Twain

When Clemens arrived in San Francisco in 1864, he went to work for a local newspaper, the *Call,* as a full-time reporter. He also retained his affiliation with the *Territorial Enterprise* by becoming its Pacific correspondent. Clemens eventually worked for a number of San Francisco newspapers, including the *Golden Era* and the *Californian.* He also became a central figure in the literary scene, joining other West Coast writers such as Bret Harte and C. H. Webb. During this time, he also became a popular public speaker and traveled to Hawaii as a correspondent for the *Sacramento Union.*

In 1866, Clemens left California for New York City. His trip east included a lengthy lecture tour, stopping in towns across the country where he retold many of the stories that had made him so popular in California lecture halls. Shortly after arriving in New York, he booked passage on a ship headed to Europe, Russia, and the Middle East as a correspondent for the *San Francisco Alta Californian.* However, before departing, he made arrangements to publish his first book, *The Celebrated Jumping Frog of Calaveras County, and Other Sketches,* a collection of stories inspired by his life in the West. Clemens, already a well-known lecturer and author, was rapidly becoming a celebrity.

After returning from his trip overseas, the American Publishing Company commissioned Clemens to write a book about his travels. *Innocents Abroad* was the result. Meanwhile, he continued his travels around the country, lecturing and writing about his experiences as he went.

After his marriage to Olivia Langdon in 1870, Clemens's lifestyle changed dramatically. He and his bride settled down in Buffalo, New York, and Samuel became editor of the *Buffalo Express,* a newspaper that he owned an interest in. About this time, *Roughing It,* a record of his experiences in California and Nevada, was published. It was about this time that Susy, his

paid Bixby $500 and became Bixby's apprentice. Two years later, Samuel received his river pilot's license. Unfortunately, in 1861, the Civil War ended civilian traffic on the Mississippi River, and Clemens's career as a river pilot came to an end. Later that year, he followed his brother Orion west to the Nevada Territory. After they arrived, Samuel was caught up in the gold frenzy brought on by the discovery of the Comstock Lode. He found no success as a prospector, eventually going to work in a quartz mill to support himself.

Along the way, Clemens began contributing humorous letters, mostly about life in the mining camps, to the *Virginia City Territorial Enterprise.* He eventually went to work for the newspaper as a reporter covering the territorial legislature. He also wrote about local news and contributed humorous pieces.

After working for the *Virginia City Territorial Enterprise* for a year and a half, he left Nevada suddenly to avoid being arrested for challenging a rival editor to a duel.

first daughter, was born. Olivia and Samuel eventually had three daughters—Susy, Clara, and Jean.

Though now married and a father, Clemens's life remained a busy one. Now a full-fledged literary icon, he continued to travel, expanding his lecture tour to England in 1873. Eventually, he and Olivia moved to Hartford, Connecticut, where he enjoyed his greatest concentrated literary output. Tapping into his childhood experiences in Hannibal, Clemens wrote some of his most famous and influential novels, including *The Adventures of Tom Sawyer* and *The Adventures of Huckleberry Finn.*

In the 1880s, Clemens suffered several personal and financial tragedies. He became more and more despondent and pessimistic. His writing reflected this, becoming darker and more cynical in tone. In 1891, in near financial ruin, he closed his home in Hartford and moved his family to Europe. Adding to his tragedy, in 1896, Clemens's oldest daughter, Susy, died. During this period, he wrote several books and stories, many reflecting his new cynicism, including *Pudd'nhead Wilson* and "The Man That Corrupted Hadleyburg."

By 1901, his finances back in order, Clemens was back in New York City, lecturing widely and participating actively in New York society. However, his happiness was short-lived. His wife Olivia died after a long illness in 1904. After Olivia's death, Clemens renewed his fast-paced life, writing and making countless personal appearances until 1909, when Clemen's youngest daughter, Jean, died. After Jean's death, Clemens's health rapidly deteriorated. Samuel Clemens died on April 21, 1910.

An interesting coincidence surrounds Clemens's birth and death. When he was born in 1835, Halley's Comet was in the sky. Throughout his life, Clemens insisted that he "came in on the comet" and would "go out on the comet." Ironically, when Clemens died in 1910, Halley's Comet had completed its 75 year journey and was once again in the sky.

Mark Twain (Samuel Clemens) is considered by many to be the father of modern American Literature. Although he is known widely as a humorist and children's writer, the subjects of his stories and their themes are often very serious. One of his most famous books, *The Adventures of Huckleberry Finn*, is a story of racial prejudice and of a young boy's initiation into the harsh realities of life. In it, the Mississippi River is a metaphor for life as the young protagonist, Huck, navigates his way down the river and out of innocence. Twain's style represents a significant departure from other writers of his time. Twain wrote with a caustic, often ironic wit. Unlike his contemporaries, Twain based his stories on common people in prosaic situations and settings and endowed his narratives with natural, often very colorful and thickly colloquial language. Twain's stories preserve a fading snapshot of America during a time of dramatic social change. His was the voice of America, trapped between the old and the new.

◆ OVERVIEW ◆

"The Man That Corrupted Hadleyburg" is about an arrogant and pious town that believes itself immune from corruption. A stranger passing through Hadleyburg is mistreated by its self-righteous citizens. This stranger vows to get even and sets in motion an elaborate scheme that draws the town's leading citizens into a complex hoax that ultimately results in the destruction of Hadleyburg's pristine reputation for honesty.

Hadleyburg is a small town with a big ego. Over three generations its citizens have cultivated and protected the notion that their community is the most moral, most honest, most incorruptible one in the world, certainly in the country. The principals of honesty so precious to the town are taught to infants and to children all through their formative years. The children are also shielded from temptations of any sort, so that their honesty and integrity can mature and become a permanent part of their being.

Neighboring towns are jealous of Hadleyburg's spotless reputation and put off by their arrogance, but they are also forced to admit the truth in Hadleyburg's claim to be an incorruptible town. Though Twain gives few clues as to the geographic location of this fictitious village, he does mention that one of its jealous neighbors is a town called Brixton.

Hadleyburg has a post office, a bank, a newspaper named the *Missionary Herald,* a town hall with 412 permanent seats, a public square, a telegraph office, a Baptist church and a Presbyterian church. Hadleyburg is the kind of small town where everyone knows everyone else's business. It is the kind of small town where people do not lock their doors unless they have something to hide. It is the kind of small town where houses and lawns and lives are neat and tidy, and people sit on their porches in the evening, sipping tea and humming hymns. It is the kind of town where everyone knows who does not go to church. Hadleyburg has nineteen leading citizens, and everyone knows who they are.

◆ THEMES AND CHARACTERS ◆

Twain wrote "The Man That Corrupted Hadleyburg" during a period of hardship and disillusionment. Loss and disillusion-

ment in his own life had caused him to become increasingly cynical about the world and society in general. "The Man That Corrupted Hadleyburg," often thought to be Twain's finest short story, reflects this disillusionment. The central characters in the story, though they are the pillars of their community and attend church every Sunday, turn out to be greedy, deceitful, and easily tempted. Even so, through all of this, Twain still manages to allow readers a muffled, somewhat guilty chuckle here and there.

"The Man That Corrupted Hadleyburg" has several dominant themes. Among them are weakness in the face of temptation, rationalization of guilt, vanity, and revenge. Twain develops these themes with a compelling and artistic construct of interesting characters, revealing dialogue and an intricate plot.

It is difficult to designate a protagonist or an antagonist in this story. Though readers may sympathize with the stranger, they are not given any specifics about him or the injury done to him by the citizens of Hadleyburg. It is not clear how many of the town's good citizens were involved, or even if their actions warranted such retribution. What is clear is the stranger's depth of resolve and the lengths to which he will go in order to have his revenge on Hadleyburg. Though readers may marvel at the stranger's cleverness and identify with his disdain for vain, self-righteous people, it would be difficult to consider such a shadowy and cynical character, whom the narrator labels "bitter and revengeful," a protagonist.

The reader might even consider the late Barclay Goodson a protagonistic figure. Though a long-time resident of the village, Goodson was an outsider, neither born nor raised in Hadleyburg, and therefore immune to its pious pride. The citizens of Hadleyburg hated him for this and for his regular public criticism of the town's excessive self-righteousness, but they also grudgingly admit that he was the only one in their community capable of the kind of selfless generosity and humanity described in the stranger's letter. Additionally, he was known for the quality and readiness of his advice, something his neighbors granted but did not always properly appreciate. The character of Goodson is in contrast to the typical Hadleyburg citizen. Unfortunately, Barclay Goodson is dead at the beginning of the story and is not involved at all in the action of the plot.

If there is a protagonist, it would have to be Edward Richards, the old bank cashier with whom the stranger leaves the sack of gold coins, setting the plot into motion. He is at the center of the action throughout the story, and readers find themselves constantly identifying, second-guessing, and criticizing his behavior. Like most of the citizens of Hadleyburg, Richards seems to be an essentially good and honest person, but not a perfect one. Whatever the stranger's motives, his plot to embarrass Hadleyburg simply brought to light human weaknesses that were always there, buried just below the surface. He merely demonstrated to the world that Richards and the other good citizens of Hadleyburg were susceptible to the same lures of temptation and greed that afflict the rest of the world.

Richards's wife, Mary, is at home alone when the stranger knocks on her front door, delivering what appears to be a large, very heavy bag of money and a letter. According to the accompanying letter, the bag contains a fortune. The bag is sealed, discouraging inspection or tampering. The letter goes on to relate an incredible story about a down and out gambler who, as the result of an act of kindness and generosity, has become rich and now wants to settle matters by rewarding the man who had committed that act of kindness before returning to his home in Europe. Unfortunately, the drifter

never knew the name of his benefactor, and so has designed a clever plan to assure that the money goes to the right person. The generous citizen of Hadleyburg had, in addition to a gift of twenty dollars, offered the gambler a bit of parting advice. The remark was so memorable that the gambler was certain the man would remember uttering it. The letter also explains that a sealed envelope containing that remark is inside the money sack. That remark would be the proof needed to claim the reward.

The Richardses are very poor, and Mary is at once sorely tempted by the money, believing she is the only one who knows about the money and thus could simply claim it for herself and her husband. However, even before her husband returns from a trip to a nearby town, she rejects the idea, rationalizing that it is tainted, the result of gambling, "the wages of sin." Mary's ethics survive their first test.

Edward Richards returns home exhausted, complaining about the dismal quality of his life as a salaried laborer. Edward has worked hard all his life and has been a trusted and loyal employee. Even so, he resents working while Mr. Pinkerton, the owner of Hadleyburg's bank and Edward's boss, just sits "at home in his slippers, rich and comfortable." Edward's first response is the same as his wife's. He imagines he and Mary keeping the bag of money for themselves, rationalizing that they could simply deny any knowledge of the stranger or his money if he ever returns. However, before his reverie could crystallize into action, Mary breaks his trance by reminding him the danger of keeping that much money in their home. (This seems rather ironic in a town known for its honesty.) Coming to his senses, Edward rushes from the house, on his way to publish the stranger's letter in the newspaper, beginning the process of finding its rightful recipient. This time, though Mary and Edward are both sorely tempted, they manage to resist the promise of a comfortable retirement and do the right thing.

The only person the Richardses can think of in the entire village with the goodness and generosity to have given an indigent stranger twenty dollars is Barclay Goodson. Ironically, the good Barclay Goodson is universally disliked in the village because he had insisted publicly, on many occasions that Hadleyburg is not only honest but also "narrow, self-righteous, and stingy." The only problem is that Barclay Goodson is dead.

Other Hadleyburg citizens who hear the story also conclude that the bag's proper owner must be Barclay Goodson. At one point, at the urging of his wife, the newspaper editor, Cox, came to Richards and propose they pull the letter from the paper and split the contents of the bag, since no one else knows about it and Goodson is not around to collect. They might have gone through with the plan, but the letter has already been printed and distributed. So far, the stranger's plan was working perfectly. Every "honest citizen" that has knowledge of the bag of money has at least considered fraud and deceit.

The letter named Reverend Burgess, the "second best hated man" in Hadleyburg, to be the man responsible for opening the sealed envelope and making sure that the bag of money went only to the person to which it is intended. This rather surprises Mary, as she knows Burgess to be a less than honorable man who had lost his entire congregation following some kind of terrible scandal. Ironically, Edward Richards knew that Burgess was innocent of the charges against him, but, fearing retribution from the rest of the village, did not offer the evidence that would have cleared Burgess's name. To his credit, when it appeared that Burgess's life might be in dan-

ger, Edward had gone to him, warning him to leave town until passions waned. For this, Burgess was forever grateful to Edward. Prior to confessing this to Mary, Edward had never told a soul. At first Mary is shocked, then she rationalizes Edward's behavior, thinking it probably would not have changed what happened to Burgess.

The stranger remains in Hadleyburg, monitoring the effect of his efforts. He then draws the remainder of Hadleyburg's leading citizens into his trap by sending identical letters to each of them under the signature of a fictitious fellow named "Stephenson." "Stephenson" claims to have been an acquaintance of the late Barclay Goodson and to have knowledge of all the events leading up to the current moral dilemma in Hadleyburg. Each believes that they are the sole recipient. "Stephenson" claims to have been present at the time of the generous act, confirming that it was indeed Goodson who had been the drifter's benefactor. He also claims to know the memorable remark that Goodson had uttered at the time. "Stephenson" explains that he knows Mr. Goodson is deceased and without an heir and goes on to explain that the person to whom the letter is sent has done some unspecified but significant good deed for Goodson in the past and is, therefore, most qualified to collect Goodson's prize. He suggests the addressee submit a claim using the motto he has provided as if he is the one to whom the money is intended. All of Hadleyburg's nineteen leading citizens, including Edward Richards, fall for the trap; each sends Reverend Burgess a note claiming to be the rightful owner of the bag of money. Each of Hadleyburg's leading citizens has committed an act of fraud and deceit. Now the stranger must only find a way to reveal Hadleyburg's hypocrisy to the world.

At the appointed time and place, the town of Hadleyburg gathered to witness what now has become a spectacle, the award-ing of a fortune in gold to one of Hadleyburg's upright and respected citizens. As the event has attracted considerable outside interest, in addition to most all of Hadleyburg's citizens, reporters from newspapers all over the country are present. Reverend Burgess draws the sealed envelope from the bag, opens it and reads the first part of the letter inside. Then Burgess begins to read the nineteen notes claiming the prize. It soon becomes obvious that all are guilty. The town is shocked and embarrassed. When Burgess reaches for the nineteenth note, he cannot find it, concluding that he must have miscounted the number of claims. Of all the nineteen leading citizens of Hadleyburg, only Richards's name remains without dishonor.

At this time, Burgess read the rest of the letter from the bag, which explains the hoax and its purpose and the bag is found to contain only worthless, gilt-covered lead coins. A citizen suggests they auction off the contents of the bag to the highest bid-der, the proceeds to be given to Richards, the only leading citizen in Hadleyburg whose honor remains intact. The Richardses cringe, embarrassed and afraid that Edward's note will turn up any minute.

The stranger and perpetrator of the hoax sits in the crowd, disguised to look like an English nobleman. He too is shocked that one of his victims has actually resisted his bait, and resolves to show his admiration for Richards's moral strength. Since none of the eighteen disgraced citizens is bidding, he takes it upon himself to stir the pot and inflate the bidding. He eventually purchases the bag for a bid of $1282. He then proposes that he be allowed to strike the coins with the likenesses of the eighteen men whose names had been sullied by their deceit and greed, thus increasing their value. The stranger promises to donate part of his earnings to Richards, whom he now deeply

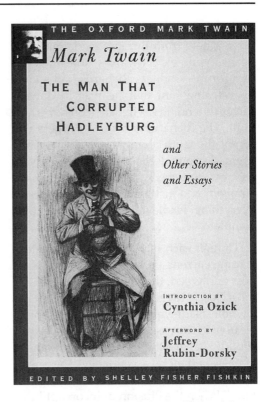

Book cover illustration by Lucius Hitchcock for *The Man That Corrupted Hadleyburg and Other Stories and Essays* by Mark Twain.

respects, believing Richards to be the only truly honest man in Hadleyburg.

"Dr." Clay Harkness, the proprietor of a patent medicine and one of the richest men in Hadleyburg, is one of the unfortunate men whose face is to appear on the coins. He is running for the legislature and stands to gain tremendous wealth in land dealings if he wins the seat. To prevent further dam-age to his reputation, Harkness secretly purchases the coins from the stranger for $40,000. Chagrined that his plan is not com-pletely successful and believing Richards is a truly honest man, worthy of reward, the stranger then delivers $38,500 to Richards and disappears without a word.

Along with the money, the stranger left a note expressing his admiration of Richards's singular honesty. The Richardses also receive a note from Burgess explaining that he has withheld Edward's note to repay him for the kindness Richards had shown by warning him that he was in danger. Richards and his wife are consumed by guilt. The Richardses believe Burgess will reveal the truth about them. Their health begins a steady decline. Eventually, Edward destroys the check given to them by the stranger, and just before he dies confesses everything. Hadleyburg's dishonor is then complete.

Though each of Hadleyburg's nineteen leading citizens suffers from human weakness and greed, the theme of vanity is tied most closely to the village of Hadleyburg as a whole. Hadleyburg's identity is inseparable from its citizens. The people of Hadleyburg proudly believe themselves the epitome of honesty and moral ascendancy. The town's motto had been "Lead us not into temptation." When the illusion of incorruptibility is dispelled by the fall of its leading citizens, Hadleyburg's carefully cultivated self-image crumbles. The town is changed forever. Shortly after its embarrassing disgrace, the town changes its name and its motto. The town's new motto, "Lead us into temptation," offers a hint as to the direction that it may have gone.

◆ LITERARY QUALITIES ◆

Like all of Twain's stories, the characters in "The Man That Corrupted Hadleyburg," are unique, the plot is intricate and carefully crafted, and the dialogue is brisk and believable. However, "The Man That Corrupted Hadleyburg" represents at least two departures from Twain's previous short stories. First, instead of the more typical first person narration chosen for most of his stories, Twain elected to use a third person

omniscient teller, lending the tale more objectivity and allowing the reader to consider the thoughts and feelings of several key characters. Also, "The Man That Corrupted Hadleyburg" is very long for a short story. At over 17,000 words, it is almost three times as long as Twain's typical short narrative. Some publishers would consider it a novella.

The story's exceptional length allows Twain to develop the characters with a depth and fullness beyond what is seen in most short stories. Notable are the main characters of Edward and Mary Richards. They are long-suffering people whose social position in the community has been earned by a lifetime of deeds and hard work. They are old and poor and devoted to each other. They have been married so long that they seem to think as one. Twain's masterful use of dialogue and the omniscient point of view opens their minds and makes readers aware of the Richardses' secret desires, their struggles with temptation, and their depth of disillusionment. When Edward and Mary are doing the right things, such as when Mary first rejects the temptation of the money, calling it the "wages of sin," readers know the secret fears, regrets, and fits of indecision that accompany their actions. When they finally give in to temptation, hiding the truth or falsely claiming the sack of gold, readers see their twisted logic, their rampant imaginings, their creative rationalization, and their growing feelings of guilt.

Minor characters like Barclay Goodman and Jack Halliday lend texture to the story. They add context, massage the tone, and shade the mood of the story. It is characters such as these that have always set Mark Twain apart as a writer. Although Jack Halliday plays no real role in the plot of the story, his character lends a needed counterpoint to the self-serving, self-righteous majority in Hadleyburg. Like Barclay Goodman, his character stands in striking contrast to the righteous nineteen. Every town has a Jack Halliday. Jack Halliday is the "loafing, good-natured, no-account, irreverent fisherman, hunter, boy's friend, stray dog's friend, typical 'Sam Lawson' of the town." He is the sole citizen of Hadleyburg that notices the change that comes over the town after the arrival of the sack of gold. Jack notices everything, and makes fun of everything he notices. He notices when gold and avarice creep into everyone's head, making them moody and absent-minded, and he jokes about it. No one takes him seriously. When the nineteen leading citizens each believe they are about to claim the fortune in gold, Jack Halliday notices their expressions change to contentment and happiness. Again he makes jokes, and again no one listens. Jack Halliday's character and role in life seems a close parallel to that of his creator. Mark Twain would not be the first writer to cast himself as a character in one of his stories.

The only suspense in the plot of "The Man That Corrupted Hadleyburg" is related to how the stranger intends to embarrass an entire town. Twain answers this question and he develops the plot of the story slowly, a piece at a time, using each plot element as an engine for developing and fine-tuning character and setting. The stranger's three letters mark divisions in the plot development, developing the conflict and providing motivation for the characters. The first letter, the one that was given to Mary along with the sack of gold, begins the action by introducing the central conflict, the internal struggle between greed and honesty. Stephenson's letter broadens the plot to involve more characters and adds conflict in the form of jealousy and guilt. The third letter, sealed within the bag of gold, provides the first elements of resolution as it reveals the dishonesty and corruption of Hadleyburg's finest citizens, marks the climax, and sets the denouement into motion.

◆ SOCIAL SENSITIVITY ◆

"The Man That Corrupted Hadleyburg" is Twain's *Tartuffe*. Like Moliere's 17th century French satire, it is an indictment of those who too loudly profess their piety and, in this case, their honesty. Twain recognizes that even the best among us is human, and thus has human weaknesses and is corruptible. In fact, this story would suggest that those who claim to be incorruptible are, in fact, the most easily corrupted. The story also demonstrates that people have the power to control their own destiny and are capable of making the right choices, even if they do not always do the right thing.

"The Man That Corrupted Hadleyburg" indicts blinding self-righteousness that loses sight of compassion and true charity. Ironically, in a town priding itself for its goodness and piety, only one man, Barclay Goodman, was capable of such an act of selfless generosity.

Twain also examines the nature of honesty, and how outwardly righteous people like Mary and Edward Richards find ways to rationalize their deceit and hide it from their own conscience. He demonstrates that good never exists without its share of evil. The people of Hadleyburg tried to ignore the reality of evil and had sheltered their children from corruption. In changing the motto at the end of the story, Twain suggests that children would be better served by teaching them the fallible nature of man, rather than trying to protect them from it.

◆ TOPICS FOR DISCUSSION ◆

1. Were the people of Hadleyburg as honest and incorruptible as they claimed?

Why do you suppose they believe they were? What did they do to reinforce that image and to perpetuate it?

2. What do you suppose happened to the stranger in Hadleyburg that would cause him to go to such extreme ends to seek his revenge? Why do you suppose he chose to get his revenge on the entire town instead of the individual or individuals that injured him?

3. Why do you think that all of the nineteen fell into the stranger's trap? What do you think the stranger would have done if none had sent a note to Reverend Burgess?

4. Why do you think the town changed its name at the end of the story?

5. Mark Twain is known for his colorful diction. Locate an example of this and explain how you think diction influences the overall effect of the story?

6. Why do you think Twain kept the setting of the story so vague? Besides its name, what else do you know about Hadleyburg?

7. Explain how the gilt-covered lead coins in the stranger's sack might be a metaphor for the citizens of Hadleyburg.

8. Who are the leading citizens of Hadleyburg? Compare them to the leading citizens of your community. What are the similarities? Differences?

9. What caused Edward and Mary Richards to lose their health at the end of the story? Why do you think they never cashed the check given to them by the stranger?

10. At the end of the story, the town not only changes its name, it changes its motto to "Lead us into temptation."

Why would they change the motto to one that invites temptation?

◆ IDEAS FOR REPORTS AND PAPERS ◆

1. The plot of "The Man That Corrupted Hadleyburg" ends pretty much as the stranger had planned it. Rewrite the end of the story in such a way that the town is somehow saved from dishonor. Which ending do you think is more realistic? Why?

2. Twain often invents interesting characters such as Jack Halliday to spice up the plot and give the setting context. Invent another character that would fit into the story. Using a combination of action, dialogue, and description, write a new section of the story, integrating your new character into the plot.

3. Hadleyburg is not unique in the changing of its name. Discover the name of two real villages, towns, or cities that have changed their names. Write a report detailing the circumstances leading up to the change and how and why they chose new names for their communities.

4. Mark Twain is not the only writer who is critical of society. Historically, writers have long believed that they have a responsibility to critique human behavior and expose the ills of society. Write a report on contemporary poets, novelists, or short story writers that are known for taking political stands and for their social satire. Include short abstracts of their most satirical works, explaining their favorite issues and the nature of their social criticism.

5. Write a report comparing the town of Hadleyburg to a school or business with

which you have personal and direct experience. Include parallels to the characters in the story and to the issues involved, including those of arrogance, power, and greed.

6. The citizens of Hadleyburg all rationalized their dishonest decision to claim the stranger's sack of gold in a number of ways. They created arguments and convinced themselves that doing so was not immoral. One argument was that no one would be hurt by his or her actions. Is that true? What other arguments did they use to rationalize their deceit? Is there evidence they have done this in the past?

7. The stranger's plot centers on a fictitious gambler who uses the twenty dollars given to him in Hadleyburg to win more money and become a wealthy man. Why was this ironically appropriate? What does this suggest about social standing of gamblers in the late-nineteenth century? What kind of gambling would he likely have been involved in? How has gambling and its degree of social acceptance changed in the past hundred years?

8. Having a motto is not unique to Hadleyburg. Mottoes are found everywhere—on money, on emblems, in churches, and above doorways. Chances are that your school, your town, your state, even your country has a motto. What are these mottoes? What do they say about the people who adopt them? Who creates mottoes? What is their purpose? Create a family motto, one that you believe reflects both you and your family.

◆ RELATED TITLES ◆

In Twain's later works, his natural sarcasm gradually grows into a general bitterness, disillusionment, and pessimism toward the basic nature of God and the human race. This growing cynicism influenced much of his later writing, emerging in his writing as increasingly sharp and biting social criticism.

In addition to "The Man That Corrupted Hadleyburg," many of Twain's most famous works can also be characterized as social criticism. Often considered his greatest novel, *The Adventures of Huckleberry Finn* (1884), tells the adventures of a young boy and a runaway Negro slave as together they search for truth and freedom on the Mississippi River. The novel does more than tell a compelling story of action and adventure. It lays bare the blatant and pervasive social and racial prejudice of nineteenth-century America. It also questions the individual's responsibility to society and the extent to which people must shape themselves to fit the mold of social expectation.

Twain's growing bitterness can also be seen in *A Connecticut Yankee in King Arthur's Court*, which was published in 1889. *A Connecticut Yankee in King Arthur's Court* is a novel about a young man who, after a blow to his head, is magically transported across time and space from his home in nineteenth-century America to medieval England and the mythical kingdom of King Arthur. Though the book certainly offers the clever narrative and special brand of homespun humor expected from Twain, it is also a broad sweeping social satire. Among other issues, the book takes to task the inflated ego of nineteenth-century industrialists and misuse of power, no matter the source. Like many of Twain's other works, it also offers an indictment of such universal ills as excessive personal ego, arrogance, and social injustice.

In 1980, "The Man That Corrupted Hadleyburg" was dramatized on the television series *American Short Story*. The episode featured Robert Preston as the stranger.

◆ FOR FURTHER REFERENCE ◆

"Mark Twain." In *Short Story Writers*, vol. 3. Pasadena: Salem Press, Inc., 1997: pp. 907–908. Provides helpful insights into many Twain's short works, including useful criticism and analysis.

"Mark Twain." In *Twentieth Century Literary Criticism*, vol. 12. Detroit: Gale Research, 1984: pp. 423–424. Limited biographical sketch with some publishing details and brief comments on selected works.

Rasmussen, R. Kent, editor. *Mark Twain A to Z: The Essential Reference to His Life and Writings*. New York: Facts on File, 1995: p. 188. Just as the title suggests, a complete Twain reference.

◆ RELATED WEBSITE ◆

Waisman, Scott. "Sam Clemens—A Life." *About Mark Twain* http://www.geocities.com/swaisman (December 2001). Provides a thorough discussion of the author's life, including a time line and publications.

Robert Redmon

MARTHA GRAHAM: A DANCER'S LIFE

Biography

1998

Author: Russell Freedman

◆

Major Books for Young Adults

Teenagers Who Made History, 1961

2000 Years of Space Travel, 1963

Jules Verne: Portrait of a Prophet, 1965 (biography)

Thomas Alva Edison, 1966 (biography)

Scouting with Baden Powell, 1967

How Animals Learn, 1968 (with James E. Morriss)

Animal Instincts, 1970 (with James E. Morriss)

Animal Architects, 1971 (with James E. Morriss)

The Brains of Animals and Men, 1972

The First Days of Life, 1974

Growing Up Wild: How Animals Survive, 1975

Animal Fathers, 1976

Animal Homes, 1976

How Birds Fly, 1977

Hanging On: How Animals Carry Their Young, 1977

Getting Born, 1978

How Animals Defend Their Young, 1978

Tooth and Claw: A Look at Animal Weapons, 1980

Immigrant Kids, 1980

Farm Babies, 1981

Animal Superstars: Biggest, Strongest, Fastest, Smartest, 1981

When Winter Comes, 1981

Children of the Wild West, 1983

Rattlesnakes, 1984

Cowboys of the Wild West, 1985

Sharks, 1985

Indian Chiefs, 1987

Lincoln: A Photobiography, 1987 (biography)

Buffalo Hunt, 1988

Franklin Delano Roosevelt, 1990 (biography)

Eleanor Roosevelt: A Life of Discovery, 1990 (biography)

The Wright Brothers: How They Invented the Airplane, 1991

An Indian Winter, 1992

Kids at Work: Lewis Hine and the Crusade against Child Labor, 1994

The Life and Death of Crazy Horse, 1996 (biography)

Out of Darkness: The Story of Louis Braille, 1997 (biography)

Martha Graham: A Dancer's Life, 1998 (biography)

Give Me Liberty: The Story of the Declaration of Independence, 2000

◆ ABOUT THE AUTHOR ◆

Notable among Russell Freedman's many honors are the 1988 Newbery Medal for *Lincoln: A Photobiography*, the first non-fiction book awarded this distinction, and Newbery Honor citations for *The Wright Brothers: How They Invented the Airplane* (1992) and *Eleanor Roosevelt: A Life of Discovery* (1993). In 1998, he was given the Laura Ingalls Wilder Medal by the American Library Association for his contributions to children's literature.

Russell Bruce Freedman was born on October 11, 1929, the son of Louis N. Freedman (a sales representative for MacMillan Publishing Company) and Irene Gordon Freedman (an actress). He attended San Jose State College (now University) from 1947 to 1949 and the University of California, Berkeley, earning his Bachelor of Arts degree in 1951. He served in Korea in the Army's Counter Intelligence Corps from 1951 to 1953. He worked from 1953 to 1956 for the Associated Press as reporter and editor, from 1956 to 1961 for an advertising company, and for Columbia University Press from 1961 to 1963.

Though he acknowledges his writing skills were honed in these journalistic endeavors, Freedman found his real destiny in the field of children's nonfiction. Reading that Louis Braille was only sixteen when he invented the Braille alphabet and typewriter, Freedman researched other significant contributions made by the young. Braille, along with Sam Colt, Edna St. Vincent Millay, Wernher von Braun, Toscanini, Lafayette, Babe Didrikson Zaharias, and Galileo comprised Freedman's first book, *Teenagers Who Made History*, (1961). *Two Thousand Years of Space Travel* (1963) and *Jules Verne: Portrait of a Prophet* (1965) followed.

Freedman then became interested in animal behavior. From 1969's *How Animals Learn* to 1985's *Sharks*, he won acclaim for

explaining complex scientific concepts simply and understandably in nearly two dozen books. His trademark integration of photographs with the book's narrative developed during this time.

In the 1980s Freeman's interest ventured beyond the animal kingdom. *Immigrant Kids* (1980), *Children of the Wild West* (1983), and *Cowboys of the Wild West* (1985) were lauded for their accurate portrayal of subjects in both the East and West.

His *Lincoln: A Photobiography* followed in 1987, winning distinction for its meticulous and balanced portrayal of the sixteenth president. Since then, Freedman has continued developing his photobiographies, publishing *Franklin Delano Roosevelt* (1990), *The Wright Brothers: How They Invented the Airplane* (1991), *Eleanor Roosevelt: A Life of Discovery* (1993), *Out of Darkness: The Story of Louis Braille* (1997), *Martha Graham: A Dancer's Life* (1998), and *Babe Didrikson Zaharias* (1999). The drama of the West continues in his books *Indian Chiefs* (1987), *Buffalo Hunt* (1988), *An Indian Winter* (1992), and *The Life and Death of Crazy Horse* (1996). Freedman took a look at early twentieth-century children in *Kids at Work: Lewis Hine and the Crusade against Child Labor* (1994).

Freedman has found his destiny, writing for children. He says, "A writer of books for children has an impact on readers' minds and imaginations that very few writers for adults can match."

◆ OVERVIEW ◆

A biography by Russell Freedman is always more than just a story of one person's life. Freedman details Martha Graham's creative as well as her chronological life. He carefully portrays both the cost and the rewards of genius. Readers finish *Martha Graham: A Dancer's Life* with a feeling for the evolution of dance in America and the cultural forces which determined it. The photographs Freedman includes offer readers a visual image of the artist, complimenting the written portrait the author develops in his text.

◆ SETTING ◆

The world Martha Graham was born into was too small and too tight for her. She grew up during Victorian times which restricted an individual's expression, and imposed strict behavioral rules. For a revolutionary dancer, the determination to express her dance had to be strong in order to break free of the confines of strong approval and disapproval.

Martha Graham seeks out places which were most conducive to her vision. When the repetitive nature of the exotic dances she was performing in Ruth St. Denis's company and the Greenwich Village Follies in New York City became too confining, Graham fashioned her own environment. In her dance studio Graham is free to create her innovations. On the stage, Graham is free to express them. These two settings are important in the life of Martha Graham. Freedman describes Graham sitting on the floor, sewing costumes and instructing her students in executing "contractions" and pushing down on the floor to give strength to their movements. Using description and quotations of eyewitnesses, and remarkable photographs, Freedman puts Graham on stage so that the reader can see the grief, the pioneer spirit, and the passion which Graham personified. As Graham invents modern dance, she embellishes the bare stage with men, with scenery which is itself nearly a work of art, with the spoken word, and with music written especially for dance. Freedman painstakingly chronicles Graham as she evolves as dancer, company director, and choreographer in the only setting Graham wanted, "The Theater of Martha Gra-

Russell Freedman

ham." Once a critical success in New York City, the rest of the geographic world is Graham's for the taking.

◆ THEMES AND CHARACTERS ◆

Martha Graham: A Dancer's Life holds important messages for all readers about realizing their ambitions. Once she had seen Ruth St. Denis dance, Graham had found her destiny. She is determined to achieve it at the cost of any obstacle in her way. She began her training late for a dancer. She was not physically attractive and her body shape and size (a mere five foot, two inches) did not fit into traditional dance norms. However, these physical limitations did not deter her single-mindedness about becoming a dancer. Freedman includes Graham's early financial troubles which forced to her to borrow money from her mentor and lover Louis Horst, make her own clothes, and become a vegetarian. Her fiery temperament incinerates anything—even friendships—that might interfere with her life's work. She purposefully avoids bearing children. "I couldn't control being a dancer," she said. "I knew I had to choose between a child and dance, and I chose dance."

Freedman also shows the dark side of genius. As a perfectionist, she is harsh, demanding, disciplined, and driven. Graham insults those who have offended her; she tears costumes that do not meet her standards; she scraps dances that do not satisfy her. In a furious display of temper, she rips a telephone from the wall and later yanks a tablecloth from a table, sending silverware and glassware to the floor.

Graham had intense personal relationships with Louis Horst and Erick Hawkins. Horst, who played the piano for her first audition, is both lover and mentor to the dancer. Freedman quotes Horst saying, "I gave her discipline. I was the tail to her kite, because she was a wild one. . . . I was her thread to earth." He loans her money, gives her advice, and provides a sounding board for her ideas. Their relationship spans three decades before an argument over one of Graham's dances causes him to walk out. Bringing dancer Erick Hawkins into her all-female company allows Graham to expand the emotions and themes on the stage. Passionately in love with him, Graham eventually marries Hawkins. Agnes de Mille says "He was the man for her." But the marriage between the two fiery artists collapses when Hawkins belittles Graham's dancing. There was little room on the stage for any one else when Martha Graham stood in the spotlight.

The only thing Graham could not dominate by the force of her will was age. Graham reluctantly adapts in order to stay near dance. Hampered by arthritis, she nonetheless reinvents herself from dancer to company director to choreographer.

As a woman and as a dancer, she provoked her audience beyond the pretty sto-
ries of classical ballet. John Martin wrote, "Audiences who come to be amused and entertained will go away disappointed, for Miss Graham's programs are alive with passion and protest. She does the unforgivable thing for a dancer to do—she makes you think."

After "The Three Gopi Maidens," "Maid with the Flaxen Hair," and "Clair de Lune" which reviewers labeled "decorative" and "undisturbing," Graham's dances began to embrace social protest and the strong human passions of ordinary people. She speaks against war, reveals fears of the young, embodies grief, and condemns intolerance. Graham tells in story form the life of Emily Dickinson and Charlotte Brontë, strong and independent women like herself who found the interior world gratifying.

Freedman includes chapters on the new language of movement Graham invents and describes the process in which Graham creates a dance—from her initial inspiration through rehearsal and scenery design to performance. No reader leaves this biography of Graham's life without realizing the rigors of the creative process.

◆ LITERARY QUALITIES ◆

Freedman draws on nearly forty references to construct his portrait of Martha Graham. The details he uses from these sources create an intricate picture of Graham's life. Freedman's descriptions of Graham as a child quickly allow young readers to identify with her. What little girl has not played dress up with her mother's "junk jewelry" or made a theater curtain with a bed sheet like Graham did?

Likewise, Freedman's attention to minutiae captures the world around Graham. The Victorian era of Graham's childhood is perfectly explained by Freedman's comment that little girls were expected to wear "spotless white gloves when they went to church."

His use of quotations from critics, admirers, friends, lovers, and even Graham herself creates an immediacy that also draws both the young adult or mature reader into Graham's life, into her rehearsal studio, and on to the performance stage. Dancing in "Frontier," during the period Graham expressed what being an American was to her, she smiles. Walter Terry writes, "I was there, and it was the most ravishing smile I have ever seen in my life."

Freedman's biography provides balance, including both the praise and the criticism her early work and her later dancing received. He mentions, but does not belabor, her bouts of alcoholism and depression.

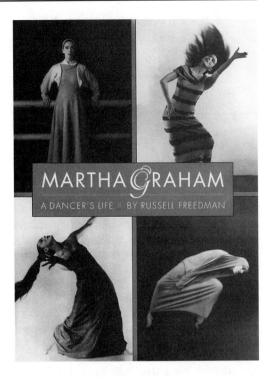

Book jacket photographs by Barbara Morgan and Soichi Sunami for *Martha Graham: A Dancer's Life* written by Russell Freedman.

◆ SOCIAL SENSITIVITY ◆

Martha Graham's life spanned nearly a century. The world Martha Graham was born into was too small and too tight for her. Freedman gives the reader a history lesson in Victorian attitudes. Children were expected to sit up straight and wait for adults to direct them. Though George Graham was a loving man, he still was a Victorian father whose approval or disapproval would have impacted Martha's determination to study dance.

Absorbed in her own work, Graham was little affected by major events in society. But young readers receive a mini lesson in the Nazi persecution of the Jews, the 1936 Olympics, and a glimpse of the censorship which attempted to stifle the avant guard. But seeing them for what they are—prejudice and tyranny—Graham distances herself and her dance company from them.

The dance world Graham revolutionized had been determined by the geometric patterns and narrow, prescribed positions of the body. Ballet feet were tightly bound in order to perform that most unnatural feat of balancing *en pointe,* that is, on the tips of a woman's toes, to tell fluffy, decorative stories. In contrast, Graham's passions were as bare as the feet with which she danced. Her dances explored feelings and conflicts of the "interior landscape." "I did not dance the way that other people danced," she once said. "In many ways I showed onstage what most people came to the theater to avoid."

Martha Graham: A Dancer's Life can be read on several levels. It can be seen as the retelling of one woman's life. It can also be viewed as a chronicle of the cost and the reward of actuating a great ambition. Or it can be considered a history of the evolution of modern dance.

1. How did Martha Graham's ideas of dance differ from the traditions of classical ballet?

2. Part of Graham's success came from surrounding herself with supportive associates. What did Louis Horst, Erick Hawkins, Isamu Noguchi, and Ron Protas contribute to her development as a dancer/creator?

3. Genius is said to be one percent inspiration and ninety-nine percent perspiration. Give examples of Graham's sacrifices in building her dance company.

4. What aspects of her personality as a child and young girl marked the certainty that she was destined to pioneer a new way of dancing?

5. Discuss how the themes in Graham's dances shifted focus over her long career. Cite examples.

6. Women had just earned the right to vote as Graham began her critical success as a dancer. In what ways would she be considered a feminist in today's society?

7. What things did Martha Graham give up that you would not be willing to sacrifice to reach your own ambitions. Explain why.

8. Cite ways Graham adapted to accommodate the limitations age imposed on her ability to dance.

◆ IDEAS FOR REPORTS AND PAPERS ◆

1. Ruth St. Denis and Isadora Duncan were forerunners in the modern dance. How did their styles depart from the established dance of the time?

2. Paul Taylor and Merce Cunningham were students of Martha Graham. Discover how they departed from her teaching, creating distinctive styles of their own.

3. Who is Aaron Copland? Research and listen to the music he composed. What common ground do you think he and Graham shared? Why would he and Graham have collaborated so well?

4. Congressmen objected to the use of federal funds to help support "Phaedra." How does the National Council for the Endowment of the Arts function today? Research recent instances where federal funding of art has become controversial.

5. New expressions of art often cause controversy among the public. Investigate the current definitions and boundaries of art and how it can be distinguished from the profane and obscene.

6. Compare and contrast Freedman's account of Graham's life with Graham's autobiography, *Blood Memory*.

7. Without limiting yourself to the world of dance, pick a pioneer or tradition breaker. Research that person's life, seeing if any common qualities exist with Martha Graham.

8. What issues and themes are dominant in modern dance at present? Is Graham's once ground breaking style and technique still performed on stage?

9. Create a time line recording the accomplishments in Martha Graham's life.

◆ RELATED TITLES ◆

In his annotated bibliography, Freedman lists nearly forty sources about and by Martha Graham which he used for *Martha Graham: A Dancer's Life*. These include other books about her, books about dance, magazine and newspaper articles, and film references.

The Life and Dances of Martha Graham by Trudy Garfunkel, *Frontiers of Dance: The Life of Martha Graham* by Terry Walter, and *The Importance of Martha Graham* by Pamela Pratt are books specifically written for young people. Freedman book's, however, is written in a manner appealing to older readers as well as young ones.

Fellow dancer Agnes De Mille wrote *Martha: The Life and Work of Martha Graham.* Herself a colorful figure of dance, De Mille provides an insider's view of her friend of sixty years. Don McDonah's *Martha Graham: A Biography* was published two years after her death and is described by Freedman as "the most carefully documented biography of Graham."

Martha Graham's autobiography, *Blood Memory,* includes material not found in other biographies. Graham's version of her life reconfirms what analyses and photographs catch: the scope of a great talent and the confidence it inspires.

Those interested in investigating the scope of modern dance might use Jack Anderson's *Ballet and Modern Dance: A Concise History* or Joseph H. Mazo's *Prime Movers: The Makers of Modern Dance in America* as starting points in their search for information about famous dancers.

◆ FOR FURTHER REFERENCE ◆

Giblin, James Cross. "Freedman, Russell." *Horn Book* (July–August, 2000): 473. Giblin quotes Russell about his philosophy of writing, about writing for children, and the influence of photographs in aspects of his career.

Horning, Kathleen T. Review of *Author Talk: Conversations with Judy Blume, Bruce Brooks, Karen Cushman, Russell Freedman, Lee Bennett Hopkins, James How, Johanna Hurwitz, E. L. Konigsburg, Lois Lowry . . . Horn Book* (July–August, 2000): 473. Horning praises author Leonard S. Marcus for focusing the conversations with authors on the creative process. She also likes the way Marcus questions the authors from the standpoint of an adult researcher asking questions children would not think to ask but would be interested in learning the answers.

Review of *Martha Graham: A Dancer's Life. Publishers Weekly* (April 6, 1998): 80. Freedman is praised for his balanced view of the genius/artist, gleaned from exhaustive sources.

Rochman, Hazel. Review of *Martha Graham: A Dancer's Life. Booklist* (April 1, 1998): 1324. Rochman appreciates this first Freedman book about an artist and Freedman's efforts to focus on Graham's creation of a modern dance language. The reviewer finds that Freedman's descriptions lead naturally to photographs.

Striggles, Theodore W. Review of *Martha Graham: A Dancer's Life. New York Times Book Review* (May 17, 1998): 29. While Striggles gently complains Freedman could have made more of Graham's legendary temper and bouts with alcoholism and depression, he praises him for the "fine introduction" the book gives to readers about an icon of modern dance.

Zvirin, Stephanie. Review of *Martha Graham: A Dancer's Life. Booklist* (June 1 & 15, 1998): 1716. *Martha Graham* is included in *Booklist*'s "Crossover" selections because it appeals to both young readers and adults. Zvirin praises Freedman's books as "speaking eloquently" about Graham's personal life and including "electrifying photographs."

Vicki Cox

THE MERLIN EFFECT

Novel

1994

Author: T. A. Barron

Major Books for Young Adults

Heartlight, 1990
The Ancient One, 1992
The Merlin Effect, 1994
The Lost Years of Merlin, 1996
The Seven Songs of Merlin, 1997

The Fires of Merlin, 1998
The Mirror of Merlin, 1999
The Wings of Merlin, 2000
Where Is Grandpa?, 2000
Tree Girl, 2001

◆ ABOUT THE AUTHOR ◆

T. A. Barron was born on March 26, 1952 in Colorado Springs, Colorado. As a boy growing up surrounded by the mountains of Colorado, Barron developed a great respect for the natural world. Always an avid reader, he also loved to write down his own thoughts and feelings, and as a fifth grader even produced a personal magazine for his family and friends entitled "The Idiot's Odyssey." After receiving a bachelor's degree from Princeton University, he spent several years in Europe traveling and studying at Oxford University on a Rhodes scholarship. During this period, he also continued to write and completed his first novel. He abandoned his plans to be a professional writer after over forty publishers rejected this manuscript, and returned to the United States to pursue a law degree at Harvard University. However, instead of completing his law degree, he eventually moved to New York to seek success in the business world working for a small venture capital firm.

Although he temporarily stopped writing fiction, Barron continued to dream of one day becoming a writer. In 1990, a number of life changing events including the death of a close friend, marriage, and the birth of a child happened in rapid succession and prompted him to begin writing again in earnest. At this point he was also fortunate enough to meet Madeleine L'Engle, who asked to read the novel he was working on, a book that would eventually be *Heartlight*. L'Engle was so favorably impressed with Barron's work that she passed the manuscript on to her agent who in turn submitted it to Philomel, the children's di-

T. A. Barron

Effect won the 1997 Texas Lone Star Award, the 2000 Best of the Texas Lone Star Reading Lists, and the 1998 Utah Book Award, among others. Barron's "Lost Years of Merlin" series continues to be cited by such groups as the American Library Association, the New York Public Library, and the Children's Book Council.

Barron says that he writes because it allows him to explore any place and any time period he chooses; he can travel into space, back in time, or under the ocean. Writing for him is not only a way of telling stories, but also thoughtfully exploring the big questions of life. Before he can write his stories, he does extensive research so that he can successfully convince the reader of the reality of a fantastic place or time. For example, prior to writing *The Merlin Effect*, he learned about the legends of Merlin, the history of Spanish galleons (sailing ships), and the lives of gray whales, as wells as the sights, sounds, motion, and smells of the ocean.

vision of Putnam Publishing, where *Heartlight* was published in the fall of 1990.

With the publication of *Heartlight,* Barron decided to take a chance on pursuing his longtime dream of becoming a full-time writer. So, in 1990, he moved back to Colorado and started writing from his home office in Boulder. Since 1990, he has written and published nine young adult novels, two nature books (*To Walk in Wilderness: A Rocky Mountain Journal*, 1993 and *Rocky Mountain National Park: A 100 Year Perspective*, 1995), and a picture book (*Where Is Grandpa?*, 2000).

Barron's books have been well received by critics and young adult readers alike. *The Ancient One* and *The Merlin Effect* have both appeared frequently on lists of best books chosen by young adult readers, as well as those selected by adults. For example, *The Ancient One* was selected for the International Reading Association's Young Adult Choices list and the Voice of Youth Advocates' Best Books of 1992 list. *The Merlin*

◆ OVERVIEW ◆

The Merlin Effect combines scientific research procedures with the mythical stories of Merlin the magician and the conventions of modern fantasy. It tells the story of Kate Gordon and her father and their expedition to the coast of Baja California to search for a sunken Spanish galleon said to contain the lost horn of Merlin. Their research site also reveals unusual undersea volcanic activity, ancient fish that should be long extinct, local villagers with unusual longevity, and a group of ever-singing gray whales guarding a mysterious and dangerous whirlpool. Always willing to test her limits, Kate gets sucked into the whirlpool where she meets Merlin himself, finds the horn, and battles with Merlin against the world's mortal enemy. Along the way, she resolves her relationship with her father, learns to make choices, and comes to understand her own powers of creation.

◆ SETTING ◆

Setting is one of the most important elements in Barron's writing; he believes strongly that readers must experience the world depicted in the story through all their senses. To establish a tone of realism, he uses vivid and highly accurate descriptions of the natural world that look, feel, and smell true. Then, once readers thoroughly believe in the reality of the story, Barron moves them gradually into the fantasy world of his book.

The Merlin Effect is set on the coast of Baja California and off shore in the Pacific Ocean. The story opens with Kate Gordon—alone, paddling out to sea in a kayak, and pondering the state of her relationship with her father. Her isolation in the ocean intensifies her anger at her father. She feels he is ignoring and excluding her, and she dares herself to sprint beyond the second buoy in hopes of attracting his attention. When she reaches the second buoy, she has her first encounter with one of the inhabitants of the ocean, a gray whale caught in the wiring of the sonar transmitter. As Kate struggles to set the trapped whale free, she must also battle the cold, wet, and painful reality of the ocean until she is rescued by her father.

As the story unfolds and the setting is developed, it becomes clear that the amazing beauty of the Pacific Ocean is not the only awe-inspiring quality of this place. Not only do the whales sing continuously, but there are local legends that claim these creatures have actually rescued sailors from drowning for centuries. The other sea life in the area is also strange; some of the fish resemble creatures that have been extinct for centuries. When Isabella (marine biologist and oceanographer) conducts genetic testing on specimens she buys from village fishermen, she discovers that not only the species but also the individual fish are actually hundreds of years old. The whirlpool, called "Remolino de la Muerte" by the villagers, is surrounded by mysterious mists reminiscent of Arthurian Avalon, and protected by the whales. Legends say that there is a Spanish galleon on the ocean floor, but no one has been able to penetrate the whirlpool to find it. Efforts by the research team to record a picture of it have been to no avail. Barron lends additional authenticity to the setting by providing a map of the lagoon and the ocean printed on the end papers of *The Merlin Effect*. By the end of "Part One: Beyond the Lagoon," the author has effectively established the real world and the challenges it poses for the research team.

By the time Kate is swept away in the whirlpool to the underwater world of the Spanish galleon, the reader is well prepared to experience this fantasy. In the murky and misty rooms inside the whirlpool, real and mystical time blend and become confused. At first, Kate and Sir Geoffrey have trouble communicating because she speaks in contemporary idiomatic English that he takes literally; his difficulty is her first clue that time is confused. The air is very humid and full of mist, recalling the mists of Avalon that hid the magical island in Arthurian times. By the time Merlin's nemesis Nimue shows up, Barron has convinced his readers of the believability of the story and the reader has become fully engaged in the narrative.

◆ THEMES AND CHARACTERS ◆

Barron develops the major themes of the novel through the character of Kate Gordon and the story of her inner struggles and her relationships with the other characters. In the course of her adventures, Kate explores the value of choosing, the importance of power, the ability to create, and the best way to determine truth.

The novel's main character, Kate Gordon, is an adventurous thirteen-year-old girl who is spending her summer vacation assisting her historian father on a scientific expedition to Baja California. Kate (who has had other fantastic adventures in Barron's previous novels, *Heartlight* and *The Ancient One*) feels somewhat distant and alienated from her father and longs to be closer to him. Like many adolescents, Kate feels powerless to create her own life, is seeking some goals and direction through her relationship with her father, and would like to be creative, but does not know where to start. She hopes that spending time with her father will make them closer, but as the story begins she feels that he is so wrapped up in his work that he barely notices her existence. After he rescues her from the ocean, Kate and her father do experience a moment of closeness, but it is quickly shattered when she tells him that, in rescuing the whale, she damaged the sonar equipment so critical to the research project. After this incident, Kate is so despondent that she remarks to Isabella that "sometimes being alive does not feel so great" and believes the break in the relationship with her father is her fault.

Jim Gordon, Isabella, and Terry each introduce Kate to a different way of examining the world and determining the truth. Jim is a historian who has spent his career trying to prove the historical truth of the legends of King Arthur and, more specifically, the existence of Merlin. Since myths cannot be definitively proved, his work requires that a certain amount of faith be mixed with fact. At the other extreme, Terry is a geologist who believes in the fundamentals of science and has figured out how to use sonar imaging with thermal sensing to measure volcanic activity. If he cannot see something, he does not believe it. When

Kate is transported to the undersea world, she understands the limitations of this approach. Isabella is a marine biologist and oceanographer who uses genetic analysis to study the theory of evolutionary biology, but she understands that her data does not explain everything she is discovering. Her work enables her to understand creation as an ongoing process with all the possibilities for the future lying within the present. Her explanations of the continuing renewal of cells help Kate to understand that she has the power to create her own life by making choices.

When Kate falls overboard and is swept into the whirlpool, she encounters another group of characters who lead her through life-changing adventures at the bottom of the ocean. First, she meets a curious old Englishman named Sir Geoffrey of Birdseye who has been imprisoned in the whirlpool since the *Resurreccion* sank in 1547. As it turns out, he is actually Merlin and has been hiding in the whirlpool for almost five hundred years to protect the Horn of Merlin from the evil Nimue. Nimue craves the Horn of Merlin so strongly that she has been waiting outside the whirlpool for centuries so that she may steal it, drink from it, and become immortal. In order to lure Merlin out of the whirlpool, she captures Jim and Isabella and holds them prisoner. Merlin transforms Kate into a fish and even allows her to experience the beginning of life as a water spirit, preparing her for the choices she must make to triumph. Using her evil ring to control Kate, Nimue commands Kate to kill her father. Ultimately, however, Kate is able to resist and joins in the battle with Merlin and her father to defeat Nimue and save the Horn.

Through her adventures with these characters, Kate learns that the power of free will and the ability to create your own life is the most important power of all. When she finally gets control of the Horn, she decides not to drink from it because she realizes that she has these powers within herself. She also comes to understand that although she might like to live forever, she actually prefers the chance to continue to grow and change. Her new found wisdom has given her multiple ways of arriving at truth, a skill she can use to keep on growing.

◆ LITERARY QUALITIES ◆

In *The Merlin Effect*, Barron weaves many traditional elements of the fantasy genre with mythology, scientific issues, and a contemporary setting to create a fresh, original story. *The Merlin Effect* includes a hero who must make difficult personal choices that have profound meaning, a quest, the discovery of the credible in the incredible, and the use of legendary materials to tell a new story. Kate's quests, both personal and universal, are most important to the story because she is the central character, but the other characters are also pursuing their own quests. Kate's mission is to find and save the Horn of Merlin to protect the world from evil, but she also seeks to find meaning and direction in her own life as well. For Kate, a trip to the incredible undersea world of Merlin and Nimue is the key to finding the answers to her own personal dilemmas. Most quest fantasies for children and young adults tell the story of a male hero. Barron's use of a female hero who experiences adventure, danger, and a successful quest distinguishes his work from other fantasies and provides a strong role model for adolescent girls struggling with their own questions of identity and purpose. Finally, although there are a number of fantasies for young adults based on Arthurian legends, few, if any, combine those legends with a contemporary setting. This use of myth and legends connects the present with the past and provides a unique venue for exploring questions of adolescent identity.

Book cover illustration by Darrell K. Sweet for *The Merlin Effect* by T. A. Barron.

Barron makes important use of symbols to tell his story and enrich its meaning. The central symbol of the novel is the spiral. It appears first as a code associated with the *Resurreccion* that is found in the Spanish archives. The whirlpool is a spiral that both hides the Treasures of Merlin and sweeps the characters to their adventures. Later, the image is found in the strands of DNA, which hold the basic elements to create life, and finally in the Horn of Merlin itself, which can grant immortal life. This spiral not only ties the story together, but it also symbolizes the vast, continuing nature of creation and life itself. The whirlpool is named the place of death, but the sunken galleon is named as a place of resurrection or rebirth. Barron also makes use of cold and warmth to symbolize evil and good or danger and safety, while he use images of light and dark to signify good and evil.

Barron uses the "Ballad of the *Resurreccion*" to provide a sense of connection among all the elements of the story. The words of the ballad begin and end the novel. For Jim Gordon, the ballad is evidence that the sunken galleon, the Horn of Merlin, and Merlin himself did exist, although others may dismiss it as just a song. The ballad also creates a historical context for the strange occurrences in the lagoon and around the whirlpool. Kate has heard the ballad so often that she frequently recites lines from it to explain what is happening to her and comes to understand the truth of Merlin's story through the poetry of the ballad.

◆ SOCIAL SENSITIVITY ◆

While *The Merlin Effect* poses few if any controversial issues requiring social sensitivity, it does raise some philosophical and scientific questions which students may find interesting to discuss. Terry, Isabella, and Jim disagree on the best way to discover what is "true" and they each bring the methods of different disciplines to their work. Barron also raises the question of whether truth can be discovered not only through facts but also through faith. The research project team seeks to find and retrieve the wreck of a sunken galleon. There is controversy in this field concerning whether remains of this type should be salvaged or left as graves. Finally, Kate's choice to rescue the whale, even though it causes the destruction of the research equipment, poses questions about the impact of scientific research on the environment.

◆ TOPICS FOR DISCUSSION ◆

1. What is the Merlin Effect? How does it affect each of the characters in the story?

2. Choice is an important theme in the story. What choices do Kate, Merlin, Jim, and Terry make throughout the story? Why is Merlin's Horn so tied to choice?

3. Does Kate think power is important? How is power represented in the story?

4. When Isabella asks Kate what her goals are, Kate tells her she would like to create something. When Kate chooses to return the Horn to the ocean, what do you think she has decided about her goals?

5. Barron uses figurative language to create the setting and characters in this story. Find examples of figurative language devices, including simile, metaphor, and personification and explain how they are used in the text.

6. Barron says that he was very conscious of needing to create an authentic female voice for Kate. Do you think he succeeded? In what ways are Kate's voice and character distinctively female? How would this story be different if Kate were a boy?

7. Barron says that words contain powerful magic to create moods. What is the most important word in the story? Prepare a list of reasons that defends your choice.

8. What are the major conflicts in this book? Which conflicts are the most difficult for Kate to overcome? How does conflict advance the story?

1. The stories of King Arthur and his court have a long history. Research the following elements of Arthurian legend that are mentioned in this book: Merlin, Arthur, Isle of Bardsey, Emrys, Thirteen Treasures of Britain, Nimue, and Avalon.

2. Jim Gordon, Terry, and Isabella are all engaged in research projects in Baja California. Jim is a historian, Terry is a geologist, and Isabella is a marine biologist. Find out more about these careers and what other types of research they might do.

3. Write a ballad or poem about Kate and the Horn of Merlin.

4. What kind of marine life really lives off the coast of Baja California? Does Barron describe his setting and its inhabitants accurately?

5. This story ends with many questions. Will the team get a permit to continue its research? Is Terry dead? What will happen to the wreck of the *Resurreccion* now that is has been discovered? Will Merlin return again? Write another chapter that continues the story.

6. Research the biology and ecology of gray whales.

7. The news of this research expedition could be reported for a number of audiences: a national newspaper, a newsletter for historians, Kate's essay on what she did on her summer vacation, and scientific research article. Choose one of these audiences and write a report on what happened in the story.

8. *The Merlin Effect* is a sequel to both *Heartlight* and *The Ancient One*. Read one or more of these books and decide how Kate applied what she learned in the first two books to her challenges in this story.

Kate Gordon's adventures continue in two other novels, *Heartlight* and *The Ancient One*. In *Heartlight*, the first novel in this trilogy, Kate and her grandfather travel to a distant star to save the earth's sun from extinction. In *The Ancient One*, Kate finds herself helping her great-aunt battle loggers to save an old growth redwood forest by traveling back in time to fight the forces of evil. Like *The Merlin Effect*, these two novels combine science, fantasy, and myth with a strong female heroine who has extraordinary adventures in remarkable and intriguing settings. All three books explore connections: between people and other people, people and other cultures, and people and other forms of life.

Barron's research into the legends of Merlin for *The Merlin Effect* inspired him to explore the character of Merlin more deeply. Many of the conflicts and themes introduced in Kate Gordon's adventures appear again in Barron's series "The Lost Years of Merlin Epic." These five volumes explore the childhood and young adult years of the great enchanter as he learns who he is and comes into his magical powers.

Barron, T.A. "The Remarkable Metaphor of Merlin." *Book Links* (January 1998): 29–34.

Beers, Kylene. "Portraits: An Interview with T.A. Barron." *Emergency Librarian* (March-April 1997): 61–63. Interview with Barron about his life as a writer.

Cassada, Jackie. Review of *The Merlin Effect*. *Library Journal* (September 1994): 94.

Contemporary Authors, vol. 150. Detroit: Gale,

1996. Brief introduction to Barron's early work.

Cuthbertson, Ken. *Authors and Artists for Young Adults,* vol. 30. Detroit: Gale, 1999. Brief biographical and critical introduction.

Dennis, Lisa. Review of *The Merlin Effect. School Library Journal* (November 1994): 118.

Estes, Sally. Review of *The Merlin Effect. Booklist* (November 1994): 491.

"Fantasy and Realism: Two Topics, One Author's Talk with T.A. Barron." *Journal of Adolescent and Adult Literacy* (1998): 588–594. Interview with Barron focusing on his view of genre of fantasy and how his works are created.

Feicht, Sylvia. Review of *The Merlin Effect. Book Report* (January 1995): 42.

Lesene, Terry. "Words . . . Words . . . Words." *Teacher Librarian.* (December 2000): 54–56. Brief interview about the craft of writing with Barron and eight other young adult authors.

Perkins, Linda. "Caught Between: Review of *The Merlin Effect.*" *Wilson Library Bulletin* (January 1995): 117–118.

Review of *The Merlin Effect. Publishers Weekly* (August 1994): 80.

Something about the Author, vol. 83. Detroit: Gale, 1996. Brief introduction to Barron's early work.

St. James Guide to Young Adult Writers. Second edition. Detroit: St. James Press, 1999. Brief biographical and critical introduction to Barron's work.

Sullivan, Edward. "Arthurian Literature for Young People." *Book Links* (May 1999): 29–34.

"T.A. Barron: Glowing Like a Crystal." *School Library Media Activities Monthly* (June 1995): 38–43. Interview with Barron.

◆ RELATED WEBSITES ◆

"T. A. Barron." *Amazon.com talks to Thomas A. (T.A.) Barron.* http://www.amazon.com/exec/obidos/show-interview/b-t-arronhomasata/ref=pm_dp_ln_b_8/102–3896211-8570513. (February 27, 2001). Interview with Barron about his approach to writing and his view of his work.

"T. A. Barron." *The World of T. A. Barron: The Official Web Site.* http://www.tabarron.com. Accessed 22 March 2001. Excellent website created and maintained by Barron, includes copies of articles written about him, curriculum materials, maps, and news about forthcoming work.

Susan Swords Steffen

THE MOST DANGEROUS GAME

Short Story

1924

Author: Richard Connell

◆

Major Works for Young Adults

"The Most Dangerous Game," 1924

◆ ABOUT THE AUTHOR ◆

Richard Connell was born October 17, 1893, in Duchess County near the Hudson River in New York State—not far from Theodore Roosevelt's homestead. At the age of ten, he started writing for the *Poughkeepsie News-Press*, his father's newspaper, as a baseball reporter. Later, while attending Georgetown College in Washington D.C., Richard served as secretary to his father in Congress. Following his father's death in 1912, Connell enrolled at Harvard University where he served as editor for both the *Daily Crimson* and the *Lampoon*. After Harvard, Connell went to work for the *New York American*, a newspaper in New York City. He also served with American forces in World War I. In 1925, following the publication of "The Most Dangerous Game," which won him the O'Henry Memorial Award for short fiction, Connell moved to Beverly Hills, California, where he continued his career as a freelance writer.

Richard Connell was one of the most prolific short story writers of the early-twentieth-century, writing more than three hundred stories, many of which were published in popular magazines of the day, such as *The Saturday Evening Post* and *Colliers*. His most widely known story is "The Most Dangerous Game," which has been in print continuously since 1924. Many of his stories were published in three collections: *The Sin of Monsieur Petipon* (1922), *Apes and Angels* (1924), and *Ironies* (1930). Though Connell did not target young adult readers with his stories or books, "The Most Dangerous Game" is often read by young adults and is often included in collections of stories for young adults.

Connell lived in California writing short stories, novels, and motion picture scripts until his death in 1949. He wrote three novels: *Mad Lover*, *Playboy*, and *What Ho!* Among Connell's many screenplays are *Seven Faces* and *Brother Orchid*, which starred Hollywood legends Edward G. Robinson and Humphry Bogart.

Connell was a professional writer for forty-six years. It was the only life he knew. A trained reporter, he drew not only from his own experiences and imaginations, but also from all those he had interviewed and written about over the years. As a veteran of World War I, he witnessed first hand man's inhumanity to man and the horrors of war. "The Most Dangerous Game" reflects Connell's intense social consciousness, addressing some of the most pressing issues of the early twentieth century in a thoughtful and provocative manner.

◆ OVERVIEW ◆

"The Most Dangerous Game" is a story about hunting and about human nature. It explores the fine line between the hunter and the hunted, between hunting and bloodlust, between killing and murder. In the story, the author challenges readers to reflect on their own convictions regarding hunting as a sport and what it means to be civilized. The title of the story has two meanings. It speaks of the game-like, competitive nature of hunting for sport and personal pleasure while also referring to the object of the hunt. Since the most cunning and resourceful animal on earth is man, he is "The Most Dangerous Game".

◆ SETTING ◆

"The Most Dangerous Game" is set sometime after the First World War on a remote, tropical island in the Caribbean, known by sailors as Ship-Trap Island. Among those sailors, it has a mysteriously ominous reputation and is given a wide birth by knowledgeable sea captains. Those passing near it sense an elusive, indefinable sense of evil. Ship-Trap Island is somewhat removed from the regular sea route between New York and Rio de Janeiro, but not so far to avoid

the occasional passing ship. The island is covered with a dense jungle that extends all the way down to its treacherous, rocky shoreline. On one side of the island, a line of giant, jagged rocks, capable of sinking any ship that ventures into them, extends from the shore, lurking just below the surface of the sea. It is this line of rocks that gives Ship-Trap Island its name.

The protagonist in this narrative is a celebrated big game hunter named Sangor Rainsford. Rainsford and a friend are aboard a yacht enroute to Brazil to hunt the jaguar. On the deck of the ship alone, after midnight, Rainsford hears what he believes to be gunshots from the mysterious island they are passing. Standing on the railing and leaning out to listen more closely, he loses his balance and falls overboard. Unable to attract the attention of anyone on the rapidly retreating ship, Rainsford resolves to swim in the direction of the gun-shots, eventually pulling himself from the sea onto Ship-Trap Island.

On a high bluff overlooking the sea, sits a single enormous structure with tall towers. The architecture of the building is cold and forbidding. An iron gate and stone steps lead up the side of the cliff to large, heavy doors. It is the residence of General Zaroff, a rich and eccentric Russian aristocrat in exile. Upon his first sighting of the building, Rainsford describes it as a "palatial chateau." Later, Rainsford discovers that the interior of the structure is as sophisticated and refined as any of the finest residences in Europe or America. Inside the residence, Rainsford finds grand marble steps, enormous high-ceilinged rooms, elegant furnishing, richly paneled walls, luxurious draperies and all the comforts associated with an elegant and sophisticated lifestyle.

A generator on the island provides electricity, not only for lighting the chateau, but also to power a trap. Extending out along the line of dangerous rocks is a series of electric lights arranged in such a way as to mimic the marking of a channel and the pretense of safe passage through the rocks. In fact, they lead directly into the rocks, and any ship foolish enough to fall into the trap is ripped open and sunk, forcing the crew to swim to the island, where they are taken prisoner by General Zaroff. In the cellar of the chateau is a prison that General Zaroff calls his "training school." In it, men from ships that have been caught in Zaroff's trap are treated for their injuries, fed well, and prepared physically to be hunted by Zaroff. In a large, locked courtyard, Zaroff keeps an army of hungry, ferocious dogs.

◆ THEMES AND CHARACTERS ◆

A central theme of "The Most Dangerous Game" is hunting. Connell invites the reader to actively and critically reflect on hunting as a sport, as a way of life, and as a metaphor for man's inherently violent and primitive nature.

The moral and political climate in the world during the years immediately following WWI influenced and contributed to both the meaning and impact of this story. At the time "The Most Dangerous Game" was written, big game hunting was a sport promoted and enjoyed by many of the world's powerful and elite. Notable among these famous hunters was President Theodore Roosevelt, who pursued the pastime with a zealous passion. Roosevelt hunted and killed an impressive variety of animals in incredible numbers. He led many widely publicized hunting expeditions around the globe. Grand hunting expeditions were common in South America during this period, and the jaguar was a common and highly prized trophy. Roosevelt himself partici-

pated in one such safari. On the other hand, Roosevelt is also remembered as a great conservationist, using his power to establish the National Park Service, preserving many vast wildernesses and the animals in them for prosperity. Also, the terrible and bloody carnage of WWI was fresh in the minds of people all over the world, tending to desensitize many to the value of human life while galvanizing others to seek the preservation of all living things. It was within this atmosphere of stark contrast and ideological conflict that Connell wrote the "The Most Dangerous Game."

Sangor Rainsford, the protagonist, is both a veteran of WWI and a celebrated American big game hunter. Rainsford has devoted his life to hunting all sorts of animals, all over the world, always searching for bigger, more challenging prey. Contrasting with the rough and tumble outdoorsman image conjured by his hunting prowess, Rainsford is also a man of letters, the author of books on hunting that have made him known to hunters worldwide. Rainsford is intelligent, resourceful, and in excellent physical condition. When Rainsford's companion, Whitney, questions the morality of hunting, Rainsford counters by contending that animals have no feelings, no understanding of life or death. When Whitney replies that they likely feel pain and fear of death, Rainsford rejects the notion and rationalizes that "the world is made up of two classes—the hunters and the hunted."

General Zaroff is himself a study in contrasts. Like Rainsford, he is also a veteran of both war and of a lifetime of hunting. He is a gracious and genteel host that extends a warm and grand welcome to Rainsford, an unexpected guest. Zaroff is well-traveled, well-educated, well-read, and has mastered several languages. The General's speech and dress suggest he is a gentleman and the product of wealth and social ascendancy. Zaroff's home and his refined hospitality reflect Old World sophistication and civility. Yet, under this facade is a viscous killer who, bored with the lack of challenge offered by more traditional "big game," turns to hunting human beings in order to satisfy his insatiable need for killing and to insure his continued amusement. Zaroff considers the men whom he captures with his ship trap to be little more than animals, inferior to him to the extent that he feels no guilt for what he does. He justifies his actions with an allusion to Darwin, where he asserts that "Life is for the strong, to be lived by the strong, and, if need be, taken by the strong." Zaroff sees himself as one of the strong. In fact, he considers himself the perfect hunter, superior to any animal or any man in the hunt. Zaroff is obviously an intelligent man, but he is just as obviously insane. His trophy room is lined with the heads of his human victims.

Zaroff recognizes Rainsford immediately. Having read one of Rainsford's books, he recalls Rainsford's picture from the flyleaf. Zaroff is both pleased and excited to be joined on his island by someone with whom he shares so many common interests and experiences. He seems anxious to share his exploits and accomplishments with a man he believes will be able to properly appreciate them.

Ivan, a minor character in the narrative, is also a study in contrasts. Ivan is a giant of a man and a deaf mute. Besides Zaroff and the captives in the cellar, he is the only person living on the island. He has served Zaroff loyally for many years, coming with him from Russia. Ivan's role is complicated. He seems to be Zaroff's butler, his bodyguard, his trusted companion, and his jailer/enforcer. Ivan's personal coarseness and lack of social refinement provide an effective foil for the sophistication of his master Zaroff. When one of Zaroff's captives refuses to participate in his "game," Zaroff hands him over to Ivan, who amuses himself by torturing the victim to death before killing him and then feeding him to Zaroff's dogs. Ironically, Zaroff considers Ivan's treatment of the men he is given to torture much more harsh and cruel than his own. Apparently, so do the captives, as they invariably elect to be hunted by Zaroff rather than submit to Ivan's ministrations.

Both Rainsford and Zaroff justify killing in much the same way. They both believe themselves superior to their prey, providing each of them the necessary moral prerogative to kill without compunction. Zaroff's decision to hunt humans parallels Rainsford's reasons for seeking increasingly more cunning and challenging game. Eager to share his accomplishments with someone who would understand and appreciate them, Zaroff proudly describes his motivation for hunting human quarry, how he came to the island, and his ingenious ship trap. However, after Zaroff enthusiastically explains the way he hunts down and kills the unfortunate men who have fallen into his trap, Rainsford vigorously declines an invitation to join Zaroff in a hunt. Rainsford condemns Zaroff's actions as uncivilized and immoral. Since Rainsford refuses to join him in the hunt and since Zaroff is once again becoming bored by the feeble challenge offered by his inferior prey, Zaroff elects that Rainsford should be the object of his next hunt. Zaroff considers Rainsford to be the ultimate adversary, as he is also an outdoorsman and also an experienced hunter of dangerous prey.

There is powerful irony in the hunter suddenly becoming the hunted, suddenly helpless and at the mercy of his pursuer. Initially filled with fear and panic, Rainsford, at first, identifies with many of the animals he has hunted over the years, running blindly away from his pursuer. His first impulse is simply to get as far as possible away from Zaroff. His attempts to evade Zaroff are futile, and Zaroff finds him on the first day, hiding in a tree. However, evidently to prolong the hunt, Zaroff retreats, leaving Rainsford alive but feeling helpless and terrified. It was at this point that Rainsford begins to transition from his role as hunted to one of hunter. Between fits of desperation, he sets several traps intended to stop or kill Zaroff. They are partially successful, injuring Zaroff while killing Ivan and one of Zaroff's dogs.

Eventually, Rainsford evades Zaroff by playing into Zaroff's conviction that his prey is always inferior and weak. Rainsford jumps from a precipice into the sea, feigning suicide. Zaroff retreats to the chateau, assuming he has won the game. Though he claims to be "a beast at bay," Rainsford has now fully reverted to hunter mode, swimming across a small bay to Zaroff's chateau to arrive there before the general can make it back through the jungle. He uses Zaroff's bedroom as a blind, patiently awaiting Zaroff's return. As Zaroff steps into his room, locking the door behind him, Rainsford renews the game on his own terms, engaging the general in a fight to the death. Rainsford survives, winning the game. Though he identifies constantly with animals he has hunted while being pursued by Zaroff, Rainsford ultimately corroborates Zaroff's argument that life is for the strong, to be taken by the strong. Rainsford's hunter instinct overpowers the moral barriers separating murder from the kill of the hunt. Rainsford and Zaroff are not so different after all. Killing Zaroff comes naturally.

Central to this story is the ironic contradiction that allows us to believe that it is right to kill what many believe the lower animals for sport and pleasure, but wrong to kill other human beings under any circumstances, except that of war. The story raises many questions: "Why is it morally right to hunt and kill animals, but not man?" "When is killing morally wrong; when is it murder?"

◆ LITERARY QUALITIES ◆

Richard Connell is a master of short narrative. He makes effective use of a number of literary devices traditionally associated with great short stories, including historical allusion, powerful foreshadowing, vivid imagery, and clever plot reversals. "The Most Dangerous Game" is written from the third person, omniscient point of view. In addition to meticulous observations, the narrative reveals Rainsford's thoughts and feelings throughout the story, further developing his character and adding to the intensity of the action and suspense.

Connell uses an old newspaper man's sensitivity to current affairs to give credibility to an incredible story. He uses frequent references to WWI and to the Russian Revolution to lend a sense of history to "The Most Dangerous Game." Many of the story's original readers were veterans of WWI and thus identified readily with Rainsford's musings about foxholes.

The social upheaval and eventual communist revolution in Russia captured the imagination of the world during the first two decades of the twentieth century. Newspaper headlines were filled with news of the Czar and the Communist Revolution. Connell uses this to his advantage, referring frequently to things his readers would recognize as Russian. Zaroff and Ivan, both obviously Russian names, are cast as Cossacks, notoriously loyal supporters of the Czar. To augment the authenticity of Zaroff and Ivan, an ethnic Russian dish, borsch, is on Zaroff's dinner menu, and the general's ancestral home is placed in the Crimea.

The story's verisimilitude is further enhanced by Connell's choice of setting. The Caribbean was close enough to be almost familiar, but far enough away to be exotic and mysterious. Regular newspaper coverage chronicled a procession of grand hunting safaris and famous big game hunters.

After all, had not President Roosevelt just returned from just such an expedition where he had been charged, not unlike Zaroff, by an angry cape buffalo?

These allusions also serve to reinforce the story's irony and social contrast. During the 1920s, people filed into movies to see the biggest stars of the day slogging down jungle trails, elephant guns in hand, following comfortably behind an army of native porters dutifully carrying silver tea services, mosquito netting, and all the comforts of home. Ironically, they also cheered as Tarzan, the prototype animal rights activist, ripped rifles from the hands of would-be killers, saving countless innocent animals from a certain date with the taxidermist.

The plot of "The Most Dangerous Game" is skillfully paced and carefully guided by Connell's use of foreshadowing. The discussion between Rainsford and Whitney hints early that the story might focus on the morality of hunting. Careful diction and elaborate imagery rapidly build an atmosphere of danger and menace. Both the crew and passengers aboard Rainsford's yacht seem preoccupied with the island they are passing, making repeated references to its mystery and its ominous reputation. Readers suspect that Ship-Trap Island will play a major role in the story long before Rainsford falls overboard. Connell goes out of his way to present Zaroff as the consummate gentleman, leading the reader to assume that he must be hiding some insidious secret. Readers are also provided with a myriad of gentle hints pointing toward Rainsford's eventual reversal of roles from master hunter to frightened prey. Connell uses foreshadowing to draw readers into the story and to built suspense and intensity in the final stages of the hunt. He teases readers with a false climax, making it appear that Zaroff is victorious when he walks directly up to the tree where Rainsford is hiding. However, when Zaroff walks away and Rainsford climbs down out of the tree, the reader senses that some form of reversal has begun, but must continue to read to discover just how the plot will evolve. Connell treats readers to a true "cliff hanger" when Zaroff's ferocious dogs pursue Rainsford to the edge of a precipice overlooking the island's rocky shore. Rainsford, with nowhere else to run, leaps into the sea. In the end, when Rainsford kills Zaroff, many readers are surprised. However, careful reading reveals many clues pointing to that outcome. Readers can trace a steady erosion of Rainsford's sense of morality from the moment that he met Zaroff.

The atmosphere of mystery and the rich texture of the physical setting are both enhanced by Connell's skilled and generous use of imagery. In addition to careful and effective diction, Connell makes frequent use of metaphor, simile, and personification to enhance his elaborate imagery. In the opening paragraphs, Connell personifies the "dank tropical night" as "palpable," pressing "its thick, warm blackness in upon the yacht." He uses simile to augment the visual, tactile impression adding, "It's like moist black velvet," referring to the night air and describes the stillness of the sea as being "flat as a plate glass window." Examples such as these are found throughout the story, describing characters, establishing mood, and adding fine detail to the exotic setting. Strong imagery draws readers into the atmosphere of the story and allows them to experience the characters, the action, and the setting more vividly and more personally. Such powerful imagery is more common to poetry than short narrative, but Connell uses it masterfully, constructing an elaborate sensory framework within which to stage his story.

Connell keeps the narrative interesting by keeping the reader guessing. Woven into the story are a series of contradictions and reversals that add interest and intrigue to the story. These reversals impact all aspects of the story—setting, characters, and plot.

Rainsford suffers several such reversals. At the beginning of the story, he is calm, comfortable, and in complete control. Suddenly he finds himself in the sea, alone and lost—his plight unknown to his friends. After struggling onto Ship-Trap Island and finding his way to Zaroff's mansion, he once again finds himself in control and in the lap of luxury.

The most dramatic reversal occurs when Zaroff sends Rainsford out to be hunted. Suddenly, and with tremendous irony, the famous big-game hunter finds himself the object of the hunt, running for his life and hiding like an animal.

Midway in the hunt, Zaroff tracks Rainsford down, but instead of bringing the game to its logical end by killing Rainsford, Zaroff turns and walks away, presumably to prolong the hunt. After this, Rainsford adopts a more aggressive posture, becoming a hunter again, setting traps and plotting the death of his new quarry: Zaroff. In the end, Rainsford once again finds himself in control, relaxing in the comfort of Zaroff's bed, surely plotting his next hunt.

♦ SOCIAL SENSITIVITY ♦

The morality of hunting is the primary issue of social consequence addressed by "The Most Dangerous Game." The author portrays hunters as compulsive killers who are intrinsically bloodthirsty and cruel. Both Zaroff and Rainsford seem to have an insatiable need to find greater and greater challenges and more and more creatures to kill. That Rainsford initially stops short of adding human beings to his catalog of desirable prey does little to separate him from the unapologetic Zaroff. In the end, Rainsford succumbs to the same temptation as Zaroff, quenching his hunter's need for ever greater adventure, ever higher danger, and ever greater satisfaction of the kill.

Readers who hunt for sport may take offense at being associated with Zaroff's bloodlust and murderous tendencies. Readers who oppose hunting and the killing of innocent creatures will find themselves identifying with the author's obvious condemnation of such sport.

In an effort to provoke reflection and debate, Connell singles out certain races and ethnic groups who were, at the time of writing, the subject of considerable prejudice by those opposed to immigration, both in the United States and in Europe. They were often treated as sub-human and denied the basic rights afforded other members of society. These people are the pawns in Zaroff's game. Believing himself superior to them in all respects, Zaroff refers to the unfortunate sailors he traps and hunts to death as the "scum of the earth—sailors from tramp ships—lascars, blacks, Chinese, whites, mongrels," placing less value on their lives than on one of his hounds. People still struggle with such misplaced prejudice today.

♦ TOPICS FOR DISCUSSION ♦

1. How did Rainsford's character change in the course of the story?

2. What is the relationship between the hunter and the hunted? Is hunting animals morally right?

3. Is it ever morally right to kill another human being? How is killing in a war different from what Zaroff did?

4. Does exposure to violence and killing make people less sensitive to those things and more likely to be violent or to kill?

5. Would sending a man like Zaroff to prison for murder change his moral

attitude toward killing? How should murderers be punished?

6. Instead of returning to kill Zaroff, what other options did Rainsford have?

7. Could this sort of thing actually happen? What part of the world do you think a real-life Zaroff would choose for his "hunting lodge?" Why would he choose that location?

8. How is this story related to the animal rights movement? How might an animal rights organization use this story to support its cause?

9. How is this story related to the death penalty and legal abortion? What are the arguments for and against the institutionally sanctioned killing of human beings?

10. How is this story related to gun control legislation? What side do you believe Richard Connell would support? Why do you think that?

◆ IDEAS FOR REPORTS AND PAPERS ◆

1. Imagine that Rainsford discovers Zaroff's diary and decides to add a final entry. What would it be?

2. How do laws governing the killing of animals for sport differ around the world? Compare and contrast hunting regulations on several continents. Why do you think there are so many differences?

3. Compare and contrast laws governing the killing of human beings around the world. Murder is a socially constructed idea and is understood differently by different people in different places. Discover laws that identify legalized killing— such as self-defense, euthanasia, and government execution. When is a sol-

dier or policeman given the right to kill another human being?

4. How have ethical constraints against the killing of human beings changed over time? In what cultures have they changed the most?

5. Rainsford fought in WWI. What brought the United States into the war, and what was the experience like for the soldiers that fought it?

6. The Cossacks protected the Russian Czar during the social upheavals leading to the Russian Revolution. General Zaroff and Ivan were both Cossacks. Why might they have left Russia when they did?

7. Zaroff argued that "Life is for the strong, to be lived by the strong, and, if need be, taken by the strong," to justify his killing. Explain the Darwinian theory to which this alludes. Did Zaroff misinterpret it? How did Charles Darwin arrive at his theory.

8. Richard Connell began his writing career as a newspaper reporter. Write a newspaper article based on an interview of Rainsford, reporting the entire, incredible experience from Rainsford's point of view. Use the standard newspaper "inverted pyramid" format, answering the questions who, what, when, where, and why in the first sentence of the story.

◆ RELATED TITLES/ADAPTATIONS ◆

"The Most Dangerous Game" gained significant recognition and popularity at the time it was written. A film version of the story was released in 1932, eight years after the story was originally published. The movie was distributed under two titles, *The Most Dangerous Game*, and *The Hounds of Zaroff*. Though the central theme of the story, the hunter becoming the hunted, was kept intact, the film's plot was somewhat different from that of the original story. The most notable difference was the addition of a female character who, along with her brother, teams up with Rainsford to defeat Zaroff. Two later films were also based on the stories: *A Game of Death* (1945) and *Run for the Sun* (1956). The story has had an extraordinary influence on the study of literature. Over the years, "The Most Dangerous Game" has found its way into countless literature textbooks, and many other stories, books, television programs, and movies have revisited Connell's compelling theme.

♦ FOR FURTHER REFERENCE ♦

Dunleavy, Gweneth A. "The Most Dangerous Game." In *Masterplots II: Short Stories,* Series 4, *Lon-Pro.* Pasadena: Salem Press, 1986: pp. 1535–1537.

"The Most Dangerous Game." In *Literature and Its Times,* vol. 3. Detroit: Gale Research, 1997: pp. 231–235. Includes a discussion on Darwinism and how it influences the story.

"The Most Dangerous Game." In *Short Stories for Students,* vol. 1. Detroit: Gale Research, 1997: pp. 155–169. A thorough analysis with historical background and plot summary.

Robert Redmon

MY BROTHER, MY SISTER, AND I

Autobiographical Novel

1994

Author: Yoko Kawashima Watkins

$$\blacklozenge$$

Major Books for Young Adults

So Far from the Bamboo Grove, 1986
Tales from the Bamboo Grove, 1992
My Brother, My Sister, and I, 1994

◆ ABOUT THE AUTHOR ◆

Yoko Kawashima Watkins is of Japanese ancestry but was born in Harbin, Manchuria in 1933, then moved to North Korea where she lived with her family while her father worked as a Japanese government official during World War II. She lived in a bamboo grove in Nanam until 1945, when the Russian and Korean Communist forces, angered at years of Japanese oppression, escalated their warfare and drove hordes of Japanese people out of the country. Yoko lived a comfortable life in the bamboo grove until the age of eleven, when she, her mother, and her sister Ko were forced to flee to Japan and leave her father and brother Hideyo behind. After her harrowing ordeal as a refugee she learned how to survive and persevere. Watkins worked hard, became educated in Kyoto, and learned English well enough to work as a translator at an American air force base. She married an American pilot named Donald Watkins in 1953, moved with him to America in 1958, then settled in Massachusetts and raised six children, two of them Taiwanese orphans. In 1976, thirty-one years after her escape from Korea, Watkins began writing her story. She published *So Far from the Bamboo Grove* in 1986, then continued her story in *My Brother, My Sister, and I*, which she published in 1994. Watkins' vivid portrayal of life as a Korean refugee won her praise as a young adult writer, and she won numerous awards for both books. She also wrote a book of Japanese folk tales, and she continues to educate young people about the horrors of war by lecturing about her experiences.

◆ OVERVIEW ◆

In this sequel to Watkins' fictionalized autobiography *So Far from the Bamboo Grove*,

Yoko Kawashima Watkins

poverty and prejudice to make a place for themselves in the world. It is a story of survival, and Yoko, Ko, and Hideyo conquer hardship after hardship by relying on each other for love and support, and by helping each other tap their own strength. During their life in Kyoto, the children endure both physical pain and mental anguish, and they fall prey to false accusations of arson and murder. But their story is more about love than about hardship, and it is more about fortitude than misfortune. At the end of the novel, we cannot help but rejoice in their accomplishments and marvel at their fortunate change of events. Their father returns to them, battered but whole after his years as a prisoner of war, and Yoko, Ko, and Hideyo make a warm, comfortable home, finish their education, and eventually marry and lead happy, successful lives.

thirteen-year-old Yoko, her sister Ko, and her brother Hideyo live together in post–World War II Japan, struggling to make a life for themselves after their harrowing escape from Korea. Yoko's family was stationed in North Korea during World War II while Yoko's father worked as a Japanese government official in nearby Manchuria, but they were forced to flee the country when Russian and Korean Communists escalated their war against Japan and drove the Japanese people out of Korea. Yoko and her sister Ko escaped with their mother, who later died, and Hideyo escaped alone and later reunited with his sisters in Kyoto. Yoko's father remained behind, working in Manchuria, and is now imprisoned in Siberia.

Like *So Far from the Bamboo Grove, My Brother, My Sister, and I* paints a picture of courageous young adults struggling against

◆ SETTING ◆

The book is set in Kyoto, Japan in the late 1940s and early 1950s. The war is over, and though Kyoto escaped the demolition that Tokyo and other Japanese cities suffered, it did not escape the poverty. Watkins takes us to Kyoto's back streets where the homeless roam hungry and cold and dig through garbage for food and seek shelter in warehouses and under bridges. This world contrasts greatly with the world Yoko and her family knew in Nanam, Korea, before their escape, where Watkins says she lived in "a beautiful big house . . surrounded by a graceful bamboo grove." The war devastated both the land and the people, and Watkins' vivid descriptions of Yoko's world in post-war Kyoto makes the desolation of war painfully obvious.

The places Yoko calls home include a cold, drafty clog warehouse with couple of futons for beds and an apple box for a table, a hospital with an iron cot for Ko and no place for Yoko to sleep but underneath the cot, and a lean-to shack under a bridge with no protection from cold weather or burglars. When the Minatos, a kindly couple who rescue Yoko and her family from under the bridge, invite them to share their small house in the Tanaka area, Yoko feels blessed. But Yoko's cruel classmate points out that Burakumin live in the Tanaka area. Burakumin, Watkins explains, are social outcasts, labeled by some as four-legged animals or dirty people. By order of the Shogun in twelfth-century Japan, they were forced out of the village communities and into small shacks, relegated to jobs such as digging graves and butchering animals, and excluded from attending prestigious schools or marrying outside their social stratum. The environment where Yoko lives helps reinforce Watkins' message that she felt like a social outcast—forced out of her home in Korea and condemned to a life far removed from that of her classmates and shunned by the upper classes. Watkins' descriptions of her "home" under the bridge and her experiences on the streets makes us understand where this woman gained her humility, and how she came to view the Minato's small house as a palace, and a fresh piece of cake as a treat worthy of queens. The impoverished world in which Yoko lives teaches her that home is where the heart is. She learns to value love, to appreciate simple pleasures, to rejoice in small comforts, and to respect kind, hardworking people who give selflessly and expect nothing in return.

◆ THEMES AND CHARACTERS ◆

In this sequel to *So Far from the Bamboo Grove*, Watkins chronicles Yoko's maturation process as she recounts the story of her struggle to survive in Kyoto with her brother Hideyo and her sister Ko. Yoko is thirteen now, and she is trying to make it in the world with meager possessions and little money. Ko works as a seamstress sewing aprons and kimonos, Hideyo works as a laborer, and Yoko finds work wherever she can and must attend school as well. Their mother is dead and their father is a prisoner of war in Siberia. We understand the fear and longing these children must have experienced during this time of their lives. They survived the war, but they lost their mother, have no idea if they will ever see their father again, and they must constantly worry whether or not they will be able to make enough money for food and clothing. They have only themselves to rely on, and they succeed admirably, even as hardship after hardship challenge their strength and resolve time and time again.

When the Kawashimas first arrive in Kyoto they have hope for the future. They made it out of Korea alive, and they look forward to a happy reunion with their family. But shortly after arriving in Japan, they learn that their grandparents were killed and their home destroyed. Then they experience the death of their own mother, who expires in the train station after learning the devastating news of her parents' death. Alone and frightened, the children feel fortunate when they meet the Masudas at the train station and are offered a place to live in a clog warehouse in return for guarding the place against burglars. They settle in a small room there and begin their daily struggle to survive.

Early in the novel, the Kawashimas do encounter a burglar in the warehouse, and shortly after that, fire breaks out and destroys their home. Braving smoke and flames, Ko races upstairs to retrieve their few precious possessions and suffers a terrible accident. She falls from the top of the stairs onto the concrete floor. Yoko hears her sister's bones crack, and she fears that

Ko might die. Ko does not die, but her right knee is shattered, her left leg broken in three places, and her right wrist and three ribs are broken. She must remain in the hospital for months. Leaving their home once again, Yoko and Hideyo pick up what belongings they have, move them into the doctor's shed, and set their sights on helping their sister.

Life gets harder for the Kawashimas after Ko's accident. Ko is in terrible pain and can no longer work, Hideyo must struggle to pay hospital bills, and Yoko must suspend her schooling to care for her sister. They then learn that the Masudas died in the fire, and Junko Masuda, their niece, accuses the Kawashimas of setting fire to the factory, killing her aunt and uncle, and stealing their cash box. Yoko is outraged at these accusations and deeply insulted that her integrity is in question. Watkins makes clear Yoko's pride. We are "at the bottom of the bottom," she says, but "the Kawashima children would never steal, harm or destroy things that belong to others." Nevertheless, Junko Masuda reports the children to the police, and an investigation begins. When we read Watkins' story we marvel at the fact that anyone can maintain their resolve after suffering so many setbacks. Just when they appear to conquer one setback, another one slaps them in the face; yet they manage to conquer and keep their goals in sight. The children get frustrated with life and with each other, but they never give up hope for a better future. All three children find work wherever they can, whether it be cleaning toilets, shining shoes, or collecting cans—and they manage to scrape up enough money for Yoko's schooling and Ko's hospital bills. They learn to prioritize, and they look after each other's needs. When Yoko gets money from selling aprons and kimonos, she must choose between buying toothpaste and three toothbrushes or a bottle of calcium pills for Ko. She decides that the pills are more important. We listen to Yoko contemplate this decision and ask herself, "which is the more important thing now?" We realize then that she has learned to think and act responsibly. We also realize that she has learned to act selflessly. Yoko knows that Ko needs the calcium pills for her bones to heal properly so she does not hesitate to spend her hard-earned money on them. From the minute they left Korea, Ko tended to Yoko's needs and now Yoko returns the gift. It is this supportive attitude that sees them through the most difficult times.

Ko is deeply touched when Yoko gives her the calcium pills, but at first she lashes out at her, complaining that Yoko she must learn to manage money. This is often how Ko reacts when Yoko makes a sacrifice for Ko. But we know that these children never consider their kindnesses sacrifices. Ko acts angry, but then cries, deeply touched. She remembers a time during their escape from Korea when Yoko was whining and complaining and Ko had blurted out that she wished Yoko were dead. Ko feels ashamed of herself. But Yoko knows that her sister loves her more than anything and that their bond is unbreakable, their support for each other never-ending. Yoko soothes her sister's guilt by telling her that she knew Ko did not mean what she said. "War makes people mean and ugly," she explains, "and robs everyone's gentle heart."

In both of her books, Watkins intends to convey the futility of war, but perhaps the strongest message she conveys is the power of pride and determination. The Kawashimas refuse to let war rob their gentle hearts. Watkins makes it clear that the children help each other hold on to their pride and their determination, and that the love and support they give each other makes even the most challenging situations surmountable. But Ko bosses Yoko around and Yoko resents it. Ko calls Yoko a spoiled brat. They experience the same tensions other siblings experience. We know that whatever spats they have, however, the Kawashimas love and depend on each other more than anything in the world. Readers can relate to the dual nature of their relationship, the conflicting emotions of sibling love. These sisters experience love and hate, joy and anger, jealousy and adoration; but they stick together, and that is what counts. In the face of adversity, neither of them is ever alone. This bond gets them through the worst of times.

Watkins hints at the horrors the Kawashimas experienced together during their escape from Korea (she covers this in detail in her first book, *So Far from the Bamboo Grove*), but here in Kyoto they face new horrors. That these children survived their escape at all seems miraculous, and that they survive the poverty and humiliation they suffer in Kyoto attests to their resolve. Yoko attends classes at the Sagano Girls' School, and her classmates ridicule her for living in poverty and call her names such as "Rag Doll" and "Trash Picker." That hurts her deeply, but when they unjustly accuse her of stealing a watch, it humiliates her. "I pitied myself," she said. "I wondered which was worse. Walking on the bombshell? The awful trek on an empty stomach? Being wounded by bombing? Or was it worse being constantly picked on by the girls in the school, accused of things I knew nothing about?" The problems at school continue, but Yoko comes to realize that however hurtful, these people can not undermine her resolve or shake the Kawashima pride. They knew nothing about love. Once, after seeing a picture the girls at school hung on the bulletin board to ridicule Yoko, she realizes that these girls know nothing about being hungry and homeless, or about missing a father they fear they may never see again. "As I looked at the drawing, I wanted to yank it down," Yoko said.

"Then, standing there, I suddenly realized that in spite of our cruel condition, Hideyo, Ko, and I were helping one another live day by day. We kept the hope of Father's return alive. I had absolutely nothing material, but I had a brother and a sister who gave me their love. They were teaching me the value of human life. We had not done anything to be ashamed of. I was proud of what we'd been doing."

Yoko's classmates show her no mercy and no kindness, but she manages to live with their cruelty and finish her schooling— and even graduate with top honors. Her classmates still ostracize her, and they do not want her in the school photo. Again, Yoko feels humiliated, but she does not wallow in self-pity. She knows that she has succeeded in ways these children never will. She has learned how to be courageous, strong, and proud. She has experienced a side of life that made her recognize what is truly important; "the value of human life," she said. She has gained insights that these rich, spoiled children will never learn. Watkins contrasts Yoko's depth with her classmates shallowness. The classmates may have material wealth, but the Kawashimas have spiritual wealth. Because of this, they are able to preserve their moral character and hold their head high.

Previously published plot summaries of *My Brother, My Sister, and I* mention that Watkins builds suspense as to who set fire to the warehouse and how the children are going to exonerate themselves. But as one reviewer points out, "the mystery of who set fire to the factory and killed the owners seems almost tangential to the more central mystery of how Yoko will find enough food to stay alive and enough fortitude to fight the prejudice she suffers at school because of her poverty." (Hearne 1994) Yoko survives because she and her brother and sister have all the qualities they need to survive. They are strong. They are courageous.

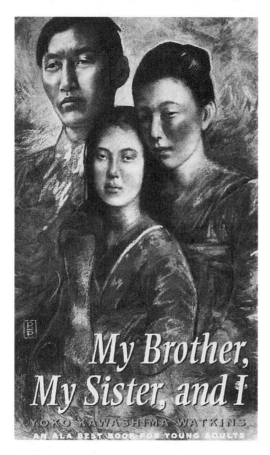

Book cover illustration by Pamela Patrick for *My Brother, My Sister, and I* by Yoko Kawashima Watkins.

Yoko is continuing with school, and all signs point to emergence from the depths of despair. ''My brother, my sister, and I emerged from the depth because we simply cooperated, accepted our responsibilities, and kept our dreams and hopes alive,'' Watkins explains. Yoko learns that true contentment comes not from material wealth but from love and kindness, and from sharing your life with people who give that same love and kindness in return.

It must be difficult for three young people living alone on the streets to retain their cultural identity and to hold on to family traditions. Yet through all their suffering, the Kawashimas dig deep into their past and find comfort in the life they once knew. Watkins recounts incidents from happier times to help us understand the strength of their family bonds. She uses flashbacks to recount the horrific story of her struggle, but she also uses them to relay pieces of advice her father and sister once gave her—words of wisdom that impressed her when she was young, and that helped her carry the Kawashima pride and develop a set of values later in life. She also recounts instances when Ko and Hideyo imitate gestures or actions they learned from their parents, or instances when she imitates actions she learned from Ko. Watkins includes these incidents to show us how much she was influenced by her family, their values, and their philosophy of life.

With no relatives living or available to help give the children a sense of cultural identity, the Kawashimas still manage to retain their identity, and one way Watkins divulges this is by revealing the bond with nature that characterizes Japanese culture. When Watkins uses nature imagery she

They are forthright. And they have spiritual resolve. When Yoko's shoes are destroyed in the fire, Hideyo sends the shoes down the river, says a prayer for them, and tells them to send a message to their father. The Kawashimas all have an amazing ability to turn adversity to opportunity, and to find hope in desperate situations. By the end of the novel, things start looking up for Yoko and her siblings, and we know that however tragic their life has been, they feel truly blessed. Their father returns from his imprisonment. They have a warm, comfortable home with the Minatos, with bamboo growing all around it. Ko is getting better,

shows how deeply this philosophy permeates their lives. Yoko says "the sun goes to sleep quickly in winter," to explain the darkness, and she speaks of the winter wind behaving itself. Hideyo, in trying to teach a lesson in patience says, "Remember, for today, today's wind blows, and for tomorrow, tomorrow's wind blows." "Why do you worry when you cannot do much?" The Japanese are in awe of nature; they believe spirit manifests itself in natural wonders. Yoko marvels at the flowers. "I could be like the humble wildflowers that grew along the stream bank during the spring, summer, and fall," she says. "If tramped on, they would always spring back, and give a bit of pleasure to the passersby."

Perhaps the most poignant reference to nature's wonder is Watkins' explanation of a silkworm project she is assigned in school for biology class. Mr. Iwai, the biology teacher, asked Yoko to watch the worms grow, write a report about their growth and transformation, cook the cocoons and spin silk thread, and exhibit her project at the city science fair. Watkins realizes that she gained important life perspective while observing the silkworms, and she uses the development of the silkworms as a metaphor for the development of her own character. Watching the silkworms reinforced her hope for a better future. "I took a peek at the worms," she said. "They were very ugly. Still, they had accepted their burden and lived as best they could. From the worms would come beautiful, strong, pure white threads! Will I be a beautiful person if I, too, accept and endure burdens and go through life calmly? I wondered. If a silkworm can, then I, as a human being, certainly can!" Yoko always had the ability to realize her potential, as did Ko and Hideyo, and all of them strove to internalize the beauty in the world. Using nature imagery once again, Hideyo said that though they could not change their past, they could strive for a better future. "The Kawashima children can become a few drops of water in the ocean," he said, "and make ripples that will spread humanity."

◆ SOCIAL SENSITIVITY ◆

Anyone who reads about Watkins' experiences understands how deeply they must have molded her values and changed her outlook on life. As both a refugee fleeing from Korea and as an indigent scraping by in Kyoto she was an outcast, yet she managed to hold her head high, finish her schooling, and become the successful and confident woman she is today. The hardships Watkins faced were likely more severe than any those of us will ever know, yet we all face hardship. The stories she tells gives us hope that with determination, we can survive the most difficult of times.

In *My Brother, My Sister, and I*, Watkins continues to relay her message from *So Far from the Bamboo Grove*: that love and kindness is important, that values are important, and that with strength and willpower, we can overcome adversity. In *So Far from the Bamboo Grove* Yoko, Ko, and Hideyo survive their hellish escape from Korea, and in *My Brother, My Sister, and I* they survive the hardship of living in poverty with no parents and little money with which to buy food. What money they do make is hard-earned, and they suffer the humiliation of others who see them not for the upstanding and hard-working people they are, but as street bums, unworthy of consideration and respect. Yoko is ostracized by her classmates, yet she must face them every day in order to continue her schooling and improve her position in life. Though not many of us can relate to the pain Yoko suffered, some of us have experienced poverty and prejudice. Watkins story gives us hope that we can rise above it and conquer it, and move on to be successful, happy people.

Readers of Watkins' novels understand that hardship breeds strength, and that those who suffer hardship learn the value of love and support from others. Yoko, Ko, and Hideyo support each other every step of the way, and they never take for granted the kindness of others. It may amaze us to learn how grateful these children are for small kindnesses that we so easily take for granted. A pair of shoes, a pile of wilted greens, a piece of cake from a neighbor—these are all gifts that touch the children greatly; they are thankful for small favors and appreciative of anyone who helps them. Perhaps Yoko knows, even as she faces the cruel children at school each day, that these children have a distorted view of life, that they have their priorities reversed, and that they would never know the value of sharing. Amazingly, Yoko never loses sight of her values or loses faith in herself, even as she suffers with poverty and humiliation. She has the love and support of Ko and Hideyo always, and that love gives her the strength she needs to cope.

Watkins paints a vivid picture of sibling relationships as she details the tensions that complicate the bond between Yoko, Ko, and Hideyo. They argue and find fault with each other as any siblings do, but their love is strong in ways we will never know. We can understand Yoko's fear when she thinks that Ko might die and leave her, but can we truly understand her desperation? This is a young girl who lives a brutal existence and has lost everything dear to her except her brother and sister. Yoko loves Ko and Hideyo more than anything in the world. The Japanese culture places high value on family bonds, and the bond Yoko, Ko, and Hideyo share is strengthened tenfold by the severity of their struggle. Watkins lets us marvel at the unconditional love these children show each other as they fight for life's

most basic needs. Watkins' book teaches us lessons about the importance of working together and about acting generously and selflessly toward others. It would have been easy for any of the three of them to give up trying—to withdraw from school, to lash out at the people who ridicule and humiliate them, or to engage in dishonest practices to get what they need. But these three young people have high standards, and Watkins conveys the message that they help each other hold onto their values. They encourage each other to carry on, tackle adversity, and tap their stores of courage and strength. They know it's not easy, but they have each other. This makes them more determined than ever to succeed.

◆ TOPICS FOR DISCUSSION ◆

1. When Yoko first sees her father at the train station, she does not recognize him. Why do you suppose that in a few short minutes she no longer sees him as the "a tired, worn old man," she saw when he arrived, but as "a strong, wise, kind father?"

2. Why do you suppose Junko Masuda accused the Kawashimas of arson, theft, and murder?

3. Why does Ko act angry when Yoko surprises her with touching kindnesses?

4. What do you think bothers Yoko more: the constant humiliation of her peers or the accusations of arson, theft, and murder?

5. When Kyoko accuses Yoko of stealing her watch, the teacher takes Kyoko's accusation seriously and strip searches Yoko. Do you think if Yoko accused Kyoko of stealing the teacher would have taken Yoko seriously? Why or why not?

My Brother, My Sister, and I

6. What do the children's efforts to find their father say about their character?

7. Give instances from the story that show how the Mr. and Mrs. Kawashima instilled values in their children.

◆ IDEAS FOR REPORTS AND PAPERS ◆

1. Write a paper using the development of a silkworm as a metaphor to explain Yoko's development into a strong, selfless person.

2. Write a paper on homelessness and how Yoko's outlook helped her manage on the streets.

3. Watkins points out that Burakumin have been discriminated against since the twelfth century and that they have carried their burden from generation to generation. Compare and contrast the discrimination the Burakumin suffer in Japan to the kind of discrimination that occurs today in America.

4. Yoko, Ko, and Hideyo survive and persevere because they never give up. Discuss some of the ways each of them persisted to chase their dreams, despite their hardships.

5. The Japanese people traditionally have a strong sense of family pride. Using instances from the story, discuss the family pride Yoko, Ko, and Hideyo feel and the ways in which they exhibit it.

6. Discuss several instances in the novel that reveal the Kawashima's qualities of determination, courage, and selflessness.

7. There are several instances in the novel when Watkins recalls wise words, or advice, from her father. Discuss these wise words and how Yoko, Ko, and Hideyo follow their father's advice in their lives alone in Kyoto.

8. Write a paper to support Watkins' message that "home is where the heart is."

◆ RELATED TITLES/ADAPTATIONS ◆

Yoko Kawashima Watkins began telling the story of her childhood experiences in *So Far from the Bamboo Grove* (1986), a fictionalized account of her harrowing escape from Korea with her mother and sister and their subsequent arrival in Kyoto.

◆ FOR FURTHER REFERENCE ◆

Hearne, Betsy. *Bulletin of the Center for Children's Books* (July–August 1994): 376. A review of *My Brother, My Sister, and I.*

Mori, Kyoko. *New York Times Book Review.* (October 9, 1994): 26. A review of *My Brother, My Sister, and I.*

Philbrook, John. *School Library Journal* (September 1994): 224. A review of *My Brother, My Sister, and I.*

Rochman, Hazel. *Booklist* (May 1, 1994): 1594. A review of *My Brother, My Sister, and I.*

"Watkins, Yoko Kawashima." In *Contemporary Authors*, Volume 153. Detroit: Gale, 1997, pp. 244–246. A biographical sketch that describes Watkins' life and her books.

"Watkins, Yoko Kawashima." In *Something about the Author*, Volume 93. Detroit: Gale, 1997, pp. 209–212. A biographical essay that describes Watkins' life and her books.

Tamra Andrews

MY FATHER, DANCING

Short Stories

1998

Author: Bliss Broyard

◆

Major Books for Young Adults

My Father, Dancing, 1998

◆ ABOUT THE AUTHOR ◆

Bliss Broyard was born to Anatole Broyard, the noted essayist and *New York Times Book Review* critic, and to Alexandra, his wife, who edited her husband's memoir, *Kafka Was the Rage,* and published it after his death. Anatole Broyard was a prolific writer and a charismatic man and was obviously quite an influence on his daughter. Not only did he inspire her to write, but to write passionately and affectionately about fathers. Bliss Broyard wrote poetry as a young child, and short stories in college. The title story of her book, *My Father, Dancing,* is the tale of a young woman reminiscing about earlier days dancing with her father who is now lying on his deathbed. Broyard began writing this story when her own father was dying of prostate cancer, and she took three years to complete it. Anatole Broyard passed away in 1990, and since that time Broyard finished her book and succeeded in creating a vivid portrait

of father figures as influential and dynamic as her own.

Bliss Broyard is the Henry Hoyns Fellow at the University of Virginia's creative writing program, and her stories have appeared in *Best American Short Stories 1998, The Pushcart Prize Anthology,* and the magazine *Grand Street.* She was also an editor for an MTV series that profiled presidential candidates. Today, Broyard lives in New York and is working on another book, which focuses entirely on her own father. Because Anatole Broyard was an African American who kept his racial identity hidden for most of his life, his daughter's new work discusses the impact of race on her father's life.

◆ OVERVIEW ◆

This collection of eight short stories deals with the complex emotions women experience in relationships, particularly in relationships with their fathers. Some of the

Bliss Broyard

Because Broyard's book consists of eight separate stories, each story has its own setting, but they flash back to the upper-middle-class neighborhoods these women lived in as children, places that help characterize the fathers as worldly professional men and the daughters as privileged young women who have lived rather sheltered lives. These young women all grew up in New England, and they all attended elite, private schools. The school setting comes into play in several stories, revealing the bond young women often develop with older male teachers in their desire for father figures in their lives.

Broyard emphasizes the everlasting bond between fathers and daughters by exploring their relationships in both past and present contexts. The cabin in "At the Bottom of the Lake" is a place of the past, as are the kitchen and barrooms where the young woman shared intimate moments with her father in "My Father, Dancing." The present environment in which these characters live contrasts with the world they existed in as young adults and helps to explain the difficulty these women have adjusting to the move to other worlds inhabited by new, younger men with less money, less influence, and less panache. The scenes the characters recall from the past stress the tenderness and intimacy they felt at the time, while the scenes from the present stress the harsh realities they come to recognize. In "My Father, Dancing," for instance, the horrors of the present-day hospital room contrast with the pleasures of the dance floors of the past, and in "At the Bottom of the Lake," the reality of times in the cabin today contrasts with the memories of the cabin remembered from the past. Similarly, the abrupt scene of the car accident in "Ugliest Faces" and the disturbing scene in the cabin in "Snowed In" contrast with the

stories are tearjerkers, others light and uplifting, but all of them are poignant portraits of the special bond fathers and daughters share. All of Broyard's stories emphasize the father-daughter bond, but they also explore the wide range of human emotions experienced by women in close relationships with other people of the opposite sex. Broyard outlines the feelings her young characters have regarding their sexuality and she focuses on the problems these characters experience in communicating and in learning to understand the changes in themselves. The young women in this work are coming-of-age and dealing with the complexities of the process. In each of the stories in this collection, Broyard explores how fathers influence their daughters' lives and how relationships between fathers and daughters affect how these women grow and learn to relate to the men they encounter in their adult lives.

warmth and tenderness remembered from past times.

◆ THEMES AND CHARACTERS ◆

The protagonists in all the stories are young women coming-of-age and exploring their relationships with men, particularly with their fathers. All these women fit into the same mold as Broyard: they all come from upper-middle-class backgrounds and they all have fathers who are charismatic, worldly, and wise. Essentially, the father in each of Broyard's stories could be the same man. The father in "The Trouble with Mr. Leopold" is a writer, the father in "A Day in the Country" and "Snowed In" is an orchestra conductor, and the father in "At The Bottom of the Lake" is a lawyer. All of these men are smart, literary, and articulate, like Broyard's own father, and as their stories unfold, they all reveal a side of themselves that their daughters never before recognized. It is difficult to see our fathers in contexts other than as fathers, but Broyard explores the father figure as a man of many faces. She explores the complexities and human weaknesses these men possess as their daughters discover these frailties for the first time. Because the women in Broyard's stories have idealized their fathers but come to see them in a new light, they must deal with debunking their ideal. As these women grow into adults, they begin to see their fathers as complex characters; no longer solely protectors and providers, but real men with desires and needs disturbingly similar to those of other men these young women have come to know.

Developing an altered view of the father figure is a necessary step in the maturation process. As young women pull away from their parents and move toward independence, not only must they come to terms with their own individuality, but with the individuality of their fathers as well. Grow-ing up, in this sense, means that women must relinquish the father-daughter connection to some extent in order to relate to other men. The daughters actually get help doing this from their fathers, who inadvertently assist by revealing a side of themselves that feels foreign to their daughters. These women must learn to relate to men in new ways and to accept the concept of foreignness with regard to understanding the male psyche. The relationships these women form with other men feel odd and rather uncomfortable in comparison with the familiar relationship they share with their father. It is ironic that it is the fathers themselves who validate the concept of the foreign male to their daughters.

Inherent in the process of debunking the notion of father as infallible male is affirming the notion of father as betrayer. All of the fathers, in a sense, betray their daughters. The father's death in "My Father, Dancing" is the ultimate betrayal. It says, "I will no longer be there for you. I can no longer protect you. I am fallible, weak, and mortal." The fathers in the other stories all betray their daughters in lesser ways. In "Mr. Sweetly Indecent" the father betrays his daughter by exposing his selfishness and his willingness to deceive. This man, the young woman realizes, is no different from any other man. He is a sexual being, separate from her and her mother, and he is capable of hurting the women he loves. The father in "At the Bottom of the Lake" betrays his daughter when the young woman realizes that it is he, not her stepmother, who has remained aloof over the years. The father in "The Trouble with Mr. Leopold" betrays his daughter when he exposes his vanity and his vengefulness, and the fact that he is not perfect and can damage his daughter even when trying to help her.

The fathers in Broyard's collection loom larger than life, even in those stories where the fathers never figure as characters in the story. In "Snowed In", for instance, Lily's father never appears, yet his influence is strong enough for readers to feel his presence. The fathers in the stories are clearly the most appealing of the male characters. They are strong and passionate despite their flaws. But by exposing their flaws, Broyard conveys the message that women must stop idolizing their fathers and learn to recognize their imperfections. Unless these women can do this, she seems to be saying, the other men who come into their lives will never live up to the ideal man they imagine.

In Broyard's stories, the fathers have greater depth of character than the other men who come into the protagonists' lives. The same holds true for the women. The women in Broyard's collection are strong and resilient, yet still they appear more passive than their fathers, and all of the young heroines crave their fathers' attention. Only five of the eight stories feature fathers as main characters. Yet two of the other three stories seem to center on the search for father figures. "Ugliest Faces" and "The Trouble with Mr. Leopold" both involve male teachers who fill the father role, and both women protagonists crave their teacher's attention. The boyfriends in the stories—such as Sam, Ethan and Ted—appear rather flat, and none of them seem as vibrant or as interesting as the fathers. In "At the Bottom of the Lake," for instance, Broyard neglects to give us much information about Sam's character at all.

"If Sam, Ethan, and Ted seem at times like stick figures, it's because the father dancing here blows them off the page," says Allegra Goodman in her commentary on Broyard's book. Lucy in "At the Bottom of the Lake" struggles to relate to Sam, but keeps him constantly in the shadow of her father. Pilar of "Loose Talk" cannot commit to her lover Max because he does not live up to her image of the perfect man. The heroines in the other stories also struggle

with new relationships, and with the realization that their fathers are no longer their primary male companions. All of these women must learn to receive the love and security they got from their fathers from the new men who enter their lives, but they have difficulty doing so. These young women must reconcile their desire for their fathers' approval with their desire to move away from parental influence. They must learn to see their fathers in a different light in order to grow into mature male-female relationships.

The fathers in all of Broyard's stories are far from "ideal." They exhibit human flaws and appear to be manipulative and vain, but intelligent and charming at the same time. In light of these contradictions, the women in the stories seem to feel ambivalent about men, and they struggle to reconcile their idealistic views of male-female intimacy with the reality they come to experience in love relationships of their own. In advancing her coming-of-age theme, Broyard emphasizes awakenings. Her stories are about awakening to the fact that fathers are fallible. The stories are also about awakening to the fact that women must learn to let go of the most important man in their lives in order to relate to men in new ways. And Broyard's stories deal with sexual awakenings—sexual awakenings that seem oddly, yet at the same time predictably, connected to how these women feel about their fathers.

Elizabeth Lenhard, in her review of Broyard's collection, refers to the women in the stories as exhibiting "an overindulged Electra complex," and Susie Linfield in her review comments that these young women are "obsessed with their fathers, and filled with longing, muted anger, bewilderment and love." All children must awaken to the fact that their parents exist as people in their own right, and part of this awakening involves recognizing their parents' sexuality. They have roles other than parents, just

My Father, Dancing

as the women themselves have roles other than daughters. It is no accident that the young woman in "Mr. Sweetly Indecent" is just returning from an affair of her own when she sees her father kissing another woman. The daughter must confront the shocking possibility that not only is her father cheating on her mother, but he has a sexual side she never before recognized, a side that allows him to love other women in ways he can never love her.

Does the young woman in "Mr. Sweetly Indecent" recognize that however harsh this encounter with her father seemed, it served to validate the affair she herself was having? Perhaps Broyard is saying that women subconsciously feel as if they are betraying their fathers when they get involved with other men. If that be the case, the father in "Mr. Sweetly Indecent" allowed his daughter to accept her own intimate connection with another man by revealing his own intimate connection with another woman. It does no good to undermine the sexual overtones that exist in relationships between fathers and daughters, and Broyard makes no attempt to do so. Rather, she lets us know that it is natural for this first male-female relationship to affect how women develop into sexual beings.

Anatole Broyard was reputedly quite a womanizer, and so is the man in "Mr. Sweetly Indecent." But all the fathers in this collection are weak and flawed, and they all have the ability to harm as well as to love, to feel sexual passion and to indulge in self-serving behavior as well as to be affectionate and caring. The young women in Broyard's stories must learn to recognize their fathers as fallible, sexual beings. If, indeed, they were the first and, therefore, the most influential men in their daughters' lives, it is inevitable that it is the fathers who must teach their daughters lessons about the complexities of male-female relationships. It is also inevitable that it is the fathers who

must teach their daughters about loss. For if, indeed, these women must let go of their fathers, they must also experience a feeling of loss. In each of the stories the pain of relinquishing a father is evident.

◆ LITERARY QUALITIES ◆

The title story, "My Father, Dancing," seems to encapsulate the symbolism Broyard herself recognizes in the nature of relationships. The fathers in her collection are indeed dancing; they are the ones who move and who seem most alive, particularly in their daughters' minds. Dancing can be seen as a metaphor for movement, and also as a metaphor for human emotion. The act of dancing involves an intimate exchange, a give and take that marks the continuing bond between fathers and daughters. Looking back on her experiences dancing with her father—in the kitchen, then in the bars—the young woman realizes that during those moments her father not only taught her to dance but he taught her about life. The father in this story moved his daughter, slowly and intimately, into adulthood. When he danced with her, he talked with her. And when they talked, they revealed things about themselves.

"Father was my first male audience, and I used him as a mirror to understand what I looked like to the world," the young woman in the title story relates. "Once my father told me that he wanted to be the first man to break my heart," she continues, "because then he could ensure that at least it would be done gently." Poignant, powerful words from a woman (both author and character), who considered her father's love gentle, nurturing, and everlasting and her relationship with him one long, continual dance. But death is not gentle, nor is any of the other ways in which fathers break their daughter's hearts. In the course of life, women all lose their fathers, and they lose

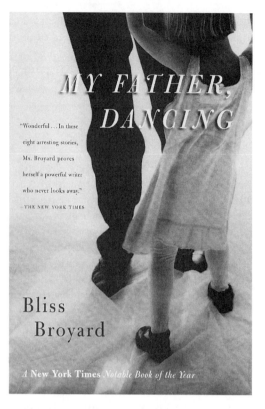

Book cover photograph by Mary Javorek for *My Father, Dancing* by Bliss Broyard.

them in many ways. As these women grow and change, they lose the men they knew and recognized through a child's eyes.

Broyard's characters are faced with the challenge of finding men to live up to the men they idealized as children, and unless they let go of the hold their fathers have on them, no man will ever be able to compete. The symbolism of the father's death in "My Father, Dancing" is significant. The women in all of the stories must come to terms with the "death" of their fathers; that is, the death of the father they knew as perfect, their own private protector. They must do this in order to accept their fathers as fallible human beings, as men not gods, and as men with human frailties that these women never could recognize as a young girls.

The concept of death in the literary tradition quite appropriately includes the concept of rebirth. Broyard's death symbolism implies rebirth as well: the rebirth of a woman from her childhood state, and the rebirth of an adult ready to cope with adult relationships. "My Father, Dancing" goes backward in time, from the father's deathbed to places in the young woman's childhood where she danced with her father when he was young and vibrant. Accepting her father's mortality is one way of accepting his fallibility. His death is the ultimate betrayal.

The women in each of Broyard's stories are betrayed by their fathers in some way. They are not intentionally betrayed, but they feel betrayed as they recognize, sometimes abruptly, that their fathers have never been what they imagined them to be. Now wise to their fathers' weaknesses, these young women feel both betrayed and abandoned. They experience the death of an ideal, the death of naivete, and the death of the father they immortalized in their minds.

The reconciliation of father-as-father with father-as-man naturally leads Broyard to present a set of contrasts. In "My Father, Dancing," for instance, she contrasts her images of her helpless dying father with her memories of a strong younger man dancing his daughter into adulthood. In "The Trouble with Mr. Leopold," she contrasts the intelligent, literate father with the father capable of getting a "C" on an English paper, and the helpful, guiding father with the self-serving father concerned primarily with preserving his own vanity. In "The Trouble with Mr. Leopold, " the conflict between these two men allows Celia to recognize the perversity in Mr. Leopold rather than in her own father. But by pitting these two against each other, Broyard subtly reduces Celia's father to Mr. Leopold's level. Broyard is constantly contrasting the young boyfriends with the fathers as well,

My Father, Dancing

and by doing so she contrasts realism with idealism, the search for perfection with realization that perfection does not exist.

Though Broyard's collection is highly symbolic, it is also realistic in that it portrays the complex emotions of everyday life. Broyard appears to have a keen understanding of human behavior and a talent for revealing unspoken depth and meaning in ordinary conversations, intercourses, and gestures. Some of the stories read like an autobiography, written in first-person narrative. The others, written in third person, still appear autobiographical, with Broyard detailing small moments to convey enormous concepts. Broyard uses descriptive language to create vivid pictures of the meaningful moments in these women's lives, so we see their relationships in a series of images, arguably the most powerful of which is Kate dancing with her father. We get glimpses of the father-daughter interchange in the past and in the present, which helps us understand the strength of the father-daughter bond and the inevitability of breaking it.

The young women in these stories are naïve in many ways, and they all seek acceptance from their fathers. Both the fathers and the daughters are similar in so many ways that they could almost be the same person. In this way Broyard gives her stories a sense of continuity. The fathers are all affluent, intelligent, and vibrant, while the women all appear shy and insecure. The fact that Broyard included women in all stages of life, from young girls to married women, seems to reveal the continuing influence of the father-daughter relationship. The relationship is ongoing like a dance, and the movement inherent in that dance naturally leads women through the stages of their lives.

Broyard seems to be a master at creating poignant images that convey powerful emotions. The image of the daughter dancing with her father evokes a far different emotion than does the image of Mr. Leopold lining the girls up outside his office so he can give them lessons in fashion and style, or the image of the boy in "Snowed In" removing a drunken Lily's clothes and fondling her body. Broyard allows her characters to recognize the flaws in the other men in their lives on purpose. In doing so, she lets us know that these women are learning to recognize that men are capable of deception. Recognizing that their own fathers are also capable of deception is simply the next step.

Anatole Broyard was literary and articulate, like the father in "The Trouble with Mr. Leopold," and given that Bliss Broyard began writing "My Father, Dancing" when Anatole was dying, what could be more autobiographical than the image of a father lying in his hospital bed? As autobiographical as the book may be, Broyard succeeds in revealing universal needs and emotions. All fathers dance in the minds of their daughters, and those daughters fortunate enough to have a close relationship with their fathers allow these men to dance them gently into adulthood.

◆ SOCIAL SENSITIVITY ◆

The women in all the stories come from the same privileged position. But not everyone is fortunate enough to have a father dance her gently into adulthood. People have a completely different view of father. Many have fathers who are abusive or absent, and these people may have difficulty recognizing the father figure Broyard presents. Broyard's book is clearly slanted toward the upper middle class, to professionals who are articulate and literary, influential and charming, and extremely complex. This is her world, and her view of father.

Broyard's themes in all her stories revolve around the complexity of men. We have to wonder if she presents the adult male in unreal proportions. Because she focuses on the father-daughter relationship, readers get the sense that men have a much greater impact than women on their daughters' sense of identity. This leads us to examine our views of sexual identity. Some critics have said that the women in these stories seem passive, at least in comparison to their fathers. Their fathers overshadow them. The fathers also appear much more complex and charismatic than their wives, and much more in control.

Lenhard's comment about the "overindulged Electra complex"(the female counterpart to the Oedipus complex) begs the question of who might find this work offensive. The young women do indeed appear "obsessed with their fathers," as Linfield says, but does this mean that Broyard presents the sexual dimension of the father-daughter relationship in an inappropriate manner? "In Loose Talk," "Snowed In," and "Ugliest Faces," the young women are coming to terms with their sexuality and wishing to establish an intimacy with their lovers and boyfriends like the intimacy they imagined with their fathers. But until they remove their fathers from their pedestals, the urgency of desire can never be as caring, as intimate, or as innocent.

It appears that Broyard sees nothing inappropriate about the sexual element of the father-daughter bond because she presents any sexual awakenings as natural steps in the growing up process. It is only natural that these fathers influence their daughters' sexual development just as they influence their daughter's feelings about love and loss. Broyard stresses the tenderness of the connection. In "My Father, Dancing," Broyard expresses true compassion for a child's pain as she witnesses the physical deterioration of her father. Broyard presents this scenario with tenderness, and what emerges is a recognition of the affection this father and daughter share.

◆ TOPICS FOR DISCUSSION ◆

1. Do you think of the women in Broyard's collection as passive or submissive? How does this make you feel?

2. Do you believe the young women in the collection have unrealistic views of male/female intimacy? Why or why not?

3. Do you recognize each of the young women characters in the collection as individuals? Do you think Broyard does a good job in distinguishing the difference between them? Explain.

4. Does Broyard do a good job of distinguishing the differences between the fathers in the collection? What sets one apart from the other?

5. Which of the stories did you consider the most poignant and why?

6. To what extent does miscommunication serve as a theme in the stories?

7. Which of the young women characters do you believe changes the most in their perspective of men? How does she change?

8. What kind of relationship do you think these women had with their mothers? How did they view their mothers?

9. Who do you consider the protagonists of these stories, the young women or their fathers? Why?

10. Write a paper on the symbolism of death in the title story, "My Father, Dancing."

11. Write a paper on the symbolism of dance, and discuss how it applies to the

title story in particular and the collection in general.

12. Discuss the theme of betrayal in three or more of the stories.

13. Using the two stories that involve male teachers, discuss how the heroines of these stories perceive these teachers as father figures.

14. Choose one of the stories that omit the father from the plot. How is the presence of this father felt and what do you know about him?

♦ IDEAS FOR REPORTS AND PAPERS ♦

1. Do some research on Anatole Broyard. Compare his personality traits with one of the fathers from this collection.

2. Do research on families without the father present and compare the girls growing up in these families with those who grow up in families with the father present. What are some of the differences you discover? Similarities?

3. The author seems to focus on upper-middle class families. Compare families in this class with those in the lower-class. How different, or similar, are the father-daughter relationships?

4. Discuss the contrasting personality traits of the fathers in the collection. All these men are both charming and vain, charismatic and weak. Expand on these contrasts.

5. Discuss Broyard's view of women, based on her characterizations of the daughters and mothers in her stories. Research families without mothers present and compare them to families with mothers. What differences and/or similarities are there in the girls growing up in families without mothers compared to those who had mothers growing up?

6. Elizabeth Lenhard in her book review in the *Atlanta Journal and Constitution* refers to the concept of an "overindulged Electra complex." To what degree to you believe the young women are obsessed with their fathers? Do they have a healthy love for their fathers, or does their love border on impropriety? Discuss the Electra complex as a mythological and a psychological concept and detail to what extent you believe it applies to the women in Broyard's collection.

7. Research the Oedipus complex and compare it to the Electra complex.

♦ RELATED TITLES ♦

Richard Bausch explores similar themes in his collection of short stories entitled *Someone to Watch Over Me*. These stories, like the ones in *My Father, Dancing*, stress the impact of intimate relationships and the different ways in which we establish connections. The collection offers insight into the nature of human longing, the human desire for love, and the universal need to establish emotional bonds with other people.

Can You Wave Bye Bye, Baby by Elyse Gasco is another collection of short stories focusing on the bond between mothers and daughters. Like *My Father, Dancing*, Gasco's book explores the nature of the parent-child bond while at the same time highlighting the complexities of human emotions.

♦ FOR FURTHER REFERENCE ♦

Goodman, Allegra. "I Remember Papa." *New York Times Book Review*. August 15, 1999: 8. Goodman discusses the similarities between the characters in Broyard's debut collection and the characters in Broyard's own life. She summarizes the plot in each of the stories, and points out the influence Anatole Broyard had on his daughter's life and work.

Lenhard, Elizabeth. "Bloodlines, Not Plot Lines Carry Weight in *Dancing*." *The Atlanta Journal and Constitution* (August 8, 1999): 11L. Lenhard presents a more critical view of the book, referring to Broyard's lack of imagination, her "over-indulged Electra complex," and, with the exception of "The Trouble With Mr. Leopold," the book's dearth of believable characters and subtle symbolism.

Linfield, Susie. "Stories of Father Obsession and Betrayal: *My Father Dancing* by Bliss Broyard." *Los Angeles Times* (August 26, 1999): E5. Linfield discusses the passivity of Broyard's women characters, the similarities of the fathers in the collection to Anatole Broyard, and the "tonal monotony" of the stories. She discusses in particular "My Father, Dancing," "Mr. Sweetly Indecent," and "The Trouble with Mr. Leopold."

Tamra Andrews

THE NECKLACE

Short Story

1882

Author: Guy de Maupassant

◆

Major Books for Young Adults

The Best Stories of Guy de
Maupassant, 1945

La Maison Tellier (published in English
as *The Tellier House*), 1881

◆ ABOUT THE AUTHOR ◆

Author Henri Rene Albert Guy de Maupassant was born on August 5, 1850, in any of several locations in Normandy, France, according to whether one believes his death certificate or various biographers. He spent his entire youth in Normandy, and never allowed that fact to be forgotten.

He was the elder son of Laure Lepoitevin de Maupassant and Gustave de Maupassant. The intimate friendship his mother and maternal uncle had with Gustave Flaubert, the author of *Madame Bovary,* became of utmost importance in Maupassant's early literary development. Laure de Maupassant divorced her gay-blade of a husband and devoted herself and the considerable settlement she received to the upbringing of her two sons. Maupassant was educated at the school of Etretat and by his mother until the age of thirteen; she was a highly lettered

person and conveyed to him a strong enthusiasm for Shakespeare. He studied briefly at the seminary of Yvetot, where his anti-religious and amorous verses earned him many rebukes, before being expelled as an insubordinate pupil for stealing and drinking the faculty's choice wines. Subsequently, at a lycee in Rouen, he had Louis Bouilhet for a teacher, who (with the help of Gustave Flaubert's letters, in a kind of correspondence-school) gave direction to Maupassant's increasing interest in literary expression.

During the Prussian invasion in 1870, Maupassant served in the army, gathering experiences and observations which were of great use in his future writing. Eight months after the armistice was signed, he returned to civilian life. In endless literary discussions with French writers in Flaubert's home, Maupassant resolved to commit himself to a literary career as a poet, a precarious existence that would need the support of a job with regular income. He became a

Guy de Maupassant

"Boule de Suif" (title means "Ball of Fat") appeared in a collection with stories by four other obscure writers and perhaps the most controversial name in French letters, Emile Zola.

The columns of the most popular newspapers were immediately opened to Maupassant, and overnight he became, with Zola, the highest paid writer of the day. He left behind ten years of poverty and a seven-year apprenticeship that had made him at best an indifferent poet. Stories and prose flowed from his pen. Maupassant was grateful above all else that his success gave him independence, material as well as literary. This was encouraged in him by Flaubert, whose death a few weeks after the release of "Boule de Suif" set Maupassant free from any lingering artistic dominance.

With the royalties from his first short story collection, *La Maison Tellier* (published in English as *The Tellier House*), he built a villa in his hometown of Etretat on the coast of Normandy. Part of the proceeds from his novel *Bel Ami* (title means "Good Friend") were used to buy a yacht with which he explored the Mediterranean coast. With each new best-seller, Maupassant improved his living quarters, eventually arriving at the fashionable Avenue Victor Hugo. He also contributed substantially to the support of his mother and younger brother, Herve, and came to the aid of several indigent writers.

For the next decade, Maupassant dedicated himself to producing a steady flow of writing: nearly three hundred short stories, a half-dozen novels, several other books, and over two hundred miscellaneous articles which were not collected in book form. Frequent excursions for rest or escape from society did not interrupt his work.

His writing was introduced to America by the translator Lafcadio Hearn and by Henry James, and he was compared to Walt Whitman and other American literary lu-

clerk doing routine printing and distribution of stationery supplies for the Ministry of Marine in Paris, a position he both detested and depicted in his stories. At this time he was happy to take intensive boat excursions on the river Seine with carefree companions, rowing and swimming and indulging in physical excesses.

Maupassant spent a rigid apprenticeship under Gustave Flaubert for seven years. He was neither his nephew nor godson as is sometimes reported, but he was almost completely under his master's thumb. In spite of being forbidden to seek publication of his work until it was perfected, Maupassant employed a pseudonym to see some of his verse published and plays performed.

With a transfer to the Ministry of Education, Maupassant's work as a clerk became more congenial, and a little later in 1880, he left behind the pseudonyms under which he had contributed a few poems, tales, and studies to various periodicals. His story

minaries. He became a classic author, taught in schools, almost instantly in both French and English.

Unfortunately, Maupassant had contracted syphilis when he was a young man, and the disease was further aggravated by his incessant literary work. His eyes hurt intensely, and splitting migraines sent him to every specialist in France in search of a possible remedy. He undertook journeys to Africa, Italy, Sicily, and Corsica in efforts to overcome his terror of blindness and other disabilities. From these journeys came his travel books and many stories with striking images of foreign lands. Medical treatment at that time was not highly effective, and the robust young man dwindled to a shadow of his former self. He read and wrote less because of eyestrain. The acute pessimism he had shared with Flaubert became even stronger, intensifying in 1889 when Maupassant's younger brother, Herve, had to be interned in an insane asylum.

Maupassant could see that insanity was to be his own future and was determined to avoid it at any cost. In December 1891, when the deterioration of his mind was apparent, Maupassant tried to commit suicide. He was stopped by his faithful valet Francois, who had been in his service for eight years and loved him dearly. Maupassant tried again in January 1892 to commit suicide, but Francois saved him again. The devoted servant was unable, however, to save his master from being committed to a mental institution in Passy. There he was watched by vigilant keepers, and there Maupassant died eighteen months later on July 6, 1893 at the age of forty-three.

◆ OVERVIEW ◆

A young, pretty woman from a family of clerks marries a petty clerk in the office of the Board of Education in Paris. She feels keenly the lack of luxuries and adornments, and is disappointed by their plain apartment. Her husband's tastes are simple, but she envies the fine trappings of the rich and their elegant attentions. Consequently, she does not like to visit her school friend, who is wealthy.

Her husband manages to secure an invitation for both of the Loisels to spend an evening at the home of the Minister and his wife, but this news does not make her happy. She desires a suitable dress; and her husband gives her all the money that he has saved for a hunting gun so that she can have a dress made.

As the day of the ball approaches, Madame Loisel is still unhappy to be without a jewel; "nothing to adorn myself with." Her husband's suggestion that natural flowers are *chic* does not convince her; but then he suggests that she ask her wealthy friend Madame Forestier to lend her jewels. Upon request, Madame Forestier willingly loans to Madame Loisel a superb necklace of diamonds.

Madame Loisel is a great success at the ball: "the prettiest of all, elegant, gracious, smiling, and full of joy." All the men notice her, and she dances with enthusiasm until four o'clock in the morning, while her husband dozes "in one of the little salons with three other gentlemen whose wives were enjoying themselves very much."

When they leave, Madame insists on rushing away on foot; eventually they find a cheap, shabby cab and return to their apartment. There she realizes that the necklace is missing. It is not to be found anywhere.

Loisel uses all of his inheritance (18,000 francs) and borrows an equal amount to buy a replacement necklace. To pay back the frightful debt and interest, the Loisels take cheaper lodgings and Madame does all their housework without the help of a maid. She dresses simply and haggles to stretch their pennies. Loisel keeps his job, works evenings, and does copying at night.

After ten years they have paid all that they owe. When Madame Loisel sees her friend Madame Forestier one day, still young, still pretty, she speaks to her and tells her story, being decently content that it is finished.

But Madame Forestier takes her hands and explains that her diamonds are fakes, worth only five hundred francs.

◆ SETTING ◆

Maupassant wrote this story set in a present that he knew and had lately lived: Paris in 1880. There, a Breton could find honest labor as a government clerk, and people of modest means or desperate straits could see the jeweled rich living in luxury just out of reach.

By Maupassant's descriptions of Madame Loisel's envies and daydreams and one glorious ball at the house of the Minister, readers get a picture of what Paris looked like for the wealthy, and how elegant and comfortable their lives must have been. By his descriptions of the Loisels' modest and economical apartment, their visits to the theater, and Monsieur Loisel's wish to go shooting with some friends, readers know what Paris looked like for working people, and that their lives were not luxurious but comfortable and far from desperate.

However, working people crippled by debt shared the lifestyle of the uneducated, the unskilled, and the unlucky: the poor. Living in cheap rooms under a mansard roof, the Loisels would have roasted in summer and shivered in winter. With no running water, the simple hauling up four or five flights of stairs every bucket of water for cooking and cleaning and bathing was enough to exhaust a person. Buying the most economical foodstuffs, cooking meals and cleaning afterwards, and doing laundry by hand was for one person more than a modern full-time job.

The office work done by Loisel would have been tedious, repetitive, and unsatisfying for a literate man who enjoyed occasional visits to the theater. Neither modern nor classical working conditions were common in 1880; Loisel would have worked in a poorly-lit room with bad ventilation among people who bathed infrequently, and he could have been fired without cause or notice or recourse.

◆ THEMES AND CHARACTERS ◆

It is a fallacy to assume that a story must contain only action, particularly if it is written by Maupassant. In this, as in many of his stories, there is little or no "action" and very little actually "happens" from the viewpoint of many readers. Yet in "The Necklace," mood and atmosphere are brilliantly created; in this and in many other stories by Maupassant, the sense of life is not diminished when no earth-shattering events happen.

When this story was written, the French Revolution loomed much closer in memory than it does now, and egalitarianism was still a fashionable idea. Though many aristocrats had been executed during the Revolution, a de facto aristocracy of wealth had sprung up. It should not escape the reader's notice that the wealthy Madame Forestier's name translates as "Mrs. Forest-Worker," a name that invokes images of men earning money by the sweat of their brow, not inheriting it.

One of Maupassant's themes in this story is that wealth is admired beyond reason. Matilda deserved the luxuries and leisure and pleasure of wealth no more and no less than anyone does. But when such trappings are hoarded by some and witheld from others, people invest far too much significance in them, as Matilda does. Her envy blinded her to the pleasure her husband took in a simple, but well-prepared meal.

Loisel is shown simply but clearly to be a man of modest talents and appetites, whom any reader should not only understand but would be well advised to attempt to emulate. An insensitive man would not take his wife to the theater, nor would he scheme to get an invitation to an event that would please her. A greedy man would not give his own recreational savings for her dress rather than a gun for hunting with his friends. An ineffectual husband would not search for the necklace or the cab in which it might have fallen, nor would he be able to handle the usurers. A lout would have left his wife to face the consequences alone, without help. A weakling could not have sustained ten year's work at three jobs and monthly renewal of his loans. Loisel is not to be faulted therefore, for being mild and quiet in his habits, without grand ambitions.

The most astonishing technique used by Maupassant in "The Necklace" is that he does not introduce his characters by name as they are brought into the story. They are only named at significant moments in the narrative. The Loisels are not named until their invitation to the Minister's ball is read. The wife's given name, Matilda, is not used until her husband asks her how much a suitable dress would cost. Her given name is not used again until the last page of the story. Her wealthy friend from school is not named until Monsieur Loisel suggests asking Madame Forestier for the loan of a jewel, and Mme. Forestier's given name, Jeanne, is used only once by Matilda in the final scene, where they recognize each other after ten years.

Monsieur Loisel's given name is never used at all. Perhaps this could be seen as depersonalizing this character, and some readers may think that Maupassant is leaving this character unfinished, unreal, or unimportant. This is not true, however. In France in 1880 (and to some extent even to this day) a man's family name is used by almost everyone whom he contacts, far more often than his given name, which is used only by his most intimate friends and family. A boy in a story or in real life would be addressed by his given name, and almost everyone would address a grown man of any social standing at all by his family name.

When the author refers to the little Breton clerk only by his surname, the intention is to represent this character as a grown man with a respectable occupation, rather than as an unskilled laborer or a simpleton. The author may also have intended to show by omission that the wife is not deeply affectionate or emotionally linked with her husband, as she never addresses him by his given name.

Far from Loisel being diminished by being referred to only by his surname, it is Madame Loisel who is depersonalized by being referred to almost always as "Mrs. Loisel" rather than Matilda and never by her maiden name. She is a de facto Loisel property, rather than an independent being. It is only at the end of the story, when she has learned "a proud and simple joy" at the completion of their desperate labors, that she is truly a helpmate and complement for her spouse; then they truly share a name. For the first time, she identifies herself as Matilda Loisel.

Their marriage was a reasonable and suitable match: he had an honest though modest profession, and she had no dowry or prospects for an inheritance when she married him. There was no reason for Matilda to hope for marriage to or attentions from a wealthy suitor of high social status. Her "sad regrets and desperate dreams" for luxuries are justified only by her personal charms and graces, not by any status of birth or achievement.

Matilda's envy is not a positive element in her life. Far from inspiring her to achieve goals worthy of admiration, her desires of status and wealth merely make her dissatisfied with the virtues of the modest, but sufficient, life that she and her husband actually have. As the story begins she does not, for example, make drawings or embroideries of the finery she imagines. She does not sing songs or write poetry. She does no generous kind deeds for children or the church or the less fortunate. She makes no effort to be any kind of a great lady, because there is only one kind of status she wants: material wealth. Her envy leads her to beg for the loan of an adornment which she does not own, has not earned, and which she covets immoderately.

Ultimately, Matilda's envy leads her to pride, when neither she nor her husband even consider confessing the loss of the borrowed necklace. If she had the courage to come to her friend with her husband's inheritance of 18,000 francs in hand and a written promise to pay the other half she owed, admitting the loss of the necklace, her life would have gone very differently. If Madame Forestier was a loving friend, she would have instantly admitted that the necklace's true value was not double that of Loisel's inheritance, but only five hundred francs. There is no reason in the text to assume that Madame Forestier would cheat her friend out of more than the necklace's actual value.

Even if the necklace had contained real diamonds, a loving and generous friend might have recognized the effort necessary for the Loisels to pay another 18,000 francs, and allowed payments to be made directly to her, rather than insisting upon a lump sum. It was the interest charged by usurers that kept the Loisels in debt for so many years. A truly loving and generous friend may have declared her diamond necklace

to have been of inferior quality, worth only 18,000 or 20,000 francs, and silently accepted the loss of half her diamonds' value for the sake of a friendship.

Thus it is clear that Matilda has done her friend a great wrong: she has assumed that her friend would not be loving and generous. She has deprived Madame Forestier of the opportunity to be kind to her. Madame Forestier is clearly able to be kind, as she willingly lent the necklace when asked. When the two women meet after ten years apart, she is willing to talk with Matilda immediately, though Matilda is careworn and roughened by years of work and deprivation. She even takes Matilda's hands and immediately confesses without vanity that her diamonds had been false.

The true value of the necklace then is not the 500 francs that Madame Forestier's husband had paid for the false diamonds, nor even the 36,000 which the Loisels paid for the real diamonds. The true value of the necklace, according to Maupassant, is that to buy one, you must pay with every moment of leisure and work, every bucket of water hauled up four or more flights of stairs, every basket of vegetables haggled over in the market for five or ten coins, every chance to be generous enough to hire a part-time maid, every worn pen and cramped writing hand and eyestrain from inadequate candles . . . for ten long years. That is what a diamond necklace is truly worth, the author tells readers. And an appalling portion of that effort goes to pay usurers, not jewelers or diamond-miners.

One would think that an egalitarian citizen of the French Republic would have been embarrassed to wear diamonds while a child starved in the gutters of Paris. Perhaps Maupassant is suggesting this.

It should not be forgotten that Madame Forestier's necklace was a fake. Readers are never told if Madame Forestier has done any worthy deeds in her life, other than her friendship with Matilda. She coveted the trappings of wealth as much as Matilda did. She settled for the appearance rather than the reality. The reader is left to wonder how many of the trappings of material wealth are also fakes, just pretending to look like diamonds.

Book illustration by Gary Kelley for *The Necklace* by Guy de Maupassant.

◆ LITERARY QUALITIES ◆

In a few words, Maupassant could portray a figure, in a few pages he could describe a fate. Some of his stories in translation fired the imagination of short story authors around the world.

Maupassant's name has become coupled with the "trick ending" in the short story tradition (his admirer O. Henry took this technique to extreme lengths). It is not fair to associate Maupassant exclusively with the "trick ending," however, as he rarely employed it. This link is probably due to the frequency with which his story "The Necklace" has been anthologized. It is likely that "The Necklace" has been anthologized so often because it has no overt sexual element, and so publishers may feel safe about including it in books intended for young students.

"It is a grave error, and a greater injustice, to associate Maupassant with the naturalists, that all too easy label of the manuals of literature," wrote Professor Artine Artinian in his introduction to *The Complete Short Stories of Guy Maupassant*. "He shared Flaubert's burning aversion to 'schools,' and he deplored Zola's noisy proclamation of esthetic theories. His was the craftsman's cult of art in practice rather than in theorizing."

◆ SOCIAL SENSITIVITY ◆

Maupassant never married, and after reading this story one can guess that at least part of the reason may have been that for ten years he was unwilling to take on the responsibility for supporting a wife and family on the wages of a government clerk. After his writing brought him wealth, Maupassant still did not marry; perhaps because he knew then that he had syphilis or perhaps because he knew that he was unsuited to married life. He wrote like a man obsessed and indulged himself in athletic and carnal excesses. He would not have made a good spouse—a better husband by far would be the little Breton Loisel from this story, who schemed to get an invitation to please his wife, gave his entertainment savings to have her dress made, searched on foot for hours for the missing necklace, spent his inheritance and took on a staggering debt to buy a new piece of jewelry, and worked at three jobs for ten years to pay the interest on the loans.

The author never needs to tell the audience in so many words that Loisel is a good, honest man and a good husband. The reader knows this by what the man does.

Maupassant goes to a great deal of effort to describe Madame Loisel's experiences, as a discontented young wife of modest means, as a social butterfly for one night, and as a penny-pinching household drudge. He even mentions her proud and simple joy when the debt is paid.

Monsieur Loisel's labors are summed up in three modest sentences:

> Every month it was necessary to renew some notes, thus obtaining time, and to pay others.

> The husband worked evenings, putting the books of some merchants in order, and nights he often did copying at five sous a page.

> And this life lasted for ten years.

This statement is particularly significant when one remembers that Maupassant spent ten years living in poverty as a government clerk, and only three of those years working at a better job in the Department of Education. The little Breton he makes seem first an object of humor and then an earnest, desperate worker, is himself. Maupassant may not have known "the horrible life of necessity" that the Loisels learned, but he certainly knew their modest circumstances described at the beginning of the story. And while he did not keep books and do copying by night, Maupassant labored at his literary apprenticeship.

It is especially meaningful that Maupassant does not tell the story from the viewpoint that one would expect, knowing his own life experiences. It would be natural for a writer to tell a story from the viewpoint most like his own. While in his novel *A Clockwork Orange* Anthony Burgess told the horrifying incident of a home invasion, assault, and rape, much like that actually endured by Burgess and his wife, from the viewpoint of an attacker, in "The Necklace" Maupassant tells the story from the viewpoint of the wife. That is where Maupassant's talent shines best in this story.

The wife's labors are no less significant than her husband's work, and her viewpoint is no less "valid" or "real." A writer of lesser talent would have told the story from the husband's viewpoint, tolerant of his wife's selfishness. Perhaps a writer with a more prosperous background would have told the tale from the viewpoint of Madame Forestier, forgiving of her friend's envy. But either alternative would have suggested that this was the true perspective that mattered on the events that happened. Writing from the viewpoint of Madame Loisel as she learns pride and joy in her honest labors is an affirmation to the reader: first, that such people exist in any class, women with profound desires and ambitions; and second, that their lives are worth living, and therefore worthy of attention in the arts and literature.

This is a profoundly feminist and humanist story, and it is as supportive of the working classes as it is supportive of women.

Maupassant said of himself and his stories, "We have but one objective: Man and Life, which must be interpreted artistically."

1. What does Matilda covet? How does her desire affect her life?

2. What is ambition? Why is it a good servant but a poor master?

3. What was the slogan of the French Revolution? Which aspects are being explored in this story?

4. What are the goals and ambitions of Loisel as the story begins? What has he accomplished by the story's end?

5. What sort of school must Matilda Loisel and Jeanne Forestier have attended? How important is it culturally that the one girl grew up to marry a man of means, and the other married a clerk?

6. What can you guess about the economy in Paris and France at the time the story is set?

7. Why, for a story set in the crowded city of Paris in 1880, are there so few characters in this story?

8. How has technology made this story possible? Why could it not have been set in fourteenth-century France?

◆ IDEAS FOR REPORTS AND PAPERS ◆

1. What virtue does Madame Loisel learn in her sustained efforts to run her household with the utmost economy? What has this lesson cost her? Is this price fair or just or necessary? Could she have learned a similar lesson without spending all her youth and prettiness?

2. What does Madame Forestier know of the life experienced by her friend Madame Loisel before and after the loan of the necklace? How truly sophisticated is she to tell her friend that the jewels she worked so hard to replace were paste? What do we know of her from the text, and what can we guess of her personal qualities such as integrity and intelligence? What would a loving friend or a true great lady have done to honor such long, honest labor, rather than make that effort worthless with a single sentence?

3. Why does Maupassant spend so little effort on the character of Monsieur Loisel? Is he unworthy of the reader's attention? Or is his nature and experience so understandable and customary to the reader that it does not need puffed-up explanations? Is Maupassant describing a virtuous man?

4. What were the goals and ideals of the French Revolution? How does Maupassant explore the ideal of "Equality" in this story? Does Matilda believe in equality? What does she do because of her beliefs?

5. What is jealousy? How is it distinct from envy and desire? Are these entirely negative emotions? What good, if any, can these emotions bring to a person's life?

6. What kind of people are the wealthy people envied by Madame Loisel? What do we learn of them from the text? What can we infer from the societal and cultural situations which are presented as common in Paris? Are these people truly great ladies and men of wit and intelligence as well as money?

7. Sketch out a rewrite of the story from the viewpoint of Monsieur Loisel. How is our understanding of the story affected by this viewpoint shift?

8. Discuss whether "The Necklace" is an example of what Henry David Thoreau was meaning when he wrote: "The vast majority of men lead lives of quiet desperation."

9. Which of these characters are motivated by love? What kind of love? What does this motivation lead them to do? Does this love have a positive effect for this character or anyone else?

◆ RELATED TITLES/ADAPTATIONS ◆

Readers who have enjoyed this story would be particularly advised to read Maupassant's story "Boule de Suif" and any of dozens of his short stories. A teacher would be well advised to assign both this story and "The Ones Who Walk Away from Omelas" by Ursula K. Le Guin in her short story collection *The Wind's Twelve Quarters* for comparative study, as both stories discuss the relative and absolute values of material wealth as compared to human misery.

◆ FOR FURTHER REFERENCE ◆

Artinian, Artine, editor. *The Complete Short Stories of Guy de Maupassant.* Garden City, NY: Hanover House/Doubleday, 1955. The introduction discusses Maupassant's writing from a critical viewpoint, praising the artistic merit of this author's many works.

Le Guin, Ursula K. "The Ones Who Walk Away from Omelas." In *The Wind's Twelve Quarters.* New York: Harper & Row, 1975. A short story describing a fantasy city of great wealth, and the misery of one child whose captivity preserves that wealth by magic.

Maupassant, Guy de. *The Best Stories of Guy de Maupassant.* Edited by Saxe Commins. New York: Random House, 1945. Includes a fine introduction describing the life and experiences of Maupassant.

Paula Johanson

The Necklace

NO-NO BOY

Novel

1957

Author: John Okada

◆

Major Books for Young Adults

No-No Boy, 1957

◆ ABOUT THE AUTHOR ◆

John Okada, a *nisei* (a person of Japanese descent born in America), was born in Seattle, Washington in 1923 to Japanese parents. He attended the University of Washington where he received two Bachelor of Arts degrees, then moved to Columbia University and earned a Masters of Art in English. Like many Japanese Americans who came of age during World War II, Okada was interned after the bombing of Pearl Harbor and called by the United States government to either join the U.S. Armed Forces and pledge loyalty to the United States or remain in prison. He chose to fight. He was released from his internment in Minidoka, Idaho, became a sergeant in the U.S. armed forces, and was discharged in 1946.

Okada's experience during the war years influenced him to write *No-No Boy* and shed light on the catch-22 situation and the subsequent identity crisis many Japanese Americans suffered after the bombing of Pearl Harbor. *No-No Boy* was published in 1957, and it hit home for all who had themselves either experienced the horrors of internment or the feelings of conflict that arose from fighting for a country that considered them second-class citizens at best. At the time of its publication in 1957, the novel was underappreciated, just as Japanese Americans were at that time. But it became a classic in the 1970s, regrettably, only after Okada's death in 1971. The fact that Okada's book received little recognition in 1957 was not surprising, because for a long time the plight of Japanese Americans who lived in the aftermath of World War II was a neglected part of American history. Unfortunately, Okada spent much of his life feeling disappointed because his own people disregarded his work. Not much is known about Okada's life other than what can be inferred from his novel. His wife destroyed much of his work after his death.

John Okada

◆ OVERVIEW ◆

No-No Boy details the plight of Japanese-American citizens who lived the nightmare of internment in prison camps following the bombing of Pearl Harbor. The novel centers on a young man named Ichiro who was raised Japanese but born in America, and who chose not to join the Armed Forces and pledge his loyalty to the United States. Had he done so, he would have escaped the internment camp where he and his family were sent after Pearl Harbor; but as a result of his decision not to fight, he remains imprisoned in the camp for two years. Okada's story begins after Ichiro's release from prison. He returns home to his family in Seattle, Washington, and struggles for acceptance in postwar America. The book is a historical novel based on Okada's own experiences during this time, and it details the painful conflicts that arose within the minds of many Japanese Americans who were forced to either pledge their loyalty to a country that had no respect for them as citizens, or remain imprisoned.

◆ SETTING ◆

The setting of Okada's novel is post-World War II Seattle, immediately after the bombing of Pearl Harbor. Ichiro returns to his family, who are living in a lower-middle-class Japanese community. Okada embellishes his text with enough historical facts to place Ichiro in his fictional setting. In the preface, Okada sheds light on the postwar environment. He recounts the story of a young man—like Okada himself at the time of the war—who answered "yes" to the loyalty questions, donned a U.S. army uniform, and fought against his native country. When this young man tells an American soldier, his copilot, that his parents are in an internment camp, the American wonders out loud why on earth this young Japanese soldier is fighting. This question, and the postwar setting, is crucial to Okada's message. The notion of America as a model of acceptance and tolerance is less than true. In the Japanese communities during the postwar era, many people felt that their American citizenship would never truly afford them the rights and privileges that America professed to offer them.

Okada calls attention to the contradiction that while the United States government professes to practice integration and tolerance, it enforces racist policies. Setting his novel in the Japanese community helps Okada define the rift between policy and practice and underscores the resultant racial injustice. Ichiro's parents, as *issei* (first generation immigrants) were denied U.S. citizenship, which confined them and other families like them to their own communities. The discriminatory practices of the U.S. government also denied these families the opportunity for well-paying jobs and prevented them from moving up the socioeconomic ladder. Integration into American society was not a possibility, at least not during this time in history.

Several crucial incidents take place on the night Ichiro returns home from prison. Ichiro and his mother visit several *nikkei* (native-born Japanese living outside Japan) families and their homes provide the appropriate setting to highlight the Japanese traditions and customs that Ichiro starts to reject. Homecomings are celebrated with festivity in Japan, and Mrs. Yamada, Ichiro's mother, gleefully celebrates her son's homecoming. She is elated that her son answered "no" to the obligatory questions because in her mind, this declared his loyalty to his culture. But Ichiro loathes what he witnesses in the *nikkei* homes. These people live in poverty and hold what he considers to be undesirable jobs, and he recognizes how severe the rift is between the rich Americans and the impoverished Japanese. He becomes disillusioned and dismayed that the job opportunities afforded him are less than satisfactory, and he recognizes—painfully—the blatant discrimination he and his people will continue to face.

Ichiro's visit to the Ashidas and his subsequent visit to the Kumasakas bring to light yet another side of the issue. Ichiro finds himself hating the Ashidas for their poverty, and for their apparent willingness to accept their role as second-class citizens. The Kumasakas have achieved more success than the Ashidas economically, but their son was a yes-yes boy, served in the army, and died in the war. Ichiro becomes incensed when he realizes that his mother knew of the Kumasaka's son's death yet bragged to them of her son's loyalty. She seemed to be saying that the Kumasaka's son was dead because he denounced Japan, and her own son was alive because he remained loyal. Depicting this type of incident, Okada underscores the divisions within the Japanese community.

◆ THEMES AND CHARACTERS ◆

Details of Executive Order 9066 help place Okada's book in its historical context. The executive order, signed by President Franklin Delano Roosevelt on February 19, 1942, resulted in the internment of over one hundred thousand Japanese Americans in prison camps throughout the United States. The title *No-No Boy* refers to two questions the U.S. government required all internees to answer in order to secure their release: "Are you willing to serve in the armed forces of the United States on combat duty, wherever ordered?" and "Will you swear unqualified allegiance to the United States of America and faithfully defend the United States from any or all attacks by foreign or domestic forces, and foreswear any form of allegiance to the Japanese emperor, or any other foreign government, power, or organization?" Those who answered "yes" to both questions were released and enlisted in the U.S. armed forces. Those who answered "no" to both questions remained in prison. Ichiro, the central character in the novel, answered "no," and thus became a "no-no boy." But Okada makes it clear that neither answer provided any resolution. The Japanese Americans caught in the aftermath of World War II found themselves in a continual struggle for self-acceptance, acceptance within American society, and acceptance within their own communities. Some Japanese pledged their allegiance to the U.S. and considered themselves Americans, while others remained loyal to their Japanese roots. Almost all of them felt displaced and confused.

Ichiro is twenty-five years old when he is finally released from prison and returns home to his disinterred family in Seattle. He finds himself facing his own identity crisis, which arose when, after the war, his confusion over race and nationality intensified. He is a man caught between cultures, hostile toward the U.S. government that imprisoned him, yet hostile toward his own Japanese culture as well. He is full of self-hatred. Ichiro returns to a divided community and a divided family. His mother is devoutly loyal to Japan and believes that Japan has won the war. His brother Taro is devoutly loyal to the United States and disrespects Ichiro for his no-no status. Ichiro's father is an alcoholic struggling with issues of his own, including a domineering wife. Thus begins Okada's novel, Ichiro's struggle, and the confusion over identity and nationality that plagued Okada himself in postwar America.

Ichiro's choice to answer "no" to both questions forces him to analyze his loyalties. Raised by a traditional Japanese mother, and a domineering one at that, Ichiro himself embraced the traditional concept of filial piety—loyalty to one's family above all else. Mrs. Yamada, Ichiro's mother, praises Ichiro's choice and views his actions as a show of pride in his Japanese heritage. But Ichiro feels conflicted. He realizes that whether he identifies himself as Japanese or American, he is doomed to a life of racial discrimination. He cannot identify with his mother, who falsely believes that Japan emerged from the war victorious, and he cannot identify with his brother, who professes to be an American and discounts their Japanese status. Ichiro cannot distance himself from his family or from his culture, but at the same time, he feels that he can never live in America and be truly free from discrimination.

The issue of filial piety is one that Okada addresses in the novel, in part by referring to the Japanese fairy tale "Momotaro: The Peach Boy." In the fairy tale, the son proves his willingness to sacrifice his life to save his parents. Ichiro proves this willingness by becoming a no-no boy and remaining in prison with his parents. He acted out of respect for his parents, out of filial piety. Clearly, his mother expected him to remain

loyal to Japan, even if it cost him his freedom. Yet not only does he lose his freedom, he is ostracized both by the Japanese-American community and by American society for the remainder of his life.

Okada's novel points to the American treatment of Japanese citizens after the bombing of Pearl Harbor as constituting a violation of their constitutional rights. The Japanese prisoners were unable to express their opinions, and required to simply answer "yes" or "no" to the questions. Were they loyal to the U.S. government or to the emperor of Japan? Neither choice offered them resolution or freedom in any real sense. In the novel, Okada creates characters who choose different courses of action and embrace different beliefs. All these characters suffer the same confusion; all feel that they will lose their rights as citizens, no matter what choice they make. Mike fights in the war, and believes that he demonstrates his loyalty to America by doing so. Bull continually harasses Ichiro for his no-no status and his avowed "disloyalty" to the United States. Kenji becomes a yes-yes boy, but unlike Bull, instead of treating Ichiro with contempt for his no-no status, Kenji treats him with respect. But both Ichiro and Kenji question their decisions and suffer guilt for making them. Ichiro's guilt is reinforced by the discrimination he suffers at the hands of those Japanese Americans who consider him a traitor to America; Kenji's guilt is reinforced by those Japanese loyalists who consider him a traitor to his own heritage.

Perhaps because Okada himself was a yes-yes boy, Kenji's turmoil likely parallels Okada's anguish. Kenji is a wounded war veteran who dies little by little when he loses his leg. Consider the symbolism of Kenji's war wound. He literally loses more and more of himself, just as Japanese Americans lose themselves figuratively by discounting their culture. Kenji's family has become Americanized; they have adopted American customs and attitudes, and Kenji sacrifices himself for the American cause. The theme of self-sacrifice recurs throughout the novel.

Several incidents that take place at the Club Oriental underscore the divisions within the Japanese community and clarify the racial hierarchy inherent in postwar America. The Club Oriental is a hangout for *nisei*, and during the postwar years, an obvious setting for young people to play out the tensions between Japanese and American loyalists. One scene involves a young man named Bull who enters the bar with a white woman and makes it obvious that he considers her superior to him. Another scene involves *nisei* discriminating against several African Americans who enter the bar and are turned away. Both of these incidents reflect the self-hatred with which the young *nisei* struggle. It is ironic that Kenji feels comfortable at the Club Oriental because he does not feel prejudice there, yet the Chinese owners of the club prevent two African American from entering. It is ironic that Bull boasts of escorting a white woman, because this reveals his own reticence to accept minorities like himself as social equals to white Americans. This appeared to be a common attitude among Japanese Americans. Kenji tells Ichiro to move away from the Japanese community and marry a white girl—essentially to dissimulate himself—to interbreed with whites to the point of Japanese extinction, as if this is the only way that integration in America will ever insure equality. The notion of Japanese extinction—of the death of one culture for the survival of another—clearly emerges as another theme. Kenji's death, Mrs. Yamada's death, and, at the end of the novel, Freddie's death, all exemplify this. Kenji and Freddie are literally broken apart, symbolically alluding to the fractured lives and feelings these people faced as they witnessed outright hatred for their native culture.

By highlighting his characters' ambivalence about their native culture, Okada not only explores the theme of racial tension, but also the theme of self-hatred. Ichiro's search for self-acceptance and the impossibility of the postwar situation lead to his own self-hatred. The issue stems from the fact that *nisei* who identified themselves (or wished to identify themselves) as American found themselves hating and resenting their parents and their culture—and themselves. Ichiro's relationship with his mother is problematic. True to Japanese tradition, he was taught to demonstrate unconditional loyalty to his family, and Mrs. Yamada clearly expects her son to be fiercely loyal to Japan. Yet Ichiro feels he must distance himself from his mother's loyalty to become integrated into American society. He resents her for her inability to accept Japan's loss in the war. Because Ichiro's conditioning to embrace Japanese culture and values is at odds with his need to become integrated into American society, his relationship with his mother suffers. It is only after Mrs. Yamada's death that Ichiro feels comfortable enough to move toward integration and finds it possible to truly identify himself with both cultures.

Mrs. Yamada's death represents a crucial turning point in the novel. She commits suicide when she can no longer deny Japan's loss in the war, as if she knows that by accepting the loss, she will never feel comfortable as a Japanese woman living in America. Again the theme of self-sacrifice surfaces. Ichiro has mixed emotions about his mother's death. In one way it gives him the freedom to integrate into American culture, but on the other hand, it forces him to recognize the value of his Japanese culture. His mother, Ichiro knew, could never be comfortable living as an American, nor was

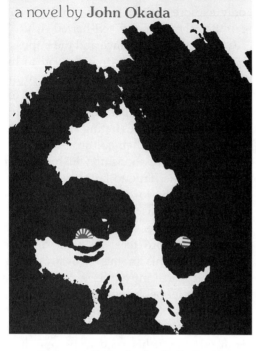

NO-NO BOY

a novel by **John Okada**

Book cover illustration for *No-No Boy* by
John Okada.

she ever accepted as an American (because *issei* were denied citizenship.) If she had accepted herself as American, Ichiro realizes, she would be a woman with no country, displaced and homeless and unable to ever feel at peace in her new land. Though Ichiro is still conflicted at the end of the novel, he has come to an understanding of his mother's loyalties and has forgiven her for instilling in him a Japanese identity he felt pressure to shed. By the end of the novel, and through his mother's death, Ichiro has also learned to accept responsibility for answering "no" to the loyalty questions. He looks toward a more positive future, though he knows he will continue to live in a fractured community.

◆ LITERARY QUALITIES ◆

Okada uses Ichiro's personal journey to accept his "Americanness" as an allegory for the overall integration of Japanese Americans (and perhaps all immigrants) into American society. Ichiro and his contemporaries, like Okada and his, were forced to embark on this journey. In order to achieve personal identity, they had to accept themselves as both Japanese and American. Ichiro's struggle to do this and the identity crisis he suffers underscores the difficulty, if not the impossibility, of the task. Okada uses the death of several key characters to allude to the "death" of Japanese culture. He uses the notion of self-sacrifice to parallel the self-sacrifice that Japanese internees had to experience in order to feel accepted in American society. Through these themes, Okada reveals his opinion that reconciling the two cultures could never have occurred during this time in history, because in order to integrate into American society, these Japanese people had to renounce their Japanese heritage. The hatred that Okada's characters experience, both toward themselves and others, alludes to the overall atmosphere of hatred that existed during the war. The Japanese were the enemy, and any Japanese living in America had difficulty shaking that image.

Though the novel is written in third person, from the perspective of Ichiro, readers gain clear insight into the thoughts and feelings of many other characters in the book, all of whom reveal their own perspectives of the wartime situation. Ichiro represents the Japanese Americans who chose not to fight for America and went to jail for their decision. Mike and Bull represent the Japanese-Americans who fought in the war and came to despise those who chose otherwise. Kenji represents the Japanese Americans who fought in the war but held no hostility against those who did not fight. Mrs. Yamada represents the Japanese-

American citizens·who continued to embrace traditional Confucian principles and continued to remain fiercely loyal to Japan. Okada uses these characters individually to highlight the confusion of the Japanese-American people, and in doing so, he creates a mosaic of life in the West Coast Japanese communities. All the people living in these communities, regardless of their personal choices, experienced a sense of displacement. All of them appeared to question the meaning of loyalty. Upon analysis of Okada's treatment of the issue of loyalty, we begin to recognize that both his references to Confucian practice and to Japanese literature reinforce the discrepancy between what the Japanese people associate with the word "loyalty" and what the American people associate with the word. Loyalty, to the Japanese, encompasses the concept of filial piety, of dedication to one's family. This is but one of the cultural differences that keep the notions of "Japanese" and "American" in opposition.

No-No Boy is a study in contrasts, and it is both a political commentary and a realistic account of racial discrimination in America. Okada contrasts the ideal of America as a melting pot and the reality of America as a place of bigotry and hatred. The United States government prides itself on welcoming immigrants into their country, but how does America truly feel about racial integration? Do immigrants feel accepted as American citizens or do they feel more like victims of discriminatory practices that will cause them to feel forever alienated? Okada explores these questions while driving home his own view that Japanese Americans who lived through the internment following the bombing of Pearl Harbor will always struggle with their identity and never feel truly part of the American nation.

Okada draws a strict dividing line between "Japanese" and "American." He develops the characters and attitudes of Ichiro's mother, his father, Kenji, Emi, and the other people in the community to delineate a contrast between those who feel loyal to Japan and those who feel loyal to America. By showing that Ichiro and the other characters feel the split between cultures, Okada makes it known that contrasts exist within the Japanese communities themselves as well as in America as a whole. He makes the divisions clear. The conflicts between the no-no boys and the yes-yes boys are similar to the conflicts between the *nisei* (American-born Japanese) and the *nikkei* (native-born Japanese living outside Japan). Furthermore, those conflicts seem to parallel the general conflicts between two vastly different cultures; the wartime conflicts between America and Japan, and the conflicts that exist when people have no choice but to tolerate the guise of racial equality, yet experience the reality of bigotry and hatred. Though *No-No Boy* deals with a uniquely Japanese experience, it details the plight of all immigrants searching for identity and acceptance in America.

◆ SOCIAL SENSITIVITY ◆

No-No Boy forces readers to examine the issue of racial inequality. The racial tensions experienced between Okada's Japanese and American characters (or those who label them as such) closely parallels the racial tensions experienced today between blacks and whites. The message is disturbing, because Okada's book paints a negative portrayal of America. It brings to the surface the prevalent idea that many Americans largely ignore racial injustice and often discount class divisions, resulting in hypocritical viewpoints. If America welcomes immigrants into the country, why do Americans treat the Japanese and other racial minorities as second-class citizens? If America is the land of opportunity, why do these minorities have difficulty acquiring high-paying jobs?

Okada's book is about civil rights, and civil rights for all people of any race living in America. The writing of *No-No Boy* coincided with civil rights campaigns run by African Americans who suffered the same discrimination the Japanese Americans suffered. But a Japanese civil rights movement never occurred, and the civil rights of those interned after the bombing of Pearl Harbor were certainly violated. No matter which choice the Japanese prisoners made, they lost. America won. If Japanese Americans declared their loyalty to America, they still knew that America considered them noncitizens. If they did not declare loyalty to America, but to the Emperor of Japan instead, they would be imprisoned. Either way, they were considered inferior in the country in which they lived, and for a long time they would be considered the enemy. Okada's book pits Japan against America. But it also emphasizes that the wartime situation and the internment of Japanese-American citizens made enemies among the citizens living within the Japanese communities themselves. Okada's cast of characters demonstrate the opposing Japanese-American viewpoints about what it meant to be American. Okada's characters also act out the hatred that arose from a situation where many of Japanese-American people lived their lives feeling imprisoned by their feelings of displacement—both from the land of their birth and the land of their choice. Okada's novel makes it clear that the notion of America as a model of racial diversity never occurred, that none of the Japanese people who lived during the horrors of the World War II truly experienced America as the "land of the free."

♦ TOPICS FOR DISCUSSION ♦

1. To what extent do you believe Mrs. Yamada was responsible for Ichiro's confused sense of identity?

2. Put yourself in the place of Okada or Ichiro or anyone else forced to answer the loyalty questions. Which choice do you believe you would have made and what factors do you think would have influenced your decision?

3. Do you think Okada regretted his decision to pledge loyalty to the United States and fight in the war?

4. What purpose does Emi serve in the novel?

5. What resolution, if any, do you recognize in the novel?

6. How does Ichiro relate to his mother after his return from prison?

7. Why do you think Mrs. Yamada and others cling to the belief that Japan has won the war?

8. Why do you think that Okada's novel was not well-received by the Japanese-American community?

9. Why do you think Ichiro was ostracized by his friends?

♦ IDEAS FOR REPORTS AND PAPERS ♦

1. Compare the racial discrimination experienced by Japanese Americans versus the discrimination experienced by African Americans.

2. Discuss the contradictory notions of Japanese Americans as model minorities versus the view of them as anti-American.

3. Compare and contrast Ichiro and Kenji.

4. Write a character analysis of Mrs. Yamada.

No-No Boy

5. Discuss the concept of filial piety in relation to Ichiro's actions, the actions of Momotaro in the fairy tale "Momotaro: The Peach Boy," and the actions of Mulan in the Japanese story remade by Disney several years ago.

6. Recap and analyze the events that occurred from the bombing of Pearl Harbor to the enactment of Roosevelt's Executive Order 9066.

7. Discuss Mrs. Yamada's death and expound on the purpose you believe it served in the novel.

8. Based on Okada's characterization of Ichiro as a no-no boy, detail how you believe Okada himself felt about being a yes-yes boy.

9. Read Joy Kogawa's *Obasan* and compare and contrast this novel with *No-No Boy*.

◆ RELATED TITLES/ADAPTATIONS ◆

Aiiieeeee!: An Anthology of Asian-American Writers is a collection that includes works of fiction by Japanese, Chinese, and Filipino authors who have been given little voice in the literary genres. It includes a lengthy introduction to Chinese- and Japanese-American literature, and it presents works of prose, poetry, plays, and excerpts from novels. An excerpt from Okada's *No-No Boy* is included.

Like *No-No Boy*, Joy Kogawa's *Obasan* explores the effect of postwar internment and racial discrimination on the Japanese people. Kogawa's book, however, deals with Japanese Canadians while Okada's book deals with Japanese Americans, and it has been argued that Kogawa presents a more positive viewpoint than Okada. Beginning after the bombing of Pearl Harbor, Kogawa details the struggles of these minorities to come to terms with both their Canadian and Japanese identities.

Monica Hoi Sone has written an account of her life as a young Japanese American living in Seattle before World War II and confined to an internment camp after Pearl Harbor entitled *Nisei Daughter*. It details the efforts of Japanese Americans to hold on to their dignity and their traditions during this time, while living in a country that disregarded them as citizens.

◆ FOR FURTHER REFERENCE ◆

Ling, Jinqi. "Race, Power, and Cultural Politics in John Okada's *No-No Boy*." *American Literature* 67 (June 1995): 359–381. Ling analyzes *No-No Boy* and the contradictory notions that affect Ichiro's experience in postwar Seattle.

McDonald, Dorothy Ritsuko. "After Imprisonment: Ichiro's Search for Redemption in *No-No Boy*." *Melus* 6(3) (1979): 19–26. McDonald discusses the problems Ichiro encounters in his search for redemption and self-identity. She feels that Ichiro represents the many Japanese Americans who faced racial discrimination and cultural confusion after their release from prison during World War II.

Sato, Gayle K. Fajita. "Momotaro's Exile: John Okada's *No-No Boy*." In *Reading the Literatures of Asian America*. Edited by Shirley Geok-lin Lim and Amy Ling. Philadelphia: Temple University Press, 1992: 238–258. Sato refers to the Japanese legend of "Momotaro: The Peach Boy" and discusses the theme of filial piety in the legend and in Okada's novel.

Sumida, Stephen H. "Japanese American Moral Dilemmas in John Okada's *No-No Boy* and Milton Urayama's *All I Asking for Is My Body*." In *Frontiers of Asian American Studies: Writing, Research, and*

Commentary. Edited by Gail M. Nomura, Russell Endo, Stephen H. Sumida, and Russell C. Leong. Pullman: Washington State University Press, 1989: 222–233. Sumida analyzes the questions of loyalty faced by Japanese Americans as he compares Okada's novel to Milton's.

Yeh, William. "To Belong or Not to Belong: The Liminality of John Okada's *No-No Boy*." *Amerasia Journal* (Winter 1993): 121–134. Yeh presents his critical analysis of Okada's novel and discusses the problems Japanese Americans faced during the postwar period in defining their loyalties and trying to mend their fractured sense of identity.

Yogi, Stan. "You Had to Be One or the Other: Oppositions and Reconciliation in John Okada's *No-No Boy*." *Melus* 21(2) (Summer 1996): 63–77. Yogi explores the problems of self-identification among the Japanese Americans after the war, and he discusses the tension and conflicting loyalties within the Japanese communities.

Tamra Andrews

P.S. LONGER LETTER LATER

Novel

1998

Authors: Paula Danziger and Ann M. Martin

◆

Major Books for Young Adults

P. S. Longer Letter Later, 1998
Snail Mail No More, 2000

◆ ABOUT THE AUTHORS ◆

Paula Danziger was born on August 18, 1944 in Washington D.C. and was raised in New York. She wanted to be a writer as early as second grade, but became a teacher first, and worked teaching high school, junior high school, and college. Danziger studied to be a teacher at Montclair State College and graduated in 1967. It was in graduate school that Danziger wrote her first novel, *The Cat Ate My Gymsuit*, which became a best-seller and endeared her to young adult readers. Eventually she chose writing over teaching, and dedicated herself to her writing full-time. Danziger remains active traveling around the country giving lectures and talking to school groups. In part because she bases her stories on her own life experiences, particularly as a teacher, Danziger succeeds in portraying adolescent life realistically, and with empathy and humor. She deals with common difficulties young teenagers face growing up,

such as the struggle for self-acceptance, problems with friendships and boyfriends, and the pain of dealing with difficult family situations. Today, Danziger has a long list of titles to her credit and has won multiple awards, including the Parents' Choice Award, the Children's Book Council Award, the IRA-CBC Children's Choice Award, and the California Young Readers Medal. She has a home in London where she is a guest contributor and host of a segment on books for children on the BBC's "Live and Kicking," and has become one of today's most popular novelists for young adults.

Ann Mathews Martin was born on August 12, 1955 in Princeton, New Jersey. She, too, was a schoolteacher before becoming a writer, and has worked in the book publishing industry as an editorial assistant, a copywriter, an associate editor, and an editor. Martin has been a freelance writer and editor since 1985, and today is one of the most prolific best-selling novelists for

Paula Danziger

young adults. She says that she has loved to write since childhood, and she took creative writing classes at a young age. Like Danziger, Martin injects humor into her writing but she touches on serious themes such as coping with physical disabilities and dealing with divorce. Martin says that she draws on her excellent memory to reach into the past and weave memorable personal experiences into her novels.

Martin is dedicated to her writing, producing one or two novels a month. She is perhaps most noted for the popular "Baby Sitter's Club" series and its spin-offs, twenty million copies of which are in print today. Recently Martin has begun a new series written in diary format, called "The California Diaries," starring Dawn of the Babysitter's Club as the main character. Some of Martin's books have been trans-

lated to foreign languages and various "Baby Sitters Club" books have been produced as television programs, board games, and videos. Martin channels much of her money into community services and into the Ann M. Martin Foundation, established to help children and homeless people and to fund education and literacy programs.

◆ OVERVIEW ◆

P.S. Longer Letter Later is a novel written in letters, depicting the friendship between twelve-year-old pen pals. Paula Danziger and Ann Martin, as authors, portray Tara and Elizabeth. Tara (portrayed by Danziger) has moved to another town, but the two girls maintain their relationship through letters and continue to share their thoughts and feelings. Tara and Elizabeth are compatible, but different in many ways. Tara is outspoken and free spirited and Elizabeth is shy and reserved. Tara comes from young parents with little money or assets and Elizabeth comes from older, stable, wealthy parents. During the course of the novel, however, the girls' situations change. Each of them struggles with problems as they learn to adjust to life without each other, to cope with the pains of growing up, and to make sense of the changing events within their households. A reviewer for *Publisher's Weekly* calls the book "a celebration of friendship." Through the girls' correspondence, Danziger and Martin create a poignant, realistic novel that chronicles the joys and pains of adolescence.

◆ SETTING ◆

The novel consists solely of letters and spans the course of seventh grade, a difficult time for both Tara and Elizabeth, particularly because they are apart from each other and can rarely communicate by telephone. Tara has moved to Ohio and is adjusting to life in a new school. Elizabeth is adjusting to life in her old school without Tara to help her through the aches and pains of her newly tumultuous home life.

Danziger says she likes to write about school settings because all teens can relate to them. Tara speaks to Elizabeth about the different groups or cliques in her school and the girls share stories of their school experiences. But the home setting plays a large part in the novel, too. Elizabeth lives in a large, expensive house during the first part of the novel, then she moves into a small apartment after their family loses their money. Tara has always lived in a small place, as her parents are just beginning to save money to buy a house. The authors use the girls' home settings to contrast their socioeconomic status and to help define their differences as characters.

◆ THEMES AND CHARACTERS ◆

Elizabeth and Tara are opposites in many ways. Tara is outgoing and impulsive, and she wears unconventional clothes and streaks her hair purple. Elizabeth is shy and reserved and prefers jeans and loafers to anything chic. Tara has young, free-spirited parents who are just learning to become responsible adults and earn a steady income, and Elizabeth has older, upper-middle-class parents who make enough money to hire maids and gardeners and live in a six-hundred-thousand-dollar house. Early on in the novel, Tara appears to have a rather unstable home life and Elizabeth appears to have security and stability. Then the girls undergo a reversal of fortunes. Over the course of the novel, the girls' situations change drastically, and by the end of the story, the authors have defined the nature of true friendship.

The girls remain close despite their differences because they continue to show each other respect, kindness, empathy, and genuine concern for each other's happiness. These similarities far outshine their differences. Yet the contrasts in the girls' lives move beyond their personalities and socioeconomic status as these characters begin to deal with their reversal of fortunes. Both girls' lives change significantly during the course of the novel, and the authors successfully chronicle their characters' responses to the changes. No conversations take place in the novel except between Tara and Elizabeth, yet through their letters, much is revealed about their relationships with other people. We come to understand their relationships with others because the authors so successfully express their characters' feelings. The only other character in the novel who has an active voice at any point is Tara's mother, who writes to Elizabeth to express her concerns and give her support when Elizabeth experiences hardship.

Tara and Elizabeth share a special kind of friendship and they manage to remain close despite the distance between them. These girls love each other and trust each other, yet they have the typical arguments best friends have in seventh grade. Their relationship begins to dissolve when the girls become volatile because of their tense home situations and they exchange angry words. Tara's frustration at not knowing how to help Elizabeth understand her father increases the tension. But neither long distance, nor petty arguments, nor angry words over sensitive issues undermines their friendship. They use each other as sounding boards, testing their own actions and reactions to life's complexities. Readers recognize much of what transpires between Tara and Elizabeth from the close friendships in their own lives. The authors make it clear that close friendships, like any long-term relationships, involve ups and downs, pains and joys. They convey the message that friendships are not always easy, but if two people respect and genuinely care about each other, they can resolve their problems together.

Some of the difficulties the girls face in the novel are typical adolescent problems that arise in school situations everywhere. Tara worries about making friends in her new school, for instance, and Elizabeth worries about navigating through her old school without Tara. They both discuss situations that arise with boys. But some of the problems the girls face are serious and disturbing. Change in itself can be disturbing for young teenagers, and having a best friend suddenly move miles away is a big adjustment. The girls must soon make other adjustments to situations within their families. Elizabeth becomes disillusioned by her father's irresponsible behavior, and Tara becomes worried when she sees her parents settling into patterns that feel unfamiliar. Both of these girls experience rude awakenings when they recognize that things are not always as they seem and change is inevitable and not always positive.

The authors underscore the difference in the girls' lives from the start of the novel. Before Tara moved away, Elizabeth's life was always predictable, and she always felt that her family's financial situation was stable and her parents had a good, solid relationship. Then her parents' finances and their relationship disintegrate. Her father loses his job and abandons his family. Elizabeth knows there are problems even before her father leaves, but she can not positively identify them. Her fear escalates as her parents continue to suffer, but neglect to tell Elizabeth the full story. She expresses her concern and her confusion to Tara, and the girls try to analyze the situation together.

Although Elizabeth's life was stable before these changes occurred, Tara's life was rather chaotic. Tara's parents begin to settle down just as Elizabeth's stability begins to crumble. Tara's parents begin to act more responsibly, set household rules, and make plans to have a baby. It becomes clear early in the novel that Danziger and Martin intend to make change a primary theme. As adolescents, Tara and Elizabeth are in a natural state of change, but the events that turn their homes inside out make the passage from childhood to adulthood particularly difficult.

As the girls progress through the passage, they struggle with conflicting emotions and their relationship becomes volatile. So not only do the girls' lives change, but their friendship changes as well. What Tara and Elizabeth appear to fear most is that their relationship could die as they each establish new friends and lives in different cities. As Tara and Elizabeth share their joys and hardships in their letters, the process of navigating through their lives seems to parallel the process of navigating through their friendship. In both cases, the girls' emotions evolve through the stages of contentment, confusion, disillusionment, and renewal. They undergo tests of loyalty, strength, and perseverance in both their home situations and in their relationship with each other. The story begins with the girls' physical separation and ends with their emotional union. The conflicts in their lives begin with the fracture of set patterns and end with a rebirth of security and self-confidence.

Tara and Elizabeth learn how to cope with their problems by giving each other sympathy and support. But they also learn how to cope with their problems by observing their parents' methods of coping with them. When times get rough in Elizabeth's house, her father turns to alcohol and abandons his family, while her mother takes action to solve the problem rather than retreat from it. She gets a job for the first time and takes over the role of breadwinner. Elizabeth gains a new kind of respect for her mother when she witnesses this. As a result, Elizabeth quite naturally follows suit and settles rather comfortably into her small apartment, learns how to cook, and tries to act maturely and help her little sister through this confusing time.

Danziger and Martin deal with the issue of parenting in the novel, as the actions of the parents teach Tara and Elizabeth lessons in responsibility. Tara's family struggles with money, but her mother is communicative with her daughter and with Elizabeth and is sensitive to their needs. Perhaps, in part, being such a young mother led to her sensitivity, but Tara's mother also appears to be naturally empathetic and sympathetic. Elizabeth has a much easier time talking to Tara's mother about her problems than she does talking to her own mother. An examination of Tara's relationship with her mother and Elizabeth's relationship with hers forces the issue of what is important in life—possessing material things or the freedom to express feelings. This applies to the relationship between Tara and Elizabeth, too. It does not matter that one is rich and one is poor, or that one is shy and one is outgoing. What matters is that they respect each other as individuals and take the time to communicate with each other.

Danziger is often criticized for offering simple solutions to complex problems. Her books are humorous and upbeat, yet she often deals with disturbing issues; Elizabeth's father resorts to alcoholism to cope and abandons his family, leaving them bankrupt. But the authors do not seem to be offering any simple solutions to these problems; they seem to be stressing that people can tap into their own strengths and survive most difficulties. By the end of the novel, the girls have navigated through their hardships, dealt effectively with the rifts that occurred in their friendship, and emerged as stronger people and better friends.

◆ LITERARY QUALITIES ◆

Biographical information written about Danziger and Martin reveals that their personalities are much like the personalities of the girls they portray. It appears that developing a voice to connect to their characters came easily for both writers, then the plot simply fell into place. The first-person narrative flows easily, and the authors have no problem creating strong voices that readers can easily distinguish. Perhaps because of the spontaneity of the character's interchange, they able to carry the plot and introduce the various plot twists effectively. Suspension builds as the girls' letters get more serious and their lives and their friendship threaten to explode.

The spontaneous dialogue allows Danziger and Martin to develop a realistic account of a friendship between two adolescent girls. The authors incorporate their individual styles to create two contrasting personalities, and the letter format allows Tara and Elizabeth to define the characteristics of other people in their lives in their own words. Readers come to know the girls' parents even though these characters never speak. It is true that we only see the parents through the eyes of their children, but this allows Danziger and Martin to stress the confusion the girls feel about their relationships. The letter format also helps the authors to clarify the intensity of the girls' feelings. Letters give the authors an advantage in a way, because they know that the girls writing the letters have the opportunity to think through their thoughts more clearly than they could if they were speaking. Yet the letters are conversational and incorporate typical teenage expressions.

A Novel in Letters

PAULA DANZIGER
& ANN M. MARTIN

Book jacket illustration by Paul Colin for *P. S. Longer Letter Later* by Paula Danziger and Ann M. Martin.

It is unclear whether Danziger and Martin intentionally use irony as a literary device, but certainly the adults in the novel act in ways that seem inconsistent with their images. Elizabeth's father, cast in the role of successful breadwinner, presumably acts stable and responsible but turns out to be the most irresponsible adult of all. Elizabeth's mother, who has always assumed a passive role in the family, turns out to be the one capable of taking charge and pulling it together when things get rough. Tara's parents, who were young and not emotionally prepared to have children when they did, rise to the occasion and prove capable of providing for Tara's emotional needs. Their carefree and rather unstructured life-

style does not, as it would be easy to assume, lead them to act irresponsibly.

The authors tell their story through the protagonists' viewpoints, alternating between voices to create lively dialogue. Distinct characters emerge early in the novel as Danziger and Martin breathe life into their letters to create two vibrant individuals who appear amazingly real. Their conversations are animated and reveal familiar teen emotions. The authors have said that they began this novel by beginning to write their own letters to each other in the voices of Tara and Elizabeth. In the beginning, the writers had only a basic knowledge of the plot, then developed characters strong enough to propel the story to its conclusion. The story moves through a linear plot and letters are the only style of narration the authors use to present a situation, introduce a series of conflicts, and arrive at a resolution.

◆ SOCIAL SENSITIVITY ◆

Tara and Elizabeth come from different socioeconomic backgrounds, and Danziger and Martin make it a point to express that these differences are not a barrier to their friendship. It is never clear why Elizabeth's father dislikes Tara, but we have to wonder whether his hostility toward her stems from her lower socioeconomic status or from Tara's rather unconventional ways. But it is Elizabeth's father's character that comes into question. We find out that he was never able to save money, relies on alcohol to escape from his financial problems, and deserts his family, leaving his wife and children to struggle with these problems alone. So Elizabeth is left to reevaluate her perceptions of him.

Elizabeth is also forced to reevaluate her perceptions of her mother. Elizabeth is proud of her mother when she takes charge of her life and gets a job to support the family. The strength of this woman is inspirational to

Elizabeth, and she emerges from the ordeal feeling positive and empowered. Danziger and Martin clearly seem to be giving young girls the message that women are strong. They are capable of pulling their lives together, tapping their strengths, and doing what is necessary to get themselves back on track when things go wrong. Once Elizabeth realizes this, she is able to accept that their lifestyle will change, and she can handle it with maturity. Not that Danziger and Martin intentionally criticize men, but in this situation, the woman proves to be a source of strength and the man a model of weakness.

Tara's mother also proves to be a source of strength. Despite the fact that this woman had her daughter at the age of seventeen, she accepts responsibility, pulls her life together, and acts as a loving, available, communicative mother. Elizabeth turns to her for support. Tara trusts her opinions. This woman may have not been ready for motherhood as a teenager, but she rose to the occasion. Then she waited to have another baby until she was older, more experienced and stable, and more confident in her parenting ability.

Danziger and Martin succeed in showing empathy and sympathy for young adult problems, and they inject humor into their dialogue to make these problems seem surmountable. As mentioned previously, Danziger has been criticized for making light of serious situations, but teens do get the message that they can overcome serious difficulties. They learn that it is okay to have problems and to share their feelings about them. In this novel, Danziger and Martin cover two of the most prevalent challenges young people face today: moving from close friends and familiar surroundings and dealing with divorce. These situations trigger strong emotions and introduce major changes, and the friendship between Tara and Elizabeth weathers both.

It becomes clear as the girls share their thoughts and concerns, that communication makes coping with change much easier.

◆ TOPICS FOR DISCUSSION ◆

1. Why do you think Tara is so upset about her new baby brother or sister?

2. What lessons do Tara and Elizabeth learn about responsibility?

3. How does Elizabeth react when she learns that her father is leaving?

4. What lessons does Elizabeth learn from her mother?

5. Why do you think Elizabeth's father is so hostile to Tara?

6. The novel clearly outlines the differences in the girls' personalities. What personality traits do they have in common?

7. Think about the disagreements the girls have. Do they serve a purpose?

8. How do you feel about Tara's reaction to Elizabeth's problems? Do you think Elizabeth was justified in getting angry about Tara's hostility toward Elizabeth's father?

9. Why do you think the girls' relationship nearly deteriorated?

10. Contrast Tara's relationship with her parents with Elizabeth's relationship with hers.

11. Write a character analysis of Elizabeth's father. Based on your observations, how do you think he will act in the future? Will he resurface and act more responsibly?

12. Discuss the theme of change the authors address in the novel. What kind of changes do the girls experience in their lives?

13. Discuss the ways each of the characters in the book exhibit strength.

◆ IDEAS FOR REPORTS AND PAPERS ◆

1. Do you know anyone whose parents are divorced? How do you think it affects their family? Their friendships?

2. Write a character analysis of either Tara or Elizabeth and explain what you believe influenced them to think and act the way they do.

3. Analyze the arguments the girls have in their letters and explain what you believe causes their angry reactions.

4. Research the problem of alcoholism in the United States. How does it relate to divorce? Financial problems? How does it affect families? What else does it affect?

5. Research school culture. What's it like being new to a school? How do some individuals try to fit in? Talk about the various groups and cliques in schools. Compare American schools with schools, say, in Europe or India or China. How are they different?

6. In our present society a lot of mothers are working. Discuss how this changes the family environment. How does this impact the mother-daughter relationship? What about the other relationships in the family? The financial situation? What about the mothers themselves?

7. Write a short story in a series of letters between you and an "imaginary friend." Give your characters strong voices, allow them to speak with clarity and emotion, and develop a plot from there.

8. Based on the relationships in the novel and the problems that arise, write a paper on the importance of communication.

◆ RELATED TITLES ◆

In the sequel to *P.S. Longer Letter Later* entitled *Snail Mail No More*, Tara and Elizabeth continue their correspondence through e-mail. The girls are in eighth grade now, and their lives are changing once again. Tara's mother is pregnant, and Elizabeth's father has returned and is causing problems in his family's lives. Again, this is an analysis of friendship, as the girls share their joys and troubles and navigate through the ups and downs of life.

◆ FOR FURTHER REFERENCE ◆

Authors and Artists for Young Adults, vol. 4. Detroit, Gale, 1990. A biographical essay about Paula Danziger.

Children's Books and Their Creators. Boston: Houghton Mifflin Co., 1995. Contains information about Ann M. Martin.

Children's Literature Review, vol. 20. Detroit: Gale, 1990. Contains information about Paula Danziger's books.

Comerford, Lynda Drill Lynda."A True Test of Friendship: Epistolary Fiction Written by Ann M. Martin and Paula Danziger." *Publishers Weekly* (March 9, 1998): 26. An article about the challenges of coauthoring books.

Contemporary Authors, vol. 115. Detroit: Gale, 1985. A biographical essay detailing Paula Danziger's life and work.

Contemporary Authors, New Revision Series, vol. 32. Detroit: Gale, 1991. A biographical essay detailing Ann M. Martin's life and work.

Contemporary Literary Criticism, vol. 21. Detroit: Gale, 1982. A compilation of reviews relating to Paula Danziger's work.

Elders, Ann. Review of *P.S. Longer Letter Later. School Library Journal* (July 1999): 54.

Koertge, Ron. "Please Mr. Postman." *New York Times Book Review* (May 17, 1998): 27. A review of *P. S. Longer Letter Later.*

Krull, Kathleen. *Presenting Paula Danziger.* New York: Twayne, 1995. An in-depth look at Paula Danziger and her writing.

Nilsen, Alleen Pace and Kenneth L. Donelson. *Literature for Today's Young Adults.* Second edition. Scott, Foresman, 1985. Contains a discussion of Paula Danziger's books.

The One Hundred Most Popular Young Adult Authors. Englewood, CO: Libraries Unlimited, 1996. Discusses Ann M. Martin.

Review of *P.S. Longer Letter Later. Publishers Weekly* (June 7, 1999): 53.

Rochman, Hazel. Review of *P.S. Longer Letter Later. Booklist* (June 1, 1998): 1765.

Science Fiction and Fantasy Literature, 1975–1991. Detroit: Gale, 1992. An essay about Ann M. Martin's work.

Something about the Author, vol.70. Detroit: Gale, 1993. A biographical essay about Ann M. Martin and her books.

Something about the Author, vol. 102. Detroit: Gale, 1999. A biographical essay about Paula Danziger and her writing.

Steinberg, Renee. Review of *P. S. Longer Letter Later. School Library Journal* (May 1998): 141.

Twentieth-Century Young Adult Writers. First edition. Detroit: St. James Press, 1994. An essay about Paula Danziger's life.

Tamra Andrews

THE QUEEN OF ATTOLIA

Novel

2000

Author: Megan Whalen Turner

◆

Major Books for Young Adults

Instead of Three Wishes, 1995 (short
stories)

The Thief, 1996
The Queen of Attolia, 2000

◆ ABOUT THE AUTHOR ◆

Megan Whalen Turner was born on November 21, 1965, in Fort Sill, Oklahoma, when her father, Donald Peyton Whalen, was stationed there with the United States Army. As a child, Megan read widely. Like many would-be writers, when she ran out of stories she wanted to read she decided to write her own. Unfortunately, she did not quite know how to get started at this point. She tried Roald Dahl's advice to young writers to keep a notebook of story ideas, but in her case "the idea just sat there on the page. It did not magically turn into a story the way it was supposed to." So she gave up on writing books for quite a while, turning her attention back to reading them instead.

At the University of Chicago she was an English major. For a senior project she decided to work on children's literature and wrote children's stories as part of it.

She claims they turned out "almost uniformly horrible." This she attributes to her perfectionism. She thought everything was supposed to come out perfect the first time around, a trick which very few writers can accomplish. Her efforts were not wasted, though, earning a bachelor's degree with honors.

When she married Mark Bernard Turner in 1987, she found that his research as a professor meant frequent relocation. For several years she worked as a children's book buyer in bookstores in Chicago and Washington, D.C. On a summer trip to Greece, the landscape caught her imagination as a setting for a book, but she did not start writing *The Thief*, which like *The Queen of Attolia* uses a fantasy world setting based on ancient Greece, until later.

Then, living in California, the state's olive groves provided a reminder of the book she wanted to write. This young adult fantasy adventure, *The Thief*, was an immedi-

Megan Whalen Turner

ate success and received a Newbery Honor in 1997. Meanwhile, a book of her short stories for children, *Instead of Three Wishes*, had been published and drawn praise from reviewers.

Turner credits her mother, Nora Courtenay Whalen, for giving her high standards in her writing. Her mother always supervised her written homework and even made sure she wrote thank-you notes. Her father's profession perhaps influenced her writing too, judging by the focus on military and geopolitical strategy in this latter novel. Turner and her husband have two sons, John and Donald. She continues to work on fiction for young adults.

◆ OVERVIEW ◆

In a genre crowded with series whose heroes and adventures seem much the same from one book to the next, *The Queen of Attolia* stands out. It is a sequel to the au-

thor's much acclaimed previous novel *The Thief*. While it has the same protagonist—Eugenides, the Thief of Eddis—the young hero has changed significantly since his quest for the legendary Hamiathes' Gift. He is not so apt to spout off wry comments or insults simply to get a reaction, and he has learned that the world does not revolve around him. He still has a healthy pride in his work and his judgement, however. In the sequel, this trait both gets him into worse straits than he has ever been in before and leads him to an exquisite revenge—or redemption. After having his hand cut off by the cold, beautiful Queen of Attolia, he manipulates affairs of state so that he can do the incredible—first kidnap the Queen, then marry her.

This book is full of political intrigue and military plans, but even those readers not fascinated by such topics can appreciate Eugenides' quicksilver wit, the mystery of a beautiful queen whose evil deeds mask her fear, and a group of other unique characters first met during Gen's quest for the Gift. These characters and courts are seen from a different angle this time too, as the book's scope widens and a third person narrative replaces the young thief's personal-view-point tale.

Behind it all, but integral enough that it colors every scene vividly, is the background, a sort of alternate-universe ancient Greece. The book will be most meaningful to those readers who are already familiar with its prequel, but even those who are not will easily fall under the spell of this intriguing story and world.

◆ SETTING ◆

Like most fantasy novels, *The Queen of Attolia* takes place in an imagined world which shares some features with a real place and era in history. The historical setting it draws on is the ancient Mediterranean world, especially ancient Greece.

The terrain bears a marked resemblance to that of Greece and Asia Minor. Eddis, Attolia, and Sounis, the three countries where the story's actions take place, share a rugged peninsula. Attolia and Sounis have seacoasts and harbors, enabling both countries to deploy naval forces and prosper from seaborne trade. Most of Eddis's territory lies at the top of mountain ranges; only one province seems to be lowland and have coastal frontage. Eddis has other resources. Its capital and environs, located on the heights, are easily defensible. The one pass and land route between the other two countries runs through Eddis, which can easily inspect or delay traffic at its Main Bridge. Eddis also controls the dam across the Aracthus River and can lock the sluice gates so that no water flows to irrigate the farmlands of Attolia. Because of the importance of such geographic features to the story, they are described in much detail.

The plot revolves around war and threats of war among the three nations, complicated by the threat of the Mede Empire, which has ambitions to control the peninsula. Eddis uses all her resources in the course of the hostilities, as well as destroying ships in Sounis's harbor and taking an Attolian coastal fortress by stealth. A map on the inside covers or frontispiece would have helped the reader visualize these operations, but unfortunately none is given. The landscapes and cityscapes also evoke ancient, and in some cases, archaic, Greece. All the larger cities have grown up around a megaron or royal fortress, which has been expanded from a one-room stronghold built in ages past. Now they are much roomier, but they still keep up their dungeons and raised walks behind battlements. The countryside has forests and olive groves, and Attolia has a wasteland of volcanic ash called the dystopia. Ocean water laps mysteriously in coves along the Attolian coast at night. All these images add to the book's atmosphere and sense of place, although they are not described as fully as the strategic factors.

If the physical setting reflects the ancient world, the cultural landscape makes some rather large departures from it. Both Eddis and Attolia are governed by queens. The queen of Eddis inherited her throne without struggle. The Attolian ruler came to hers by a more devious and bloody route. There is no hint of Athenian democracy in the book, but neither is there the aura of state militarism that is associated with Sparta. The various courts seem to function more like those of medieval Europe, with royal relatives, unrelated barons, and other councilors providing input—and sometimes headaches—to the monarch.

The greatest discrepancies occur in technology. Many aspects of this world's material culture are standard low-tech: horses and carts for land transport, oil lamps for light, and so on. But some material objects postdate ancient Greece by many centuries. Among these are pocket watches, cannon and guns, and matches. Except for the cannon, which is used in a military ruse, these items play no great role in the story. Most fights and battles are still fought with swords, as guns are said to be less reliable. (This was true in "real" history too for many decades.) It is hard to tell whether these anomalies are just curiosities or if they will prove important in a later volume. Given the author's penchant for surprises, the latter is definitely possible.

Names in the novel are often drawn from ancient Greece. Sometimes there is a rough parallel between a character's name and its original holder. For example, Eddis's court physician is named Galen, and an army commander is called Xenophon. Other names simply "sound Greek," without connections to actual historical personages.

The religions are partly derived from Greek sources but with many unique twists. There are two pantheons, of the old gods and of the new, and which group is worshiped seems to be a matter of political choice. The head deity, at least in Eddis, is the goddess Hesperia. She is a goddess of fire and volcanoes; her sacred mountain is the holiest place in Eddis. The deities do manifest themselves to mortals, but rarely. When they do, they provide the "magic" or otherworldly element that is otherwise lacking in this fantasy world.

Despite the mix of historical and invented elements, this world "works" quite well. The reader is shown enough to build a vivid mental image of places where the book's exciting events are happening. Often the "why" of events depends upon the setting too. The author has shown considerable skill in interweaving the two. It is a talent uniquely important to writers—and readers—of fantasy and science fiction. Even within these fields, it is rare to find a story where so much of the plot revolves around setting.

◆ THEMES AND CHARACTERS ◆

Eugenides, the Thief of Eddis, is the book's main character. Almost equally important is Irene, the Queen of Attolia. In the course of the story, the two go through a complex dance of hate and love, intrigue and longing that carries out the book's major themes.

At first glance, there seems no reason the two would have much to do with each other. Eugenides is a cousin of Eddis's queen. The office he holds has been in his family for generations. His proudest boast is that he can steal anything. This is close enough to the truth that his very presence makes many people uneasy. It is also a trait that makes him useful to his own queen, who values him both as a friend and a somewhat disreputable member of her court.

So what is he doing hiding in Attolia's palace as the story begins? The text never says for certain. Discovered, he flees through flues and across rooftops, under the city's walls, and into the countryside. The desperate chase ends with him cornered by dogs and then imprisoned. This opening sequence is riveting enough that only later is a reader likely to wonder why Eugenides was there. He does not take anything valuable. Perhaps he was sent on a mission by the Eddisian queen? Perhaps he thought it would be a grand adventure to sneak into Attolia's palace and tease its queen with hints of his presence?

As it turns out, both explanations are true. But neither of them are the whole truth. Not until far into the novel does it become clear that Eugenides is obsessed with the Queen of Attolia. Even after she cuts off his hand and sends him home in a blur of pain and depression, he plans to go back. He works out an elaborate scheme by which he can sneak into a lightly guarded coastal castle where she is staying and kidnap her. By this time the two countries are at war. Eugenides' plan will be a preemptive strike—if he can make it work.

Strangely enough, in his plans Eugenides intends to marry the Queen. Ridiculous as it sounds, his idea has a chance of working. It is in both countries' strategic interests to ally against the larger threat of the Mede Empire, rather than to fight each other. A marriage between the two houses would cement a treaty. Moreover, in Eugenides' mind, at least, it would not be only a dynastic marriage, but a romantic one, for he is in love with Attolia's queen.

This chain of reasoning reflects the novel's most important theme. Things are seldom only what they seem to be. The theme seems suitable for a book whose hero is a thief. It turns out to be equally valid in the life of a queen. Attolia, who wears a mask of silence and rationality in public, has secured her power by actions which would normally be thought immoral: poisoning her first husband and his father, who planned to use her as a mere puppet; hanging rebellious barons to teach a lesson to others; never letting her gentler emotions show, if indeed she has them. Yet after she orders Eugenides' hand cut off, sleeplessness afflicts her. She looks out over the night-darkened ocean and broods. Even if she never admits or even fully realizes it, she is obsessed with the thief. Why else would she have her spies keep watch on him at Eddis's court, where he has supposedly sequestered himself in the library, unable to accept the enormity of his pain and loss?

On one level, Attolia's plight is that of someone who has always had to suppress her better impulses in order to keep power or perhaps in order to do her duty—in her mind, the two are probably interchangeable. Eugenides evokes these impulses and emotions from her almost in spite of himself. He is younger, handicapped by her own order, and seemingly untrustworthy—by most standards a very unsuitable mate for a queen. Yet she recognizes in him a sort of kindred spirit. Here is a man as devious and clever as she, and he jars her conscience in ways she has seldom felt before. By taking up his offer, she may be grasping her one chance to become a reasonably moral and balanced person. All these factors show the complexity of the characters' interaction.

Somewhat clearer, if not simpler, is the role of the Queen of Eddis. Friends since childhood, she and Eugenides trust each other perhaps more than either can trust anyone else. Eddis, who is short and stout, has never thought of Eugenides in a romantic way, although she is not above giving that impression to mislead political enemies. The two also share a talent for strategy and intrigue. This queen brings some additional thematic notes to the fore. Well-thought-out plans can trump superior force.

In fact, the most desirable trait in a ruler may be strategic thinking, cleverly applied. When she (or he) can do so, she is less likely to use cruelty to maintain her power.

Other characters play lesser parts in the story. The magus, a major character in the book's prequel *The Thief*, is back again. Eugenides kidnaps him from the court of Sounis, largely to make a point with its king. He spends most of the war detained in Eddis's capital, where he and Eugenides jockey for work space in the library but enjoy each other's company more than either would admit. The magus has lived long enough to appreciate his captivity in a relatively benign place. It is far from the worst thing that might have befallen him in time of war.

Gods and goddesses do not readily enter the affairs of humans, but near the end one appears, in response to Eugenides' sacrifice. She remains nameless, even as he is sure he has worshiped her before. As she talks, she brings into relief things he still has to accept. The actions of deities are beyond human understanding, but they too have limits on their power. She cannot grant his wish to have his hand back. But if he thinks about what has happened since, he may have some of the answers to his perpetual "Why?"

◆ LITERARY QUALITIES ◆

In structure the book is a departure from its prequel as well as from the majority of fantasy novels. *The Thief* is a fast-moving quest-adventure tale in which the suspense centers around "Will they get the magic artifact?" and "What danger lurks just ahead?" *The Queen of Attolia* starts off with a tense, suspenseful opening, but when Eugenides returns to Eddis, the story's focus widens. He is still the main character, but the novel begins to deal with the affairs of state of at least two countries.

This shift results in a change of pace. Whereas the first part of the book is headlong action, the rest of it mixes ordinary scenes of dialogue and event with two other, quieter types of narrative. A great deal of information is given on strategic factors and the shifting alliances among the countries. Some of it comes out in conversation, but the author also uses flashbacks and straight explication for this purpose. There are scenes where Eugenides walks the halls of Eddis's palace in the dead of night, struggling to come to terms with his loss. There are other scenes in which Attolia's queen looks out over the water, brooding in painful solitude. Although it may seem that nothing much is happening in these passages, the plot twists that follow show them as incubators for a change of heart or direction. The story sometimes jumps abruptly to a new locale and event in progress, without the usual foreshadowing or transition. Again, the earlier text does not wholly fail to give cues, but they are subtle. Altogether, in this book the author has chosen to build tension in ways other than a simple sequence of increasing dangers. That she succeeds so well in doing this is a tribute to her skill.

The point of view is a limited third-person. Most scenes are shown either from Eugenides' perspective or that of the Attolian queen. Unlike *The Thief*, which is told in first person with readers privy to Gen's every ache and hunger pang, a fair amount of distance is maintained between the unseen narrator and the point-of-view character.

Indeed, if the novel has a fault, it is the way its characters' emotions stay masked or underplayed. Clearly Eugenides is suffering from the loss of his hand. But on most other matters, the reader must look for tiny clues to figure out what a character is feeling.

Such a "flat affect" style has been standard in many circles of twentieth-century "serious" literature. However, it is unusual in fantasy fiction, and even more so in young adult literature. Given Turner's very different approach in her previous novel, it is likely she uses the technique for its effect in heightening the surprise value of her characters' changes of heart.

Even after these unfold, the author springs other surprises. Mede soldiers "rescue" Attolia's queen after Eugenides captures her. She then orders her own troops to ally with the Eddisians, and sends the oily Mede ambassador fleeing across the sea. Then the proposed marriage almost falls through, over the small issue of Eugenides wanting an altar to the goddess Hesperia. Like every other development in the book, this point has multiple interpretations and offers room for unpredictable plot twists in the next volume. As the book closes, it leads to a spectacular scene where Eugenides accuses the Goddess's messenger of betraying him. Glass shatters and a future volcanic explosion erupts around him. When he regains consciousness, Eugenides is amazed to find himself alive, with the Queen of Attolia keeping watch over him. The one touch of magic in a fantasy story otherwise devoid of the supernatural, it is a fitting ending for a novel that revels in the unexpected.

◆ SOCIAL SENSITIVITY ◆

Two story threads raise perplexing questions of ethics and human behavior. First, the Queen of Attolia has committed many acts that would usually be considered evil. Eddis's queen, who has not had to use violence to keep her throne, nonetheless says that in the other queen's place, she would have done the same. Modern democracies pride themselves in believing that their political leaders reject such drastic means of holding power. Yet a case can be made that a ruler needs a touch of ruthlessness to be effective. Some parts of the world still sometimes impose the death penalty for treason, which is in essence what Attolia's rebel barons were accused of. Readers must ask themselves whether they use different standards in judging state actions (like the queens') than those of individuals.

Similarly, Eugenides says that the Queen of Attolia is "like a prisoner within stone walls" herself. Is this a natural consequence of being afraid and emotionally suppressed, and having to live with the aftermath of her acts? Her biggest worry about marrying Eugenides is whether she could ever trust him to tell her the truth. Is this because of his character or her own reputation for revenge?

There are no easy answers to these questions; they raise profound philosophical and psychological issues. Parallels can be found in current events, in the many public debates over cases of police brutality, the death penalty, and character assassination in political campaigns.

The other perplexing question is how Eugenides could love a woman who ordered his hand cut off. Occasionally a similar case happens in the real world—a woman marries a man who has earlier attacked and blinded her with acid, for example. There are also women who repeatedly marry abusive men, and, occasionally, men who are drawn to abusive women. Some readers may find the novel's love story too reflective of such unhealthy matches. Others may wonder if the Queen represents the fascination of evil.

These reactions may well be valid. The arguments against them include Eugenides' belief—also psychologically valid—that without him, she will never break free of her self-imposed prison of coldness and calculation. To be able to love, one needs to receive love. In many ways she needs him more than he needs her. After all, Eugenides can always return to his place at Eddis's

court. The Queen would have a hard time finding another husband she can trust even as much as Eugenides.

Readers who are very literal about rules might stumble on the book's hero being a liar and a professional thief. But the skillful and likeable thief is a frequent character in fantasy tales. Like Robin Hood, Eugenides never takes from those who cannot afford it; in fact at one point he brags that he only steals items which their owners do not need. He also illustrates how even a thief can have pride in his work.

◆ TOPICS FOR DISCUSSION ◆

1. Why does Eugenides say the Queen of Attolia is "like a prisoner within stone walls?" Does she herself feel this way?

2. What does Eugenides hope to accomplish when he sets fire to Sounis's fleet? Does he succeed?

3. Eugenides is a master thief, but the reader never sees exactly how he accomplishes his thefts. Why not?

4. When he first comes home to Eddis without his hand, Eugenides locks himself in his room and library, not wanting to face his relatives and other members of the court. Do you think this is a natural reaction? Does Eugenides have reasons for doing so besides his pain and awkwardness?

5. How does Eugenides know that the Queen of Attolia is staying in the fortress at Ephrata rather than her capital city? Is his plan to capture and kidnap her there realistic?

6. Eugenides cannot understand the King of Sounis's desire to marry the Queen of Eddis. Although he is close to her, he describes her as "ugly, short, broad-shouldered, and hawk-faced." The magus

responds that she is brilliant and has a lovely smile, in addition to the match's political advantages. Which one gives the better reasons?

7. Why do you think Eugenides really does not want his Queen to marry the King of Sounis?

8. Although the book's setting is based on ancient Greece, the world's inhabitants have some technology unknown to the Greeks, including rifles, cannons, matches, and watches. Do any of these items make a difference in events?

9. Would it be hard to be a ruling queen in a world like this? Why or why not?

10. Several times after his hand has been cut off, Eugenides says he wishes Attolia's queen had just executed him instead. Do you think he means it?

◆ IDEAS FOR REPORTS AND PAPERS ◆

1. Eugenides survives the loss of his hand, but he almost dies afterwards from infected bites. What are some of the measures that ancient-world physicians could take to treat amputations, infections, and other serious ailments? After doing some research, write a report about your findings.

2. Draw a map of the lands of Attolia, Eddis, and Sounis and the adjacent sea. Show mountain ranges, important rivers, the dystopia, and the cove and castle at Ephrata. Draw in the route the Eddisian soldiers took down the course of the Aracthus to Attolia.

3. The Queen of Eddis tells a story about Horreon, a goddess's son who lives at his forge deep within the Sacred Mountain. He needs a wife, but no one will

marry him until Hespira is tricked into going to his cave. While she spends the winter there, her mother wanders the earth looking for her. This story has some elements in common with two Greek myths: Hades' abduction of Persephone and Aphrodite's marriage to Hephaestus. Read one or both of these myths and compare them to the story the Queen tells.

4. How does the story about Horreon and Hespira foreshadow events at the end of the novel?

5. Do you think a marriage between Eugenides and the Queen of Attolia will last? Will they be happy? Explain your reasons, and write or draw a scene showing them at some time in the future.

6. If you have read Turner's *The Thief,* describe how its story's focus or structure differs from that of *The Queen of Attolia.* Which type of book do you prefer? Has Eugenides changed much from the boy in *The Thief?* Write a report comparing and contrasting the two books.

7. Explore other strategies the Queen of Eddis might have taken to get the Medes out of Attolia and work out a treaty with that country's Queen. Would they work?

8. There are quite a few fantasy novels based on Greek myths. After reading one, explain how the myths and magic are treated differently from Turner's approach.

9. The author received the inspiration for *The Queen of Attolia* and its prequel while on a trip to Greece. Have you ever been to a place which made you want to write or create another type of art based on it? Try and use that inspiration for a work of your own.

◆ RELATED TITLES ◆

The novel is a direct sequel to Turner's 1997 Newbery honor book *The Thief.* In that book, Eugenides is rescued from the King of Sounis's prison by his magus, who needs his talents as a thief on a quest for the Hamiathes Gift, a magically-charged stone. After many adventures, including detainment by the Queen of Attolia, Eugenides surprises his own queen by bringing her the stone.

◆ FOR FURTHER REFERENCE ◆

Estes, Sally. Review of *The Queen of Attolia. Booklist* (April 15, 2000): 1534. Favorable review with a short plot summary and some keen observations about the major characters. Recommends the book, especially for readers who liked *The Thief.*

Shook, Bruce Anne. Review of *The Queen of Attolia. School Library Journal* (May, 2000): 176–177. Short review which praises the situation and opening sequence, but feels Eugenides' infatuation with the Queen is not quite believable and that the book slows down too much as it goes on.

"Turner, Megan Whalen." In *Contemporary Authors,* vol. 156. Detroit: Gale, 1997. Biographical article including the author's explanation of how, after feeling like a failure in her childhood and college attempts to write stories, she tried again as an adult and succeeded. Contains commentary on her first published volume, the story collection *Instead of Three Wishes.*

Emily Alward

QUIDDITCH THROUGH THE AGES

Fantasy

2001

Author: J. K. Rowling

◆

Major Books for Young Adults

Harry Potter and the Philosopher's Stone,
 1997 (also published as *Harry Potter*
 and the Sorcerer's Stone)
Harry Potter and the Chamber of
 Secrets, 1998

Harry Potter and the Prisoner of
 Azkaban, 1999
Harry Potter and the Goblet of Fire, 2000
Fantastic Beasts and Where to Find
 Them, 2001
Quidditch Through the Ages, 2001

◆ ABOUT THE AUTHOR ◆

J. K. (Joanne Kathleen) Rowling was born in Gloucestershire, England on July 31, 1966. She attended Exeter University and worked as a teacher in Edinburgh, Scotland and in Portugal before publishing her first Harry Potter book in 1997. She wrote this book while she was a single mother supported by public assistance, unable to work and pay for child care at the same time. After the publication of this first book, entitled *Harry Potter and the Sorcerer's Stone,* Rowling's situation changed from rags to riches. The first three books in her seven-book series sold over 30 million copies, they were printed in 35 languages, and Rowling earned over $400 million.

Rowling has received numerous awards for her Harry Potter books, and because of her tremendous success stimulating children to read, she was awarded an honorary doctorate from St. Andrews, Scotland in 2000. Because Rowling's Harry Potter books dominated the top slots on the *New York Times* Best-Seller list, the decision was made to create a separate best-seller's list for children's books. This of course, was an honor to Rowling as well as a boon for children's authors. Rowling is an inspiration for children's authors. She achieved stardom with her first published book, she sold Warner Bros. the film rights to her first two books, and she sold all seven volumes of Harry Potter's adventures as a series, each volume focusing on one year of Harry's training at the Hogwarts School of Witchcraft and Wizardry. The publication of *Quidditch Through the Ages* (under the pseudonym Kennilworthy Whisp) and *Fantastic Beasts and Where to Find Them* came about after the British charity Comic Relief, dedicated to helping poor children all over the world, asked Rowling to write something for them. They suggested a short story at first, but Rowling instead suggested the idea of producing two of Harry's textbooks from the Hogwarts School. Not surprisingly, these two "textbooks" achieved remarkable success. They are distributed all over the world, and most of the money from these titles goes to charity.

◆ OVERVIEW ◆

Quidditch Through the Ages is a spin-off from the books in Rowling's Harry Potter series and is intended to be one of the books Harry and his friends use themselves. This book is a history of the magical sport, Quidditch, played by witches and wizards and enjoyed by Harry Potter and his friends in Rowling's books. This book is purportedly borrowed from the library of Harry's school, the Hogwarts School of Witchcraft and Wizardry, and is intended to be comprehensive in scope, beginning with the history of broomsticks, covering the changes in the game over the centuries, and ending with an overview of Quidditch today. *Quidditch Through the Ages* serves as an actual sports handbook written in the same style as any sports handbook, and it provides detailed information about Quidditch teams, players, and past matches.

◆ SETTING ◆

The setting of this book is within the fantasy world Rowling created for Harry Potter and his friends; a place where witches and wizards engage in all sorts of magic, including games that involve the use of magical broomsticks and that engage players with extraordinary powers. When J. K. Rowling brought Harry Potter and his friends to life, she created a world in which the rules of logic no longer exist. Because children of all ages found themselves immersed in Rowling's magic world, she embellished that world with enough details to sustain the magic. The setting of this book therefore, as well as its companion book *Fantastic Beasts and Where to Find Them,* is in the imagination. Rowling takes readers back into Harry's imaginary world, to the library of the Hogwarts' school, and to places such as Moose Jaw, Saskachewan, the home of Canada's three most celebrated Quidditch teams.

◆ THEMES AND CHARACTERS ◆

Quidditch is a game similar to soccer but played in the air on broomsticks, and Rowling wrote the book under the pen name Kennilworthy Whisp, a wizard who claims to be a Quidditch expert. Though readers of the Harry Potter books know nothing of Kennilworthy Whisp until the publication of *Quidditch Through the Ages,* they were familiar with the book and with the sport itself. Harry is a Quidditch player, and he learned how to play the game by reading this very book, which was mentioned in several books in the series.

As with *Fantastic Beasts and Where to Find Them,* the theme of *Quidditch Through the Ages* seems to be simply that magic exists, based on the underlying presumption that wizards can transcend the boundaries of the mortal world. In the game of Quidditch, they fly through the air on broomsticks, a feat that Rowling (a.k.a. Whisp) says witches and wizards have been performing as early as AD 962. The book is filled with "fictional facts" about the sport in order to explain the rules of the game and the evolution of the game over centuries. For example, she tells us that a wizard named Bowman Wright has been credited with the invention of the Golden Snitch, a walnut-sized ball that was "bewitched" to remain within the boundaries of the playing field, and she tells us that a wizard named Zacharias Mumps has been credited with first developing a description of the game.

Bowman Wright and Zacharias Mumps serve as characters in this unconventional work as do Kennilworthy Whisp, some Quidditch players, and Gertie Keddle, the witch who lived on Queerditch Marsh in the eleventh century and who wrote a diary detailing important information about the beginnings of Quiddith. Rowling does not truly develop these characters, yet she does give them substance by embellishing her story with details. We understand that Zacharias Mumps is concerned with hiding the sport from Muggles (non-magic folk), and that Gertie Keddle "only knew the name of one of the days of the week." Kennilworthy Whisp, the fictional author of this book, can certainly be labeled a principal character, even though Kennilworthy Whisp is simply a pen name for J. K. Rowling, who created Whisp's character to maintain the suspension of disbelief. She provides information about Whisp's life and work in a few brief paragraphs about the author. Whisp, she tells us, is a self-proclaimed Quidditch fanatic who collects vintage broomsticks and is the author of many Quidditch-related works.

Rowling created the character of Kennilworthy Whisp to write the book, but she used a character from her past books, Albus Dumbledore, to write the book's foreword. Harry Potter fans already thoroughly know Dumbledore; he's the headmaster of Hogwarts School of Witchcraft and Wizardry, and he also wrote the foreword to *Fantastic Beasts and Where to Find Them*. Dumbledore personally asked Madam Pince, the librarian of the Hogwarts school, to make this book available to Muggles. He explains in the foreword that even though he tells Madam Pince that proceeds from the sale of this book would go to charity, the librarian was shocked and speechless about lending it to Muggles. Madam Pince appears to be dedicated to maintaining the secrecy of the magic world and "has been known to add unusual jinxes to the books in her care." Kennilworthy Whisp, Albus Dumbledore, and Madam Pince all frequent the world of Harry Potter and all emerge as well-respected wizards dedicated to upholding tradition. The characters in *Quiddich Through the Ages* belong to one of two categories; those like Whisp and Dumbledore and Pince who purportedly live in the world today (that is, in the world today as created by Rowling), and those who purportedly lived in the world of the past and played some role in the development of Quidditch through the ages.

◆ LITERARY QUALITIES ◆

Rowling uses numerous devices to make her book a credible representation of an actual book from the Hogwarts' library. First and foremost, she does not identify herself as the author, but rather she creates a fictional character who anyone immersed in the magic world of Harry Potter can believe had the proper credentials to write the book. Then she embellishes her story with other colorful characters who, like Whisp, add to the suspension of disbelief. The creation of a network of secret societies also adds to the suspension of disbelief. Rowling mentions the regulations on the game of Quidditch imposed by the Department of Magical Games and Sports, for instance. She explains that this department developed as a result of the International Statute of Wizarding Secrecy of 1692, which made every Ministry of Magic "directly responsible for the consequences of magical sports played within their territories."

Furthermore, all the characters including Kennilworthy Whisp, Madam Pince, Gertie Keddle, and the Quidditch players of the past all appear to be dedicated to maintaining the "secrecy" of their wizarding ways.

Quidditch Through the Ages and *Fantastic Beasts and Where to Find Them* came about long after Rowling succeeded in captivating children worldwide with her use of enchantment. She clearly knows the world she has created so well that details seem to come effortlessly. She can recount statistics of the game, she can detail the rules, and she can provide humorous accounts of past players and past matches. In order to maintain the suspension of disbelief, Rowling also includes diagrams and illustrations, copies of fictional newspaper articles, excerpts from letters and diaries purportedly archived in places such as the Norwegian Ministry of Magic, and copies of items on display in the Museum of Quidditch in London.

◆ SOCIAL SENSITIVITY ◆

The wide appeal of Rowling's books and the success she has had in creating a world of magic influenced this author to create both *Quidditch Through the Ages* and *Fantastic Beasts and Where to Find Them*. Both of these books are geared to Harry Potter fans specifically, but they are unique and amusing enough to appeal to anyone who peruses fantasy books and to anyone who finds themselves captivated by the idea of a world that transcends the rules of logic.

There has been some criticism of Rowling's motives for writing *Quidditch Through the Ages* and its companion book *Fantastic Beasts and Where to Find Them*. Due to the popularity of her Harry Potter books, Rowling probably felt confident that people would devour anything that kept them captivated by Harry Potter's world, and she published these two books at a time when readers were eagerly awaiting another fix of Harry Potter's magic. Though these two books certainly boosted Rowling's popularity, she wrote them after Comic Relief approached her about writing something for charity. Proceeds from both *Quidditch Through the Ages* and *Fantastic Beasts and Where to Find Them* support Comic Relief, and have provided funds to needy children around the world.

◆ TOPICS FOR DISCUSSION ◆

1. By comparing Quidditch to soccer, what literary techniques does Rowling use to make Quidditch seem like a credible sport?

2. Explain your interpretation of Dumbledore's comment in the foreword: "All that remains is for me to . . . beg Muggles not to try playing Quidditch at home; it is, of course, an entirely fictional sport and nobody really plays it."

3. Using examples from the book, explain Rowling's use of humor and what purpose you believe it serves.

◆ IDEAS FOR REPORTS AND PAPERS ◆

1. Choose several of the "characters" in the book and explain how they add to Rowling's creation of an enchanted world.

2. Explain the term "suspension of disbelief" and explain how Rowling achieves this in *Quidditch Through the Ages*.

3. Read *Fantastic Beasts and Where to Find Them* and compare and contrast these two books in terms of style and content.

4. Explain the stylistic devices Rowling uses to make Quidditch appear like a real sport and her book appear like a credible sports history.

◆ RELATED TITLES ◆

Fantastic Beasts and Where to Find Them, the companion book to *Quidditch Through the Ages* is another of Harry Potter's schoolbooks, this one purportedly a facsimile of Harry's personal copy. Both of these books were written by fictional authors created by Rowling, and both of them further describe the enchanted world of Harry Potter.

◆ FOR FURTHER REFERENCE ◆

Bethune, Brian. "Fun and Games with Harry." *MacLean's* 114(12) (March 19, 2001): 50. Review of *Quidditch Through the Ages* and *Fantastic Beasts and Where to Find Them.*

Cooper, Ilene. *Booklist* (May 1, 2001): 1683–1684. Review of *Quidditch Through the Ages* and *Fantastic Beasts and Where to Find Them.*

Gleick, Elizabeth. "The Wizard of Hogwarts." *Time* 153(14) (April 12, 1999): 86. Discusses Rowling's success as an author, gives brief biographical information about her, and some information on the appeal of her books.

Gray, Paul. "Magic 101." *Time* (March 19, 2001): 77. Review of *Quidditch Through the Ages* and *Fantastic Beasts and Where to Find Them.*

Jones, Malcolm. *Newsweek* (March 19, 2001): 62. Review of *Quidditch Through the Ages* and *Fantastic Beasts and Where to Find Them.*

◆ RELATED WEBSITES ◆

Maduran, Jane. "Textbooks for Wizards." The Tech 121(16) www.tech.mit.edu.

Richards, Linda. "Spellbinding Textbooks." Januarymagazine www.januarymagazine.com/ kidsbooks/rowlingcomicrelief/html.

Tamra Andrews

RATS

Novel

2000

Author: Paul Zindel

◆

Major Books for Young Adults

The Pigman, 1968
My Darling, My Hamburger, 1969
I Never Loved Your Mind, 1970
The Effect of Gamma Rays on Man-in-the-
  Moon Marigolds, 1970 (play)
Pardon Me, You're Stepping on My
  Eyeball!, 1974
I Love My Mother, 1975
Confessions of a Teenage Baboon, 1977
The Undertaker's Gone Bananas, 1979
A Star for the Latecomer, 1980 (with
  Bonnie Zindel)
The Pigman's Legacy, 1980
The Girl Who Wanted a Boy, 1981
Harry and Hortense at Hormone
  High, 1984

The Amazing & Death-Defying Diary of
  Eugene Dingman, 1987
A Begonia for Miss Applebaum, 1989
The Pigman & Me, 1992
Fright Party, 1993
Attack of the Killer Fishsticks, 1993
David & Della, 1993
The 100% Laugh Riot, 1994
Loch, 1994
The Doom Stone, 1995
Reef of Death, 1998
Raptor, 1998
Night of the Bat, 2000
Rats, 2000
The Gadget, 2001

◆ ABOUT THE AUTHOR ◆

Paul Zindel was born on Staten Island, New York, on May 15, 1936. His father abandoned his family when he was still very young, and this abandonment may by the source of the many broken families in his writings. His family moved around frequently in New York, dogged by poverty. At fifteen years old, Zindel was diagnosed with tuberculosis and was placed in a sanatorium for a year and a half, delaying his graduation from high school by a year. He attended Wagner College, earning a bachelor's degree in chemistry in 1958, and eventually a master's degree in chemistry. After a brief stint as a technical writer, he became a high school chemistry teacher, teaching on Staten Island from 1959 to 1969. Zindel married on October 25, 1973, and has two children. He presently lives in New York and has become one of the most admired writers for young adults.

He had already begun writing plays while in college, and his interest in writing combined with his interest in his teenage students resulted in *The Pigman,* a novel for young adults that was well received and ended up on several best-books-for-children lists. Although he published additional well-received novels for young adults, it was a play that brought him national stature as an important writer. Produced off-Broadway, *The Effect of Gamma Rays on Man-in-the-Moon Marigolds* was a notable success, winning several drama awards and the 1971 Pulitzer Prize for drama. Although generally regarded as a play for grownups when it was first produced, *The Effect of Gamma Rays on Man-in-the-Moon Marigolds* has since been recommended as a best-of-the-best work for young adults by the American Library Association.

◆ OVERVIEW ◆

Rats is a thrilling page-turner with a fast, exciting narrative that makes it hard to put down. In a landfill near New York City, a horde of rats has something that other rats lack—a leader with the cunning of Attila the Hun. When humans cover the mounds of the dump with thick layers of tar, the rats are cut off from their food supply. With their existence threatened, they react with ferocity and a sense of purpose. Zindel says that in real life large packs of rats are known to have leaders and a leadership hierarchy such as that of the rats portrayed in the novel. He works this and other bits of the natural history of rats into his plot, giving it a sense of possibility and making readers believe that the events could really happen. Against the rat horde stand two youngsters, whose knowledge of the behavior of

rats is pitted against a clever, ruthless adversary.

◆ SETTING ◆

Among the strong points of *Rats* are the descriptions of its settings. Zindel creates a strong sense of place, as in this passage:

> The pier stretched out into the Hudson River, thousands of pilings reaching up from the black water like dark fingers clutching the main pier and its extensions. The beginning of the pier was covered with a flow, like dark lava. Sarah stared down from the chopper window at the lights and vast nets of the golf range. Everything was ablaze with floodlights except for the amusement park annex. Its metal-tube roller coaster, Ferris wheel—all the rides—sat in darkness like the skeleton of a leviathan carcass.

As this description shows, creating a feel for a place depends on more than just identifying what can be seen. It requires words chosen for their connotations, so that not only is the place described, but its meaning for the characters observing it—in this case, Sarah and Michael—comes through. Zindel achieves this with metaphorical language such as "pilings reaching up from the black water like dark fingers clutching the main pier." In this description, the commonplace becomes ominous, as if the pilings were alive. The apprehension felt by the youngsters is echoed in the description of the darkened amusement park as a "skeleton of a leviathan carcass." It is not only a vivid way of showing what the amusement park looks like, it is also a reminder of death and the crawling mass that brings it, looking like "a flow, like dark lava."

It is tempting to skip descriptive passages in any book—especially a thriller in which action is an important element—but one would be missing a treat by skipping the descriptive passages in *Rats.* Anyone who wishes to write fiction could learn much from Zindel's technique. For instance, note how Zindel makes the description of the area in which Sarah and Michael live work for him, advancing his ideas and the narrative:

> She and Michael started their trek through their sprawling housing development. There was no end to split-level ranch houses lining the east border of the garbage dump. Richmond Estates was the next development to Springville Gardens— and that was all Cape Cod-style homes. The other major housing tract was Holly Farm Homes, the cheapest built of them all, on the south side of the dump. Sarah knew for a fact that the walls of the houses there were paper-thin.

Zindel needs his main characters to be involved in the description, to show the setting as part of their lives. He does this by choosing an everyday activity: Sarah and Michael are selling candy to earn money for the Woodland Bird Sanctuary. This means that they must walk through their neighborhood and nearby neighborhoods—an excellent excuse for a quick description of how the neighborhoods fit together. The passage avoids being forced, instead seeming a natural outcome of something schoolchildren often do. When the rats flow out of their mound and into the neighborhoods, their movements will be easier to follow because of this passage.

In a *Globe* article, "How I Write My Books," Wilkie Collins, author of *The Woman in White* and *The Moonstone*, remarked that he thought it the job of an author of fiction to show the romance in everyday life. In *Rats*, Zindel chooses an everyday American setting. In other thrillers such as *Reef of Death* and *Raptor*, the author has sometimes chosen exotic settings for the adventures of his main characters. In *Rats*, the adventure takes place in a suburb of ranch houses, a city dump, and the edges of New York City. This helps make Sarah and Michael seem

Paul Zindel

like fairly ordinary young people living fairly ordinary lives in a fairly ordinary place. Using a setting common to many readers, Zindel makes his characters' experiences in *Rats* seem like experiences that Zindel's audience could have also.

Further, his description of settings invites people to reconsider their own surroundings, to see where the mystery and romance may be found in the sights that they have taken for granted. For instance, in one paragraph, Sarah and Michael make their getaway in a motor boat:

> She threw the throttle wide open. The prop of the outboard screamed as it bit into the water and threw a wake of bubbles and oil out behind the boat. Sarah sat behind the wheel, flicked on the head and safety lights, and steered the boat away from the pier. Michael scooted about after the few rats in the boat with a fishing net. He caught them one by one and dropped them into the black oil-slicked water.

The tone is intense, here, because Sarah and Michael are barely escaping the rampaging rats, some of which have pursued them right onto their boat. In this intense action, Zindel slips into a description, seamlessly, as if it were only natural to consider the setting for a moment:

> Strings of lights came on suddenly across the huge mounds of asphalt. Crude street-lights lined the main roads linking the mounds. Sarah slowed the boat. She didn't want to run into any flotsam, planks of wood, or tin cans and bottles—anything that could shatter the cotter pin of the prop. The last of the twilight made the Jersey side of the river surreal. Factory lights burned brightly. Smokestacks coughed forth tremendous white streams of smoke, ghostly fingers reaching high into the black-ening sky. The tops of the refinery chimneys shot out flames and ripples of yellow sulfur. Circles of light marked the several platforms that clung to the enormous Staten Island Con Ed plant.

Mentioning the flotsam is an especially effective touch, because it makes the point that Sarah must consider the setting in order to safely navigate her boat. In addition, the setting is eerie, with "ghostly fingers reaching high into the sky." Even further, the description of the setting promotes the themes of the novel. The wood, tin cans, and bottles, as well as the smoke and flames are reminders of the polluted environment that fosters the rats but threatens the habitat of other, some might say more desirable, animals.

◆ THEMES AND CHARACTERS ◆

The main theme of *Rats* is that of a corrupted environment. Sarah believes that the rebellion of the rats is a logical outcome of people despoiling the land: "People had ruined the water and the land and the air for as far as she could see. Oil-and-grease-covered barges lined a dead black shore.

Everything was endangered. Crawling. Dying." Sarah and Michael are shown to be on the right side of the battle over the environment by their selling candy to raise money for a bird sanctuary. Sarah in particular has a strong interest in natural history and wildlife, and Michael's research into wild rats proves essential in the war against the rats from the local dump.

Environmental issues appear in other Zindel novels. For instance, in *Loch*, youngsters try to save some ancient animals from extinction at the hands of adventurers, and in *Reef of Death*, the destruction of Australia's wild lands by unscrupulous international corporations is an important motif. Even so, in *Rats*, the idea of environmental destruction is taken to new extremes. New Jersey and New York are portrayed as areas of poisonous ruin caused by poor disposal of urban wastes, festering with polluted air and water caused by factories and people who live along the Hudson River. In this context, the rats are symbolic: They represent the natural world rebelling against human despoilment of the land and water. Where few other animals can exist, the rats have thrived on garbage. When humans pave over their dump the way the land around them has been paved for homes, schools, and roads, the rats fight back.

This helps to explain the gruesome opening of the novel. Leroy Sabiesiak is a killer of the rats, taking pleasure in shooting them while he is riding his bulldozer. This makes him a representative of all the people who treat the lives of the rats as worthless, as well as representative of the people who intend to encase the dump and its rats in asphalt. In terms of the environmental theme, his death suggests that the poisoning of the land will eventually affect human beings. It also suggests that there are more frightful thrills to come.

Central to the plot are Sarah and Michael Macafee, whose father Mack is in charge of the local dump. Sarah is the novel's main character and point-of-view character, meaning most events are seen through her perspective. She is smart, tough, and quick to take action, all good qualities to have for the main character of a thriller. Her brother, Michael, is harder to understand, because he is unusually immature for a ten-year-old. His fifteen-year-old sister spends a lot of time dealing with his childish ways, because their mother is dead and their father works long hours. Near the end of *Rats*, he insists on pursuing Surfer, his pet rat, in the rat-infested dump, even though common sense says that it would be a wasted effort. His sister, obliged to follow him, nearly dies because of his foolishness. Sarah thinks that he remains immature because of the shock of losing his mother. The young boy also exhibits strange behavior, such as fixating on his pet rat to perhaps compensate for his absent mother. In any case, he is fortunate that his sister is forgiving, courageous, and quick witted.

Surfer is Michael's pet rat or "Michael's friend," as Sarah reminds herself. That something strange is occurring is evidenced by Surfer's behavior. When he and the youngsters watch television, he will change channels with the remote control, settling on shows about nature. When taken outside, he often rushes into the dump. This is one reason why he has been equipped with a transmitter, to help Michael find him after he runs off. Further, he seems to talk to other rats: "He's been making sounds like that a lot lately," Michael says to Sarah. Surfer functions as a spy in the enemy camp of humans, learning about wildlife and humans and telling the landfill rats what he has learned. Although he seemingly saves Sarah and Michael's lives at one point in *Rats*, he is vengeful and has Sarah endure a physical examination the way he did when she brought him to school to teach other youngsters about rats. He pays for his vengeance in a nice turn of events involving methane gas and his transmitter.

Other characters in the novel are not particularly well developed. Mack Macafee is a kindly father but a bit befuddled by the rats' behavior. In fact, the only official who seems to apply common sense to the crisis of the invading rats is the local mayor, in a reversal of stereotype common for thrillers. Usually, politicians are villains, but Zindel avoids the stereotype, perhaps because he wants to make the corruption of the environment the fault of everybody, rather than just politicians.

Most of the rest of the characters exist mostly to be victims of the rats. Like Miss Lefkowitz, an English teacher, they are killed and devoured. On the other hand, Mrs. Carson defies the pattern of terrified victims by fighting back, defending her child. Aunt B uses good sense in her handling of the rat invasion, but most characters serve as grisly reminders of the hatred of the rats, as Hippy does, whose cadaver is devoured in the rats' caves.

Given that multitudes of people are killed, individually or in mass in New York City, death is an inescapable theme. Although not as important as the main theme of environmental corruption, it is important in how it supports the main theme. Although *Rats* is a thriller, meant more to entertain then enlighten, the idea that humans polluting the environment will eventually result in the deaths of humans is significant.

◆ LITERARY QUALITIES ◆

It takes talent and skill to write truly frightening scenes. The writer has only ink on paper to work with, without sound effects, scary voices, or other advantages a live performance offers. Zindel is one of only a few writers for any age group who

Book jacket illustration by Dan Horne for *Rats* by
Paul Zindel.

can compose prose that actually frightens.
For instance, Mrs. Carson and her son Kyle
confront a rat in their bathroom. The scene
begins with a common human response to
a surprise: hesitation. "By the time it was
clear that it was a living thing it was too
late," Zindel notes. "In a flash, Mrs. Carson's instincts interpreted the movement as
beyond the parameters of anything inanimate. Concern, apprehension, and even
fright raced electrically through her as the
thing swam upward in the bowl." In this
brief passage, Zindel accomplishes three
things: He foreshadows the thrills to come
by mentioning "it was too late"; he ties in
his environmental theme by mentioning
Mrs. Carson having "instincts," putting her
into a violent natural world for which her
experiences have left her unprepared; and
Zindel places his characters in a vulnerable

position likely to be familiar to his readers—
using the bathroom.

Further, Mrs. Carson is a mother with a
child to protect; this makes her even more
vulnerable to the rat than she would otherwise be. She was stunned "as she realized a
head with snout and teeth was exploding—
erupting!—straight at her." Then, "Mrs.
Carson jerked her head back and away, but
the large rat had launched itself into the air
now. Its body was sleek, with powerful legs
and claws digging into the air." Zindel
says, "She had a single moment to push
Kyle away from the bowl into a pile of
laundry and get to her feet." By now, the
nature of the threat has been established,
and Mrs. Carson's dire situation is plain.
She has neither powerful legs nor claws.
What can she do?

> Before she could get to Kyle, the powerful
> and wet writhing body of the huge rat was
> half out of the toilet and heading for her.
> She held Kyle as the rat leaped from the
> bowl and charged at her. With her free
> hand she grabbed a broken mop and swung
> it with full force.

Here, Mrs. Carson has become primeval
woman, determined to protect her young,
and she does what human beings have
done for thousands of years, she tries to
compensate for her lack of claws by using a
tool, whatever her environment offers: in
this case, a broken mop. Earlier passages
have made clear what the rats can do when
they surprise and overwhelm people, but
in Mrs. Carson's case, the human assesses
her situation and replaces surprise with an
aggressive defense:

> At first she missed, stroke after stroke, and
> she settled instead for diverting the dark,
> snarling mass. It scooted like a shadow, a
> horrible stalking shadow that closed on
> her feet. She leaped and stepped to one
> side faster than she knew, and an innate
> ability to battle replaced any thought of
> fleeing. Blood rushed into her head, and
> her brain pounded as she brought the

Rats

stick down on top of the rat. Again. And again.

There is a master hand at work in this passage, because it not only contains frightening and captivating action, but also because the author's few words speak volumes about Mrs. Carson. A character about whom little can be known at the start of the scene, Mrs. Carson immediately becomes a fleshed-out figure. Through her behavior, without any explanation from Zindel, Mrs. Carson is shown to be passionate about the welfare of her child, as well as courageous, smart, and quick witted.

Occasionally, *Rats* seems somewhat mechanical. For instance, Zindel hammers on foreshadowing for creating suspense. That Surfer's collar can spark is mentioned often enough that readers should notice this must be an important detail to remember. Other instances include the "moaning" in the mound, Surfer's penchant for visiting the dump, taking boats across the river—showing that the rats are right by the river, and "the real nightmare was just beginning." These instances of foreshadowing are sometimes awkward enough to affect the style of the narrative because they become a distraction from events, making *Rats* somewhat inferior to novels such as *Raptor* and *Loch.*

◆ SOCIAL SENSITIVITY ◆

Environmental issues frequently appear in Zindel's thrillers. For instance, the destruction of Australia's natural environment is a prominent issue in *Reef of Death,* in which unscrupulous corporations despoil the land and coastal waters. In *Rats* human beings have despoiled much—perhaps most—of the land in and near New York City. The landfill in which the rats live has been placed in a bad spot, right next to a community of homes. Its smell is foul and it is infested with vermin. Zindel contrasts this with the Woodland Bird Sanctuary, a place that represents hope for undoing the destruction that people have wrought on the land.

This environmental theme is nicely worked into the plot of *Rats* so that it appears to be a natural part of the novel. The rats themselves have adapted to the polluted landscape, becoming creatures who can survive where others cannot. Without natural checks on their population, the rats have swarmed through the dump and the city. Zindel has Sarah mention what she has learned about rat behavior in order to underscore the point that the rats are behaving much as they would in the wild. The problem is that the human habitat has become so unbalanced that a single rapacious species of animal can come to dominate its part of the land.

By having the rats turn on humans in a fury of destruction, Zindel makes two points. One is that the natural world can fight back; the other is that a poisoned land will poison human beings as well as animals. The furious rending apart of human beings is a consequence of human carelessness, of many years of ruining the environment to the point that humans become the only available prey. Therefore, when the rats attack and overwhelm human technological defenses such as the fishing boat, they represent the wretched, polluted natural world in conflict with the modern human environment—a spasm of violence doomed by humanity's superior brain and ability to adapt to a corrupted environment in which kill-or-be-killed is the only choice left for animals.

Like other of Zindel's thrillers (*Loch, Reef of Death, The Doom Stone,* and *Raptor*), *Rats* has scenes of grotesque violence like this one where Sarah struggles to free herself from Hippy's rotten corpse:

> As though alive, the bones and flesh of the body followed her, followed her screams and terror, and she felt as if her heart

would shatter. She pulled and yanked at the legs and disembodied arms, until finally she was free of it and the snake and the sickening stench of rotting flesh.

Terrifying stuff, the material is perhaps more explicit than some readers would care for, although most teenagers would take this and other such scenes in stride. *Rats* also has scenes in which people are eaten alive, as well as scenes of dismemberment as the rats swarm through city streets in search of revenge, prey, and a new home. These scenes add to the dramatic intensity of the novel. In addition, these incidents make the rats' efforts to enter Manhattan menacing and suspenseful because their potential for destruction has been made clear. Even so, some parents may wish to read the novel before they decide whether it is suitable for their youngsters. Sensitive younger readers may find the images of rats swarming into automobiles and homes, while devouring people, to be the stuff of nightmares.

◆ TOPICS FOR DISCUSSION ◆

1. Does the brutal violence of *Rats* make it unsuitable for children? In your opinion, what should be the appropriate age for readers of this book?

2. How well does Zindel show what he means as opposed to telling what he means, especially when speculating on the rats' motivations?

3. How intense are the scenes in the rats' caves? Why would Zindel send Sarah and Michael into the caves? Did you enjoy those scenes?

4. Why would Zindel include scenes of goo and slime in Rats?

5. What is the point for having the rat leader examine Sarah the way Surfer was examined?

6. Why would workers at the landfill not realize that they had a serious rat problem, one much worse than usual for a dump?

7. What purpose does the absence of Sarah and Michael's mother serve in the plot of *Rats?*

8. When does it become apparent that Surfer is up to no good? What are the clues Zindel provides before the scenes in the caves?

9. Mentioning that Surfer's collar can spark is called "foreshadowing" because it sets up the scene in which the mound is blown up. What other instances of foreshadowing are there in *Rats?*

10. Why do people in *Rats* underestimate the rats?

11. Why would Michael, supposedly an intelligent youngster, insist on going into the rats' lair to find Surfer?

◆ IDEAS FOR REPORTS AND PAPERS ◆

1. Real-life rat behavior is mentioned now and again in *Rats.* How accurate is Zindel's portrayal of rat behavior?

2. What are Norwegian rats? Where are they to be found? Why would people be afraid of them?

3. What is the situation for rats in New York City? Where in the city are they to be found? What problems do they create? Do they do anything beneficial to the city? How successful have efforts been to control them?

4. From Zindel's description of the area along the Hudson River, locate where Sarah and Michael's home should be. Draw a map showing where their house, their aunt's house, and New York City are in relation to each other.

5. How polluted is the Hudson River area near New York City? Who or what is doing the polluting? What are the pollutants?

6. Sarah's research into the natural history of rats says that Malaysia has large packs of rats like those described in *Rats*. Look up the real-life accounts of the Malaysian rats. Is Sarah accurate in her depiction of their social structure?

7. What actually happens to old dumps when they have outlived their usefulness? Are any paved over like the dump in *Rats*? Would the people in *Rats* have had alternatives to paving over and sealing their dump?

8. Do fishing boats such as the *Parsifal* actually exist. If so, how do they function? If not, what sort of boats would come close to being like the *Parsifal*?

9. What bird or wildlife sanctuaries are there on the New Jersey side of the Hudson River? What animals are to be found in them? Is there a place like the Woodland Bird Sanctuary?

◆ RELATED TITLES ◆

Rats is one of a series of thrillers that Zindel has recently written. The others, so far, are *Loch, Reef of Death, The Doom Stone*, and *Raptor*. These novels feature frightful monsters, but *Rats* finds its chills in a common animal. Like that of *Rats*, the plots of *The Doom Stone, Loch*, and *Raptor* turn on the fates of their monsters; in *Reef of Death*, the monster fills a secondary role as one among several sources of chills. In *Loch*, three youngsters defy a rapacious research expedition bent on capturing the plesiosaurs dead or alive—more likely dead. In *Reef of Death*, two young adults and an elderly man confront an illegal mining operation that is disguised as a research ship. The bloody scenes in *Reef of Death, Loch*, and *Raptor* equal or exceed those in *Rats*, providing vivid descriptions of dismemberment and gore. *The Doom Stone* is more circumspect about gory scenes, relying on a hideous monster and perilous situations for its scares. Of *Loch, Reef of Death, The Doom Stone, Raptor*, and *Rats, Loch* has the most complex plot, one into which the characterizations are seamlessly woven. *Reef of Death* and *Raptor* feature somewhat more common plots, familiar from numerous monster movies. Of the novels, *The Doom Stone* and *Raptor* surpass the others in sheer, gripping suspense, although those who enjoyed reading them are likely to enjoy *Loch, Reef of Death*, and *Rats* as well.

◆ FOR FURTHER REFERENCE ◆

Review of *Rats. Publishers Weekly* (August 2, 1999): 86. The reviewer insists that ideas are secondary to violence in Rats, claiming, "The book does contain a somewhat watered-down message about environmentalism, but readers caught up in the fast-paced, blood-spewing action may not take time to ponder the moral."

Kirk H. Beetz

REALM OF THE REAPER

Novel

1999

Author: K. A. Applegate

◆

Major Books for Young Adults

The Story of Two American Generals:
    Benjamin O. Davis, Jr., and Colin L.
    Powell, 1992
The Boyfriend Mix-Up, 1994
Sharing Sam, 1995
Listen to My Heart, 1996

Boyfriends and Girlfriends series,
    including:
Zoey Fools Around, 1994
Lucas Gets Hurt, 1998
Claire Can't Lose, 1999
Who Loves Kate, 1999

Animorphs series, including:
The Message, 1996
The Stranger, 1997

The Reunion, 1999
The Prophecy, 2000
The Ultimate, 2001

Everworld series
Search for Senna, 1999
Land of Loss, 1999
Enter the Enchanted, 1999
Realm of the Reaper, 1999
Discover the Destroyer, 2000
Fear the Fantastic, 2000
Gateway to the Gods, 2000
Brave the Betrayal, 2000
Inside the Illusion, 2000
Understand the Unknown, 2000
Mystify the Magician, 2001
Entertain the End, 2001

◆ ABOUT THE AUTHOR ◆

Katherine Alice Applegate is simultaneously one of America's most famous authors and one of America's most mysterious. She guards her privacy, as does her publisher, Scholastic, which has brilliantly marketed her Animorphs and Everworld series for astounding sales. Applegate was already a well-established writer of books for young readers, mostly romance novels, when she proposed the Animorphs series to Scholastic, where the proposal was met with enthusiasm. She wanted to write a series of books that showed how the world might look from the perspectives of different animals; the result has been a series of fascinating novellas for late elementary to junior high school students.

Having moved several times around the United States, the Michigan-born writer now resides in Minneapolis. She has published more than one hundred books, and she has written them at an amazing pace. Begun in 1996, her Animorphs series numbered more than forty books plus several spin-offs by 2001. Her twelve-volume series intended for adolescents, *Everworld*, begun in 1999, was completed in 2001. Sally Lodge, in *Publishers Weekly*, quotes Applegate:

> A series writer has to develop plotting and pacing that become a well-oiled machine. You don't have the luxury of spending a year on a book and absolutely cannot indulge in writer's block. Yet I knew I had to write in perfect language and choose just the right images, to make sure that my middle readers fell in love with the characters and returned again and again.

The two hundred letters from young readers that Applegate receives per week, as well as the one hundred e-mails she receives per day, attest to the success she has had in reaching her intended audience. Readers love her characters.

In spite of the success of Applegate's writings, they have received scant attention in the press, perhaps because of a prevailing view that books written so quickly cannot be worth writing about, or perhaps because of the immense difficulty in keeping current with all the books Applegate publishes. But despite the great pace at which Applegate has written her books, they tend to be of higher quality than other mass-market writings. The Animorphs series provide artful and informative perspectives of characters as animals, whether fleas or birds. The Everworld novels offer suspense and tales of adventure with fine introductions to the mythologies of the world.

Applegate does not shy away from the tough questions about growing up and building sound, honest relationships with others. For instance, the non-series title *Sharing Sam* deals with the prospect of a close friend dying and how to love in spite of the pain of the loss of loved ones. In *Everworld*, the relationships among the principal characters are essential to the appeal of the novels. Applegate has mastered the art of characterization, and this is perhaps the most important reason her rapidly-written works are considered both good literature and entertaining reading.

◆ OVERVIEW ◆

In Everworld, the gods of ancient mythologies live and rule over their human subjects, brought with the gods when they left the Old World, Earth. Some of the wandering nature of L. Frank Baum's Oz stories is found in the fourth Everworld novel, *Realm of the Reaper*. In this novel, Jalil, David, Christopher, and April roam the countryside and enter a city called Her City that in its own way is as weird as the city of upside-down people in Oz. Her City is a place in which people live in fear and men are never allowed to leave. A beast stalks the city at night, leaving death in its wake, and men are the preferred prey. Jalil (the narrator) and his companions solve the mystery of the Terror Queen, and in the process find themselves unwillingly delving deep into the mysteries of life and death in Everworld.

◆ SETTING ◆

Jalil and his companions wander into Her City, an Everworld city that is surrounded by huge walls and guarded by fierce eunuchs. Her City is an embodiment of anti-maleness, guarded by men who have been neutered, and housing men to be given to Her. But even in a city where men are victims, April does not get a break. The Terror Queen wants all the men for herself, and, as one man says, "She's [April is] a beauty, and hell will brook no competition."

Jalil, David, Christopher, and April not only visit a hellish city, they end up in hell itself—as the ancient Norse viewed it—run by Hel, daughter of Loki. There are horrors aplenty in it. For instance, there is a floor paved with living, suffering heads and a great pit filled with people, one of them Senna, whom the four had followed into Everworld in the first novel of the series, *Search for Senna*, dangling from its walls. Hel imprisoned two important Norse gods: The first god is Baldur. As Hel pauses to admire her captive, she describes Baldur: "Most beloved of the gods of Asgard. Odin's favorite. And now? All mine. A pity he isn't more cooperative. He is such a fine figure of a god." The other god is Thor:

> It was a god, not a man. Big. Bigger than Loki at his most extreme. Bare arms like tree trunks. Booted legs that could have supported a brachiosaurus. He had long, wild red-blond hair, a full blond beard, blue eyes, and angry, feral mouth.

Matters already looked bad in Everworld. With the discovery that Thor is trapped in hell, matters appear even bleaker than before.

As in the previous novels, the Everworld setting is contrasted with the real world. The four teens find that when they go to sleep in Everworld they are back in their old lives on Earth. In fact, they are living two lives, one of everyday experiences at home on Earth and the other of fantastic adventures in Everworld.

Jalil asserts that Everworld is a "lunatic asylum," because he suffers from a mental disorder on a supposedly sane Earth but does not in the supposedly insane Everworld. This contest of sanity and insanity, taking place between Earth and Everworld and associated with Jalil's mental state, gives the narrative much of its tension.

In Jalil, Applegate presents an extraordinary figure whose contradictions motivate him and can destroy him. Jalil suffers from obsessive-compulsive disorder, a disorder that he recognizes and is educated about, that compels him to wash his hands seven times in a row. It is part of what makes him miserable while on Earth, but it does not afflict him in Everworld:

> Over there, in Everworld, in that mad place, that lunatic asylum, that universe where gods feed on human hearts, where wolves could grow to the size of city buses, that universe of dragons where Senna Wales had drawn me, over there I could lie asleep, aware of the itching of fleas, aware of the dirt under my fingernails, aware of the filth all around me, and still sleep.

Yet, Everworld makes Jalil miserable because it defies his desire for logic and order in life, both reactions to his obsessive-compulsive disorder. Even where he should feel free, he feels bad. Further, when Senna offers him lasting relief from his compulsions, he refuses her help because it means that he would have to do her bidding.

Jalil responds to his disorder by trying to place everything in order, and he takes pride in being a rationalist probably because he knows that his behavior is fundamentally irrational. Thus, when he proclaims his atheism and demands proof of God, it is not so much a conviction that there is no God as it is a matter of having no neat, clean, orderly place into which he can fit God. Jalil offers a notable contrast to April, who believes in God and who narrated the previous novel, *Enter the Enchanted*.

Jalil, in *Realm of the Reaper*, does not seem to grow as much as April does in *Enter the Enchanted* as she learns to take the initiative—something that saves her companions, Jalil especially—when she takes action against Hel. Perhaps Jalil's mental disorder requires too much work to be overcome in only one novel. He whines a bit, but he is not all gloom. His understated humor lightens his narrative: "We were dirty. We smelled. We were four nasty teenagers in lousy moods." In any case, after what Jalil and the others have achieved, they are four teenagers not to be messed with, as Hel learns.

Largely unknown to the other teenagers, Jalil has his own special contest with Senna. Senna is only a teenager on Earth but the focus of titanic rivalries in Everworld, where she supposedly can open a passage from Everworld to the Old World, Earth. When Senna offers Jalil freedom from the "voice" in his head that tells him what to do, in exchange for her controlling him, he surprises her by refusing her. "'You think I'm weak, Senna,' I managed to say. 'You think I'm weak because I can't control this part of myself. You're wrong. My own brain messes with me, but I am still who I am.'" Until *Realm of the Reaper*, it has been a mystery why Senna chose Jalil as one of the four teenagers she took with her to Everworld. He seems to have been selected because Senna thought that he would submit to her control in exchange for release from his unending mental torment on Earth.

Before *Realm of the Reaper* even begins, Jalil is already a complex figure, and, as he narrates the novel, his complexities deepen, resulting in a portrait of a full, three-dimensional character.

According to Jalil, Senna is the crux of the conflicts in Everworld, "And it all comes down to possession of Senna Wales, the gateway between universes." Through three novels in the Everworld series, Senna has managed to keep much of herself private, but April and Christopher have noted some qualities of her character, such as her manipulation of others and her arrogance. In *Realm of the Reaper*, more is revealed because she is finally in a position in which

she is helpless, stripped of her defenses: "Senna hung helpless above Hel's own Hell." She asks Christopher and April to kill her rather than leave her hanging; she is in despair, and at that moment she is not the witch Senna, but the teenaged girl Senna.

She later shows herself to be a good observer of her surroundings, as she figures out where she and the others are and explains some of the figures beneath hell. Even so, vulnerability does not mean that she has lost her cunning or her penchant for verbal contests. "Power. That's it for you, Senna. That's the drug for you, isn't it? You want the power. You've gone crazy with it," Jalil says to her. She fires right back with, "It's reasonable, Jalil—that's your drug, isn't it? Reason? Everything has to be neat and orderly and make sense?" During her verbal sparring with Jalil, she reveals her own deep plans for Everworld, proclaiming that it is only reasonable that she should rule the world rather than Loki or Merlin. How she intends to deal with "Ka Anor: the god eater" is not clear.

Of himself, David, Christopher, and April, Jalil declares, "We are four high school kids from a suburb north of Chicago." Four "nasty" kids, he means. David narrated the first novel in the Everworld series and is big and tough. He puts up with a large amount of sarcasm from Jalil, but Jalil admits, "Maybe David isn't a hero but there are times when he sure looks like one."

Although David wants to be the hero, in *Realm of the Reaper* April steals some of his thunder. By the end of *Enter the Enchanted* April had made the choice to take action on her own behalf and on behalf of others by defying Senna's sarcastic putdowns and walking forward to battle the trolls. She is quick-witted and quick to seize opportunities. Before, David had been the one to size up opponents and assess their weaknesses, but when Hel leaves herself open for a moment, April is at her with Galahad's sword, stabbing and hacking like any noble knight. It is one of the highlights of *Realm of the Reaper*.

Christopher thinks of himself as a spear-carrier in a movie about everyone else, so it is not entirely surprising that he spends more time commenting on the action than taking action. As is typical of him, he makes wisecracks and sarcastic jokes but, whether he realizes it or not, often sizes up what is actually happening in Everworld. He even can be prophetic. "Where are the leprechauns?" he asks, only later to have Nidhoggr proclaim that leprechauns had stolen four of his most valued treasures. The other teenagers look at him in surprise, and Christopher says, "Sooner or later, there had to be leprechauns."

The reaper of *Realm of the Reaper* is Hel, a supernatural figure from Norse mythology. The right side of Hel is incomparably beautiful, the other so hideous that Jalil is paralyzed by his own screaming. The Terror Queen shouts "I am Hel! Ruler of Nifleheim! Daughter of Loki! No mortal tells me I *must*!" when April tries to appeal to her womanly side. She is suitably wicked and terrifying, so frightening that "Hel doesn't have a lot of friends. Even Loki is afraid of her."

Nidhoggr the dragon makes a brief but important appearance. When he sees that he has Senna in his power, he realizes that he can use her to bargain for the return of items stolen from him. His hoard is already immense, but, like the dragons of medieval European folklore, he lusts after more wealth. In exchange for Senna, whom they do not wish to fall into the clutches of Loki, the teenagers promise to find four mystical items stolen from Nidhoggr by leprechauns. They will pay a terrible price for this promise at the beginning of the next novel, *The Destroyer*.

Book cover illustration by Greg Spalenka for *Everworld: Realm of the Reaper* by K. A. Applegate.

◆ LITERARY QUALITIES ◆

Applegate likes to experiment, and her novels tend to be lively exercises in ideas and techniques. In the case of Everworld, she creates a place where all the world's ancient mythologies coexist, and she has fun creating adventures that involve mixing the mythologies. For the Everworld series, she creates four adventurers who are snatched from fairly ordinary teenaged American lives, although Jalil's psychological problems are somewhat out of the ordinary. Through these characters she experiments with techniques of narration by having each one narrate novels.

The personality of each narrator shows through in the telling of each book, and Jalil proves himself an able narrator whose analytical approach to narration helps to explain how events in Everworld may be related to one another. The shifting of narrators allows Everworld to be described through David's love of action and interest in logistics in *Search for Senna,* through Christopher's acidic humor and tendency to see below the surface of events to find what is really going on in *Land of Loss,* through April's good sense and practicality in *Enter the Enchanted,* and through Jalil's analytical mind that finds the logic linking events in *Realm of the Reaper.*

In *Search for Senna,* David notes that the stars in the sky of Everworld are different from the ones he would see from earth. This serves to assure him that he truly is in a different world from the one of Lake Michigan and Chicago. For Jalil, looking at the heavens is an experience different from that of David. He sees stars, and he doubts they are stars at all, but he offers no good reason why the sun, moon, and stars should not be real, thereby undercutting his own claim to rationality.

Applegate's detailed description of Everworld in *Realm of the Reaper* works in two ways. First, it informs about Everworld and outlines a few of its mysteries. Second, it tells about the state of mind of Jalil. Always doubting, always wondering what is real and what is a product of his obsessive-compulsive disorder, Jalil provides a narrative not only of an amazing adventure, but also of a young man's struggle to redefine himself, to defy the bizarre demands of his own mind.

◆ SOCIAL SENSITIVITY ◆

Jalil's atheism is significant to understanding his personality, but it is not a theme in *Realm of the Reaper.* April's own belief in God has more influence on her behavior in *Enter the Enchanted* than Jalil's atheism has on his behavior in *Realm of the Reaper.* Of more importance for the narrative is the obsessive-compulsive disorder that is the source of his atheism and of his insistence on being a rationalist. This disorder was identified by Sigmund Freud, who characterized it as a form of "objectification," in which an object is substituted in the mind for another object or emotion; in obsessive-compulsive disorder the compulsive behavior would be a substitute for something else, perhaps another form of behavior. Views on compulsions have become more complex since Freud's time, with the behavior being seen sometimes as a substitute for a memory (or memories) or an emotion (or emotions). In Jalil's case, the reasons for his compulsive behavior are not clarified in *Realm of the Reaper.* In terms of literary technique, this use of suspense in regard to the source of Jalil's disorder and whether he can overcome it provides another reason among many for continuing to read the Everworld series. It seems likely that, since Everworld affords Jalil relief from his disorder, Everworld provides answers to questions about his condition.

◆ TOPICS FOR DISCUSSION ◆

1. Would you have gone into the city if you were with Jalil, David, Christopher, and April? Why or why not?

2. What does April's attack on Hel say about April's personality?

3. Does Applegate exploit Jalil's obsessive-compulsive disorder?

4. How dangerous does Senna seem at the end of *Realm of the Reaper*? Explain.

5. How does Hel control Jalil's mind even though he is able to resist Senna?

6. Is Senna on the side of good or of evil, or some other side altogether? How do you know?

7. Do you miss anything in Jalil's descriptions that you wish he had told you? If so, what?

8. Are there dreamlike passages in *Realm of the Reaper*? Describe them.

9. Does Jalil's character grow at all during *Realm of the Reaper*? Why or why not?

10. Why would Nidhoggr give Senna to Loki even though he despises Loki? Does this reveal a weakness in Nidhoggr that could be exploited?

11. Why is Hel obsessed with men?

◆ IDEAS FOR REPORTS AND PAPERS ◆

1. What is Nifleheim in Norse mythology? Where would it be found? What happens there?

2. Who is Hel in Norse mythology? What are her powers? How did she come to have Baldur as her captive? In Norse mythology, who is Jormungand? Why would he be associated with Hel?

3. What characteristics does Nidhoggr have in common with the dragons of medieval European folklore? Or in common with the dragon in *Beowulf*? Or in common with dragons in Norse mythology?

4. What is rationalism? What are its strengths? What are its weaknesses?

5. Compare the narratives of *Realm of the Reaper*, *Enter the Enchanted*, *Land of Loss*, and *Search for Senna*. Are there notable differences in how the stories are told? Are there notable similarities? What does this tell you about Applegate's artistic achievement in *Realm of the Reaper*?

6. Draw a picture of Her City, including all the notable places and what the walls and buildings would look like.

7. What are the common characteristics of dragons in medieval European folktales? Are any of these characteristics reflected in *Realm of the Reaper*?

8. In what ways is Her City like a police state?

9. Describe the similarities between Jalil's view of Everworld and C. S. Lewis's description of the world of Narnia in *The Chronicles of Narnia*.

◆ RELATED TITLES ◆

The Everworld novels introduce mythologies, and in the process, Applegate creates a new mythology of her own, in which human endeavors are placed in a vast cosmic scheme in which everyone is important, even though in any individual novel they may seem like pawns. *Search for Senna* introduces Vikings, Loki, and Norse mythology. *Realm of the Reaper* delves more deeply into Norse myths about life and death and the underworld. *Land of Loss* focuses more on Aztec mythology than Norse mythology and introduces the Coo-Hatch, aliens from yet another world. *Enter the Enchanted* tells of the survival of Arthurian culture in Everworld and shows how the various cultures and their gods know about each other and mix with each other. This helps explain the intrusion of leprechauns into Nidhoggr's den, even though the leprechauns come from Irish folklore while Nidhoggr comes from Norse mythology.

Once the teens meet Merlin in *Land of Loss*, the grand contest of universe-shaking powers begins to reveal itself, and dreams in fact do seem more real than real life. *Realm of the Reaper* advances the unifying plot of the Everworld series by showing some of Senna's vulnerability. When she is hung from the wall of Hel's pit, although she is still arrogant and manipulative, she is seen to be not only human, but at least partly the teenager she appears to be.

◆ FOR FURTHER REFERENCE ◆

"Applegate, K. A. (K. A. Applegate)." In *Something about the Author,* Vol. 109. Detroit: The Gale Group, 2000. An essay that includes biographical information about Applegate and information about her writing.

"K. A. Applegate." In *Authors and Artists for Young Adults,* Vol. 37. Detroit: The Gale Group, 2000. A biographical essay with comments on Applegate's life and work.

Lodge, Sally. "Scholastic's Animorphs Series Has Legs." In *Publishers Weekly* 244, 45 (November 3, 1997): 36–37.

Publishers Weekly 246, 25 (June 21, 1999): 69. In this review of *Search for Senna,* the reviewer says, "With her blend of accessible story and mythological cast of characters, Applegate is sure to attract a host of new fans."

Kirk H. Beetz

REBELLION

Novel

1988

Author: Nora Roberts

◆

Major Books for Young Adults

Rebellion, 1999

Prolific romance writer Nora Roberts owes her career to a blizzard and a bad case of cabin fever. In 1979, while snowed in with her two young sons at their home in Maryland, Roberts decided to try writing down one of the stories she had made up in her mind since childhood. She put pencil to paper and the result, according to Roberts, "was really bad, but I got hooked, and it changed my life." She spent the next three years collecting rejection slips before her first manuscript was accepted.

Born in Silver Spring, Maryland, on October 10, 1950, Roberts is the youngest of five children. Her Roman Catholic upbringing plays a role in her first published work, *Irish Thoroughbred* (1981), and in several later books, including a minor one in *Rebellion*. Her first marriage ended in divorce, leaving her with two sons, Daniel and Jason. She remarried in 1985 in true storybook romance style by finding love with Bruce Wilder, the carpenter who came to make repairs and additions to her home in Keedysville, Maryland. Roberts's novels revolve around family and relationships, which is not surprising considering her extended family. Many of her novels are interconnected along family relationships, including *Rebellion*, which is her first historical romance tying in with her contemporary romance series about the MacGregor family.

Roberts spends anywhere from six to eight hours a day honing her craft, and her dedication to her chosen career has paid off. She is a charter member of the Romance Writers of America, an organization supporting and networking published and aspiring romance novelists, and she was the first author inducted into the RWA Hall of Fame in 1986. Her career achievements include five Golden Medallion awards from RWA from 1982 to 1986; Reviewer's Choice Awards from *Romantic Times* each year from 1984 to 1986; a Silver Certificate from *Affaire de Coeur* in 1985 for her MacGregor series; three Rita awards from RWA from 1990 to

Nora Roberts

1992; and numerous bookseller awards. In addition, she was the first author to receive RWA's Centennial Award for her one hundredth novel, *Montana Sky*, and the RWA Lifetime Achievement Award in 1997.

With the publication of *Heart of the Sea* in December 2000, Roberts landed on the *New York Times* bestseller list for the fifty-sixth time under her own name and her pseudonym, J. D. Robb. By December 2001, she had published 141 novels that had been translated into twenty-five languages. According to her website, one of her books sells every four minutes in the United States.

◆ OVERVIEW ◆

Serena MacGregor, a young Scottish woman, refuses to believe her brother Coll's friend Brigham Langston, an Englishman, is loyal to the plan to place Bonnie Prince Charlie on the throne of Scotland and overthrow the hated English troops who have caused her family so much pain in the past. Brigham refuses to let Serena's antagonistic attitude keep him from pursuing her and winning her love. As he reveals his heart to her, Serena learns to look beyond labels to see the true heart awaiting her if she only will let go of her fears.

◆ SETTING ◆

Rebellion starts with a prologue set in 1735 at the family home in Glenroe Forest in Scotland, ten years before the main part of the novel. Serena MacGregor is a pre-adolescent bemoaning the fact that she did not get to go hunting with her father, Ian, and older brother, Coll. When she sees riders approaching, she starts to greet them, but a warning from her mother, Fiona, sends her and the other two children upstairs as English dragoons in red coats sweep into the yard. The dragoons, under the command of the sadistic Captain Standish, torch villagers' homes and plan to make an example of the MacGregor men, whom the captain accuses of conspiring against the British ruler, Queen Caroline. With the men out hunting, he vents his anger on Fiona by raping her then throwing her naked into the room with her children. Serena's hatred of the English grows in an instant from a child's mimicry of her parents' political views to an intense hatred rooted in her soul for all things English.

The plot skips forward to 1745 and the drawing room of Brigham Langston, the fourth earl of Ashburn, at his country estate. Brigham and his friend Coll MacGregor are quietly discussing the brewing rebellion in Scotland when he receives a note informing him Bonnie Prince Charlie is on his way to Scotland. The two men immediately make plans to leave for Coll's home in the Glenroe Forest.

As they travel through the wild Highlands of Scotland, bandits from the Campbell clan attack and seriously wound Coll. Brigham receives a minor wound to his arm while routing the bandits and takes Coll the rest of the way home as quickly as possible so his wound can be treated. Serena is the first one to greet them, and she immediately accuses Brigham of causing Coll's wound by refusing to fight. He treats her with extreme politeness, which enrages her until her mother's sharp words make her mind her manners.

The majority of the rest of the relationship highs and lows take place in Glenroe Forest in the family home and surrounding woods against a backdrop of rising unrest and bitterness towards the English. Near the end of the novel, Brigham, Coll, and Ian leave to join the prince's army as it moves to Edinburgh, Newcastle, Manchester, and Derby. By this time, the promised aid from France has failed to materialize, and the Highlanders realize their dream is dying. The British troops under the command of the duke of Cumberland follow the remaining supporters of Bonnie Prince Charlie to Inverness where they meet in battle for the last time in April 1746 on Drumossie Moor in the Battle of Culloden.

Brigham realizes the futility of fighting British troops that outnumber the Scots almost three to one, and decides to leave the battlefield taking a wounded Coll with him. The men make for home where they find the surviving MacGregors camped in a cave in the hills above the family home where the dragoons will have a hard time finding them. When a few dragoons do find them, the MacGregors fight back and realize they need to find another hiding place. Coll plans to stay in the Highlands with his wife and child, but Brigham and Serena, married in a hurried ceremony before Culloden, plan to travel to the Americas. Too many people know of Brigham's part in the rebellion for him to return to England.

Overall, the setting takes second place to the romance and lacks the detail to fully draw a reader into the time period. This same story could have taken place in almost any setting and any time period—only surface details such as clothing, housing, and a few historically significant names tie it specifically to Scotland and the Third Jacobite Rebellion.

◆ THEMES AND CHARACTERS ◆

The heroine, Serena MacGregor, is a redheaded, hot-tempered shrew who is at the same time a stereotypical redhead and a character based on the freedoms of more modern women. Stuck in a rut of hating the English for most of the book, she lacks the depth of Brigham's character. Only at the end does Serena start to blossom from child to woman.

Brigham Langston, fourth earl of Ashburn, is a strong character who steadily develops over the course of the book. His initial portrayal as an English dandy, supported by his immaculate clothing and lace cuffs, is offset by the quiet strength of his convictions and his sword arm. He looks past the labels that trip up Serena, sees the woman who will haunt his dreams for the rest of his life, and goes after her. He is constantly in forward motion waiting for Serena to get out her rut.

Serena's oldest brother Coll fills the role of stolid sidekick to Brigham's more flamboyant personality. He still teases Serena and calls her "pest," but he has a healthy respect for her temper. When Serena's friend Maggie MacDonald pays a visit, Coll prepares to tolerate her presence, but she has grown into a woman since he last saw her, and he falls in love at first sight. The exquisitely beautiful Maggie resembles a porcelain doll and is a real lady, as opposed to Serena's tomboy image. Serena and Brigham's romance pales in comparison to Coll and Maggie's, which is more entertaining.

Love is perhaps the strongest theme in *Rebellion* because it motivates the characters. Love of a country and an ideal sets events in motion leading to the final battle at Culloden. Serena and Brigham share the passionate side of love as they battle to establish their relationship. Coll and Maggie share a quieter, but no less intense, new love that is accepted without question. Ian and Fiona share a love tempered by time and trial, as they have raised a family together and dealt with the aftermath of her rape. The MacGregors also share the love of parent for child and sibling for sibling.

Loss is also present as Brigham and Coll physically lose the battle for Scotland and mentally say goodbye to their dreams. Ian dies in battle for his beliefs. Fiona loses a piece of herself after being raped by Captain Standish, and she loses her heart when Ian dies. Serena loses the certainty of childhood when she sees her mother broken after the rape. In the end, Brigham and Serena lose even Scotland itself as they head for a new world and a new beginning.

◆ LITERARY QUALITIES ◆

Rebellion is an apt title that catches the rebellious nature of the main characters and the state of Scotland during the course of the novel. The viewpoint shifts numerous times so the reader sees parts of the story through almost every major character's eyes at some time, even if only briefly. Serena and Brigham are the primary focuses for the point of view, though, so the transitions are not confusing.

Roberts uses relatively few colloquialisms to add authenticity to the characters. After Serena calls Brigham an "English pig" during their first meeting, everyone tends to speak casually, more like modern Americans.

◆ SOCIAL SENSITIVITY ◆

The political background of the time is turbulent, with the majority of the fighting and political upheaval taking place on Scottish soil. The Jacobite Rebellion of 1745 is the third such uprising as the Stuarts attempt to regain the throne of Scotland. The last time a Stuart held the throne was during the reign of Queen Elizabeth I of England (1558 to 1603) when Mary, Queen of Scots, angered her cousin Elizabeth with her claims to the throne and was beheaded. Unfortunately for Bonnie Prince Charlie, his ties to the French government are not strong enough for them to risk a war with the British Empire, at this time, still one of the strongest political and military forces in the world. Roberts captures the political issues swirling around Serena and Brigham in an evenhanded manner.

In the prologue, Roberts obliquely leads the reader to infer that Fiona MacGregor was raped by Captain Standish. She does not describe the physical act of the rape, mentioning instead Standish's anger at not finding the men at home to punish and his anger at Fiona for not fearing him. The scene then skips to dragoons throwing Fiona's naked and battered body into the room where her children are held. Later in the novel, Brigham is enraged to learn of the attack even though it took place ten years before, and he gets even with Standish by maneuvering him into a duel so he can kill him. Roberts makes the impact of the rape stronger by not discussing and dissecting it at length. Rape is a silent crime, and victims of rape tend to hide their physical and mental scars because they believe they somehow invited the attack. Roberts uses Standish to show rape is a crime against women.

The trend in adult romance novels since the 1970s is for the characters to indulge in premarital sex with the understanding that marriage will be the end result of the story. This sexual freedom is a reflection of changing societal mores, making the discussion of premarital sex more open in society if not in the family home. However, premarital sex is not a new discovery, and Roberts's depiction of Serena and Brigham making love is not surprising. The main difference between 1745 and modern times is the man would be expected to marry the woman if she was a virgin. A woman's virginity was often her only dowry, and if the man refused to marry her, she would be considered shamed and wantonly.

◆ TOPICS FOR DISCUSSION ◆

1. How does Serena MacGregor act differently from the average upper-class lady of her time, as portrayed by her friend Maggie MacDonald? Does she fit in with her time or is she a more modern woman?

2. How do Brigham Langston's background and appearance help him act as a spy for the growing rebellion in Scotland?

3. Was Brigham a coward for leaving the battle at Culloden when he knew it was hopeless? Or was he following the adage, "He who fights and runs away, lives to fight another day"?

4. Serena MacGregor was not allowed to fight at Culloden. Do you believe women should be allowed to fight in combat? Why or why not?

5. How does the rape of Fiona MacGregor affect Serena? Brigham? The rest of her family?

6. Even though Fiona MacGregor's rape is only hinted at in the prologue, rape is a consequence of war. Did Captain Standish receive a just punishment for the acts he committed? How else could Brigham have handled the matter?

7. Did Ian MacGregor's death make the battle at Culloden seem more real and personal after having read about his character throughout the novel? Why or why not? Would it have been realistic for everyone in the MacGregor family to survive?

8. Malcolm MacGregor is too young to fight at Culloden, yet he is left as the "man in charge" of his family when the others leave for war. Should a teenager, male or female, be responsible for an entire family's welfare? Why or why not?

◆ IDEAS FOR REPORTS AND PAPERS ◆

1. How realistic is the description of life in Scotland in 1745? For the upper classes? For the lower classes?

2. What is the role of the clans in Scottish history? What drove some clans to fight for England in 1745 while others followed Prince Charles?

3. Who was Prince Charles? Why would the clans follow him into battle? When did the other Jacobite rebellions take place, and what were their outcomes?

4. Serena MacGregor was not allowed to fight at Culloden. Do you believe women should be allowed to fight in combat? Why or why not?

5. Rape is often a consequence of war. How has rape been treated in the Serbian-Bosnian conflict in recent years? Has anyone been punished for their actions?

6. Describe how warfare has changed since the 1700s. When did gunpowder, pistols, rifles, and cannons replace swords, shields, and knives?

7. Was Culloden and the fight to restore Prince Charles to the throne the only time Scotland rebelled against British rule? Who were some other famous Scottish leaders?

8. Queen Caroline sat on the throne in England. What was her policy towards Scotland and its people? Was she a strong ruler or a weak one?

9. Standards of beauty change with time. Is Serena MacGregor an example of the "standard of beauty" in 1745, or does she fit a more modern standard? How has beauty and fashion changed for women through the centuries?

10. The British Empire was so vast at one time that the sun supposedly never set on it. What other countries did Britain control in the 1700s and 1800s? Did any rebel like the Scots did?

◆ RELATED TITLES ◆

Rebellion offers readers a glimpse into the history of the modern family depicted in Roberts's MacGregor saga. The original five stories from the mid-1980s have been repackaged: *The MacGregors: Serena and Caine* contains *Playing the Odds* and *Tempting Fate; The MacGregors: Alan and Grant* contains *All the Possibilities* and *One Man's Art; The MacGregors: Daniel and Ian* contains *For Now, Forever* and *In from the Cold,* a historical novella. Other titles in the series are *The MacGregor Brides, The Winning Hand, The MacGregor Grooms,* and *The Perfect Neighbor.* The books are listed here in reading order.

Older readers interested in the Scottish setting may want to tackle Diana Gabaldon's "Outlander" series, the story of a woman who time travels back to an earlier Scotland to find the man of her dreams. Younger readers may want to investigate the titles of Ann Rinaldi, whose historical fiction covers a wide variety of time periods and settings.

◆ FOR FURTHER REFERENCE ◆

Dyer, Lucinda, and Charles Hix. "LOVE: It Ain't What It Used to Be." *Publishers Weekly* 246 (June 21, 1999): 26–33. Overview of efforts of romance authors and publishers to maintain sales, with details on Roberts's career.

Gray, Paul, and Andrea Sachs. "Passion on the Pages." *Time* 155 (March 20, 2000): 76–79. Discusses Roberts's background, primarily in relation to her transition from paperback to hardback markets, and her book *Carolina Moon,* in addition to the appeal of romance novels.

McMurran, Kristin. "Page Churner." *People* 46 (July 1, 1996): 31. Brief look at Roberts and how her career started.

Quinn, Judy. "Nora Roberts: A Celebration of Emotions." *Publishers Weekly* 245 (February 23, 1998): 46–47. Profiles Roberts.

"Roberts, Nora (Nora Roberts)." In *Contemporary Authors New Revision,* vol. 45. Detroit: Gale Research, 1995. Brief biographical information, now somewhat dated, with an incomplete listing of titles published through 1994. Updates information from *Contemporary Authors,* vol. 123.

"Roving Editor." *Writer* 113 (Sept. 2000): 4. Provides update on status of romance novel industry in the United States during preceding year with a brief focus on Roberts's career.

Melanie C. Duncan

SABRIEL

Novel

1996

Author: Garth Nix

◆

Major Books for Young Adults

The Ragwitch, 1995
Sabriel, 1996

Shade's Children, 1997
Lirael: Daughter of the Clayr, 2001

◆ ABOUT THE AUTHOR ◆

Award-winning author Garth Nix took the fantasy world by storm with the publication of his second young adult novel, *Sabriel*, in 1996. A native of Australia, Nix was born in Melbourne in 1963 and eventually settled in Sydney. He put his bachelor's degree in professional writing from the University of Canberra to good use, working as a sales representative, publicist, and senior editor in the publishing field. He also worked in a bookstore, served four years in the Australian Army Reserve, and established a marketing agency. Nix has focused solely on his writing since 1998. His background in the Australian Army Reserve adds a dose of realism to the border scenes and fighting in *Sabriel*.

According to Nix, his hobbies include "fishing, bodysurfing, collecting books of all kinds, reading, films, writing and lunch." In the "How I Write" section of his website,

Nix says his ideas "stem from a single image or thought that lodges in [his] brain and slowly grows into something that needs to be expressed." His idea for *Sabriel* came from a photograph of Hadrian's Wall. Using a Waterman fountain pen, Nix writes his first draft in longhand in small, easy-to-carry notebooks. When he types his second draft on the computer, he makes revisions as he goes.

Sabriel won Best Fantasy Novel and Best YA Novel in the 1995 Aurealis Awards for Excellence in Australian Speculative Fiction, and was nominated for an Australian fan award the same year. It is an American Library Association Notable Book, an ALA Best Book for Young Adults, and a LOCUS magazine Recommended Fantasy novel. The New York Public Library listed it as a Book for the Teen Age in 1997, and *VOYA: The Voice of Youth Advocates* listed it with the Best Science Fiction, Fantasy and Horror.

Garth Nix

Six states in the United States short-listed it for awards.

◆ OVERVIEW ◆

Sabriel receives an otherworldly message from her father, Abhorsen, which leads her on a quest into the Old Kingdom and through the Gates of Death to find him and prevent a malevolent creature called Kerrigor from destroying the Land of the Living. Along the way, she learns to look beyond appearances for the true faces of friends and enemies, and grows to accept that Death comes for everyone at some point.

◆ SETTING ◆

Sabriel opens with a prologue detailing the title character's birth and first encounter with Kerrigor. Almost before she takes her first breath, Sabriel slips past the First Gate of Death to be snatched up by Kerrigor from the stream flowing through the Second Gate. The Abhorsen, her father, follows close on her heels, managing to rescue her and banish Kerrigor for a short period of time. The prologue gives the book a definite fantasy flavor with a magical battle that sets the stage for later events and provides a glimpse into the enmity between man and demon.

The switch from fantasy prologue to a seemingly modern setting jars the senses momentarily until Sabriel secretly resurrects a younger classmate's pet rabbit that was hit by a car. This day, eighteen years later in Ancelstierre at the Wyverly College for Young Ladies of Quality, a messenger from beyond the Gates gives Sabriel her father's sword and bandolier which is holstered with seven bells of increasing size. Abhorsen would only pass on the tools of his trade if he were unable to help himself, or if he were dead. Sabriel immediately makes plans to find him or his body, leaving behind the genteel, almost cloistered air of her school. Even though magic is on the curriculum at Wyverly because the school is so close to the border of the Old Kingdom, young ladies must receive special permission from their parents to take the class. Sabriel's ease with magic sets her on a level with the teacher of the class.

The country of Ancelstierre is reminiscent of the English countryside before World War II. Towns have electricity and motor vehicles, but Ancelstierre is still mainly an agrarian society with most people living in small villages and farming the land around them. The countryside close to the border between Ancelstierre and the Old Kingdom, however, is affected by the magic leaking through the protective barriers, and monsters occasionally roam in the night. Charter Mages help guard the border and protect the citizens. If Ancelstierre possessed a higher level of technology, computers, and biological and chemical warfare, it would change the entire flavor of the book by taking the focus off the people.

The Perimeter Command guards the border at a fortified barrier resembling Hadrian's Wall. The soldiers possess an odd mix of technological and medieval weaponry as they parade around in battle fatigues toting guns, with swords strapped to their waists or backs. When technology fails without warning at the border, the swords are their backup weapons. They also rely on the Charter Mages' magic and the binding power of Charter symbols to defeat the Dead that do not stay dead. The wall also symbolizes the gradual change from magic and superstition to technology by providing a physical point of change from which the characters move further into magic or technology. Because technology is pure science and reason, and magic relies heavily on belief, magic refuses to work around technology. Reason can defeat belief, and vice versa, which is why Ancelstierre and the Old Kingdom are polar opposites.

Time moves differently in Ancelstierre and the Old Kingdom, emphasizing the technology versus magic debate. A patrol can spend two weeks in the Old Kingdom and return to find their comrades think they have been gone only eight days: the soldiers left back at base rely on their clocks to keep track of time, while the soldiers on patrol in the Old Kingdom have to rely upon the physical changes in their environment from night to day.

Sabriel's encounter with Kerrigor takes place in a waterway beneath the ruins of the castle in the crumbling capitol city of the Old Kingdom. There has not been a ruler for four hundred years, nor a regent for the past twenty. The water is a pale imitation of the various streams, rivers, and oceans flowing through the Nine Gates of Death, but Sabriel carefully treads them using secrets

learned by Abhorsens in the past to find her father and free him.

Large stretches of unpopulated, desolate land might have been inspired by Nix's travels through the Middle East while writing *Sabriel*. The description of Sabriel's robe-like armor and helmet also has a Middle Eastern flair. Nix also wrote parts of this novel at the beach, and Sabriel's journey takes her to the ocean as she nears the end of her quest.

◆ THEMES AND CHARACTERS ◆

"A year ago, I turned the final page of *The Book of the Dead*. I don't feel young any more," Sabriel says to Colonel Horyse when they meet for the first time at the border. The title character is tall and slender with ghostly pale skin and raven-black hair. She has been fighting undead creatures since childhood, and her eighteen years weigh heavily on her shoulders. Her burden grows heavier when her father disappears and she realizes his name, "Abhorsen," is a title that has been passed along to her. Like her father, Sabriel is "an uncommon necromancer": she sends the Dead back to Death rather than calling them forth to serve her as most necromancers do. Her journey to find her father shows her curious blend of wisdom and innocence as she takes the prodigious amounts of book learning she has amassed over the years and puts it to practical use. Her situation is learn or die, and she learns quickly, but at no time does she become a larger-than-life heroine who is unbeatable. There is always an element of chance in her battles that could just as easily shift to favor the other side. Her flaws make her more accessible as a character.

The Abhorsen, her father, actually appears only briefly, but readers still get the sense of a man of honor and strongly held convictions who does not abuse his power as a necromancer. He sends Sabriel to school in Ancelstierre to protect her from the Dead creatures he fights, but he faithfully visits with her through a spell on the full moon every month. Sabriel's memories show him as a loving father, and he only drags her into battle as a final resort. He accepts his own death, but he fights to keep his only daughter alive.

Colonel Horyse realizes who Sabriel is almost from the moment they meet. By calling her Abhorsen, he accords her the support and honor her position expects, but he relates to her in a father-daughter manner saying she reminds him of his own daughter who is Sabriel's age. A tough, battle-hardened warrior, Horyse is not surprised by much anymore except the appearance of a teenage girl as defender of the realm.

At her father's home, Sabriel inherits Mogget, a creature appearing to be a large cat wearing a collar saturated with binding spells. The spells force Mogget to serve Sabriel, but it does so at its own pace in its own sly manner. The semblance of a cat bestows a cuddly, domesticated image on what turns out to be a wild creature composed of Free Magic that only wants the Abhorsen dead so it will be freed.

In a hidden valley, Sabriel and Mogget find the funeral barges of the royal family. One figurehead of a nude young man catches Sabriel's eye, but when she examines him closer she feels faint emanations of magic running beneath his wooden frame. The magic leads past the First Gate of Death where she realizes the young man has been trapped half in, half out of Death. Following her gut instincts, she returns him fully to life. The young man claims to have been a member of the Royal Guard, but the only name he is willing to give is "Touchstone," the name commonly given to the fool in folktales. Throughout the novel, he is the stiffest character in actions and demeanor, perhaps as an offshoot of so many years

trapped as a wooden man. Only as his feelings for Sabriel bring him back to life does he begin to relax somewhat, but he still carries a burden of guilt as a result of his unwitting betrayal of the royal family he served.

Kerrigor embodies the evil Sabriel fights. He is absolute evil without even a hint of compassion to link him to the humanity he cast aside hundreds of years ago. His quest for power corrupted his soul and made him anathema to the Land of the Living. His goal is to open the Gates of Death and conquer the living.

The primary theme of *Sabriel* is the quest, or journey. Sabriel undertakes a journey to find her father, and life is a journey towards death. Even though Sabriel has dealt with death and the undead since her birth, when it comes to her own father, she is as much in denial as anyone facing the loss of a loved one. Her quest is not to defeat death per se, because it is a natural part of the life cycle, but to face her own fears of death and loss and, if not conquer, at least learn to accept them.

◆ LITERARY QUALITIES ◆

Nix tells the story almost solely through the point of view of Sabriel. Her thoughts, her fears, her triumphs are foremost. The only change in point of view occurs near the end when Touchstone begins to awaken from his melancholy state and begins to let go of his guilt and self-recrimination.

Water appears as a recurring motif. It is a source of life when it falls as rain, and it stands as a barrier to the undead preventing their passage. The undead cannot cross the rivers or ocean waters without a bridge. At the same time, each Gate of Death is represented by some form of water, whether the seductively, gentle danger hidden in the fast-flowing stream of the First Gate or the crashing waves, hidden eddies, and rampaging rivers of the later gates.

Keys also appear as a motif. The Abhorsen's surcoat is woven in a pattern of keys reflecting the fact that Sabriel, as the latest one to bear the title, is a key to banishing the undead, a key to the Gates of Death, and a key to the survival of Ancelstierre and the Old Kingdom. She is a key in that only her touch can release Mogget's collar, and only her skills can release Touchstone from his wooden tomb.

Nix takes imagery to new heights as he deftly captures the essence of a character or the look of a background with vivid descriptions that are deceptively simple:

> The final confirmation of strangeness lay beyond the Wall. It was clear and cool on the Ancelstierre side, and the sun was shining—but Sabriel could see snow falling steadily behind the Wall, and snow-heavy clouds clustered right up to the Wall, where they suddenly stopped, as if some mighty weather-knife had simply sheared through the sky.

◆ SOCIAL SENSITIVITY ◆

At eighteen, Sabriel is a confused mixture of woman and child, learning to be confident of her own abilities yet still wanting and needing her father's guidance and advice. In this way, she typifies older teens who want to be treated as adults but have second thoughts and doubts when the time comes.

Sabriel's reaction when she first sees Touchstone as a nude wooden figurehead is perfectly normal. She experiences an embarrassed fascination with his complete nudity, having only seen pictures in textbooks. His exposed body conversely makes her aware of her own, covered by clothes and armor in the beginning of a sexual awakening only hinted at in this book.

Sabriel's fight against death for the life of her father is also a normal reaction. Death is something that happens to other people, other families. Teens especially blind themselves to the possibility of death as a consequence of their actions as they experiment with greater freedom and new experiences. *Sabriel* shows an obsession with how death ends life and action, but when Colonel Horyse steps into battle after experiencing a vision foretelling his death, he emphasizes the point that everyone has a time and place to die. Worry will not change the future, but action will.

Another sensitive topic for teens is the separation Sabriel experiences from her father. With high divorce rates today, many teens are separated from one parent or the other. Sabriel's longing to be with her father is offset by her understanding that he left her at Wyverly for her safety and benefit. Many teens do not have her reassurance and lose touch completely with a parent after divorce due to distance or lack of concern on the parent's part.

◆ TOPICS FOR DISCUSSION ◆

1. Sabriel is torn between two worlds yet comfortable in both. How do teens (or children) now deal with the pull of two cultures?

2. Colonel Horyse compares Sabriel to his daughter. Does this make him underestimate her capability as the Abhorsen?

3. How does the Charter work? Does it compare to religion in any way?

4. How does the idea of nine gates in *Sabriel* compare/contrast with Dante's vision of the levels of Hell in *The Inferno*?

5. What purpose does magic serve? What are the differences between Free Magic and Charter Magic?

6. Do people still believe in magic? Or do most people associate magic with witchcraft?

7. Is the Paperwing truly alive, or is it merely animated by the spells cast upon it?

8. Why does Touchstone conceal his true identity?

9. Does the Perimeter Command fit your idea of a military outpost? What peculiarities exist here that are not seen in the modern foot soldiers?

10. What is the importance of the recurring theme of water?

11. Is the Abhorsen a suitable father figure, or does he abandon his responsibilities to Sabriel? Would you want the Abhorsen for your father? Why or why not?

◆ IDEAS FOR REPORTS AND PAPERS ◆

1. When was Hadrian's Wall built? Who built it, and why? Would you compare it to the Berlin Wall in Germany or the Great Wall of China?

2. Describe the history and the purpose of boarding schools. How have they changed over time?

3. What is the purpose of a border patrol? What are some borders that are still being patrolled today?

4. How does the idea of nine gates in *Sabriel* compare/contrast with Dante's vision of the levels of Hell in *The Inferno*?

5. Discuss the history of—and belief in—magic and mysticism through one culture or group of people such as the Druids, the Native Americans, or the African tribes.

6. Sabriel uses skis to reach the Perimeter Command crossing. What is the history of skiing as a form of travel? When did it become more of a sport?

7. The Perimeter Command uses swords in addition to guns. Discuss the history of either weapon.

◆ RELATED TITLES ◆

The second title in Nix's trilogy beginning with *Sabriel* was released in 2001. *Lirael: Daughter of the Clayr* focuses on a group of people only briefly mentioned in *Sabriel*. Nix's science fiction title, *Shade's Children*, also offers a strong female teen protagonist leading a band of teens into battle against a menace taking over Earth.

Sally Estes, in her review for *Booklist*, suggests fans of the fantasy *The Golden Compass*, book one of Philip Pullman's "His Dark Materials" trilogy, will enjoy the adventures of Sabriel and her companions. Lyra, the main character in Pullman's trilogy, has a demon named Pantalaimon as a companion, although Pantalaimon is not looking for a chance to escape like Mogget. The setting combines the real and fantasy, starting out at Oxford University in England and mentioning modern countries with a blend of historically extinct peoples and countries mixed with fantasy. Both Sabriel and Lyra lack the influence of an immediate parental figure of either sex, yet both are pivotal to events shaping their worlds.

Other fantasy adventures with appeal for readers of *Sabriel* are Robin McKinley's *The Blue Sword*, which follows the adventures of a young woman named Harry who is kidnapped into a foreign culture to become one of their greatest heroines when she saves them from total annihilation. A prequel tale, *The Hero and the Crown*, tells of the Princess Aerin who originally wielded the Blue Sword in defense of her country. In Mercedes Lackey's *Arrows of the Queen*, a young farm girl is chosen by one of the magical horse-like Companions to be the Queen's Own, a position of tremendous power for a fourteen-year-old insecure about herself and her future.

◆ FOR FURTHER REFERENCE ◆

A. A. F. Review of *Sabriel. Horn Book* 73 (January/February 1997): 64. Positive review of "a compelling fantasy."

Cushman, Carolyn. Review of *Sabriel. LOCUS* (July 1995). Positive review.

Decker, Charlotte. Review of *Sabriel. Book Report* 15 (March/April 1997): 39. Refers to Nix as "an exciting new voice in the fantasy field."

Estes, Sally. Review of *Sabriel. Booklist* 93 (October 1, 1996): 350. Starred review.

"Nix, Garth (Garth Nix)." In *Contemporary Authors*, Vol. 164. Detroit: Gale Research, 1998. Brief biographical information with comments focusing mainly on *Sabriel* and *Shade's Children*.

"Nix, Garth (Garth Nix)." In *Something about the Author*, Vol. 97. Detroit: Gale Research, 1998. Same essay as in *Contemporary Authors*.

White, Kerry. "Know the Author." *Magpies* 12 (September 1997): 10–12. Profiles Nix, mainly with reference to *Shade's Children*.

◆ RELATED WEBSITES ◆

Nix, Garth, http://www.eidolon.net/garth_nix/). June 16, 2001. Author's website.

Melanie C. Duncan

SAMMY SOSA: A BIOGRAPHY

Biography

1999

Author: Bill Gutman

◆

Major Books for Young Adults

Staubach, Landry, Plunkett, Gabriel, 1972

Kilmer, Hale, Bradshaw, Phipps, 1973

Pistol Pete Maravich: The Making of a Basketball Superstar, 1972

World Series Classics, 1973 (with Dan Gutman)

Hank Aaron, 1973

Famous Baseball Stars, 1973

Jim Plunkett, 1973

Aaron, Murcer, Bench, and Jackson at Bat, 1973

Csonka, 1974

O.J., 1974

Cedeno, Rose, Bonds, and Fish, 1974

Giants of Baseball, 1975

Pele, 1976

Munson, Garvey, Brock, Carew, 1976

My Father the Coach and Other Sports Stories, 1976

Mark Fidrych, 1977

Harlem Globetrotters: Basketball's Funniest Team, 1977

Dr. J., 1977

Walton, Thompson, Lanier, Collins, 1977

Payton, Jones, Haden, Dorsett, 1978

The Picture Life of Reggie Jackson, 1978

Great Basketball Stories: Today and Yesterday, 1978

Grand Slammers: Rice, Luzinski, Foster and Hisle, 1979

Gridiron Greats: Campbell, Zorn, Swann,

Grogan, 1979

The Signal Callers: Sipe, Jaworski, Ferguson, Bartowski, 1981

Baseball's Belters: Jackson, Schmidt, Parker, Brett, 1981

Flame Throwers: Carlton and Gossage, 1982

Summer Dreams, 1985

Refrigerator Perry and the Super Bowl Bears, 1987

Sports Illustrated's Great Moments in Pro Football, 1987

Sports Illustrated's Pro Football's Record Breakers, 1987

Smitty, 1988

Rookie Summer, 1988

Pictorial History of Baseball, 1988

Great Sports Upsets, 1988

Sports Illustrated Baseball's Record Breakers, 1988

Great World Series, 1989

Sports Illustrated Great Moments in Baseball, 1989

Sports Illustrated Strange and Amazing Football Stories, 1989

Great All-Star Games, 1989

Smitty II: the Olympics, 1990

Sports Illustrated Growing Up Painfully, 1990

Sports Illustrated Baseball Records, 1990

Sports Illustrated Strange and Amazing

Baseball Stories, 1990

Bo Jackson, 1991

The Giants Win the Pennant! The Giants Win the Pennant!, 1991

Pro Sports Champions, 1991

From Worst to First, 1991

Jim Abbott: Star Pitcher, 1992

Baseball Super Teams, 1992

Michael Jordan: Basketball Champ, 1992

Magic Johnson: Hero on and off the Court, 1992

Mario Lemieux: Wizard with a Puck, 1992

Ken Griffey, Sr., and Ken Griffey, Jr.: Father and Son Teammates, 1993

Barry Sanders: Football's Rushing Champ, 1993

Shaquille O'Neal: A Biography, 1993

David Robinson: NBA Super Center, 1993

Jennifer Capriati: Teenage Tennis Star, 1993

The Golden Age of Baseball 1941–1964 , 1994

The Kids' World Almanac of Football, 1994

Reggie White: Star Defensive Lineman, 1994

Larry Johnson: King of the Court, 1995

Hakeem Olajuwon: Superstar Center, 1995

Juan Gonzalez: Outstanding Outfielder, 1995

Michael Jordan: A Biography, 1995

The Kids' World Almanac of Basketball, 1995

Emmitt Smith: NFL Super Runner, 1995

Jim Eisenreich, 1996

Julie Krone, 1996

Frank Thomas: Power Hitter, 1996

Grant Hill: Basketball's High Flier, 1996

Troy Aikman: Super Quarterback, 1996

Gail Deevers, 1996

Steve Young: NFL Passing Wizard, 1996

Alonzo Mourning: Center of Attention, 1997

Anfernee Hardaway: Super Guard, 1997

Tiger Woods: A Biography, 1997

Deion Sanders: Mr. Prime Time, 1997

Scottie Pippen: The Do-Everything Superstar, 1997

Dan O'Brien, 1998

Greg LeMond, 1998

Paul Azinger, 1998

Shooting Stars: The Women of Pro Basketball, 1998

Ken Griffey, Jr.: A Biography, 1998

Brett Favre: A Biography, 1998

Baseball Bloopers, 1998

Basketball Bloopers, 1998

Cal Ripken, Jr.: Baseball's Iron Man, 1998

Teammates: Michael Jordan, Scottie Pippen, 1998

Sammy Sosa: A Biography, 1999

Changing Face of Sports, 1999

Greg Maddux: Master of the Mound, 1999

Tara Lipinski: Queen of the Ice, 1999

Gridiron Scholar, 1999

Michael Jordan: Basketball to Baseball and Back, 1999

Parcells: A Biography, 2000

Marion Jones: The Fastest Woman in the World, 2000

Venus and Serena: The Grand Slam Williams Sisters, 2001

Bill Gutman is a veteran writer of sports books for children and young adults, as well as adults. His research for *Sammy Sosa: A Biography* included long interviews with Sosa himself, coaches he played with, and ballplayers such as Mark Grace. Gutman's long record of publications about sports and his reputation for treating his subjects fairly has resulted in his having access to athletes who might not otherwise talk to other sportswriters. On the other hand, his flood of sports biographies for young adults has resulted in a diffident attitude among book reviewers, with some titles such as *Sammy Sosa* being overlooked, in spite of their popularity. One of the significant issues that arises when studying Gutman's writings is whether his works suffer from his writing too many during a given year.

Born in New York, but raised in Stamford, Connecticut, Gutman originally intended to become a dentist. Yet, while attending Washington College in Maryland, he majored in English. Upon graduation, he became a sports reporter, working for the *Greenwich Time*. He tried working in advertising, but by then his sports books were proving successful, and since the 1970s he has followed sports figures, famous or unrecognized, and devoted himself to writing books about them.

◆ OVERVIEW ◆

The focus of *Sammy Sosa: A Biography* is on the 1998 baseball season during which Sosa hit sixty-six home runs. Most aspects of his life prior to 1998 are only sketched and not presented in detail. Gutman points out the pitfalls of Sosa's career, but they and Sosa's early successes are all treated as preludes to Sosa's superb 1998 season. *Sammy*

Sosa is written as a popular biography, not a definitive one, and young adult readers may be interested primarily in Sosa's actions during the season that made him a prominent public figure, as well as establishing him as one of baseball's greatest players.

◆ SETTING ◆

Samuel Peralta Sosa was born November 12, 1968, in San Pedro de Macoris in the Dominican Republic. In 1975, Sammy's father Juan Montero Sosa died, and Sammy's mother Mireya Sosa took a job in the textile district, delivering food to the workers. Sosa and his siblings had to find work, ending his hopes for an education. Sosa's mother and her seven children lived in a one-room home until Sammy bought them a new home when he became a major-league baseball player.

In about 1983, at age fourteen, Sosa was persuaded by a brother to play baseball for the first time. He proved adept at the game while using an inside-out milk carton for a fielder's glove. In 1985, Sosa attended a baseball camp run in the Dominican Republic by the Toronto Blue Jays, but it was a scout for the Texas Rangers, Amado Dinzey, who saw him and asked a minor-league coach for the Rangers, Omar Minaya, to come look at a kid with a strong arm and home run power. Minaya invited Sosa to a tryout and was impressed by the raw talent in the young man; he offered Sosa a professional contract with a $3,000 signing bonus, but Sosa asked for $4,000. They settled on $3,500, and Sosa bought himself his first bicycle, giving the rest of the money to his mother.

From 1986 through 1989, Sosa bounced around the Rangers' minor league system, showing much promise, but much inconsistency as well. A low batting average and numerous strikeouts hampered his advancement. He began his career in Florida, where Latinos helped him adjust to American customs and taught him to speak English. On June 19, 1989, Sosa moved to the big leagues, playing right field for the Texas Rangers, but he developed a reputation as uncooperative with his coaches, and he was returned to the minor leagues.

Later in 1989, Sosa and two other players were traded to the Chicago White Sox. In August, Sosa returned to the major leagues and performed well. The White Sox played Sosa for an entire season in 1990, but he struggled to hit consistently, striking out too often. In the field, he often threw to the wrong base. His coaches were frustrated with him because he seemed unwilling to learn what they had to teach him. He ornamented himself in jewelry, and seemed self-centered and uninterested in helping his team, so in July 1991, the White Sox sent Sosa to their AAA minor league club in Vancouver, and he seemed destined for a career as a backup player—as someone who plays mostly in the minor leagues and only occasionally joins a major league club to replace an injured player.

In 1992, the White Sox traded Sosa to the Chicago Cubs, where Sosa worked with hitting coach Billy Williams. Under the gentle teaching of Williams and other coaches, Sosa began to learn how to play baseball intelligently. His strong throwing arm became a big asset; his base running improved; and his big looping swing became compact and smooth. All this is quickly outlined by Gutman, whose focus is on the 1998 baseball season and how Sosa performed during that season. Sosa became a romantic public figure—a hero without conceit or envy. He greeted the enormous publicity that his home runs engendered with a smile and happy banter with the hundreds of reporters who followed him around.

◆ THEMES AND CHARACTERS ◆

The unifying theme of *Sammy Sosa: A Biography* comes from a remark Sosa made: "My life is kind of like a miracle." He adds, "Pressure is when you have to shine shoes and sell oranges just to make sure there's enough to eat at the next meal." Gutman builds on this comment, noting how Sosa's family struggled to make ends meet, with the earnings of the children sometimes making the difference between eating and not eating on any given day. "My dream was to get to the United States any way I could," Sosa says. Part of his miracle is that he was noticed by scouts and that one of them, Omar Minaya, was willing to take a chance that his raw talent could be shaped into the skills a professional ballplayer needs to have. To emphasize what a wonderful bit of luck this was for a poor boy, Gutman notes that Sosa gave most of his signing bonus to his mother, but "His only indulgence was to buy a bicycle, the first one he had ever owned." Sosa would have to learn how to make a big leap from a life of poverty to one in which he would become wealthy and famous.

Part of Sosa's miracle involves his overcoming not only poverty but himself. Chicago White Sox general manager Ron Schueler, explaining why he traded Sosa to the Cubs, says, "If I had to identify one problem, it was that he had no discipline." Sosa was considered selfish, obsessed with building his statistics at the cost of his team, and ignorant of the basics of baseball such as what base he should throw to when he fielded a ball.

The young man who joined the Cubs in 1992 was on the verge of losing his opportunity to be a major league player when Billy Williams, the Chicago Cubs hitting coach, began working with him. Although Gutman does not go into great detail about the relationship, he points out their differences.

Williams had been a suave, sophisticated ballplayer who overcame liabilities, such as slow foot speed, that Sosa did not share. According to Gutman and Sosa, Williams took the time to explain matters to Sosa without reproaching him. Sosa says that he did not like being yelled at by other coaches and that he appreciated how the Cubs' coaches would not embarrass him in front of the rest of the team but would take him aside to explain that he had made a mistake.

Under the tutelage of Williams and other coaches, Sammy's attitude changed. He worked harder and became more of a team player. In 1998, Sosa explained the change in his play: "I'm trying to make contact; I'm more patient; I'm more relaxed. That's what I've been doing and you see the results. . . . I want to be known as a good person more than I do a good baseball player," he said. Gutman insists that such sentiments reflect the true Sosa and are not just for publicity.

One of the themes running through *Sammy Sosa: A Biography* is "Good things were happening to a genuinely nice guy." For Gutman, Sosa's goodness had a powerful affect on those around him and on major league baseball. He likens Sosa to Babe Ruth, whose astonishing feats drew fans back to baseball after the Black Sox scandal, in which several Chicago White Sox ballplayers conspired with gamblers to throw the 1919 World Series to the Cincinnati Reds. Ruth had an ebullient, larger-than-life personality that enhanced the records that he set.

Gutman sees Sosa as doing something similar to what Ruth did. A wage strike by ballplayers in 1994, almost all millionaires, marred the image of the players, making them seem greedy and selfish. According to Gutman, Sosa changed the public image of ballplayers with his good humor and graciousness: "He [Sosa] was still smiling, still gracious, still willing to talk to everybody," even after months of intense scrutiny of his every move by public media. Billy Williams explains about Sosa, "He's a person who is at peace with himself. And when you're at peace with yourself, you can handle a lot of stuff." Sosa's admiration for Mark McGwire (Cardinal player who broke Sosa's home run record of 66 by hitting 70) set the tone for their race to set a new home run record, and his sportsmanship attracted disenchanted fans back to the game. Gutman declares, "They [Sosa and McGwire] really liked each other, and the compliments that passed between them made the home run chase even more of a feel-good situation."

Another theme that runs through *Sammy Sosa* is Sosa's love for one's country. Sosa loves the Dominican Republic. He is proud of the baseball stars from there who had made names for themselves in the United States. Sosa realized that he too could inspire young athletes who would, in turn, help the people of the Dominican Republic as he did when he put his money into ambulances for communities in his homeland.

◆ LITERARY QUALITIES ◆

According to Gutman, Sosa is a true sports hero, who "not only emerged as a genuine superstar of his sport, but also as a man to be universally admired for his humility, his sportsmanship, his competitiveness, his humor, and perhaps most importantly, his humanity." Even when Gutman discusses some negative aspects of Sosa's personality, they tend to be part of the fairy tale. Gutman implies that the impressions of Sosa as selfish and not a team player were misunderstandings, that he had been playing baseball for only a few years before the Rangers signed him and thus had not had time to learn the skills of baseball. Also, he at first had trouble learning to speak English, and he was an unsophisticated kid for whom the United States presented daunting complexity.

Reading between the lines, one may form the impression that Sosa, until he reached the Chicago Cubs, thought he could do everything easily and required no coaching—an adolescent attitude from someone who was an adolescent when he signed his first professional contract. Gutman handles these negative aspects of Sosa's career gracefully, working them into a narrative of a poor boy who through talent, hard work, and good fortune rises out of poverty and returns to help his people. Even Texas Rangers scout Omar Minaya appears in Sosa's life like a fairy godfather, giving Sosa a chance to escape his poverty. Throughout *Sammy Sosa*, Gutman accentuates the positive, presenting negatives either as misunderstandings or as examples of how much Sosa has matured and how far he has come from the days when he shined shoes.

With the emphasis on the positive in this biography, Sosa's apparently numerous conflicts with his coaches and teammates in the years before he joined the Chicago Cubs are mentioned but not detailed. That Sosa was deemed uncooperative is clear enough, but the particulars are absent. With whom was he in conflict? Was he sullen, did he bicker, did he ignore his coaches? What made him such a hard pill to swallow that two major league organizations gave up on him in spite of his great talent? Neither Gutman nor Sosa go into these details in *Sammy Sosa*, although Sosa insists that he was not difficult to coach. Gutman suggests that previous coaches yelled at Sosa every time he made a mistake, whereas Williams and other Cubs coaches would take Sosa aside and quietly explain to him what he should be doing.

◆ SOCIAL SENSITIVITY ◆

Sammy Sosa is primarily an invitation to enjoy Sosa's 1998 season, yet the issue of poverty is unavoidable in any full account of Sosa's life. In this biography, he is representative of many boys in the Dominican Republic who struggle to help their families survive, and Sosa seems to see himself as representative of other boys in the Dominican Republic. He recalls admiring George Bell and other players from the Dominican Republic who were successes in the major leagues and who built big houses in their homeland. Upon becoming a major league player, he may have emphasized his wealth more than he should, exhibiting gold chains and expensive jewelry, although buying his family a big home seems a worthy deed. Sosa eventually quit his ostentatious displays of wealth and put his money into ambulances for communities in his homeland. He says he sees himself as a hopeful example, that through hard work and good will, poverty can be overcome. His numerous contributions to the well being of impoverished youngsters may be his example of how the well-to-do should behave toward those who are poor.

◆ TOPICS FOR DISCUSSION ◆

1. Why did Sosa seem spoiled and unmanageable during his first years in professional baseball?

2. How was Sosa transformed from self-indulgence into the generous, thoughtful man who chased Roger Maris's home run record?

3. Why would Gutman favor Sosa's exploits on the baseball field over Sosa's private life? What do you think Sosa is like in his private life?

4. What purpose is served by devoting most of *Sammy Sosa: A Biography* to the 1998 baseball season?

5. Is Sosa an admirable man? What does Gutman say about Sosa's being or not

being admirable? Should Gutman's point of view on this matter be trusted?

6. Why do you think Gutman wrote *Sammy Sosa: A Biography*?

7. Why would Gutman shift back and forth between past tense and present tense at the end of the biography?

8. What made Sosa's cheerfulness during the 1998 baseball season appealing to fellow players, sportswriters, and fans? What lesson do you think can be drawn from Sosa's behavior?

9. What is unique about Sosa's quest for sixty home runs in a season?

◆ IDEAS FOR REPORTS AND PAPERS ◆

1. A host of popular biographies of Sammy Sosa were published after his titanic 1998 baseball season. Compare them to Gutman's *Sammy Sosa: A Biography*. Do they portray Sosa differently? If so, how do they differ in his portrayal?

2. During the 1998 baseball season, the Cardinal's Mark McGwire hit 70 home runs, surpassing Sosa's mark of 66, but Sosa won the Most Valuable Player award for the season. Why did he receive it instead of McGwire? How do these two players compare in personality and skill?

3. In 1927, an aging Babe Ruth, thinking his best years as an athlete were passing away, tried to set a special record, one that would leave a permanent mark on the history of baseball. He managed to hit 60 home runs and had an incredibly productive period during August and September. Research his 1927 season and compare it to Sammy Sosa's 1998 season.

4. Babe Ruth's childhood and early life have much in common with those of

Sosa. What similarities do the early lives of the men have? How did they respond to their early lives?

5. Gutman notes that some people believe Sosa was a selfish player when he entered the major leagues. Why did they think this? What do you think?

6. What is the "Sammy Claus World Tour"? What does it do?

7. What has Sosa accomplished in his baseball career that would merit induction into the Hall of Fame, or does he fall short of meriting induction?

8. How has Sammy Sosa affected the Dominican Republic? Give examples.

◆ RELATED TITLES ◆

There was a flood of Sammy Sosa and Mark McGwire books after the 1998 season, with some appearing only two or three weeks after the end of the season, and others appearing throughout 1999. Most of these books are minor, often little more than brief collections of photographs, but some have enough substance to be of long-term interest. Laura Driscoll's *Sammy Sosa: He's the Man* (1999) emphasizes Sosa's on-field achievements and, like Gutman's book, offers some color photographs. Matt Christopher's *At the Plate with . . . Sammy Sosa* (1999) is part of a series of *At the Plate with . . .* books about baseball players. As with other books in this series, it is somewhat slight and best suited to younger readers. This is also true of P. J. Duncan's *Sosa!: Baseball's Home Run Hero* (1999; please see separate entry), which is also available in Spanish (*El Heroe del Jonron*). Duncan places Sosa's 1998 season in the context of Roger Maris's record and the history of baseball over the last few decades.

Merrell Noden's *Home Run Heroes: Mark McGwire, Sammy Sosa, and a Season for the*

Ages (1998) appeared in November 1998, almost immediately after the 1998 baseball season ended. It is an account of the 1998 home run race with statistics and photographs. William F. McNeil's *Ruth, Maris, McGwire and Sosa: Baseball's Single Season Home Run Champions* (1999) is a thoughtful comparison of the achievements of the four players in baseball's history to hit sixty home runs in a single season, and he evaluates Sosa against a strong historical background. George Castle's *Sammy Sosa: Slammin'*

Sammy (1999) emphasizes Sosa's positive characteristics and presents him as a role model.

♦ FOR FURTHER REFERENCE ♦

Olendorf, Donna. "Gutman, Bill." In *Something about the Author*. Volume 67. Detroit: Gale Research, 1992.

Kirk H. Beetz

SANDWRITER

Novel

1985

Author: Monica Hughes

◆

Major Books for Young Adults

Gold-Fever Trail, 1974
Crisis on Conshelf Ten, 1975
The Keeper of the Isis Light, 1980
The Guardian of Isis, 1981
The Isis Pedlar, 1982
Ring-Rise, Ring-Set, 1982
My Name Is Paula Popowich, 1983
Sandwriter, 1985
Log Jam, 1987
The Promise, 1989
Invitation to the Game, 1990
The Crystal Drop, 1992
The Golden Aquarians, 1994

Where Have You Been, Billy Boy, 1995
Castle Tourmandyne, 1995
The Faces of Fear, 1997
Jan's Big Bag, 1997
What if. . .?, 1998 (anthology edited
    by Hughes)
The Story Box, 1998
Jan and Patch, 1998
The Other Place, 1999
Jan on the Trail, 2000
Storm Warning, 2001
Jan's Awesome Party, 2001

◆ ABOUT THE AUTHOR ◆

Monica Hughes was born Monica Ince in Liverpool, England, on November 3, 1925. Her parents both worked at the University of Liverpool, her father (E.L. Ince, a Welshman) in mathematics and her mother (Phyllis Ince, an Englishwoman) in biology. A few months after Hughes's birth, her parents left Liverpool so that her father could take up a new position as head of the department of mathematics at the new University of Cairo in Egypt.

Hughes's first memories are of Egypt: their first house in Heliopolis, walks in the desert with the nanny for Hughes and her younger sister, and seeing mirages of palm trees and buildings floating in the sky. Later they lived in an apartment in Cairo, with a spectacular view of the pyramids, which they visited on weekends. Her parents climbed the Great Pyramid for the view, while the girls played with bottle caps littered in the sand at its base. "So much for history," sighed Hughes. She still remembers little lizards, birds of prey and the

Monica Hughes

wind-blown sand; these and other memories became elements in her novels *Sandwriter* and *The Promise*.

The Ince family returned to England in 1931 so the girls could attend school in a suburb of London, England. Hughes was pleased and excited by the exposure to music and a wider range of books, particularly Norse mythology and the works of E. Nesbit. For a while she wanted to be an archaeologist and Egyptologist, but seeing Boris Karloff in the film *The Mummy* gave her nightmares for weeks and put an end to that ambition.

When the Ince family moved to Edinburgh in 1936, Hughes found refuge from the plain, cold city and boring school in the nearby Carnegie library. She plunged into the dramas of nineteenth-century writers and the works of Jules Verne. All of her small allowance went on hardcover blank books in which she would write exciting titles and "Chapter One." Then she would sit and dream of being a famous writer. That and a journal kept when she went on vacations was all the writing she did at that time.

When the war began in 1939, Hughes and her sister were sent away to school, first to an isolated hunting lodge in Scotland, and later to a boarding school in Harrogate, not far from the Yorkshire moors where the Brontë sisters had lived. There she was encouraged to write fiction, as well as essays and compositions.

After her father died, Hughes could no longer plan to go to Oxford; Edinburgh University was the best the family could afford. At age sixteen she began an honors mathematics degree, though the English lecturers were far more interesting to her. At eighteen, she volunteered for service in the Royal Navy, was sent down to London, and spent two years working with thousands of other service women in the Women's Royal Navy Service (called Wrens) on the secret project of breaking the German code. Every free moment she had, Hughes spent in the gallery of the New Theatre watching ballet.

After the war, Hughes transferred into meteorology, first in Scotland and then Belfast, Ireland where she was delighted to find food rationing a thing of the past. When she left the WRNS in 1946, she lived in Chelsea, London with her mother and sister. For a few years she worked freelance as a dress designer, before taking a friend's advice and travelling to visit South Africa and Rhodesia (now called Zimbabwe). Hughes lived and worked with that friend's sister and husband for two years, making first-run dresses for a local factory, and later working in a bank. Her journey to Africa and back stayed long in her memory, and her experiences filtered into many of the books she was later to write, including *Sandwriter* and *The Promise*.

Living once again with her mother and sister in an unheated London apartment got her thinking about the sun. Australia seemed to be the place to emigrate, but the waiting list was three years long. Hughes left for Canada instead, in April of 1952, intending to work her way across to the West Coast and pick up a ship across the Pacific to Australia. Working in Ottawa, Ontario, in the National Research Council, she began writing stories to combat the loneliness she felt.

At a writing class at the YMCA Hughes met a woman who became her best friend in Canada, and who introduced her to Glen Hughes, who became her husband in 1957.

The Hughes lived in Ontario, moving from Cornwall to Toronto and London with Glen's work. Hughes began writing again in the late evening and early morning, as well as caring for their four children. When the youngest was a week old in 1964, they moved to Edmonton, Alberta, driving on the new TransCanada Highway across the seemingly endless prairies—a trip that she remembered twelve years later when writing her novel *Earthdark*.

This began a furiously creative time for Hughes: she painted in oils, embroidered wall hangings, wove tapestries and wrote, but never sold a single short story, article or novel.

With the death of her mother and sister, and as her children grew older, Hughes had few touchstones to her past memories. In 1971 she resolved to spend a year writing for four hours each day. She read armloads of books by the best writers for young people. After some unfruitful efforts, she was inspired by a Jacques Cousteau movie, *The Silent World,* to begin her novel *Crisis on Conshelf Ten.* In 1974, it was accepted by a British publisher, who asked for another story about the lead character.

Since then, Hughes has written over thirty books for young people. Her works have been translated into over a dozen languages. Though she did eventually tour Australia and New Zealand in 1990 with her husband, she feels firmly settled in Canada with her husband, grown children and grandchildren. In the spring of 2001, with new projects in hand, she fully intends to write as long as she possibly can.

◆ OVERVIEW ◆

Antia, princess of the twin continents of Kamalant and Komilant, is surprised by a visitor to the palace of her uncle the King. Lady Sofi has come for her husband Chief Hamrab, to invite Antia to visit their desert island of Roshan.

Antia does not want to go, nor does she want the marriage that her aunt the Queen is arranging for her with the Chief's son. But Antia's tutor Eskoril persuades her to make the journey and to write to him of all she sees and hears in Roshan.

The sailing ship is slow, Antia's nurse, Nan, is miserable in the heat, and the town of Lohat in Roshan is small and simple. Antia is nonplussed to see the simplicity of Chief Hamrab's house and the room set aside for her and Nan. The humble and fiercely loyal people of Roshan and their Chief confuse her. Antia will have nothing to do with Jodril, the Chief's son, but he makes friends with Antia's nurse; meanwhile Lady Sofi is kind, showing Antia around Lohat and the market, and saving her from a runaway beast of burden.

Eskoril's reply to Antia's letters is curt, asking about the rest of Roshan. She is confused, but asks Chief Hamrab to arrange for her to travel with a caravan, to see more of the desert. Jodril is set to be her guide.

The open desert and a small oasis affects Antia more than she is willing to admit. She is caught in a sandstorm, and awakens in a village at the next oasis by the Great Dune.

Dimly she remembers, as in a dream, someone bathing her in cool water, and another pool where the water seemed on fire. Jodril is relieved to find her alive in the village, and they resolve to be friends; but he later reads her diary and destroys pages describing her dream.

Antia stalks off, climbing to the top of the Great Dune, where she briefly meets the Sandwriter, a mysterious old woman.

In spite of her introspective experiences in the desert and on the Dune, Antia writes to Eskoril of her journey.

His reply alarms her, and she shows it to Jodril. They inform the Chief, who directs them to consult the Sandwriter.

When they return to the Great Dune with the next caravan, Sandwriter listens to Antia and Jodril, and shows them the secret heart of Roshan, and tells them to wait. But Eskoril came with the caravan in disguise. He forces Antia to show him the secret—a deep pool of water, and another of petroleum—which he has been looking for, to exploit for personal gain.

When Eskoril sets out at top speed to cross the desert, Antia tells Sandwriter, who calls up a sandstorm. After it passes, Jodril and Antia and the village headman bring Eskoril's body to the village for burial. Sandwriter is exhausted, but pledges Antia and Jodril to each other, and tells them that she is looking for a child from their union to come to her.

◆ SETTING ◆

Throughout the novel, Hughes gives details of landscape, buildings, clothing and food, all of which combine to create clear and intense images of Kamalant and Roshan. The effect is gradual, though stronger as Antia writes her letters to Eskoril, and the descriptions of where things are happening never interferes with the narrative of what

is happening. Though exact and profusely described, the setting is clearly not just one of the African countries that Hughes has visited with a fantasy name. From zaramint bushes to little slima snakes, the details are what make this a unique and independent world.

When Antia leaves the palace of her uncle and aunt, King Rangor and Queen Sankath of Kamalant, in the city of Malan in Kamalant, she leaves the trappings of material wealth behind. There are no ornamental fountains in the town of Lohat in Roshan; and instead of an ostentatious palace filled with riches and servants and courtiers, the Chief's home is a large, though simple house, with curtains for interior doors and nothing but two beds, a shelf and five pegs in the wall of the room that Antia is to share with her nurse.

All the clothes her nurse has packed for her are wrong, too: gauze gowns embroidered with jewels, and tight embroidered slippers. No wonder Jodril mistook Antia for a dancing girl at first glance. The people of Roshan, even the Chief and his lady, wear simple, loose robes for comfort. The villagers and Sandwriter wear rough homespun clothing.

The town and market are different from anything Antia has seen: rough cobbles, noisy merchants hawking their goods, and the hairy kroklyns (beasts of burden) are frightening. Even the wells of the oasis and the walls of the underground village are an unfamiliar dressed stone, strange to the eyes of a pampered and sheltered princess.

Most of the people she meets in Roshan are lean, with hands hardened by work and skin browned by the sun. This is a strong contrast to the pale, idle nobles she knew in her uncle's court, where fat Nan and the plumpness of her other uncle are not unusual. Antia is used to seeing simple garments and lean, brown skin as marks of a servant or peasant, so every person she sees is a contradiction of her past. A leader who lives simply and humbly is as confusing for her as the workers who are confident and self-directed.

Clearly, in this novel Hughes is making some pointed comments about real world nations and cultures with similar contrasts in material goods and the trappings of monetary wealth. The reader may enjoy deciding if Kamalant and Komilant are meant to symbolize America and Europe, or if Roshan is meant to be Africa or Arabia or Australia. Hughes has taken great care not to introduce the spectre of racism into the novel: these people are one race, though some are tanned and some of the idle rich are pale. Metaphors of Earth's nations and cultures will go only so far in an interpretation of *Sandwriter*.

◆ THEMES AND CHARACTERS ◆

Early on in Hughes' work on *Sandwriter*, she determined that there were two countries in this world, one rich in natural resources, and the other a desert. "Then suddenly my heroine Antia appears," Hughes says—in an essay on the origins of the novel *Sandwriter*—"stamps her foot and says, 'Dust and flies. It's nothing but dust and flies! I won't go!'" The story is overturned by the strong-willed princess Antia, heir of Kamalant and Komilant. Hughes could not force her, but had to think of a way to persuade her to change her mind.

Hughes has read the works of Robertson Davies, who talks in his novel *Fifth Business* about the character in opera story-telling who is "Fifth Business": the character who alters the balance of the story. That is what Hughes needed: a Machiavellian tutor with his own secret agenda, which is later proved to be dastardly. Eskoril persuades Antia to write to him of all that she sees and hears, and so help him rise to a station where he can pay court to her. "A spy? How glamorous! And since she is a little bit in love with her tutor, she agrees to go," says Hughes of her heroine. Thus the journey is made and the story begins.

Antia travels to Roshan with Nan, her nurse (who is loving and fat and a gossip) in the company of Lady Sofi, wife of Chief Hamrab.

Lady Sofi is a calm, confident woman—a strong contrast to talkative, fluttery Nan and the Queen Sankath (who always finds fault with Antia). The Chief is wise and more than a match for the headstrong young princess. Their son, Jodril, is a worthy young man and no more interested in an arranged marriage than Antia is; when they finally resolve their differences at the village by the Great Dune, they become good friends.

The one character who is completely out of the ordinary for a young adult adventure novel or romance is the Sandwriter, the mysterious old woman who saves Antia's life and calls up the sandstorm to kill Eskoril. She is a hermit priestess who holds not only the land of Roshan, but the entire world of Rokam in her hands. Her understanding of the natural world is simple and powerful. When the princess writes her name and royal titles in the sand on the top of the Great Dune, only to see the words blow away, Sandwriter says Antia is of the sand. She calls up the best in Antia, and thus when Eskoril threatens the headstrong princess, Anita is able to rely on the confidence taught to her by Sandwriter.

In this novel, Hughes uses the theme of environmentalism to make her plot seem not only natural, but necessary. Those who do not care for the environment, like Eskoril, do not care for people either. All things—natural resources, people, plants and animals—are to Eskoril only tools to be used for his own gain, without respect or husbandry or forethought.

The people in the village at the oasis protect and respect the Sandwriter in her isolated cave in a cliff behind the Great Dune. Chief Hamrab, Lady Sofi, and their son respect the people, and so they offer and are offered every courtesy and consideration that these marginal living conditions can support. Together they live as lightly and responsibly on their planet Rokam as they can manage.

But Eskoril shows his true colors when he threatens Antia in Sandwriter's cave and reveals his plan to do away with the king and rule through the queen, or possibly Antia, in the future. Eskoril and others like him in Komilant and Kamalant are spendthrifts and wasters of the abundance of their nation; they are opportunists and profiteers. They destroy themselves and what has been entrusted to them. Those who care for the environment can be good caretakers of their own minds and bodies, of the people and natural world around them, and one day Antia and Jodril become worthy rulers of the world.

◆ LITERARY QUALITIES ◆

Hughes has a natural writing style, which is sustained throughout all of her novels. Descriptions of settings do not delay the action of Sandwriter, but inform the reader where the characters are. Setting is always important in a novel by Hughes, and nowhere more important than in Sandwriter. People think and often behave differently in a desert or in a simple house than they do in a market or a luxurious palace.

When writing her book The Tomorrow City, Hughes developed an awareness of two halves of her mind: the right brain (imaginative, holistic, in touch with one's dreams and subconscious) and the left brain (linear, logical, source of language, without which stories cannot be written). From this understanding came Hughes's ability to construct a story which would be of inter-

est, make sense, and mean something important to the reader.

Hughes finds story ideas everywhere: thoughts drifting through her head, the question "What if. . . ," and the curiosity about a passer-by—these can be the tiny seed out of which grows a novel. In 1974, she read a newspaper article about a boy condemned to an isolated life because of a faulty immune system. She kept the clipping in her ideas file for five years, read it at least ten times, and from her thoughts about isolation and loneliness came her novel The Keeper of the Isis Light and two sequels. These are her most popular and celebrated works to date.

The genesis of Sandwriter was a casual image on television of a tall sandstone pillar, apparently in a desert setting. Into Hughes's head came the thought: "Oh, that must be the entrance to one of their houses." She had no clue whose houses, where or why, but scribbled down the thought for her ideas file. Some time later she went to the library and combed the card file for "Deserts." She came upon a remarkable book by a woman journalist who climbed Mount Sinai at night in order to be there for the sunrise. In her long vigil the journalist meditated on the significance of desert places in the Judeo-Christian tradition, these lonely places where prophets met Jehovah, where leaders were confirmed in their mission.

"Suddenly there appeared in my head the picture of a female shaman, all powerful, living near an oasis in the midst of a desert land, and her name was Sandwriter," reported Hughes. "That was all. I had a single character." That was not enough for a story, though.

Hughes knew this desert was not on Earth. "I got a piece of blank paper and stared at it. Terra Incognita. Then I began to doodle. To the west a continent, similar in shape to the Americas; to the east a very large island, somewhat like Australia." Since contrast invites conflict and conflict is the essence of story to Hughes, she imagined the western continent as richly endowed, while she saw the island as an almost barren land, with towns clustered only around the edges, and the occasional oasis in the interior. Between these two lay the ocean, inviting travel and movement.

Hughes thought that travel from desert to the western land would be like a trip to paradise; delightful, but not very challenging for the writer. Travel to the desert, on the other hand. . . "But why would anyone want to go?" Hughes wondered. "Perhaps they are forced to. I think of arranged marriages, and this implies royalty. Maybe my protagonist is a princess being cajoled into a marriage with the son of the chief of the desert lands." So her story began to take shape, with logic balancing imagination.

She took her story from *terra incognita* to a land mapped and peopled, with a spunky heroine and a dark counterforce. "As for the sandstone pillar," Hughes added, "I found it marking the entrance to Sandwriter's cave home."

◆ SOCIAL SENSITIVITY ◆

Hughes has been called "Canada's finest writer of science fiction for children" by critic Sarah Ellis. Ellis goes on to say: "There is a gentleness to her books that is rare in science fiction. The hairsbreadth escapes, the exotic flora and fauna,. . . the villains and the heroes—all are enclosed in one overriding concern, subtle but ever-present: the value of kindness. This theme seems rather a nonrobust one for science fiction. But Hughes manages to clothe the homey quality in flesh and blood . . . to give it strength and resilience."

The work of Hughes, like most science fiction, is international in its scope. She deals with global issues, but gives them substance in a way that makes them immediate and connects the personal with the political; the best example of this is how Hughes links the environmental theme of *Sandwriter* with the theme of Antia's loyalty (both personal and patriotic).

When Antia has explained to Jodril about the letters she was writing to her tutor, Eskoril, Jodril is furious.

"And you accepted my father's invitation into our home as a spy?"

She felt her cheeks grow hot. How loyal and unbending were these Roshanites. Against Jodril she felt flighty and good-for-nothing. "But it wasn't like that. It didn't seem . . ." She stumbled, remembering her feelings beneath the desert night sky. She dredged up a word out of her past. It was statecraft.

"Statecraft? What is that but a powerful word to make you feel in the right? After you have betrayed the hospitality of our house—my own feelings."

Even so, Jodril comes to understand that Antia was led astray by her tutor, and, at his father the Chief's direction, he brings her to Sandwriter. She listens to Antia's explanation of her letters to Eskoril.

"Did you not think that you were destroying truth when you deceived us, as our guest and friend?"

"Yes. No. A little maybe. But he is my friend, too. I wanted to help him."

"There was no truth in you, was there?"

"No. I. . ."

"Though you had been bathed in the water of Roshan?"

"I didn't know it was something special. I thought it was just water."

"And so it is. Just water. The most precious thing on Roshan. The wellspring. The heartland of the world."

Hughes speaks most directly and plainly through the words of the woman Shudi in the sunken village Ahman at the oasis by the Great Dune, after Eskoril's body has been recovered. "Waste is sad. That is the saddest thing about evil, that it wastes what could have been good."

◆ TOPICS FOR DISCUSSION ◆

1. What is statecraft?

2. When is loyalty a virtue? Is there any kind of loyalty which is not a virtue?

3. How splendid is the wealth of the King and Queen of Kamalant?

4. How practical is the wealth of the Chief and Lady of Roshan?

5. How necessary is the wealth of Sandwriter's understanding of the natural world?

6. When is Antia in danger? From what or whom?

7. When does Antia discover her strength and talents?

8. What good has Antia ever done in the past for herself or anyone?

9. What has Antia accomplished to remedy her betrayal of the secret of Roshan?

10. What actual countries, modern or in the past, is Hughes writing about in her descriptions of Kamalant and Komilant, and Roshan?

◆ IDEAS FOR REPORTS AND PAPERS ◆

1. How is statecraft practised by the King and Queen of Kamalant and Komilant? Or by Chief Hamrab of Roshan? Or their advisors?

2. What is patriotism? Does it supercede loyalty to friends as Antia first thought? When it does, who or what is being served?

3. Define and discuss responsible resource management in terms of animal husbandry, agriculture and non-renewable resources. What are the responsibilities of a modest-sized nation such as Roshan, with marginal resources? What are the responsibilities of a nation or empire that is blessed with abundant resources?

4. What is respectable social and ethical behaviour for the leader of a nation? How should lesser authorities behave? What about their trainees and heirs?

5. Compare the merits of steam versus sail in ocean transport. What factors will you consider: time, personnel, resources, weather, or other factors? When is one alternative to be preferred over the other?

6. Architecture and housing changes in different areas of the world. Describe the buildings and homes that Antia sees at home and during her travels. What needs are being met by these constructions? Where is environment or climate a concern? What about vanity and display?

7. Though it looks as though the Queen's intent was to send away the heir of Kamalant and Komilant to marry the son of a desert chief, far from anywhere that matters, what has really happened? How will it change the corrupt court of Kamalant when Antia brings home Jodril as her Prince Consort? Could this be, instead of Eskoril's plan to steal and profit from Roshan's petroleum resoures, a serendipitous elevation of a responsible ruler to the throne?

8. How important to the story is Antia's romantic attraction to Eskoril and to Jodril? From the viewpoint of statecraft, is the romance story necessary at all? From the viewpoint of Sandwriter, does

it belong? When does Antia see that anything else at all is happening?

9. Compare the character of Nan to the Nurse in Shakespeare's *Romeo and Juliet*. In what ways is Nan clearly derivative of the Nurse? How is she independent of the other? Is she a lesser creation, or more fully realized? Why does Hughes write her into the story at all, or keep her in after the voyage to Roshan?

◆ RELATED TITLES/ADAPTATIONS ◆

Readers who have enjoyed *Sandwriter* can look to the sequel *The Promise* for answers to some questions raised by the first novel. In the sequel, Rania, the daughter of Antia and Jodril, is brought to Roshan to be trained as the heir of Sandwriter.

Also to be recommended for their environmental and ethical themes are Hughes's novels *The Golden Aquarians* and *The Crystal Drop*.

Other contemporary authors whose works may be enjoyed by fans of Hughes are Julie Lawson, Dave Duncan (especially the three young adult novels in his series *The King's Daggers*), and Eileen Kernaghan (*Dance of the Snow Dragon* and *The Snow Queen*).

◆ FOR FURTHER REFERENCE ◆

Duncan, Dave. *Sir Stalwart*, Avon Books, 1999. Volume one in the series *The King's Daggers* which runs parallel to the author's *The King's Blades*. The setting is a little like the England of Henry the Eighth, but with sorcery as well as swords and court intrigue.

Ellis, Sarah. "News from the North." *The Horn Book* (October 1984): 661. Contains a positive analysis of Hughes's merit as an author of imaginative writing for young people.

Hughes, Monica. *The Crystal Drop*, Stoddard, 1992. In this near-future science fiction novel, an orphaned brother and sister must leave their drought-stricken farm to look for their uncle and his land.

Hughes, Monica. *The Golden Aquarians*, Stoddard, 1994. A boy from Earth goes with his father to be part of a terraforming project on the planet Aqua.

Hughes, Monica. *The Promise*, Stoddard, 1989. Sequel to *Sandwriter*. The daughter of Antia and Jodril becomes Sandwriter's apprentice.

Kernaghan, Eileen. *Dance of the Snow Dragon*, Thistledown Press, 1982. A historical fantasy set in Bhutan, telling the life and adventures of a boy who becomes a Buddhist monk and follows a spiritual quest. A grand adventure linking faith and the natural world.

Kernaghan, Eileen. *The Snow Queen*, Thistledown Press, 2000. Winner of the 2000 Prix Aurora Award for Canadian speculative fiction, English long-form work category. A re-telling of the Hans Christian Andersen tale, set in the Victorian era. Feminist in a positive way, this novel integrates spirituality with science.

"Monica Hughes." In *Something about the Author Autobiography Series*, Volume 11, Detroit: Gale Research, 1992. Insight into the life of this author who has lived on four continents and written over thirty books for young adult readers.

Parker, Douglas H. "The Alien Within," *Canadian Children's Literature* 73 (1994): 69. Review of Hughes's novel *The Golden Aquarians*, with the comment: "Those who know Hughes's other work will understand that she never allows her readers the facile satisfaction of witnessing a 180 degree turn in her characters' behaviour just to bring things to a 'happier ever after' conclusion."

Review of "Sandwriter," *Canberra Times,* Australia (July 10, 1985). "Acclaimed as a powerful writer of popular science-fiction for young readers, Monica Hughes has triumphed again with this intriguing novel... Most characters are well depicted, while Antia grows in strength as her purpose in the strange sequence of events becomes clear to her. Hughes shows her considerable skill in powerful, descriptive writing."

Review of "Sandwriter," *The Northern Echo,* United Kingdom (December 10, 1985). "An outstanding novel, interwoven with snippets of timeless wisdom."

Van Luven, Lynne. "And Here's Novel No. 25," *The Edmonton Journal* Sunday Books Pages (February 23, 1992): C4. Interview with photo of Hughes. Local writer is famous, and rightly so for her accomplishments; still, she leads a practical, quiet life.

◆ RELATED WEBSITES ◆

www.ecn.ab.ca/mhughes. The author's personal website, with interviews, listings for each of her novels, including *Sandwriter,* and her home e-mail address. Includes a series of personal essays on the origins of many of her books.)

www.yabs.ab.ca.hughesm.html. The website for the Young Alberta Books Society, which has a listing for Monica Hughes as an author resident in Alberta, Canada.

Paula Johanson

SEARCH FOR SENNA

Novel

1999

Author: K. A. Applegate

◆

Major Books for Young Adults

The Story of Two American Generals:
    Benjamin O. Davis, Jr., and Colin L.
    Powell, 1992
The Boyfriend Mix-up, 1994
Sharing Sam, 1995
Listen to My Heart, 1996

Boyfriends and Girlfriends series,
    including:
Zoey Fools Around, 1994
Lucas Gets Hurt, 1998
Claire Can't Lose, 1999
Who Loves Kate, 1999

Animorphs series, including:
The Message, 1996
The Stranger, 1997

The Reunion, 1999
The Prophecy, 2000
The Ultimate, 2001

Everworld series
Search for Senna, 1999
Land of Loss, 1999
Enter the Enchanted, 1999
Realm of the Reaper, 1999
Discover the Destroyer, 2000
Fear the Fantastic, 2000
Gateway to the Gods, 2000
Brave the Betrayal, 2000
Inside the Illusion, 2000
Understand the Unknown, 2000
Mystify the Magician, 2001
Entertain the End, 2001

◆ ABOUT THE AUTHOR ◆

Katherine Alice Applegate is simultaneously one of America's most famous authors and one of America's most mysterious. She guards her privacy, as does her publisher, Scholastic, which has brilliantly marketed her Animorphs and Everworld series for astounding sales. Applegate was already a well-established writer of books for young readers, mostly romance novels, when she proposed the Animorphs series to Scholastic, where the proposal was met with enthusiasm. She wanted to write a series of books that showed how the world might look from the perspectives of different animals; the result has been a series of fascinating novellas for late elementary to junior high school students.

Having moved several times around the United States, the Michigan-born writer now resides in Minneapolis. She has published more than one hundred books, and she has written them at an amazing pace. Begun in 1996, her Animorphs series numbered more than forty books plus several spin-offs by 2001. Her twelve-volume series intended for adolescents, Everworld, begun in 1999, was completed in 2001. Sally Lodge, in *Publishers Weekly*, quotes Applegate:

> A series writer has to develop plotting and pacing that become a well-oiled machine. You don't have the luxury of spending a year on a book and absolutely cannot indulge in writer's block. Yet I knew I had to write in perfect language and choose just the right images, to make sure that my middle readers fell in love with the characters and returned again and again.

The two hundred letters from young readers Applegate receives per week, as well as the one hundred e-mails she receives per day, attest to the success she has had in reaching her intended audience. Readers love her characters.

In spite of the success of Applegate's writings, they have received scant attention in the press, perhaps because of a prevailing view that books written so quickly cannot be worth writing about, or perhaps because of the immense difficulty in keeping current with all the books Applegate publishes. But despite the great pace at which Applegate has written her books, they tend to be of higher quality than other mass-market writings. The Animorphs series provide artful and informative perspectives of characters as animals, whether fleas or birds. The Everworld novels offer suspense and tales of adventure with fine introductions to the mythologies of the world.

Applegate does not shy away from the tough questions about growing up and building sound, honest relationships with others. For instance, the non-series title *Sharing Sam* deals with the prospect of a close friend dying and how to love in spite of the pain of the loss of loved ones. In Everworld, the relationships among the principal characters are essential to the appeal of the novels. Applegate has mastered the art of characterization, and this is perhaps the most important reason her rapidly-written works are considered both good literature and entertaining reading.

◆ OVERVIEW ◆

In Everworld, the gods of ancient mythologies live and rule over their human subjects, brought with the gods when they left the Old World, Earth. The natural laws that David, Christopher, April, and Jalil are used to shift and change in Everworld. Gravity in particular behaves in mysterious ways. In *Search for Senna*, Everworld is faced with a terrible crisis: it is being invaded by a being that can consume the gods themselves, and they need a way to fight or escape this enemy who is more terrible than even the most terrifying of the gods. This becomes the problem of the four teens because Loki, Viking god of destruction, hoping to escape the invader, is scheming to use their friend Senna, a witch, to open a way back to the Old World so that the gods may return there and rule Earth once again. An ordinary teenager on Earth, Senna is a magical being in Everworld, seemingly the one person who can open Earth to the gods of Everworld.

Given the brutality that some of the gods inflict upon the people of Everworld, the return of the gods to Earth would be horrible, but can Loki be stopped? In addition, the Hetwan, beings from outside Everworld, have their own secret plans, and the enigmatic Senna is either hiding from Loki or possibly pursuing her own plans for ruling and destroying—while controlling the actions of David and Christopher. Meanwhile, the teens have to find ways to survive in a world where most people want to kill them, as well as figure out how they can live in Everworld and on Earth simultaneously. In this first Everworld novel, the complications are many, danger is everywhere, and only four teenagers stand between Earth and the unprecedented threat from Everworld.

In *Search for Senna*, the settings contribute much to the suspense and the fantasy-escapism of the story. Everworld as a whole is full of surprises for David, Jalil, Christopher, and April. David says they were all near a pier, where Senna was, then,

> The clouds twisted as if a tornado were forming. The pier seemed almost to curl, like a pig's tail. I looked at Jalil. His face was turning inside out. Inside out! I could see the back of his eyes, the gray wrinkled brain, the heaving, gasping trachea in his throat.

Later, David revives and discovers himself in a bad situation: "I was hanging by my arms. My back was against a stone wall. Stones as big as cars. Chains were attached to my wrists with shackles. The chains and shackles could have held King Kong." This is his unfriendly introduction to Everworld.

At first, David and his companions are in a weird version of the culture of the ancient Vikings. There are both real-life Vikings and ancient Norse gods and other supernatural beings, including Loki and a giant wolf. Eventually, Harald Goldtooth, one of the Vikings, explains a little about what happened: "When Everworld was born, the gods left the Old World and came to this new place. And they carried their people with them; Zeus and his children, Huitzilopoctli and his foul brood, Odin and his own. All the gods." This means that

Everworld is a place where ancient religions and mythologies are true; it is where gods and heroes live as they did in ancient stories.

Contrasted with the Everworld setting is the real world. The four teens find that when they go to sleep in Everworld they are back in their old lives on Earth. In fact, they are living two lives, one of everyday experiences at home on Earth and the other of fantastic adventures in Everworld.

The principal characters of the Everworld novels are David, Jalil, Christopher, April, and Senna. David Levin narrates the first novel, *Search for Senna*. He is about sixteen years old and says, "I have a rep as a fairly tough guy." He likes being "tough" but dislikes the fact that other people expect him to be stupid because of it. As he tells the tale of *Search for Senna*, he reveals a good, logical mind—one that is well suited to military logistics. Whether his companions like it or not, they often need his ability to spot weaknesses in an opponent's defenses, as well as his talent for finding something to do when all hope appears lost.

Ever the man of action, David is eager to knock heads and defeat foes. As he works an oar of the Dragonshield, a Viking longboat, he notes, "And it occurred to me then that at that moment I was as happy as I've ever been in my life." Yet, although he loves physical activity, he is introspective enough to be an interesting narrator. "Maybe a hand was guiding me," he says, "and all of us. Maybe, even, it was Senna's own hand. Life's so much easier if you think that way. So much easier to blame some unseen force." He realizes his weakness for Senna, and the fact of this realization suggests that he may eventually overcome this weakness, no matter how much he enjoys being the hero protecting the fair damsel. David also knows his limitations. For example, he observes that Sven Swordeater is a man, "And I'm a boy." Tough guy or not, David realizes that he has yet to become what Swordeater is already. This is one of David's strengths: not only does he spot the weaknesses of others, but he also knows his own and is able to judge what he can do and should not try to do.

According to David, Jalil doesn't believe the truth should offend anyone but offending people is something Jalil does very well. It will take until the first novel Jalil narrates, *Realm of the Reaper,* to reveal exactly why he is at once very intelligent and thoughtless, but in *Search for Senna* he has a tendency to state the obvious and to unnecessarily point out other people's flaws to them. He comes from an upper-middle-class family, and is a sharp-minded high school student. In spite of being thin-skinned and choosing bitter words to express himself, he points out significant aspects of the environment that are clues to what may be happening. For instance, he asks, "Why does a Norse god speak English?" It may irritate David that Jalil does not have answers for his questions, but formulating the questions is important for seeking the answers. It also shows that Applegate is alert to the contradictions in her story and sensitive to the powers of thought in her teenage characters. Thus, Jalil is not only an interesting character, he serves to ask questions readers themselves may ask, and he serves to provide foreshadowing—that is, he asks questions that will eventually be answered.

Christopher is somewhat similar to Jalil in that he is intelligent and tends to irritate David, but Christopher's remarks tend to be sarcastic attempts at dry wit. Whereas Jalil asks questions, Christopher tends to make observations such as "Hell of a coincidence having two different universes where so much is the same." He tends to be better at figuring out what is going on, but

spends too much of his time thinking of himself as a rival to David, especially for the affections of Senna.

April just happens to be better prepared for adventuring in Everworld than her companions. When sucked through a vortex into Everworld, she had her backpack, which has some useful supplies. She tends to be introspective and makes remarks such as "Maybe dreams are memories of another universe." One of April's functions in *Search for Senna* is to stand apart from Senna's influence and offer some common sense when the boys lose their own common sense to the schemes and controlling power of Senna."

The device of having the characters sleep and dream that they are living their former lives on Earth until reawakening in Everworld offers a chance to explore the personalities of each character deeply, because the characters have time to reflect, and also because their behavior when they are under great stress is contrasted with their behavior when they are living the somewhat boring though stressful lives teenagers on Earth normally live.

David's reaction to the way of life on Everworld is "Real seemed unreal. Familiar was strange. I'd gone to sleep in living color and woken to black and white and all the shades of gray." He thrives on the challenges of Everworld and likes Everworld better than Earth. The others are not so sure; Everworld is an uncomfortable place far from the showers, beds, and foods they like. The switching from Everworld to Earth and back again confuses them, although Christopher soon realizes that returning to Earth is a valuable opportunity and he studies books about the figures he is meeting in Everworld, remembering his reading when he wakes up in Everworld.

The crux of *Search for Senna* is Senna herself. She appears to be an ordinary teenager—April's half sister. But in Everworld

Senna is a different person, becoming diffident and remote in her personality. Further, she exerts a greater than usual influence over the boys. David is in her thrall, focused more than anything on protecting her. Christopher resists but cannot break from her influence, wishing to be first in her affections. Jalil finds her annoying, as he does just about everyone. April realizes that Senna's influence is more like mind control than the ordinary effect a pretty girl has on a young man. Who Senna is and why the gods view her as the key to their survival are central mysteries of the Everworld series.

The villains, drawn in broad strokes and vivid colors, are part of the fun of *Search for Senna*. For instance, there is "Great Loki," god of destruction: "His hair was blond, long, and combed. His face was thin, cruel but not stupid. He was handsome in a way. Handsome like a poisonous snake can be beautiful. But he was nervous, too, drumming his fingers on stone. Rocking just slightly back and forth. Yeah, nervous. Afraid despite his power." David notices Loki's fear, which means Loki has a weakness of some sort. Even so, Loki is a formidable figure, for "the man [Loki] and the wolf were each impossibly large."

Loki and the wolf are taken from ancient Norse mythology. Loki was a villainous figure, a trickster who contrived the death of Baldur, the most beloved of the gods, and who eventually helped bring about the destruction of Asgard, the heavenly home of the gods, as well as the destruction of Earth. The wolf who snatches Senna and who appears with Loki is a reference to Fenris, a gigantic wolf who is placed in dwarf-made chains and imprisoned in the ground by the gods, but who is released by Loki and who eventually kills and eats the chief of the gods, Odin, during the last battle that destroys the world. Both are evil figures.

But what of the good gods? In Norse mythology, Thor is sympathetic to human beings, but in Everworld he has been imprisoned. "With Thor lost to us, who else will save us from the Hetwan?" asks Thorolf, a Viking. Thor and Odin are absent; the Vikings must find a way to free them. "My father [Harald] says you [David] come from the Old World. The world of before," says Sven Swordeater. The Vikings may be forgiven if they hope David and the others can help.

◆ LITERARY QUALITIES ◆

Applegate likes to experiment, and her novels tend to be lively exercises in ideas and techniques. In the case of Everworld, she creates a place where all the world's ancient mythologies coexist, and she has fun creating adventures that involve mixing the mythologies. For the Everworld series, she creates four adventurers who are snatched from fairly ordinary teenaged American lives, although Jalil's psychological problems are somewhat out of the ordinary. Through these characters she experiments with techniques of narration by having each one narrate novels. The personality of each narrator shows through in the telling of each book, so that Everworld is described through David's love of action and interest in logistics in *Search for Senna*, through Christopher's acidic humor and tendency to see below the surface of events to find what is really going on in *Land of Loss*, through April's good sense and practicality in *Enter the Enchanted*, and through Jalil's analytical mind that orders events to find the logic of their organization in *Realm of the Reaper*. The cycle of narrators is repeated through the subsequent novels, but Senna narrates the ninth, *Inside the Illusion*.

This can be disconcerting. David is an engaging narrator, and losing his storytelling voice for *Land of Loss* is disappointing, although Christopher manages to make *Land of Loss* his own novel. Once the reader gets used to the rhythm of the shifting narrators, however, Applegate's experimentation becomes fun.

Applegate paints remarkable scenes with her words. Take, for instance, narrator David's description of the fearsome city of Huitzilopoctli:

> The city looked ancient and modern all at once. The walls of shining white stone were perhaps a hundred feet high. I saw no towers. It wasn't a castle built for defensive war; it was a wall raised against the jungle that pressed in all around the wall, a sea of dark, almost black-green that flowed down from distant mountains. Green, unbroken green, as far as the eye could see.

This offers an impressive view of an ancient Mezo-American city, but notice how Applegate stretches beyond merely putting her words into David's mouth. Instead, the description is vintage David, bearing the hallmarks of his character. The man-of-action of the young adults who have been sucked into Everworld, he thinks in terms of strengths and weaknesses. He is the one who most easily adapts to new weapons. Thus, his description of Huitzilopoctli is one of offense and defense, and the picture he paints is of a city defending against the jungle. This is typical of Applegate's achievement in the Everworld series—sharp, inspiring descriptive passages expressed in terms that are in keeping with the personalities of her narrators.

Applegate is a keen observer of telling details. Note her description of the wolf: "It was a huge gray beast the size of an elephant, but it moved with the easy grace that comes from tremendous strength. It watched us with yellow eyes that burned with more than canine intelligence. The same eyes that had gloated as it snatched Senna from the end of the pier." There may be a touch of

Animorphs, here, in her description of an animal that has human intelligence, but her words convey the size and menace of the beast. It is more than a giant animal—it thinks, and its shining eyes betray its intelligence.

Such descriptions combined with dire events make *Search for Senna* a rich, full experience, reminiscent of the organization of the Oz stories of L. Frank Baum, which feature a large, strange place with bizarre creatures, new adventures, and threats everywhere to life and limb. In *Search for Senna*, David, Jalil, Christopher, and April wander through Everworld much as Dorothy and the other characters wandered through Oz, sometimes lost, sometimes thinking they knew where they were going.

On the other hand, the Everworld books have a harder edge to their narratives. In *Search for Senna*, people die. When the Vikings charge the Aztecs, they confront an ancient, frightening god:

> He was shaped like a man. Blue, the blue of the sky late on a summer day. His face was striped horizontally with bands of blue and yellow. Around his eyes were glittering white stars, stars that seemed real and hot and explosive. Iridescent feathers grew from his head, spreading down across his shoulders and back. In his left hand he held a disk, a mirror that smoked and burned. In the right hand was a snake, a twisting, writhing snake that breathed fire and almost seemed an extension of his hand. His other hand, the one that held the mirror, dripped red. It dripped red and you knew, knew deep down, that it could never, would never be wiped clean.

Everworld is home not just to the bizarre, but to true horrors. David looks up at the gigantic god and notes, "This was the heart and soul of evil. This was corruption and filth and torture and madness." Passages such as this make for excellent cliffhangers, and Applegate manages to end her chapters with good ones, and the novel, first in a series, with a magnificent one.

◆ SOCIAL SENSITIVITY ◆

In *Search for Senna*, Applegate incorporates parts of two ancient mythologies into her tale of adventure. One is that of the ancient Norse, the Vikings, who populated much of the North Atlantic and terrorized Europe and central Asia during the Middle Ages. Although Applegate works significant aspects of the Norse tales into *Search for Senna*, her purpose is not to explain Norse religious beliefs, but instead to tell a thrilling adventure in which the tales are a part. Thus, she does not explain much about such figures as the giant wolf, although anyone familiar with Norse mythology will recognize not only the gods and the wolf, but the snake, as well.

Ancient Aztec beliefs receive fuller coverage in *Land of Loss*, the second novel in the Everworld series. In *Search for Senna*, the Aztecs first appear to be the victims of a Viking raid intended to acquire the ransom needed to release their favorite god. The Vikings do not realize that they are part of a larger plan that includes their destruction. As in the mythology of the Norse, the gods are not always mindful of the welfare of human beings, and people are often pawns in a game they do not realize exists. For the purposes of the plot in *Search for Senna*, the Aztec culture is only sketched from the perspective of David, who is mindful of strengths and weaknesses, of walls and warriors. The Aztecs are no match for the large, well-armed Vikings, but *Search for Senna* is the story of people caught up in events larger than themselves. Just as David, Jalil, Christopher, and April are part of a plan that they do not yet understand, involving Senna, Loki, and others, so, too,

are the Vikings and Aztecs caught up in the plans of their gods. It is enough to know that the god Huitzilopoctli demanded blood sacrifices, and that at his worst Loki never demanded what the Aztecs were expected to give.

◆ TOPICS FOR DISCUSSION ◆

1. Why does David feel insecure?

2. Why does David feel happy while rowing the Dragonshield?

3. What does Christopher contribute to the adventure? What does this say about his personality?

4. What does April contribute to the adventure? What does this say about her personality?

5. What does Jalil contribute to the adventure? What does this say about his personality?

6. What is David's attitude toward each of his companions: Christopher, April, and Jalil? What does this tell about David's personality?

7. Why does Huitzilopoctli frighten David more than Loki does?

8. Why do the adventurers fall slowly into a pool? Could this be foreshadowing anything? Is it like any common part of human experience?

9. Why does Applegate seem to be beginning a new story more than ending one in the final passages of *Search for Senna*?

10. What advantage does David have as a storyteller over Christopher, April, and Jalil?

11. Why would Applegate make the gods huge in *Search for Senna*?

12. Which passages are dreamlike in *Search for Senna*?

♦ IDEAS FOR REPORTS AND PAPERS ♦

1. Exactly who is the giant wolf in Norse mythology? Is he like the wolf portrayed in *Search for Senna*?

2. What is the relationship between Loki, the wolf, and the snake in Norse mythology? Does knowing this relationship help clarify their relationship in *Search for Senna*?

3. What part do blood sacrifices play in Aztec religious beliefs? What did their neighbors think about these practices? Would their neighbors have welcomed the Viking attack on the Aztecs?

4. What are some cliff-hangers in *Search for Senna*? Where does Applegate use them? How effective are they?

5. David looks for descriptions of Viking longboats in *Search for Senna*. What were they? What did they look like? David is particularly interested in how to make them sail best; how effective were they in sailing the ocean? What in their design affected their effectiveness?

6. Why would the Vikings miss Thor in particular? What is he like in Norse mythology?

7. What are the best descriptive passages in *Search for Senna*? What makes them the best?

8. Some of the Vikings in *Search for Senna* live on farms. What were real Viking farms like? Do the ones in *Search for Senna* resemble the real-life farms?

9. April thinks that Senna has a witchlike power over the boys. What are some examples in folktales and mythology of girls or women who could supernaturally control boys or men? (You might start with *The Odyssey*.)

10. How does *Search for Senna* compare with the best books of the Animorphs series? Does the fact that *Search for Senna* is intended for an audience older than that of the Animorphs books affect its quality?

♦ RELATED TITLES ♦

The subsequent Everworld novels continue to introduce mythologies, and in the process, Applegate creates a new mythology of her own, in which human endeavors are placed in a vast cosmic scheme in which everyone is important, even though in any individual novel they may seem like pawns. *Land of Loss* focuses more on Aztec mythology than Norse mythology and introduces the Coo-Hatch, aliens from yet another world. *Enter the Enchanted* tells of the survival of Arthurian culture in Everworld and shows that the various cultures and their gods know about each other and mix with each other. *Realm of the Reaper* delves more deeply into Norse myths about life and death and the underworld. Once the teens meet Merlin in *Land of Loss*, the grand contest of universe-shaking powers begins to reveal itself, and dreams do seem more real than real life.

♦ FOR FURTHER REFERENCE ♦

"Applegate, K. A. " In *Something about the Author*, Vol. 109. Detroit: The Gale Group, 2000. An essay that includes biographical information about Applegate and information about her writing.

"K. A. Applegate." In *Authors and Artists for Young Adults*, Vol. 37. Detroit: The Gale

Group, 2000. A biographical essay with comments on Applegate's life and work.

Lodge, Sally. "Scholastic's Animorphs Series Has Legs." In *Publishers Weekly* 244, 45 (November 3, 1997): 36–37.

Review of *Search for Senna.* In *Publishers Weekly* 246, 25 (June 21, 1999): 69. The reviewer says, "With her blend of accessible story and mythological cast of characters, Applegate is sure to attract a host of new fans."

Kirk H. Beetz

SHADE'S CHILDREN

Novel

1997

Author: Garth Nix

Major Books for Young Adults

The Ragwitch, 1990
Sabriel, 1995

Shade's Children, 1997
Lirael, 2001

◆ ABOUT THE AUTHOR ◆

Garth Nix was born in 1963 in Melbourne, Australia. He grew up in Canberra, the federal capital of Australia. When he finished secondary school, he traveled in Europe for several years. In 1983 he returned to Australia where he enrolled at the University of Canberra in a professional writing program. He also joined the Australian Army Reserve. After graduating from the university in 1986, Nix worked for several years in the publishing industry, eventually becoming a senior editor with a large publisher in 1991. In 1993, Nix quit his job as an editor to travel in Eastern Europe, the Middle East, and Asia. He returned to Sydney in 1994, and began working for a public relations firm. In 1996, with two partners, he started his own public relations company—Gotley Nix Evans Pty Ltd.

In January 1998 Nix stopped working actively at Gotley Nix Evans and wrote full-time until May 1999 when he also began to work part-time as a literary agent for Curtis Brown, Australia's largest literary agency.

◆ OVERVIEW ◆

Shade's Children is a science fiction novel that portrays a world that has been taken over by seemingly alien beings, called overlords, who have made all of the adults on the planet disappear. The aliens raise children in order to harvest their body parts. A guerilla team of children—some of Shade's children—overthrow the overlords and restore their society. The novel is fast-paced, suspenseful, and full of action, and addresses some important ideas about identity and the role of children in society.

◆ SETTING ◆

The setting of this futuristic novel is particularly convincing. The novel opens fifteen years after the sudden disappearance of the adults during the commuter rush hour one morning. This event is called The Change. None of the characters except Shade, the leader of the rebel children, and Ella, a guerilla team leader, remember life before the overlords. Children are raised in dormitories and each child is controlled by a computer chip implanted in the wrist. On their fourteenth birthday, the day the children call their Sad Birthday, the children are removed from the dorms. Some girls are taken to another location for breeding purposes. However, most children are taken to the Meat Factory where they are sedated until their body parts, particularly their brains, can be harvested and put into the bodies of the overlords' creatures. The central characters of *Shade's Children* have escaped the dorms by using a Change Talent unique to each which they discover at about the time they reach puberty. They live together in a partially submerged submarine that functions as Shade's headquarters.

The characters move through an abandoned urban landscape. Urban infrastructure still exists: buildings have operating electricity, water, heating and cooling, and security systems. The streetlights and traffic signals still work, though many of the streets are clogged with abandoned vehicles. Because the overlords and their beasts and soldiers control the surface of the city, the teams of children use the water and sewer system to move about the city when they pursue their guerilla operations against the armies of the overlords.

The overlords and their armies are the most dangerous element of the setting. The six overlords and their armies are identified by color: Red Diamond, Black Banner, Gold Claw, Blue Star, Emerald Crown, Gray Crescent. Each overlord has multitudes of creatures that form into armies, do battle with the creatures of other overlords, and

hunt for escaped children. Myrmidons travel in groups of seven. Myrmidons are "Seven-foot-tall, barrel-chested monsters with long arms ending in spade-shaped hands. Six-fingered hands, with thick, oversized thumbs." They are armored and helmeted and are the most powerful of the creatures. Trackers are less powerful than Myrmidons, but frightening nonetheless: "Thin, spindly stick-humans that looked like half-melted plastic soldiers. Bright, bulbous eyes, too large for their almost-human eye-sockets. Long pointed noses that were almost all red-flared nostril. . . They could smell a human out with those noses . . . . No matter where he hid." Wingers are gigantic flying creatures that are also semihuman: "[A] human body stretched out with arms stretched longer still; the taloned hands; the stumpy legs ending well above the knees; and the great leather-bellows bat wings spanning twenty feet or more." These creatures can pick up a child who has been restrained by a net and take him or her to the Meat Factory. Screamers are also flying creatures. They function primarily as scouts, hunting for children or enemies and then screaming to alert their respective leaders. Gigantic ferrets roam the city at night, sucking the blood from their prey, whether they are children, wild dogs, or each other. During the day they rest in the dry tunnels of the water and sewer system, so they pose a threat to the guerrilla teams of children as they travel throughout the city. The creatures, rather than the abandoned landscape itself, threaten the existence of the children.

While the setting of the novel is convincing for the most part, the unnamed city is isolated and separate, leaving the reader to wonder about the rest of the world. *Shade's Children* seems to be set on Earth, but we only see the events of one city. Have the overlords destroyed every city? What has happened to the rest of humanity?

Though other guerilla teams composed of escaped children exist, we get to know the members of one team best. At nineteen, the leader Ella is, she believes, the oldest human being on the planet. The other young adults her age who managed to escape the Meat Factory have all died on guerilla missions ordered by Shade. As the oldest, Ella takes on the responsibility of keeping her team alive. However, there is nothing maternal about her. She is a hardened warrior who kills without regret or guilt. The younger members of the team are not yet so hardened.

Ella's Change Talent is the ability to create a physical object from an image in her mind. To effect such a change requires a great deal of energy, sometimes leaving Ella physically drained to the point of immobility. "It took three months of practice for me to build that picture into something real, a hard, sharp object to hold in my hand. Then one day, it wasn't just a thought. It was there in my hand. Real. Sharp." The object Ella creates is a razor blade which she then uses to cut her wrist and remove the tracer capsule "from where it nestles between veins and bones." Ella also creates a grenade later in the story which, used at a climactic moment, rescues her teammates.

Drum is the next oldest member of the team, although we do not know his exact age because he quit counting his birthdays after he left the Training Grounds. Unlike most children, Drum was removed from the dorms to the Training Grounds when he was eight years old and fed a constant diet of steroids. The overlords intended to harvest his artificially enhanced muscles for use in their creatures. However, he strangles a guard and escapes the Training Ground just before his fourteenth birthday.

His escape does not undo the results of the steroid treatment, however. He is a large, muscular human, but the steroids have prevented any sexual maturity from taking place. Consequently, despite his imposing masculine physique, he has the high, unchanged voice and the genitals of a prepubescent boy—he is neither boy nor man. He can see no future for himself nor imagine a society in which he might live. Responding to Shade in a videotaped interview, Drum remarks, "I don't expect any brave new world will have career openings for harem guards or gelded civil servants."

Drum's Change Talent is the mental version of his physical strength. He is able to move things by thinking about them. When he and Ella jump/fall from a bridge, Drum exerts his Talent to prevent them from hitting the water too forcefully:

> He'd never lifted anything heavier than a cat before, and the muscles in his arms strained as if he were trying to pull himself and Ella up a rope without using his feet, strained till they felt as if they would burst out of his skin, and his brain explode with them. . . .

> But he did slow their fall, perhaps enough . . . and in the last few seconds he twisted both of them around, shielding Ella as his back smacked into the water with a tremendous force.

Ninde is a younger member of the team. She is only about fifteen years old and is clearly more immature than Drum or Ella. She has fantasies of becoming a doctor or a movie star after the overlords have been defeated. She is fascinated by films from "the old days" which she has seen repeatedly via videotape, and they influence her behavior because they are her only conception of adults. She often speaks before she thinks. She is impatient, less committed to the cause of overthrowing the overlords, and more willing to break the rules Shade has established; unlike Drum and Ella who have had to take on adult responsibility for so many years that they have become adultlike.

Ninde's Change Talent is her ability to know what people and creatures are thinking. In an odd, almost psychic connection she chews on the knuckle of her forefinger and is able to concentrate and hear what creatures are thinking. She finds hearing the thoughts of the creatures easier than those of human beings.

The youngest member of the team is Gold-Eye whose name comes from his unusual eyes: "They weren't normal human eyes at all, blue or brown or green irises against the white. His pupils and irises were gold, bright gold." As the book opens, he is escaping from creatures when Ella, Drum, and Ninde rescue him. He had escaped from the dorms with his brother Petar several years earlier and had been hiding from the creatures since then. His years of living on his own have turned him into a kind of primitive. He can hardly speak in complete sentences, and he does not really understand how to behave around other human beings.

Gold-Eye's Change Talent is an ability to see into the immediate future, what he calls the "soon-to-be-now." Unlike the other members of the team, Gold-Eye cannot control his talent. It simply comes over him, immobilizing him until the vision passes.

The children have been formed into a community by Shade. Shade's existence is one of the most interesting elements of the novel, for his character distills many of the identity conflicts of the team members. His explanation to Gold-Eye of his existence suggests his character as well:

> What I am, Gold-Eye, is a human personality stored in a computer's memory. I have the memories of that real person. I think like a real person. But no flesh, save the holographic appearance you have seen—which I must confess is partly based on a twentieth-century actor—so I look rather better than I did in the flesh. A conceit that possibly shows my continuing humanity. . . .

Ironically, it is in his existence as a good-looking, suave gentleman that Shade is most deceptive, to the children and to himself. He sends various teams out on suicide missions in order to gain information that will help him attain a more physical level of existence. He is able to download himself (or parts of himself, that is, enough consciousness to spy) into mechanical objects, which are, significantly, mechanical rats and a mechanical spider, in order to achieve his ends. At the climax of the book, when he is a mechanical spider, he betrays the team to the overlords in hopes of exchanging them for information that might allow him to create a more humanlike body in which he might reside. Despite the fact that the overlords eventually destroy the mechanical object (The Thinker) that contains the computer that holds Shade's personality, he is able to download aspects of himself into various devices. After the destruction of The Thinker, Shade takes responsibility for the deaths he has caused and returns to Ella and Drum as a holographic image of his original self—Robert Ingman. In that identity he provides Ella and Drum with the necessary information to destroy the mechanical devices which allow the overlords to control the world.

Given the centrality of character in this novel, it is no surprise that issues of identity are prominent themes in the novel. The rather straightforward adolescent psychological quest of discovering an identity is made a physical fact in this novel. The individual Change Talents highlight the uniqueness of the individual and provide a role for that individual within the guerilla teams. However, the novel also emphasizes that the team members must work together in order to survive, thereby emphasizing the social nature of identity. Each Change Talent makes the individual vulnerable for a period of time, thereby requiring the team to protect the individual in order to take advantage of the talent. Furthermore, the novel makes it clear that no one person can accomplish what the team is able to do together.

Nix does not avoid the complications and difficulties of interpersonal relationships. Being a friend is often dangerous, as events in the novel show. Gold-Eye reports to Shade that Petar, his brother, sacrificed his life so that Gold-Eye could escape the dormitories. Ninde, Ella, and Gold-Eye risk their lives to rescue Drum from the Meat Factory against Shade's wishes. Even within the relatively safe community that Shade has established for the children, close friendship is heart-wrenching and painful. When Ella reflects on her first sexual experiences, she focuses on the loss of loved ones: "sex only made her closer to people, made it easier to love them, made it so much harder to bear when they were lost." Despite these difficulties, Nix is able to present characters who do create a family with surrogate (unconventional) parents; who do learn to work together, despite their differences; and who do grow to love one another in ways that can be expressed sexually (between Gold-Eye and Ninde) and in ways that are platonic (between Ella and Drum).

Nix heightens this theme when Shade sacrifices Ella's team to bargain with the overlords. Though Shade appears to be a loyal paternal figure, throughout the novel Nix lays clues that Shade should not be trusted. When he finally leads the children into the trap, his completely self-serving nature becomes evident. Shade's disloyalty to the children is parallel to the children's recognition late in the novel that the overlords are human. Ninde cries in despair at this discovery, but Drum points out to her that "What they've done has made them something else. Not human . . . not people . . . overlords." To be human, in this novel, is not to have a human shape, but to treat others humanely.

These issues are further complicated by issues of existence. What is a human being? Is Shade/Robert Ingman a human being? Is a Myrmidon or Tracker a human being because it has a human brain implanted in its body? Is an overlord a human being? The novel asks readers to consider these questions carefully. If they are human beings, should they be expected to behave according to human standards of decency and compassion? If they are not human beings, can there be expectations regarding their behavior? Do the Change Talents make the children no longer human? Gold-Eye has been mistaken for a creature because of his golden eyes, and he is quick to remind Shade that he is not a creature. Nix handles these questions and issues deftly, neither philosophizing nor discoursing about these ideas, which would impede the brisk rate of the narrative.

◆ LITERARY QUALITIES ◆

Nix uses multiple documents to construct the novel. Interspersed among chapters of straightforward narration are transcriptions of video and audio recordings and other documents. The latter include interviews with characters, training lessons, reports from other guerilla teams, overheard (i.e., bugged) conversations and comments, Shade's self-examination sessions, lists, and records of team activity. The effect of these documents is to call into question the accounts of the characters who are often only guessing or surmising circumstances or situations—or, in the case of Shade, deliberately deceiving the other characters. The different typeface and related computer visuals of the interspersed documents contribute to the futuristic setting.

Nix is an accomplished storyteller. The plot of this novel is so action-packed and well paced that readers will have a hard time putting it down. The characters move from one adventure or crisis to another, always in danger. Yet the action is always clearly conveyed, stripped down to its essentials so that readers can easily see the events in the mind's eye. Nix builds the thematic content of the novel into the action and the brief bits of dialogue between the characters rather than in the voice of the narrator or the use of symbols or metaphorical imagery.

◆ SOCIAL SENSITIVITY ◆

The issues of identity and existence that are central to the novel have been discussed above. However, *Shade's Children* also obliquely addresses the role of children in society and the relationships between adults and children. The overlords treat the children as objects, as a commodity to be produced or a natural resource to be mined. Nix's novel goes to the heart of current controversies about children's rights and their role in society.

Also, *Shade's Children* comments, again obliquely, on the beneficial role of parents in the development of a child's life. In this futuristic world we see what happens to children who grow up without adults. In the restored world at the end of the novel, the nuclear family is again central to the child's experience.

◆ TOPICS FOR DISCUSSION ◆

1. How is technology portrayed in the novel? Do you think that Shade's ability to download himself into various computers is a way of keeping him alive? The advanced technology of the overlords allows them to create dangerous creatures. Do you think that this technology is out of control?

2. Is Shade human? Is the Winger who has Brat's brain human? What charac-

teristics determine whether one is a human being?

3. Ninde and Gold-Eye are parents at the end of the novel. But they have not grown up in families with parents, so they may not know how to act like parents. Do you think that they will be good parents? Why or why not? What advice would you give to them about being parents?

4. What are the differences between the character of Shade and the character of Robert Ingman? Where do you discover those differences? How do those differences help to explain his involvement in the destruction of vital overlord technology?

5. What kind of information do we gain from the documents included in the narrative? How do those documents help us to understand the story, the characters, and their motivations?

6. The overlords view the battles of the creatures as games. They do not take seriously the amount of destruction that they cause. Are there ways in which we play "games" with the natural world or creatures who are less powerful than us? To what degree do we destroy to support our habits of living?

7. Do you think that the Change Talents the characters have make them more human or less? What do you think of someone who is very different from everyone else? What does it mean to be an individual or to fit in with the crowd?

8. Do you think Shade was wrong to send the children on difficult missions? Consider the fact that, although some died, he did protect them and eventually they were able to overthrow the overlords.

9. Why must Drum and Ella die at the end of the novel?

1. How do holographs work?

2. What is Artificial Intelligence? How does it work? Can computers think like human beings?

3. How do prostheses or artificial limbs work?

4. What are the effects of steroid use?

5. If young adults from the future only had American movies of the 1990s to understand adult behavior, what would society be like? What kinds of behaviors would they assume are normal? Discuss several titles and the ways in which they portray adults.

6. How do weather patterns work? What technology would we need in order to create storms or fog as the overlords are able to do in the novel?

7. Research the history of orphanages and/or changing social policy regarding children whose parents have died or who have been abandoned.

8. What is the history of the technology of spying?

9. How has technology affected human relationships in today's society?

♦ RELATED TITLES/ADAPTATIONS ♦

Though no film adaptation has been developed for *Shade's Children*, a number of other books do address similar themes and issues. Lois Lowry's *The Giver*, Nancy Farmer's *The Ear, the Eye, and the Arm*, and Peter Dickinson's *Eva* are novels for young adults that depict future societies in which technology has reshaped human relationships. For a related title on out-of-control computers, you need look no farther than the film *2001: A Space Odyssey*.

♦ FOR FURTHER REFERENCE ♦

Gross, Melissa. "*The Giver* and *Shade's Children*: Future Views of Child Abandonment and Murder." *Children's Literature in Education* 30 (1999): 103–117. Discussion of the ways in which *Shade's Children* departs from the normal pattern of child abandonment in literature.

Jones, J. Sydney. "Garth Nix." *Authors and Artists for Young Adults*, vol. 27. Detroit: Gale, 1999. Provides background information and summarizes reviews of *Shade's Children*.

Something about the Author, vol. 97. Detroit: Gale, 1998. Brief biographical sketch and a short paragraph discussing *Shade's Children*.

♦ RELATED WEBSITES ♦

"Garth Nix." http://members.ozemail.com.au/ ~garthnix/December 2001. Garth Nix's homepage. It includes book covers, descriptions of each of his novels, an interview, a brief biographical note, photographs and drawings of Nix, as well as a great site about his writing process, including scanned images of pages of his handwritten notebooks. Nix has also included at the site an interactive text adventure called "Down to the Scum Quarter" that might be appropriate for older students.

Ellen Donovan

SO FAR FROM THE BAMBOO GROVE

Autobiographical Novel

1986

Author: Yoko Kawashima Watkins

◆

Major Books for Young Adults

So Far from the Bamboo Grove, 1986
Tales From the Bamboo Grove, 1992
My Brother, My Sister, and I, 1994

◆ ABOUT THE AUTHOR ◆

Yoko Kawashima Watkins is of Japanese ancestry but was born in Harbin, Manchuria in 1933, then moved to North Korea where she lived with her family while her father worked as a Japanese government official during World War II. She lived in a bamboo grove in Nanam until 1945, when the Russian and Korean Communist forces, angered at years of Japanese oppression, escalated their warfare and drove hordes of Japanese people out of the country. Yoko lived a comfortable life in the bamboo grove until the age of eleven, when she, her mother, and her sister Ko were forced to flee to Japan and leave her father and brother Hideyo behind. After her harrowing ordeal as a refugee she learned how to survive and persevere. Watkins worked hard, became educated in Kyoto, and learned English well enough to work as a typist and a translator at Misawa American Air Force base. She married a pilot named Donald Watkins in 1953, moved with him to America in 1958, then settled in Massachusetts and raised six children, two of them Taiwanese orphans. In 1976, thirty-one years after her escape from Korea, Watkins began writing her story. She spent the next eleven years reliving anguished memories and finally published her first book in 1986. Once again she was rewarded for her strength. Her vivid portrayal of life as a Korean refugee won her praise as a young adult writer, and she won numerous awards both for *So Far from the Bamboo Grove* and for its sequel, *My Brother, My Sister, and I.* Watkins also wrote a book of Japanese folk tales, and she continues to educate young people about the horrors of war by lecturing about her experiences.

Eleven-year-old Yoko and her family are stationed in North Korea during World War II while Yoko's father works as a Japanese government official in nearby Manchuria. They live in a bamboo grove in Nanam until the Russian and Korean Communists invade their country and escalate their war against Japan. Because Yoko's father protects Japanese interests, the family knows they are in particular danger and must flee the country as soon as possible. *So Far from the Bamboo Grove* tells the story of their escape. Yoko, her mother, and her sister Ko learn of the urgency of their escape one night as Corporal Matsumura comes to their house and instructs them to leave immediately. Frightened and heartsick at having to leave Yoko's father at work in Manchuria and her brother Hideyo at work in an ammunitions factory, the three women embark on their journey alone. They travel by train and on foot. They hide by day and they walk by night. They withstand gunfire, disease, poverty, and near starvation. Finally, they arrive in Seoul, travel by train to Pusan, and board a ship to Japan. Once in Japan, however, Yoko's mother dies from exhaustion and defeat, and Yoko and her sister Ko must learn to survive on their own. Their strength and determination leads them to success. Japan loses the war, but Yoko emerges victorious. Watkins's gripping tale of courage and strength recounts the plight of refugees through the story of Yoko, Ko, and Hideyo, many of whom withstood similar harrowing ordeals and struggled to survive during years of political unrest.

◆ SETTING ◆

Watkins begins her story in North Korea, moves into Seoul, South Korea, then into Pusan, a port city of Japan, and finally into Kyoto. These areas have been ravaged by war, and Watkins takes us behind the scenes and introduces us to the filthiest trains, the filthiest stations, and the filthiest people on both sides of the war. Her vivid descriptions of the devastation, the blood, and the stench allude to the ugliness of war. We picture the wreckage, and we feel the fear Yoko experiences when trying to navigate through such horrors without getting killed.

If we study the myths and traditions of Japan, we learn that the Japanese have a deep respect for the environment and the natural features of the land. Watkins describes how Yoko and her family use the Asian landscape to provide relief and protection. They bathe in the ponds and rivers, they hide in the brush, and they find food growing in the fields to sustain them. Watkins uses the setting of her novel to highlight the contrast between war and peace, love and hate, evil and goodness. During war, everything of beauty is destroyed, and the land that protects and provides for them crumbles, but eventually renews itself.

◆ THEMES AND CHARACTERS ◆

So Far from the Bamboo Grove is a story about strength, perseverance, and personal victory. At the start of the novel, Yoko, her sister Ko, and her brother Hideyo live with their mother in Nanam, North Korea, during a time of political upheaval when hostilities are raging between the Koreans and the Japanese. It is 1945, and word has just reached Korea that Japan is losing the war. Tokyo has been bombed, Russian communist troops have invaded North Korea, and angry Koreans have vowed revenge against the Japanese for years of political oppression. The Japanese people living in Korea must flee for their lives, and as the family of a Japanese government official, Yoko and her mother and sister are among the first to flee. Devastated and frightened, the three of them embark on a harrowing journey. In describing that journey Watkins tells a poignant tale of endurance and survival.

During this time in history, anger and hatred toward Japan led the Korean communists to commit horrible human rights violations against the Japanese people. Japan had ruled Korea for thirty-five years, and as soon as Japan lost the war, Korean communists forced the Japanese out of the country. They raped them and killed them. They dropped bombs from airplanes and ravaged them in the fields as they tried to escape. Japanese refugees had a long and dangerous journey before they reached Seoul, South Korea and then Japan. Thousands were killed or died of starvation or disease. But thousands more reached the port cities of Japan each day and faced the task of re-establishing their identity and building new lives in a country that had been devastated by Allied bombs. Yoko and her sister are fortunate; they survive. Watkins lived this nightmarish adventure as the young Yoko, and the experience molded her life view forever.

So Far from the Bamboo Grove is classified an autobiographical novel, and Watkins reveals her thoughts as she describes her journey across the war-ravaged land. We understand Yoko's plight and we ache for her. At eleven years of age she has seen more death and destruction than most people see in their lives. Trapped in a hostile country and surrounded by enemies, Yoko has to remain strong and fight to survive. She learns about love and strength and values in the process. Watkins concentrates primarily on her escape with her mother and her sister Ko, but then she flashes to the escape of her brother Hideyo. Hideyo makes his escape after the women, traveling by himself to Seoul in a nightmarish adventure of his own. Hideyo shared his personal horrors with his sister years later, shortly before he died, and Watkins incorporates them into her book to further illustrate the devastating effects of war.

Watkins reveals little about Hideyo's character but she lets us know that he was loyal to both his family and to his people. He planned to join the armed forces, but failed the written exam—Ko says on purpose. But he left shortly thereafter to work in an ammunitions factory where he could serve his people in a less dangerous way. While Hideyo is away at the factory, Yoko, Ko and their mother get word that they must flee Korea immediately. The Russians have landed, and because Yoko's father works for Japanese interests, their family is in imminent danger. With not a minute to spare, Yoko, Ko, and their mother have no alternative but to leave without Mr. Kawashima and Hideyo. They write Hideyo a note telling him to meet them at the train station in Seoul. Then they slip out into the night, the three of them tied together with a rope.

It seems fitting that the three women begin their venture at night because the minute they leave the bamboo grove in Nanam they enter a dark, dangerous world. Once Japan came close to defeat, life became increasingly tough in Nanam, and Yoko lived in constant fear of bombings and air raids. But never once did she imagine what lay beyond the bamboo grove; and she soon witnesses horrors far beyond her wildest dreams. It is not surprising that Watkins could not write about her escape for more than thirty years. We can imagine how she must have been haunted by the sights and sounds that characterized her world as a refugee.

The moans of injured people, dead bodies tossed from trains, the stench of tired and battered soldiers, and the warmth of blood-soaked clothing sticking to her skin—these were the sights and sounds of Yoko's world. Her experience in many ways typified the experience of thousands of other Japanese women forced out of Korea. Leaving the home in the bamboo grove must have been painful, knowing that they had to leave Hideyo, Mr. Kawashima, and their entire life behind them. Yoko had no understanding of how difficult it would be to make it safely out of the country and back to Japan. Watkins conveys the sense of fear she and all the refugees felt embarking on this journey. She makes clear the overwhelming sense of loss the refugees felt facing an unknown future and leaving their life and their loved ones behind them.

Corporal Matsumura, a friend from the Japanese army who warns Yoko and her family to flee Nanam, has ensured that Yoko and her family be allowed to board a medical train for Seoul. As they are crammed in the women's compartment with the injured, they see people sucking urine from toilets to quench their thirst, they see a dead baby tossed from the train, and they see the women and children suffering from pain and near starvation. The next day the Korean Communist Army invades their compartment looking for Yoko and her family and other political fugitives. The medic and the nurse throw Yoko roughly on the floor and they smear Ko and her mother with blood so they look like the other injured passengers. Their persecutors leave, but that night the Koreans attack the train. Yoko, Ko, and their mother generously leave their precious provisions of food and water for an injured woman who just gave birth, and they jump out of their compartment.

The medical train is disabled forty-five miles from Seoul, and Yoko, Ko, and their mother have no choice but to continue their journey on foot. To remain safe, they travel by night, in darkness, and they sleep by day, hidden in wild rushes. In vivid detail Watkins describes the treacherous journey that lies ahead of them, and she makes us painfully aware of the horrifying plight of all Japanese refugees trying to escape. She outlines the dangers for girls, particularly, relating an especially frightening experience for sixteen-year-old Ko. When Korean soldiers appear out of nowhere and find the women en route to Seoul, they threaten to rape Ko, and the only thing that saves her is a bomb that drops from an airplane killing the soldiers. The incident leaves them shaken and terrified. Yoko sustains a piece of metal in her chest and another one in her ear. After Ko's narrow escape with the soldiers, Yoko's mother shaves the girls' heads and orders them to don the smelly uniforms of the dead soldiers to protect themselves.

Life changes drastically for Yoko during her journey. At the age of eleven she must learn to live with constant pain and fear, and she learns lessons about survival that most of us never learn. Yoko is a strong child, but her sister Ko appears to be stronger, perhaps because at the time of their flight, Ko is sixteen years old and Yoko is still a young child. She is used to being pampered. Before the communists invaded North Korea, Yoko lived a comfortable life in the bamboo grove, and for a while, she whines and complains at her unfortunate change of circumstances. She soon learns that she must remain strong. Ko is the model of strength, and she often speaks harshly to Yoko and Yoko resents it. But she also protects Yoko, carrying her on her back when she gets tired and sharing food with her when she is hungry. Watkins briefly describes the tensions that rage between Yoko and Ko, but she also describes the deep love they share.

When the three finally reach the station at Seoul, Yoko and her family join the other escapees waiting for trains to Pusan, the port city where they will board a ship for Japan. The war is over, and thousands of other Japanese refugees are feeling the same pain Yoko is feeling, and they are facing the same challenges. Yoko discovers that her chest wound is infected and she is deaf in one ear where the piece of metal punctured her eardrum. She is treated by the doctors, and must remain there two weeks in a hospital tent. They live at the station for over a month. Hideyo never arrives, and they must finally board a freight train to Pusan without him. Watkins goes on to describe their fears and concerns on the train and at the station in Pusan. Rape is a constant worry; many of the Koreans are drunk—celebrating their independence from Japan—and they are after the women. So the women have to do whatever they can to protect themselves. They have to bind their breasts and stand to urinate like boys. Male refugees had equally horrendous experiences, and these are recounted via Hideyo, who has a harrowing escape. Men and women both must dig through garbage for food. The nearly die from hunger and thirst and exhaustion, and they are sick with fear. Watkins recounts the suffering she endured and the pain she felt at leaving her old life behind and not knowing if she would ever again see Hideyo or her father. But at the same time she lets us know that she was never without hope. Battered and broken, she boards the ship for Japan with Ko and her mother and they feel an incredible sense of relief. After months of suffering, they will finally reach their beloved homeland and be reunited with their loved ones.

Yoko had imagined that Japan as a beautiful country full of cheerful people who would welcome them and make them feel safe. But when she arrives she finds her homeland devastated by bombs and reduced to rubble. Watkins's vivid descriptions of the wreckage conveys the message that war devastates both the land and the people. Not only do Yoko and her family find the Japanese cities demolished, but they discover that their grandparents have been killed. Mrs. Kawashima had left her children in Kyoto to attend school while she went to find her parents and discovered the loss. Battered and grief-stricken, she

returns to Kyoto but dies shortly thereafter. Yoko and Ko are then left alone in a strange city to fend for themselves.

They say that tragedy brings people together, and Watkins stresses the bond that develops between Yoko and Ko. With no money, no assets, and no place to live, they face new trials every day, and they face a desperate struggle simply to survive. But they do manage to survive and to pull their lives together. They find shelter above a clog warehouse, curl together to keep warm, and they manage to continue with their schooling and find food to eat, often by digging through garbage cans like they did on their journey. Ko takes on the role of protector, but during their time in Kyoto, Yoko matures and learns to become self-reliant. Watkins describes several instances when she becomes aware of her sister's selflessness. A particularly touching incident occurs near the end of the book when Yoko discovers her sister shining shoes to make money to pay for Yoko's food. At this point she wants nothing more than to show her sister her appreciation. She scrapes together what money she has and she buys food for a New Year's feast. As a special treat, she buys tea and a "cheaply made" teapot. Then for the first time, she prepares a meal herself. When Ko returns home to the warehouse, Yoko welcomes her warmly and serves her the feast. When at the end of the meal Yoko bows to Ko and pours her a cup of green tea, Ko is overwhelmed. We understand that the simple act of pouring tea, in Japanese culture, is a sincere gesture of respect.

Watkins succeeds in writing a gripping novel of tragedy and survival, and she chronicles both the horrors of war and Yoko's growth into a loving and respectful young woman. "I competed with life and death when young, and I won," Watkins says later in life. She won in many more ways. Not only did she survive her experience as a refugee but she also learned the true value of love and respect. She learned not to take life or life's comforts for granted, and she emerged from her experience with a profound sense of pride and a true understanding of the significance of sisterly and familial bonds.

◆ LITERARY QUALITIES ◆

So Far from the Bamboo Grove pits good against evil, war against peace, strength against weakness, and creation against destruction. Unintentionally perhaps, Watkins uses the symbolism of the bamboo to emphasize the contrast. Before Yoko and her family are forced to flee their home, they live peacefully and comfortably in a bamboo grove, so it seems relevant to relate the role that bamboo plays in Japanese symbolism, an evergreen plant that symbolizes constancy. It is also a hearty plant and it lives an exceedingly long time, so it symbolizes longevity. Because the bamboo has strong roots and it always grows upright, it appears to show strength of character. It perseveres, even during hard times: the roots of the bamboo thrive, even in ice and snow, and they sprout multiple stems, which further indicate its strength and vitality. Long ago, the Japanese took note of the bamboo's long life and perpetual foliage, and they labeled it not only a symbol of strength but a symbol of friendship as well. Like friendship, it remains steadfast and true. Watkins may not have intentionally incorporated the symbolism of bamboo into her novel, but in analyzing the themes, it appears that Yoko and Ko embody the same qualities the Japanese attribute to their sacred plant. They too remain strong and they too persevere, even during hard times. And their love for each other remains steadfast and true. Furthermore, their peaceful life in the bamboo grove contrasts greatly with the violence they experience traveling through the war-ravaged areas of Korea.

Watkins draws parallels to compare the devastation of the land to the devastation of people's lives, and to compare the persecution she suffered as an escapee in Korea to the persecution she suffered as a destitute student in Kyoto. She seems to be alluding to the wreckage in her heart when she describes the wreckage caused by bombs and guns and when she describes the destructive comments made by Yoko's insensitive classmates. The death of Mrs. Kawashima is highly symbolic. Did the wreckage in her heart not also stem from the loss of her childhood world? Did Yoko not experience the death of innocence and the death of her old life? It is significant that the first task the sisters face after their mother's death is disposing of their mother's body. They manage to get a ride to a crematorium and pay for the cremation and urn for the ashes. They watch as the men in charge place their mother in the furnace. According to Japanese tradition, Yoko and Ko are given the opportunity to light the fire, and Ko bravely lights it. Watkins then describes how the girls walk away from the furnace, down the hill in the twilight, and watch the smoke rise slowly and spread into the sky. This death and cremation seems symbolic of what Yoko and Ko and all the other Japanese refugees faced at the end of World War II. Their old life reduced to ashes, they had to move forward, painfully, and rebuild a new life in a new land, leaving everything they knew and loved behind.

◆ SOCIAL SENSITIVITY ◆

The memories of her escape were so painful that it took Watkins thirty-one years before she could begin to write her story. Her story is riveting and her message poignant, and anyone who reads about Watkins's experiences understands how deeply they must have molded her values and changed her outlook on life. Today Watkins lectures to children and young adults throughout the country and in other parts of the world as well. The stories she tells teach all of us important lessons about the sanctity of life, the value of love and kindness, and the necessity of world peace.

Both *So Far from the Bamboo Grove* and its sequel *My Brother, My Sister, and I* stress the importance of strength and perseverance in the face of tragedy. In this first book Yoko, Ko, and Hideyo brave hellish conditions and they survive amazing odds. Not only do they face gunfire and bombs and threats from hostile soldiers, but they face poverty and prejudice. These are problems many children struggle with today. Young people today who read Watkins's novel get the message that hardship breeds strength and fortitude. Yoko and Ko do what it takes to survive. They dress like boys to avoid being raped and they eat from garbage cans to avoid starvation. Forced into dire circumstances, these two girls learn how to be resourceful and how to take care of each other's needs. Ko sets an admirable example and Yoko follows suit. When the girls move into the warehouse in Kyoto, they have no coats to keep them warm, no money to buy food, and not even a bed to sleep on. But Ko can sew. She cuts the uniforms they stole from the dead soldiers into small strips, and she uses them to make a coat for Yoko. Yoko can shine shoes, and she uses the money she makes to buy a special dinner and green tea for Ko.

Watkins lived the most difficult years of her life without parents, but with an older sister who not only shared her determination to survive but who showed her unconditional love. Watkins's book teaches important lessons about love between siblings and about the importance of working to-gether. Yoko and Ko leaned on each other and supported each other; they braved the world together and conquered it. The two sisters had lived a comfortable life in the bamboo grove in Nanam, and they never imagined they would spend years of their life fighting for life's most basic needs. Ko acts generously and selflessly and Yoko learns from her example. By the end of the book she has learned the importance of sharing, she has learned not to take comfort for granted, and she has learned that with strength and determination, she can survive. She has also learned the power of love. Strong familial bonds are typical in Japanese society, and the bond Yoko and Ko share becomes virtually unbreakable during their hardship. At the end of the novel, Hideyo finds them in Kyoto, and we know that the bonds among the three of them will only strengthen as they navigate through life together.

Yoko's experience as a refugee tested her strength and endurance, and she passed the test. By contemplating this test, we understand that through hardship we learn values. Many of these values Mrs. Kawashima taught her daughters while she was running with them; she certainly helped them recognize the value of love and family ties, but she helped them also recognize the value of education. It was not easy for Yoko to go to school in Kyoto; she was ridiculed by her schoolmates, called "rag doll" for coming to school in tattered clothes and a blanket for a coat, and called "trash picker" for having to search for food in garbage cans. But this made Yoko more determined than ever to succeed. Ko worked hard so that Yoko could go to school, and we know that her education and determination paid off. Readers will marvel at Yoko's courage and at the strength it must have taken for her to rise above the humiliation she felt, both in Korea and in Kyoto, and become the proud and successful woman she is today.

◆ TOPICS FOR DISCUSSION ◆

1. Ko said that Hideyo purposely failed the written test to join the armed forces. Do you think she was right? Why or why not?

2. Name several ways in which Yoko shows her gratitude to Ko.

3. What do you suppose drove Yoko to make friends with the stuttering man?

4. Why is Yoko so determined to do well in school?

5. How do Yoko and her family feel when they first arrive in Japan?

6. Often seeing so much violence and death desensitizes people. Do you think Yoko and Ko became desensitized? Why or why not?

7. Consider the plight of the Koreans who suffered for years under Japanese rule. Does Watkins make any attempt to portray Koreans as sympathetic?

◆ IDEAS FOR REPORTS AND PAPERS ◆

1. Gain some background to the Japanese-Korean relations during World War II. Do you think that Watkins realistically portrayed this situation in Korea or do you believe her account was biased?

2. Describe the different escape routes from Korea to Japan and outline some of the hardships the refugees may have faced along each route.

3. Discuss the Treaty of Portsmouth and outline its ramifications for families like Yoko's.

4. Discuss the ways the Japanese controlled the Koreans and treated them as second-class citizens in their own country. Find instances from Watkins's book to support this.

5. Advance an argument for why the Japanese took control of Korea.

6. Describe some of the human rights violations Yoko witnessed on the escape route to Japan.

7. How did Hideyo's experience as a refugee differ from Yoko's? How was it different for men and for women?

8. Describe what Hideyo might have witnessed at the 38th parallel.

9. Choose another survival story from the related titles below. Compare and contrast Yoko's experience with the experience of one of the characters in these books.

◆ RELATED TITLES/ADAPTATIONS ◆

My Brother, My Sister and I (Simon and Schuster, 1994) is the highly praised sequel to *So Far from the Bamboo Grove*. In this work, Watkins continues her story of Yoko, Ko, and Hideyo as they build a new life in Kyoto. *Year of Impossible Goodbyes*, by Sook Choi (Econo-clad Books, 1999) also recounts a young girl's harrowing escape from Korea and details the horrifying experiences she had along the way.

One reviewer compared *So Far from the Bamboo Grove* to two notable holocaust survival stories. Aranka Siegal's *Upon the Head of the Goat* (Farrar, Straus and Giroux, 1982) describes the suffering and bewilderment of a young Jewish child living in Hungary during its German occupation during World War II, and Ester Hautzig's *The Endless Steppe* (HarperTrophy, 1989) describes the experience of a young Siberian girl taken prisoner by the Russians and moved to a forced labor camp where she and her mother and grandmother must struggle to stay together and survive.

◆ FOR FURTHER REFERENCE ◆

Bulletin of the Center for Children Books (June 1986): 199. A brief review of *So Far from the Bamboo Grove.*

Contemporary Authors, vol. 153. Detroit: Gale, 2000.

Fujita Sato, Gayle K. "Watkins, Yoko Kawashima." In *Oxford Companion to Women's Writing.* Edited by Cathy N. Davidson and Linda Wagner-Martin. Oxford University Press, 1995. This biographical entry on Watkins briefly describes the harrowing experiences she wrote about in *So Far From the Bamboo Grove* and it praises her success in reaching children and young adults with her messages about life, values, and world peace.

Sherman, Louise L. *School Library Journal* (September 1986): 147. A review of *So Far from the Bamboo Grove.*

Something about the Author, vol. 93. Detroit: Gale, 1997.

Twitchell, Ethel R. *Horn Book* (July-August 1986): 453. A review of *So Far from the Bamboo Grove.*

Ward, Nel. *Voice Youth Advocates* (August-October 1986): 152. A review of *So Far from the Bamboo Grove.*

"Yoko Kawashima Watkins: *So Far from the Bamboo Grove.*" In *Literature and Its Times: Profiles of 300 Notable Literary Works and the Historical Events That Influenced Them*, Vol. 4: *World War II to the Affluent Fifties (1940's–1950's).* Edited by Joyce Moss and George Wilson. Detroit: Gale Research, 1997. In addition to providing biographical information on Watkins and a synopsis of the plot, this essay includes a thorough overview of the historical events that took place at the time the novel was written, and a list of seven suggested readings that may help students understand the hostile relationship between Korea and Japan that Watkins speaks of in her novels.

Tamra Andrews

SOUL CATCHER

Novel

1972

Author: Frank Herbert

◆

Major Books for Young Adults

Dune, 1965
Dune Messiah, 1969
The Worlds of Frank Herbert, 1970
Soul Catcher, 1972

The Godmakers, 1972
The Book of Frank Herbert, 1973
Children of Dune, 1976

◆ ABOUT THE AUTHOR ◆

Author Frank Herbert was born in 1920 in Tacoma, Washington. He served in the U.S. Navy in World War II.

Frank Herbert worked for many years as a newspaper journalist on the west coast of the United States, from Los Angeles to Seattle. He spent more than ten years writing for the San Francisco *Examiner*. Herbert wrote over twenty books of science fiction from the 1950s until his death in 1986. His work has been translated into many languages, and almost all his novels remain in print. His novel *Dune* won both the Hugo and Nebula awards and is one of the all-time bestsellers in the science fiction field, with over ten million copies sold. He wrote a total of six books in the *Dune* series, which is still the best-selling science fiction book series (by a single author) ever.

When writing his books, Herbert drew on his studies of Oriental philosophy and undersea geology, as well as his own experiences which have included working as a professional photographer, television cameraman, radio news commentator, oyster diver, and lay analyst. He also taught creative writing. As an authority on ecology, he was an active lecturer and campaigned for the preservation of the world's resources. On six wooded acres in northwest Washington state, Herbert developed an ecological demonstration project to show how a high quality of life can be maintained with a minimum drain on the total energy system.

He lived in the states of Washington and California with his wife Bev and their three children until his death in 1986.

Frank Herbert

◆ OVERVIEW ◆

Grieving for his sister's death, Charles Hobuhet rejects his university education and takes on the name and role of Katsuk. He kidnaps David Marshall, the son of an American diplomat, and brings him on a journey through the back country to be ritually sacrificed as an innocent.

The young man and the boy travel for several days, and spend some time in the company of friends and relatives of Hobuhet in a Wilderness Area. Gradually their relationship shifts slightly from captor and victim as the boy begins to learn some wilderness survival skills; the last days they spend together David actually looks after Hobuhet/Katsuk, who has fallen ill.

Through inserts into the narrative at each scene break, the reader is made aware of the search going on and of the statements made by searchers, consultants and Hobuhet. As the searchers close in on the fugitive and his captive, Hobuhet completes his plan as

Katsuk to send the authorities a message through the death of this innocent boy.

◆ SETTING ◆

The novel is set in Washington State, largely in the Wilderness Area, a large undeveloped park on the Olympic Peninsula. Published in 1972, the novel is consistent with 1969 to 1971 in terms of cultural indicators.

Herbert lived for years near where the novel is set, and his intimate familiarity with the flora and fauna of the area gives authenticity to his storytelling. "A stroll in the park" in this story takes two weeks of hard hiking and sleeping in rain forest.

It is hard for city dwellers, or people from other climates, to realize just how dense the rain forest can be in northern Washington State. It is entirely plausible for the author to place his characters a few yards away from a hiking path and have them be entirely invisible to searchers. When Hobuhet/Katsuk murders a hiker, the few sounds would not be audible to other people nearby; the hiker's body and the marks on the ground would be easy to obscure.

In such a dense, damp forest growing out of uneven ground sloping down from the Olympic Mountains, it is possible to be completely lost within two hundred yards of a highway, river or seashore. It is not surprising that David becomes disoriented, lost and completely dependent upon his captor for food, shelter and survival. Neither is it surprising how much David learns about wilderness survival and how competent he becomes; in real life a single-day hike in this area can be a profoundly moving experience that forever changes a person's attitude towards the natural world.

It might also be difficult for a reader in the twenty-first century, accustomed to books and music and films composed by or containing characters who are indigenous people, to realize just how unfamiliar it might be to most readers in 1972.

◆ THEMES AND CHARACTERS ◆

This novel is told from multiple viewpoints, mostly from the viewpoints of the two protagonists: Charles Hobuhet and David Marshall. The internal voices of their thoughts are as distinct as their external voices. Young man and boy become tied to each other, first by Hobuhet/Katsuk's obsession, then by familiarity. By the end of their journey, neither bears the other any ill will, but Katsuk completes his dangerous vision as the reader has known he would from the very first page of the book.

David is first introduced to the reader as a child, even less mature than one might expect because he has been raised with little parental guidance and mostly by servants in an affluent household. As the novel begins, David is just emerging as a personality. Though he has had few formative experiences, he is bright and nimble enough to be capable of a future in his father's diplomatic career field. He is certainly formed and changed by a few days of wilderness experiences as a captive. It is hard to imagine a boy could reach adolescence while remaining so naïve and sheltered ... but then, that is exactly what sort of innocent that Katsuk was seeking.

When first introduced, Hobuhet is glad to leave behind his grief and incomplete ventures in order to take up his role as Katsuk. He begins the novel as a far more rounded character than David; Hobuhet has a past of studying and caring for his sister, a long effort that has come to nothing. Not only has his sister committed suicide after a brutal rape, but Hobuhet walks away from his university studies into the backcountry. As days go on, he fits himself more and more deeply into his image of

Katsuk until there is nothing left of Hobuhet. By the story's end, he can see no future ahead for himself and David but the end of both their lives: one by death and the other by loss.

Both David and Hobuhet/Katsuk fall into the pattern of behavior which psychologists call the Stockholm Syndrome. Their experiences bring to mind those of Patty Hearst when she was kidnapped by terrorists who called themselves the Symbionese Liberation Army. The hostage comes to identify with the kidnapper to an extent that would never be expected before their captivity. In *Soul Catcher*, Herbert has not written a work of fiction about an imaginary psychological condition, he has written a novel about fictional characters in a realistic situation, behaving in a psychologically realistic fashion. This is the most contemporary of all Herbert's writing, dealing with issues of great importance in the American cultural psyche at that time.

From time to time, the narrative is interrupted by a piece of text: a note left by Charles Hobuhet/Katsuk, statements by his professors, press releases by David Marshall's parents, and statements by the police and park rangers. This is a hallmark element of Frank Herbert's writing style, used to great effect in his novel *Dune* to convey a sense of commentary from the future upon the events being narrated in that novel. In *Soul Catcher*, the effect is more like the structure of the popular novel *Looking for Mr. Goodbar* by Judith Rossner. The reader knows from the beginning of the novel what the end of the story will be, and everything works towards that point with a growing sense that the final fate is becoming unavoidable.

Throughout many of his books, Frank Herbert touches repeatedly upon the theme of responsibility for the environment (whether a fantasy planet, a country or the actual Earth) and the people who live there. This is overtly and abruptly true in *Soul Catcher*. Katsuk lectures on this theme repeatedly and incorporates it in the many notes found by the park rangers and police.

People are responsible, in this novel and in all Herbert's works, for the consequences of what they do. Those who do not act responsibly will visit the consequences upon their neighbors, their community of fellow living beings, and (in what should be the most motivating result) upon their descendants. It is justice when his characters reap the folly they have sown, and die; it is tragic when their families and communities suffer.

◆ LITERARY QUALITIES ◆

This novel is a paradox: the least well-written book by this master of cultural science fiction. This book would never have been published in 1972 as a first novel because it is deeply political and opinionated, though it is of superior quality on an absolute scale for plot, structure and characterization. Though the novel has substantial merit, the storytelling fades in comparison to talents the author has shown in other novels written before and after *Soul Catcher*. It's simply not Herbert's best; and his best can move the hearts and minds of people around the world. This novel needed a rewrite to further develop the character of David in the latter part of his journey, and to quote other commentators than Katsuk on American colonial imperialism.

Herbert was far better known for his grand series of *Dune* and its many sequels than for the stand-alone novel *Soul Catcher*. This series is the most celebrated work of science fiction in the world to elevate politics from a minor plot twist to an integral story element. Other writers have since tried to imitate Herbert's world-creating vision, but have not captured his dense imagery and character development (common to all

his novels). By comparison, *Soul Catcher* is a less effective novel than the *Dune* series and comes across as an argument rather than a revelation. It is not the tool for social change that Herbert seems to have intended it to be.

Still, Herbert's writing talents elevate *Soul Catcher* above the crop of popular thriller/horror novels published in 1999 and 2000, which focus on planned ritual murder and which are told from both the victim's and the killer's viewpoints as is Herbert's 1974 novel. Most of the newer novels are mere "death pornography" and highly unsuited to young adult readers. Few writers have the skills to present images from all the senses as clearly as Herbert does, or to put an incident in a context that makes it seem wholly unnecessary but tragically inevitable by the story's end. Twenty-five years of publishing have not yet brought the world a better book in this style.

In 1972, Herbert was not writing just to meet the market for his books, or to be a commercial success. In *Soul Catcher*, he was being true to the kind of story he wanted to tell. "I was a writer and I was writing. The success meant I could spend more time writing," Herbert said of that time in his life, in his foreword to *Heretics of Dune* (1984). "Looking back on it, I realize I did the right thing instinctively. You don't write for success. That takes part of your attention away from the writing. If you're really doing it, that's all you're doing: writing."

◆ SOCIAL SENSITIVITY ◆

With its contemporary setting, this is the most overtly socially relevant of Frank Herbert's novels. In this work of fiction, only realistic things happen, only believable reasons motivate his characters, and the dialogue is well suited to the situations. Some fiction is hard to read because it is unrealistic, but this book is not easy to read precisely because it is painfully accurate in many ways.

The grief and rage felt by Hobuhet/ Katsuk, and the confusion and wilderness education of David are made clear to us in not only their dialogue but their thoughts, actions, appetites and emotions. Their feelings seemed somewhat exotic to readers in 1972, but have become more familiar to the average North American reader some twenty or thirty years after the book was first released.

This book is the least popular novel written by Herbert, and has had the least effect upon culture, critics and the book industry. That is a paradox, as the setting and subject have much to do with real life in twentieth-Century North America, unlike Herbert's other fiction. It is probable that the setting and story mattered so much to Herbert personally that he could not bear forceful statements and reiterated condemnations. Perhaps Herbert's message, reiterated again and again in the ravings and notes of Katsuk, is simply unpalatable now as it was then: many Americans do not wish to face these kinds of statements, Aboriginal Americans do not need to have their consciousness raised on these issues, and some people simply do not care to read a novel on this topic. One could say after all, the character Hobuhet/Katsuk was driven mad by grief; the manifest destiny of the Americas was to be colonized; and the novel is a work of fiction anyway.

The novel addresses social issues that should be of great concern to anyone living in the Americas, and it presents attitudes that were not widely represented in fiction in 1972. These issues and attitudes must be resolved. Any discussion of this novel in a classroom would by necessity include an analysis of the treaty process, colonization, the grievances Hobuhet had, and appropriate responses that could have been made. The multicultural tolerance being taught in classrooms today must include not only new immigrants, but First Nations people. From a modern viewpoint, murder seems so completely unnecessary.

◆ TOPICS FOR DISCUSSION ◆

1. What are the crimes committed by Charles Hobuhet/Katsuk?

2. What is the genesis for Charles Hobuhet's decision to commit these crimes? What did he believe he would accomplish?

3. Why does Katsuk not attempt to escape after his crimes?

4. What is an "Indian militant"? How is this different from being a social activist?

5. How old is David? How much does this matter to Hobuhet/Katsuk?

6. How old is Charles Hobuhet? How old does he feel as Katsuk?

7. Is it likely that Charles Hobuhet would have the same reaction to his sister's death if he had been younger than David? What if he had been her father or grandfather instead?

8. What factors led to Hobuhet/Katsuk's decision to murder the hiker?

9. Why didn't David escape from his kidnapper, even when he was left alone?

10. Who is accountable now for the actions of the American government as it asserts sovereignty over what is now the western United States of America? Who is Katsuk trying to hold accountable, and for what?

11. What world events were happening as Herbert wrote this novel? What influence could the Energy Crisis, Greenpeace

or the Vietnam War have had upon the writer as he worked?

◆ IDEAS FOR REPORTS AND PAPERS ◆

1. What are the old traditions of the Wakashan-speaking Makah people of the Olympic Peninsula in northwestern Washington state regarding captives from other peoples? Are any of these traditions being observed today? Are the First Nations characters in this novel a fair representation of the actual First Nations people living in that area today?

2. Does the story of Charles Hobuhet/ Katsuk bear any resemblance to the lives of the actual Makah people, in the same way that the novels of Jane Austen bear some resemblance to the lives of the people she knew in England? Is the novel *Soul Catcher* a work of realistic fiction, or more of a fantasy than it appears?

3. Writers in Canada have debated very seriously the problem of "appropriation of voice": when a writer (particularly a male of European descent) appropriates the stories and characters of a marginalized culture, and uses them beyond fair comment. A particular example is the fictional writings of W.P. Kinsella about people of the Ermineskin Band in Alberta. Has Frank Herbert similarly "appropriated the voice" of a character? Does Herbert have the cultural background to write authentically and honestly from the viewpoint of Charles Hobuhet/Katsuk? Does it matter that Herbert's novel is written from multiple viewpoints, unlike Kinsella's novels? Does it matter that this is the only novel Herbert wrote with realistic characters from a contemporary culture different from his own, while Kinsella

wrote seven books from the viewpoint of a man similar to the men he once drove in a cab?

4. Discuss the theme of cultural interactions and conflict in Frank Herbert's novels. How does Herbert incorporate realism in developing this theme? Does he have greater license in his fantasy/ science fiction novels than in *Soul Catcher*?

5. What is cultural imperialism? How does it affect the Hoh people in this novel? How is Charles Hobuhet affected? How is David changed by it, living in the natural world and under Katsuk's control for a few days?

6. If David had been released, how would he have been changed by his experiences? What could this son of a diplomat have learned to bring to the world in which his father lives? How would Hobuhet/Katsuk have been changed by releasing the boy? What could he possibly have contributed to the world from prison and from the ruins of his university career?

7. Charles Hobuhet's people are not activist demonstrators, but they hunt and spend time in the Wilderness park and work to get their aboriginal land rights recognized by the State and Federal governments. They do not overcome Charles Hobuhet by sheer numbers, but they do not embrace his vision as Katsuk. Are they cowards? Are they brave? What are they accomplishing that Hobuhet/Katsuk does not? What have they lost (or retained tenuously) which he has found?

8. Discuss how Hobuhet/Katsuk feeds and shelters his captive, and later, how David takes care of his captor who has fallen ill. What does this caretaking and physical closeness mean? Is Katsuk wholly destructive and evil? Was David

Soul Catcher

completely ignorant of responsible behavior before being kidnapped? Was murder the only choice that would finish the pattern that Katsuk insisted upon? What other choices did their closeness and sharing make possible? Could releasing the boy be true to Hobuhet's beliefs, and satisfy his grief and rage?

9. Discuss the female characters appearing in *Soul Catcher*. Compare them to the male characters by their numbers, amount of dialogue, and their activities. When do women have an active voice in this story? What kinds of choices and actions do they make? If you replaced all the gender-specific words in this story (i.e., he, she, her, his, mother, father, sister, brother, etc.) with non-gendered equivalents (i.e., parent, sibling), could you tell which was a female character and which was male?

10. How would the story be changed if gender roles were less defined for the characters? What if one or more characters had a different gender? Does sexual orientation count when determining gender roles in this story, particularly since the shamans of North American aboriginal groups were sometimes homosexual or bisexual?

♦ RELATED TITLES/ADAPTATIONS ♦

There have been no adaptations made of *Soul Catcher* in other media. There is a film adaptation of Frank Herbert's most celebrated novel *Dune*, rated R. The film was directed by David Lynch.Raffaella Di Laurentis was the films producer. Visually, the special effects are striking and were state-of-the-art at the time of the film's release in 1984. The script was less successful than the setting or the acting; where the dialogue departed from the novel it disap-

pointed the audience of loyal Herbert readers. But video copies of the film are still available in libraries and video rental stores.

Readers who have read all of Frank Herbert's novels and wish for more will be interested to know that Herbert's son Brian is co-writing new novels in the *Dune* series. The first two prequels to *Dune* are now in print and have received some critical acclaim. Brian Herbert has not announced any intentions to write prequels or sequels for *Soul Catcher* or for any of his father's other science fiction novels.

♦ FOR FURTHER REFERENCE ♦

Benet's Readers' Encyclopedia of American Literature, vol. 1. HarperCollins, 1991. Biographical notes about Frank Herbert and discussion of his Dune series in particular.

"Frank Herbert." *Mother Earth News.* (May-June 1981): 16. A thoughtful article on Herbert discussing the realism in his fantasy and science fiction writing.

Herbert, Frank. *The Book of Frank Herbert.* Berkeley, 1973. Author's statements provide some insight into his thoughts and intentions when he wrote this story collection, and at the time he was writing Soul Catcher.

Herbert, Frank. *Heretics of Dune.* Berkeley, 1984. Author's statements on his experiences and intentions as an author, particularly when writing his Dune series.

Herbert, Frank & Bill Ransom. *The Jesus Incident*, Berkeley, 1979.

Herbert, Brian & Kevin J. Anderson. *Prelude to Dune: House Atreides.* Hodder & Stoughton, 2000. A prequel to Herbert's Dune series, written by his son and another author.

Herbert, Brian & Kevin J. Anderson. *Prelude to Dune II: House Harkonnen.* Hodder &

Stoughton, 2001. A second prequel to Herbert's Dune series, written by his son and another author.

McDowell, Edwin. "Frank Herbert" *New York Times Book Review* (May 13, 1981): 54. Includes retrospective statements on Herbert, and mostly on his Dune series.

McKernan, Brian. "Dune." *Omni* 7 (November 1984): 94. Treats Herbert as a master of the genre, and the novel Dune as a classic.

Stagner, Ross. "Master of Dune." *Psychology Today* (October 1984): 68. Discusses the author and his character development in the Dune series.

Paula Johanson

TWO SUNS IN THE SKY

Novel

1999

Author: Miriam Bat-Ami

◆

Major Books for Young Adults

Dear Elijah, 1995
Two Suns in the Sky, 1999

◆ ABOUT THE AUTHOR ◆

Miriam Bat-Ami was born on June 26, 1950 in Scranton, Pennsylvania. She grew up in a Jewish home—her father, Simon, was a rabbi—and she attended college at Hebrew University in Jerusalem where she received her bachelor of arts degree in 1974. She married Ronald Rubens in 1976, and continued her education in America. She obtained a master of arts from California State University in 1980 and a doctorate degree from the University of Pittsburgh in 1989.

Bat-Ami has always been interested in teaching young adults and increasing their awareness of multicultural issues. She worked as a tutor and a teacher of English as a Second Language (ESL), and as an executive assistant at the Israeli Consulate in Los Angeles. Since 1994, she has been an English professor at Western Michigan University in Kalamazoo. Today, Bat-Ami lives in Mattawan, Michigan, with her husband Ronald and two sons, Aaron and Daniel, and she continues to research and publish multicultural short stories, books for children and young adults, journal articles, and literary criticism. She has achieved acclaim for her historical fiction and nonfiction for children and young adults. Bat-Ami won first prize in the CELERY Short Story Award for "Nielah," and, in 1999, she received the Scott O'Dell Award for Historical Fiction for *Two Suns in the Sky*. She continues to write and to travel around the country and speak to school groups, using her experience researching and writing *Two Suns in the Sky* to teach young writers about the investigative work necessary to write historical fiction.

◆ OVERVIEW ◆

Two Suns in the Sky is both a historical telling of the Jews' plight in post-World

Miriam Bat-Ami

War II America and a love story between two fifteen-year-olds, Christine (Chris) Cook, a Catholic American, and Adam Bornstein, a Jewish Holocaust survivor from Yugoslavia. Adam and his family live with nearly a thousand other refugees in Fort Ontario, a refugee camp in Oswego, New York, and Chris lives in the town of Oswego, among narrow-minded and prejudiced people, like her father, who feel a hostility toward the refugees and a hatred of their culture. Bat-Ami's book is about a culture clash, and it chronicles the tense relations between Jews and Americans at a place and time in history when both groups had to struggle to reconcile two worlds. Chris and Adam ignore the culture clash and create a world of their own when Chris sneaks into the camp, meets Adam, and the two begin a passionate romance. Chris and Adam are not unlike other fictional star-crossed lovers: Romeo

and Juliet, Catherine and Heathcliff, Pyramus and Thisbe, and Tony and Maria. Their love transcends cultures and religions, and the story of their struggle touches the hearts of anyone wishing to believe in the power of love and hoping to find acceptance and tolerance in a prejudiced world.

◆ SETTING ◆

Bat-Ami sets her story in a refugee shelter at Fort Ontario in Oswego, New York. This was a real refugee center, but a little-known one, established by the United States government in the fall of 1944 to house about one thousand refugees from Italy and help these people escape from Hitler's persecution. The novel begins in the last year of World War II, after Italy has been liberated and the Jewish people have been released. But Adam and the other Jews who left Rome for the shelter in America find nothing liberating about living in the refugee camp in a country they believed to be "the home of the free." Chris and Adam find that persecution against the Jews continues in America, and they discover that they are in for quite a battle as they attempt to nurture a love amidst prejudice and intolerance.

The refugee camp of *Two Suns in the Sky* is bleak and grim, and in sharp contrast to the love Chris and Adam share. Both of them live in a gray world until they come together; Chris lives outside the camp, but sneaks in and falls in love with Adam. She is as susceptible to cultural intolerance as Adam, whose life behind a barbed wire fence attests to the hypocrisy in the notion of freedom in America. Hazel Rochman in her review of Bat-Ami's book in *Booklist* refers to *Two Suns in the Sky* as documentary fiction. Both the realistic setting of the story and the author's note document the political environment at the end of the war, with Bat-Ami using actual camp records and quotes from President Roosevelt, the refugees, and townspeople to add historical significance to the text.

◆ THEMES AND CHARACTERS ◆

Two Suns in the Sky is a complex novel in which Bat-Ami spins a poignant love story that captures the culture clash characteristic of post-World War II America. Chris Cook is a Catholic girl who lives in Oswego, New York, and Adam Bornstein is a Yugoslavian Jew who fled to Rome under threat of persecution, then escaped to America after Italy was liberated. The lives and experiences of these two characters could not be more different. But though Chris and Adam come from different worlds, they experience universal emotions.

The first chapter begins with Chris, and we find out quickly that she is bored living in a small town and that she is experiencing the restlessness typical of fifteen-year-old girls. She longs for adventure, she longs for romance. Chris says that she is fed up with the boys her age and that she wants someone older and more mature. "I want to really be kissed," she says. Bat-Ami lets us know right away that Chris is on the brink, ready to do something. She is ready to express strong emotion, to feel something passionately, to fall in love.

When Adam enters the story he, too, is on the brink. He is ready to explore new worlds, both literally and figuratively. He is ready to define himself in news ways and to explore his sexual and cultural identity. Adam is just fifteen, like Chris, but he has experienced pain to last a lifetime and he knows war from the inside. Adam is confused by America, and Chris is intrigued by the strangers in her town and fascinated with the war she knows little about.

Two Suns in the Sky is a coming-of-age novel, so in the book Bat-Ami dissects the teenage psyche. She allows Chris and Adam to reveal their thoughts and dreams and, in doing so, she reveals universal concerns while contrasting the American teenager with a teenager touched deeply by war. Adam worries about his missing relatives and he agonizes over living in secrecy, whereas Chris worries about her annoying parents and agonizes over what kind of clothes to buy. It is clear, though, that these two young people are open to new perspectives and capable of understanding ways of life different from their own. Poised on the edge of childhood and adulthood, they are easily moldable; their attitudes about life and love are not yet developed enough to restrict them from moving the world.

Faced with the possibility of exploring foreign concepts, Chris and Adam suddenly find the world a new and intriguing place. Chris feels curious and captivated with the refugees as Adam feels curious and captivated with the Americans. The willingness of these teenagers to explore each other's world lets us know that Bat-Ami's vision extends far beyond the narrow-mindedness of the townspeople. All of the people of Oswego get excited when the refugee camp opens, but many of them have already been tainted by prejudice and have decided that these immigrants do not belong in their town. Bat-Ami uses Chris's father as a model of the American bigot. He warns his daughter to stay away from the refugees, and he refers to them as "somebody else's dirt." If at first Chris appears to be in danger of becoming narrow-minded and materialistic like her father, we quickly realize that she is simply naïve and has no understanding of human suffering. Chris feels compelled to sneak down to the camp and find out what these people are all about. That is when she meets Adam, and she is instantly captivated with him.

Eventually, Adam and the other refugees are allowed to leave the camp and go to the local school, and the relationship between Adam and Chris escalates. Though both of these young people are fascinated by the unknown and willing to explore each other's world, they live in an intolerant society, and encounter numerous barriers—barriers they need to break in order to explore their own sexuality and their own racial and religious identity. Chris's parents are strict Catholics and Adam's parents are Jewish. Chris's father is narrow-minded and controlling, and he forbids his daughter from seeing Adam. At one point he strikes her and he kicks Chris out of the house. But because love knows no bounds, she sees Adam anyway. Both of these young adults are at a crossroads in life and, like any adolescent, eager to broaden their horizons. Both Adam and Chris want excitement and independence, and as they venture out on their own to find these things, they develop a bond that bridges cultures and religions.

To Chris's father, and to all the people he represents, Jews and Catholics should remain separate, like night and day, sun and moon. The refugees should remain inside the fence that surrounds their camp, and the Americans should remain outside it. But Chris and Adam both feel trapped on their side of the fence; Chris feels trapped in the boring life of Oswego and Adam feels trapped in the camp. Feeling trapped is one theme Bat-Ami advances in the novel. As these young teenagers keep encountering metaphorical fences that keep them confined in separate worlds, they become more and more determined to break down the barriers and to find holes under the fences.

Chris and Adam add freshness to this novel by introducing the promise of love in a world full of hatred. In their search for love, they romanticize the world, so what Bat-Ami wishes to convey here is the power of love in a more general sense. What could be more contrasting than love and war? If love knows no bounds, and if Chris and Adam represent separate identities, then the love that Chris and Adam share represents not just a bond between two people, but a bond between two cultures and two religions. This is their dream for a postwar America. It begs the question of whether the love of two hopeful teenagers can survive in the postwar world as it truly is, not in the postwar world of their dreams.

In telling her story, Bat-Ami contrasts the real with the ideal, the optimistic with the disenchanted. Her subplots involving Chris's and Adam's lives clarify the contrast between worldviews. The war means different things to Chris than to Adam. To Chris the war is "an abstraction"—something that happened "over there" that she could easily ignore because it never touched her life in any significant way. To a large extent, Chris romanticized the war, just as Adam romanticized America. Though Adam and Chris have vastly different pasts and therefore vastly different life-views, the bond they share allows them to influence each other and broaden each other's perspectives. Though in the end, the two characters move in separate directions, the relationship they shared changed them forever. They found a commonality among difference, recognized the likeness in divergent worlds. It must have been Bat-Ami's intent to introduce this possibility. As Martha Walke says in her review of the book for *Horn Book Magazine*, "the relationship Chris and Adam shared led them to an understanding of who they are, what they mean to each other, and what they want in a postwar world." What they want is what they saw when they opened themselves up to each other—not a sun and moon, but two suns in the sky.

◆ LITERARY QUALITIES ◆

Bat-Ami manages to present both sides of the immigrant issue—that of the American residents and that of the refugees—by telling her story in two first-person narratives. She relates the American viewpoint in the voice of Chris, and she relates the immigrant viewpoint in the voice of Adam. The story therefore unfolds in alternating perspectives, and the individual voices of the two main characters are as distinct and diverse as their cultures, their language, and their religion. Bat-Ami seems to have a talent for creating realistic dialogue, and she uses that talent to give depth and substance to her characters. Using two first person narratives not only gives readers insight into the private thoughts of both an American citizen and a Jewish refugee, but it allows Bat-Ami to explain the culture clash that permeates the novel and defines the political environment of the time she revisits.

Bat-Ami's novel is both a historical documentary fiction novel and a tale of personal experience. She allows Chris and Adam to tell their stories, but then she intertwines the plots. She also embellishes her story with quotations from former residents of the refugee camp and from President Roosevelt. These quotations, as well as a detailed Author's Note, place the novel in historical perspective. Bat-Ami's gift for characterization, her realistic dialogue, and her sense of drama all add to the book's authenticity.

The story of Chris and Adam emerges as a realistic portrayal of youthful optimism as well as a realistic account of historical strife and the isolation the Jewish refugees experienced when they arrived in the New

Book jacket illustration by Hilary Mosberg for *Two Suns in the Sky* by Miriam Bat-Ami.

World. The love between Chris and Adam transcends the boundaries that relegate them to separate worlds. The existence of such boundaries revolves around the symbolism of the fence. The fence is the most prominent symbol in the novel, and the first image of America the refugees encounter when they arrive at the camp. Bat-Ami describes the barbed wire and the armed guards surrounding the refugee center, and she makes it clear that the immigrants recognize this place from the disturbingly similar concentration camps in Europe. Arriving at the refugee center and seeing the fence lead the Jewish refugees to the painful conclusion that their dream of finding freedom in America is only an illusion. In reality, they left one set of barriers only to encounter a new one, and though they did

Two Suns in the Sky

manage to escape Hitler's persecution, they could never escape their feelings of isolation.

The symbolism of the fence extends beyond the refugee camp to the town, where the residents of Oswego put up other metaphorical fences to separate themselves from the immigrants. Chris and Adam both feel fenced in by their separate worlds, and language, religion, family, and society are all metaphorical fences that keep Chris and Adam apart. But determined lovers can scale fences, and they can find ways to break barriers. Chris and Adam use the hole under the fence that surrounds the refugee center to sneak in and out of the camp.

The image of two suns in the sky appears to refer to the commonality of separate worlds, and Chris and Adam find those two suns. On the boat to America, Adam recalls a legend his father told him when Adam witnessed a sunset and believed the sun and the moon to be two suns: "On the water was a reflection of the setting sun. In the sky was the rising moon, which appeared orange because of the sun's reflection shining back on it. With the orange moon rising and the sun descending, there seemed to be two suns in the sky." Adam continues: "Then I was reminded of a legend Papa once told Villi and me: A man who sees two suns in the sky is never the same."

◆ SOCIAL SENSITIVITY ◆

Bat-Ami's book takes one group of people victimized by ethnic cleansing and explores their experiences adjusting to life in America. But in using this one example— the Jews at Fort Ontario—she underscores the difficulty all groups of people victimized by ethnic cleansing experience when they encounter American intolerance. From Bat-Ami's story, readers can make generalizations about America's attitude toward immigrants and refugees and form their own opinions as to how this attitude affects the development of a multicultural nation. Many groups of people came to America expecting to live in a free land, but their dreams were shattered. True, they did attain freedom from Hitler, or from mass extermination from any dictator, but they would never be truly free from prejudice. In America, as well as in Europe, these refugees felt like second-class citizens.

Bat-Ami addresses the reality of American intolerance by making Chris's father an example of the American bigot. He hates anything foreign, anything different from himself, yet he seems to justify his prejudice toward the Jews because he lives in America and not in Germany. Chris's father helps explain American attitudes during World War II, and Bat-Ami explains the effects this attitude had on the Jewish immigrants. She shows sensitivity to the plight of the Jews by revealing Adam's inner thoughts, and she introduces the possibility of a tolerant nation by emphasizing Chris's willingness to share her thoughts and her love with Adam.

Bat-Ami is a natural teacher, and she has succeeded in writing a thought-provoking novel that instructs without being moralistic. She has always been sensitive to differences in people and cultures, so she created characters like Chris and Adam who show that same sensitivity and who embody the hope of a tolerant nation. Chris and Adam manage to find the commonality between them and they learn from each other's life experiences. By focusing on their love in the face of hatred, Bat-Ami fosters an acceptance of other worlds and a sensitivity toward other cultures and other ways of life.

To help readers accept diversity and work toward becoming a truly multicultural nation, it is essential that Bat-Ami define the political environment of the times. She explores the refugee issue sensitively, revealing not only the thoughts and attitudes of

Chris and Adam, but also of the other Jews in the camp, of Chris's father, and of the townspeople in Oswego. Probing the views of all these people brings to light sociopolitical issues that urge readers to examine their own views about tolerance. Her book stimulates people to think about how immigrants feel when they come to America struggling to be free and yearning to affirm their cultural identity in a prejudiced society. Chris, in her love for Adam, affirms his Jewishness and disregards stereotypes. The struggle of these two people to unite leads them not only to accept diversity, but also to better understand themselves. Chris and Adam embody the ideal of a world where people from diverse cultures can overcome their prejudices and transcend socioreligious hatred and other conflicts. By making her story a love story, Bat-Ami's poignant message rings clear—we must all search for what binds us together rather than dwell on what drives us apart.

◆ TOPICS FOR DISCUSSION ◆

1. What attracts Chris to the refugee camp?

2. Discuss the various groups of people victimized by ethnic cleansing.

3. Why do you suppose that few people knew about the refugee camp in Oswego?

4. Do you think that the Jews who came to America and lived in the refugee center considered themselves Americans? Why or why not?

5. How does Christine's father justify his attitude toward the Jews?

6. Who acts more maturely in the novel, the young adult protagonists or their parents? Explain the definition of maturity you consider in answering this question.

7. Was the outcome of Chris and Adam's relationship predictable? Why or why not?

8. What significance does Mira play in the story?

◆ IDEAS FOR REPORTS AND PAPERS ◆

1. Write a comparison of the romance between Chris and Adam and either Shakespeare's Romeo and Juliet, or Tony and Maria from West Side Story. Discuss the forces that tear them apart and the forces that bring them together.

2. Contrast Adam's view of World War II with Chris's view.

3. Clearly, Adam and Christine come from backgrounds that could not be more different. Do they find common ground? Detail the similarities these teenagers share when it appears that their differences are overpowering.

4. Discuss point of view in Two Suns in the Sky. Do you think the story would be as poignant if Bat-Ami chose to tell her story from one perspective—either Chris's or Adam's? Why or why not?

5. Compare the Jewish immigrant experience in the Oswego refugee camp to the Japanese experience in and after their stay in internment camps.

6. Compare the Jewish immigrant experience during World War II with the Albanian refugee experience, wherein thousands of refugees are arriving in America from Kosovo.

7. The Emergency Refugee Center at Fort Ontario (that is, the Jewish refugee camp in Oswego) is not well known. Research the camp and write a paper that captures the experiences of the immigrants who resided there.

8. Discuss the symbolism of fences in the novel.

9. Compare the Jewish experience in concentration camps in Europe to the Jewish experience in the refugee camp in Oswego.

10. How would you compare America's treatment of the Jewish refugees with homeless people? Do you feel they are both homeless?

11. How did the refugee experience contribute to the establishment of the state of Israel?

◆ RELATED TITLES ◆

Perhaps the title most closely related to *Two Suns in the Sky* is *Good Night, Maman,* by Norma Fox Mazer. Like Bat-Ami, Mazer focuses on the camp in Oswego, but Mazer tells the refugee story through the eyes of Karin Levi, who had to leave Europe without her ailing mother or her father, who was captive at Auschwitz. In first-person narrative, Mazer discusses Karin's wartime experiences: her escape to America, her arrival at Oswego, and her struggle to adjust to American culture while dealing with the pain of leaving loved ones behind. Other young adult novels that help bring the Holocaust into focus include *The Diary of Anne Frank,* Lois Lowry's *Number the Stars,* and Ida Vos's *Anna Is Still Here* and *Dancing on the Bridge of Avignon.* The protagonists in all of these books are Jewish, and they all recount their experiences of persecution by the Nazi regime.

Another book that focuses on the immigrant experience is *The Melting Pot: An Adventure in New York,* a novel set at the turn of the century that recounts the life of a young Russian immigrant in New York. Sonia Levitin's *Journey to America* and its two sequels, *Silver Days* and *Annie's Prom-*

ise, tell the story of a young girl named Lisa Platt and the hardships she experiences escaping from Berlin, then living in Switzerland during the Nazi era and waiting with her mother and two sisters for her father to come and get her. *Farewell to Manzanar* by Jeanne and James Houston *and No-No Boy* by John Okada talk about the wartime experiences of Japanese Americans who were imprisoned in internment camps during the war then, like the Jews, were released into a prejudiced, intolerant society that treated them like second-class citizens.

◆ FOR FURTHER REFERENCE ◆

Clarke, Kate. Review of *Two Suns in the Sky. Book Report* (November/December 1999): 57.

Contemporary Authors, vol. 150. Detroit: Gale, 1996.

Morning, Todd. Review of *Two Suns in the Sky. School Library Journal* (July 1999): 92.

Roback, Diane, Jennifer M. Brown, and Cindi De Marzo. Review of *Two Suns in the Sky. Publishers Weekly* (May 17, 1999): 92.

Rochman, Hazel. Review of *Two Suns in the Sky. Booklist* (April 15, 1999): 1523.

Something about the Author, vol. 82. Detroit: Gale, 1995.

Walke, Martha. Review of *Two Suns in the Sky. Horn Book* (July 1999): 460–461.

Tamra Andrews

THE VOYAGE OF THE SPACE BEAGLE

Novel

1950

Author: A. E. van Vogt

Major Books for Young Adults

Slan, 1946
The Voyage of the Space Beagle, 1950
Triad: The Voyage of the Space Beagle,
    Slan, The World of A, 1959
The Silkie, 1973

◆ ABOUT THE AUTHOR ◆

Alfred Elton van Vogt was born April 26, 1912 on a farm near Winnipeg, Manitoba, Canada, the son of Henry van Vogt, an attorney, and Agnes (Buhr) van Vogt, a homemaker. His father seems to have been unstable financially and the writer's early life was marked by frequent migrations to and from various towns and villages in Saskatchewan and Manitoba.

Young Alfred was an enthusiastic reader of fairy tales until he was twelve, when a teacher's sarcastic comment made him ashamed of his taste in literature. When Alfred was fourteen, the family returned to Winnipeg. The shock of city life turned him into an introvert. He read two books a day for years, mostly detective stories.

Because of the family's poverty, young Alfred was unable to go to college, but he educated himself as best he could by haphazard but wide and intense reading—as many as five hundred books a year. He later studied at the University of Ottawa and the University of California.

Van Vogt began writing while employed in Ottawa by the Canadian census bureau in 1931. His early ambition was to win one of the prizes offered by McFadden's *True Story* magazine, and, in fact, it was not long before he had received a prize of $1,000, an amount equal to his yearly salary as an employee of the census bureau. Despite this reward and his understandable euphoria, he developed a revulsion against this type of fiction and turned to other ways of making a living. Among these was the writing of plays for Canadian radio, for which he received about $10 each—making a total of only $600 for fifty plays, a sum which included bonuses and some resales in the United States.

Perhaps not many would have said at this point that van Vogt had much future as a writer. But in 1938, in McKnight's Drugstore in Winnipeg, he casually picked up the August issue of *Astounding Stories* and read the first half of a novella by Don A. Stuart. He wrote the editor, John W. Campbell, Jr., not knowing that Campbell was himself the author of "Who Goes There?", and briefly outlined a story more or less inspired by it. Campbell replied with words of encouragement and advice and subsequently accepted "Vault of the Beast," although he wisely withheld it until some stronger pieces by the new writer had been published.

Shortly after this, in 1939 van Vogt married Edna Mayne Hull, daughter of a Canadian economist and herself a writer, and they began living what was to be for some time a precarious existence. Canada was already at war with Germany, and van Vogt was drawn into service as a clerk for the government, working long days and weeks for barely subsistence wages, and writing *Slan* in the late evening hours.

A. E. van Vogt was recognized as a major science fiction talent with the publication of his first story, "Black Destroyer"—later to become part of *The Voyage of the Space Beagle*—in the July 1939 issue of *Astounding*. This verdict was confirmed the following year when his first novel, *Slan*, was serialized in the same magazine.

Within a year and a half he had become an important figure in science fiction, the only writer at that time approximating the stature of Robert A. Heinlein; and, after Heinlein had left to fight in World War II, van Vogt easily and happily dominated *Astounding*, the most important science fiction magazine of its day, for several years.

After the acceptance of *Slan*, van Vogt quit his job and began slowly but very industriously to turn out stories for *Astounding*. He wrote by the Gallishaw method: in 800-word scenes, the action in each developing through five carefully delineated steps. This technique was much discussed in the 1940s and 1950s, perhaps because, in contrast to the vague statements offered by other writers about their methods of composition, it could be discussed. The method sounds mechanical, but van Vogt supplemented it with work habits that were anything but prosaic. Like some writers, he slept on his stories, but, unlike those others, he purposely dreamed them—he would awaken himself every hour and a half during the night with an alarm clock to fix the new incidents in his mind.

Slan, published as a book in 1946, is still widely regarded as a classic, and continues to be the mainstay of his fame.

Van Vogt's second published novel, *The Weapon Makers*, was serialized in 1943 and published as a book in 1947. This story did not engage the interest and affections of readers to the same extent as his first novel, but it was good-humored, colorful, and uninhibitedly inventive.

In 1944 the van Vogts moved to Los Angeles, and the number of van Vogt's publications fell off in 1945 because he was at work on a 90,000-word serial, *World of A*. Editor John W. Campbell spoke of this novel as "one of the truly great stories of science fiction," and he was never careless with his praise. But for the first time, dissenting voices were heard and antagonistic reviews appeared.

A. E. van Vogt's science fiction career divides into two distinct phases: the period when he was published in *Astounding* science fiction magazine (1939–1950) and the modern period (1962–present). During the gap from 1950 to 1962, he was heavily involved in dianetics, a system of psychology invented by the science fiction writer L. Ron Hubbard, who later founded the Church of Scientology. He was the first managing director of the Hubbard Dianetic Research Foundation of California, Los Angeles from 1950–53, and co-owner of the Hubbard Dianetic Center in Los Angeles from 1953–61. Van Vogt had only one wholly new work published during this time, *The Mind Cage* (1957), but he also released several "fix-up novels," as he terms them: magazine pieces stitched together to form more or less coherent narratives. He became a naturalized American citizen in 1952.

He returned to full-scale writing in 1962, with the publication of *The Violent Man,* a book that is not science fiction but was of crucial importance in the development of his career. It was meant to expose the psychogenesis of violence, a subject he felt to be of such importance that the book would necessarily become a best-seller. But, though the book was carefully constructed and undoubtedly his most serious piece of writing, his hopes for it were not realized. Instead, van Vogt returned to science fiction with some rather safe and unadventurous magazine pieces. He wrote a series of paperback novels, most of which were published in the 1970s, reflecting his growing preoccupation with the nature of violence. This seemed to be a topic of inexhaustible interest to this gentle man who said in many fanzine interviews that he turned inward and to writing because of the remorse he suffered when, at the age of seventeen, he pursued and killed a harmless snake.

Van Vogt was still writing in the 1980s. He not only produced four new books from 1978 through 1980, but set about learning what seemed to be virtually every language of this planet. He was a Founder of the 200 Language Club in 1974.

His first wife died in 1975; he later married Lydia I. Brayman (a linguist and superior court interpreter) in 1979. Van Vogt died of Alzheimer's disease on January 26, 2000, in Los Angeles, California and is buried in Holy Cross Cemetery, Culver City, California.

◆ OVERVIEW ◆

As the novel begins, Coeurl is prowling his desolate planet looking for food. The arrival of beings in a spaceship, beings who can be his food, inspires ravenous hunger.

The beings are humans on a scientific expedition. They are curious about this vaguely cat-like alien and carefully bring the caged alien into their ship. On board, the alien proceeds to kill as many of the humans as it can, and to take over the engine room. The ship is saved only after one of the crew, the Nexial Science department head Grosvenor, devises a plan to trick Coeurl into stealing a lifeboat. The alien is fooled into following the ship instead of returning to his own planet, and commits suicide rather than be destroyed.

The Space Beagle is a ship staffed with nearly a thousand men, travelling from Earth on a deep exploration mission through our Milky Way galaxy and beyond it. The crew intend to spend four or five years travelling before eventually returning to Earth, but only half of these exploration missions return. Grosvenor is the first Nexial scientist to be sent on this type of mission, in hopes that his integrated knowledge of all sciences may improve the odds for survival.

The attrition rate may be understandable, not only because of internal politics but also because the number of dangerous alien races seems particularly high. While Grosvenor is coping with a rival science department head, the ship must cope with what appears to be a mental attack from telepathic aliens. Grosvenor has to invent a way to communicate with the aliens, who are actually friendly and peaceful, and tell the Riim to quit sending these confusing telepathic images—or else the captain will steer the spaceship into a star to keep it out of the hands of the scientists fighting him for control.

The humans have barely settled their dispute over who will be director of the mission when they meet another alien. Ixtl (as it calls itself) has been marooned in intergalactic space for an immeasureable amount of time. This tough, strong alien has survived unprotected in space, and one of the crew calls it a "blood-red devil spawned out of a nightmare." When the crew traps the alien Ixtl and brings it into the ship to be examined, Ixtl moves freely through the ship, walking at will through bulkheads, decks and everything but the dense outer shell of the ship. Ixtl kills some crew members and takes others as host incubators for its eggs. The humans' only hope is to follow Grosvenor's plan: to evacuate the ship and irradiate it. Ixtl escapes the radiation to drift once again in intergalactic space, unaware that the humans have returned to their ship.

On arrival at the next galaxy, M31, the crew becomes aware of the Anabis, a planet-changing alien which modifies planets so that they will be covered with dense jungles of living plants and animals. The alien, in the form of a gaseous cloud suffusing the entire galaxy, then envelops the planet and consumes all the life. It wishes, driven by the tropism of hunger, to follow the humans' spaceship to their own galaxy and graze there. Grosvenor devises a plan to trick it into following them in the direction of an impossibly distant galaxy until it starves; then the humans will return to their own galaxy in about five years. He applies all the persuasions of his Nexialist training, and not only is given his way, but begins a successful series of lectures teaching the Nexialist methods to his fellow scientists,

including the department head who used to be his rival and enemy.

◆ SETTING ◆

The novel takes place in deep outer space, after months of travel from Earth's own solar system. The characters are travelling in a space ship among star systems across the Milky Way galaxy, and even to the neighbouring galaxy, M31, in Andromeda.

The Space Beagle is a spaceship of grand proportions, larger than any aircraft carrier which actually existed at the end of the twentieth century, but smaller than the fictional "Death Star" from the *Star Wars* movies. The duties of only a few characters are described, or even sketched out, among the crew of 180 officers and soldiers and 804 scientists.

The planets and beings encountered by the crew of the Space Beagle are intended to be plausible, scientific speculations of what could possibly be discovered during such a journey. The places and cultures described are also intended to be interesting and educational for the reader. A great deal of facts, as well as the author's opinions, are inserted into every scenic description of ruined cities or analysis of the motives of tentacled aliens.

With courageous explorers moving their high-tech equipment from planet to planet as easily as an automobile is driven, the novel is easy to identify as a classic example of pulp fiction published serially in America before World War II, and as a seminal influence upon the space opera sub-genre of science fiction writing. The reader will be overwhelmingly aware that all post-1950 films and television series set on a spaceship are at least as heavily influenced by *The Voyage of the Space Beagle* as van Vogt was influenced by Jules Verne's *Voyage to the Moon* and *Twenty Thousand Leagues Under the Sea.*

◆ THEMES AND CHARACTERS ◆

The only character well fleshed out in this novel is Elliot Grosvenor (pronounced ell-yot grow-venn-er), sometimes called Grove by his crewmates. He is some five or six years younger than any other science department head on the Space Beagle, perhaps thirty-five years old, and that is the only physical characteristic which the reader is told about him. Apparently he is healthy, strong and active, as would be expected of any astronaut.

All the other crewmates exist as foils for Grosvenor to interact with; they are knowledgeable in only one field, helpful or interfering as they see fit, and all of them are eventually deeply impressed by Grosvenor's Nexial training.

What the reader is told about Grosvenor is that he has been thoroughly trained in Nexialism, or to understand all the sciences. The author seems to have intended to impress the reader with Grosvenor's analytical ability, rather than inform the reader with the knowledge of how to be so capable and well-trained.

In short, Grosvenor's character is like that of Mr. Spock or Data from the *Star Trek* television series, and he is probably at least as hard to get along with as either of them. Like them though, he does have some friends. Grosvenor has only good intentions for everyone on board his ship. He never misuses his knowledge and talents to gain any personal benefits. It may seem that he does, in the latter part of the novel, when Grosvenor takes over the entire ship and applies his persuasive techniques for a short while; but he does so only to ensure that the crew will seriously consider his methods to defeat the current alien menace and save

the ship. Then Grosvenor gives up control of the ship. He is, of course, achieving the goal he was placed on the ship to do: keep the people alive in the face of great danger, and teach them Nexialism while doing so. He has always been working toward this goal, all along.

In this novel van Vogt originated and explored ideas and themes that have since become mainstays of science fiction writing. Donald A. Wolheim says of van Vogt:

> From the first, his stories have concerned themselves with extraordinary powers, with new concepts in science or in mental gymnastics, and he constantly seems to strive to create new systems of thought and mental order which will permit the creation of supermen.

"Fascination with a system of thought—in this case, general semantics—is characteristic of van Vogt's writing," says Jeffrey M. Elliot. It is an attempt to explain the thought process that goes on in a person's mind when a word is spoken or heard. In this novel, Grosvenor has learned a great deal of science by verbal means, through hypnotic instruction and subliminal recordings when he is asleep. He is quite capable of manipulating his crewmates through overt application of words, sounds, hypnotic gases and assorted technology. He is far less effective at affecting his crewmates' behavior through mere conversation or displaying a poster.

There is a strong theme throughout *The Voyage of the Space Beagle*, which is reinforced every time the ship meets an alien being. That theme is rejection and hatred of the female.

The spaceship is crewed entirely by men—nearly a thousand of them, all given drugs to reduce their sex drive. This is emotionally unsatisfying, though, and the reader is told baldly early in the book that the men's favorite topic of conversation at breakfast and lunch is to discuss women and sex. They do not describe these women in positive terms, though; as one of the men puts it: "What defenseless woman's character shall we assassinate today?" That is the only time women are mentioned at all during the course of the novel, except when Grosvenor plays a mind-control machine which makes a man remember his mother—a technique Grosvenor discards as too manipulative.

This alone is not unusual for a pulp science fiction novel written in the 1930s or 1940s. But the ship is not referred to as "she." Not only are there no women in this novel, but the aliens are not referred to as female either. Male pronouns are used for Coeurl and Ixtl, and the Riim and the Anabis are called "it." This in spite of the fact that Ixtl is an egg-layer, the Riim reproduce by parthenogenetic budding (reproduction by development of an unfertilized, usually female, gamete [germ cell] that occurs especially among lower plants and invertebrate animals), the Anabis envelops the objects of its desire, and Coeurl is a feline, graceful being actually named *pussy* by the crew of the Space Beagle.

These alien beings have many feminine characteristics, and it is at least in part because of these feminine characteristics that the men of the Space Beagle want to kill every alien being they meet. It is only with disappointment that they leave Coeurl's people to starve to death on their planet; the crew would much rather go back and kill them all. The crew is similarly disappointed that they cannot blame the Riim sufficiently for causing insurrection on board the Space Beagle with telepathic messages; there really is no excuse to go back and kill them all. Ixtl and the Anabis are stranded in intergalactic space to starve—only because they are too hard to kill by shooting.

Ultimately, *The Voyage of the Space Beagle* is the story of a boy's clubhouse travelling through space with a metaphorical sign saying "No Girls Allowed" hung from each of the (non-metaphorical) weapons.

Many critics find van Vogt's later work less impressive than *The Voyage of the Space Beagle* and other pieces which he did for *Astounding* in the 1940s. Various stylistic oddities tend to detract from the story line. The author himself explained to Jeffrey Elliot:

> For years, until the 1960s, I consciously wrote pulp-style sentences. They have a certain lush poetry in them. In the late 1960s, I began to concentrate on content and even allowed my protagonist to be neurotic, also. However, these current stories don't seem to win the same approval as when I followed the earlier system.

Elliot is not alone in his assertion that

> there are few science fiction writers alive today who can boast the singular achievements of A. E. Van Vogt, a long-time talent in the field, who has spent his lifetime giving meaning and import to the shape of things to come.

◆ LITERARY QUALITIES ◆

The Voyage of the Space Beagle was a popular novel when it was published, because it combined interesting scientific speculations with a plot that leapt from crisis to crisis, written in the plain language style of the Golden Age science fiction pulp magazines. The novel's flat characterization and Anglo-American-centered worldview were expected by the editors and writers of that time. It is no longer as popular, because the dialogue has very little emotion or personal content; this and the abrupt transitions from scene to scene make this novel old-fashioned.

Readers may find this novel emotionally flat and didactic. The author tends to "tell" the reader that actions have happened, instead of "showing" the reader what is happening through the thoughts and reactions of the characters. A few energetic fight scenes and high-tech tools are no longer enough to keep the attention of most young readers engaged for an entire book.

As one of the influential works of sociological science fiction, this was primarily a novel of ideas, in which the author showcased several science concepts without cluttering up the narrative with too many motivations or metaphors. *The Voyage of the Space Beagle* has spawned many intellectual grandchildren. But during the more than sixty years since "Black Destroyer" (the first published portion of the novel) appeared in print, there have been several literary movements in the science fiction genre. Sociological science fiction published in the twenty-first century now relies considerably more on characterization, foreshadowing and symbolism than can be found in van Vogt's first novel.

Van Vogt's decline in popularity may have been caused by many of his stories of recent years not having the same degree of narrative interest as his early ones. Arthur Coax suggests in a biographical essay that van Vogt had become

> more and more interested in conveying his ideas to the reader, and the result is a loss of narrative credibility that causes the startling transitions and violent actions of the plots sometimes to seem insufficiently motivated and therefore out of focus or even comic.

The genesis of this later trend in van Vogt's writing can be seen even in this first novel, in which the violent actions and startling transitions do at times seem insufficiently motivated. The author is conveying science ideas instead of making his narrative credible. It is hard for a reader to summon up fear for the survival of the crew of the Beagle when few of them have names or distinguishing habits, and they endure successive attacks by aliens instead of making useful discoveries.

◆ SOCIAL SENSITIVITY ◆

Teachers using this novel in a classroom must be acutely aware that the first alien met by the crew of the Space Beagle is named *pussy* by them. There will be no escaping the scorn and hilarity of adolescents, an understandable reaction. There was no need for the author to use this particular word with its associated obscene and denigrating meanings when naming a beast which appears vaguely feline in shape: in 1939, "kitty" was used at least as often to name cats in print and in polite conversation. The author, who never spent time in the company of men at a university, in the Armed Forces or the work force, clearly was unfamiliar with the common, informal vocabulary of grown men. He may be excused for his inexperience, but his editor can be blamed for perpetrating the woman-hating theme of this novel through bad editing.

In this novel, the reader can see all the essential traits of van Vogt's writing throughout his career, and even his later obsession with ethics and violence.

In his latter years, van Vogt no longer wrote in the action/adventure style as he did in *The Voyage of the Space Beagle,* when that style of pulp science fiction writing was popular. It seems that during the years of his absence from the field of science fiction publishing, van Vogt's involvement with dianetics brought him into contact with questions concerning the health and happiness of human beings. Contact with a bustling movement addressing itself to matters of large import changed his perspective. He could not go back, innocently, to writing pulp-magazine stories. He was troubled by the feeling that such "unreality writing" is "aberrated."

But there was a way in which science fiction could be worthy —it could become a vehicle for his ideas. By suggesting to the reader something of the underlying dynamics of life and the universe, van Vogt could affect him in a more basic and permanent way. Van Vogt is quoted as saying in Arthur Coax's biographical essay:

> My feeling is, that once a reader has read any science fiction of mine, his brain will no longer be the same. That's my mark on the sands of time; several million readers all over the world changed (for better or worse—I think for better) without their even noticing it.

In numerous magazine interviews, van Vogt claimed immortality as a writer—based on the quality of his fiction of ideas, his speculations on the psychology of violence, the character of women, and the politics of totalitarianism. Even the misogynistic theme of *The Voyage of the Space Beagle* can be read as feminist in that it regards females as active, powerful characters in a narrative, and that it gives any consideration at all to the existence of females (unlike much pulp fiction of the 1930s and 1940s). His insistence on the idea component of his work invests him, as a science-fiction writer, with a peculiar authenticity. His life as a writer and his life as a man are linked by the ideas which dominated his later writing. But his most striking work results from his translating figurative ideas into literal realities; and he is remembered above all else as the author of *Slan, The World of Null-A,* and *The Voyage of the Space Beagle.*

◆ TOPICS FOR DISCUSSION ◆

1. Where have you heard before of a ship full of men going into uncharted regions, looking for knowledge?

2. How is this journey different from others you have heard about? Is the futuristic setting the important difference? Is the fictional element the important difference?

3. What do these travellers intend to accomplish on their journey?

4. What is revealed to the reader through the story, which may not be part of the traveller's intended goals?

5. Why does the story focus on Grosvenor rather than the Captain or the Director?

6. What is Grosvenor's major accomplishment during the voyage? Is it overt or subtle?

7. Why does the author tell the reader so little about his characters? Is it hard to guess how these men look, sound, dress or move?

8. How does the crew react to crisis situations?

9. How does Grosvenor react to opposition? How does he behave in a crisis?

10. Can you make any guesses about why half of the interstellar expeditions sent out in the last two hundred years have not returned?

◆ IDEAS FOR REPORTS AND PAPERS ◆

1. Who was Darwin? What voyage did he make? Is van Vogt drawing any comparisons between the journey of his character Grosvenor and the voyage that Darwin made? What were the goals of Darwin and Grosvenor, and what did they achieve during their travels?

2. The process of democratic elections being held aboard the Space Beagle during the course of this novel are more reminiscent of votes held aboard pirate ships in the Caribbean and the South Seas than like the power structure in the ships of the British Navy. Are the

explorers on this spacecraft really privateers seeking plunder and personal gain, or are they soldiers on a reconnaissance mission? Explain.

3. Grosvenor behaves as though he wishes to be treated like a scientist and scholar, dedicated to sharing knowledge and learning whatever he can. Does he actually live up to the idealized image of himself which he tries to present? Are his motives as pure as he tries to make them? What disparity is there between his actions and his stated goals?

4. Compare Kurt Vonnegut's novel *Breakfast of Champions* with A. E. van Vogt's novel *The Voyage of the Space Beagle*. What elements of science fiction are employed by one, or both, of these authors? How important is technology in each of these novels? What is the reader intended by the author to learn about human nature in each of these novels? What is your own reaction to the author's voice in these novels? Do you find the writing style of Vonnegut or of van Vogt to assist in your understanding of the story, or does it interfere?

5. What does the crew of the Space Beagle do each time that it meets an alien being during this voyage? Discuss what this tells the reader about the actions and culture of the crew and its leaders, whatever their stated intentions may be. Is this journey truly a scientific voyage of discovery? Is this journey more like Columbus's than Darwin's?

6. Choose one of the aliens described in *The Voyage of the Space Beagle*. Select two or more passages which describe the creature's physical appearance, usually including external color, limbs, and sensory organs. Draw a picture of the alien as described in one of the scenes. Will you show the alien in its own setting, or

on board the Space Beagle? Will there be human figures nearby for comparison? Prepare your picture for display, with the excerpts from the novel.

7. In *The Voyage of the Space Beagle*, A. E. van Vogt goes to considerable lengths to tell the reader about the physical appearance of each alien race described in the novel. Yet he makes only minimal references to the physical appearances of the human beings on board the Space Beagle. Also, all of his characters are referred to by male pronouns (except the neuter Anabis), whether they are human, near-immortal non-breeding alien, egg-laying alien or parthenogenetic budding aliens. Some of the aliens are referred to as "red devil" or "Black Destroyer." Is van Vogt writing a racist manifesto or a pulp sci-fi novel? How much is racism a factor in this novel? Or sexism? Is van Vogt simply writing in the style common to the genre and period, or is he writing to meet a cultural agenda? What can the reader infer about the author, the magazine he was writing for, and the time and place in which he was writing?

8. Van Vogt writes in this novel that all the interstellar expeditions that are being sent from Earth, as the Space Beagle was sent, are "proving grounds for sociological experiments: Nexialists, elections, split command—these and innumerable small changes were being tried out in the hope that man's expansion into space could somehow be made less costly." Half of the ships sent out in the last two hundred years never came back. If half of the ships blew up when the engines were first started, engineers would investigate the problem and redesign the engines. What are the sociological problems being investigated, by whom, and how successful does the redesigning process appear to be?

9. Compare Grosvenor's manipulation of his crew mates through verbal means (assisted with hypnotic gas and other technical tricks) with the manipulations done by the linguists in Suzette Haden Elgin's books *Native Tongue* and *The Judas Rose: Native Tongue II*. Why can the linguists have such profound effects upon the emotions of the people with whom they converse, while Grosvenor is comparatively ineffectual in conversation?

◆ RELATED TITLES/ADAPTATIONS ◆

The Voyage of the Space Beagle is credited by James Cameron as being the inspiration for the movie *Alien*.

The character of Grosvenor in this novel definitely inspired the character of Mr. Spock in the television series *Star Trek,* produced and created by Gene Roddenberry. There are some overt references to this novel in the *Star Trek* novels published by Pocket Books, especially the novels which are also derivative of small-press fan-fiction.

The character of Grosvenor was also a clear inspiration for John Brunner's novel called *Polymath,* featuring characters who are polymaths—multi-talented individuals who have been trained as experts in very nearly every field of human learning.

◆ FOR FURTHER REFERENCE ◆

Coax, Arthur Jean. *Dictionary of Literary Biography, Vol. 8: Twentieth-Century American Science-Fiction Writers.* Editors David Cowart & Thomas L. Wyner. Detroit: Gale Research, 1981. A useful and complete biography of A. E. van Vogt.

Elliot, Jeffrey M. *Science Fiction Voices #2,* Borgo Press, 1979. A literary discussion of van Vogt's fiction.

Knight, Damon. *In Search of Wonder.* Advent Press, 1956. Author puts van Vogt's writing in context with that of his science fiction writer contemporaries.

Moskowitz, Sam. *Seekers of Tomorrow: Masters of Modern Science Fiction.* Cleveland: World, Hyperion Press 1966, pp. 213–228. Moskowitz discusses how van Vogt's writing fits in among that of his fellow science fiction writers.

Platt, Charles. *Dream Makers: The Uncommon People Who Write Science Fiction.* 1980. Platt's scholarly viewpoint of Berkly Books, renders a portrait of van Vogt as an author.

Shepherd, Kenneth R. *Contemporary Authors Online.* Farmington Hills: Gale Group, 2000. A useful biography with bibliographic notes.

van Vogt, A. E. *Reflections of A. E. Van Vogt: The Autobiography of a Science Fiction Giant, with a Complete Bibliography.* Fictioneer Books, 1975.

van Vogt, A. E. *The Silkie.* New York: Ace, 1969; London: New English Library, 1973. This is the story of a shape-changing being on Earth. One of the better novels written by van Vogt after the Golden Age of SF faded, this is also probably the one most accessible to modern readers.

van Vogt, A. E. *Slan.* Arkham, 1946. Revised edition, Simon & Schuster, 1951. Reprinted, Berkley, 1982. A novel of mutants who are superior to humans, but wish to live in peace.

van Vogt, A. E. *Triad: The Voyage of the Space Beagle, Slan, The World of A.* New York: Simon & Schuster, 1959. A spaceship embarks on a five-year scientific expedition through the galaxy and beyond.

Wollheim, Donald A. *The Universe Makers,* Harper, 1971. Discussion of van Vogt and his fellow Golden Age science fiction writers. Interesting because Wollheim went on to become editor of DAW Books.

Paula Johanson

WHEN JEFF COMES HOME

Novel

1999

Author: Catherine Atkins

◆

Major Books for Young Adults

When Jeff Comes Home, 1999

◆ ABOUT THE AUTHOR ◆

Catherine Atkins has enjoyed a career as a news reporter, a talk show host, a teacher, and a writer. She taught alternative education programs and worked with people on improving their writing skills. Atkins has worked with students of all ages, from very young children to adults. During the course of her career, she learned that she especially likes working with teenagers, and *When Jeff Comes Home* attests to her ability to empathize with teenage problems and concerns. Atkins says that she enjoys working with teenagers because they have empathy, as well as childlike curiosity mixed with an intellect that amazes her. She says that teenagers can be mature one minute and naïve the next, qualities that help define the teen characters in *When Jeff Comes Home*. *When Jeff Comes Home* is Atkins's first novel and it reveals to readers the insights she has gained into teenage emotional trauma.

◆ OVERVIEW ◆

This novel, about the kidnapping and sexual abuse of a young teenage boy, is reputedly based on the true story of Steven Stayner, a California teen who was kidnapped in 1972 and returned to his parents in 1980. In Atkins's book, thirteen-year-old Jeff Hart and his family are at a roadside rest stop when a disturbed man named Ray kidnaps the boy at knife-point and then abuses him both physically and psychologically for the next two and a half years. The story begins after Jeff has returned home, but Atkins reveals the feelings of anguish, terror, and humiliation he continues to experience as he remembers what happened during his time with Ray. The book not only focuses on Jeff's struggle to find himself, but it focuses on the struggle of Jeff's father, who becomes so driven to heal his son that he creates serious rifts in his family. Atkins's descriptions of the painful emotions people feel in situations as dire as this one makes this book a heart-wrenching portrait of child abduction and sexual abuse and their lasting effects. Though Jeff was returned to his family, Atkins describes the boy's attempts to readjust to a "normal" life, to deal with the questions and assumptions of others, and to come to terms with what happened to him during the terrifying ordeal that robbed his innocence and changed him forever.

◆ SETTING ◆

The primary action of the book takes place in Jeff's California hometown after he is returned to his family. Atkins underscores the foreignness of this setting to Jeff, although this "normal" home, "normal" school and "normal" community once felt very comfortable and familiar to him. When Jeff first enters his home he is immediately sensitive to light and sound. We soon learn that he was locked in a dark basement for years and frequently blindfolded. The light and noise inside Jeff's old home immediately overloads his senses.

When Jeff first enters his old room, he gets glimpses of the boy he once was. He was thirteen years old at the time of his abduction, and he returns to a thirteen-year-old's room. Everything is the same as it was when he disappeared. His homework and eighth grade school books are still sitting on his desk. Again, all of this feels strange and Jeff feels out of place. Atkins uses descriptions of the setting to help convey Jeff's feelings of isolation. Later on in the novel, Jeff's father, Ken, shows some sensitivity to Jeff's needs by changing things in his environment and agrees to get rid of his eighth-grade room. Perhaps Ken Hart is beginning to get the picture, but he seems to be reducing Jeff's problem down to the fact that he's grown up and feels out of place in the room of a younger boy. What truly makes Jeff want to change his room is not that he's no longer a young boy, but that

he's no longer the same boy. Nothing feels familiar to him, in part because he lives within his own mind. His tortured memories of his home with Ray seem more real to him than his family home, and it will take a long time before Jeff can feel comfortable in the strange, "normal" world where he once belonged.

◆ THEMES AND CHARACTERS ◆

Atkins' story of Jeff Hart is a portrait of a teenage boy living a nightmare. Jeff's life changed abruptly and permanently the day at the rest stop when a man named Ray held a knife to his throat, forced him into a van, and took him away to be his personal sex slave. On that day, the life Jeff had as a normal young boy ceased to exist. His innocence ended and his perception of self disintegrated. Atkins's book focuses on Jeff's struggle to find himself after Ray returns him to his family. The primary themes that arise during the course of the novel are the power of mental conditioning, the stigma of sexual abuse, and the corruption of the innocent.

During the course of the book, Atkins reveals some chilling insights into the nature of mental conditioning. She begins in Chapter One in describing Jeff's drive back to his home, when Jeff tells Ray not only that he loves him, but that he does not have to go home. "Are you sure you want me to?" Jeff asks Ray. "It's what you want, kid. You can stay, I told you that," Ray replies. This gives us a taste of the brainwashing that occurred during the time he lived with Ray. Jeff has a twisted view of love and loyalty, as does an abused child who has been battered and broken and conditioned to love his parents despite their cruelty. Ray is, in essence, a parental figure to Jeff, albeit a sick and twisted one. Jeff confuses his feelings for Ray. Ray becomes Jeff's lover, protector, provider, and abuser. By the time

When Jeff Comes Home

Jeff returns home, he can no longer distinguish between love and hatred, pain and pleasure, weakness and strength. He no longer had any idea how to think for himself.

Jeff is returned home and left to face a world in which he no longer feels connected. His father is determined to integrate Jeff back into the world and obsessed with removing any vestiges of his son's other life. We find out right away that Jeff's father treats Jeff differently than his brother and sister; he's warmer with Jeff and much more attentive. In narrating his story, Jeff says that Connie, his stepmother, "spent most of her energy trying to keep [her husband] happy." So she failed to notice their children's neglect. The two and half years Jeff is missing take a deadly toll on his family, one that can never be fully repaired. Healing will take a lifetime. The physical scars Jeff carries on his back are only a brutal reminder of the emotional scars that he and everyone close to him will carry with them forever.

In narrating his feelings about returning to normal life, Jeff remains constantly haunted by the life he feels he can never reveal. To make things worse, Jeff is inundated with questions from the police and the FBI. The press fire extremely personal questions at him, then his friends and family begin to question him as well. The questions from his family and friends are not intentionally insensitive; they're simply indicative of the fact that no one can comprehend the extent of Jeff's psychological trauma. For a long time Jeff defends Ray and denies any sexual relationship with him. He remains uncooperative and emotionally distant, frozen by the fear and guilt that molded his conscience.

Jeff constructs a wall around himself that keeps him forever imprisoned within his own mind. The fact that everyone wonders what happened to him is too painful for Jeff to deal with. He is living with shame and guilt most of us can never imagine. We understand that Jeff was beaten, and that he was forced to perform sexual acts with Ray in order to eat. In narrating his story and in a few haunting flashbacks, Jeff reveals just enough to help us imagine. We understand that he was raped on the night of his abduction and that he was raped repeatedly after that. We also understand that after a while Jeff engaged in sex with Ray willingly because he had no other choice. He had to play Ray's games in order to survive.

Jeff has so many mental obstacles to overcome, but his overwhelming feelings of guilt and shame rule his life. Jeff's father's guilt rules his life too. Ken seems unable to deal with the fact that he could not protect his son. Atkins begins her prologue with Jeff's unspoken thought: "Dad never believed me later, when I told him there was nothing he could have done." This lets us know right away that the thoughts and feelings of Jeff's father are central to the plot. Ken Hart is a powerful character in the book, and he and Ray, like no one else, are the two people who have the ability to control Jeff's emotions.

Jeff has to fight unconscious comparisons between his father and Ray. For two years Ray served as Jeff's father, though he became a "father" who gave Jeff a lethal mixture of abuse and love. Aside from Ray, no one can ruffle Jeff's feathers like Ken can. Jeff worries about what everyone thinks of his "relationship" with Ray, but he worries most about what his father thinks happened and how his father views him because of it. Because he has been trained to please his father figure yet beaten to let him know he never can, Jeff struggles with feelings that tell him he can never please his own father. He thinks that his father finds him effeminate and repulsive. At one point, Jeff mentions the "unimaginable picture" of his father and Ray in the same room. On more than one occasion Jeff becomes painfully aware of similarities in the mannerisms of his father and Ray; parental gestures, for instance, such as putting a hand under Jeff's chin and raising his head to meet his eyes. Any outburst of emotion, anger, or excitement from his father makes Jeff flinch.

Jeff speaks once or twice about the mixture of pleasure and pain he felt with Ray, and we understand where his guilt is coming from. He is confused about his views of himself and unable to intellectualize the fact that he gave in to Ray's demands and acted as a willing participant because he had no other choice. Later in the novel, after Jeff reveals his sexual willingness to his father, his father understands what Jeff has yet to understand himself. Ray won the mind games he played with him and Jeff lost the ability to control his thoughts.

In one particularly disturbing scene from the novel, we get a glimpse of the kind of mind games Ray played. In a story Jeff tells to Brian and Charlie one day when they question him about life with Ray, we learn about Staredown, a game that Brian was familiar with but to which Ray added a sick twist. "Hey, Brian. You remember 'Staredown'?" Jeff asks. "Sure," Brian replies. "Well, Ray used to play that with me a lot. He played it different than we used to, though. You want me to show you?" Jeff backs Brian up against a wall and tells him to look him in the eye. "The first one to break the stare gets slapped," Jeff explains. " ... That's how Ray plays ... You get slapped every time you look away from him, so the only way to win is to never look away." Brian, by this time, is crying, and Jeff feels disgusted with himself. Here again, Jeff's father obsession surfaces. Charlie asks him if there is anything they can do to help. "One thing," Jeff responds. "Don't tell Dad."

Ken Hart is driven, intelligent, and fiercely determined to heal his son. Though he is well intentioned, he has no idea what he is dealing with, and he fails to recognize Jeff's desperate desire to please him. Yet the bond between father and son shouts out from every page. Ken spent two and a half years obsessed with finding Jeff and his obsession affects everyone in the family. Aside from Ken and Jeff, Brian suffers most of all. Brian became mentally absent to his father from the minute Jeff became physically absent. Both of these boys will have father issues to deal with for the rest of their lives.

Ken's loyalty to his son is fierce and unbending, but because Jeff feels so much shame about what he knows happened with Ray, he is repulsed by himself and believes that his father must be repulsed by him too. When his father demands that Jeff take his earring off, Jeff immediately thinks that his father must have been looking at him repugnance. Jeff looks at himself in the mirror and feels sick. Jeff is an attractive boy, but he hates the way he looks because Ray loved it. He hates who he is, because Ray loved him. He defines himself only in relation to Ray, because for two and a half years, that was all he knew how to do. Jeff lost himself during that time; he lost his identity, his self-respect, and his ability to love and be loved by others. Anything remotely related to sex embarrasses him, for instance, a poster of a pin-up girl in his room, the attention from a sales clerk at the Gap, a wink from a waiter in a restaurant, and he shudders from any kind of physical contact, especially any kind of physical affection from his father.

For a long time, Jeff vehemently denies that anything sexual happened with Ray. He is overwhelmed with shame. Jeff even defends Ray, saying that he is not "a sick rapist pervert." When the FBI agent tells Jeff that in law enforcement it is generally assumed that missing kids over 14 years old have run away, Jeff lets us know that this is his "fear made flesh." Jeff assumes that everyone will think that what happened was by choice, because he eventually consented to the sex. Jeff is momentarily relieved when they finally arrest Ray and learn that he had a record for assault, not for sexual abuse or rape. Then the FBI agent tells Jeff and his parents that they often reduce the crime of sexual assault against children down to assault presumably to protect the victim. Yet, when the FBI, the press, and his friends and family ask him about the sexual abuse, he continues to deny that any occurred. This causes him to remain imprisoned by Ray. Then when Vinny, Jeff's best friend, finds out that Jeff has been lying to him he lashes out, and Jeff retreats further into his own isolated world.

The novel changes focus when Ray is caught and arrested. At this point, Jeff can no longer deny his sexual molestation and he must gain the strength to tell his story because Ray is telling a story of Jeff as a willing sex partner. Ray knows that Jeff will not talk, in fact, he is counting on it. So he readily admits that he had a sexual relationship with the boy but that Jeff was an eager participant. "Are you going to let Ray Slaight do your talking for you?" the FBI officer asks Jeff, and Jeff knows that he has to tell his story. Furthermore, the FBI agent lays guilt on Jeff when he will not talk by saying that Jeff will be responsible if Ray abducts another child.

Though the novel ends with Jeff moving out of his denial, we feel less than optimistic that his problems will be resolved. Throughout the book Atkins stresses Jeff's loss of identity. When he first arrives at the door of his old house, a man opens the door and asks him if he is Jeff Hart. Jeff tells us that he wanted to say "not exactly," but he just nodded. He did not feel like Jeff Hart anymore and can never be the same boy again. To further stress this loss of identity, Jeff says that during his first conversation with Vinny, he does not recognize his friend's deep voice. "He grew up, stu-

pid." Jeff tells himself. ". . . Just like you would have."

Except for the chilling image we get of Ray, Jeff and his father are the only characters we gain a true understanding of in the novel, though we get the idea that everyone in Jeff's life has suffered psychological damage from Ray's abuse. Vinny has some problems with Jeff's dishonesty, but he appears more ignorant than callous. Brian and Charlie try to be supportive, but they are naturally curious, as is everyone else, and they cannot possibly understand what Jeff needs from them at this time. They want the old Jeff back again, but no one has a clue as to how they can help Jeff through his psychological distress. Connie, Jeff's stepmother, tries to be understanding but she remains a passive character throughout the story. Atkins gives her no true voice, nor does she give us much insight into her thoughts and feelings. Where is Jeff's biological mother? We never find out what happened to her, but we get the impression that Connie has mothered these children since they were little. Were Brian and Charlie her children or her stepchildren? These questions are never answered because Atkins is so intent on making Jeff's personal anguish the focus of her story. What emerges is a chilling portrait of a sick man's penchant for psychological torture and corruption of the innocent.

◆ LITERARY QUALITIES ◆

Through Atkins' use of the first person narrative, *When Jeff Comes Home* achieves a chilling reality. The fact that Atkins leaves most of the grim details unstated does nothing to undermine the impact of what we understand was Jeff's terror. We do not know exactly what happened to him, but we can imagine. Jeff tells bits and pieces of his story throughout the novel, and he reverts to flashbacks when the terror in his past becomes too real to ignore. Atkins puts words in italics when Jeff thinks deep, unspoken thoughts that he is not yet ready to come to terms with or voice out loud. These italicized phrases are particularly insightful, and we quickly begin to understand the devastating effect Ray had on Jeff's psyche.

The book can essentially be broken down into two parts. In the first part, Atkins builds suspense as to how and when Ray will appear and how and when he will be caught and arrested. She peppers the novel with tense scenes as Ray stalks Jeff to sustain his control over him. Early on in the novel we find out that Ray had been at Jeff's house the night before, after Jeff's arrival home, and that he set the bag of clothes Jeff was wearing when he disappeared on the porch steps of the boy's house. There are several instances when Jeff thinks he sees Ray. Then Ray truly resurfaces in Jeff's life in person. In the scene when Jeff and his father leave the barber shop and go to his father's office, Ray is there, dressed in a suit rather than his usual jeans and T-shirt, but this time Jeff knows it is him. Ray turns around, walks over to them, and asks Jeff's father for directions. This incident, as well as the incident with the clothes on the front porch, serves as a chilling reminder of the psychological games Ray played with Jeff for years.

It is just after Ray's conversation with Jeff's dad when Jeff begins to break down. Though Jeff was too paralyzed with fear to identify Ray when he was talking with his father, he does identify him later that day in the FBI office. He reveals Ray's last name. During the first part of the novel, Jeff remains paralyzed with fear and unable to turn his back on Ray. He remains in denial about the sexual abuse that occurred and he refuses to give the authorities much information at all. In the second part of the novel, once Jeff begins to talk, Ray is caught and the tension eases. Then Atkins concen-trates largely on Jeff's psychological development. Once Ray begins to talk, Jeff must move from denial to acceptance. He begins to do so, but we understand that there is a long road ahead.

◆ SOCIAL SENSITIVITY ◆

Jeff says that his primary fear is that people will think that he engaged in sex with Ray willingly. He also fears that they will label him a "fag". Given the coercion he suffered and the mind-bending that occurred, his fears certainly seem legitimate. But the homophobia that plagues Jeff's father, Vinny, and the boys at school seem way off the mark. If Atkins were indeed recounting the actual experiences of the boy kidnapped in 1972, this would be simply a sign of the times. But she sets her story in California in the 1990s, making the extreme homophobic attitudes of Jeff's peers seem unrealistic. Furthermore, sensitizing children and teenagers to the feelings of peers who have experienced severe trauma seems to be rather commonplace in school counseling practice in recent years, and the boys at school should have some awareness of what they are dealing with.

The reactions of everyone in Jeff's life make it painfully clear that counseling should be made available to everyone affected by situations as critical as this one. Yet Atkins does not address the necessity for therapy. Jeff should have seen a therapist immediately, for instance, someone who could have prepared him for the probing questions of the FBI and the press, not to mention someone who could help him through his psychological distress. Perhaps the high school students should have received counseling before Jeff returned to school, and perhaps Brian and Charlie should have been sent to a therapist who could help them relate to the Jeff they now see who no longer feels like the Jeff they remember. Given that much of her book is a kind of psychological analysis, it seems logical that therapy should have been made readily available to Jeff and to everyone else affected by what happened.

◆ TOPICS FOR DISCUSSION ◆

1. Do you think the reactions of the kids at school were realistic? Would they truly be so callous and uncaring?

2. Do you think Vinny acted as a good friend to Jeff? Why do you suppose he acted the way he did when he realized that Jeff lied to him about the sexual abuse?

3. Did you get a clear picture of what life was like for Jeff during the time he was with Ray even though Atkins relates very few details? Why or why not?

4. What was it in the end that led Jeff to make the decision to talk?

5. Does Atkins give readers a clear understanding of what emotions Brian and Charlie were experiencing after their brother returned? Explain.

6. What would you say would be Jeff's greatest challenge as he moves on with his life?

7. Do you think Dave Stephens, the FBI officer, treated Jeff appropriately? Why or why not?

8. Do you have a clear understanding of Ray Slaight's motives for kidnapping Jeff?

9. What do you think Jeff means when he refers to "the unimaginable picture" of Ray and his father in the same room?

10. What kind of issues do you think Jeff's brother Brian might have in the future?

◆ IDEAS FOR REPORTS AND PAPERS ◆

1. Do some research on the characteristics of child molesters, then using your research and what information Atkins reveals about Ray, write a character analysis of this man.

2. Write a character analysis of Jeff's father, using his reactions to Jeff to explain the emotions he feels. Find examples from the story that illustrate how guilty Ken feels about being unable to protect his son.

3. In When Jeff Comes Home, Atkins concentrates primarily on Jeff's emotions and she touches on Jeff's father's emotions after his son's return. Read Sue Beth Pfeffer's The Year Without Michael, which concentrates on the emotions experienced during the time their son is missing. Compare the emotional experience of this family to the emotional experience Jeff's family must have had during the time they knew nothing of their son's whereabouts.

4. Do some research on the trials faced by victims of childhood sexual abuse. How does Jeff fit the mold of the "abused child?"

5. Explain some of the fears Jeff has as he attempts to re-adjust to normal teenage life and explain some of the things you think will help him combat those fears.

6. Give your analysis of the relationship Jeff has with his father. Discuss what binds them together and what keeps a distance between them.

7. Write a paper outlining what kinds of psychological support exists for people like Jeff. This may include personal therapists, support groups, school counseling sessions, etc.

It has been surmised that Atkins based her fictional story of Jeff Hart on the true story of Steven Stayner, the California teen who was kidnapped in 1972. This heart-wrenching story prompted NBC to air a miniseries about the boy, entitled "I Know My First Name is Steven," which aired on May 22 and 23, 1989, and lengthy stories about Steven have appeared in numerous magazines and newspapers over the years. *Time* magazine of August 9, 1999 briefly recounts the story in relation to what happened to Steven's brother Cary. Cary was sentenced to life later that year for the brutal killing of a naturalist in Yosemite National Park and has been accused of killing three other women as well. The story of Cary Stayner helps explain the extent of the trauma Brian in Atkins's novel suffers, and has been recounted in a book by Dennis McDougal entitled *The Yosemite Murders* (Ballantine Books 2000). The television movie "I Know My First Name is Steven" was remade into a book of the same name, written by Mike Nichols (Pinnacle Books 1999).

Quite a few young adult novels have been published about child abduction. Elaine Marie Alphin's *Counterfeit Son* tells the story of Cameron Miller, a fifteen-year-old boy whose father kidnaps, abuses, then kills young boys. Cameron himself is a victim of his father's abuse, and while imprisoned in the basement of his home reads his father's files on the lives and deaths of his victims. After his father dies, Cameron assumes the identity of one of these victims and joins the victims family as their missing son. Like Atkins, Alphin writes a terrifying tale of the psychological trauma experienced by victims of child abduction.

Caroline Cooney presents a different angle on child abduction in *The Face on the Milk Carton*, which like Atkins's book, was also made into a TV movie. In this story,

fifteen-year-old Janie recognizes herself as a missing child on a milk carton and comes to find out that she was kidnapped from her biological parents when she was three years old. Cooney's book concentrates on Janie's inner turmoil and describes her struggle to discover her past and learn the truth about what happened.

Harry Mazer's book *Who Is Eddie Leonard*? focuses on a fifteen-year-old boy who believes he is the missing child he sees on the TV news. He has lived with his grandmother for years, and after she dies, he returns to the family he believes was once his and struggles to feel at home there. Mazer's book details the emotions of Eddie, who longs to be a part of this family, and of the other family members who long to have their son back but are not sure that Eddie is their true son.

In another heartbreaking tale of child abduction, Sue Beth Pfeffer's *The Year Without Michael* is told primarily from the perspective of sixteen-year-old Jody, and it details her family's pain and frustration after Jody's brother Michael mysteriously disappeared. While *When Jeff Comes Home* focuses on the family's feelings after their son returns, *The Year Without Michael* focuses on the family's feelings during their son's absence. Then, presenting another angle to the incident of child abduction, Pfeffer's *Twice Taken* focuses on the feelings of a young boy who believes he was kidnapped by his father.

♦ FOR FURTHER REFERENCE ♦

Fakolt, Jennifer. Review of *When Jeff Comes Home*. *School Library Journal* (February 2000): 117.

Fass, Paula S. *Kidnapped: Child Abduction in America*. London: Oxford University Press, 1997. Recounts compelling stories of true cases of child abduction and discusses the public reaction to these cases.

Peters, John. Review of *When Jeff Comes Home. Booklist* (October 15, 1999): 428.

Review of *When Jeff Comes Home. Publishers Weekly* (September 20, 1999): 89.

Zvirin, Stephanie. Review of *When Jeff Comes Home. Booklist* (November 15, 1999): 618.

Tamra Andrews

THE WIND'S TWELVE QUARTERS

Short Stories

1975

Author: Ursula K. LeGuin

◆

Major Books for Young Adults

Rocannon's World, 1966
The Left Hand of Darkness, 1969
The Lathe of Heaven, 1971
The Dispossessed, 1974
The Wind's Twelve Quarters, 1975
The Language of the Night, 1975 (essays)
The Word for World Is Forest, 1976
Always Coming Home, 1985
Unlocking the Air and Other

Stories, 1996

Earthsea series
A Wizard of Earthsea, 1968
The Tombs of Atuan, 1971
The Farthest Shore, 1972
Tehanu, 1990
The Other Wind, 2001

◆ ABOUT THE AUTHOR ◆

Ursula K. Le Guin was born on October 21, 1929, in Berkeley, California. Her parents were the famed anthropologist Alfred Louis Kroeber and Theodora (Kracaw) Kroeber, who authored the ethnology classic *Ishi in Two Worlds* and several children's books published by Parnassus Press. The bond of empathy and respect that existed between Alfred Kroeber and the Amerindians he studied led to his friendship with Ishi, the last remaining aboriginal raised without contact with "Americans" and the subject of Theodora Kroeber's classic book. The Kroebers raised all their children according to their progressive and non-sexist beliefs.

Young Ursula had two older brothers, Theodore Charles and Karl, and an older half-brother, Clifton, from her mother's previous marriage to Clifton Spencer Brown.

Throughout her childhood, young Ursula was exposed to Celtic and Teutonic folklore and magic from cultures around the world. She learned to respect cultural diversity and human unity, and appreciate the virtues and vices of the academic community. Young Ursula was inspired as well by authors such as Hans Christian Andersen, Lord Dunsany, Padraic Colum, and J. R. R. Tolkien (a writer to whom she is often favorably compared), and by the anthropological views of Sir James Frazer, whose

Ursula K. Le Guin

Golden Bough first thrilled her as a child when she discovered a juvenile adaptation written by his wife.

Le Guin wrote her first fantasy story at nine, about a man persecuted by evil elves, and she submitted her first science fiction work, a story about time travel that she wrote when she was ten or eleven, to *Amazing Stories*. It was rejected, but *Amazing Stories* was to publish her first science fiction story, "April in Paris," over twenty years later. Lord Dunsany's *A Dreamer's Tales,* which she encountered at age twelve, was a revelation to her. She recalls that moment in her nonfiction collection *The Language of the Night:* "What I hadn't realized, I guess, is that people were still making up myths. One made up stories oneself, of course; but here was a grownup doing it, for grownups, without a single apology to common sense, without an explanation, just

dropping us straight into the Inner Lands. . . . I had discovered my native country."

Unlike the earlier generation of "Golden Age" science fiction writers who learned their craft on the job, writing for pulp magazines, this writer calls herself "an intellectual born and bred." Ursula Kroeber graduated Phi Beta Kappa from Radcliffe in 1951 and earned her master's degree in Romance Literatures of the Middle Ages and Renaissance at Columbia University in 1952. She won a Fulbright fellowship to study in Paris, where she met Charles Le Guin and married him in December, 1953.

Keeping in step with her husband's academic itinerary, she left her own post-graduate studies and taught French at Mercer University in Macon, Georgia, in 1954 and at the University of Idaho in 1956. In 1959 the Le Guins settled in Portland, Oregon, where Charles Le Guin teaches history at Portland State University. Together the Le Guins have raised three children, Elizabeth, Caroline, and Theodore.

By the early 1960s, Le Guin had published a few poems and one story in small magazines, but she also had five unpublished novels, written over ten years, mostly set in the imaginary central European country of Orsinia. She turned to science fiction at that point out of a desire to be published, and her work quickly grew in power. Two of her first short stories were set on islands and dealt with, among other things, the rules of magic. In 1967 the publisher of Parnassus Press asked her for a manuscript and suggested to her that she might try her hand at writing for young people, giving her complete freedom to write anything she liked. As she let her imagination roam, Le Guin found herself remembering the islands and magic of her earlier stories, and she began to wonder how wizards—traditionally depicted as wise, white-haired old men—learned their magic arts. From this came *A Wizard of Earthsea*, Ursula Le Guin's first book for young people, published in 1968.

She has written over twenty-five novels and short story collections, four non-fiction books and several works of poetry. Her best-known and best-loved works, most notably the "Earthsea" series, are on school curriculums across the continent.

Though she identified (in 1976) as her influences eight romantic poets, four English and four Russian novelists, and a handful of contemporary speculative fiction writers, in 1973 she had named as her earliest preferences the Lord Dunsany and the trashiest pulp magazines she could find. She denies all connection with the magazine *Astounding Science-Fiction*, and indeed her writing bears little resemblance to the works of "Golden Age" authors. The writers she most admires are Charles Dickens, Leo Tolstoy, Tolkien, Virginia Woolf, and the Brontë sisters.

It is obvious that much of her parents' anthropological studies filtered into her young mind, not only from the subjects of her writing but from overt elements like the use of "the Dreamtime" in her novel *The Word for World is Forest*, and the Jungian elements in her "Earthsea" writing. Le Guin's critical writing for literary journals, fanzines, writers' workshops, and public lectures (much of it collected in *The Language of the Night*) shows that there is abundant material for academic and formal intellectual study of modern science fiction and fantasy works.

A highly respected author of fantasy fiction, Le Guin expands the scope of the genre by combining conventional elements of science fiction with more traditional literary techniques. When she offers thought-provoking speculations on alternative societies and philosophies, she is encouraging commentary on existing cultural beliefs and behaviors. One of the most distinguished authors of our time, she is the winner of numerous awards, including a Newbery Honor, the National Book Award, three Nebula Awards from the Science Fiction Writers of America, and four Hugo Awards from the annual World Science Fiction Convention.

The first science fiction convention Le Guin ever attended was V-Con One in 1975, the annual SF convention held in Vancouver, Canada. Now she is a regular participant in conventions and Internet discussion groups, and a strong supporter of the James Tiptree Memorial Award for exploration of gender roles in science fiction. She is also the judge for the new Ursula K. Le Guin Award for Speculative Fiction.

Le Guin has taught writing workshops at Portland State University and the University of Washington, among other universities. Consonant with her antiwar activism in the 1960s, she worked in the Portland area in the presidential campaigns of Democratic candidates Eugene McCarthy and George McGovern. She lives in a roomy old frame house on the banks of the Willamette River in Portland, Oregon, with her husband, Charles Le Guin.

◆ OVERVIEW ◆

The Wind's Twelve Quarters was published in 1975, collecting into a retrospective Le Guin's short stories that had been published over the previous twelve years. The stories are: "Semley's Necklace," "April in Paris," "The Masters," "Darkness Box," "The Word of Unbinding," "The Rule of Names," "Winter's King," "The Good Trip," "Nine Lives," "Things," "A Trip to the Head," "Vaster Than Empires and More Slow," "The Stars Below," "The Field of Vision," "Direction of the Road," "The Ones Who Walk Away from Omelas," and "The Day before the Revolution."

In "Semley's Necklace," Semley is a young noble of the planet Fomalhaut II, as poor in material goods as the noble husband who "loves no gold but the gold of her hair." Semley goes on a quest for the lost treasure of her family, among the Fiia and the Clayfolk and the Starlords. She makes a relativistic journey to the museum planet of the Starlords, a trip that takes her one long night but lasts seventeen years for the planet she returns to at last.

"April in Paris" brings together four lonely people on an island in Paris. Each is brought from a different century by a magic spell, finding what they need most in their new company.

"Darkness Box" is set in a sunless fantasy world, where gryphons fly and dead soldiers come alive again to follow their prince, until he opens a small box washed up by the sea, restoring time and daylight as well the darkness and mortality that his father the king had trapped in the box.

"The Word of Unbinding" tells of the struggles of the wizard Festin, imprisoned by an invading wizard who ruins islands and all that live there.

"The Rule of Names" shows that a comical, inept wizard may have a true name, showing him to be something far different from what his village neighbors expect.

In "Winter's King," the young King Argaven of Karhide on Gethen is kidnaped, drugged, and brainwashed so that she (the Gethenians are all androgynes) will, subconsciously, rule the country in a way so as to favor the fraction who kidnaped her. She escapes from this plot by traveling to another planet of the Hainish Ekumen, where her mind is restored. After an education as a diplomat of the Ekumen, she returns to Gethen. Her heir—an infant when she left, but now old due to Argaven's relativistic journey—is an incompetent ruler. So, backed by both the Ekumen and the Karhidish people, King Argaven resumes her reign.

"The Good Trip" is a story about a man who has had to watch his wife slowly go insane. He is now on drugs, but this time he goes off on a better trip—without the drugs— which reaches not only to his wife's mind in the sanatorium but also their future together, well and content.

When "Nine Lives" begins, Martin and Pugh have been isolated on the sterile planet Libra, setting up a mining operation there. Then a working team arrives: five men and five women, all cloned from the same man. The ten-clone is very efficient, but does have some peculiarities unique to clones. When nine of the ten are killed in an accident, the only survivor has to learn how to cope with being alone, as singleton humans are all alone.

In "Things," the end is nigh on an island. Nothing new is being built, made, grown or bred, including children. The Ragers are killing off the animals and burning the fields. "It is well to be free of Things." But there is one man who still has a dream of the islands said to exist somewhere out there. And so he tips his huge stock of bricks into the sea—much to the Ragers' pleasure. But secretly, under water, he arranges the bricks into an underwater causeway, a sea road.

"A Trip to the Head" is a strange, surrealistic tale of someone who has lost the names of things and does not know who he or she is or what he is looking for. But then again, neither does her or his companion.

"Vaster Than Empires and More Slow" tells of ten misfit explorers sent to investigate an unreasonably distant planet. The strangest of the crew is Osden, an empath who feels exactly what everybody else really thinks about him and each other. The planet they come to has no animal life, just one interconnected mess of plants, trees, and vines of different kinds. This huge biosphere learns from them fear of the Other, but comes to accept Osden.

In "The Stars Below" an astronomer, Guennar, hides in the cellar when his observatory is burned to the ground. He is hidden by a friend in a mine, and survives there when the few miners come to trust him. His search for knowledge continues, even underground, and eventually before disappearing, he tells the miners where he has seen stars in the rock, a great wealth of silver undiscovered.

"The Field of Vision" tells of astronauts returning with strange effects from a visit in a mysterious 600 million-year-old city on Mars. One of them sees things and another hears things. After a long struggle, they learn to make sense of their sounds and visions. They see and hear the immanence of God in everything.

"Direction of the Road" is an old oak tree's story about itself, growing beside a road as a living being interacting as it is perceived by all who pass.

In "The Ones Who Walk Away from Omelas," the narrator speaks to the reader, asking him or her to imagine Omelas, city of joy, and the scapegoat whose misery keeps all the rest in peace and plenty. But then, there are some who cannot stand the thought of the suffering child—the ones who walk away from Omelas.

The final story in this collection is "The Day before the Revolution," in which readers are introduced to Laia Aseio Odo, hero and founder of a political philosophy. She is seventy-two, living in an Odonian collective, and putting together in her mind all her memories of life.

◆ SETTING ◆

When Le Guin wrote these stories, they appeared first in numerous science fiction and literary magazines and anthologies be-fore being collected in *The Wind's Twelve Quarters*. Some of these stories are strongly imaginative and fantastic, while others are more mainstream in setting. But in all the stories, Le Guin uses realism and believable settings to depict real-life issues within the realms of the fantastic.

The first of her stories to appear in print was "April in Paris" (September 1962), a time-travel story, more fantasy than science fiction, in which black magic romantically unites four lonely people from different eras.

The second was "The Masters" (February 1963), her first genuine science fiction story, set in a post-catastrophic world where science is proscribed because of the havoc it has wrought. Its heroes are two defiant adventurers brought to inquisitorial justice for secretly studying mathematics.

The third published was "Darkness Box" (November 1963), a moody fantasy, with the child of a witch and the son of a king, gryphons and a talking cat. The king halts time, change, and mortality, at least temporarily, by shutting darkness into a box and throwing it in the sea.

The fourth, "The Word of Unbinding" (January 1964), was, along with a later story, "The Rule of Names," the prelude to the "Earthsea" trilogy. Both stories were set on the islands of Earthsea. "Darkness Box" and "Things" may be set on islands of Earthsea, as well, a reasonable assumption for any of Le Guin's stories written in this decade and set on islands.

Another story, published in *Amazing* in September 1964, was "The Dowry of Angyar," later retitled "Semley's Necklace," the first of her "Hainish" stories. In this story Le Guin lays out not only four cultures of humanity on the planet later to be known as "Rocannon's World" (in the novel of the same name), but also establishes the consideration of the Hainish people that stars represent all of their scattered brethren.

Le Guin's imaginary worlds tend to be utilitarian, not mere flights of fantasy. They teach the reader, in the utopian tradition. In the two "Earthsea" stories in *The Wind's Twelve Quarters*, the lessons are subtle and far below the surface.

"A Trip to the Head" is set in an unspecified forest, a nowhere space that confuses the viewpoint character. For some of these stories, especially "The Ones Who Walk Away from Omelas," the setting is merely elsewhere, described with a technique reminiscent of Jorge Luis Borges. Remember that "utopia" translates into English literally as "noplace."

In "The Stars Below," a setting much like that in "The Masters," the astronomer learns not only the movements of the stars in the sky, but the ways of the dark places of the deep earth, hidden and forgotten and frightening.

The hospital setting of "The Field of Vision" is quarantined from the wide world of Earth, but it is "a blooming, buzzing confusion" to Hughes after his return from investigating a lost, empty city on Mars. His perceptions have been forever altered.

In contrast with all the stories that have gone before, "Direction of the Road" is a refreshing pastorale, with a realistic setting by the side of a country road in Oregon and enough activity to engage the reader even though the viewpoint character is an oak tree.

"The Day before the Revolution" is similarly realistic as well, set on the planet Urras but in a city far too much like any major American city (old buildings, busy squares, and ghettoes) to be at all unfamiliar.

By contrasting fantasy with reality in an imaginative fashion, Le Guin has developed her narrative skills which enable her to express alienation, the individual's haunting feeling of belonging neither here nor there, as a fundamental quality of the human condition.

◆ THEMES AND CHARACTERS ◆

The first story in the collection, "Semley's Necklace," was actually the eighth story she sold; Le Guin calls this "the most characteristic of my early science fiction and fantasy works, the most romantic of them all." When Semley returns from her relativistic journey, she brings home her family's necklace in triumph only to find that her husband has died in the war, for "he had little armor for his body, and none at all for his spirit." Semley gives the necklace to her now-grown daughter and flees to her husband's grave. In her quest, Semley has learned resolution and triumph, and now she understands regret for desiring her family's rightful treasure, which had been lost in her grandmother's time. She had thought to leave her husband and child for only a few days, and is devastated to learn that her journey lasted years.

Le Guin was a dedicated mother to her children as they grew, as well as being a prolific author. Far from using up her intellect and talents, Le Guin's children were a source of inspiration and human understanding. In her introduction to "Darkness Box," she describes an event that occurred when her daughter Caroline was three years old. "She came to me with a small wooden box in her small hands and said, 'Guess fwat is in this bockus.' I guessed caterpillars, mice, elephants, etc. She shook her head, smiled an unspeakably eldritch smile, opened the box slightly so that I could just see in, and said: 'Darkness.'" That simple exchange started Le Guin writing this story, showing how mortality cannot be rejected just by a king putting it into a box and throwing it away. When darkness and death are given up, time and achievement are cast out as well. The prince counts the cost of darkness and mortality as well-paid if the sun shines again and an end (any end) will come to the interminable war with his brother.

"The Masters" is Le Guin's first story using the figure of the lonely scientist, wishing to learn more in his chosen craft and about the world. Though she used this theme later in other stories and novels with considerably better equipment, this story has the show-stopping line: "He had been trying to measure the distance between the earth and God." Simple trigonometry is an arcane study by heretics, in this story.

In writing these stories, Le Guin employed as a plot element psychic phenomena, including telepathy, clairvoyance, and precognition, and incorporated some of the philosophies of Taoism and Zen, resulting in themes of reciprocity, unity, and holism. By presenting complex, often paradoxical symbols, images, and allusions, Le Guin stressed the need for individuals and societies to balance such dualities as order with chaos and harmony with rebellion to achieve wholeness.

Le Guin claims that she does not plan her works but must discover them in her subconscious. The discovery of Earthsea began with a story about a wizard, "The Word of Unbinding," published in *Fantastic* in 1964. A later story, "The Rule of Names," developed further both the islands of Earthsea and the rules of its magic and introduced a dragon. The whole of the "Earthsea" world is encapsulated in these two stories.

Her "Earthsea" writings have been strongly influenced by Tolkien, George MacDonald, M. R. James, and C. S. Lewis's fantasies, although Le Guin has been praised for her original allegory which has none of the theological quiddities of C. S. Lewis. In fact, Le Guin creates a world without a deity, although magic exists, along with tremendous powers for good and evil. Hers is a modern, existential, humanistic universe where the weight of responsibility rests on the individual to act wisely, for by acting otherwise he or she can imperil the balance of the world. The emphasis of balance—of good and evil, light and dark, life and death—in the "Earthsea" works have led many critics to see the influence of Taoist notions of dynamic equilibrium, of the necessity for a balance of yin and yang, on the author.

Critic Darrell Schweitzer says that Le Guin's "Earthsea" works are "central to twentieth-century fantasy, probably more influential than anything other than *The Lord of the Rings,* often taken as models by other writers because they create a world as vivid as Tolkien's, but on a smaller, more intimate scale." Schweitzer goes on to add that

Le Guin has turned Tolkien's epic into a novel of character, with a smaller, more sharply realized cast; and, for all the Earthsea books were published as ostensible juveniles, they are in every sense more adult, fully willing to admit that even beloved characters fade and die or come to nasty, abrupt ends, where Tolkien hedges mortality in endless appendices, reluctant to let go.

Le Guin emphasizes in some of these stories a favorite theme of hers: the idea that unity is achieved through the interaction and tension of such paired terms as likeness and unlikeness, native and alien, male and female. Her short story "Winter's King" provided the seed for Le Guin's *The Left Hand of Darkness,* which was the crowning achievement of the *Hainish* series, marking the author's attainment of a full measure of complexity, characterization, and ingenuity. She has described the novel as, in part, a feminist "thought experiment," exploring what would happen in a society free of sexual role-playing, although her main concern was not with sexuality but with fidelity and betrayal. Even this brief short story, "Winter's King," shows that the human motivations of the King are not bound by gender roles, but rather by love for her child and responsibility for her nation.

Also fitting into the "Hainish" series was the novella "Vaster Than Empires and

More Slow." In it, Osden, the misanthropic interplanetary explorer with "wide-range bioempathic receptivity" can finally leave the rejection and pity of other humans behind when he finds contentment in being accepted by the semi-sentient vegetation of an Edenic planet.

The astronomer in "The Stars Below" is traumatized, not only by having his observatory burnt over his head by zealots, but also by going underground in an almost-abandoned mine. Living almost without light, almost without company, he learns the science of geology and what could be called geomancy. He can reveal a hidden vein of silver for his trusted friends, the miners, but he cannot come up into the wide world of life and humanity, even for a night or for a meal. He is lost in the dark, having become a mystic and learned about things in the dark places of the Earth that are also told in Le Guin's "Earthsea" novel *The Tombs of Atuan*.

Learning to see the truth about the world is not always to be wished. The two returned astronauts in "The Field of Vision" see and hear the immanence of God in everything, and at least one of the two would dearly prefer to return to normal perceptions of the surfaces of things: "All I have to do is open my eyes and I see the Face of God. And I'd give all my life just to see one human face again, to see a tree, just a tree. . . . " says the astronaut Hughes. "They can keep their God, they can keep their Light. I want the world back. I want questions, not the answer."

The surface world is described more clearly in "Direction of the Road." Le Guin herself has pointed out her obsession with trees, and in this story a tree takes the leading role. It is a monologue held by an old oak tree, which tells readers about how it strives to uphold the "Order of Things." It has much to do: growing and looming high over anybody who passes by, and then diminishing again until the spectator is gone.

In "The Ones Who Walk Away from Omelas," Le Guin carefully creates for the reader a word picture of the town of Omelas, as the festival of Summer begins. There are happy people everywhere; there is horse-racing and rich pastries, music and beer, and Le Guin asks the reader if they can imagine this place, if they can believe in its peace and plenty. Just as the picture is complete, she takes readers to a basement or cellar underneath the city, to a dark cupboard where old, dirty mops are stored. There, a child is kept in misery, shut away from light and air and human contact. All who live in Omelas know of this child's misery, and have been taken to see it when they reach the age of reason. Through a magical economy, all of Omelas prospers because this child is kept in misery. "The terms are clear. Not even a kind word may be spoken to the child."

All who live in Omelas have come to accept this bargain, but a very few leave when they learn of it, or later after much thought. Le Guin cannot tell readers where they go. It is a place even harder to imagine than Omelas, especially for readers who live in an actual Omelas of their own making and complicity.

A more "realistic" story in this collection is the final story, the portrait of Laia Aseio Odo, the anarchist philosopher who founded the culture of the planet Anarres, in the story "The Day before the Revolution." The story tells of the last day in Odo's life, using flashbacks from her childhood in a working-class slum and her daring political activism as an adult in and out of prison. Gradually her efforts and inability to live fully in keeping with her egalitarian ideals are shown. It is always "the day before the revolution," but the revolution is never over.

A biographical essay on Le Guin in *Science Fiction Writers* suggests that "Taoism,

Jungian psychology, anarchism, ecology, and human liberation resonate in Le Guin's visions of humankind's potential for unity and balance in the individual, in society, and perhaps in the galaxy." Essentially the same themes dominate Le Guin's utopian, dystopian, and surrealistic stories that she wrote for this collection, when she was also writing her most celebrated novels of "Earthsea," "Orsinia" and the "Hainish" cycle.

The stories in this collection which did not presage her novels, or fit into the erratic "future history" which all her science fiction books follow, are her early fantasies. Also included are the later ones Le Guin calls psychomyths: "more or less surrealistic tales, which share with fantasy the quality of taking place outside any history, outside of time, in that region of the living mind which—without invoking any consideration of immortality—seems to be without spatial or temporal limits at all."

◆ LITERARY QUALITIES ◆

Science fiction is defined differently by each person who reads or writes it, but Le Guin resists making distinctions between science fiction and fantasy. Even so, it is fantasy that she defends more wholeheartedly, arguing in her nonfiction writings on behalf of language rather than technology, of characterizing "the Other" rather than creating alien worlds, and of writing literature for children rather than for adults.

Le Guin is a writer of great versatility and power, as shown by the range of storytelling in this one volume. All her fiction is distinguished by careful craftsmanship, a limpid prose style, realistic detail (shown here in the creation of the imaginary worlds of Gethen, Libra, and the Hainish League, and the depiction of Earth in various present and future guises), profound ethical concerns portrayed here in characters as varied as Odo and Osden and

in actions such as arson and witch-burning, and mythical reverberations created through the use of symbolic and archetypal patterns. Her typical story involves a hero's quest for maturity and psychological integration, and her major theme is the need for balance and wholeness.

"A Trip to the Head" started in quiet desperation for the author. At a time when some writers abandon their craft (the Le Guins were in England; she remembers that "it was November and dark at two in the afternoon and raining, and the suitcase containing all my manuscripts had been stolen at the dock in Southampton and I hadn't written anything for months.") Le Guin sat down and began scribbling words, hopelessly. She got about as far as "'Try being Amanda,' the other said sourly." A year later, at home in Oregon with her suitcase of manuscripts recovered, she found the scribble on a rainy day and completed it. This is the kind of story Le Guin describes in her introduction to the story as a "Bung Puller." "The author for one reason or another has been stuck, can't work; and gets started again suddenly, with a pop and a lot of beer comes leaping out of the keg and foaming all over the floor."

Le Guin won the Hugo Award in 1973 for her story "The Ones Who Walk Away from Omelas," included in this collection. It is less of a story than a meditation on an idea of William James, to the effect that some people could not accept even universal prosperity and happiness if it depended on the deliberate subjection of even a single idiot child to abuse it could barely understand.

Le Guin's introduction to the story quotes James's *The Moral Philosopher and the Moral Life:* "All the higher, more penetrating ideals are revolutionary. They present themselves far less in the guise of effects of past experience than in that of probable causes of future experience, factors to which the environment and the lessons it has so far taught us must learn to bend." Le Guin herself adds, "The application of those two sentences to this story, and to science fiction, and to all thinking about the future, is quite direct."

Logan Hill, in his overview of this story for *Short Stories for Students*, states that:

> The story presents not a fully-developed fantastic world but a work-in-progress. . . .
> In this story the reader consciously follows the narrator's attempt to create a believable world with Utopian characteristics. The story can be read as a story about storytelling, a story about the act of creating an alternate, plausible reality.

In contrast to the standard assumption that a story must proceed according to a single narrative, Le Guin overtly requires each reader to envision his or her own narrative and his or her own personal Utopia, forcing the reader to consciously create the story with the narrator. The idea of such awesome responsibility is rarely admitted (though it is always the way stories are created), says Hill, before adding: "Le Guin softens her request by writing, in relation to technology, 'Or they could have none of that: it doesn't matter. As you like it.' She eases the readers' sense of responsibility while exploiting it and implicating the reader more thoroughly into the act of writing."

A highly respected author of fantasy fiction, Le Guin is praised for expanding the scope of the genre by combining conventional elements of science fiction with more traditional literary techniques, while offering thought-provoking speculations on alternative societies and philosophies. Her works employ psychic phenomena, including telepathy, clairvoyance, and precognition, and commonly incorporate the philosophies of Taoism and Zen, resulting in themes of reciprocity, unity, and holism. By presenting complex, often paradoxical symbols, images, and allusions, Le Guin stresses the need for individuals and societies to balance such dualities as order with chaos

and harmony with rebellion to achieve wholeness.

◆ SOCIAL SENSITIVITY ◆

The ten cloned siblings of John Chow in the story "Nine Lives" are less impossible than they seemed in 1969, when the story first appeared in *Playboy* magazine, under the byline U.K. Le Guin (the only time the author was ever asked to publish under gender-neutral initials). The cloned siblings' mutual understanding is far more a product of their shared upbringing than their shared genetics alone. In one of Le Guin's few actual speculations about scientific matters or human relations which she does not herself understand, this story proposes that cloned siblings raised together would be totally simpatico, by means of ordinary human communication; that is, with no imaginary extrasensory powers necessary.

This speculation is one of the few times Le Guin puts her foot wrong in this volume. Yes, Mr. Underhill is a silly little man, and the introspective characters in "A Trip to the Head" and "The Good Trip" are self-indulgent in their search for self-knowledge. But twins, triplets, and other multiple siblings are simply *not* dependably seamless teams who understand each other perfectly and have no emotional ties to other people. Not dependably enough, at any rate, to make raising clone teams a good investment at three million dollars per cloned sibling. Most of the positive aspects to the teamwork of the cloned siblings of John Chow could be gained by similar fostering of naturally conceived children (probably even unrelated children). There would be negative aspects as well, unrecognized in this story. Le Guin is correct that there would be no cloned armies, only a few exceptional individuals in the cautiously expanding population of Earth, and she is right to treat these ten clones as one self-reinforcing union.

In "The Day before the Revolution" Le Guin makes it clear that the process matters as a person or a nation approaches but never reaches the ideals being attempted. This reminder earned Le Guin another Hugo Award in 1974, at least partly because the story is inseparable from Le Guin's popular utopian novel *The Dispossessed*. From time to time, anarchism is a fashionable philosophy in Western countries. It is a rare anarchist who is as understandable as Laia Odo in this story, going about the business of her last day alive as the world steps into a revolutionary change.

One of the stories in this collection, "The Ones Who Walk Away from Omelas," is a masterpiece, unsurpassed at both creating a fantasy world and shifting in a heartbeat from delight to horror. For inspiring a sense of wonder it is matched only by Theodore Sturgeon's short story "The Silken-Swift" or possibly one of Ray Bradbury's most sensitive pieces from *Dandelion Wine*. As social commentary it is on a par with James Blish's short story "Who Steals My Purse." Far too many fantasy stories create unbelievable societies and settings with little or no consideration given to the supports that allow a noble to be rich or a minstrel to have the leisure to create beautiful music. Even fewer manage to infer, not state baldly, that readers ought to be aware of whose miseries support them in luxury. That awareness is called by Le Guin herself, in the introduction to this story, "the dilemma of the American conscience."

That dilemma is discussed very thoroughly by Logan Hill in his overview of this story for *Short Stories for Students*. "That the reader consciously collaborates with Le Guin to create this story becomes crucially important. The reader knowingly becomes an accomplice in the writing of this story and as a responsible creator must accept the results. Once the reader has imagined her Utopian Omelas, the narrator slowly begins to take control of the story." Hill goes on to suggest that

> By forcing the reader to create Omelas with her, she forces us to understand that while we do not live in ideal worlds, we live with ideals every day of our lives, and that even by not walking away, we support the ideals and the society we live in. That Le Guin cannot imagine a world not based on oppression forces one to face the oppression of one's own society.

Le Guin explains her philosophy of writing fantasy for children in *The Language of the Night*. She believes that Americans have a moral disapproval of fantasy "which comes from fear" and is related to "our Puritanism, our work ethic, our profit-mindedness, and even our sexual mores." As a result, Americans are taught "to repress their imagination, to reject it as something childish or effeminate, unprofitable, and probably sinful."

Le Guin's own belief is just the opposite:

> I believe that maturity is not an outgrowing, but a growing up: that an adult is not a dead child, but a child who survived. I believe that all the best faculties of a mature human being exist in the child, and that if these faculties are encouraged in youth they will act well and wisely in the adult, but if they are repressed and denied in the child they will stunt and cripple the adult personality.

For that reason, she believes it is the pleasant duty of librarians, teachers, parents, and writers to stimulate and encourage the humanizing power of the imagination "by giving it the best, absolutely the best and purest, nourishment that it can absorb."

What the child needs to grow up, Le Guin asserted in *The Language of the Night*, "is reality, the wholeness which exceeds all our virtue and all our vice. He needs knowledge; he needs self-knowledge. He needs to see himself and the shadow he casts. That is something he can face, his own shadow, and he can learn to control it and to be guided by it." Le Guin sees fantasy as a psychic and a moral journey "to self-knowledge, to adulthood, to the light." The goal of that journey is psychic wholeness.

◆ TOPICS FOR DISCUSSION ◆

1. What makes a story a fantasy?

2. Is it necessary to set a fantasy in a distant time or place?

3. What is the primary function of a fantasy story, as opposed to a contemporary realistic story?

4. How do you define science fiction and fantasy stories, as opposed to "mainstream" literature?

5. Is it necessary for a story to have a crisis or emergency in order for it to have events and conflict and change?

6. How does a fantasy story teach us to think about our real lives?

7. How has the author incorporated her real-life experiences raising her own children into some of these stories?

8. What are some of the standard mythic story elements which the author has integrated into some of these stories?

9. What ethical and moral issues does Le Guin cover in these stories?

10. How seriously can readers take a story with a fantasy setting? How much do these ideas matter, compared with real life?

◆ IDEAS FOR REPORTS AND PAPERS ◆

1. Outline a fantasy story of your own, one that should end up no more than two thousand words long. Will you begin with an outline, a "brainstorming" page with notes expanding outwards from the center, or a list of free-associations? Make paragraph-long character studies, or small sketches of your characters. Does your story have a theme or a goal? Can you visualize where your story takes place better if you make a sketch map? Display all your materials on a bulletin board near a writing desk. Does the outline help you write your story?

2. Choose one of the stories from *The Wind's Twelve Quarters* and create a similar bulletin board display to the one described above. Will you outline the story in point form notes, a "brainstorming" page or a list of free-associations? Make a few paragraph-long character studies or small sketches of the characters. Draw a sketch map of the place where the story occurs. Does the outline and display help you understand the story better?

3. Compare a story from *The Wind's Twelve Quarters* with a story by an author you admire. Who are the protagonists of these stories? Who are the viewpoint characters? Are these stories primarily driven by the plot, the theme, or the beliefs of the author? What do these stories tell you about the process of fantasy? What do they tell you about real life?

4. In what ways is it apparent to you as a reader that this author is female? American? Caucasian? Educated? How does this affect the stories she tells?

5. Choose one of these stories and summarize it, in the style of the short stories of Ernest Hemingway. How would the vocabulary change in the text and the title? How would the story feel differ-

ent, even though the same incident and actions occur?

6. Retell one of these stories in the style of a newspaper article. Compose an appropriate headline and quotes from witnesses. What will your news article's lead paragraph be? Will it be short and to the point, with a sidebar summarizing statistics or necessary information, or will it be detailed as if the journalist were trying for a Pulitzer Prize nomination?

7. Read a daily newspaper. Choose a moral or ethical situation which appears in one (or more) article(s) in the newspaper and in a story from this anthology. (An example would be cloning.) Make a photocopy of the article and of the story and highlight key words. Compare the people in the article with the characters in the story. How do the actions of the people relate to those of the characters? What can you learn from the crafted narrative of a story that you can only guess from a newspaper article? What did Le Guin understand, in the 1960s and 1970s, about this moral or ethical situation? Has much been learned about this issue in thirty or more years to contradict her?

8. Compare "Semley's Necklace" with "The Diamond Necklace" by Guy de Maupassant. What evidence can you find to indicate that Le Guin had read Maupassant's story? What changes has Le Guin rung on the classic story? How are the characters of the husbands (Loisel and Durhal) alike? What is their role in the story? How are both these stories profoundly egalitarian and humanist and feminist? How is the sin of pride explored by these authors? Does it matter that one story has a fantasy setting and the other is realistic?

9. How do Le Guin's characters face the end of the world as they know it? Who falls into despair in her stories, and who rises to battle? Who moves at her or his own center, having found *wu wei*? What, ultimately, do they achieve?

◆ RELATED TITLES ◆

The last story in this collection, "The Day before the Revolution," is the tale of the last day in the life of Odo, the philosopher whose beliefs became the core of the world of Anarres in Le Guin's novel *The Dispossessed*. As a literary one-two punch, the novel is an excellent companion piece to read either before or after this short story collection. Both works are particularly to be recommended as a tonic for adolescent angst and dissatisfaction with world events, politics and "the establishment."

The story "Winter's King" is a good introduction to Le Guin's novel *The Left Hand of Darkness*, which is a discussion of gender and human nature. It is a classic in the genre and highly recommended by many critics. A very readable novel, not a rant.

The story "Semley's Necklace" introduces the reader to the setting of *Rocannon's World,* one of Le Guin's early (and less celebrated) novels in her "Hainish" cycle. "Vaster Than Empires and More Slow" also takes place in the Hainish future galactic setting, and introduces two minor characters from the Cetian planet system, where *The Dispossessed* is set.

This story collection is the best entry point for a study of Le Guin's writings. The reader will know if she or he has any interest in following any of these settings, or characters, or ideas to a more fully-realized creation such as a novel or series of novels. A teacher with little time to read the collected works of this fine American author can at least begin the study and analysis of Le Guin with this book.

◆ FOR FURTHER REFERENCE ◆

Cumming, Elizabeth. "The Hand-Lady's Homebirth: Revisiting Ursula K. Le Guin's Worlds." *Science-Fiction Studies* (July, 1990): 153–166. A discussion of the world-building in Le Guin's fiction.

Cumming, Elizabeth. *Understanding Ursula K. Le Guin,* revised edition. Columbia: University of South Carolina Press, 1993.

Hill, Logan. "'The Ones Who Walk Away from Omelas.'" In *Short Stories for Students.* Detroit: Gale, 1997. Hill is a scholar specializing in American literature. In his essay, he discusses the possible parallels between Omelas and America, and the moral implications of this story where the reader collaborates with the author.

Knapp, Shoshana. "The Morality of Creation: Dostoevsky and William James in Le Guin's 'Omelas.'" *The Journal of Narrative Technique* (winter, 1985): 7581.

Le Guin, Ursula K. *Always Coming Home.* New York: Harper & Row, 1985. A collection of short and long stories, poems, drawings, plays, and music detailing the culture of the Kesh people, who live in a river valley on the California coast in the future.

Le Guin, Ursula K. *The Dispossessed: An Ambiguous Utopia.* New York: Harper and Row, 1974. A novel outlining both the utopian world of Anarres and the learnings done by one man in both sociology and physics and mathematics. A modern classic.

Le Guin, Ursula K. *The Language of the Night: Essays on Fantasy and Science Fiction.* Edited by Susan Wood. New York: Putnam, 1979. An accessible and authoritative discussion of literature, giving both the history and a working vocabulary.

Schweitzer, Darrell. "Ursula K. Le Guin." In *St. James Guide to Fantasy Writers.* Detroit: St. James Press, 1996.

Wood, Susan. "Discovering Worlds: The Fiction of Ursula K. LeGuin." In *Voices for the Future,* vol. 2. Edited by Thomas D. Clareson. Bowling Green, OH: Bowling Green University Popular Press, 1978. A Canadian critic's perspective on Le Guin's fiction.

Paula Johanson

YOU WANT WOMEN TO VOTE, LIZZIE STANTON?

Biography

1995

Author: Jean Fritz

◆

Major Books for Young Adults

The Cabin Faced West, 1958
Story of Eli Whitney, 1962
George Washington's Breakfast, 1969
Cast for a Revolution, 1972
*Who's That Stepping on Plymouth
    Rock?*, 1975
Will You Sign Here, John Hancock?, 1976
What's the Big Idea, Ben Franklin?, 1976
*Where Do You Think You're Going,
    Christopher Columbus?*, 1980
*Traitor: The Case of Benedict
    Arnold*, 1981
Homesick: My Own Story, 1982
*Can't You Make Them Behave, King
    George?*, 1982

The Double Life of Pocahontas, 1983
China Homecoming, 1985
*Shh! We're Writing the
    Constitution*, 1987
*China's Long March: 6,000 Miles of
    Danger*, 1988
The Great Little Madison, 1991
Surprising Myself, 1993
*Around the World in a Hundred
    Years*, 1994
*Harriet Beecher Stowe and the Beecher
    Preachers*, 1994
*You Want Women to Vote, Lizzie
    Stanton?* 1995
Why Not, Lafayette?, 1999

◆ ABOUT THE AUTHOR ◆

Jean Guttery was born in Hankow, China, on November 16, 1915. Her parents, Arthur and Myrtle Guttery, were missionaries for the Young Men's Christian Association (Y.M.C.A.). Around 1928, she and her family left China to escape the warfare following the revolution that removed the old monarchy and replaced it with a fragile civilian government. While in China, Jean kept a notebook of her thoughts and observations that later served as a basis for writing about China, writings that reveal a nostalgia for China.

After she graduated from Wheaton College in 1937, Jean took a job with an advertising agency in New York, but left to work for a textbook publisher, Silver Burdett Company. She married Michael Fritz on November 1, 1941. Soon after, he was called to military service and sent to San Francisco after Japan bombed Pearl Harbor and America entered into World War II. Jean, her husband, and their two children moved to Dobbs Ferry, New York, in 1953. There, she found a job as a librarian and created a children's literature section.

During the 1960s, she researched the history of the American Revolution and wrote a book intended for adults but suitable for teenagers, *Cast for a Revolution*, and several works for young readers such as *Will You Sign Here, John Hancock?* Although she has written distinguished fiction, Fritz is plainly drawn to biography, particularly lives presented in the context of the history of their times. In 1986, she received the Laura Ingalls Wilder Award for her lifetime of writing. Although published after Fritz won the award, *Harriet Beecher Stowe and the Beecher Preachers* may be the most universally praised of her books.

Fritz won the National Book Award several times. The Children's Book Guild gave her its honor award in 1978 for her many historical writings. In 1982, her autobiography *Homesick: My Own Story* was named a Newbery Honor Book and a *Boston Globe-Horn Book* Honor Book, and it won the American Book Award (what the National Book Award was called for a brief period). *The Double Life of Pocahontas* won the *Boston Globe-Horn Book* Nonfiction Award for 1984, and *The Great Little Madison* won the same award in 1990. The Madison biography also received the Orbis Pictus Award from the National Council of English Teachers.

◆ OVERVIEW ◆

Elizabeth Cady Stanton led a life of privilege, enjoyed cooking for her family and, in her later years, looked like a lovable grandmother, speaking soft, friendly words to strangers and friends alike. She was also one of history's most outspoken advocates of women's rights who chose to endure hardship and hostility to spread her ideas about the equality of men and women, and the need to allow women to vote. She faced down the hoots and howls of her enemies, risked her life, and uttered words that shaped public debate in her day. Her ideas about civil liberties for women have formed part of the foundation of the modern women's movement.

"As a child," says Fritz, "[Elizabeth Cady] knew that girls didn't count for much, but she didn't expect to change that." The child who did not expect to change how America treated its women became one of the people who influenced change. She wrote many of the speeches delivered by the firebrand Susan B. Anthony; she delivered many others herself. The sweet, loving woman with the disarming appearance created firestorms of controversy, wore trousers in public, likened women's lives to those of slaves, and was one of the first people to articulate the idea that "white men" were to blame. Even after her death, mention of her name could spark heated debate among friends as well as foes. In *You Want Women to Vote, Lizzie Stanton?* Jean Fritz presents the woman in her contradictions and humanity, while showing how she became one of the titans of American social history.

◆ SETTING ◆

Lizzie Stanton led an active, often adventurous life, and the settings change in *You Want Women to Vote, Lizzie Stanton?* as she moves from place to place. She lived most of her adult life in New York State, much of her middle years in a country house, and her later years in New York City, where she entertained social reformers. According to Fritz, Stanton was unhappy for awhile living in the country, far from the social activists she liked to meet. During that period, she also found her children to be more annoyance than pleasure, and she did not adjust to her country life until she found outlets for her many ideas about reforming American society. Thereafter, Fritz observes, Stanton started to take pleasure in what then would have been considered womanly arts, such as cooking and caring for children. According to Fritz, this is something Stanton's friend Susan B. Anthony did not understand, believing that Stanton should be unencumbered by children in order to focus on writing about women's social and political rights. Stanton had several children, sometimes bemoaned the time she spent on their care, yet produced an enormous body of writings. Until she found a housekeeper-nanny who proved trustworthy, loyal, and capable, Stanton bore the responsibility for her household chores.

Her husband lived mostly in New York City, visiting the home in the country only a few months a year. This, Fritz says, became a habit for Henry and Elizabeth. After she moved the family to New York City, they found that they were comfortable living apart for much of the year, even though they could live under the same roof all the time if they chose. In New York City, Stanton formed alliances with other social reformers, often entertaining them in her home, and she thrived on the attention she received.

You Want Women to Vote, Lizzie Stanton? has two other major settings: London and Kansas. Stanton had been elected to attend a world abolitionist meeting in London. While voyaging there, she embarrassed some of the other American delegates with her fearless behavior, such as requesting to be hoisted in a chair up the main mast just because she wanted to see what the view was like from the top of the mast. This would form a pattern for her, perpetually defying stereotypes about what women should not do and what they could do. Later in her life she would travel by train

across America and scandalize others with behavior deemed unsuitable for a sweet old woman, such as playing cards with soldiers while traveling across Texas. In London, Stanton met with prejudice against women that was more severe than what she encountered in America. Even male American delegates were outraged when the duly elected female representatives were at first denied admittance to the meeting hall and then were allowed in an area once reserved for slaves and told to be silent. For the outspoken Stanton, this had to be very trying. Even so, she would visit London again in later years to meet with friends and supporters there.

Although the campaign for woman's right to vote in Kansas took up a short period of Stanton's life, Fritz covers it in detail, perhaps so that it may serve as an example of how determined Stanton was as a campaigner. The Supreme Court ruled that the enfranchisement of women was up to the individual states, and a proposition giving Kansas women the right to vote had been offered. Stanton endured, in various humorous scenes, noisy pigs, bedbugs, mice walking across her while she tried to sleep, and uncomfortable carriages. Journeying across rivers and into remote parts of Kansas, she learned to ask the nearest farmstead for a place to sleep when the sun was setting. The Kansas proposition lost, but Stanton developed the fortitude that was to enable her to crisscross the United States for many years, campaigning for woman's suffrage.

◆ THEMES AND CHARACTERS ◆

The central figure of *You Want Women to Vote, Lizzie Stanton?* was born Elizabeth Cady in 1815 in Johnstown, New York, which was "a gloomy-looking town that cowered beneath poplar trees." Elizabeth had four sisters—Harriet, Margaret, Tryphena, and Catherine—three dead brothers, and another brother, Eleazar, who died just after college. This grieved her father, Judge Cady, greatly, and Elizabeth wanted to make him happy. She was a girl, but Fritz says, "Still, perhaps she could make it up to her father if she became just as good as a boy, as smart and brave as Eleazar had been. So that's what she'd do. To be smart, she would study Greek. To be brave, she would learn to ride a horse so well that she would be able to jump fences—even high fences." By this account, Elizabeth was a remarkable child, for she learned to be an accomplished equestrienne, and "Elizabeth was put into the highest class of mathematics and languages at Johnstown Academy," graduating at age sixteen.

Even so, her father wished she had been a boy. She remembered being in her father's office once when a woman who had purchased a farm and run it with her own money came for legal help, saying that she had married and that her husband later died and left the farm to a wastrel son who mistreated her. Judge Cady told the woman that she had no legal recourse, that her husband automatically owned everything that was hers and could do with it what he wanted. Elizabeth was outraged, but her father showed her the law and told her that the law had to be changed by a legislature that was elected. Fritz implies that this was a lesson Elizabeth learned well and never forgot— that male legislators elected by men had made a law that denied a woman the right to her own property.

The pivotal moments in Stanton's life are emphasized in *You Want Women to Vote, Lizzie Stanton?* One of these, according to Fritz, was Elizabeth's visit to a house owned by abolitionists: "People at the Smith house didn't talk about obeying laws; they talked about justice." Here, then, is the theme of *You Want Women to Vote, Lizzie Stanton?*: justice. Fritz's account of Stanton's life is

one of a lifetime devoted to justice. Stanton begins by becoming an abolitionist, against her father's wishes. Her decision to defy her father in this and other social issues may have been prompted, at least in part, by her love for someone she met at the Smith's home. Henry Stanton "was a fiery abolitionist who hoped to go into politics one day." Although he was "[t]en years older than Elizabeth, Henry was tall, handsome, and dramatic looking." Impulsively, she accepted his marriage proposal the moment he made it. This seems out of keeping with Elizabeth's character, because she seems careful and calculating throughout *You Want Women to Vote, Lizzie Stanton?*, but perhaps that impetuousness that makes her decide to vote one day when a Republican carriage stops at her home, offer rides to voters, and have herself hauled to the top of a ship's mast for the view, would better help explain how the studious, rational young woman would leap at Henry's proposal. After withstanding a long period of Judge Cady's disapproval of the marriage, Elizabeth and Henry eloped on May 1, 1840.

This began a strange marriage in which the spouses were more often apart than together, in which neither really supported the other in the pursuit of her or his interests, yet which produced several children over a period of twenty years and seems to have been loving. Early in the marriage, Stanton formulated ideas that would become the foundation of her work for women's rights. For instance, she noticed, "In everyday life woman's rights seemed always to take second place to woman's work." Henry complained that such attitudes embarrassed him and could hinder his political career. It seems odd that an abolitionist, someone who wanted to liberate slaves, should oppose the liberation of women, Elizabeth pointed out to her husband. In fact, she expected the liberation of the slave to coincide with the liberation of women.

When this did not happen, she was very disappointed.

Yet, Fritz remarks, "Elizabeth Cady Stanton prided herself on her ability to cope with difficulties." Much of the first half of *You Want Women to Vote, Lizzie Stanton?* is an account of Stanton's increasing frustrations. "What angered her," writes Fritz, "was the general condition of women who had no say in anything." It is extraordinary how Stanton could turn her views into action. For instance, when she and some friends decide to hold a convention on women's rights, they are ready in one week to stage the convention and persuade such renowned civil rights figures as Frederick Douglass to attend. They even draw up a document of principles. It shows Stanton's predilection for striking, controversial statements that are sure to draw attention: "'The history of mankind,' they wrote, 'is a history of repeated injuries . . . of man toward woman.'" What Stanton wanted most was "women to have the right to vote." A radical idea, Fritz says, that even Stanton's comrades thought might be too far-fetched.

Even so, Stanton's flair for words put her at the center of controversy all of her life. "A woman, [Elizabeth] would later say, was a woman first, and a wife and mother second," Fritz writes, but "'A woman is nobody,' a Philadelphia paper declared. 'A wife is everything.'" This is a mild attack compared to some of the others launched at Stanton, but it summarizes what her opposition believed. According to Fritz, Stanton replied to every newspaper attack on her, telling her friends that the papers would print her replies to their columns and thus allow her to reach an audience otherwise closed to her. This shows her to be a wise strategist who learned to take advantage of even slim opportunities to get her ideas across to Americans. As Fritz notes, "Elizabeth was quick, daring, charismatic, and she had a way with words."

Another important figure in *You Want Women to Vote, Lizzie Stanton?* is Susan B. Anthony, still one of America's best-known historical figures. Stanton and Anthony bumped into each other on a New York City street corner in 1851 and from that moment formed an abiding friendship. Not that they did not try each other's patience. Stanton had children and took pride in raising them, even though she sometimes yearned to be free of her responsibilities toward them. Anthony vowed not to marry so that she could devote herself to the cause of women's rights, especially the right to vote, and she urged Stanton to stop having children so that she could devote her energies to social campaigning. Fritz says that Stanton did, at one time, vow that her next child would be her last. This was not to be. Stanton continued to have children into her forties and, although she complained to Anthony about the time they required from her, they remembered their mother with fondness.

Even though, Fritz asserts, Stanton was an advocate of women's rights, she did not necessarily disparage household activities. In fact, except for a short frustrating period before she found some reliable household help, she enjoyed some aspects of keeping house, especially cooking. She liked to entertain, and took pleasure in making dishes to eat. Apparently, Stanton even convinced Anthony into helping in the kitchen. None of this seemed demeaning to Stanton, for she believed that "No matter what anyone said or didn't say, she really was as good as a man."

Under Fritz's pen, Stanton becomes a compellingly engrossing figure. Sometimes contradictory, sometimes giving in to social pressure—as she does when she stops wearing pants even though she liked them very much—often defiant, and ready to do battle, Stanton takes shape as one of the most radical feminists of her day while retaining her own personal loves and interests. "Indeed," Fritz remarks about the aging Stanton, "it was hard for strangers to believe that this plump, motherly lady with the white hair was the radical Mrs. Stanton." Motherly, gentle, and tougher than steel, Stanton eventually strides across Fritz's stage as someone whose determination changed America's culture. She passed her determination to younger women who carried on her battle for decades after her death, and she passed on her spirit to her own children. The best line in *You Want Women to Vote, Lizzie Stanton?* is given to Stanton's daughter Harriot: "When she was a little girl her father once told her to come down from a high tree limb, but she replied, 'Tell Bob. He's three years younger and one branch higher.'" A delicious line!

◆ LITERARY QUALITIES ◆

You Want Women to Vote, Lizzie Stanton? is a short biography, with a great deal of information condensed into a short space. It is probably intended for readers at the younger end of young adulthood, but it is written so well that it is actually a pleasure for grownups to read. As such, it is one of Fritz's best works, a triumph of sparkling diction and concision. However, there are drawbacks to concision, one being that not all the events of a life can be told. What Fritz does is focus on significant incidents in Stanton's life that tell much about what she did at other times. For example, Stanton's campaign in Kansas is told at length. Fritz tends to include humor in her writings, so the odd inconveniences such as loud, curious pigs are highlighted. Yet, her account shows Stanton's sense of humor and fortitude when trying to overcome a daunting task, comparing incidents of her childhood with events in her adult life. This gives the biography a fine continuity from chapter to chapter without the need to go into detail about every one of Stanton's many campaigns.

◆ SOCIAL SENSITIVITY ◆

Lizzie Stanton was a very controversial person in her own day, and some of her opinions would be considered radical even today. She began her public career as an abolitionist, someone who tried to abolish slavery worldwide. She insisted that women were also slaves, and Fritz notes that "when the slaves got their freedom, she figured, women would get theirs too." She tried to have the Fourteenth Amendment to the Constitution include women in its declaration of rights for African Americans and was bitterly disappointed when this failed to happen.

Most readers would be hesitant to compare Stanton's relatively comfortable life with the lives of America's slaves, whose living conditions were beyond appalling. A question asked in her own day was "what about black women"? What white woman lives a life nearly as bad as that of a black woman slave? Fritz does not go into this issue in detail, but she points out that Stanton was focusing on the laws governing women's lives, laws that declared wives to be the property of their husbands. Further, Stanton was not just talking about the lives of upper-middle-class women such as herself, but the life of any woman who could be beaten by her husband while laws specified what men were allowed to beat women with. She was stirred by the plight of women rendered destitute because their property and earnings belonged to their husbands and their sons; by women who suffered abuse sanctioned by laws; by women, as a Philadelphia paper declared, who counted for nothing.

Also likely to stir debate is Stanton's hostility toward clergymen. According to

Fritz, "Elizabeth blamed preachers for holding women down." Fritz writes, "And men believed that they were the 'lords of creation,' Elizabeth said. They claimed that the minds of men and women were different, each suited only to its own 'sphere.'" Stanton blamed the clergy for promoting this view, for giving what she considered to be a biased view of the Bible. Stanton even wrote a book about the passages in the Bible where women are mentioned, and she asserts their equality with men before God. There are many modern-day Americans who would disagree with Stanton's view, claiming that their religious faith requires women to submit to men. This issue is still one that can spark angry debate because religious faith is a deeply personal matter that shapes people's lives. For her part, Stanton refused to "obey" her husband, and she inspired some women to have the "obey" taken out of their wedding vows, commonplace today, but a radical departure from custom during Stanton's lifetime.

Although Stanton campaigned for revision of laws that made women subject to men, Fritz says that she emphasized the enfranchisement of women, that is, the right of women to vote. Stanton and Susan B. Anthony and other women actually tried to vote, insisting that the Fourteenth Amendment to the Constitution gave the vote to American citizens and that women were explicitly included in law and the Constitution as citizens. Those who actually cast ballots in elections were arrested and convicted in a kangaroo court in which the judge forbade the jury to even consider the women's defense. When Stanton tried to vote, a man wrapped his arms around the ballot box, covering the slot with his body. These efforts by Stanton and others to claim their rights as citizens to vote in public elections helped lay the foundation for the eventual success of the women's suffrage movement.

Stanton believed that the right to vote was the key to the liberation of women from legal and social restrictions on their civil rights. The right to vote meant being able to elect the people who would write America's laws. When she was invited to speak to Congress, some senators treated her with contempt, chatting with one another or reading a newspaper while she spoke. When she addressed a Senate committee, the chairman and other committee members pointedly conducted other business while she spoke. It is worth noting that there were always senators sympathetic to her cause, men who introduced bills to give women equal rights with men, and these bills always drew supporting votes, although never enough for passage. Ulysses S. Grant even lent his prestige as a war hero and President of the United States to Stanton's cause by hosting her and other women of the women's civil rights movement at the White House. Eventually, Stanton ran for the House of Representatives, arguing that the law may bar women from voting (although she did not think so), but the law plainly did not bar women citizens of America from being elected to public office by the votes of men. She lost, but her campaign brought her much satisfaction because some men did vote for her.

One of the most controversial aspects of Stanton's long career advocating women's rights was her insistence that men be excluded from women's rights organizations. As Fritz notes, this caused a split in the women's rights movement that lasted decades. Stanton wanted women to take as radical a stance on women's issues as possible, and she thought men would make women's rights organizations too conservative. In 1869, this resulted in a major division of resources between two national organizations, the National Woman Suffrage Association, founded by Stanton and Anthony, and the American Woman Suffrage Association, founded by the prominent suffragist Lucy Stone and others. The exclusion of men from Stanton and Anthony's association could be seen as hateful, as well as an unsound campaign tactic in a legal system in which the cooperation of men was necessary in order to have laws changed. Stone, who was viewed as very radical in her day, wanted male supporters to be recognized and included in a social revolution.

A revolution was what Stanton wanted, and she used the word "revolution" in her writings and speeches. As she aged into a stout, grandmotherly woman, she became ever more radical. She seems to have wanted to recreate the American social system. According to Fritz's account, Stanton's worry about Stone's American Woman Suffrage Association being more conservative than the National Woman Suffrage Association may have been valid, for the word "revolution" was disturbing to the rival organization. When the two organizations united in 1890 in the National American Women's Suffrage Association, Stanton remained opposed to men being members of the organization. When she was nominated to be the united association's president, Fritz says, "She did not decline. But she did leave for Europe right away." That Stanton discriminated against male supporters may well be disturbing, not only for what it says about her attitudes toward men, but because it seems in retrospect to have been a grave tactical error. Just as her insistence on comparing the lives of white women to those of slaves may have alienated potential supporters, her rejection of men in her organization may have alienated other potential supporters—men whose votes were needed to change laws.

On the other hand, Stanton's uncompromising attitude may have been an inspiration to other women. Furthermore, her pleasure in her family and her pleasure in cooking, as well as her friendly appearance, may have lent credence to the idea that a woman could be assertive and adventurous and committed to women's rights, while enjoying family life. As Fritz writes it, about the kitchen "Henry used to say that Susan [Anthony] stirred the pudding, Elizabeth stirred up Susan, and Susan stirred up the world."

◆ TOPICS FOR DISCUSSION ◆

1. Why would Elizabeth Cady Stanton want to exclude men from her women's rights organization?

2. Why would Susan B. Anthony choose to remain unmarried throughout her life? Could it have some relationship to laws that cost a woman her farm early in *You Want Women to Vote, Lizzie Stanton?*

3. How could Stanton like both her home life and her passion for campaigning for women's rights?

4. Does Fritz do a good job of showing how Stanton's family influenced her life and her work?

5. Why would Stanton expect women's liberation to coincide with the liberation of slaves?

6. What does Stanton's campaign in Kansas tell us about her personality?

7. Which of Stanton's views as presented in *You Want Women to Vote, Lizzie Stanton?* would still be controversial? What makes them controversial?

8. Why would Stanton refuse to hear anything bad about her father in public, even though he disapproved of her work to change the status of women in America?

9. Why would Elizabeth think she could be as good as a boy to her father?

10. Why would Stanton think that the right to vote was crucial for women's liberation?

11. Why would Stanton say she wanted no more children yet continue to have them?

12. What specifically were Stanton's views on women and housekeeping?

◆ IDEAS FOR REPORTS AND PAPERS ◆

1. Was Stanton or Anthony the more successful advocate of women's rights?

2. Fritz mentions that by the 1890s three states had given women full enfranchisement. Choose one of these states and write a short history of how women gained their voting rights in it. Be sure to discuss why they were successful.

3. What aspect of Stanton's life do you miss from *You Want Women to Vote, Lizzie Stanton?* What would you like to know more about?

4. Fritz mentions that many years passed after Stanton's death before a Constitutional amendment was passed that assured women the right to vote. How did the amendment come to be written and then passed?

5. What has been Stanton's influence on American society?

6. Women elected by Americans to attend an international convention on the abolition of slavery were not allowed by the English to participate in the gathering in London. What was the status of women in England at the time? How did it compare to the status of women in America? Why would American men accept women as important participants in abolitionism while Englishmen would not?

7. Why was Susan B. Anthony chosen to appear on an American coin?

8. Fritz mentions that Stanton's children participated in the women's rights movement. Which ones did? What did they do?

9. Look up the document Stanton and her comrades wrote for the women's convention they first held. What does it say? Is any of it true now? Have any of its objectives been achieved? Which ones have not? Are they still important?

10. How important is the written word for social change in America? What does the life of Stanton reveal about this?

◆ RELATED TITLES ◆

Of Fritz's other works, the book that most closely parallels *You Want Women to Vote, Lizzie Stanton?* is *Harriet Beecher Stowe and the Beecher Preachers*. In this biography, Fritz traces the life of another woman whose independence of spirit began when she tried to be the boy her father wanted. Where Lizzie took to feats of physical courage such as horse jumping, Harriet tried to please her father with her skillful writings and her ability to write a good sermon. In both *You Want Women to Vote, Lizzie Stanton?* and *Harriet Beecher Stowe and the Beecher Preachers*, the father just declares that he wished his daughter had been a boy. In each life, the daughter was circumspect about her father's response to her work, although in *You Want Women to Vote, Lizzie Stanton?* Fritz says Judge Cady strongly disapproved of his daughter's efforts to alter the status of women in society.

Both Stanton and Stowe were women of words, using their writings as their weapons in campaigns for social reform. Stowe became world famous and an intimate of presidents, senators, and royalty, but Stanton evidently did not, even though President Grant took an interest in her advocacy of civil rights for women. Both women were hated bitterly by opponents. Defenders of slavery openly advocated the murder of Stowe; Fritz does not mention much violence against Stanton, although she notes that the mayor of Albany, New York, held a gun while he sat beside her as she gave a speech, apparently to keep men in the audience in line. Both women had effects on American society, helping to shape what America would become. Stowe was given more credit in her day, perhaps because her influence on attitudes about the Civil War was more obvious than Stanton's effects on attitudes toward women's rights. Even so, both women had many accomplishments to look back upon when they reached great old age. Late in life, Stowe, like Stanton, advocated more civil rights for women and was an inspiring figure for the suffragist movement. In the 1890s, Stanton could rejoice that three states—Wyoming, Oklahoma, and Oregon—had given women full enfranchisement, as well as other states that had taken small steps to recognizing the full rights of citizenship for women.

Nowadays, both Stowe and Stanton remain controversial. Fritz goes into more depth in her account of Stowe's life and influence than she does in her account of Stanton's, and she seems to give more weight to Stowe's achievements, perhaps because Stowe remains esteemed for the artfulness of her novels, whereas Stanton's writings are somewhat obscure. On the other hand, Fritz makes her admiration for both women plain, and she suggests that their influence on how modern Americans live their lives is pervasive. Stanton has long been in the shadow of her close friend Susan B. Anthony—whose image has even appeared on an American coin—but perhaps the knowledge that many of Anthony's speeches were written by Stanton will encourage readers of *You Want Women to Vote, Lizzie Stanton?* to take an interest in what she had to say.

Another interesting aspect of both *You Want Women to Vote, Lizzie Stanton?* and *Harriet Beecher Stowe and the Beecher Preachers* is Fritz's coverage of their influence on their children. Stanton's children, boys and girls, seem to have loved her very much. Stanton's daughters were, in Fritz's account, liberated for their day, especially in their marriages. Stowe's children loved her, and two daughters devoted themselves to helping her mother in her campaign for women's rights, becoming important leaders even after their mother's death.

◆ FOR FURTHER REFERENCE ◆

Burns, Mary M. *Horn Book Magazine* (January–February 1996): 89–90. About *You Want Women to Vote, Lizzie Stanton?* Burns declares, "As Jean Fritz demonstrates in her inimitable style, Lizzie Stanton not only wanted women to vote but, in her passion to secure that right, helped to change history as well as make it."

Foner, Eric. *New York Times Book Review* (November 12, 1995): 36. The reviewer thinks that *You Want Women to Vote, Lizzie Stanton?* is unremarkable.

O'Connell, Rebecca. *School Library Journal* (September 1995): 208. O'Connell praises *You Want Women to Vote, Lizzie Stanton?* and recommends it.

Review of *So You Want Women to Vote, Lizzie Stanton? Publishers Weekly* (August 28, 1995): 114. "Fritz maintains her reputation for fresh and lively historical writing with this biography of the 19th-century American feminist" declares this reviewer, "imparting to her readers not just a sense of Stanton's accomplishments but a picture of the greater society Stanton strove to change."

Rochman, Hazel. *Booklist* (August 1995): 1948. Rochman says that *You Want Women to Vote, Lizzie Stanton?* "is Fritz at her ebullient best, writing a historical biography that weaves together the life of a spirited leader and the fight for her cause."

Kirk H. Beetz

APPENDIX: GLOSSARY OF LITERARY TERMS

─────────────◆─────────────

allegory: A metaphorical work in which characters and events represent abstract ideas and in which the story is usually intended to teach a moral. Hans Peter Richter's *Friedrich* is allegorical in that it is meant to teach the dangers of inaction in the face of evil and in that each character represents the attitudes of a particular segment of World War II German society.

allusion: A literary allusion is an indirect reference to other works of literature. For example, in Irene Hunt's *Across Five Aprils* the references to lilacs allude to Walt Whitman's famous poem "When Lilacs Last in the Dooryard Bloom'd" Through literary allusions, authors enrich their writing by drawing on earlier works.

analogy: The process of explaining one idea by comparing it to a dissimilar but usually more concrete idea. Metaphors and similes are types of analogies.

antagonist: An antagonist is anything that opposes a protagonist. Antagonists come in four forms: 1) a person 2) the natural world 3) society 4) a force or emotion within the protagonist (for example, Huck wrestles with his conscience in Mark Twain's *Adventures of Huckleberry Finn*, and Daniel learns to deal with his anger in Elizabeth George Speare's *Bronze Bow*).

bildungsroman: A novel that is primarily concerned with the coming of age of an idealistic protagonist. As such, the novel explores the conflict between the protagonist's romantic or even impractical outlook and the realities that he or she must eventually face. J. D. Salinger's *The Catcher in the Rye* is an example of a *bildungsroman*.

biographical novel: A work in which the author presents the known facts of a real person's life. The author builds on this foundation to create fictional dialogue and descriptions of characters' emotions, and occasionally offers a psychological analysis of characters' motivations.

catharsis: The process by which a reader, moved to pity or fear by a work of literature, releases pent-up emotions and sometimes undergoes a change of heart. The term was originally applied to ancient Greek drama by Aristotle.

characterization: The process by which a character is developed in a narrative or drama. Often the character's personality is revealed through conflict or stress in the plot.

climax: The moment when the conflict in the plot reaches its peak of intensity and characters must face the consequences of their actions.

comedy: A literary work that is intended to please, amuse, and entertain, often by being funny. Comedies often have happy endings, but readers should remember that some comedy is grim or tragic, as in Joseph Heller's novel *Catch-22*.

coming of age: A theme in a narrative in which a young person takes a significant step away from childhood and into adulthood.

conflict: The struggle that results from the interaction of the protagonist and the antagonist.

critic: A person, often a scholar, who attempts to explain and evaluate works of literature or other art.

dialogue: Conversation between two or more characters.

didacticism: The practice of including clearly stated ideas, morals, sermons, or other forms of instruction in a literary work. Usually a didactic work is meant to teach its readers a moral lesson.

drama: Deriving its origins from theatrical presentations, the term "drama" in fiction refers to the actions that cause the climax. "Dramatic action" refers to a series of events leading to an inevitable outcome.

epic: A work of literature that celebrates a people's heroic traditions. Homer's *Iliad* is an epic about the war of ancient Greek heroes against the city of Troy. The ancient Greeks thought of the *Iliad* as the embodiment of the ideals of their society. By its narrowest definition, the epic is a narrative poem, but many prose works that celebrate a people's heroic tradition, such as the stories of King Arthur, are now called epics.

fable: A narrative that is intended to provide moral instruction, often featuring as main characters animals who speak and act like people.

fairy tale: A fanciful tale that usually employs magic and mystical creatures. Fairy tales are a subcategory of folktales.

fiction: A prose story that is produced from the imagination rather than from fact, although some works of fiction are based on historical or biographical information.

first-person narrator: A character who tells a story. This kind of narrator typically refers to himself or herself as "I." The first-person narrator tells the story from the *first-person point of view*.

flashback: A jump backward in the chronological order of the narrative, usually accomplished in literature through recollection or dream sequences.

foil: In literature, a foil is a character whose marked difference from another character, often the protagonist, highlights the other character's distinctive personality traits. Settings or events may also act as foils.

folktale: A story that usually has its origin in the oral tradition, having been passed on from one storyteller to the next by word of mouth. Folktales are often fanciful and romantic. The term "folktale" is also sometimes applied to short stories that imitate folktales, even though they were composed originally in written form.

foreshadowing: The process of hinting at the outcome of the story by placing literal or symbolic clues about what will happen before the events actually take place.

Gothic: A kind of literature that emphasizes the mysterious and grotesque. In popular fiction, this often takes the form of the horror novel, which emphasizes a frightening supernatural world.

hero: A character, usually a person or animal, who confronts a chain of potentially tragic events. In classical literature the hero, through his courage, integrity or nobility, may reverse the course of tragedy; other heroes risk or sacrifice their lives for some noble or divine cause. However, readers should remember that while heroes are often "good" people, they are not always so, especially in contemporary literature. Sometimes a hero begins as the villain but through self-discovery changes his view of life, as does Scrooge in Charles Dickens's *A Christmas Carol*. The hero might also be unaware that he or she is acting heroically, thus becoming a naive or passive hero, such as Anne Frank or Anthony Bums. Usually a hero's actions result in an outcome that society considers "morally correct," but there is a body of fiction in which the "hero" works against society, as in Joseph Heller's *Catch-22*. This type of character is called an "anti-hero." In some regards even Huck Finn is an anti-hero.

historical novel: A work of fiction that uses historical facts as the basis for the story but adds imaginative material, such as dialogue.

imagery: The use of colorful description to produce vivid mental images. Often these images hold symbolic significance in the book, such as Holden Caulfield's "image" of children falling off a cliff in J.D. Salinger's *The Catcher in the Rye*.

irony: The use of words to convey the opposite of their literal meaning. A reader's understanding of the characters and plot prepares him to understand that a statement is ironic. Similarly, a scene in a work contains "dramatic irony" when the words or acts of a character or group of characters have meanings that the characters do not perceive but which the audience or readers do understand. For instance, in Mark Twain's *Huckleberry Finn*, the reader knows that Huck and Jim's voyage down the river is taking Jim into slavery, while the characters believe they are escaping to freedom.

metaphor: A figure of speech that draws a comparison between two unlike objects. "His face is a bright red tomato" is an example of a metaphor.

moral: This is the lesson that a literary work—most often a fable or allegory—is meant to teach. Most literary works do not have explicit morals.

narrative: The narrator's account or interpretation of a sequence of events in a novel or short story.

narrator: The person who relates the events of a story. A first-person narrator refers to himself or herself as "I," and usually participates in the events of the story. A third-person narrator is usually not involved in the story and refers to all the characters as "he" or "she." An omniscient narrator is a third-person narrator who reveals the thoughts of the characters. A narrator who reveals the thoughts of just one character, usually the protagonist, is referred to as "limited omniscient."

novel: A long work of fiction that has both a main plot and subplots. It often, but not always, features many characters. A novel always builds to a climax, the moment when the characters must face the consequences of their actions.

novelette/novella: These terms are sometimes used to distinguish a short novel from a long novel or a short story. But a novelette or novella's length is not as important a characteristic as the number of characters it includes or the moment at which the climax occurs.

personification: A literary device by which human qualities are attributed to inanimate objects or abstract ideas. "The ocean crashed against the shore in a violent rage" is an example of personification because rage is a human emotion that oceans cannot experience.

plot: The actions that derive from conflict in a narrative or drama. In a novel, these usually build to one major climax. Novels that depend too much on plot and not enough on theme and characterization are considered inferior works of literature. Novels that contain a series of loosely connected plots are called "episodic."

point of view: In literature, this refers to the particular perspective of the narrator of the story. An omniscient narrator has a broad, all-knowing point of view; a first-person narrator has a much more limited point of view. A "shifting point of view" alternates the narrative perspectives of at least two characters.

protagonist: The main character in a work of fiction, biography, or other literary work. The protagonist can be the hero but does not have to be. Instead, the protagonist can be villainous and not at all heroic; he or she just needs to be the focus of the work. Sometimes the protagonist is not even a person but is instead an animal, a place, or even a building. For instance, in David Macaulay's *Cathedral*, the cathedral itself is a kind of protagonist because the book is about how the structure grows and changes during its construction.

satire: A literary work that ridicules its subject. It is often meant to inspire social or political change.

short story: A short work of fiction that is tightly focused on a central plot and a small number of characters. The climax always occurs at the end of the story, whereas in a novel it occurs about two-thirds through.

simile: A figure of speech that directly compares two dissimilar objects through the use of "like" or "as." One famous simile is "My love is like a red, red rose," by which the poet describes the qualities of a woman by comparing her to a red rose.

symbolism: The use of specific images, objects, incidents, names or places to suggest abstract ideas, such as love, faith, or wisdom. In Cynthia Voigt's *Solitary Blue*, the blue heron is a symbol that represents Jeff's withdrawal from people and his preference for the solitude of nature.

tone: The overall mood evoked by the narrative voice in the story.

tragedy: An account of a series of related events that end in catastrophe for the protagonist.

villain: The character who works against the good of the other characters or society. Often in fiction the protagonist is the hero and the antagonist the villain. In Charles Dickens's *A Christmas Carol*, Scrooge begins as the villain and ends as the hero.

APPENDIX: TITLES GROUPED BY THEMES

VOLUME 14

◆

Abandonment/Desertion

Armageddon Summer
Discover the Destroyer
Land of Loss
Martha Graham: A Dancer
P.S. Longer Letter Later
Rebellion
Sabriel
Search for Senna
The Wind's Twelve Quarters

Abortion

Armageddon Summer
Beyond Dreams

Absurdity

Athletic Shorts
Discover the Destroyer
Don Quixote
Enter the Enchanted
Fantastic Beasts and Where to Find Them
Gulliver's Travels
Harrison Bergeron
Harry Potter and the Goblet of Fire
The Hitchhiker's Guide to the Galaxy
Quidditch Through the Ages
Search for Senna

Abuse

Armageddon Summer
Athletic Shorts
Beyond Dreams
"A Boy and His Dog"
Don Quixote
Gathering Blue

Gooseberries
Harrison Bergeron
Harry Potter and the Goblet of Fire
My Brother, My Sister, and I
Shade's Children
When Jeff Comes Home
You Want Women to Vote, Lizzie Stanton?

Acceptance and Belonging

Armageddon Summer
Confessions of an Ugly Stepsister
Forty Acres and Maybe a Mule
Gathering Blue
Go Ask Alice
The Grass Dancer
Great Expectations
Gulliver's Travels
*Harriet Beecher Stowe and the Beecher
  Preachers*
Harry Potter and the Goblet of Fire
Josh Gibson
"The Lesson"
My Brother, My Sister, and I
My Father, Dancing
P.S. Longer Letter Later
Shade's Children
Two Suns in the Sky

Activity and Passivity

Armageddon Summer
Athletic Shorts
Beyond Dreams
Discover the Destroyer
Don Quixote
Forty Acres and Maybe a Mule

Gathering Blue
Go Ask Alice
Gooseberries
Great Expectations
Gulliver's Travels
Harriet Beecher Stowe and the Beecher
   Preachers
Harrison Bergeron
The Hitchhiker's Guide to the Galaxy
Land of Loss
"The Lesson"
"The Man That Corrupted Hadleyburg"
Martha Graham: A Dancer
"The Most Dangerous Game"
My Brother, My Sister, and I
"The Necklace"
No-No Boy
P.S. Longer Letter Later
The Queen of Attolia
Rats
Realm of the Reaper
Rebellion
Search for Senna
The Voyage of the Space Beagle
When Jeff Comes Home
The Wind's Twelve Quarters
You Want Women to Vote, Lizzie Stanton?

Adolescence and Youth

Armageddon Summer
Athletic Shorts
Beyond Dreams
The Black Stallion
"A Boy and His Dog"
Confessions of an Ugly Stepsister
Discover the Destroyer
Enter the Enchanted
Forty Acres and Maybe a Mule
Go Ask Alice
The Grass Dancer
Great Expectations
Harriet Beecher Stowe and the Beecher
   Preachers
Harrison Bergeron
Land of Loss
"The Lesson"
The Merlin Effect

My Brother, My Sister, and I
My Father, Dancing
P.S. Longer Letter Later
Rats
Realm of the Reaper
Sabriel
Sammy Sosa: A Biography
Search for Senna
Shade's Children
So Far from the Bamboo Grove
Two Suns in the Sky
When Jeff Comes Home

Adultery

Armageddon Summer
My Father, Dancing
"The Necklace"

Adulthood

Beyond Dreams
Great Expectations
Harriet Beecher Stowe and the Beecher
   Preachers
Harry Potter and the Goblet of Fire
Josh Gibson
Martha Graham: A Dancer
My Father, Dancing
Rebellion
Sammy Sosa: A Biography
You Want Women to Vote, Lizzie Stanton?

Adventure

The Black Stallion
"A Boy and His Dog"
Discover the Destroyer
Don Quixote
Enter the Enchanted
Gulliver's Travels
Harry Potter and the Goblet of Fire
The Hitchhiker's Guide to the Galaxy
Land of Loss
The Merlin Effect
"The Most Dangerous Game"
The Queen of Attolia
Rats
Realm of the Reaper
Rebellion

Sabriel
Sandwriter
Search for Senna
Shade's Children
So Far from the Bamboo Grove
Soul Catcher
The Voyage of the Space Beagle
The Wind's Twelve Quarters

African-American Life and Thought

Forty Acres and Maybe a Mule
Harriet Beecher Stowe and the Beecher
     Preachers
Josh Gibson
Land of Loss
"The Lesson"
Realm of the Reaper

Age of Reason

Gulliver's Travels
Rebellion

Aging

Gathering Blue
Harriet Beecher Stowe and the Beecher
     Preachers
My Father, Dancing
Shade's Children

Agriculture

Forty Acres and Maybe a Mule
Gooseberries

Aids

Athletic Shorts

Alchemy

The Merlin Effect
Quidditch Through the Ages

Alcoholism and Addiction

Josh Gibson
"The Lesson"
No-No Boy
P.S. Longer Letter Later

The Wind's Twelve Quarters

Alienation

Armageddon Summer
Athletic Shorts
Beyond Dreams
"A Boy and His Dog"
Discover the Destroyer
Don Quixote
Enter the Enchanted
Forty Acres and Maybe a Mule
Gathering Blue
Go Ask Alice
Gooseberries
Gulliver's Travels
Harriet Beecher Stowe and the Beecher
     Preachers
Harrison Bergeron
Josh Gibson
Land of Loss
"The Lesson"
"The Man That Corrupted Hadleyburg"
"The Most Dangerous Game"
My Brother, My Sister, and I
No-No Boy
Rebellion
Sandwriter
Search for Senna
Shade's Children
Soul Catcher
Two Suns in the Sky
When Jeff Comes Home
The Wind's Twelve Quarters

Alternative Societies

Armageddon Summer
"A Boy and His Dog"
Confessions of an Ugly Stepsister
Discover the Destroyer
Enter the Enchanted
Fantastic Beasts and Where to Find Them
Forty Acres and Maybe a Mule
Gathering Blue
Gooseberries
The Grass Dancer
Gulliver's Travels
Harrison Bergeron

Harry Potter and the Goblet of Fire
The Hitchhiker's Guide to the Galaxy
Land of Loss
"The Most Dangerous Game"
My Brother, My Sister, and I
The Queen of Attolia
Quidditch Through the Ages
Realm of the Reaper
Sabriel
Sandwriter
Search for Senna
Shade's Children
The Voyage of the Space Beagle
The Wind's Twelve Quarters

Altruism

Discover the Destroyer
Don Quixote
Enter the Enchanted
Forty Acres and Maybe a Mule
Gathering Blue
Gooseberries
Great Expectations
Harriet Beecher Stowe and the Beecher
    Preachers
Harry Potter and the Goblet of Fire
Land of Loss
"The Man That Corrupted Hadleyburg"
The Merlin Effect
My Brother, My Sister, and I
Rats
Sabriel
Sammy Sosa: A Biography
Sandwriter
Two Suns in the Sky
The Voyage of the Space Beagle
The Wind's Twelve Quarters
You Want Women to Vote, Lizzie Stanton?

Ambiguity

Armageddon Summer
Confessions of an Ugly Stepsister
Discover the Destroyer
Don Quixote
Enter the Enchanted
Fantastic Beasts and Where to Find Them
Gathering Blue

Gooseberries
Great Expectations
Gulliver's Travels
The Hitchhiker's Guide to the Galaxy
Land of Loss
"The Lesson"
"The Man That Corrupted Hadleyburg"
The Merlin Effect
My Father, Dancing
"The Necklace"
The Queen of Attolia
Realm of the Reaper
Sandwriter
Search for Senna
Shade's Children
When Jeff Comes Home
The Wind's Twelve Quarters

Ambition

Confessions of an Ugly Stepsister
Discover the Destroyer
Don Quixote
Forty Acres and Maybe a Mule
Gooseberries
Great Expectations
Harriet Beecher Stowe and the Beecher
    Preachers
Harrison Bergeron
Harry Potter and the Goblet of Fire
Josh Gibson
"The Lesson"
Martha Graham: A Dancer
The Merlin Effect
My Brother, My Sister, and I
P.S. Longer Letter Later
The Queen of Attolia
Rebellion
Sabriel
Sammy Sosa: A Biography
Sandwriter
The Voyage of the Space Beagle
The Wind's Twelve Quarters
You Want Women to Vote, Lizzie Stanton?

American Dream

Beyond Dreams
Forty Acres and Maybe a Mule

Harriet Beecher Stowe and the Beecher
    Preachers
Harrison Bergeron
Josh Gibson
"The Lesson"
Martha Graham: A Dancer
P.S. Longer Letter Later
Sammy Sosa: A Biography
You Want Women to Vote, Lizzie Stanton?

American East

Armageddon Summer
Harriet Beecher Stowe and the Beecher
    Preachers
Josh Gibson
"The Lesson"
Martha Graham: A Dancer
My Father, Dancing
Rats
Two Suns in the Sky
You Want Women to Vote, Lizzie Stanton?

American Midwest

Athletic Shorts
Discover the Destroyer
Enter the Enchanted
The Grass Dancer
Harriet Beecher Stowe and the Beecher
    Preachers
Land of Loss
P.S. Longer Letter Later
Realm of the Reaper
Search for Senna

American Northwest

No-No Boy
Soul Catcher

American South

Forty Acres and Maybe a Mule
Josh Gibson
You Want Women to Vote, Lizzie Stanton?

American Southwest

Beyond Dreams
The Merlin Effect

American West

Athletic Shorts
The Merlin Effect

Anarchism

"A Boy and His Dog"

Ancient World

Land of Loss
The Queen of Attolia

Anger

Beyond Dreams
Discover the Destroyer
Enter the Enchanted
Forty Acres and Maybe a Mule
Gulliver's Travels
Harriet Beecher Stowe and the Beecher
    Preachers
Harrison Bergeron
Harry Potter and the Goblet of Fire
The Hitchhiker's Guide to the Galaxy
Josh Gibson
Land of Loss
"The Lesson"
Martha Graham: A Dancer
"The Most Dangerous Game"
My Brother, My Sister, and I
No-No Boy
Realm of the Reaper
Rebellion
Search for Senna
Shade's Children
Soul Catcher
Two Suns in the Sky
The Voyage of the Space Beagle
When Jeff Comes Home

Angry Young Men

Armageddon Summer
Athletic Shorts
Beyond Dreams
"A Boy and His Dog"
Discover the Destroyer
Forty Acres and Maybe a Mule
Gathering Blue

The Grass Dancer
Harrison Bergeron
Land of Loss
No-No Boy
Realm of the Reaper
Search for Senna
Shade's Children
Soul Catcher
Two Suns in the Sky
When Jeff Comes Home

Angry Young Women

Confessions of an Ugly Stepsister
Discover the Destroyer
Don Quixote
Enter the Enchanted
Gathering Blue
Go Ask Alice
Harriet Beecher Stowe and the Beecher
    Preachers
Land of Loss
"The Lesson"
Martha Graham: A Dancer
My Brother, My Sister, and I
My Father, Dancing
P.S. Longer Letter Later
Realm of the Reaper
Rebellion
Sabriel
Sandwriter
Search for Senna
Shade's Children
Two Suns in the Sky
You Want Women to Vote, Lizzie Stanton?

Animals/Beasts

The Black Stallion
"A Boy and His Dog"
Discover the Destroyer
Don Quixote
Gulliver's Travels
The Merlin Effect
Rats
Sandwriter
You Want Women to Vote, Lizzie Stanton?

Antebellum South

Forty Acres and Maybe a Mule

Anthropomorphism

"A Boy and His Dog"
Discover the Destroyer
Fantastic Beasts and Where to Find Them
Gulliver's Travels
The Merlin Effect
Rats
Search for Senna
Shade's Children

Anticulture

Armageddon Summer
Athletic Shorts
"A Boy and His Dog"
Don Quixote
Fantastic Beasts and Where to Find Them
Go Ask Alice
Gooseberries
Gulliver's Travels
Harriet Beecher Stowe and the Beecher
    Preachers
Harrison Bergeron
"The Lesson"
"The Man That Corrupted Hadleyburg"
"The Most Dangerous Game"
"The Necklace"
No-No Boy
So Far from the Bamboo Grove
Soul Catcher
Two Suns in the Sky

Anti-Semitism

Two Suns in the Sky

Antiwar Protest

Gulliver's Travels

Anxiety

Armageddon Summer
Discover the Destroyer
Enter the Enchanted
Forty Acres and Maybe a Mule
Go Ask Alice

The Hitchhiker's Guide to the Galaxy
Land of Loss
"The Lesson"
"The Man That Corrupted Hadleyburg"
The Merlin Effect
"The Most Dangerous Game"
My Brother, My Sister, and I
My Father, Dancing
P.S. Longer Letter Later
Rats
Realm of the Reaper
Sabriel
Sandwriter
Search for Senna
Shade's Children
So Far from the Bamboo Grove
When Jeff Comes Home
The Wind's Twelve Quarters

Apathy
Harrison Bergeron

Apocalypse
Armageddon Summer
Shade's Children

Appearance vs. Reality
Confessions of an Ugly Stepsister
Discover the Destroyer
Don Quixote
Fantastic Beasts and Where to Find Them
Gathering Blue
Gooseberries
Great Expectations
Gulliver's Travels
Harriet Beecher Stowe and the Beecher Preachers
Harry Potter and the Goblet of Fire
Josh Gibson
Land of Loss
"The Man That Corrupted Hadleyburg"
The Merlin Effect
"The Necklace"
The Queen of Attolia
Rats
Sabriel
Shade's Children

Apprenticeship
Gathering Blue
Great Expectations
Gulliver's Travels
Harriet Beecher Stowe and the Beecher Preachers
Harry Potter and the Goblet of Fire
Martha Graham: A Dancer
The Merlin Effect
Sabriel
Sammy Sosa: A Biography
Shade's Children
Soul Catcher

Architecture
Land of Loss
Realm of the Reaper
Search for Senna

Aristocracy
The Queen of Attolia
Rebellion
Sandwriter

Arthurian Legend
Enter the Enchanted
Land of Loss
The Merlin Effect

Artificiality
Confessions of an Ugly Stepsister
Don Quixote
Gathering Blue
Great Expectations
Gulliver's Travels
Harriet Beecher Stowe and the Beecher Preachers
Harrison Bergeron
"The Lesson"
"The Man That Corrupted Hadleyburg"
"The Most Dangerous Game"
My Father, Dancing
"The Necklace"
Quidditch Through the Ages
Shade's Children
The Voyage of the Space Beagle

Artists

Confessions of an Ugly Stepsister
Gathering Blue
Harriet Beecher Stowe and the Beecher Preachers
Harrison Bergeron
Martha Graham: A Dancer

Artists and Society

Confessions of an Ugly Stepsister
Gathering Blue
Harriet Beecher Stowe and the Beecher Preachers
Harrison Bergeron
Martha Graham: A Dancer

Arts

Confessions of an Ugly Stepsister
Gathering Blue
Martha Graham: A Dancer

Asian-American Life and Thought

No-No Boy

Assimilation and Acculturation

No-No Boy
Sammy Sosa: A Biography
Sandwriter
Two Suns in the Sky

Astronomy

The Hitchhiker's Guide to the Galaxy
The Wind's Twelve Quarters

Atonement and Redemption

Great Expectations
The Queen of Attolia

Authority

Armageddon Summer
Athletic Shorts
Discover the Destroyer
Enter the Enchanted

Gathering Blue
Gulliver's Travels
Harriet Beecher Stowe and the Beecher Preachers
Harrison Bergeron
Harry Potter and the Goblet of Fire
Land of Loss
"The Man That Corrupted Hadleyburg"
The Merlin Effect
The Queen of Attolia
Rats
Sandwriter
Search for Senna
The Voyage of the Space Beagle
The Wind's Twelve Quarters

Baseball

Josh Gibson
Sammy Sosa: A Biography

Beauty and Aesthetics

Confessions of an Ugly Stepsister
Gathering Blue
Harriet Beecher Stowe and the Beecher Preachers
Harrison Bergeron
Martha Graham: A Dancer
Realm of the Reaper

Betrayal

"A Boy and His Dog"
Discover the Destroyer
Enter the Enchanted
Go Ask Alice
Gulliver's Travels
Harry Potter and the Goblet of Fire
Land of Loss
"The Lesson"
Rats
Realm of the Reaper
Sandwriter
Search for Senna

Birth

Beyond Dreams
Harriet Beecher Stowe and the Beecher Preachers

Black Identity

Forty Acres and Maybe a Mule
Josh Gibson
Land of Loss
"The Lesson"
Realm of the Reaper

Blasphemy and Heresy

Armageddon Summer
"The Man That Corrupted Hadleyburg"

Blindness

Gulliver's Travels

Bliss

Gooseberries
Gulliver's Travels
"The Necklace"

Bourgeois Life

Gooseberries
Great Expectations
Harriet Beecher Stowe and the Beecher Preachers
My Father, Dancing
"The Necklace"
P.S. Longer Letter Later
Two Suns in the Sky

Bravery

Athletic Shorts
The Black Stallion
Discover the Destroyer
Don Quixote
Enter the Enchanted
Gulliver's Travels
Land of Loss
The Merlin Effect
"The Most Dangerous Game"
Rats
Realm of the Reaper
Rebellion
Sabriel
Sandwriter
Search for Senna
Shade's Children

So Far from the Bamboo Grove
The Voyage of the Space Beagle
The Wind's Twelve Quarters

Brotherhood

Armageddon Summer
Forty Acres and Maybe a Mule
Gulliver's Travels
Harriet Beecher Stowe and the Beecher Preachers
Sammy Sosa: A Biography
Shade's Children
Two Suns in the Sky

Brutality

Athletic Shorts
The Black Stallion
"A Boy and His Dog"
Discover the Destroyer
Don Quixote
Gulliver's Travels
Harriet Beecher Stowe and the Beecher Preachers
Harrison Bergeron
Land of Loss
"The Most Dangerous Game"
The Queen of Attolia
Rats
Realm of the Reaper
Rebellion
Sabriel
Search for Senna
Shade's Children
So Far from the Bamboo Grove
Soul Catcher
When Jeff Comes Home

Bureaucracy

The Hitchhiker's Guide to the Galaxy

Business and Business Life

Discover the Destroyer
P.S. Longer Letter Later

Capitalism

Discover the Destroyer

Carpe Diem
Athletic Shorts
Beyond Dreams
The Black Stallion
Discover the Destroyer
Don Quixote
Forty Acres and Maybe a Mule
Gulliver's Travels
Harriet Beecher Stowe and the Beecher Preachers
The Hitchhiker's Guide to the Galaxy
"The Man That Corrupted Hadleyburg"
Sabriel
Sammy Sosa: A Biography
Search for Senna
The Voyage of the Space Beagle

Catastrophe
Don Quixote
Enter the Enchanted
Go Ask Alice
The Grass Dancer
Gulliver's Travels
The Hitchhiker's Guide to the Galaxy
My Brother, My Sister, and I
"The Necklace"
P.S. Longer Letter Later
Rats
Rebellion
Search for Senna
Shade's Children
So Far from the Bamboo Grove

Catharsis
Athletic Shorts
The Merlin Effect
My Father, Dancing
P.S. Longer Letter Later

Catholicism (Roman)
The Grass Dancer
Two Suns in the Sky

Celebration
Gathering Blue
The Grass Dancer

Great Expectations
Harry Potter and the Goblet of Fire
You Want Women to Vote, Lizzie Stanton?

Censorship
Harrison Bergeron

Ceremonies and Rituals
Armageddon Summer
Confessions of an Ugly Stepsister
Gathering Blue
The Grass Dancer
Harry Potter and the Goblet of Fire
Land of Loss
"The Man That Corrupted Hadleyburg"
Quidditch Through the Ages
Sabriel
Soul Catcher
Two Suns in the Sky

Change and Transformation
Armageddon Summer
Beyond Dreams
Discover the Destroyer
Gathering Blue
Go Ask Alice
Great Expectations
Gulliver's Travels
Harriet Beecher Stowe and the Beecher Preachers
Harry Potter and the Goblet of Fire
Josh Gibson
Martha Graham: A Dancer
The Merlin Effect
No-No Boy
P.S. Longer Letter Later
Sammy Sosa: A Biography
Sandwriter
Shade's Children
Soul Catcher
The Voyage of the Space Beagle
When Jeff Comes Home
The Wind's Twelve Quarters
You Want Women to Vote, Lizzie Stanton?

Chaos and Order
"A Boy and His Dog"

Don Quixote
Enter the Enchanted
Go Ask Alice
Harriet Beecher Stowe and the Beecher
    Preachers
Harrison Bergeron
Harry Potter and the Goblet of Fire
The Hitchhiker's Guide to the Galaxy
Land of Loss
"The Man That Corrupted Hadleyburg"
"The Most Dangerous Game"
P.S. Longer Letter Later
Rats
Sabriel
So Far from the Bamboo Grove
The Voyage of the Space Beagle
The Wind's Twelve Quarters

Childhood
Great Expectations
Harriet Beecher Stowe and the Beecher
    Preachers
Rebellion
Sammy Sosa: A Biography
Shade's Children
So Far from the Bamboo Grove
Soul Catcher

Chivalry
Discover the Destroyer
Don Quixote
Enter the Enchanted
The Merlin Effect

Christianity
Armageddon Summer
The Grass Dancer
Harriet Beecher Stowe and the Beecher
    Preachers
"The Man That Corrupted Hadleyburg"
Two Suns in the Sky
You Want Women to Vote, Lizzie Stanton?

Church of England
Harriet Beecher Stowe and the Beecher
    Preachers

City Life
Athletic Shorts
Beyond Dreams
Confessions of an Ugly Stepsister
Discover the Destroyer
Enter the Enchanted
Great Expectations
Harriet Beecher Stowe and the Beecher
    Preachers
Josh Gibson
"The Lesson"
Martha Graham: A Dancer
My Brother, My Sister, and I
"The Necklace"
Rats
Sammy Sosa: A Biography

Civil Rights
Forty Acres and Maybe a Mule
Harriet Beecher Stowe and the Beecher
    Preachers
Harrison Bergeron
Josh Gibson
"The Lesson"
My Brother, My Sister, and I
No-No Boy
You Want Women to Vote, Lizzie Stanton?

Civil War (American)
Forty Acres and Maybe a Mule
Harriet Beecher Stowe and the Beecher
    Preachers

Civilization
Gathering Blue
Gulliver's Travels
Land of Loss

Class Conflict
Don Quixote
Gathering Blue
Gulliver's Travels
Harriet Beecher Stowe and the Beecher
    Preachers
Josh Gibson
My Brother, My Sister, and I

Two Suns in the Sky

Class Structure

Confessions of an Ugly Stepsister
Don Quixote
Forty Acres and Maybe a Mule
Gathering Blue
Gooseberries
Great Expectations
Gulliver's Travels
Harriet Beecher Stowe and the Beecher
  Preachers
Josh Gibson
"The Lesson"
My Brother, My Sister, and I
"The Necklace"
No-No Boy
P.S. Longer Letter Later
Rebellion
Sammy Sosa: A Biography
Sandwriter
So Far from the Bamboo Grove
Two Suns in the Sky
The Wind's Twelve Quarters

Classical Greece/Rome

The Queen of Attolia

Clothing and Fashion

Great Expectations
Martha Graham: A Dancer
"The Necklace"
P.S. Longer Letter Later
Two Suns in the Sky
You Want Women to Vote, Lizzie Stanton?

Comedy of Life

Athletic Shorts
Don Quixote
Gooseberries
Great Expectations
Gulliver's Travels
The Hitchhiker's Guide to the Galaxy
"The Man That Corrupted Hadleyburg"
Quidditch Through the Ages
You Want Women to Vote, Lizzie Stanton?

Coming of Age

The Black Stallion
Confessions of an Ugly Stepsister
Great Expectations
Martha Graham: A Dancer
The Merlin Effect
My Father, Dancing
Rebellion
Sabriel
Sammy Sosa: A Biography
Shade's Children
Two Suns in the Sky

Commercialism

Confessions of an Ugly Stepsister
Discover the Destroyer
"The Lesson"

Common Man/Common Woman

Confessions of an Ugly Stepsister
Don Quixote
Forty Acres and Maybe a Mule
Great Expectations
Harrison Bergeron
"The Lesson"
"The Man That Corrupted Hadleyburg"
My Brother, My Sister, and I
"The Necklace"
Sammy Sosa: A Biography

Complacency

Harrison Bergeron
Rats

Conformity

Armageddon Summer
Athletic Shorts
Gathering Blue
Go Ask Alice
The Grass Dancer
Great Expectations
Harrison Bergeron
"The Lesson"
"The Man That Corrupted Hadleyburg"
My Brother, My Sister, and I
"The Necklace"

No-No Boy
P.S. Longer Letter Later

Confusion
Armageddon Summer
Beyond Dreams
Discover the Destroyer
Don Quixote
Enter the Enchanted
Gooseberries
Great Expectations
Harry Potter and the Goblet of Fire
The Hitchhiker's Guide to the Galaxy
Land of Loss
"The Man That Corrupted Hadleyburg"
The Merlin Effect
"The Most Dangerous Game"
My Brother, My Sister, and I
My Father, Dancing
"The Necklace"
No-No Boy
P.S. Longer Letter Later
Rats
Realm of the Reaper
Search for Senna
Shade's Children
So Far from the Bamboo Grove
When Jeff Comes Home

Conquest
Enter the Enchanted
Gulliver's Travels
Land of Loss
The Queen of Attolia
Search for Senna

Conscience
Armageddon Summer
Athletic Shorts
Discover the Destroyer
Don Quixote
Gathering Blue
Gooseberries
Great Expectations
Gulliver's Travels
Harriet Beecher Stowe and the Beecher
    Preachers

Land of Loss
"The Man That Corrupted Hadleyburg"
The Merlin Effect
My Brother, My Sister, and I
My Father, Dancing
The Queen of Attolia
Realm of the Reaper
Two Suns in the Sky

Consolation and Comfort
Athletic Shorts
Enter the Enchanted
Gathering Blue
Gulliver's Travels
Harriet Beecher Stowe and the Beecher
    Preachers
My Brother, My Sister, and I
My Father, Dancing
P.S. Longer Letter Later
Sandwriter
So Far from the Bamboo Grove

Conspiracy
Gathering Blue
Harriet Beecher Stowe and the Beecher
    Preachers
Harry Potter and the Goblet of Fire
Josh Gibson
The Queen of Attolia
Rebellion
Search for Senna

Construction
Harriet Beecher Stowe and the Beecher
    Preachers

Corruption
"A Boy and His Dog"
Discover the Destroyer
Harrison Bergeron
Harry Potter and the Goblet of Fire
Josh Gibson
"The Man That Corrupted Hadleyburg"
"The Most Dangerous Game"
Realm of the Reaper
Sandwriter
Search for Senna

Country Life

Don Quixote
Forty Acres and Maybe a Mule
Gathering Blue
Gooseberries
The Grass Dancer
Harriet Beecher Stowe and the Beecher
   Preachers

Courage

Athletic Shorts
The Black Stallion
Discover the Destroyer
Don Quixote
Enter the Enchanted
Forty Acres and Maybe a Mule
The Grass Dancer
Gulliver's Travels
Harriet Beecher Stowe and the Beecher
   Preachers
Harrison Bergeron
Harry Potter and the Goblet of Fire
The Hitchhiker's Guide to the Galaxy
Josh Gibson
Land of Loss
Martha Graham: A Dancer
The Merlin Effect
"The Most Dangerous Game"
My Brother, My Sister, and I
Rats
Realm of the Reaper
Rebellion
Sabriel
Sandwriter
Search for Senna
Shade's Children
So Far from the Bamboo Grove
Two Suns in the Sky
The Voyage of the Space Beagle
The Wind's Twelve Quarters
You Want Women to Vote, Lizzie Stanton?

Courtly Love

Confessions of an Ugly Stepsister
Don Quixote
Great Expectations
Gulliver's Travels

Harriet Beecher Stowe and the Beecher
   Preachers
Land of Loss
The Queen of Attolia
Sandwriter
Two Suns in the Sky

Covenant

Armageddon Summer
Forty Acres and Maybe a Mule
Great Expectations
Harriet Beecher Stowe and the Beecher
   Preachers
"The Most Dangerous Game"
Realm of the Reaper
Sabriel
Shade's Children

Cowardice

The Hitchhiker's Guide to the Galaxy
Land of Loss
"The Most Dangerous Game"
Realm of the Reaper
Rebellion
Soul Catcher

Creative Process

Confessions of an Ugly Stepsister
Discover the Destroyer
Gathering Blue
Gulliver's Travels
Harriet Beecher Stowe and the Beecher
   Preachers
Martha Graham: A Dancer
The Merlin Effect
You Want Women to Vote, Lizzie Stanton?

Crime and Criminals

"A Boy and His Dog"
Discover the Destroyer
Go Ask Alice
Great Expectations
Harrison Bergeron
"The Most Dangerous Game"
The Queen of Attolia
Rebellion
Soul Catcher

When Jeff Comes Home

Cruelty

Athletic Shorts
Beyond Dreams
The Black Stallion
"A Boy and His Dog"
Discover the Destroyer
Don Quixote
Enter the Enchanted
Forty Acres and Maybe a Mule
Gathering Blue
Gooseberries
Gulliver's Travels
*Harriet Beecher Stowe and the Beecher
    Preachers*
Harrison Bergeron
Harry Potter and the Goblet of Fire
The Hitchhiker's Guide to the Galaxy
Josh Gibson
Land of Loss
The Merlin Effect
"The Most Dangerous Game"
My Brother, My Sister, and I
The Queen of Attolia
Rats
Realm of the Reaper
Rebellion
Sabriel
Search for Senna
Shade's Children
Soul Catcher
Two Suns in the Sky
When Jeff Comes Home
The Wind's Twelve Quarters
You Want Women to Vote, Lizzie Stanton?

Cultural Differences

The Black Stallion
The Grass Dancer
Gulliver's Travels
Josh Gibson
Land of Loss
The Merlin Effect
No-No Boy
Sammy Sosa: A Biography
Sandwriter

Search for Senna
Soul Catcher
Two Suns in the Sky

Culture Clash

The Grass Dancer
Land of Loss
No-No Boy
Sandwriter
Soul Catcher
Two Suns in the Sky

Curiosity

"A Boy and His Dog"
Gulliver's Travels
Land of Loss
The Merlin Effect
Realm of the Reaper
Two Suns in the Sky
The Voyage of the Space Beagle

Customs and Traditions

The Black Stallion
Discover the Destroyer
Enter the Enchanted
Gathering Blue
The Grass Dancer
Gulliver's Travels
*Harriet Beecher Stowe and the Beecher
    Preachers*
Harry Potter and the Goblet of Fire
The Hitchhiker's Guide to the Galaxy
Josh Gibson
Land of Loss
Martha Graham: A Dancer
The Merlin Effect
My Brother, My Sister, and I
My Father, Dancing
No-No Boy
Quidditch Through the Ages
Sandwriter
Search for Senna
So Far from the Bamboo Grove
Soul Catcher
Two Suns in the Sky
You Want Women to Vote, Lizzie Stanton?

Cynicism

"A Boy and His Dog"
Discover the Destroyer
Go Ask Alice
Land of Loss
"The Man That Corrupted Hadleyburg"
No-No Boy
Realm of the Reaper
Rebellion
Search for Senna
Shade's Children

Dancing

Martha Graham: A Dancer
My Father, Dancing
Search for Senna

Danger

Armageddon Summer
Athletic Shorts
Beyond Dreams
The Black Stallion
"A Boy and His Dog"
Discover the Destroyer
Don Quixote
Enter the Enchanted
Forty Acres and Maybe a Mule
Gathering Blue
Go Ask Alice
The Grass Dancer
Gulliver's Travels
Harriet Beecher Stowe and the Beecher
    Preachers
Harrison Bergeron
Harry Potter and the Goblet of Fire
The Hitchhiker's Guide to the Galaxy
Josh Gibson
Land of Loss
The Merlin Effect
"The Most Dangerous Game"
My Brother, My Sister, and I
The Queen of Attolia
Rats
Realm of the Reaper
Rebellion
Sabriel
Sandwriter

Search for Senna
Shade's Children
So Far from the Bamboo Grove
Soul Catcher
Two Suns in the Sky
The Voyage of the Space Beagle
The Wind's Twelve Quarters
You Want Women to Vote, Lizzie Stanton?

Darwinism

The Merlin Effect
Rats

Daughters

My Father, Dancing

Death and Dying

Athletic Shorts
"A Boy and His Dog"
Discover the Destroyer
Don Quixote
Enter the Enchanted
Gathering Blue
Go Ask Alice
Gooseberries
The Grass Dancer
Gulliver's Travels
Harriet Beecher Stowe and the Beecher
    Preachers
Harrison Bergeron
Harry Potter and the Goblet of Fire
Josh Gibson
Land of Loss
The Merlin Effect
"The Most Dangerous Game"
My Brother, My Sister, and I
My Father, Dancing
"The Necklace"
No-No Boy
Rats
Realm of the Reaper
Rebellion
Sabriel
Sandwriter
Search for Senna
Shade's Children
So Far from the Bamboo Grove

Soul Catcher
The Voyage of the Space Beagle
The Wind's Twelve Quarters

Death of Parent

Confessions of an Ugly Stepsister
Forty Acres and Maybe a Mule
Gathering Blue
The Grass Dancer
Great Expectations
Harriet Beecher Stowe and the Beecher
    Preachers
My Brother, My Sister, and I
My Father, Dancing
No-No Boy
Sammy Sosa: A Biography
So Far from the Bamboo Grove

Death Wish

Go Ask Alice
Land of Loss
Realm of the Reaper
So Far from the Bamboo Grove

Decadence

"A Boy and His Dog"
Go Ask Alice
Gooseberries
Great Expectations
Gulliver's Travels
"The Lesson"
"The Man That Corrupted Hadleyburg"
"The Most Dangerous Game"
Two Suns in the Sky

Decay

"A Boy and His Dog"
Gathering Blue
Go Ask Alice
"The Man That Corrupted Hadleyburg"
Realm of the Reaper

Deception and Delusion

Armageddon Summer
Discover the Destroyer
Don Quixote

Fantastic Beasts and Where to Find Them
Gathering Blue
Go Ask Alice
Gooseberries
Great Expectations
Harry Potter and the Goblet of Fire
Land of Loss
"The Man That Corrupted Hadleyburg"
The Merlin Effect
"The Necklace"
Sabriel
Search for Senna
Shade's Children
When Jeff Comes Home

Deformity (Physical)

Gathering Blue
Realm of the Reaper
Shade's Children

Dehumanization

Armageddon Summer
"A Boy and His Dog"
Harrison Bergeron
"The Most Dangerous Game"
My Brother, My Sister, and I
Sabriel
Shade's Children

Deities

Enter the Enchanted
Land of Loss
Realm of the Reaper
Search for Senna

Democracy

Harriet Beecher Stowe and the Beecher
    Preachers
"The Lesson"
You Want Women to Vote, Lizzie Stanton?

Denial

Go Ask Alice
Harrison Bergeron
The Voyage of the Space Beagle
When Jeff Comes Home

Dependence

Armageddon Summer
Beyond Dreams
Confessions of an Ugly Stepsister
Go Ask Alice
Great Expectations
Harriet Beecher Stowe and the Beecher
 Preachers
Land of Loss
Martha Graham: A Dancer

Despair

Athletic Shorts
Go Ask Alice
Josh Gibson
Land of Loss
Realm of the Reaper
So Far from the Bamboo Grove

Destruction

Armageddon Summer
"A Boy and His Dog"
Discover the Destroyer
Don Quixote
Enter the Enchanted
Gulliver's Travels
Harriet Beecher Stowe and the Beecher
 Preachers
Harry Potter and the Goblet of Fire
The Hitchhiker's Guide to the Galaxy
Land of Loss
"The Man That Corrupted Hadleyburg"
My Brother, My Sister, and I
Rats
Rebellion
Sabriel
Search for Senna
Shade's Children
So Far from the Bamboo Grove
The Wind's Twelve Quarters

Deus ex Machina

Enter the Enchanted
Gulliver's Travels
Land of Loss
Shade's Children

Devil

"The Man That Corrupted Hadleyburg"

Diary Writing

Go Ask Alice
Gulliver's Travels
Sandwriter

Dignity

Athletic Shorts
Don Quixote
Gulliver's Travels
My Brother, My Sister, and I
Sammy Sosa: A Biography

Disappointment

Confessions of an Ugly Stepsister
Don Quixote
Forty Acres and Maybe a Mule
Great Expectations
Gulliver's Travels
Josh Gibson
Land of Loss
Sandwriter
Two Suns in the Sky
You Want Women to Vote, Lizzie Stanton?

Discipline

Armageddon Summer
The Black Stallion
Gathering Blue
Harriet Beecher Stowe and the Beecher
 Preachers
Land of Loss
Martha Graham: A Dancer
"The Most Dangerous Game"
My Brother, My Sister, and I
Quidditch Through the Ages
Sammy Sosa: A Biography
Shade's Children
The Voyage of the Space Beagle
You Want Women to Vote, Lizzie Stanton?

Discrimination

Armageddon Summer
Forty Acres and Maybe a Mule

Harriet Beecher Stowe and the Beecher
    Preachers
Josh Gibson
My Brother, My Sister, and I
No-No Boy
Two Suns in the Sky
You Want Women to Vote, Lizzie Stanton?

Disease
Athletic Shorts
Harriet Beecher Stowe and the Beecher
    Preachers

Disillusionment
Armageddon Summer
The Black Stallion
Don Quixote
Forty Acres and Maybe a Mule
Gathering Blue
Go Ask Alice
Great Expectations
Gulliver's Travels
Harriet Beecher Stowe and the Beecher
    Preachers
Josh Gibson
"The Lesson"
"The Necklace"
P.S. Longer Letter Later
Sandwriter
Search for Senna
So Far from the Bamboo Grove
Soul Catcher
Two Suns in the Sky

Divorce
Martha Graham: A Dancer
P.S. Longer Letter Later

Domesticity
Beyond Dreams
Harriet Beecher Stowe and the Beecher
    Preachers
Martha Graham: A Dancer
My Brother, My Sister, and I
"The Necklace"
No-No Boy
P.S. Longer Letter Later

Rats
When Jeff Comes Home
You Want Women to Vote, Lizzie Stanton?

Doubt and Self-Doubt
Armageddon Summer
Beyond Dreams
The Black Stallion
Confessions of an Ugly Stepsister
Discover the Destroyer
Enter the Enchanted
Go Ask Alice
Gooseberries
The Grass Dancer
Great Expectations
Gulliver's Travels
Harriet Beecher Stowe and the Beecher
    Preachers
The Hitchhiker's Guide to the Galaxy
Land of Loss
The Merlin Effect
"The Most Dangerous Game"
My Brother, My Sister, and I
My Father, Dancing
"The Necklace"
No-No Boy
P.S. Longer Letter Later
Rats
Realm of the Reaper
Sammy Sosa: A Biography
Search for Senna
So Far from the Bamboo Grove

Dreams and Dream Fulfillment
Beyond Dreams
Discover the Destroyer
Don Quixote
Enter the Enchanted
The Grass Dancer
Land of Loss
Realm of the Reaper
Sandwriter
Search for Senna

Drifters and Nomads
"A Boy and His Dog"
Discover the Destroyer

Don Quixote
Enter the Enchanted
Forty Acres and Maybe a Mule
Gulliver's Travels
The Hitchhiker's Guide to the Galaxy
Josh Gibson
Land of Loss
"The Most Dangerous Game"
Realm of the Reaper
Search for Senna
The Voyage of the Space Beagle
The Wind's Twelve Quarters

Drugs/Drug Culture

Go Ask Alice
Josh Gibson
The Wind's Twelve Quarters

Dualism

Confessions of an Ugly Stepsister
Discover the Destroyer
Don Quixote
Enter the Enchanted
Fantastic Beasts and Where to Find Them
Gathering Blue
Gooseberries
Harry Potter and the Goblet of Fire
Land of Loss
The Merlin Effect
"The Most Dangerous Game"
"The Necklace"
The Queen of Attolia
Realm of the Reaper
Sabriel
Search for Senna
Soul Catcher

Dueling

"The Most Dangerous Game"

Duty and Responsibility

Athletic Shorts
Beyond Dreams
Discover the Destroyer
Don Quixote
Enter the Enchanted
Gathering Blue

Gooseberries
The Grass Dancer
Gulliver's Travels
Harriet Beecher Stowe and the Beecher
  Preachers
Harry Potter and the Goblet of Fire
Land of Loss
"The Man That Corrupted Hadleyburg"
The Merlin Effect
My Brother, My Sister, and I
P.S. Longer Letter Later
Rats
Rebellion
Sabriel
Sammy Sosa: A Biography
Sandwriter
Search for Senna
Shade's Children
So Far from the Bamboo Grove
The Voyage of the Space Beagle
The Wind's Twelve Quarters
You Want Women to Vote, Lizzie Stanton?

Dystopia and Dystopian Ideas

Armageddon Summer
"A Boy and His Dog"
Discover the Destroyer
Don Quixote
Gathering Blue
Gulliver's Travels
Harrison Bergeron
Harry Potter and the Goblet of Fire
The Hitchhiker's Guide to the Galaxy
Land of Loss
"The Man That Corrupted Hadleyburg"
"The Most Dangerous Game"
My Brother, My Sister, and I
The Queen of Attolia
Realm of the Reaper
Search for Senna
Shade's Children
Two Suns in the Sky
The Voyage of the Space Beagle

Earth

Discover the Destroyer
Enter the Enchanted

The Hitchhiker's Guide to the Galaxy
Land of Loss
The Merlin Effect
The Wind's Twelve Quarters

Easter Rebellion
Eastern Traditions
My Brother, My Sister, and I
So Far from the Bamboo Grove

Ecology
The Merlin Effect
Sandwriter
Soul Catcher

Economics
Confessions of an Ugly Stepsister
Discover the Destroyer
Gulliver's Travels
"The Lesson"
My Brother, My Sister, and I
P.S. Longer Letter Later
Rats

Education
Athletic Shorts
Beyond Dreams
The Black Stallion
Fantastic Beasts and Where to Find Them
Gathering Blue
Go Ask Alice
Great Expectations
Gulliver's Travels
Harriet Beecher Stowe and the Beecher
    Preachers
Harry Potter and the Goblet of Fire
"The Lesson"
My Brother, My Sister, and I
Rats
Sabriel
Soul Catcher
The Voyage of the Space Beagle

Egotism
"A Boy and His Dog"
Discover the Destroyer

Don Quixote
Harrison Bergeron
Josh Gibson
Land of Loss
Martha Graham: A Dancer
"The Most Dangerous Game"
The Queen of Attolia
Realm of the Reaper
Sammy Sosa: A Biography
Search for Senna
Shade's Children

Emasculation
The Queen of Attolia
Shade's Children
The Voyage of the Space Beagle

Empathy
Athletic Shorts
Forty Acres and Maybe a Mule
Harriet Beecher Stowe and the Beecher
    Preachers
My Brother, My Sister, and I
My Father, Dancing
Two Suns in the Sky

Enlightenment
Gulliver's Travels

Ennui
Go Ask Alice
Great Expectations
Gulliver's Travels
Josh Gibson
Land of Loss
Realm of the Reaper
Shade's Children
When Jeff Comes Home

Enthusiasm
Discover the Destroyer
Don Quixote
Josh Gibson
Martha Graham: A Dancer
Sammy Sosa: A Biography
Search for Senna
You Want Women to Vote, Lizzie Stanton?

Environmental Issues
The Merlin Effect
Rats
Sandwriter
Soul Catcher
The Wind's Twelve Quarters

Envy
Land of Loss
"The Man That Corrupted Hadleyburg"

Epiphany
"A Boy and His Dog"
Gulliver's Travels
The Wind's Twelve Quarters

Equality
Harrison Bergeron
You Want Women to Vote, Lizzie Stanton?

Eroticism
"A Boy and His Dog"
The Grass Dancer
Realm of the Reaper
Shade's Children

Escapism
The Black Stallion
Discover the Destroyer
Don Quixote
Enter the Enchanted
Fantastic Beasts and Where to Find Them
Harry Potter and the Goblet of Fire
The Hitchhiker's Guide to the Galaxy
Land of Loss
The Merlin Effect
"The Most Dangerous Game"
The Queen of Attolia
Quidditch Through the Ages
Rats
Realm of the Reaper
Rebellion
Sabriel
Sandwriter
Search for Senna
Shade's Children

The Voyage of the Space Beagle
The Wind's Twelve Quarters

Essay Writing
Harriet Beecher Stowe and the Beecher Preachers

Establishment
Gathering Blue
Harriet Beecher Stowe and the Beecher Preachers
Harrison Bergeron
Two Suns in the Sky
You Want Women to Vote, Lizzie Stanton?

Ethics and Values
Armageddon Summer
Athletic Shorts
Discover the Destroyer
Don Quixote
Go Ask Alice
Gooseberries
The Grass Dancer
Great Expectations
Gulliver's Travels
Harriet Beecher Stowe and the Beecher Preachers
Harry Potter and the Goblet of Fire
Land of Loss
"The Lesson"
"The Man That Corrupted Hadleyburg"
"The Most Dangerous Game"
My Brother, My Sister, and I
Realm of the Reaper
Sammy Sosa: A Biography
Sandwriter
Shade's Children
When Jeff Comes Home

Evil
Armageddon Summer
"A Boy and His Dog"
Discover the Destroyer
Don Quixote
Enter the Enchanted
Forty Acres and Maybe a Mule
Go Ask Alice

Gulliver's Travels
Harriet Beecher Stowe and the Beecher
    Preachers
Harry Potter and the Goblet of Fire
Land of Loss
"The Man That Corrupted Hadleyburg"
The Merlin Effect
"The Most Dangerous Game"
My Brother, My Sister, and I
The Queen of Attolia
Rats
Realm of the Reaper
Rebellion
Sabriel
Sandwriter
Search for Senna
Shade's Children
Soul Catcher
When Jeff Comes Home
The Wind's Twelve Quarters

Execution
Harrison Bergeron
Land of Loss

Exile
Armageddon Summer
Discover the Destroyer
Enter the Enchanted
Great Expectations
The Hitchhiker's Guide to the Galaxy
Land of Loss
The Queen of Attolia
Realm of the Reaper
Sabriel
Search for Senna
Two Suns in the Sky
The Wind's Twelve Quarters

Expatriatism
Great Expectations
Sammy Sosa: A Biography
Sandwriter

Exploitation and Manipulation
Armageddon Summer
"A Boy and His Dog"

Discover the Destroyer
Enter the Enchanted
Gathering Blue
Gooseberries
Land of Loss
"The Lesson"
"The Man That Corrupted Hadleyburg"
"The Most Dangerous Game"
My Brother, My Sister, and I
The Queen of Attolia
Realm of the Reaper
Sandwriter
Search for Senna
Shade's Children
When Jeff Comes Home

Exploration
The Voyage of the Space Beagle
The Wind's Twelve Quarters

Extraterrestrials
Discover the Destroyer
Land of Loss
Shade's Children
The Voyage of the Space Beagle
The Wind's Twelve Quarters

Failure and Success
Athletic Shorts
Discover the Destroyer
Don Quixote
Forty Acres and Maybe a Mule
Josh Gibson
Land of Loss
Martha Graham: A Dancer
"The Most Dangerous Game"
Sammy Sosa: A Biography
Shade's Children
You Want Women to Vote, Lizzie Stanton?

Faith
Armageddon Summer
Don Quixote
The Grass Dancer
Harriet Beecher Stowe and the Beecher
    Preachers
"The Man That Corrupted Hadleyburg"

Sammy Sosa: A Biography
Two Suns in the Sky
You Want Women to Vote, Lizzie Stanton?

Fall of Man/Woman

Don Quixote
Go Ask Alice
Gulliver's Travels
"The Man That Corrupted Hadleyburg"

Fame

Don Quixote
*Harriet Beecher Stowe and the Beecher
    Preachers*
Josh Gibson
Martha Graham: A Dancer
"The Most Dangerous Game"
Sammy Sosa: A Biography
You Want Women to Vote, Lizzie Stanton?

Family Honor

Athletic Shorts
*Harriet Beecher Stowe and the Beecher
    Preachers*
My Brother, My Sister, and I
Rebellion
Sabriel
Sandwriter

Family Life

Athletic Shorts
Beyond Dreams
Confessions of an Ugly Stepsister
Forty Acres and Maybe a Mule
Go Ask Alice
*Harriet Beecher Stowe and the Beecher
    Preachers*
"The Lesson"
The Merlin Effect
My Brother, My Sister, and I
No-No Boy
P.S. Longer Letter Later
Rats
Rebellion
Sammy Sosa: A Biography
Sandwriter
So Far from the Bamboo Grove

Two Suns in the Sky
When Jeff Comes Home
You Want Women to Vote, Lizzie Stanton?

Family Values

Athletic Shorts
Beyond Dreams
Forty Acres and Maybe a Mule
Go Ask Alice
*Harriet Beecher Stowe and the Beecher
    Preachers*
"The Lesson"
The Merlin Effect
My Brother, My Sister, and I
My Father, Dancing
No-No Boy
Rats
Sammy Sosa: A Biography
So Far from the Bamboo Grove
Two Suns in the Sky
When Jeff Comes Home
You Want Women to Vote, Lizzie Stanton?

Fanaticism

Armageddon Summer
Don Quixote
Land of Loss
"The Lesson"
The Merlin Effect
"The Most Dangerous Game"
Rebellion
Soul Catcher
You Want Women to Vote, Lizzie Stanton?

Fantasy

"A Boy and His Dog"
Confessions of an Ugly Stepsister
Discover the Destroyer
Don Quixote
Enter the Enchanted
Fantastic Beasts and Where to Find Them
Gathering Blue
The Grass Dancer
Gulliver's Travels
Harrison Bergeron
Harry Potter and the Goblet of Fire
The Hitchhiker's Guide to the Galaxy

Land of Loss
"The Man That Corrupted Hadleyburg"
The Merlin Effect
"The Most Dangerous Game"
The Queen of Attolia
Quidditch Through the Ages
Rats
Realm of the Reaper
Sabriel
Sandwriter
Search for Senna
Shade's Children
The Voyage of the Space Beagle
The Wind's Twelve Quarters

Fantasy Life

Confessions of an Ugly Stepsister
Discover the Destroyer
Don Quixote
Enter the Enchanted
Gathering Blue
Go Ask Alice
The Grass Dancer
Gulliver's Travels
Harriet Beecher Stowe and the Beecher
    Preachers
Land of Loss
The Merlin Effect
Realm of the Reaper
Search for Senna

Far East

My Brother, My Sister, and I
So Far from the Bamboo Grove

Fate and Chance

Great Expectations
Gulliver's Travels
Land of Loss
Sammy Sosa: A Biography

Fatherhood

Beyond Dreams
"A Boy and His Dog"
Harriet Beecher Stowe and the Beecher
    Preachers
Harrison Bergeron

The Merlin Effect
My Father, Dancing
When Jeff Comes Home

Fear and Terror

Armageddon Summer
Athletic Shorts
Beyond Dreams
"A Boy and His Dog"
Discover the Destroyer
Enter the Enchanted
Forty Acres and Maybe a Mule
Gulliver's Travels
Harry Potter and the Goblet of Fire
The Hitchhiker's Guide to the Galaxy
Land of Loss
The Merlin Effect
"The Most Dangerous Game"
Rats
Realm of the Reaper
Rebellion
Sabriel
Search for Senna
Shade's Children
So Far from the Bamboo Grove
Soul Catcher
The Voyage of the Space Beagle
The Wind's Twelve Quarters

Feminism

Confessions of an Ugly Stepsister
Enter the Enchanted
Harriet Beecher Stowe and the Beecher
    Preachers
Land of Loss
You Want Women to Vote, Lizzie Stanton?

Femme Fatale

"A Boy and His Dog"
Confessions of an Ugly Stepsister
Discover the Destroyer
Don Quixote
Enter the Enchanted
Great Expectations
Land of Loss
The Merlin Effect
"The Necklace"

The Queen of Attolia
Realm of the Reaper
Sabriel
Search for Senna

Fertility
"A Boy and His Dog"
Shade's Children

Feudalism
Enter the Enchanted

Fidelity and Infidelity
Armageddon Summer
*Harriet Beecher Stowe and the Beecher
    Preachers*
My Father, Dancing
"The Necklace"

Filth and Squalor
"A Boy and His Dog"
Don Quixote
Gathering Blue
Gulliver's Travels
Land of Loss
"The Lesson"
My Brother, My Sister, and I
No-No Boy
So Far from the Bamboo Grove

First Love
Beyond Dreams
"A Boy and His Dog"
Confessions of an Ugly Stepsister
The Grass Dancer
Great Expectations
*Harriet Beecher Stowe and the Beecher
    Preachers*
Martha Graham: A Dancer
My Father, Dancing
Rebellion
Sandwriter
Search for Senna
Two Suns in the Sky

Flesh vs. Spirit
Discover the Destroyer
Don Quixote
Gulliver's Travels
Land of Loss
The Merlin Effect
Realm of the Reaper
Shade's Children
Soul Catcher
When Jeff Comes Home

Flight
"A Boy and His Dog"
Discover the Destroyer
Enter the Enchanted
Forty Acres and Maybe a Mule
Go Ask Alice
Gulliver's Travels
Land of Loss
"The Most Dangerous Game"
My Brother, My Sister, and I
The Queen of Attolia
Rats
Realm of the Reaper
Rebellion
Search for Senna
So Far from the Bamboo Grove
Soul Catcher
Two Suns in the Sky

Food
Armageddon Summer
"A Boy and His Dog"
Enter the Enchanted
Forty Acres and Maybe a Mule
Gooseberries
Gulliver's Travels
The Hitchhiker's Guide to the Galaxy
Land of Loss
Martha Graham: A Dancer
My Brother, My Sister, and I
Rats

Forgiveness
Discover the Destroyer
The Queen of Attolia

Forties

Josh Gibson
My Brother, My Sister, and I
No-No Boy
So Far from the Bamboo Grove
Two Suns in the Sky

Free Will vs. Determinism

Discover the Destroyer
Land of Loss
"The Most Dangerous Game"

Freedom

The Black Stallion
"A Boy and His Dog"
Forty Acres and Maybe a Mule
Gulliver's Travels
Harriet Beecher Stowe and the Beecher
    Preachers
Harrison Bergeron
Josh Gibson
Rebellion
Shade's Children
Two Suns in the Sky

Friendship

Armageddon Summer
Athletic Shorts
The Black Stallion
"A Boy and His Dog"
Discover the Destroyer
Don Quixote
Enter the Enchanted
Forty Acres and Maybe a Mule
Gathering Blue
Gooseberries
Great Expectations
Gulliver's Travels
Harriet Beecher Stowe and the Beecher
    Preachers
Harry Potter and the Goblet of Fire
The Hitchhiker's Guide to the Galaxy
Josh Gibson
Land of Loss
"The Lesson"
The Merlin Effect

No-No Boy
P.S. Longer Letter Later
Realm of the Reaper
Rebellion
Sabriel
Sandwriter
Search for Senna
Shade's Children
When Jeff Comes Home
The Wind's Twelve Quarters
You Want Women to Vote, Lizzie Stanton?

Frustration

Discover the Destroyer
Forty Acres and Maybe a Mule
Josh Gibson
My Brother, My Sister, and I
No-No Boy
Sammy Sosa: A Biography
Two Suns in the Sky

Futility

Don Quixote
Harrison Bergeron
Josh Gibson
Realm of the Reaper
Soul Catcher

Futurism

"A Boy and His Dog"
Gathering Blue
Harrison Bergeron
Shade's Children
The Voyage of the Space Beagle
The Wind's Twelve Quarters

Gender Warfare

Beyond Dreams
"A Boy and His Dog"
Discover the Destroyer
Enter the Enchanted
Go Ask Alice
Harriet Beecher Stowe and the Beecher
    Preachers
Land of Loss
The Queen of Attolia
Realm of the Reaper

Rebellion
You Want Women to Vote, Lizzie Stanton?

Generation Gap
Athletic Shorts
Gathering Blue
Harriet Beecher Stowe and the Beecher
    Preachers
Harrison Bergeron
My Father, Dancing
No-No Boy
Rats
Two Suns in the Sky

Genetics
The Merlin Effect

Genius
Confessions of an Ugly Stepsister
Gathering Blue
Harriet Beecher Stowe and the Beecher
    Preachers
Martha Graham: A Dancer

God
Armageddon Summer
Harriet Beecher Stowe and the Beecher
    Preachers
The Wind's Twelve Quarters

Good vs. Evil
Armageddon Summer
Discover the Destroyer
Enter the Enchanted
Harriet Beecher Stowe and the Beecher
    Preachers
Harry Potter and the Goblet of Fire
Land of Loss
The Merlin Effect
"The Most Dangerous Game"
Rats
Realm of the Reaper
Rebellion
Sabriel
Sandwriter
Search for Senna

Shade's Children

Gossip
Athletic Shorts
Gooseberries
"The Man That Corrupted Hadleyburg"
P.S. Longer Letter Later
You Want Women to Vote, Lizzie Stanton?

Grandparents
Gathering Blue
Go Ask Alice

Great Chain of Being
The Grass Dancer
Gulliver's Travels

Greed
Discover the Destroyer
Gooseberries
Josh Gibson
"The Man That Corrupted Hadleyburg"
Sandwriter

Grief and Sorrow
Enter the Enchanted
Forty Acres and Maybe a Mule
Gathering Blue
The Grass Dancer
Harriet Beecher Stowe and the Beecher
    Preachers
Harry Potter and the Goblet of Fire
My Brother, My Sister, and I
"The Necklace"
Sabriel
Shade's Children
So Far from the Bamboo Grove
Soul Catcher
The Wind's Twelve Quarters

Grotesque
Discover the Destroyer
Don Quixote
Enter the Enchanted
Land of Loss
The Merlin Effect

Realm of the Reaper
The Voyage of the Space Beagle

Growing Up
Armageddon Summer
The Black Stallion
Harriet Beecher Stowe and the Beecher
    Preachers
My Brother, My Sister, and I
Sammy Sosa: A Biography
Shade's Children

Growth and Development
Armageddon Summer
Athletic Shorts
Beyond Dreams
The Black Stallion
Confessions of an Ugly Stepsister
Discover the Destroyer
Enter the Enchanted
Forty Acres and Maybe a Mule
Gathering Blue
Gulliver's Travels
Harriet Beecher Stowe and the Beecher
    Preachers
Harry Potter and the Goblet of Fire
Land of Loss
"The Lesson"
Martha Graham: A Dancer
The Merlin Effect
My Brother, My Sister, and I
My Father, Dancing
No-No Boy
P.S. Longer Letter Later
Sabriel
Sammy Sosa: A Biography
Sandwriter
Search for Senna
Shade's Children
So Far from the Bamboo Grove
Soul Catcher
Two Suns in the Sky
The Wind's Twelve Quarters
You Want Women to Vote, Lizzie Stanton?

Guilt
Athletic Shorts

Discover the Destroyer
Gulliver's Travels
"The Man That Corrupted Hadleyburg"
My Father, Dancing
No-No Boy
The Queen of Attolia
When Jeff Comes Home
The Wind's Twelve Quarters

Hallucinations
Discover the Destroyer
Don Quixote
Go Ask Alice

Happiness and Gaiety
Gooseberries
Gulliver's Travels
Harrison Bergeron
My Brother, My Sister, and I
My Father, Dancing
"The Necklace"
Sammy Sosa: A Biography

Hatred
"A Boy and His Dog"
Discover the Destroyer
Enter the Enchanted
Forty Acres and Maybe a Mule
Gulliver's Travels
Harry Potter and the Goblet of Fire
Land of Loss
"The Man That Corrupted Hadleyburg"
The Merlin Effect
Rats
Realm of the Reaper
Rebellion
Sabriel
Shade's Children
Soul Catcher

Hedonism
Go Ask Alice
Gooseberries
Great Expectations
Gulliver's Travels
Harrison Bergeron
"The Most Dangerous Game"

Sandwriter

Hell
Realm of the Reaper

Heredity
"A Boy and His Dog"

Heritage and Ancestry
Beyond Dreams
Enter the Enchanted
Gathering Blue
The Grass Dancer
Harriet Beecher Stowe and the Beecher Preachers
Josh Gibson
"The Lesson"
"The Most Dangerous Game"
My Brother, My Sister, and I
No-No Boy
The Queen of Attolia
Rebellion
Sabriel
Sandwriter
So Far from the Bamboo Grove
Soul Catcher
Two Suns in the Sky
The Wind's Twelve Quarters

Heroes and Heroism
Athletic Shorts
The Black Stallion
Discover the Destroyer
Don Quixote
Enter the Enchanted
Gulliver's Travels
Harriet Beecher Stowe and the Beecher Preachers
Harry Potter and the Goblet of Fire
The Hitchhiker's Guide to the Galaxy
Land of Loss
The Merlin Effect
"The Most Dangerous Game"
The Queen of Attolia
Rats
Realm of the Reaper
Rebellion

Sabriel
Sammy Sosa: A Biography
Sandwriter
Search for Senna
Shade's Children
The Voyage of the Space Beagle
The Wind's Twelve Quarters
You Want Women to Vote, Lizzie Stanton?

High Society
Great Expectations
"The Lesson"
My Father, Dancing
Rebellion
You Want Women to Vote, Lizzie Stanton?

History
Confessions of an Ugly Stepsister
Enter the Enchanted
Forty Acres and Maybe a Mule
The Grass Dancer
Harriet Beecher Stowe and the Beecher Preachers
Josh Gibson
Land of Loss
Martha Graham: A Dancer
The Merlin Effect
My Brother, My Sister, and I
No-No Boy
Rebellion
So Far from the Bamboo Grove
Two Suns in the Sky
You Want Women to Vote, Lizzie Stanton?

Holidays
Harry Potter and the Goblet of Fire

Holocaust
Two Suns in the Sky

Home
Athletic Shorts
Beyond Dreams
Go Ask Alice
Gooseberries
The Grass Dancer
Great Expectations

Harriet Beecher Stowe and the Beecher
    Preachers
Harry Potter and the Goblet of Fire
Josh Gibson
Land of Loss
"The Lesson"
"The Man That Corrupted Hadleyburg"
Martha Graham: A Dancer
"The Most Dangerous Game"
My Brother, My Sister, and I
My Father, Dancing
"The Necklace"
No-No Boy
P.S. Longer Letter Later
Rats
Rebellion
Sammy Sosa: A Biography
Two Suns in the Sky
When Jeff Comes Home
The Wind's Twelve Quarters
You Want Women to Vote, Lizzie Stanton?

Homelessness
"A Boy and His Dog"
Confessions of an Ugly Stepsister
Enter the Enchanted
Forty Acres and Maybe a Mule
Go Ask Alice
The Hitchhiker's Guide to the Galaxy
"The Lesson"
My Brother, My Sister, and I
Realm of the Reaper
Rebellion
Sabriel
Search for Senna
Shade's Children
So Far from the Bamboo Grove
Two Suns in the Sky

Homosexuality
When Jeff Comes Home

Honor and Integrity
Athletic Shorts
The Black Stallion
Don Quixote

Enter the Enchanted
Gathering Blue
Gooseberries
Land of Loss
"The Man That Corrupted Hadleyburg"
The Merlin Effect
"The Most Dangerous Game"
My Brother, My Sister, and I
No-No Boy
Rebellion
Sabriel
Sammy Sosa: A Biography
Sandwriter
Search for Senna
So Far from the Bamboo Grove
The Voyage of the Space Beagle

Hope
Discover the Destroyer
Enter the Enchanted
Gathering Blue
Gulliver's Travels
Harriet Beecher Stowe and the Beecher
    Preachers
Josh Gibson
Land of Loss
"The Lesson"
"The Most Dangerous Game"
My Brother, My Sister, and I
P.S. Longer Letter Later
The Queen of Attolia
Rebellion
Sabriel
Search for Senna
Two Suns in the Sky
You Want Women to Vote, Lizzie Stanton?

Hospitalization
Go Ask Alice
My Father, Dancing

Human Body
Martha Graham: A Dancer
The Merlin Effect
The Queen of Attolia
Shade's Children

Human Condition

Athletic Shorts
Beyond Dreams
Confessions of an Ugly Stepsister
Don Quixote
Forty Acres and Maybe a Mule
Go Ask Alice
Gulliver's Travels
Harrison Bergeron
Josh Gibson
My Brother, My Sister, and I
My Father, Dancing
P.S. Longer Letter Later
Realm of the Reaper
Sammy Sosa: A Biography
Sandwriter
So Far from the Bamboo Grove
Soul Catcher
Two Suns in the Sky
When Jeff Comes Home

Human Nature

Athletic Shorts
Beyond Dreams
"A Boy and His Dog"
Discover the Destroyer
Don Quixote
Gooseberries
Gulliver's Travels
Land of Loss
"The Man That Corrupted Hadleyburg"
"The Most Dangerous Game"
"The Necklace"
Realm of the Reaper
Shade's Children
Two Suns in the Sky
The Voyage of the Space Beagle

Humanism

Don Quixote

Humiliation and Degradation

Athletic Shorts
Beyond Dreams
"A Boy and His Dog"
Discover the Destroyer

Don Quixote
Forty Acres and Maybe a Mule
Go Ask Alice
Great Expectations
Gulliver's Travels
Land of Loss
"The Man That Corrupted Hadleyburg"
My Brother, My Sister, and I
The Queen of Attolia
Realm of the Reaper
Rebellion
Shade's Children
So Far from the Bamboo Grove
When Jeff Comes Home

Humility

Gulliver's Travels
Harriet Beecher Stowe and the Beecher
    Preachers
My Brother, My Sister, and I
Sammy Sosa: A Biography

Hunger

The Black Stallion
"A Boy and His Dog"
Enter the Enchanted
Forty Acres and Maybe a Mule
Gulliver's Travels
Land of Loss
My Brother, My Sister, and I
Rats
So Far from the Bamboo Grove

Hypocrisy

"A Boy and His Dog"
Discover the Destroyer
Gooseberries
Great Expectations
Josh Gibson
Land of Loss
"The Man That Corrupted Hadleyburg"
"The Most Dangerous Game"
Soul Catcher
Two Suns in the Sky

Idealism

Armageddon Summer

The Black Stallion
Confessions of an Ugly Stepsister
Discover the Destroyer
Don Quixote
Enter the Enchanted
Forty Acres and Maybe a Mule
Gathering Blue
The Grass Dancer
Great Expectations
Gulliver's Travels
Harriet Beecher Stowe and the Beecher
   Preachers
Harry Potter and the Goblet of Fire
Josh Gibson
The Merlin Effect
Rats
Rebellion
Sabriel
Sammy Sosa: A Biography
Search for Senna
Soul Catcher
Two Suns in the Sky
The Voyage of the Space Beagle
The Wind's Twelve Quarters
You Want Women to Vote, Lizzie Stanton?

Ignorance

Beyond Dreams
Discover the Destroyer
Gathering Blue
Go Ask Alice
Great Expectations
Gulliver's Travels
The Hitchhiker's Guide to the Galaxy
Land of Loss
The Merlin Effect
"The Necklace"
Rats
Sandwriter
When Jeff Comes Home

Illegitimacy

Beyond Dreams

Illumination

Great Expectations

Illusion vs. Reality

Beyond Dreams
Confessions of an Ugly Stepsister
Discover the Destroyer
Don Quixote
Fantastic Beasts and Where to Find Them
Gathering Blue
Go Ask Alice
Gooseberries
Great Expectations
Land of Loss
"The Man That Corrupted Hadleyburg"
The Merlin Effect
Rats
Search for Senna

Imagination

Confessions of an Ugly Stepsister
Don Quixote
Gathering Blue
Harriet Beecher Stowe and the Beecher
   Preachers
Martha Graham: A Dancer
The Merlin Effect

Immigrants

No-No Boy
Two Suns in the Sky

Immortality

Enter the Enchanted
Land of Loss
The Merlin Effect

Individual and Society

Athletic Shorts
Don Quixote
Gathering Blue
Great Expectations
Harriet Beecher Stowe and the Beecher
   Preachers
Harrison Bergeron
Josh Gibson
"The Lesson"
My Brother, My Sister, and I
No-No Boy

When Jeff Comes Home
You Want Women to Vote, Lizzie Stanton?

Individualism
Athletic Shorts
The Black Stallion
"A Boy and His Dog"
Discover the Destroyer
Enter the Enchanted
Forty Acres and Maybe a Mule
Harrison Bergeron
Land of Loss
Martha Graham: A Dancer
"The Most Dangerous Game"
My Brother, My Sister, and I
Rats
Sabriel
Search for Senna
You Want Women to Vote, Lizzie Stanton?

Industry and Labor
My Brother, My Sister, and I

Inner Conflict
Armageddon Summer
Athletic Shorts
Beyond Dreams
Discover the Destroyer
Enter the Enchanted
The Grass Dancer
Great Expectations
Gulliver's Travels
Land of Loss
The Merlin Effect
My Brother, My Sister, and I
My Father, Dancing
No-No Boy
Rats
Realm of the Reaper
Search for Senna

Innocence and Experience
Armageddon Summer
Athletic Shorts
Beyond Dreams
The Black Stallion
Confessions of an Ugly Stepsister

Discover the Destroyer
Don Quixote
Enter the Enchanted
Gathering Blue
Go Ask Alice
The Grass Dancer
Great Expectations
Gulliver's Travels
Harriet Beecher Stowe and the Beecher
    Preachers
Harry Potter and the Goblet of Fire
The Hitchhiker's Guide to the Galaxy
Josh Gibson
Land of Loss
The Merlin Effect
My Brother, My Sister, and I
My Father, Dancing
"The Necklace"
P.S. Longer Letter Later
Rats
Realm of the Reaper
Rebellion
Sabriel
Sammy Sosa: A Biography
Sandwriter
Search for Senna
Shade's Children
So Far from the Bamboo Grove
Two Suns in the Sky
The Voyage of the Space Beagle
The Wind's Twelve Quarters
You Want Women to Vote, Lizzie Stanton?

Insecurity
Armageddon Summer
Beyond Dreams
Discover the Destroyer
Enter the Enchanted
Forty Acres and Maybe a Mule
Go Ask Alice
Great Expectations
Gulliver's Travels
Harriet Beecher Stowe and the Beecher
    Preachers
The Hitchhiker's Guide to the Galaxy
Land of Loss
"The Lesson"

The Merlin Effect
My Brother, My Sister, and I
My Father, Dancing
P.S. Longer Letter Later
Rats
Realm of the Reaper
Rebellion
Sammy Sosa: A Biography
Sandwriter
Search for Senna
Shade's Children
So Far from the Bamboo Grove

Instinct
Rats

Intellectuals and Intellectualism
Confessions of an Ugly Stepsister
Gathering Blue
Gulliver's Travels
Harriet Beecher Stowe and the Beecher
    Preachers
Land of Loss
The Merlin Effect
Realm of the Reaper
The Voyage of the Space Beagle
The Wind's Twelve Quarters
You Want Women to Vote, Lizzie Stanton?

Interracial Relationships
No-No Boy

Intoxication
Beyond Dreams
Josh Gibson
"The Lesson"

Isolation
Armageddon Summer
Gathering Blue
My Brother, My Sister, and I
Two Suns in the Sky
The Wind's Twelve Quarters

Jealousy
Beyond Dreams

Discover the Destroyer
Enter the Enchanted
Land of Loss
Martha Graham: A Dancer
My Brother, My Sister, and I

Jewish Life and Thought
Land of Loss
Two Suns in the Sky

Jokes and Pranks
Josh Gibson
"The Man That Corrupted Hadleyburg"

Journey
The Black Stallion
"A Boy and His Dog"
Discover the Destroyer
Enter the Enchanted
Forty Acres and Maybe a Mule
Gulliver's Travels
The Hitchhiker's Guide to the Galaxy
Land of Loss
"The Lesson"
Realm of the Reaper
Rebellion
Sabriel
Sandwriter
Search for Senna
So Far from the Bamboo Grove
Soul Catcher
The Voyage of the Space Beagle
The Wind's Twelve Quarters

Jungle
"The Most Dangerous Game"

Justice and Injustice
Forty Acres and Maybe a Mule
Gulliver's Travels
Harriet Beecher Stowe and the Beecher
    Preachers
Josh Gibson
My Brother, My Sister, and I
The Queen of Attolia
Rebellion

Kidnaping
Soul Catcher
When Jeff Comes Home

Kindness
Athletic Shorts
The Black Stallion
Confessions of an Ugly Stepsister
Don Quixote
Enter the Enchanted
Forty Acres and Maybe a Mule
Gathering Blue
Gulliver's Travels
*Harriet Beecher Stowe and the Beecher
    Preachers*
The Merlin Effect
My Brother, My Sister, and I
Sandwriter

Knowledge
The Black Stallion
Gathering Blue
The Grass Dancer
Gulliver's Travels
*Harriet Beecher Stowe and the Beecher
    Preachers*
Harry Potter and the Goblet of Fire
The Hitchhiker's Guide to the Galaxy
Land of Loss
"The Lesson"
The Merlin Effect
"The Most Dangerous Game"
The Voyage of the Space Beagle
The Wind's Twelve Quarters

Language and Meaning
Don Quixote
Gulliver's Travels
*Harriet Beecher Stowe and the Beecher
    Preachers*
The Hitchhiker's Guide to the Galaxy
Land of Loss
"The Lesson"
The Merlin Effect
P.S. Longer Letter Later
Search for Senna

The Wind's Twelve Quarters

Law and Order
Harrison Bergeron
"The Man That Corrupted Hadleyburg"

Leaders
Armageddon Summer
Discover the Destroyer
Enter the Enchanted
Forty Acres and Maybe a Mule
*Harriet Beecher Stowe and the Beecher
    Preachers*
Harrison Bergeron
Harry Potter and the Goblet of Fire
Land of Loss
"The Lesson"
The Queen of Attolia
Realm of the Reaper
Sabriel
Search for Senna
Shade's Children
The Voyage of the Space Beagle
You Want Women to Vote, Lizzie Stanton?

Leadership
Discover the Destroyer
Enter the Enchanted
*Harriet Beecher Stowe and the Beecher
    Preachers*
Land of Loss
The Queen of Attolia
Realm of the Reaper
Search for Senna
Shade's Children
You Want Women to Vote, Lizzie Stanton?

Letter Writing
P.S. Longer Letter Later

Liberation
Athletic Shorts
Forty Acres and Maybe a Mule
*Harriet Beecher Stowe and the Beecher
    Preachers*
Harrison Bergeron
Shade's Children

Two Suns in the Sky
You Want Women to Vote, Lizzie Stanton?

Life Cycle
Beyond Dreams
Go Ask Alice
The Grass Dancer
Gulliver's Travels
*Harriet Beecher Stowe and the Beecher
    Preachers*
The Merlin Effect
My Father, Dancing
Shade's Children

Literature
Enter the Enchanted
*Harriet Beecher Stowe and the Beecher
    Preachers*
The Merlin Effect

Logic
"The Most Dangerous Game"
Realm of the Reaper

Loneliness
Armageddon Summer
Athletic Shorts
The Black Stallion
Gulliver's Travels
My Brother, My Sister, and I

Loss
Armageddon Summer
The Black Stallion
Enter the Enchanted
Forty Acres and Maybe a Mule
Gathering Blue
The Grass Dancer
*Harriet Beecher Stowe and the Beecher
    Preachers*
Harry Potter and the Goblet of Fire
The Hitchhiker's Guide to the Galaxy
Martha Graham: A Dancer
My Brother, My Sister, and I
My Father, Dancing
"The Necklace"
No-No Boy

P.S. Longer Letter Later
The Queen of Attolia
Rebellion
Sabriel
Shade's Children
So Far from the Bamboo Grove
Soul Catcher
Two Suns in the Sky
The Wind's Twelve Quarters

Love and Passion
Beyond Dreams
"A Boy and His Dog"
Confessions of an Ugly Stepsister
Discover the Destroyer
Enter the Enchanted
The Grass Dancer
Great Expectations
*Harriet Beecher Stowe and the Beecher
    Preachers*
Martha Graham: A Dancer
My Father, Dancing
"The Necklace"
The Queen of Attolia
Rebellion
Search for Senna
Two Suns in the Sky
The Wind's Twelve Quarters

Loyalty
Armageddon Summer
The Black Stallion
"A Boy and His Dog"
Discover the Destroyer
Enter the Enchanted
Gathering Blue
*Harriet Beecher Stowe and the Beecher
    Preachers*
Harry Potter and the Goblet of Fire
Land of Loss
"The Lesson"
Martha Graham: A Dancer
The Merlin Effect
"The Most Dangerous Game"
My Brother, My Sister, and I
No-No Boy
P.S. Longer Letter Later

Rats
Realm of the Reaper
Rebellion
Sabriel
Sammy Sosa: A Biography
Search for Senna
Shade's Children
So Far from the Bamboo Grove
Two Suns in the Sky
When Jeff Comes Home

Lust
"A Boy and His Dog"
Martha Graham: A Dancer
Rebellion

Machismo
Athletic Shorts
"A Boy and His Dog"
Discover the Destroyer
Josh Gibson
Land of Loss
Martha Graham: A Dancer
"The Most Dangerous Game"
Realm of the Reaper
Search for Senna

Madness and Insanity
Armageddon Summer
Don Quixote
Go Ask Alice
Harriet Beecher Stowe and the Beecher
    Preachers
The Merlin Effect
"The Most Dangerous Game"
Realm of the Reaper

Magic
Confessions of an Ugly Stepsister
Discover the Destroyer
Enter the Enchanted
Fantastic Beasts and Where to Find Them
The Grass Dancer
Harry Potter and the Goblet of Fire
Land of Loss
The Merlin Effect

Quidditch Through the Ages
Realm of the Reaper
Sabriel
Sandwriter
Search for Senna

Man/Woman vs. Machine
The Hitchhiker's Guide to the Galaxy

Man/Woman vs. Nature
The Black Stallion
Discover the Destroyer
Forty Acres and Maybe a Mule
The Grass Dancer
Gulliver's Travels
The Merlin Effect
"The Most Dangerous Game"
Rats
Sandwriter
Soul Catcher
The Voyage of the Space Beagle
The Wind's Twelve Quarters

Man/Woman vs. Universe
Armageddon Summer
Discover the Destroyer
Don Quixote
Enter the Enchanted
The Grass Dancer
Gulliver's Travels
The Hitchhiker's Guide to the Galaxy
Land of Loss
"The Man That Corrupted Hadleyburg"
The Merlin Effect
Realm of the Reaper
Sabriel
Search for Senna
The Voyage of the Space Beagle

Manhood
Athletic Shorts
Discover the Destroyer
Great Expectations
Land of Loss
Sammy Sosa: A Biography
Search for Senna

Manipulation

Discover the Destroyer
Enter the Enchanted
Gathering Blue
Harry Potter and the Goblet of Fire
Land of Loss
"The Lesson"
"The Man That Corrupted Hadleyburg"
The Merlin Effect
"The Most Dangerous Game"
The Queen of Attolia
Sandwriter
Search for Senna
Shade's Children
The Voyage of the Space Beagle
When Jeff Comes Home

Manners

Athletic Shorts
Beyond Dreams
Confessions of an Ugly Stepsister
Discover the Destroyer
Don Quixote
Enter the Enchanted
The Grass Dancer
Great Expectations
Gulliver's Travels
Harriet Beecher Stowe and the Beecher
    Preachers
Harrison Bergeron
Josh Gibson
"The Lesson"
"The Man That Corrupted Hadleyburg"
Martha Graham: A Dancer
The Merlin Effect
"The Most Dangerous Game"
My Brother, My Sister, and I
My Father, Dancing
"The Necklace"
No-No Boy
P.S. Longer Letter Later
The Queen of Attolia
Rebellion
Sammy Sosa: A Biography
Sandwriter
So Far from the Bamboo Grove
Two Suns in the Sky

The Voyage of the Space Beagle
When Jeff Comes Home
You Want Women to Vote, Lizzie Stanton?

Marital Conflict

Beyond Dreams
Martha Graham: A Dancer
P.S. Longer Letter Later

Marital Relations

Harriet Beecher Stowe and the Beecher
    Preachers
Martha Graham: A Dancer
When Jeff Comes Home

Marriage and Courtship

Beyond Dreams
Confessions of an Ugly Stepsister
Great Expectations
Harriet Beecher Stowe and the Beecher
    Preachers
Martha Graham: A Dancer
"The Necklace"
The Queen of Attolia
Rebellion

Martyrdom

Enter the Enchanted
Harrison Bergeron
Harry Potter and the Goblet of Fire
Shade's Children

Mass Murder

Shade's Children

Massachusetts

Armageddon Summer

Materialism

Discover the Destroyer
Go Ask Alice
Gooseberries
Great Expectations
Josh Gibson
"The Lesson"
"The Man That Corrupted Hadleyburg"

"The Necklace"
Sandwriter

Meaning of Life

Gulliver's Travels
"The Man That Corrupted Hadleyburg"
The Merlin Effect
Soul Catcher

Media

Gulliver's Travels
Harriet Beecher Stowe and the Beecher Preachers
Harrison Bergeron
Josh Gibson
Martha Graham: A Dancer
Sammy Sosa: A Biography
When Jeff Comes Home
You Want Women to Vote, Lizzie Stanton?

Medicine

My Brother, My Sister, and I
My Father, Dancing

Memory and Reminiscence

Armageddon Summer
Athletic Shorts
Enter the Enchanted
Gooseberries
The Grass Dancer
Great Expectations
Gulliver's Travels
My Brother, My Sister, and I
My Father, Dancing
Search for Senna
Shade's Children
When Jeff Comes Home

Mental Instability

Armageddon Summer
Don Quixote
Enter the Enchanted
Go Ask Alice
Gulliver's Travels
Josh Gibson
Land of Loss
"The Most Dangerous Game"

Realm of the Reaper
Soul Catcher
When Jeff Comes Home

Mentors

Armageddon Summer
The Black Stallion
Confessions of an Ugly Stepsister
Enter the Enchanted
Forty Acres and Maybe a Mule
Gathering Blue
Gulliver's Travels
Harry Potter and the Goblet of Fire
"The Lesson"
Martha Graham: A Dancer
The Merlin Effect
My Father, Dancing
Sabriel
Sammy Sosa: A Biography
Sandwriter
Shade's Children
Soul Catcher
The Voyage of the Space Beagle

Merchants and Trade

Confessions of an Ugly Stepsister
Discover the Destroyer
Great Expectations
"The Lesson"

Messianism

Armageddon Summer

Metamorphosis

Shade's Children

Metaphysics

Armageddon Summer
Confessions of an Ugly Stepsister
Discover the Destroyer
Don Quixote
Enter the Enchanted
The Grass Dancer
Gulliver's Travels
Harry Potter and the Goblet of Fire
Land of Loss
"The Man That Corrupted Hadleyburg"

The Merlin Effect
Realm of the Reaper
Sabriel
Sandwriter
Search for Senna
Soul Catcher
The Wind's Twelve Quarters

Middle Ages
Enter the Enchanted

Middle Class
Go Ask Alice
Harriet Beecher Stowe and the Beecher
    Preachers
"The Man That Corrupted Hadleyburg"
"The Necklace"
P.S. Longer Letter Later
Two Suns in the Sky
When Jeff Comes Home
You Want Women to Vote, Lizzie Stanton?

Military and Soldier Life
Rebellion

Misanthropy
"A Boy and His Dog"
Discover the Destroyer
Don Quixote
Go Ask Alice
Gulliver's Travels
Harrison Bergeron
Harry Potter and the Goblet of Fire
Land of Loss
"The Man That Corrupted Hadleyburg"
"The Most Dangerous Game"
Rats
Rebellion
Search for Senna
Soul Catcher

Misfortune
Confessions of an Ugly Stepsister
Enter the Enchanted
Forty Acres and Maybe a Mule
Gulliver's Travels
The Hitchhiker's Guide to the Galaxy

Josh Gibson
Land of Loss
"The Most Dangerous Game"
My Brother, My Sister, and I
"The Necklace"
P.S. Longer Letter Later
The Queen of Attolia
Realm of the Reaper
Rebellion
Sabriel
Search for Senna
So Far from the Bamboo Grove
Soul Catcher
The Voyage of the Space Beagle
When Jeff Comes Home

Misogyny
Beyond Dreams
"A Boy and His Dog"
Don Quixote
Rebellion
The Voyage of the Space Beagle
You Want Women to Vote, Lizzie Stanton?

Modern Times
Athletic Shorts
Go Ask Alice

Money
Gooseberries
Great Expectations
Harriet Beecher Stowe and the Beecher
    Preachers
The Hitchhiker's Guide to the Galaxy
Josh Gibson
"The Lesson"
"The Man That Corrupted Hadleyburg"
Martha Graham: A Dancer
My Brother, My Sister, and I
"The Necklace"
P.S. Longer Letter Later
Sammy Sosa: A Biography

Monsters and Dragons
Discover the Destroyer
Don Quixote
Enter the Enchanted

Fantastic Beasts and Where to Find Them
Harry Potter and the Goblet of Fire
The Hitchhiker's Guide to the Galaxy
Land of Loss
The Merlin Effect
Realm of the Reaper
Sabriel
Search for Senna
Shade's Children
The Voyage of the Space Beagle

Montana
Athletic Shorts

Moral Confusion
Armageddon Summer
Athletic Shorts
Discover the Destroyer
Gooseberries
Gulliver's Travels
Josh Gibson
Land of Loss
"The Man That Corrupted Hadleyburg"
"The Necklace"
No-No Boy
Realm of the Reaper
When Jeff Comes Home

Moral Corruption and Decline
Beyond Dreams
"A Boy and His Dog"
Go Ask Alice
Harrison Bergeron
Josh Gibson
"The Man That Corrupted Hadleyburg"
"The Most Dangerous Game"
Rebellion
Soul Catcher

Morals and Morality
Athletic Shorts
Enter the Enchanted
Gooseberries
Gulliver's Travels
*Harriet Beecher Stowe and the Beecher
    Preachers*
Land of Loss

"The Man That Corrupted Hadleyburg"
"The Most Dangerous Game"
My Brother, My Sister, and I
Realm of the Reaper
Sammy Sosa: A Biography
You Want Women to Vote, Lizzie Stanton?

Morbidity
Athletic Shorts
"A Boy and His Dog"
Enter the Enchanted
Gathering Blue
Go Ask Alice
The Grass Dancer
*Harriet Beecher Stowe and the Beecher
    Preachers*
Harrison Bergeron
Harry Potter and the Goblet of Fire
The Hitchhiker's Guide to the Galaxy
Josh Gibson
Land of Loss
The Merlin Effect
"The Most Dangerous Game"
My Brother, My Sister, and I
My Father, Dancing
"The Necklace"
No-No Boy
Rats
Realm of the Reaper
Rebellion
Sabriel
Sandwriter
Search for Senna
Shade's Children
So Far from the Bamboo Grove
Soul Catcher
The Voyage of the Space Beagle
The Wind's Twelve Quarters

Motherhood
Armageddon Summer
Beyond Dreams
Confessions of an Ugly Stepsister
Gathering Blue
*Harriet Beecher Stowe and the Beecher
    Preachers*
Harrison Bergeron

Josh Gibson
No-No Boy
Rebellion
So Far from the Bamboo Grove
When Jeff Comes Home

Murder
"A Boy and His Dog"
Enter the Enchanted
Gathering Blue
Harrison Bergeron
The Hitchhiker's Guide to the Galaxy
"The Most Dangerous Game"
My Brother, My Sister, and I
Rats
Sandwriter
Shade's Children
Soul Catcher

Music
Gathering Blue
Harrison Bergeron

Mutilation
No-No Boy
The Queen of Attolia

Mystery and Intrigue
The Black Stallion
Gathering Blue
Great Expectations
Harry Potter and the Goblet of Fire
My Brother, My Sister, and I
"The Necklace"
The Queen of Attolia
Realm of the Reaper
Sabriel
Sandwriter
Search for Senna
Shade's Children

Mysticism
Armageddon Summer
Confessions of an Ugly Stepsister
Enter the Enchanted
The Grass Dancer
Gulliver's Travels

Harriet Beecher Stowe and the Beecher
    Preachers
Land of Loss
"The Man That Corrupted Hadleyburg"
The Merlin Effect
Realm of the Reaper
Sabriel
Sandwriter
Search for Senna
Soul Catcher
The Wind's Twelve Quarters

Myths and Legends
Confessions of an Ugly Stepsister
Discover the Destroyer
Enter the Enchanted
The Grass Dancer
Land of Loss
The Merlin Effect
Realm of the Reaper
Search for Senna
So Far from the Bamboo Grove

Narcissism
Go Ask Alice
Harrison Bergeron
Land of Loss
Martha Graham: A Dancer

Nationalism and Patriotism
Harriet Beecher Stowe and the Beecher
    Preachers
No-No Boy
Rebellion

Native-American Life and Thought
The Grass Dancer
Soul Catcher

Natural Disasters
Rats

Natural Law
"A Boy and His Dog"
"The Most Dangerous Game"

Rats
Shade's Children

Naturalism
Athletic Shorts
"A Boy and His Dog"
Go Ask Alice
"The Man That Corrupted Hadleyburg"

Nature
The Black Stallion
Land of Loss
The Merlin Effect
"The Most Dangerous Game"
Rats
Sandwriter
Soul Catcher

Nature, Return To
Armageddon Summer
The Black Stallion
My Father, Dancing
Soul Catcher

New England
Armageddon Summer
Harriet Beecher Stowe and the Beecher
  Preachers

New York City
"The Lesson"
Martha Graham: A Dancer
Rats

Nightmare
Discover the Destroyer
Enter the Enchanted
Land of Loss

Nihilism
"A Boy and His Dog"
Go Ask Alice
Harrison Bergeron
"The Man That Corrupted Hadleyburg"
"The Most Dangerous Game"
Shade's Children

Nonconformity
Armageddon Summer
Athletic Shorts
The Black Stallion
Don Quixote
Forty Acres and Maybe a Mule
Gathering Blue
Gulliver's Travels
Harriet Beecher Stowe and the Beecher
  Preachers
Harrison Bergeron
The Hitchhiker's Guide to the Galaxy
"The Lesson"
Martha Graham: A Dancer
"The Most Dangerous Game"
My Brother, My Sister, and I
P.S. Longer Letter Later
The Queen of Attolia
Rebellion
Soul Catcher
Two Suns in the Sky
You Want Women to Vote, Lizzie Stanton?

North Dakota
The Grass Dancer

Nostalgia
My Father, Dancing
Shade's Children

Nouveau Riche
Great Expectations
"The Necklace"
Sammy Sosa: A Biography

Novel Writing
Gulliver's Travels
Harriet Beecher Stowe and the Beecher
  Preachers

Obedience and Submission
Armageddon Summer
Athletic Shorts
Beyond Dreams
Gathering Blue
Harrison Bergeron

Sandwriter
Shade's Children
When Jeff Comes Home

Obsession

The Black Stallion
Confessions of an Ugly Stepsister
Don Quixote
Go Ask Alice
Gooseberries
Great Expectations
Harry Potter and the Goblet of Fire
Josh Gibson
Land of Loss
Martha Graham: A Dancer
The Merlin Effect
The Queen of Attolia
Realm of the Reaper
Rebellion
Soul Catcher
You Want Women to Vote, Lizzie Stanton?

Occult

Confessions of an Ugly Stepsister
Discover the Destroyer
Enter the Enchanted
Fantastic Beasts and Where to Find Them
The Grass Dancer
Harry Potter and the Goblet of Fire
Land of Loss
"The Man That Corrupted Hadleyburg"
Quidditch Through the Ages
Realm of the Reaper
Sandwriter
Search for Senna
Soul Catcher

Opportunism

Discover the Destroyer
Forty Acres and Maybe a Mule
Gooseberries
Josh Gibson
Land of Loss
"The Man That Corrupted Hadleyburg"
The Merlin Effect
My Brother, My Sister, and I
"The Necklace"

The Queen of Attolia
Realm of the Reaper
Sandwriter
Shade's Children

Oppression

Armageddon Summer
Athletic Shorts
Forty Acres and Maybe a Mule
Gathering Blue
Harriet Beecher Stowe and the Beecher
    Preachers
Harrison Bergeron
Josh Gibson
Land of Loss
My Brother, My Sister, and I
No-No Boy
The Queen of Attolia
Realm of the Reaper
Rebellion
Search for Senna
Shade's Children
Two Suns in the Sky
You Want Women to Vote, Lizzie Stanton?

Optimism and Pessimism

Athletic Shorts
Discover the Destroyer
Don Quixote
Land of Loss
"The Lesson"
My Brother, My Sister, and I
No-No Boy
P.S. Longer Letter Later
Realm of the Reaper
Two Suns in the Sky
The Voyage of the Space Beagle
You Want Women to Vote, Lizzie Stanton?

Oracles

The Grass Dancer
The Merlin Effect
Sandwriter

Oral Tradition

The Grass Dancer
Josh Gibson

Sandwriter
Soul Catcher

Other Worlds
Discover the Destroyer
Enter the Enchanted
The Hitchhiker's Guide to the Galaxy
Land of Loss
Realm of the Reaper
Sabriel
Sandwriter
Search for Senna
The Voyage of the Space Beagle
The Wind's Twelve Quarters

Outer Space
The Hitchhiker's Guide to the Galaxy
The Voyage of the Space Beagle
The Wind's Twelve Quarters

Outsider
Athletic Shorts
"A Boy and His Dog"
Discover the Destroyer
Don Quixote
Enter the Enchanted
Gulliver's Travels
The Hitchhiker's Guide to the Galaxy
Land of Loss
"The Man That Corrupted Hadleyburg"
"The Most Dangerous Game"
My Brother, My Sister, and I
The Queen of Attolia
Sabriel
Sammy Sosa: A Biography
Sandwriter
Search for Senna
Soul Catcher
Two Suns in the Sky
When Jeff Comes Home
The Wind's Twelve Quarters

Paganism
Land of Loss
The Queen of Attolia
Realm of the Reaper
Sandwriter

Search for Senna
Soul Catcher

Pain and Suffering
Armageddon Summer
Athletic Shorts
Beyond Dreams
Discover the Destroyer
Enter the Enchanted
Go Ask Alice
Harrison Bergeron
Land of Loss
"The Most Dangerous Game"
My Brother, My Sister, and I
The Queen of Attolia
Rats
Realm of the Reaper
Rebellion
Search for Senna
Shade's Children
So Far from the Bamboo Grove
Soul Catcher
When Jeff Comes Home

Paradise
The Black Stallion
Enter the Enchanted
Forty Acres and Maybe a Mule
Gooseberries
Gulliver's Travels
Sandwriter

Paradise Lost
Armageddon Summer
Beyond Dreams
"A Boy and His Dog"
Enter the Enchanted
Forty Acres and Maybe a Mule
Gathering Blue
Go Ask Alice
Gooseberries
The Grass Dancer
Great Expectations
Gulliver's Travels
The Hitchhiker's Guide to the Galaxy
Land of Loss
"The Man That Corrupted Hadleyburg"

"The Most Dangerous Game"
My Brother, My Sister, and I
"The Necklace"
P.S. Longer Letter Later
The Queen of Attolia
Rats
Rebellion
Sabriel
Shade's Children
Soul Catcher
When Jeff Comes Home
The Wind's Twelve Quarters

Paradise Regained

The Black Stallion
Gooseberries
Harriet Beecher Stowe and the Beecher
    Preachers
"The Most Dangerous Game"
The Queen of Attolia
Sammy Sosa: A Biography

Paranoia

Discover the Destroyer
Go Ask Alice
Rebellion

Parent-teen Relationship

Athletic Shorts
Confessions of an Ugly Stepsister
Go Ask Alice
The Merlin Effect
My Father, Dancing
P.S. Longer Letter Later
Rats
Two Suns in the Sky
When Jeff Comes Home

Passion vs. Reason

Beyond Dreams
The Black Stallion
Don Quixote
Enter the Enchanted
Gulliver's Travels
Harriet Beecher Stowe and the Beecher
    Preachers
Land of Loss

"The Most Dangerous Game"
The Queen of Attolia
Rats
Realm of the Reaper
Rebellion
Search for Senna
Soul Catcher
The Voyage of the Space Beagle

Peace

Gooseberries
Gulliver's Travels

Peer Pressure

Athletic Shorts
Go Ask Alice
"The Lesson"
My Brother, My Sister, and I
When Jeff Comes Home

Perfection and Perfectionism

Martha Graham: A Dancer

Performing Arts

Gathering Blue
Harrison Bergeron
Martha Graham: A Dancer
Search for Senna

Persecution

Athletic Shorts
Enter the Enchanted
Harriet Beecher Stowe and the Beecher
    Preachers
My Brother, My Sister, and I
So Far from the Bamboo Grove

Philosophical Ideas

Confessions of an Ugly Stepsister
Discover the Destroyer
Don Quixote
Enter the Enchanted
Forty Acres and Maybe a Mule
Gathering Blue
Gulliver's Travels

Harriet Beecher Stowe and the Beecher Preachers
Harrison Bergeron
Land of Loss
The Merlin Effect
"The Most Dangerous Game"
Realm of the Reaper
Soul Catcher
Two Suns in the Sky
The Voyage of the Space Beagle
The Wind's Twelve Quarters
You Want Women to Vote, Lizzie Stanton?

Physical Appearance

Confessions of an Ugly Stepsister
Don Quixote
Enter the Enchanted
Harriet Beecher Stowe and the Beecher Preachers
Harrison Bergeron
Land of Loss
"The Most Dangerous Game"
My Brother, My Sister, and I
P.S. Longer Letter Later
Sandwriter
Search for Senna
Shade's Children
When Jeff Comes Home
You Want Women to Vote, Lizzie Stanton?

Physical Disability

Gathering Blue
Harrison Bergeron
"The Most Dangerous Game"
My Brother, My Sister, and I
No-No Boy
The Queen of Attolia
Shade's Children

Pilgrims and Pilgrimages

"The Lesson"

Plagiarism

Fantastic Beasts and Where to Find Them
Harry Potter and the Goblet of Fire
Quidditch Through the Ages

Poetry Writing

The Hitchhiker's Guide to the Galaxy

Political Activism

Harriet Beecher Stowe and the Beecher Preachers
You Want Women to Vote, Lizzie Stanton?

Political Correctness

Confessions of an Ugly Stepsister
Land of Loss
"The Lesson"
Realm of the Reaper
Sammy Sosa: A Biography
Sandwriter

Politics and Society

Forty Acres and Maybe a Mule
Gulliver's Travels
Harriet Beecher Stowe and the Beecher Preachers
Harrison Bergeron
Josh Gibson
The Queen of Attolia
You Want Women to Vote, Lizzie Stanton?

Population Growth

Rats

Postmodertnism

"A Boy and His Dog"
The Grass Dancer
Harrison Bergeron

Poverty

"A Boy and His Dog"
Confessions of an Ugly Stepsister
Forty Acres and Maybe a Mule
Gathering Blue
The Grass Dancer
Great Expectations
"The Lesson"
Martha Graham: A Dancer
My Brother, My Sister, and I
No-No Boy
P.S. Longer Letter Later

Sammy Sosa: A Biography
So Far from the Bamboo Grove

Power
Enter the Enchanted
Gathering Blue
Harriet Beecher Stowe and the Beecher
    Preachers
Harrison Bergeron
Harry Potter and the Goblet of Fire
Land of Loss
"The Most Dangerous Game"
The Queen of Attolia
Realm of the Reaper
Rebellion
Sabriel
Search for Senna
Shade's Children
The Voyage of the Space Beagle

Pragmatism
Beyond Dreams
"A Boy and His Dog"
Forty Acres and Maybe a Mule
Great Expectations
Land of Loss
"The Most Dangerous Game"
My Brother, My Sister, and I
"The Necklace"
P.S. Longer Letter Later
Rebellion
Search for Senna
Shade's Children
So Far from the Bamboo Grove
The Voyage of the Space Beagle
You Want Women to Vote, Lizzie Stanton?

Prairies and Prairie Life
The Grass Dancer

Preachers and Prophets
Armageddon Summer
The Grass Dancer
Harriet Beecher Stowe and the Beecher
    Preachers
"The Lesson"
Shade's Children

Prejudice
Athletic Shorts
Forty Acres and Maybe a Mule
The Grass Dancer
Great Expectations
Harriet Beecher Stowe and the Beecher
    Preachers
Josh Gibson
Land of Loss
My Brother, My Sister, and I
Rebellion
Sandwriter
Two Suns in the Sky
You Want Women to Vote, Lizzie Stanton?

Pride
Don Quixote
Forty Acres and Maybe a Mule
The Grass Dancer
Great Expectations
Josh Gibson
Martha Graham: A Dancer
"The Most Dangerous Game"
My Brother, My Sister, and I
Rebellion
Sammy Sosa: A Biography
Search for Senna

Primitivism
Armageddon Summer
"A Boy and His Dog"
Gathering Blue
Gulliver's Travels
Land of Loss
"The Most Dangerous Game"
Sandwriter
Soul Catcher

Prisons and Confinement
Don Quixote
Great Expectations
Gulliver's Travels
Land of Loss
Search for Senna
Shade's Children
Two Suns in the Sky

When Jeff Comes Home

Progress
Harriet Beecher Stowe and the Beecher Preachers
Rats

Prophecy
Armageddon Summer
The Grass Dancer

Prostitution
Don Quixote
Go Ask Alice

Protestantism
Harriet Beecher Stowe and the Beecher Preachers

Psychology and The Human Mind
Confessions of an Ugly Stepsister
Discover the Destroyer
Enter the Enchanted
Go Ask Alice
Land of Loss
"The Necklace"
Realm of the Reaper
Search for Senna
Soul Catcher
Two Suns in the Sky
When Jeff Comes Home

Punishment
Harrison Bergeron
Harry Potter and the Goblet of Fire
Rebellion
When Jeff Comes Home

Puritanism
"The Man That Corrupted Hadleyburg"

Quest
Discover the Destroyer
Don Quixote
Enter the Enchanted

Forty Acres and Maybe a Mule
Land of Loss
Realm of the Reaper
Sabriel
Search for Senna
The Voyage of the Space Beagle
The Wind's Twelve Quarters

Race Relations
Forty Acres and Maybe a Mule
Harriet Beecher Stowe and the Beecher Preachers
Josh Gibson
Land of Loss
"The Lesson"
No-No Boy
Realm of the Reaper
Soul Catcher

Racism and Racial Conflict
Forty Acres and Maybe a Mule
Harriet Beecher Stowe and the Beecher Preachers
Josh Gibson
Land of Loss
No-No Boy

Rape
"A Boy and His Dog"
Rebellion
Soul Catcher
When Jeff Comes Home

Rebellion Against Parents
Athletic Shorts
"A Boy and His Dog"
Go Ask Alice
Harriet Beecher Stowe and the Beecher Preachers
No-No Boy
Two Suns in the Sky
When Jeff Comes Home

Reconciliation
Land of Loss
My Father, Dancing
The Queen of Attolia

The Voyage of the Space Beagle

Reconstruction Era
Forty Acres and Maybe a Mule

Redemption
The Queen of Attolia
Sammy Sosa: A Biography

Reform
*Harriet Beecher Stowe and the Beecher
    Preachers*
You Want Women to Vote, Lizzie Stanton?

Refugees
Forty Acres and Maybe a Mule
Land of Loss
My Brother, My Sister, and I
Realm of the Reaper
So Far from the Bamboo Grove
Two Suns in the Sky

Regression
"The Most Dangerous Game"
Soul Catcher

Rejection
Great Expectations
*Harriet Beecher Stowe and the Beecher
    Preachers*
Josh Gibson
"The Lesson"
No-No Boy
The Queen of Attolia
Rebellion
When Jeff Comes Home

Religion and Religious Thought
Armageddon Summer
The Grass Dancer
*Harriet Beecher Stowe and the Beecher
    Preachers*
"The Man That Corrupted Hadleyburg"
Two Suns in the Sky
The Wind's Twelve Quarters

Remorse and Regret
Athletic Shorts
Enter the Enchanted
Great Expectations
Gulliver's Travels
The Queen of Attolia
The Wind's Twelve Quarters

Renaissance
Confessions of an Ugly Stepsister

Repression
Armageddon Summer
Beyond Dreams
Enter the Enchanted
Gathering Blue
*Harriet Beecher Stowe and the Beecher
    Preachers*
Harrison Bergeron
Land of Loss
Realm of the Reaper
The Voyage of the Space Beagle
When Jeff Comes Home

Revenge
Enter the Enchanted
Harry Potter and the Goblet of Fire
The Queen of Attolia
Rats
Realm of the Reaper
Rebellion
Sabriel
Shade's Children
Soul Catcher

Rites of Passage
Athletic Shorts
Beyond Dreams
The Black Stallion
Discover the Destroyer
Enter the Enchanted
*Harriet Beecher Stowe and the Beecher
    Preachers*
Land of Loss
"The Lesson"
The Merlin Effect

My Brother, My Sister, and I
P.S. Longer Letter Later
Rats
Sabriel
Sammy Sosa: A Biography
Sandwriter
Search for Senna
Shade's Children
So Far from the Bamboo Grove
The Wind's Twelve Quarters

Ritual Sacrifice
Soul Catcher

Rivalry
Discover the Destroyer
Enter the Enchanted
Harriet Beecher Stowe and the Beecher
    Preachers
Harry Potter and the Goblet of Fire
Land of Loss
"The Man That Corrupted Hadleyburg"
The Merlin Effect
"The Most Dangerous Game"
My Brother, My Sister, and I
Quidditch Through the Ages
Realm of the Reaper
Sammy Sosa: A Biography
The Voyage of the Space Beagle

Romantic Love
Beyond Dreams
"A Boy and His Dog"
Confessions of an Ugly Stepsister
Discover the Destroyer
Don Quixote
Enter the Enchanted
Great Expectations
Harriet Beecher Stowe and the Beecher
    Preachers
Land of Loss
Martha Graham: A Dancer
My Father, Dancing
"The Necklace"
The Queen of Attolia
Rebellion
Sabriel

Search for Senna
Two Suns in the Sky

Romanticism
The Black Stallion
Confessions of an Ugly Stepsister
Discover the Destroyer
Don Quixote
Enter the Enchanted
Land of Loss
"The Most Dangerous Game"
Quidditch Through the Ages
Rats
Realm of the Reaper
Rebellion
Sabriel
Sandwriter
Search for Senna
The Voyage of the Space Beagle
The Wind's Twelve Quarters

Royalty
Confessions of an Ugly Stepsister
Gulliver's Travels
The Queen of Attolia
Sandwriter

Runaways
Go Ask Alice

Rural Life
Don Quixote
Forty Acres and Maybe a Mule
Gooseberries
The Grass Dancer
Harriet Beecher Stowe and the Beecher
    Preachers
Search for Senna

Sacrifice
Discover the Destroyer
Enter the Enchanted
Harriet Beecher Stowe and the Beecher
    Preachers
Land of Loss
My Brother, My Sister, and I
Rebellion

Sammy Sosa: A Biography
Shade's Children
The Voyage of the Space Beagle

Sadism and Masochism

Beyond Dreams
"A Boy and His Dog"
Harrison Bergeron
"The Most Dangerous Game"
Rebellion
When Jeff Comes Home

Salvation

Armageddon Summer
Harriet Beecher Stowe and the Beecher Preachers
Sammy Sosa: A Biography

Sanity

Discover the Destroyer
Realm of the Reaper

Savagery

The Black Stallion
Enter the Enchanted
Gulliver's Travels
Land of Loss
"The Most Dangerous Game"
Rats
Rebellion
Search for Senna
Soul Catcher

Scandal

When Jeff Comes Home
You Want Women to Vote, Lizzie Stanton?

School Life

Athletic Shorts
Beyond Dreams
Harry Potter and the Goblet of Fire
My Brother, My Sister, and I
P.S. Longer Letter Later
Sabriel

When Jeff Comes Home

Science and Technology

Armageddon Summer
Discover the Destroyer
Harrison Bergeron
The Hitchhiker's Guide to the Galaxy
The Merlin Effect
Rats
Shade's Children
The Voyage of the Space Beagle
The Wind's Twelve Quarters

Scorn

Don Quixote
"The Man That Corrupted Hadleyburg"
My Brother, My Sister, and I

Sea and Sea Adventures

The Black Stallion
Gulliver's Travels
The Merlin Effect
"The Most Dangerous Game"
Search for Senna

Self and Self-discovery

Armageddon Summer
Athletic Shorts
Beyond Dreams
The Black Stallion
Confessions of an Ugly Stepsister
Discover the Destroyer
Enter the Enchanted
Forty Acres and Maybe a Mule
Gathering Blue
The Grass Dancer
Gulliver's Travels
Land of Loss
The Merlin Effect
"The Most Dangerous Game"
My Father, Dancing
P.S. Longer Letter Later
Rebellion
Sabriel
Search for Senna
Two Suns in the Sky

Self-Destruction

Armageddon Summer
Athletic Shorts
Beyond Dreams
Don Quixote
Go Ask Alice
Harrison Bergeron
The Hitchhiker's Guide to the Galaxy
Josh Gibson
Land of Loss
"The Man That Corrupted Hadleyburg"
P.S. Longer Letter Later
Rats
Realm of the Reaper
Sammy Sosa: A Biography
Soul Catcher
When Jeff Comes Home

Self-Expression

Confessions of an Ugly Stepsister
Discover the Destroyer
Gathering Blue
Gulliver's Travels
Harriet Beecher Stowe and the Beecher
    Preachers
Harrison Bergeron
Martha Graham: A Dancer
P.S. Longer Letter Later
Sandwriter
You Want Women to Vote, Lizzie Stanton?

Self-Image

Armageddon Summer
Athletic Shorts
Beyond Dreams
The Black Stallion
Confessions of an Ugly Stepsister
Discover the Destroyer
Don Quixote
Enter the Enchanted
Forty Acres and Maybe a Mule
Gathering Blue
Go Ask Alice
The Grass Dancer
Great Expectations
Gulliver's Travels
Harrison Bergeron

Land of Loss
"The Lesson"
Martha Graham: A Dancer
The Merlin Effect
"The Most Dangerous Game"
My Brother, My Sister, and I
My Father, Dancing
No-No Boy
P.S. Longer Letter Later
The Queen of Attolia
Realm of the Reaper
Search for Senna
Soul Catcher
When Jeff Comes Home
You Want Women to Vote, Lizzie Stanton?

Selfishness

Discover the Destroyer
Go Ask Alice
Gooseberries
Great Expectations
Land of Loss
"The Man That Corrupted Hadleyburg"
Martha Graham: A Dancer
Sandwriter
The Wind's Twelve Quarters

Self-Pity

Athletic Shorts
Discover the Destroyer
Enter the Enchanted
Go Ask Alice
The Hitchhiker's Guide to the Galaxy
Land of Loss
Realm of the Reaper
Soul Catcher
When Jeff Comes Home

Self-Preservation

Beyond Dreams
The Black Stallion
"A Boy and His Dog"
Discover the Destroyer
Enter the Enchanted
Gulliver's Travels
The Hitchhiker's Guide to the Galaxy
Land of Loss

"The Most Dangerous Game"
My Brother, My Sister, and I
Rats
Realm of the Reaper
Rebellion
Shade's Children
So Far from the Bamboo Grove
The Voyage of the Space Beagle

Self-Reliance

Armageddon Summer
Athletic Shorts
The Black Stallion
Forty Acres and Maybe a Mule
Harriet Beecher Stowe and the Beecher
    Preachers
"The Most Dangerous Game"
My Brother, My Sister, and I
P.S. Longer Letter Later
Rats
Rebellion
Sabriel
So Far from the Bamboo Grove
You Want Women to Vote, Lizzie Stanton?

Sense Perception

"A Boy and His Dog"
Confessions of an Ugly Stepsister
Don Quixote
Fantastic Beasts and Where to Find Them
Gathering Blue
Go Ask Alice
Gooseberries
The Grass Dancer
Harrison Bergeron
The Hitchhiker's Guide to the Galaxy
The Merlin Effect
"The Most Dangerous Game"
Rats
Realm of the Reaper
When Jeff Comes Home
The Wind's Twelve Quarters

Sensuality

Confessions of an Ugly Stepsister
Go Ask Alice
Realm of the Reaper

Rebellion

Sentimentality

Athletic Shorts
The Black Stallion
Don Quixote
Enter the Enchanted
Gulliver's Travels
Harriet Beecher Stowe and the Beecher
    Preachers
My Father, Dancing
Sabriel
Sammy Sosa: A Biography

Separation and Estrangement

Armageddon Summer
Beyond Dreams
The Black Stallion
Enter the Enchanted
Gathering Blue
Go Ask Alice
Gulliver's Travels
Harriet Beecher Stowe and the Beecher
    Preachers
Harry Potter and the Goblet of Fire
Land of Loss
"The Man That Corrupted Hadleyburg"
Martha Graham: A Dancer
No-No Boy
P.S. Longer Letter Later
The Queen of Attolia
Rats
Sabriel
Sandwriter
Search for Senna
So Far from the Bamboo Grove
Two Suns in the Sky
The Voyage of the Space Beagle
When Jeff Comes Home
The Wind's Twelve Quarters

Separatism

Forty Acres and Maybe a Mule
Gathering Blue
The Grass Dancer
Josh Gibson
"The Lesson"

My Brother, My Sister, and I
No-No Boy
Two Suns in the Sky

Seventies

Go Ask Alice
"The Lesson"

Sex and Sexuality

Armageddon Summer
"A Boy and His Dog"
Go Ask Alice
The Grass Dancer
Martha Graham: A Dancer
My Father, Dancing
Rebellion
Shade's Children
The Voyage of the Space Beagle
When Jeff Comes Home

Sex Roles

Beyond Dreams
"A Boy and His Dog"
Don Quixote
Enter the Enchanted
Gathering Blue
Harriet Beecher Stowe and the Beecher
    Preachers
Josh Gibson
Martha Graham: A Dancer
My Father, Dancing
"The Necklace"
The Queen of Attolia
Rebellion
Sandwriter
Shade's Children
When Jeff Comes Home
You Want Women to Vote, Lizzie Stanton?

Sexual Abuse

Beyond Dreams
"A Boy and His Dog"
Rebellion
Shade's Children
When Jeff Comes Home

Sexual Equality

Harriet Beecher Stowe and the Beecher
    Preachers
You Want Women to Vote, Lizzie Stanton?

Sibling Relationships

Armageddon Summer
Confessions of an Ugly Stepsister
Forty Acres and Maybe a Mule
Gooseberries
Harriet Beecher Stowe and the Beecher
    Preachers
My Brother, My Sister, and I
No-No Boy
Rats
Rebellion
Sammy Sosa: A Biography
So Far from the Bamboo Grove
Soul Catcher
When Jeff Comes Home

Sickness and Health

Armageddon Summer
Athletic Shorts
Discover the Destroyer
Gathering Blue
Harriet Beecher Stowe and the Beecher
    Preachers
Josh Gibson
My Brother, My Sister, and I
My Father, Dancing
No-No Boy
So Far from the Bamboo Grove
Soul Catcher

Simple Life

Armageddon Summer
The Black Stallion
Gathering Blue
Gulliver's Travels
Sandwriter
Soul Catcher

Sin and Sinners

Armageddon Summer

Harriet Beecher Stowe and the Beecher
   Preachers
"The Man That Corrupted Hadleyburg"

Single Life
My Father, Dancing

Skepticism
The Merlin Effect

Slavery and Emancipation
Forty Acres and Maybe a Mule
Harriet Beecher Stowe and the Beecher
   Preachers
Shade's Children

Sleep
Discover the Destroyer
Land of Loss
"The Most Dangerous Game"
Realm of the Reaper
Sandwriter
Search for Senna

Small Town Life
Athletic Shorts
"The Man That Corrupted Hadleyburg"

Snobs and Snobbery
Great Expectations
"The Most Dangerous Game"
My Brother, My Sister, and I
Sandwriter
Two Suns in the Sky

Social Protest
Athletic Shorts
Beyond Dreams
Confessions of an Ugly Stepsister
Go Ask Alice
Great Expectations
Gulliver's Travels
Harriet Beecher Stowe and the Beecher
   Preachers
Harrison Bergeron
Josh Gibson

"The Lesson"
"The Man That Corrupted Hadleyburg"
My Brother, My Sister, and I
No-No Boy
Rats
Rebellion
Soul Catcher
Two Suns in the Sky
The Wind's Twelve Quarters
You Want Women to Vote, Lizzie Stanton?

Social Responsibility
Athletic Shorts
Gathering Blue
Gooseberries
The Grass Dancer
Harriet Beecher Stowe and the Beecher
   Preachers
Land of Loss
Rats
Sammy Sosa: A Biography
Sandwriter
You Want Women to Vote, Lizzie Stanton?

Solidarity
Land of Loss
My Brother, My Sister, and I
P.S. Longer Letter Later
Realm of the Reaper
Rebellion
Search for Senna
Shade's Children
The Voyage of the Space Beagle
You Want Women to Vote, Lizzie Stanton?

Solitude
Armageddon Summer
The Black Stallion
The Merlin Effect
"The Most Dangerous Game"
Sandwriter
Soul Catcher
When Jeff Comes Home

Soul
Armageddon Summer
The Grass Dancer

Space Travel

The Hitchhiker's Guide to the Galaxy
The Voyage of the Space Beagle
The Wind's Twelve Quarters

Spirit World

The Grass Dancer

Spirits

The Grass Dancer

Spiritual Quest

Sabriel

Spirituality

Armageddon Summer
The Grass Dancer
*Harriet Beecher Stowe and the Beecher
   Preachers*
Realm of the Reaper
Sabriel
Sammy Sosa: A Biography
Sandwriter
Soul Catcher
Two Suns in the Sky

Sports and the Sporting Life

Athletic Shorts
The Black Stallion
Josh Gibson
Quidditch Through the Ages
Sammy Sosa: A Biography

Stockholm Syndrome

Soul Catcher
When Jeff Comes Home

Strength and Endurance

The Black Stallion
Discover the Destroyer
Gulliver's Travels
Josh Gibson
Land of Loss
The Merlin Effect
"The Most Dangerous Game"
My Brother, My Sister, and I

Rats
Realm of the Reaper
Search for Senna
Shade's Children
So Far from the Bamboo Grove
Soul Catcher

Struggle and Conflict

Beyond Dreams
Discover the Destroyer
Enter the Enchanted
Forty Acres and Maybe a Mule
Gulliver's Travels
*Harriet Beecher Stowe and the Beecher
   Preachers*
Harry Potter and the Goblet of Fire
Josh Gibson
Land of Loss
The Merlin Effect
"The Most Dangerous Game"
My Brother, My Sister, and I
The Queen of Attolia
Rats
Rebellion
Sabriel
Sammy Sosa: A Biography
Search for Senna
Shade's Children
So Far from the Bamboo Grove
The Voyage of the Space Beagle
You Want Women to Vote, Lizzie Stanton?

Sublime

The Black Stallion
Confessions of an Ugly Stepsister
Discover the Destroyer
Don Quixote
Enter the Enchanted
Gulliver's Travels
*Harriet Beecher Stowe and the Beecher
   Preachers*
Land of Loss
"The Man That Corrupted Hadleyburg"
Martha Graham: A Dancer
The Merlin Effect
Quidditch Through the Ages
Sabriel

Sammy Sosa: A Biography
Sandwriter
Search for Senna

Suburban Life
Rats
Two Suns in the Sky
When Jeff Comes Home

Suicide
Go Ask Alice
*Harriet Beecher Stowe and the Beecher
    Preachers*
Harry Potter and the Goblet of Fire
No-No Boy

Superstition
Confessions of an Ugly Stepsister
Fantastic Beasts and Where to Find Them
The Grass Dancer
Harry Potter and the Goblet of Fire
Land of Loss
Quidditch Through the Ages
Search for Senna

Surrealism
Realm of the Reaper

Survival
The Black Stallion
"A Boy and His Dog"
Confessions of an Ugly Stepsister
Discover the Destroyer
Enter the Enchanted
Forty Acres and Maybe a Mule
Gathering Blue
Gulliver's Travels
The Hitchhiker's Guide to the Galaxy
Land of Loss
The Merlin Effect
"The Most Dangerous Game"
My Brother, My Sister, and I
P.S. Longer Letter Later
Rats
Realm of the Reaper
Rebellion

Sandwriter
Search for Senna
Shade's Children
So Far from the Bamboo Grove
The Voyage of the Space Beagle
When Jeff Comes Home
The Wind's Twelve Quarters

Survival in the Wilderness
Armageddon Summer
The Black Stallion
Discover the Destroyer
Enter the Enchanted
Gulliver's Travels
Land of Loss
"The Most Dangerous Game"
Rebellion
Sandwriter
Soul Catcher
The Wind's Twelve Quarters

Sympathy and Compassion
Athletic Shorts
Confessions of an Ugly Stepsister
Forty Acres and Maybe a Mule
*Harriet Beecher Stowe and the Beecher
    Preachers*
Martha Graham: A Dancer
The Merlin Effect
My Brother, My Sister, and I
Realm of the Reaper
Rebellion
Two Suns in the Sky

Teenaged Mothers
Beyond Dreams

Telekinesis
Shade's Children

Telepathy
"A Boy and His Dog"
The Wind's Twelve Quarters

Temptation
Discover the Destroyer

Thinkers and Thinking
Armageddon Summer
Discover the Destroyer
Enter the Enchanted
Forty Acres and Maybe a Mule
Gulliver's Travels
Harriet Beecher Stowe and the Beecher
  Preachers
Land of Loss
My Brother, My Sister, and I
Realm of the Reaper
Search for Senna
The Voyage of the Space Beagle
You Want Women to Vote, Lizzie Stanton?

Thirties
Josh Gibson

Thrift
My Brother, My Sister, and I
"The Necklace"

Time
The Grass Dancer
The Merlin Effect

Time Travel
The Hitchhiker's Guide to the Galaxy
The Merlin Effect

Tolerance
Athletic Shorts
The Merlin Effect
Two Suns in the Sky

Tradition
The Black Stallion
Gathering Blue
The Grass Dancer
Harriet Beecher Stowe and the Beecher
  Preachers
Martha Graham: A Dancer
My Brother, My Sister, and I
No-No Boy
Rebellion
So Far from the Bamboo Grove

Soul Catcher
Two Suns in the Sky

Tragic Flaw
Realm of the Reaper

Transportation
The Black Stallion
Don Quixote
Gulliver's Travels
The Hitchhiker's Guide to the Galaxy
Josh Gibson
"The Lesson"
The Merlin Effect
"The Most Dangerous Game"
Quidditch Through the Ages
Rats
Sandwriter
Search for Senna
So Far from the Bamboo Grove
The Voyage of the Space Beagle
The Wind's Twelve Quarters

Travel
The Black Stallion
Don Quixote
Enter the Enchanted
The Hitchhiker's Guide to the Galaxy
Josh Gibson
"The Most Dangerous Game"
My Father, Dancing
Rebellion
Sabriel
Sandwriter
Search for Senna
The Wind's Twelve Quarters
You Want Women to Vote, Lizzie Stanton?

Treachery
"A Boy and His Dog"
Discover the Destroyer
Enter the Enchanted
Gulliver's Travels
Harry Potter and the Goblet of Fire
Land of Loss
"The Man That Corrupted Hadleyburg"
The Merlin Effect

"The Most Dangerous Game"
The Queen of Attolia
Rats
Realm of the Reaper
Rebellion
Sandwriter
Search for Senna
Shade's Children
Soul Catcher

Truth
Don Quixote
Great Expectations
Harriet Beecher Stowe and the Beecher
    Preachers
Land of Loss
"The Lesson"
"The Man That Corrupted Hadleyburg"
"The Necklace"
Rebellion
Sabriel
Search for Senna
When Jeff Comes Home

Twenties
"The Most Dangerous Game"

Tyranny and Authoritarianism
"A Boy and His Dog"
Discover the Destroyer
Gathering Blue
Harrison Bergeron
Land of Loss
"The Most Dangerous Game"
The Queen of Attolia
Realm of the Reaper
Rebellion
Search for Senna
Shade's Children
So Far from the Bamboo Grove

Uebermensch ("the Superman")
Shade's Children

Underclass
Forty Acres and Maybe a Mule

Gathering Blue
Great Expectations
Josh Gibson
"The Lesson"
My Brother, My Sister, and I
No-No Boy
Shade's Children
So Far from the Bamboo Grove
Two Suns in the Sky

Universe
Discover the Destroyer
Enter the Enchanted
Land of Loss
The Merlin Effect
Search for Senna
The Voyage of the Space Beagle

Unrequited Love
"A Boy and His Dog"
Discover the Destroyer
Don Quixote
Great Expectations
Land of Loss
The Queen of Attolia
Realm of the Reaper
Rebellion
Sandwriter
Search for Senna

Upper Class
Gooseberries
Great Expectations
"The Lesson"
"The Most Dangerous Game"
Rebellion

Upper Middle Class
Two Suns in the Sky

Urban Blight
Athletic Shorts
Harriet Beecher Stowe and the Beecher
    Preachers
"The Lesson"
My Brother, My Sister, and I

Utopia and Utopian Ideas
Don Quixote

Vanity
Don Quixote
Harrison Bergeron
Josh Gibson
Land of Loss
Martha Graham: A Dancer
"The Most Dangerous Game"
Sandwriter

Vice and Virtue
Discover the Destroyer
Don Quixote
Go Ask Alice
Josh Gibson
"The Man That Corrupted Hadleyburg"

Victim and Victimization
Athletic Shorts
Beyond Dreams
The Black Stallion
"A Boy and His Dog"
Discover the Destroyer
Don Quixote
Enter the Enchanted
Forty Acres and Maybe a Mule
Go Ask Alice
Harrison Bergeron
Harry Potter and the Goblet of Fire
The Hitchhiker's Guide to the Galaxy
Josh Gibson
Land of Loss
"The Man That Corrupted Hadleyburg"
The Merlin Effect
"The Most Dangerous Game"
My Brother, My Sister, and I
No-No Boy
The Queen of Attolia
Rats
Realm of the Reaper
Rebellion
Search for Senna
Shade's Children
Soul Catcher

Two Suns in the Sky
When Jeff Comes Home
The Wind's Twelve Quarters

Victorian Age
Great Expectations
Martha Graham: A Dancer

Victory and Defeat
Athletic Shorts
The Black Stallion
Discover the Destroyer
Don Quixote
Enter the Enchanted
Harriet Beecher Stowe and the Beecher Preachers
Harry Potter and the Goblet of Fire
"The Most Dangerous Game"
Quidditch Through the Ages
Rats
Rebellion
Search for Senna
You Want Women to Vote, Lizzie Stanton?

Vigilantes and Outlaws
Forty Acres and Maybe a Mule
Rebellion

Villains, Rakes, and Rogues
The Black Stallion
"A Boy and His Dog"
Discover the Destroyer
Enter the Enchanted
Go Ask Alice
Great Expectations
Harrison Bergeron
Harry Potter and the Goblet of Fire
The Hitchhiker's Guide to the Galaxy
Land of Loss
"The Man That Corrupted Hadleyburg"
The Merlin Effect
"The Most Dangerous Game"
The Queen of Attolia
Rebellion
Sandwriter
Search for Senna
Soul Catcher

When Jeff Comes Home

Villainy

The Black Stallion
"A Boy and His Dog"
Discover the Destroyer
Enter the Enchanted
Forty Acres and Maybe a Mule
Go Ask Alice
Harry Potter and the Goblet of Fire
Land of Loss
"The Man That Corrupted Hadleyburg"
The Merlin Effect
"The Most Dangerous Game"
My Brother, My Sister, and I
The Queen of Attolia
Rebellion
Sabriel
Sandwriter
Search for Senna
Soul Catcher
When Jeff Comes Home

Violence

Armageddon Summer
Beyond Dreams
The Black Stallion
"A Boy and His Dog"
Don Quixote
Enter the Enchanted
Gulliver's Travels
Harriet Beecher Stowe and the Beecher Preachers
Harrison Bergeron
Harry Potter and the Goblet of Fire
The Hitchhiker's Guide to the Galaxy
Land of Loss
The Merlin Effect
"The Most Dangerous Game"
My Brother, My Sister, and I
The Queen of Attolia
Rats
Realm of the Reaper
Rebellion
Sabriel
Search for Senna
Shade's Children

So Far from the Bamboo Grove
Soul Catcher
The Voyage of the Space Beagle
The Wind's Twelve Quarters

Virginity and Chastity

"A Boy and His Dog"
Don Quixote
Enter the Enchanted
Rebellion

Vitality

The Grass Dancer
Harriet Beecher Stowe and the Beecher Preachers
Josh Gibson
Land of Loss
Martha Graham: A Dancer
The Merlin Effect
My Father, Dancing
Rebellion
Sammy Sosa: A Biography
Search for Senna
Shade's Children

Vulgarity

"A Boy and His Dog"
Don Quixote
Go Ask Alice
Great Expectations
Gulliver's Travels
"The Lesson"
"The Man That Corrupted Hadleyburg"
Search for Senna
Shade's Children
When Jeff Comes Home

War

Gulliver's Travels
Harriet Beecher Stowe and the Beecher Preachers
Land of Loss
My Brother, My Sister, and I
The Queen of Attolia
Rebellion
Search for Senna
Shade's Children

So Far from the Bamboo Grove
Two Suns in the Sky

Weather
Gulliver's Travels
The Merlin Effect
Sandwriter

Western Civilization
The Grass Dancer
Gulliver's Travels
The Merlin Effect

Wisdom
The Black Stallion
Gulliver's Travels
The Merlin Effect
Sammy Sosa: A Biography

Witchcraft and Magic
Discover the Destroyer
Enter the Enchanted
Fantastic Beasts and Where to Find Them
The Grass Dancer
Harry Potter and the Goblet of Fire
Land of Loss
The Merlin Effect
Quidditch Through the Ages
Realm of the Reaper
Sabriel
Sandwriter
Search for Senna
Soul Catcher

Womanhood
Confessions of an Ugly Stepsister
*Harriet Beecher Stowe and the Beecher
    Preachers*
Land of Loss
Martha Graham: A Dancer
My Father, Dancing
P.S. Longer Letter Later
Rebellion
Sabriel
You Want Women to Vote, Lizzie Stanton?

Women's Rights
Armageddon Summer
Enter the Enchanted
*Harriet Beecher Stowe and the Beecher
    Preachers*
You Want Women to Vote, Lizzie Stanton?

Work and Play
The Black Stallion
Discover the Destroyer
Gulliver's Travels
*Harriet Beecher Stowe and the Beecher
    Preachers*
Josh Gibson
Martha Graham: A Dancer
The Merlin Effect
My Brother, My Sister, and I
P.S. Longer Letter Later
Quidditch Through the Ages
Sammy Sosa: A Biography

Working Class
Confessions of an Ugly Stepsister
"The Lesson"
My Brother, My Sister, and I
Sammy Sosa: A Biography

World War II
Josh Gibson
My Brother, My Sister, and I
So Far from the Bamboo Grove
Two Suns in the Sky

Yearning
Beyond Dreams
Discover the Destroyer
Don Quixote
Forty Acres and Maybe a Mule
Josh Gibson
Land of Loss

Zeitgeist
Armageddon Summer
Athletic Shorts
Beyond Dreams
Forty Acres and Maybe a Mule

Go Ask Alice
Harriet Beecher Stowe and the Beecher
   Preachers
Josh Gibson
"The Lesson"

My Brother, My Sister, and I
No-No Boy
Rebellion
So Far from the Bamboo Grove
Two Suns in the Sky

CUMULATIVE INDEX

VOLUMES 1-14

◆

Asimov, Isaac, 4:1643–1649, 4:1707–1712, 6:3184–3197, 7:3678–3695, 7:3742–3752, 9:4931–4943
Asimov, Janet, 7:3742–3752
ASYLUM FOR NIGHTFACE, 9:4444–4451
AT THE EARTH'S CORE, 9:4452–4461
AT THE GATEWAYS OF THE DAY, 4:1572–1577
ATHLETIC SHORTS, 14:11–26
Atkins, Catherine, 14:459–468
ATLAS SHRUGGED, 12:57–66
AUNT FLORRIE, 9:4462–4468
AUNT MARIA, 6:2767–2773
Austen, Jane, 3:1062–1070
Avi, 1:409–413, 10:227–234, 10:249–258, 10:385–392
AWAKENING, THE, 11:21–34

B
Babbit, Natalie, 5:2227–2232, 5:2626–2632
BABY BE-BOP, 10:27–38
BABYLON BOYZ, 10:39–46
Bach, Richard, 5:2360–2365
Bacho, Peter, 10:235–240
Bagnold, Enid, 2:942–947
Bailey, Carolyn Sherwin, 5:2405–2409
Baldwin, James, 4:1965–1970
BALYET, 6:2774–2780
Bambara, Toni Cade, 12:325–334, **14:241–248**
Banks, Lynne Reid, 7:3581–3587
Barrie, Sir James Matthew, 4:1547–1553, 5:2185–2192
Barron, T. A., 12:249–258, 13:11–20, **14:269–276**
Bartoletti, Susan Campbell, 10:135–144
BAT POET, THE, 5:2131–2136
Bat-Ami, Miriam, 9:4544–4553, **14:439–446**
Bauer, Joan, 11:361–370
Bauer, Marion Dane, 12:45–56
BE EVER HOPEFUL, HANNALEE, 6:2788–2796
Beagle, Peter S., 9:4615–4621, 10:193–201, 10:221–226, 10:393–398
Bear, Greg, 9:4486–4494, 9:4554–4562, 9:4649–4658, 9:4889–4897, 10:145–154
BEARSTONE, 6:2781–2787
BEASTIES, THE, 9:4469–4478
Beatty, John Louis, 2:859–864
Beatty, Patricia, 2:859–864, 6:2788–2796, 8:4183–4191, 8:4289–4298
BEAUTIFUL LOSERS, 12:67–76
BEAUTY, 4:1578–1583
Bell, Clare, 6:2946–2951
Bellairs, John, 4:2011–2016, 5:2172–2178
BELLE PRATER'S BOY, 10:47–57
BELLS OF BLEECKER STREET, THE, 1:109–113

BEN, 9:4479–4485
BENJAMIN FRANKLIN: THE NEW AMERICAN, 6:2797–2803
BEOWULF THE WARRIOR, 4:1584–1591
Bernard, Jacqueline, 2:728–735
Bernardo, Anilú, 9:4419–4424, 9:4670–4677, 9:4738–4746
Berry, James, 9:4403–4409, 9:4609–4614, 9:4916–4921
BEYOND DREAMS, 14:27–38
BEYOND THE MANGO TREE, 12:77–84
BEYOND THE REEF, 6:2804–2812
Bierce, Ambrose, 11:285–292
BIRD BONES AND WOOD ASH, 11:35–42
BIRDS OF SUMMER, THE, 1:114–118
BIZOU, 6:2813–2818
BLACK ARROW, THE, 1:119–126
BLACK BEAUTY, 1:127–133
BLACK JACK, 1:134–141
BLACK PEARL, THE, 1:142–147
BLACK STALLION, THE, 14:39–50
Blackmore, R. D., 2:820–828
Blackwood, Gary L., 8:4299–4303, 10:317–323
BLESS ME, ULTIMA, 13:31–40
Block, Francesca Lia, 8:4233–4240, 10:27–38
BLOOD AND CHOCOLATE, 12:85–92
BLOOD MUSIC, 9:4486–4494
BLOOMABILITY, 11:43–50
Blos, Joan W., 1:442–447
BLOSSOM CULP AND THE SLEEP OF DEATH, 6:2819–2824
BLUE SWORD, THE, 6:2830–2834
BLUES FOR SILK GARCIA, 6:2825–2829
Blume, Judy, 1:100–108, 8:4139–4149, 12:397–406
BOAT TO NOWHERE, A, 6:2835–2843
Bohner, Charles, 6:2844–2851
BOLD JOURNEY, 6:2844–2851
BONE DANCE, 12:93–102
BONE WARS, THE, 6:2852–2861
BONE, 11:51–58
Bonham, Frank, 1:373–377, 3:1415–1419
BOOK OF MERLYN, THE, 4:1592–1598
BOOK OF THREE, THE, 5:2137–2142
BORDERLAND OF SOL, THE, 10:59–65
Borland, Hal, 10:427–437
BORNING ROOM, THE, 6:2862–2866
BOXES, THE, 10:67–74
BOY AND HIS DOG, A, 14:51–58
Bradbury, Ray, 4:1677–1682, 4:1850–1855, 5:2580–2584, 11:427–434
Brancato, Robin F., 6:3103–3107
Braymer, Marjorie, 3:1426–1431
BREAK OF DARK, 6:2867–2875
BREATHING LESSONS, 12:103–108
BRIDGE TO TERABITHIA, 1:148–154

Bridgers, Sue Ellen, 7:3753–3761, 7:3813–3821, 8:3945–3949
Brink, Carol Ryrie, 1:171–178
Brontë, Charlotte, 2:686–694
Brontë, Emily, 3:1492–1497
BRONZE BOW, THE, 1:155–162
BRONZE KING, THE, 6:2876–2882
Brooks, Bruce, 7:3619–3628, 7:3728–3733, 9:4444–4451
Brooks, Martha, 12:93–102
Brown, Christy, 13:287–292
Broyard, Bliss, 14:297–306
Bryson, Bernarda, 4:1713–1721
BUD, NOT BUDDY, 13:41–52
BULL RUN, 6:2883–2891
BUMBLEBEE FLIES ANYWAY, THE, 1:163–170
Bunting, Eve, 8:4032–4038, 8:4046–4053
Bunyan, Paul, 5:2477–2484
Burch, Robert J., 3:1077–1083
Burgess, Melvin, 12:377–386
BURIED ONIONS, 11:59–70
Burnett, Frances Hodgson, 3:1180–1185
BURNING OF NJAL, THE, 4:1599–1604
Burroughs, Edgar Rice, 4:1823–1830, 4:1990–1996, 9:4452–4461
BUT IN THE FALL I'M LEAVING, 6:2892–2900
Butterworth, Oliver, 4:2017–2023
Butterworth, W. E.
Byars, Betsy, 3:1304–1309

C
CADDIE WOODLAWN, 1:171–178
Cadnum, Michael, 9:4571–4578, 11:371–386, 13:145–154
CAESAR, 1:179–185
CALL IT COURAGE, 4:1605–1610
CALL OF THE WILD, THE, 4:1611–1616
Callaghan, Mary Rose, 7:3289–3295
Cameron, Eleanor, 3:1144–1150, 5:2165–2171
Camp, L. Sprague de, 9:4641–4648
CANDIDE, 13:53–58
Card, Orson Scott, 5:2530–2536, 5:2546–2552, 8:3855–3862
CARNIVAL IN MY MIND, THE, 13:59–64
Carroll, Lewis, 5:2117–2123, 5:2612–2619, 13:1–10, 13:453–460
CARRY ON, MR. BOWDITCH, 1:186–191
CASE OF CHARLES DEXTER WARD, THE, 5:2143–2148
CASK OF AMONTILLADO, THE, 11:71–82
CASTING AWAY OF MRS. LECKS AND MRS. ALESHINE, THE, 4:1617–1622
CASTLE IN THE AIR, 9:4495–4505

CAT WHO WENT TO HEAVEN, THE, 5:2149–2153
CAT, HERSELF, 6:2910–2917
CAT'S-EYE, THE, 10:75–81
CATALOGUE OF THE UNIVERSE, 6:2901–2909
CATCH–22, 1:192–198
CATCHER IN THE RYE, THE, 1:199–208
CATHEDRAL: THE STORY OF ITS CONSTRUCTION, 1:209–213
CATS OF SEROSTER, THE, 6:2918–2924
CATSEYE, 4:1623–1627
CAY, THE, 1:214–222
CELEBRATED JUMPING FROG OF CALAVERAS COUNTY, THE, 11:83–94
Cervantes Saavedra, Miguel de, 1:358–365, **14:79–90**
CHARLES A. LINDBERGH: A HUMAN HERO, 9:4506–4511
CHARLIE AND THE CHOCOLATE FACTORY, 5:2154–2158
CHARLOTTE'S WEB, 5:2159–2164
Charnas, Suzy McKee, 6:2876–2882
CHARTBREAKER, 9:4512–4522
CHASE ME, CATCH NOBODY, 1:223–228
CHASING REDBIRD, 12:109–118
CHATHAM SCHOOL AFFAIR, THE, 12:119–130
Chekhov, Anton, 14:135–142
CHESTRY OAK, THE, 1:229–234
CHIEF JOSEPH: WAR CHIEF OF THE NEZ PERCE, 1:235–241
CHILD IN PRISON CAMP, A, 1:242–248
CHILDREN OF THE DUST, 6:2925–2933
CHILDREN OF THE FIRE, 13:65–72
CHILDREN OF THE FOX, 1:249–254
Childress, Alice, 2:563–570
CHOCOLATE WAR, THE, 1:255–262
Chopin, Kate, 21–34
Chrisman, Arthur Bowie, 4:1937–1941
CHRISTMAS CAROL, A, 1:263–270
Christopher, John (Christopher Samuel Youd), 8:4277–4282
Christopher, John, 4:1739–1745, 4:2063–2069
Christopher, Matt, 8:4070–4073
CHRONICLE OF A DEATH FORETOLD, 12:131–138
CIRAK'S DAUGHTER, 6:2934–2939
CIRCLE OF REVENGE, 6:2940–2945
CLAN GROUND, 6:2946–2951
Clancy, Joseph P., 2:1015–1020
Clancy, Tom, 10:83–90, 10:241–248, 10:399–406, 11:293–302, 11:435–444
Clapp, Patricia, 10:369–375
Clark, Ann Nolan, 4:1925–1930
Clarke, Arthur C., 13:409–416

Delany, Samuel R., 4878–4888
Dereske, Jo, 7:3512–3520
Derleth, August, 9:4922–4930, 10:439–448
Dessen, Sarah, 12:387–396
Deuker, Carl, 7:3783–3787
Deutsch, Babette, 3:1432–1439
Diaz, Junot, 12:167–176
DICEY'S SONG, 1:336–340
Dick, Philip K., 11:109–122
Dickens, Charles, 1:263–270, 1:486–493,
    2:981–987, 3:1325–1334, 13:103–118,
    14:153–166
Dickinson, Peter, 5:2654–2659
Dicks, Terrance, 4:1650–1656
DIGGER'S GOOD-BYE, 11:159–166
DINKY HOCKER SHOOTS SMACK,
    1:341–348
DINOSAUR SUMMER, 9:4554–4562
DISCOVER THE DESTROYER, 14:69–78
DIVORCE EXPRESS, 6:3037–3041
Dixon, Franklin W., 4:1746–1751
DO ANDROIDS DREAM OF ELECTRIC
    SHEEP?, 11:109–122
DOBRY, 1:349–357
DOCTOR WHO: THE FIVE DOCTORS,
    4:1650–1656
Dodge, Mary Mapes, 2:518–525
DON QUIXOTE, 1:358–365, **14:79–90**
DON'T CALL IT PARADISE, 12:159–166
DON'T LOOK BEHIND YOU, 6:3042–3046
DOOM STONE, THE, 9:4563–4570
DOOR IN THE WALL, THE, 1:366–372
Dorris, Michael, 12:285–294, 12:477–494
Doyle, Arthur Conan (see Conan
    Doyle, Arthur)
DR. JEKYLL AND MR. HYDE, 13:119–124
DRACULA, 5:2193–2198
DRAGON OF OG, THE, 5:2199–2203
DRAGON'S BAIT, 6:3047–3052
DRAGONS IN THE WATERS, 4:1657–1662
DRAGONSONG, 5:2204–2210
Dragonwagon, Crescent, 8:4161–4167
DREADFUL FUTURE OF BLOSSOM CULP,
    6:3053–3060
DREAM OF WATER, THE, 13:125–132
DRIVER'S ED, 10:99–104
DROWN, 12:167–176
du Bois, William Péne, 4:2024–2029
du Maurier, Daphne, 5:2524–2529
Duane, Diane, 6:3030–3036, 10:83–90,
    11:293–302
DUBLINERS, 13:133–144
Dufault, Joseph-Ernest-Nephati (see
    James, Will)
DUKES, 6:3061–3065
Dumas, Alexandre, 3:1353–1360

Duncan, Dave, 13:383–388
Duncan, Lois, 6:3042–3046, 8:4192–4196
DUNE, 4:1663–1670
Dunlop, Agnes Mary Robertson (see Kyle,
    Elisabeth)
DUPLICATE, THE, 6:3066–3072
DURANGO STREET, 1:373–377
Dyer, Daniel, 13:207–216

E
EAGLE OF THE NINTH, THE, 1:378–383
EASTERN SUN, WINTER MOON,
    6:3073–3080
Eckert, Allan W., 2:622–627
EDGE, 9:4571–4578, 13:145–154
Edmonds, Walter D., 2:865–870
EDUCATION OF ROBERT NIFKIN, THE,
    9:4579–4589
Edwards, Grace F., 12:427–434
EGYPT GAME, THE, 1:384–390
EL DORADO ADVENTURE, THE,
    6:3081–3089
ELIDOR, 5:2211–2219
Eliot, T. S., 5:2449–2454
ELLA ENCHANTED, 11:123–130
Ellison, Harlan, 14:51–58
Ellison, Ralph, 2:637–643
ENCHANTED CASTLE, THE, 5:2220–2226
ENCHANTRESS FROM THE STARS
    4:1671–1676
Ende, Michael, 5:2443–2448
ENDLESS STEPPE, THE: GROWING UP IN
    SIBERIA, 1:391–396
Engdahl, Sylvia Louise, 4:1671–1676
Enright, Elizabeth, 3:1342–1347
ENTER THE ENCHANTED, 14:91–100
ESCAPE FROM WARSAW (see SILVER
    SWORD, THE)
ESCAPE THE MORNING, 9:4590–4599
ESKIMO BOY, 1:397–401
Estes, Eleanor, 1:448–454
EVERYTHING IS NOT ENOUGH,
    6:3090–3096
EXILES OF COLSEC, 6:3097–3102
EYES OF THE AMARYLLIS, THE,
    5:2227–2232

F
FACE IN THE CLOTH, THE, 11:131–138
FACE ON THE MILK CARTON, THE,
    11:139–146
FACING UP, 6:3103–3107
FADE, 6:3108–3117
FAHRENHEIT 451, 4:1677–1682

FAIR MAIDEN, 9:4600–4608
FALL OF THE HOUSE OF USHER, THE,
  5:2233–2241
FALLEN ANGEL, 10:105–111
FALLEN ANGELS, 6:3118–3126
FAMILY RESEMBLANCES, 6:3127–3134
FANSO AND GRANNY-FLO, 9:4609–4614
FANTASTIC BEASTS AND WHERE TO
  FIND THEM, 14:101–106
FAR AWAY AND LONG AGO, 1:402–408
Farber, Norma, 7:3612–3618
Farley, Walter, 14:39–50
FARM TEAM, 12:177–186
FARMER GILES OF HAM, 5:2242–2249
FARMER IN THE SKY, 4:1683–1689
Farmer, Nancy, 11:175–188
FARTHEST SHORE, THE, 5:2250–2257
FAT GIRL, 6:3142–3147
FAT: A LOVE STORY, 6:3135–3141
Faulkner, William, 5:2683–2687
Fenner, Carol, 11:523–536
Fenton, Edward, 13:275–286, 13:359–372
Field, Rachel, 5:2327–2333
FIGGS & PHANTOMS, 4:1690–1697
FIGHTING GROUND, THE, 1:409–413
FILE ON FRAULEIN BERG, THE, 12:187–196
FINE WHITE DUST, A, 6:3148–3154
Finger, Charles J., 4:1984–1989
FINGERS, 6:3155–3160
FIRE AND HEMLOCK, 6:3161–3167
FIRST A DREAM, 6:3168–3175
Fitzgerald, F. Scott, 1:494–502
FIVE SONS OF KING PANDU, THE,
  4:1698–1706
FLEDGLING, THE, 5:2258–2265
Fleischman, Paul, 5:2366–2370, 6:2862–2866,
  6:2883–2891, 8:3950–3954, 8:4168–4174,
  11:387–400, 12:467–476
Fleischman, Sid, 4:2051–2057, 11:1–10
FLOWERS FOR ALGERNON, 11:147–158
FLY LIKE AN EAGLE, 13:155–162
FLYING CHANGES, 6:3176–3183
FOOTPRINTS IN THE SNOW, 11:159–166
FOOTSTEPS, 1:414–421
Forbes, Esther, 2:695–700
FORESTWIFE, THE, 11:167–174
Forster, E. M., 12:219–226
FORTY ACRES AND MAYBE A MULE,
  14:107–114
FORWARD THE FOUNDATION, 6:3184–3197
FOUNDATION TRILOGY, THE, 4:1707–1712
FOUR HORSES FOR TISHTRY, 6:3198–3204
Fox, Paula, 3:1238–1244, 8:3837–3842
Frank, Anne, 1:73–78
FRANKENSTEIN, 5:2266–2272
FREAKY FRIDAY, 5:2273–2279

Freedman, Russell, 2:789–796, 11:241–250,
  14:261–268
French, Allen, 4:1954–1958
French, Michael, 6:2940–2945
Freuchen, Pipaluk, 1:397–401
FRIEDRICH, 1:422–428
Fritz, Jean, 2:571–576, 3:1391–1395, **14:179–188,**
  14:483–493
FROM SLAVE SHIP TO FREEDOM ROAD,
  12:197–202
FROM THE MIXED-UP FILES OF MRS.
  BASIL E. FRANKWEILER, 1:429–435
FUTURETRACK 5, 6:3205–3212

G
Gaines, Ernest James, 6:3222–3230
GAME OF EMPIRE, THE, 6:3213–3221
GANDHI, 1:436–441
Garcia Marquez, Gabriel, 12:131–138
Garden, Nancy, 7:3807–3812
Garfield, Leon, 1:134–141, 1:414–421,
  3:1245–1250
Garner, Alan, 3:1278–1284, 5:2211–2219,
  5:2463–2470, 5:2660–2667
Garst, Doris Shannon, 1:286–293
GATHERING BLUE, 14:115–124
GATHERING OF DAYS, A, 1:442–447
GATHERING OF OLD MEN, A, 6:3222–3230
GAY-NECK: THE STORY OF A PIGEON,
  5:2280–2285
George, Jean, 2:936–941, 4:1782–1787
GERONIMO'S PONIES, 6:3231–3240
GHOST TRAIN, 10:113–118
GHOST-MAKER, THE, 6:3241–3246
GIANT BONES, 9:4615–4621
Giblin, James Cross, 9:4506–4511, 10:417–425
GIFT OF SARAH BARKER, THE, 9:4622–4632
GILGAMESH: MAN'S FIRST STORY,
  4:1713–1721
Gilman, Charlotte Perkins, 11:513–522
GINGER PYE, 1:448–454
Gipson, Fred, 2:974–980
GIRL GIVES BIRTH TO OWN PROM DATE,
  9:4633–4640
GIRL NAMED DISASTER, A, 11:175–188
GIRL OF HIS DREAMS, 6:3247–3254
GIRL WITH A PEN: CHARLOTTE BRONTE,
  1:455–461
GIVER, THE, 6:3255–3263
GLASS SLIPPER, THE, 4:1722–1726
GO ASK ALICE, 14:125–134
GOATS, THE, 10:119–126
GOBLIN MARKET, 4:1727–1732
GOD'S RADAR, 6:3264–3269
Godden, Rumer, 2:526–530, 5:2199–2203
GOLDEN COMPASS, THE, 13:163–178

LIGHT IN THE FOREST, THE, 2:780–788
LINCOLN: A PHOTOBIOGRAPHY, 2:789–796
Lindgren, Astrid, 5:2485–2492
LINE OF THE SUN, THE, 12:237–248
Lingard, Joan, 12:187–196
LION, THE WITCH, AND THE WARDROBE, THE, 5:2380–2387
LITTLE HOUSE IN THE BIG WOODS, 2:797–805
LITTLE WOMEN, 2:806–812
LOCADIO'S APPRENTICE, 7:3502–3511
LOCH, 9:4764–4771
Lofting, Hugh, 5:2639–2647
London, Jack, 4:1611–1616, 4:2058–2062, 13:461–472
LONE SENTINEL, THE, 7:3512–3520
LONG WAY FROM CHICAGO, A, 11:251–258
LONG WAY FROM HOME, A, 7:3521–3528
LORD OF THE FLIES, 2:813–819
LORD OF THE RINGS, THE, 5:2388–2397
LORNA DOONE, 2:820–828
LOST WORLD, THE, 4:1843–1849
LOST YEARS OF MERLIN, THE, 12:249–258
LOUIS, 9:4772–4778
LOVE IS THE CROOKED THING, 12:259–268
Lovecraft, H. P., 5:2143–2148, 5:2572–2579
Lowry, Lois, 4:1878–1882, 6:3255–3263, **14:115–124**
LUCK OF TEXAS MCCOY, THE, 7:3529–3533
LULLABY, 12:269–276
LYDDIE, 7:3534–3543
Lyle, Katie Letcher, 6:3006–3013
Lynch, Chris, 10:325–335, 12:203–212, 12:357–366

M
M. C. HIGGINS, THE GREAT, 2:876–883
M. V. SEXTON SPEAKING, 7:3665–3670
Macaulay, David, 1:209–213
MacDonald, George, 5:2286–2292, 5:2500–2506
MACHINE GUNNERS, THE, 2:829–836
MacLachlan, Patricia, 3:1167–1172
MacLeod, Charlotte, 6:2934–2939
MADAME CURIE, 2:837–843
Magorian, Michelle, 1:472–478
Maguire, Gregory, 14:59–68
Mahy, Margaret, 6:2901–2909, 6:2996–3005, 7:3597–3604, 8:4175–4182
MAINLY IN MOONLIGHT, 5:2398–2404
MAKRA CHORIA, 7:3544–3552
MAN IN THE WOODS, THE, 7:3560–3565
MAN THAT CORRUPTED HADLEYBURG, THE, 14:249–260
MAN WHO WAS POE, THE, 10:227–234
MANIAC MAGEE, 7:3553–3559

MANY WATERS, 7:3566–3572
MAP OF NOWHERE, A, 9:4779–4789
Markandaya, Kamala, 13:293–304
MARTHA GRAHAM: A DANCER'S LIFE, 14:261–268
MARTIAN CHRONICLES, THE, 4:1850–1855
Martin, Ann M., 8:4318–4324, **14:327–336**
MASK OF APOLLO, THE, 2:844–851
MASQUE, 12:277–284
MASTER OF FIENDS, 7:3573–3580
MASTER PUPPETEER, THE, 2:852–858
MASTER ROSALIND, 2:859–864
MATCHLOCK GUN, THE, 2:865–870
MATTER OF FAITH, A, 10:235–240
MAUDIE AND ME AND THE DIRTY BOOK, 2:871–875
Maupassant, Guy de, 14:307–316
Mayhar, Ardath, 7:3544–3552
Mazer, Harry, 6:3247–3254
Mazer, Norma Fox, 1:20–25, 8:4074–4080, 4132–4138
McCaffrey, Anne, 5:2203–2210
McCay, Bill, 10:399–406
McFarlane, Leslie (see Dixon, Franklin W.)
McGreal, Elizabeth Yates (see Yates, Elizabeth)
McKillip, Patricia A., 7:3645–3652, 11:503–512
McKinley, Robin, 4:1578–1583, 5:2316–2321, 6:2830–2834, 12:149–158, 12:335–344
McLaren, Clemence, 10:203–212
Meaker, Marijane (see Kerr, M. E.)
MEET THE AUSTINS, 2:884–891
Meigs, Cornelia Lynde, 2:628–636, 2:678–685
Meltzer, Milton, 2:758–766, 6:2797–2803
MELUSINE: A MYSTERY, 7:3581–3587
MEMBER OF THE FAMILY, A, 7:3588–3596
MEMORY OF DRAGONS, A, 7:3605–3611
MEMORY, 7:3597–3604
MEN OF IRON, 2:892–900
Mercer, Charles, 1:32–37
MERCY SHORT: A WINTER JOURNAL, NORTH BOSTON, 4:1692–93, 7:3612–3618
MERLIN, 11:259–266
MERLIN EFFECT, THE, 14:269–276
Merrill, Jean, 5:2507–2512
MERRY ADVENTURES OF ROBIN HOOD, THE, 4:1856–1864
Meyer, Carolyn, 7:3529–3533, 8:4039–4045
Meyers, Harold Burton, 6:3231–3240
MICHELANGELO, 2:901–906
MIDNIGHT DREARY: THE MYSTERIOUS DEATH OF EDGAR ALLAN POE, 13:253–262
MIDNIGHT HOUR ENCORES, 7:3619–3628
MIDWIFE'S APPRENTICE, THE, 9:4790–4801, 13:263–274

Miklowitz, Gloria, 13:73–82
Miles, Betty, 2:871–875
MIRACLES ON MAPLE HILL, 2:907–915
MISS HICKORY, 5:2405–2409
MISSING MAY, 7:3629–3637
MISTRESS MASHAM'S REPOSE, 5:2410–2418
Mitchell, Margaret, 1:462–471
Momaday, N. Scott, 12:213–218
MONSTER, 11:267–274
Montgomery, Lucy Maud, 1:79–86
MONUMENT, THE, 7:3638–3644
MOON AND THE FACE, THE, 7:3645–3652
MOONWIND, 7:3653–3659
Mori, Kyoko, 13:125–132, 13:373–382
MORNING GIRL, 12:285–294
MORNING OF THE GODS, THE, 13:275–286
**MOST DANGEROUS GAME, THE,
14:277–286**
Mowat, Farley, 2:955–960
Mowry, Jess, 10:39–46, 10:113–118, 10:407–416
MRS. FRISBY AND THE RATS OF NIMH,
5:2419–2425
Mukerji, Dhan Gopal, 5:2280–2285
MURDER IN A PIG'S EYE, 7:3660–3664
MURDERS IN THE RUE MORGUE,
5:2426–2432
Murphy, Barbara Beasley, 12:11–22, 12:23–34,
13:155–162
Murphy, Jim, 10:1–10, 10:75–81, 10:127–134,
10:481–490, 11:159–166
Murphy, Shirley R., 7:3419–3425
**MY BROTHER, MY SISTER, AND I,
14:287–296**
MY BROTHER SAM IS DEAD, 2:916–922
MY DARLING, MY HAMBURGER, 2:923–928
MY FATHER, DANCING, 14:297–306
MY FRIEND FLICKA, 2:929–935
MY LEFT FOOT, 13:287–292
MY LIFE IN DOG YEARS, 11:275–284
MY SIDE OF THE MOUNTAIN, 2:936–941
Myers, Walter Dean, 6:3118–3126, 8:3966–3975,
11:267–274
MYTHS OF THE NORSEMEN, 4:1865–1870

N
NANCY DREW SERIES, 4:1871–1877
Napoli, Donna Jo, 10:353–360, 11:401–408,
11:419–426
NARGUN AND THE STARS, THE,
5:2433–2442
NATIONAL VELVET, 2:942–947
NATIVE SON, 2:948–954
Naylor, Phyllis Reynolds, 7:3432–3438,
7:3671–3677, 8:4000–4005
NECESSARY ROUGHNESS, 12:295–302
NECKLACE, THE, 14:307–316

NECTAR IN A SIEVE, 13:293–304
Nesbit, Edith, 5:2220–2226
NET FORCE, 10:241–248
NEVER CRY WOLF, 2:955–960
NEVERENDING STORY, THE, 5:2443–2448
Neville, Emily, 2:657–661
Newton, Suzanne, 7:3400–3405, 7:3665–3670
Ng, Fae Myenne, 11:51–58
Nieminen, Raija, 8:4212–4216
NIGHT CRY, 7:3671–3677
NIGHT IN DISTANT MOTION, A,
7:3696–3703
NIGHT IN QUESTION, THE, 12:303–314
NIGHT KITES, 7:3712–3720
NIGHT OF THE WHALE, 7:3721–3727
NIGHT THE HEADS CAME, THE,
9:4802–4810
NIGHTFALL, 7:3678–3695
NIGHTJOHN, 7:3704–3711
Niven, Larry, 10:19–26, 10:59–65, 10:163–169,
10:377–384
Nix, Garth, 14:377–384, 14:413–420
NO KIDDING, 7:3728–3733
NO MORE SATURDAY NIGHTS, 7:3734–3741
NO-NO BOY, 14:317–326
NORBY: THE MIXED-UP ROBOT,
7:3742–3752
North, Sterling, 3:1084–1088, 3:1348–1352
Norton, Alice Mary (see Norton, Andre)
Norton, Andre, 4:1623–1627, 4:1795–1800,
4:1831–1837, 10:11–17, 12:345–356
NOTES FOR ANOTHER LIFE, 7:3753–3761
NOTHING BUT THE TRUTH, 10:249–258
NUMBER THE STARS, 4:1878–1882

O
O'Brien, Robert, 5:2419–2425
O'Dell, Scott, 1:142–147, 2:650–656,
3:1224–1230, 5:2585–2591
O'Hara, Mary, 2:929–935
Oates, Joyce Carol, 11:475–486
OCCURRENCE AT OWL CREEK BRIDGE,
AN, 11:285–292
ODDBALLS, 9:4811–4819
OF MICE AND MEN, 2:961–967
OGRE, OGRE, 7:3762–3769
Okada, John, 14:317–326
OLD MAN AND THE SEA, THE, 2:968–973
OLD POSSUM'S BOOK OF PRACTICAL
CATS, 5:2449–2454
OLD RAMON, 4:1883–1887
OLD YELLER, 2:974–980
OLDER MEN, 7:3770–3778
OLIVER TWIST, 2:981–987
Olsen, Tillie, 11:231–240
ON FORTUNE'S WHEEL, 7:3788–3794

ON THE DEVIL'S COURT, 7:3783–3787
ONCE AND FUTURE KING, THE, 4:1888–1896
ONCE UPON A DARK NOVEMBER, 7:3779–3782
ONE IS THE LONELIEST NUMBER, 11:293–302
Oneal, Zibby, 13:241–252
ONES WHO WALK AWAY FROM OMELAS, THE, 11:303–312
ONION JOHN, 2:988–994
OPEN WINDOW, THE, 11:313–320
Orwell, George, 5:2124–2130
OSCAR CHARLESTON: WAS COBB "THE WHITE CHARLESTON"?, 9:4820–4828
OTHERS SEE US, 7:3795–3800
OTTO OF THE SILVER HAND, 2:995–1000
OUR EDDIE, 2:1001–1006
OUT OF THE DUST, 9:4829–4844
OUTSIDERS, THE, 2:1007–1014
OVER SEA, UNDER STONE, 5:2455–2462
OWL SERVICE, THE, 5:2463–2470

P
P.S. LONGER LETTER LATER, 14:327–336
PASSAGER, 10:259–265
Paterson, Katherine, 1:148–154, 2:511–517, 2:670–677, 2:852–858, 7:3534–3543
Paton Walsh, Jill, 1:249–254, 8:4150–4160
Paton, Alan, 1:294–300
Paulsen, Gary, 6:2974–2981, 6:2989–2995, 6:3073–3080, 7:3281–3288, 7:3296–3304, 7:3384–3391, 7:3638–3644, 7:3704–3711, 8:4310–4317, 8:4348–4354, 10:297–306, 10:307–315, 11:275–284, 11:409–418
PAY AS YOU EXIT, 7:3801–3806
PEACE, O RIVER, 7:3807–3812
Pearce, Phillipa, 5:2620–2625
PEARL, THE, 13:305–314
Pearson, Gayle, 12:159–166
Peck, Richard, 1:95–99, 6:2819–2824, 6:2952–2960, 6:3053–3060, 8:3863–3869, 8:3883–3889, 8:4124–4131, 11:251–258
Peck, Robert Newton, 1:315–320, 6:3061–3065
Pei, Lowry, 6:3127–3134
PENDRAGON: ARTHUR AND HIS BRITAIN, 2:1015–1020
Penman, Sharon Kay, 10:273–279
PENN, 3:1021–1027
PENROD, 3:1028–1033
PERMANENT CONNECTIONS, 7:3813–3821
Perrault, Charles, 4:1722–1726
Perry, Steve, 10:241–248
PETROS' WAR, 13:315–326
Petry, Ann, 2:531–537
Pfeffer, Susan Beth, 8:4063–4069

PHANTOM TOLLBOOTH, THE, 5:2471–2476
PHILADELPHIA ADVENTURE, THE, 7:3822–3829
PHOENIX RISING: OR HOW TO SURVIVE YOUR LIFE, 7:3830–3836
PIECE OF MIND, A, 13:327–334
Pieczenik, Steve, 10:83–90, 10:241–248, 10:399–406, 11:293–302, 11:435–444
Pierce, Meredith, 5:2179–2184
Pierce, Tamora, 8:4341–4347
PIGMAN, THE, 3:1034–1040
PILGRIM'S PROGRESS, THE, 5:2477–2484
Pinkwater, Daniel, 9:4410–4418, 9:4579–4589, 9:4755–4763, 9:4858–4865, 9:4866–4877
PIPPI LONGSTOCKING, 5:2485–2492
PIT AND THE PENDULUM, THE, 5:2493–2499
PIT, THE, 10:267–272
PLACE APART, A, 8:3837–3842
PLAYING MURDER, 8:3843–3847
PODKAYNE OF MARS, 4:1897–1904
Poe, Edgar Allan, 5:2233–2241, 5:2426–2432, 2493–2499, 5:2518–2523, 5:2599–2604, 11:71–82
POLLYANNA: THE GLAD BOOK, 3:1041–1046
Porter, Eleanor H., 3:1041–1046
PORTRAIT OF THE ARTIST AS A YOUNG MAN, A, 13:335–346
Potok, Chaim, 1:308–314
POWER AND THE GLORY, THE, 3:1047–1053
POWER, 12:315–324
Power, Susan, 14:143–152
PRAIRIE VISIONS, 8:3848–3854
PRAIRIE-TOWN BOY, 3:1054–1061
PRENTICE ALVIN, 8:3855–3862
PRIDE AND PREJUDICE, 3:1062–1070
PRINCESS AND THE GOBLIN, THE, 5:2500–2506
PRINCESS ASHLEY, 8:3863–3869
PRISONER OF PSI, 8:3870–3876
PROMISES ARE FOR KEEPING, 8:3877–3882
PROUD TASTE FOR SCARLET AND MINIVER, A, 3:1071–1076
Pullman, Philip, 8:3917–3923, 8:3985–3992, 13:163–178
PUSHCART WAR, THE, 5:2507–2512
Pyle, Howard, 2:892–900, 2:995–1000, 4:1856–1864

Q
QUEEN OF ATTOLIA, THE, 14:337–346
QUEEN'S MAN, THE, 10:273–279
QUEENIE PEAVY, 3:1077–1083

SECRET OF THE ANDES, 4:1925–1930
SECRET OF THE NINTH PLANET, THE,
    4:1931–1936
SEEDFOLKS, 11:387–400
Seeger, Elizabeth, 4:1698–1706
SEPARATE PEACE, A, 3:1186–1193
Seredy, Kate, 1:229–234, 4:2070–2076
Serraillier, Ian, 3:1218–1223, 4:1584–1591,
    4:1752–1757
Service, Robert, 4:1628–1634
Seton, Ernest Thompson, 3:1461–1465
Sevela, Ephraim, 8:4241–4249
SEVENTH SON, 5:2546–2552
Sewell, Anna, 1:127–133
SHADE'S CHILDREN, 14:413–420
SHADOW BOXER, 12:357–366
SHADOW IN THE NORTH, 8:3985–3992
SHADOW OF A BULL, 3:1194–1199
SHAKESPEARE STEALER, THE, 10:317–323
SHANE, 3:1200–1206
Shannon, Monica, 1:349–357
SHARK BITE, 12:367–376
SHE, 5:2553–2562
Shelley, Mary, 5:2266–2272
SHELLEY'S MARY: A LIFE OF MARY
    GODWIN SHELLEY, 3:1207–1212
SHEN OF THE SEA, 4:1937–1941
SHEPHERD MOON, THE, 8:3993–3999
SHILOH, 8:4000–4005
SHIZUKO'S DAUGHTER, 13:373–382
SHY STEGOSAURUS OF CRICKET CREEK,
    THE, 5:2563–2571
SIEGE AND FALL OF TROY, THE,
    4:1942–1947
SIGN OF THE BEAVER, THE, 3:1213–1217
Silko, Leslie Marmon, 12:269–276
SILVER KEY, THE, 5:2572–2579
SILVER SWORD, THE, 3:1218–1223
Silverberg, Robert, 7:3486–3495, 7:3678–3695,
    9:4436–4443
Sinclair, Upton, 2:736–741
SING DOWN THE MOON, 3:1224–1230
Singer, Isaac Bashevis, 1:321–327, 4:2083–2088
SINGULARITY, 8:4006–4012
SIR STALWART: A TALE OF THE KING'S
    DAGGERS, 13:383–388
SIRENA, 11:401–408
SLAN, 13:389–400
SLAUGHTERHOUSE-FIVE, 3:1231–1237
SLAVE DANCER, THE, 3:1238–1244
SLAVES OF SPIEGEL, 9:4858–4865
Sleator, William, 4:1770–1774, 6:3066–3072,
    6:3155–3160, 7:3795–3800, 8:4006–4012,
    9:4469–4478, 9:4535–4543, 9:4802–4810,
    9:4811–4819, 10:67–74, 10:343–351,
    11:353–360

SLOT MACHINE, 10:325–335
SMACK, 12:377–386
SMALL DEATHS, 10:337–342
SMITH, 3:1245–1250
Smith, Betty, 3:1396–1402
SMOKY THE COW HORSE, 4:1948–1953
SNAPSHOTS, 8:4013–4019
SNARKOUT BOYS AND THE AVOCADO
    OF DEATH, THE, 9:4866–4877
SNOWS OF KILIMANJARO, THE, 13:401–408
Snyder, Zilpha Keatley, 1:114–118, 1:384–390
**SO FAR FROM THE BAMBOO GROVE,
    14:421–430**
SOLDIER'S HEART, 11:409–418
SOLITARY BLUE, A, 3:1251–1257
SOLITARY, THE, 8:4020–4025
SOMEONE LIKE YOU, 12:387–396
SOMETHING WICKED THIS WAY COMES,
    5:2580–2584
Sommerfelt, Aimee, 3:1120–1126
SONG OF THE MAGDELENE, 11:419–426
Sorensen, Virginia, 2:907–915
Soto, Gary, 11:59–70
SOUL BROTHERS AND SISTER LOU, THE,
    3:1258–1264
SOUL CATCHER, 14:431–438
SOUNDER, 3:1265–1271
Southall, Ivan, 2:701–709
Sparks, Beatrice Mathews, 14:125–134
Speare, Elizabeth George, 1:155–162,
    3:1213–1217, 3:1485–1491
Sperry, Armstrong, 4:1605–1610
Spinelli, Jerry, 7:3414–3418, 7:3553–3559,
    7:3721–3727, 10:473–480
SPIRIT HOUSE, THE, 10:343–351
SPUNKWATER, SPUNKWATER!: A LIFE OF
    MARK TWAIN, 3:1272–1277
Spyri, Johanna, 2:545–554
STAR PIT, THE, 9:4878–4888
STAR, THE, 13:409–416
Steinbeck, John, 2:961–967, 3:1105–1111,
    13:305–314
Stevenson, Robert Louis, 1:119–126, 2:742–749,
    4:2004–2010, 13:119–124
Stockton, Frank R., 4:1617–1622, 13:231–240
Stoehr, Shelley, 13:83–92
Stoker, Bram, 5:2193–2198
STONE ANGEL, THE, 13:417–424
STONE BOOK QUARTET, THE, 3:1278–1284
STONES IN WATER, 10:353–360
STORY OF GRETTIR THE STRONG, THE,
    4:1954–1958
STORY OF MANKIND, THE, 4:1959–1964
STORY OF MY LIFE, THE, 3:1285–1292
STORY OF ROLAND, THE, 4:1965–1970
STOTAN!, 8:4026–4031

Treece, Henry, 4:1599–1604
Trevino, Elizabeth Borton de, 2:607–614
TRICKSTERS, THE, 8:4175–4182
TROUBLE WITH JENNY'S EAR, THE,
  2017–2023
TRUE CONFESSIONS OF CHARLOTTE
  DOYLE, THE, 10:385–392
TRUMPETER OF KRAKOW, THE,
  3:1403–1409
TUCK EVERLASTING, 5:2626–2632
Tunis, John R., 1:38–43
TURN HOMEWARD, HANNALEE,
  8:4183–4191
Turner, Ann, 8:4217–4224
Turner, Megan Whalen, 9:4907–4915,
  14:337–346
Twain, Mark, 2:583–590, 3:1384–1390,
  11:83–94, **14:249–260**
TWENTY THOUSAND LEAGUES UNDER
  THE SEA, 4:2030–2035
TWENTY-ONE BALLOONS, THE,
  4:2024–2029
TWINS, THE PIRATES, AND THE BATTLE
  OF NEW ORLEANS, THE, 13:473–480
TWISTED WINDOW, THE, 8:4192–4196
TWO SUNS IN THE SKY, 14:439–446
Tyler, Anne, 12:103–108

U
Uchida, Yoshiko, 2:717–727, 3:1159–1166
UGLY LITTLE BOY, THE, 9:4931–4943
ULTIMATE ESCAPE, THE, 11:435–444
UNICORN SONATA, THE, 10:393–398
UP A ROAD SLOWLY, 3:1410–1414
Updike, John, 12:1–10
Ure, Jean, 6:2738–2745
URN BURIAL, 8:4197–4204

V
van Loon, Hendrik, 4:1959–1964
van Vogt, A. E., 13:389–400, **14:447–458**
VANDEMARK MUMMY, THE, 8:4205–4211
Varley, John, 8:4081–4086
Velde, Vivian Vande, 6:3047–3052
Vergil, 4:1554–1563
Verne, Jules, 4:2030–2035
VIEW FROM SATURDAY, THE, 9:4944–4953
Vining, Elizabeth Gray (see Gray,
  Elizabeth Janet)
VIRTUAL VANDALS, 10:399–406
VISIT TO WILLIAM BLAKE'S INN, A,
  5:2633–2638
VIVA CHICANO, 3:1415–1419
VOICE FROM THE BORDER, A, 12:435–444

Voigt, Cynthia, 1:336–340, 3:1251–1257,
  6:2966–2973, 6:3014–3021, 7:3406–3413,
  7:3788–3794, 8:3929–3937, 8:4205–4211
Voltaire, 13:53–58
Von Canon, Claudia, 7:3372–3379
Vonnegut, Kurt, 3:1231–1237, **14:189–200**
**VOYAGE OF THE SPACE BEAGLE, THE,
  14:447–458**
VOYAGE TO THE ISLAND, 8:4212–4216
VOYAGES OF DOCTOR DOLITTLE, THE,
  5:2639–2647

W
WALDEN, 3:1420–1425
WALDO, 13:481–488
WALK TWO MOONS, 9:4954–4961
WALLS OF WINDY TROY, THE, 3:1426–1431
Walsh, Jill Paton (see Paton Walsh, Jill)
Walsh, John Evangelist, 13:253–262
WALT WHITMAN: BUILDER FOR
  AMERICA, 3:1432–1439
WAR OF THE WORLDS, THE, 4:2036–2043
Warren, Robert Penn, 1:44–53
Wartski, Maureen Crane, 6:2835–2843,
  7:3521–3528
Waterhouse, Jane, 12:139–148
WATERLESS MOUNTAIN, 3:1440–1446
WATERSHIP DOWN, 5:2648–2653
Watkins, Yoko Kawashima, **14:287–296,
  14:421–430**
WATSONS GO TO BIRMINGHAM-1963,
  THE, 11:445–452
WAY HOME, THE, 8:4217–4224
WAY PAST COOL, 10:407–416
WE ALL FALL DOWN, 8:4225–4232
WE SHALL NOT BE MOVED: THE
  WOMEN'S FACTORY STRIKE OF 1909,
  11:453–458
WE WERE NOT LIKE OTHER PEOPLE,
  8:4241–4249
WEATHERMONGER, THE, 5:2654–2659
Weaver, Will, 12:177–186
WEETZIE BAT, 8:4233–4240
WEIRDSTONE OF BRISINGAMEN, THE,
  5:2660–2667
Wells, H. G., 4:1775–1781, 4:1997–2003,
  4:2036–2043
Wells, Rosemary, 7:3560–3565, 8:4271–4276
Wersba, Barbara, 6:3135–3141, 12:67–76,
  12:259–268, 13:59–64, 13:217–224,
  13:489–498
Westall, Robert, 2:829–836, 6:2867–2875,
  6:2918–2924, 6:3205–3212, 7:3305–3313,
  8:4197–4204, 9:4462–4468
WESTING GAME, THE, 4:2044–2050
WHAT ABOUT GRANDMA?, 8:4250–4259

YOUNG PATRIOT: THE AMERICAN
REVOLUTION AS EXPERIENCED BY
ONE BOY, A, 10:481–490

Z
Zei, Alki, 13:315–326
Zemser, Amy Bronwen 12:77–84
Zindel, Paul, 2:923–928, 3:1034–1040,
8:4161–4167, 11:335–342, **14:353–362**
ZLATEH THE GOAT AND OTHER STORIES,
4:2083–2088